Environmental Governance Reconsidered

Environmental Governance Reconsidered

Challenges, Choices, and Opportunities

edited by
Robert F. Durant, Daniel J. Fiorino, and
Rosemary O'Leary

The MIT Press
Cambridge, Massachusetts
London, England

This book was set in Sabon by Interactive Composition Corporation.
Printed and bound in the United States of America.
Library of Congress Cataloging-in-Publication Data

Environmental governance reconsidered : challenges, choices, and opportunities / edited by Robert F. Durant, Daniel J. Fiorino, and Rosemary O'Leary.
    p. cm. — (American and comparative environmental policy)
Includes bibliographical references and index.
ISBN 0-262-04218-5 — ISBN 0-262-54174-2 (pbk.)
    1. Environmental policy. 2. Environmental management. I. Durant, Robert F., 1949– II. Fiorino, Daniel J. III. O'Leary, Rosemary, 1955– IV. Series.

GE170.E5754   2004
333.72—dc22   2003064741

Printed on recycled paper.

10 9 8 7 6 5 4 3 2 1

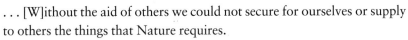

. . . [W]ithout the aid of others we could not secure for ourselves or supply to others the things that Nature requires.
—Cicero, *On Duties,* Book 1, XLIV.–XLV.

Contents

Series Foreword

More than thirty years have passed since the federal government first began to address seriously the pollution problems facing the United States. Nearly all of the environmental legislation adopted in the early and mid-1970s took the form of direct command-and-control regulation and proposed bold and ambitious deadlines and national standards. The first wave of environmental policies achieved certain immediate political aims and eventually helped improve the country's environmental quality. In addition, these policies led to the establishment of institutional and governance approaches to managing the environment. Despite these achievements, business, industry, economists, and others criticized the early laws as inefficient, burdensome, and inflexible. State and local officials often joined in the chorus, particularly on concerns over flexibility, and argued that state efforts at implementation should be judged against the divergent social, political, economic, and environmental conditions that exist across the country. Moreover, critics complained that various stakeholders, including average citizens, were being excluded from the regulatory process.

As a consequence, legislation passed in the late 1970s and afterward incorporated reforms designed to make implementation more flexible. The introduction of market mechanisms represented an attempt to increase the efficiency and cost-effectiveness of environmental regulation. State and local governments were given more say on how to manage pollution problems within their specific jurisdictions. Today, rule making in the U.S. Environmental Protection Agency regularly includes various stakeholders in the process prior to the announcement of draft regulations for public comment. In addition, citizens and community stakeholders are more involved than before in the development of environmental programs, such as watershed management plans, at the local level. These and other results-based reforms continue to be discussed and debated by scholars and practitioners.

Although much progress has been made in reducing emissions and protecting natural resources, questions are being raised about whether such regulatory reforms are capable of fully resolving the pollution and natural resource problems that the United States will face in this century. Given the amount of time that has passed, we should have enough theory, data, and information to assess accurately the success of these reforms. More generally, an opportunity exists to reevaluate the country's environmental goals and to develop pragmatic governance approaches to achieve a truly sustainable society. Analyses along these lines may help to refine existing environmental governance reform theory and identify future research avenues. Rather than allow personal impressions and politics to determine future approaches to environmental governance, we need to research carefully what works and what does not work before we decide whether we should continue to implement present reforms or adopt new ways to control pollution and manage natural resources.

Environmental Governance Reconsidered: Challenges, Choices, and Opportunities pursues this line of inquiry by providing students, scholars, and policymakers with an extensive review of research on a novel combination of topics within the environmental policy arena. In particular, the book focuses on results-based environmental governance reform initiatives. Among other things, it offers insights regarding the conditions under which governance reforms are likely to succeed, the obstacles and facilitating factors concerning their implementation, the likelihood of their continued relevance and importance, and the contradictions that arise when the reforms are viewed collectively. As the editors correctly note, current understanding about the promise and performance of the reform initiatives analyzed in the various chapters relies on impressions, interpretive case studies, and "best practices" research. Thus, future investigation will be required to advance both practice and theory building. Accordingly, the contributors to this book, all experts in their fields of specialization, suggest areas in which scholars should direct their research and analysis.

Following an in-depth, critical discussion of the perspectives taken by reform-minded policy analysts, the editors identify three primary spheres that must be considered for building the results-based sense of common purpose they see as necessary for efficient, effective, equitable, and democratically accountable environmental governance. Specifically, the chapters in the book address the need to reconceptualize purpose, reconnect with stakeholders, and redefine administrative rationality. Those who read this important study will learn how successful reformers have been in advancing their results-based environmental governance agenda as well as the likelihood that their agenda and its various elements will succeed in the new century.

The analyses represented in this book illustrate well our purpose in the MIT Press series in American and Comparative Environmental Policy. We encourage work that examines a broad range of environmental policy issues. We are particularly interested in volumes that incorporate interdisciplinary research and focus on the linkages between public policy and environmental problems and issues both within the United States and in cross-national settings. We welcome contributions that analyze the policy dimensions of relationships between humans and the environment from either a theoretical or empirical perspective. At a time when environmental policies are increasingly seen as controversial and new approaches are being implemented widely, we especially encourage studies that assess policy successes and failures, evaluate new institutional arrangements and policy tools, and clarify new directions for environmental politics and policy. The books in this series are written for a wide audience that includes academics, policymakers, environmental scientists and professionals, business and labor leaders, environmental activists, and students concerned with environmental issues. We hope they contribute to public understanding of the most important environmental problems, issues, and policies that society now faces and with which it must deal.

Sheldon Kamieniecki, University of Southern California
Michael Kraft, University of Wisconsin-Green Bay
American and Comparative Environmental Policy Series editors

Preface

The internationally renowned entomologist, Edward O. Wilson, uses an old French riddle to convey to laypersons how insidious, rapid, and unforeseen the collapse of ecosystems can be. The riddle goes like this: "At first there is only one lily pad in the pond, but the next day it doubles, and thereafter each of its descendants doubles. The pond completely fills up with lily pads in 30 days. When is the pond exactly half full? Answer: on the 29th day."[1] Whether the state of the environment is as close to the insidious "29th day" of catastrophic collapse as Wilson suggests has been the grist of typically rancorous, occasionally hyperbolic, but always thought-provoking debate worldwide over the past three decades.

Also debated with considerable passion during this era has been whether traditional "first-generation" approaches to environmental governance in the twentieth century have encountered their own version of Wilson's 29th day, steeped as they are in inordinately bureaucratic, command-and-control, and technology-based regulatory approaches. Are they, for example, up to the challenge outlined by conferees at the 2003 Third World Water Forum in Kyoto, Japan? With 2003 designated the United Nations (UN) International Year of Freshwater, conferees heard that 1.2 billion persons (more than one-sixth of the world's population) lack safe, sanitary, and secure water supplies; that approximately 5 million die yearly from waterborne diseases, including 2.2 million children under the age of five years; that water demand is increasing three times as fast as the growth rate of the world's population; and that poverty is a major factor constraining our ability to meet the 2000 UN Millennium Summit's goals of connecting 300,000–400,000 persons per day to new sanitation services. At that summit, delegates from 182 nations spoke less of command-and-control regulatory solutions to these problems and more about the necessity of forming "partnerships, joining networks, and learning from the experience of others."[2]

Nor does skepticism about the capacity of first-generation approaches end with today's and tomorrow's water supply, quality, and sanitation challenges. Are first-generation approaches, for example, capable of addressing such cross-boundary regional, national, and international environmental threats as acid rain, ozone depletion, and global warming? At a more local level, are they capable of attenuating urban runoff of toxic chemicals into streams and waterways worldwide? Are they capable of handling effectively the formidable environmental challenges posed by agricultural runoff from concentrated animal food lots? Are they able adroitly to prevent and redress inequities in the distribution of environmental burdens and benefits in societies around the globe? Can they effectively help avoid or minimize the ecological and public health threats posed by the energy production on which cities, states, and nations have grown dependent to fuel economic growth? Can they help transition fossil fuel–based economies worldwide into renewable energy-based economies? Can they be crafted in ways that protect humankind without stifling innovation whenever scientific and technological advances offer both exceptional promise and potential harm to public health, safety, and the environment? Are they capable, as Wilson deems essential, of helping societies "shift to a culture of permanence, both for ourselves and for the biosphere that sustains us"?[3]

To many, including some of the most prominent architects of first-generation approaches, the answer to each of these questions is a resounding "no." Consequently, these otherwise widely regarded friends of aggressive environmental and natural resources (ENR) protection have offered independently a disparate collection of "second-generation" environmental governance reforms over the years. These reforms, they argue, are necessary for meeting existing and emerging ENR challenges, choices, and opportunities in the twenty-first century in cost-effective, equitable, and democratically deliberative ways. The predicate for their prescriptions is that future progress in advancing ENR protection depends on building a results-based sense of common purpose among diverse public, private, and nongovernmental stakeholders, a phenomenon that historically has proven the exception rather than the rule in first-generation approaches to environmental governance.

To be sure, these critics did not set out to craft a single, explicit, and integrated progressive reform agenda in environmental governance. Nor has one since emerged, at least explicitly, from their efforts. Some critics, for example, embrace market- and information-based approaches as either substitutes for or complements to command-and-control regulation. Others tout outcomes-based management as a vastly preferable alternative to procedure-based regulation. Still others take as the predicate for ENR protection the ensconcing of sustainable development or of the precautionary principle as the central animating principle of national and international governance regimes. And yet others see mediation, third-party regulation, pollution prevention, environmental justice, the balancing of property rights and responsibilities, and civic environmentalism as preconditions for efficient, effective, democratic, equitable, and results-based environmental governance in the twenty-first century.

Yet discernible from these reform initiatives are three fundamental premises for action that are steeped in broader postmodern critiques of the contemporary administrative state: (1) the need to reconceptualize what the aims and organizing principles are of environmental governance in the twenty-first century; (2) the need to reconnect in this century with citizens estranged from or disadvantaged by the environmental governance process of the twentieth century; and (3) the need to redefine administrative rationality as we have known and practiced it historically in order to accommodate the challenges, choices, and opportunities facing environmental governance in the twenty-first century.

What have all these reform initiatives wrought? Answers to this question are evolving presently, need more systematic and rigorous analysis, and are scattered in a variety of disciplinary journals, books, and electronic venues. Therefore, our aims in this volume are fourfold. First, we wish to provide a single volume where students, scholars, managers, ENR specialists, elected officials, reformers, and interested citizens can find a comprehensive, conceptually grounded, and thematically integrated assessment of the logic, promise versus performance, and likely future of these major reform initiatives. Second, we strive not only to introduce these developments to students and lay audiences, but also to provide enough substantive and analytical depth to engage and even provoke an expert audience of scholars, practitioners, and reformers. Third, we aim at presenting these materials in ways that prompt all readers to understand environmental governance as a combination of important, interrelated, and complex issues involving environmental policy, economics, democratic theory, political science, and public administration. Finally, we seek to offer students, scholars, practitioners, and reformers both a novel combination of topics and a distinctive results-based conceptualization of the field of environmental policy studies in a collection that is more integrative and more interdisciplinary than other books in this genre.

Produced in the process is a volume that we believe will meet the needs of various audiences. It pedagogically affords an uncommonly broad, thematic, and conceptual approach to the study of environmental governance for both advanced undergraduate and graduate courses in environmental policy, environmental studies, natural resources management, and public policy courses. As such, it might serve as either a central or companion text in these types of courses, conveying a sense of the logic, the experience to date, and the future salience of various reforms. This focus is especially important, we argue, as the parameters, tools, and responsibilities facing environmental governance evolve in the decades to come. Regardless of how instructors use the volume, however, students should benefit from its thematic treatment of how economics, politics, democratic theory, science and technology, and administration interact. They also will benefit from its in-depth coverage of concepts treated less thoroughly in general texts on environmental policy because of space limitations. If after closely reading this volume students feel that they have just completed an intensive seminar on environmental governance, we have met our aims for them.

In turn, scholars, practitioners, and reformers interested in ENR policy will find the book to be a compendium of the latest thinking of some of the world's leading researchers, theorists, and practitioners of environmental governance. By summarizing the latest research on the implementation of thirteen reform initiatives, the authors here collectively offer scholars and researchers timely propositional inventories suitable for testing, elaborating, and refining in future research. Among other things offered are insights regarding the conditions under which most of the reforms are more or less likely to succeed, the obstacles and facilitating factors affecting their implementation, the likelihood of their continued salience, and the paradoxes that arise when the initiatives are viewed collectively. From this volume, scholars and researchers also can garner an appreciation for how conventional understanding of environmental governance too often is unsupported by rigorous empirical analysis. In the process, of course, they should cull insights about where future research is most needed, most dependent on more systematic data collection and more rigorous methodologies, and most ripe for future conceptual and theoretical development.

Finally, practitioners, reformers, and citizens interested in environmental governance should be able to cull from this collection a sense of the practical challenges, choices, and opportunities confronting them in the twenty-first century. As noted, too much of our understanding about the promise and performance of the reform initiatives discussed in this volume relies on impressions, interpretive case studies, and so-called best-practices research. As a consequence, both practice and theory building in this important policy arena await more rigorous research in the future. Nevertheless, the insights afforded by best practices and other research chronicled here offer perspectives, propositions, and prognostications that can serve as rebuttable "hypotheses" informing the operational, tactical, and strategic actions of practitioners and reformers alike.

A volume of this scope acquires many debts during preparation. First, and foremost, we wish to thank the authors who so generously agreed to participate in our project. Their participation was all the more impressive to us after we made it clear that we would not seek a publisher until we had the entire volume completed to our satisfaction. Without their unerring commitment to quality, receptivity to editorial direction, and patience when we occasionally moved the directional goal posts before them, this volume would never have seen the light of day. For all this, we are eternally grateful to them. Our thanks go as well to the three anonymous reviewers of our manuscript and to Don Kettl of the University of Wisconsin–Madison for their perceptive comments and suggestions. Because of their insights, this volume is much better than it otherwise would have been. We also wish to thank Jennifer Durant for her technical assistance throughout the editorial process. Most of her work was done in Chiang Mai, Thailand, as drafts and revisions of the chapters traversed the Internet during Durant's Fulbright residence at Payap University. We thank her for her patience, persistence, and dedication to keeping our project on track. Likewise, we thank the American Society for Public Administration (ASPA) for showcasing a set of thematic and topical panels organized by Bob Durant at its 2001 national conference. Commemorating the twenty-fifth anniversary of ASPA's Section on Environmental and Natural Resource Administration, these themes were later refined into the topics for this book.

Last, we wish to express our gratitude to Clay Morgan, senior acquisitions editor for environmental studies at the MIT Press, for his encouragement, support, and guidance in bringing our idea to fruition. It has truly been a joy to work with him, as well as with senior editor Katherine Almeida, marketing director Vicki Lepine, and series editors Michael Kraft and Sheldon Kamieniecki. Absent Clay's faith in us, however, this project might still be experiencing the literary equivalent of Wilson's 29th day!

Robert F. Durant, American University
Daniel J. Fiorino, U.S. Environmental Protection Agency
Rosemary O'Leary, Syracuse University

Notes

1. As cited in James Carroll, "The 29th Day for America," *Boston Globe,* January 14, 2003, www.boston.com/dailyglobe2/014/oped/, accessed January 14, 2003.

2. "100 New Commitments Pour in as Water Forum Closes," *Environment News Service,* March 23, 2003, www.ens-news.om/ens/mar2003/2003-03-24-04.asp, accessed March 24, 2003.

3. Edward O. Wilson, *The Future of Life* (New York: Vintage, 2002), p. 22.

Environmental Governance Reconsidered

Introduction

Robert F. Durant, Rosemary O'Leary, and Daniel J. Fiorino

"Queen Victoria's passing," H. G. Wells observed, "removed a great paperweight that had sat on men's minds for generations."[1] Little more than a generation has passed since the advent in the United States of the "environmental decade" of the 1970s. During that time, societies worldwide have sought to advance their legitimate interests in reducing environmental and natural resources (ENR) risks; in ensuring that citizens' rights are protected equitably from these risks; and in allocating roles, responsibilities, and resources more rationally to afford the greatest protection to all. Yet already many nations are pursuing major changes in the paradigmatic "paperweight" of the so-called first generation of regulation that "sat on the minds" of elected officials, regulators, and citizens as they pursued these ends. That paradigm was heavily bureaucratic, prescriptive, fragmented in purpose, and adversarial in nature. It offered a reactive command-and-control regulatory regime for environmental governance that focused on single-pollutant, single-medium, single-pathway, technology-driven solutions to ENR problems.[2]

Calls for a second generation of environmental governance approaches come not just from traditional critics or outright opponents of the present regime. Critics in that traditionalist genre offer a by now familiar, disparate, and sometimes contradictory agenda for regulatory reform. End it, "marketize" it, or rely on tort and nuisance law in its stead, argue critics on the political right; "mend it but don't end it," cry reformers from the political center; ratchet it up radically, "democraticize" it, and demythologize its market virtues, advise populist critics on the left; or change the metanarrative of modernism to one of postmodernism, contend various reformers at the communitarian, antistatist, or anticorporatist fringes where the extreme right and left meet.

But what is now most intriguing, and perhaps most significant politically given their stature in ENR and government circles, is that many of the architects of first-generation approaches to environmental governance are calling increasingly for major reforms of the regime they helped create. Sometimes, as the chapters in this volume illustrate, they share some of the traditional concerns of critics and opponents on the political right, center, and left. But unlike these critics, they base their concerns less on any perceived failure of the earlier paradigm they helped build. That system's achievements, after all, are not insignificant. In the United States, for example, air quality has improved significantly in almost every major city since 1970. Modest improvements also have occurred in aggregate measures or national averages of water quality, with major progress made in various locales. Moreover, although 8 billion pounds of toxic chemicals were released into the environment in 1999, a 46 percent decrease in these releases has taken place since 1986.

Rather, the concerns of many of the doyens present "at the creation" of first-generation approaches are premised more on a widely shared belief that the environmental problems remaining cannot be addressed efficiently, effectively, equitably, and accountably by the governance regimes that they helped design and implement. Nor do they see purely market-based, government-based, *or* community-based solutions as up to the task of addressing today's and tomorrow's environmental governance challenges. Theirs is a sometimes inchoate, always evolving, and decidedly pragmatic "third-way" approach to environmental governance, one that focuses on building a *results-based* (or outcomes-based) sense of common purpose as an antidote to the shortcomings of conventional bureaucratic, command-and-control, procedure-based, and adversarial approaches to ENR protection.[3] It is an approach that sees important complementary and synergistic roles in building a results-based sense of common purpose for markets *and* mandates, for experts *and* laypersons, for science *and* popular sentiments, for bureaucrats *and* communities, and for tradition *and* learning.

Applying this "third-way" synthesis, proponents argue that accountability for results, rather than accountability for compliance with rules and regulations, is a much more rational approach to environmental governance. Compliance accountability inhibits flexibility, causes risk aversion among regulators and polluters, and diminishes innovation. Moreover, results-focused performance measurement is a more rational conversation for policymakers to have than conversations about inputs and outputs untethered to work processes and the environmental outcomes these processes produce. Goal displacement can be averted, employees can become more inspired when focused on goals, and the public can become more attentive, informed, and involved in agency decision making. In the process, priority setting can be enhanced, resources can be shifted to more pressing needs, and political support for agency performance and good-faith effort can be garnered.

Make no mistake, however. The "third way" that these actors envision is grounded firmly in the realpolitik of environmental governance, not in gauzy notions of actors suddenly eschewing self-interest for the public good. As such, none see an easy or swift transition from "rule-based" (that is, compliance with rules and regulations) to "ruler-based" (that is, results-based) environmental governance.[4] Neither, however, do these reformers deny the power of normative values, premises, and ideals (such as the public good) to shape actors' perceptions of their self-interest. Consequently, they base their argument on a variety of interrelated factors that boil down to four analytically distinct, pragmatic, and normatively informed rationales for reform.

First, and on very pragmatic grounds, these critics see first-generation approaches as decidedly inappropriate for addressing ENR problems caused by small, diverse, and numerous nonpoint sources of pollution, including greenhouse gas emissions, toxic pollution runoff from urban and rural nonpoint sources, and emissions of ozone-depleting chemicals. When used to attack these types of problems, first-generation approaches can be impractical, inefficient, and unsustainable politically. They also can be problematic because they fail to recognize that many ENR risks are inherently multimedia, interactive, multiple pathway, and cumulative in nature. To treat them otherwise, critics argue, is to encourage media shifting of problems (that is, avoiding certain regulatory requirements or responsibilities in one medium by shifting waste streams to other media), costly administrative burdens, and citizens' skepticism. Moreover, as Martijn van Vliet describes the dilemma, the limits of central regulatory capacity uninformed by a results-based sense of common purpose are evident whenever flexibility and adaptability to a myriad of local circumstances, diverse regulatory targets, interdependent actors, and evolving knowledge bases are needed.[5]

Second, these reformers argue that first-generation approaches discourage behaviors deemed critical for addressing ENR problems more cooperatively, holistically, and cost-effectively in the long run. Most notable among these behaviors, they claim, are innovation, process redesign, information-based and collaborative decision making, and pollution prevention strategies.[6] Moreover, even when first-generation approaches *are* applicable (for example, when single-point-source polluters are involved), diminishing marginal returns on technological investments (for example, scrubbers on smokestacks) make building on earlier ENR successes decidedly cost-ineffective. These critics argue that collaborative partnerships imbued with a results-based sense of common purpose among the government, the private sector, and civil society make eminently more sense, especially whenever "no one is capable of enforcing coordination against the will of other actors."[7]

Third, and linked to more general postmodern critiques of bureaucracy, these critics argue that first-generation approaches to environmental governance grounded in conventional bureaucratic rationality too often produce results grounded in adversarial rather than deliberative processes. These processes, in turn, preclude the kind of critical social learning needed in an era of discontinuities, jumps, and uncertainties.[8] These reformers recognize that the sources of this dilemma are as attributable to the political environments in which agencies operate as they are to the bureaucratic cultures of ENR agencies and their staffs. Those environments, for example, often bequeath funding and staffing to ENR agencies that are incommensurate with these agencies' spiraling and complex responsibilities. Likewise, legislative gridlock can stymie both modest statutory authorization renewals and more ambitious legislation to overcome the organizational and single-media regulatory fragmentation that makes systemic learning difficult. Equally responsible for making social learning so difficult are weak, ambiguous, sometimes contradictory, and even hostile executive and legislative "signals" from Capitol Hill, chief executives, political appointees, and state legislatures. And were all this not dysfunctional enough to prevent social learning, the existence of potent, often well-healed, and litigious stakeholders flush with success in the courts encourages reactive, defensive, and adversarial behavior within ENR agencies themselves. Compromised in the process are proactive, holistic, and results-based thinking, activities, and resource reallocation within them.

Precisely because this realpolitik interacts with a protean, complex, and dynamic transformation underway worldwide in the nature of ENR problems, these critics find conventional administrative rationality inadequate to the task of advancing social learning.[9] This transformation is characterized by rapid changes that are global in implication, that make it impossible for any single institution or set of actors to control events, and that make results-oriented knowledge reflexive and contingent (that is, subject to change and reinterpretation in light of new and constantly evolving information). Under these circumstances, critics aver, conventional approaches to environmental governance that stress prescription, centralization of authority, technocratic fixes, and inflexible rules, regulations, and procedures are decidedly unsuited to effective ENR protection. As political scientist Hugh Heclo argues, policymaking under these conditions is characterized best as "collective puzzlement on society's behalf."[10]

Finally, and more normatively, these critics of conventional approaches to environmental governance argue that the administrative rationality animating them imposes burdens disproportionately on the disadvantaged in society, foils deliberative democracy, and diminishes the building of civic capital in all countries. One-way flows of expertise from government agencies to regulatory targets and citizens are seen as too hamhanded to produce positive ENR outcomes in the face of the complexity, dynamism, and diversity of ENR problems. By design or accident, they also foment or perpetuate inequalities in the ENR risks assumed by low-income communities, persons of color, and developing nations. They also foster adversarial and judicialized debates over ENR issues and marginalize citizens' participation in environmental governance. For these reasons, reformers focus on promoting the use of so-called sociopolitical governance models[11] and alternative communicative models of deliberative democracy.

Both a common premise and a common challenge link each of these rationales for change. As noted, each rationale sees the building of a results-based sense of common purpose among a miscellany of disparate interests as critical for efficient, effective, equitable, democratic, and accountable environmental governance in the twenty-first century. And each recognizes the Herculean task that reformers face in challenging a highly bureaucratized, inflexible, and hyperfragmented ENR governance regime that in the twentieth century fostered precisely the opposite tendencies. Undaunted, however, these friends of aggressive ENR protection individually, collectively, and sometimes collaboratively with traditional critics have pressed ahead over the past thirty years with a variety of results-oriented reforms that directly challenge the status quo.

Some of these reforms afford normative premises for trying to bridge differences among stakeholders in environmental governance (for example, promoting environmental justice, deliberative democracy, sustainable development, the precautionary principle, and the diminution of tragedies of the commons). Others offer specific tools for overcoming otherwise perverse legal, policy, and organizational obstacles to results-based collaboration (for example, integrating single-media statutes, civic environmentalism, alternative dispute resolution, and outcomes-based performance measures). Other initiatives offer ways to build broader support for ENR protection in the business community (for example, offering greater flexibility and certification standards for environmental management systems [EMSs]). Still others are more defensive in nature and geared toward preventing the erosion of mainstream public support for ENR protection in the face of ongoing assaults from various foes. Most significant among this group are those from the conservative right (for example, the property rights movement in the United States); from nations using the precautionary principle as a nontariff barrier to trade to protect their markets (integrated risk assessment and risk management techniques); and from anticorporatist and antiscientific elements on the left who assail and try to stymie research (for example, biotechnology) that may or may not prove beneficial to the environment in the twenty-first century.

Conceptually, however, these diverse reforms embody three primary emphases. Reformers perceive these emphases as critical for building the results-based sense of common purpose they consider essential for efficient, effective, equitable, and democratically accountable environmental governance in the twenty-first century:

1. *reconceptualizing purpose* to reflect more accurately the existing ecological, safety, and public-health risks and interdependencies at the international, national, and subnational levels of government;

2. *reconnecting with stakeholders* in the development, implementation, and assessment of any policies pursued; and

3. *redefining administrative rationality* in environmental governance.

How successful have reformers been in advancing the components of this results-based environmental governance agenda so far, and how likely are this agenda and its components to endure in the twenty-first century? Legal challenges to operationalizing various aspects of the agenda not only have been formidable, but often have produced ambiguous, contradictory, and confusing decisions. In addition, political, social, economic, organizational, and technoscientific obstacles have constrained changes substantially. Nor has it helped that regulators, environmental groups, property owners, and business interests also frequently remain skeptical. Indeed, so contentious have debates over elements of this agenda become and so formidable has resistance to them proven to be that they have not yet displaced traditional first-generation regulatory regimes. Rather, they have been grafted for flexibility on otherwise inflexible elements of existing regimes. Left as a result is a rather halting, halfway, and patchworked environmental governance regime that combines aspects of both the old and the new regimes. Moreover, this grafting occurs in ways that satisfy no one and that bequeath additional strategic challenges, choices, and opportunities to ENR reformers and policymakers worldwide in the twenty-first century.

All this, however, raises another important set of questions for policymakers and researchers grappling with the future of results-based environmental governance in the United States and abroad. First, *should* this agenda and the various reforms associated with it prosper and endure? After all, it is conceivable that the logic of the causal theories underlying these three overriding aims (reconceptualizing purpose, reconnecting with citizens, and redefining administrative rationality) and of those theories informing the various reform initiatives associated with them is flawed. They may produce conflict rather than comity. Some reforms, after all, can morph readily in stakeholders' minds into highly conflictual zero-sum redistributive choices for societies (for example, sustainable development or the precautionary principle). Even more fundamentally, they may be inherently myopic, naive, or nonimplementable. Or they may create perverse incentives for regulators or regulatory targets and thus have unintended consequences that retard rather than advance ENR protection. They even may be contradictory when considered collectively and thus work at cross-purposes. Second, is it possible that these reforms are more or less likely to be effective under differing circumstances, with different strategies, and in conjunction with other tactics? Finally, and taking these possibilities and contingencies into account, what strategic challenges, choices, and opportunities face proponents of various aspects of this results-based ENR reform agenda as they try to advance their aims in the twenty-first century?

The answers to these environmental governance questions are still evolving, disputed, and ripe for consideration as the twenty-first century dawns. Thus, each of the authors contributing to this volume agreed to join us in taking stock of and pondering the future of thirteen major reforms that have animated recent results-driven agendas and for which their expertise is internationally recognized. These topics include results-based reforms that promote the principles of sustainability, global interdependence, the precautionary principle, and common-pool resource theory; results-based decision making that promotes deliberative democracy, civic environmentalism, environmental justice, and property rights; and results-based administrative reforms that promote environmental conflict resolution, devolution, flexibility, pollution prevention, and third-party EMS auditing. These thirteen reforms by no means cover all the initiatives animating contemporary debates over results-based environmental governance. Nonetheless, most reformers view them as central to advancing or threatening efficient, effective, equitable, and accountable environmental governance in the twenty-first century. Moreover, any effort to analyze them systematically inevitably means addressing other contemporary issues in the process.

Each of the chapters in this volume addresses three primary questions. First, what is the logic of this reform proposal, and how inherently promising or complicating is it for building a results-based sense of common purpose? Second, what do the research literature, participant observation, and expert evaluation tell us about the promise, performance, and durability of this reform proposal to date? Finally, how enduring is this reform proposal likely to be, and what are the strategic challenges, choices, and opportunities facing reformers as they try to use it to build a results-based sense of common purpose in the future? Before turning to our authors for answers to these questions, however, it is important for readers to understand broadly the substance, logic, and relationships of each of the reforms discussed. They should also come to appreciate how each reform relates to the three pillars of overall environmental governance reform that are the linchpins of building a results-based sense of common purpose: reconceptualizing purpose, reconnecting with citizens, and redefining administrative rationality.

Reconceptualizing Purpose

Reformers' emphasis on reconceptualizing purpose rests in part on the idea that many pressing ENR problems emerge or have impacts on a regional or global scale that transcend the authority of traditional nation-states to solve individually. Problems such as ozone depletion, deforestation of old-growth forests, global climate change, depletion of fish stocks, marine protection, and the spread of long-dormant and dangerous diseases such as malaria and dengue fever require regional or international cooperation to resolve. As a consequence of this *global interdependence,* reformers argue that one major imperative for building a results-based sense of common purpose in environmental governance is creating international and national regimes that can deal adequately with these types of problems.

As Lynton Caldwell argues, however, progress in making the planet, rather than individual nation-states, "a center of rational loyalty for all [humanity]" has proven to be a difficult shift in value orientation.[12] Debates, after all, continue to rage over humanity's contributions to and the ultimate location and impact of wicked problems such as global warming and ozone depletion. Moreover, these debates make nation-states and their citizens nervous about abandoning too much of their sovereignty to international bodies, especially when the negative effects of these events on their citizens might be small or not occur at all and when the immediate financial costs to them seem consequential.

Although sometimes heated debate continues over the magnitude of humanity's contribution to a variety of global ecological ills, it is nonetheless difficult to dismiss the conclusion that human activities are having an unprecedented negative impact on the Earth on a global scale. As zoologist Jane Lubchenco, president of the International Council for Science, summarized in a presentation at Columbia University's Earth Institute in 2002, six major and accelerating anthropogenic impacts are cause for great scientific concern.[13] First, ecological systems on which societies worldwide depend (for example, clean air and water) are being damaged as a result of large-scale transformations of the Earth's landscapes. Second, carbon emissions from human activities (for example, from power plants and automobiles) are contributing to global warming. Third, because of agricultural runoff from factory farms, the amount of fixed nitrogen has doubled since 1992, leaving (among other things) approximately 50 "dead zones" of algae blooms that have stifled other life forms. Fourth, humanity's consumption of water is now approaching 50 percent of available supplies, with agriculture accounting for nearly 70 percent of consumption. Fifth, anthropogenic habitat degradation (for example, from logging, farming, and dam building) and overpopulation are resulting in a loss of biodiversity, with some analysts claiming that we are entering the "sixth mass extinction" event.[14] Finally, two-thirds of the world's fisheries are categorized now as depleted, overexploited, or fully exploited.

Yet even if one concedes the reality of these transnational threats and nations create a variety of international regimes to address them, reformers argue that building a results-based sense of common purpose also requires a fundamental reconceptualization of the values that traditionally have animated nations' behaviors. Two of the most prominent values that reformers offer in this regard are *sustainability* and the *precautionary principle*. In terms of the former, a growing consensus exists that decisions made today in regard to such things as energy development, economic development, and ENR protection can either narrow or expand the range of global opportunities and constraints that humanity will face in the future. As a consequence, reformers decry historical tendencies toward unbridled economic development as dangerous in the face of finite and fragile natural resources (air, water, and land, in particular). Thus, a new central animating principle must take its place: the promotion of economic development in environmentally sustainable ways.

Likewise, those touting the precautionary principle seek to reconceptualize the definition of *precaution* itself. Indeed, their regulatory approach to risk turns traditional regulatory approaches on their heads. Traditional approaches assume the safety of activities and products for commercial use unless they are proved scientifically to be harmful. But the precautionary principle shifts the burden of proof away from opponents to prove harm and toward proponents and regulators to prove safety. The rationale is straightforward, albeit controversial in many quarters: "In situations where there are threats of serious or irreversible damage, lack of full scientific certainty should not be used as reason for postponing measures to prevent environmental degradation."[15]

Finally, reconceptualizing ENR regime values also means to some that animating principles such as Garrett Hardin's "tragedy of the commons" need to be rethought. Over the past fifteen years, scholars and practitioners have concluded that the "tragedy of the commons" is no longer the only model that accurately accounts for human use of common-pool resources. For Hardin, the users of common-pool resources typically engage in an individually rational, but collectively irrational "race to the bottom" that prematurely depletes resources and leaves everyone worse off. Yet a major body of empirically grounded research (done largely in the developing world) pursued under the rubric of *common-pool resource theory* now finds that self-organizing and self-governing institutions can emerge that successfully husband the resources in question to the collective benefit of all (for example, land, irrigation, and fishery communities). Knowing the conditions under which these institutions can arise to promote sustainability, some reformers argue, will allow policymakers to further the building of a results-based sense of common purpose in environmental governance.

Reconnecting with ENR Stakeholders

Reformers' emphasis on reconnecting with stakeholders, in turn, is premised on the idea that effective environmental governance depends on valuing, promoting, nurturing, and extending *deliberative democracy* to the greatest extent possible in ENR policy formulation, implementation, and evaluation. This idea permeates, for example, the Local Agenda 21 initiatives underway in 2,000 municipalities in fifty countries. These initiatives are designed to implement sustainable development actions agreed to by the United Nations (UN) Conference on Environment and Development. Deliberative democracy also informs results-based ENR initiatives in the United States, including the Environmental Protection Agency's (EPA) Community-Based Environmental Protection program.

No longer deemed adequate, possible, or in anyone's interests are proxy models of stakeholder participation. Thus, in contrast to supporting deliberative mechanisms wherein stakeholder views and interests are articulated by others within adversarial settings, reformers want stakeholders involved early, persistently, and directly in deliberations about ENR ends and means. At the same time, some nongovernmental organizations (NGOs), in effect, are trying to buy their way into deliberations within corporate boardrooms or taking decisions about development out of company hands by purchasing lands themselves. Friends of the Earth, for instance, is among several worldwide NGOs that have bought shares in companies in the hope of changing the latter's destructive ENR practices.[16]

To appreciate the magnitude of these results-oriented deliberative approaches, one needs only to contrast them with those approaches historically informing what Michael Sandel terms the "procedural republic."[17] In the procedural republic, the legal, technical, and administrative complexity of ENR issues in the United States historically relegated citizens and other stakeholders to the periphery of agency and corporate deliberations. Advantaged inordinately in the process were large business and environmental groups that had the resources to hire legal, scientific, and administrative expertise to navigate the procedural labyrinths of regulatory agencies.

In contrast, proponents of deliberative democracy seek to promote early, informed, and substantively meaningful group-based stakeholder participation in agency decision making as a means for building common purpose. Vehicles for advancing these ends include regulatory negotiations, effective risk communication, and cooperative rangeland management agreements for critical-habitat preservation. Regardless of the approach taken, however, reconnecting with citizens presumes that any disagreements or conflicts that do develop are handled best by reasoned or probative rather than affective or prejudicial forms of argument.[18] What is more, "win-win" rather than "winner-take-all" outcomes are seen as most profitable.

The challenge of reconnecting with stakeholders also is premised on the idea that both deliberative democracy and effective ENR management can be advanced profitably by pursuing collaborative public, private, and NGO partnerships. To an extent, of course, de facto "partnerships" with regulators at other levels of government, with and among industries, and with NGOs always have existed. Many federal ENR statutes in the United States, for example, rely on the states for various aspects of implementation (for example, the Clean Air Act, the Federal Water Pollution Control Act, the Federal Land Policy and Management Act, and the Resource Conservation and Recovery Act). Governments laggard in identifying ENR problems also have been forced to respond to problems identified by angry members of local communities or by national and international NGOs. Moreover, limited funds for enforcement have always meant that even aggressive governments must rely on the private sector for ENR data collection to identify emerging or emergent problems. Consider, for example, the role that private industries play in collecting data for the Toxics Release Inventory (TRI) in the United States or in setting the "stump rate" for Douglas firs and other softwood harvesting in British Columbia's coastal temperate rain forest.[19]

Reconnecting with citizens, however, envisions a decidedly more proactive, explicit, and cooperative rather than prescriptive partnership strategy for building a results-based sense of common purpose in environmental governance. Proponents realize, for instance, that ENR protection requires adopting more environmentally benign policies in a variety of federal agencies (for example, in the U.S. Departments of

Agriculture, Energy, Transportation, and Housing and Urban Development). Consequently, they see cooperative and results-based ENR agreements across these agencies as crucial, along with revitalizing the National Environmental Policy Act in order to integrate ENR concerns into these organizations better.

Likewise, although the "partnering" relationship between federal and state ENR agencies typically has been strained if not contentious because of the federal government's tendency to limit state discretion and to impose top-down mandates on state regulators, proponents of reconnecting with citizens envision more discretion for the states in meeting ENR goals. In exchange, states must negotiate performance goals with federal regulators and agree to be held accountable for meeting them, as in the U.S. EPA's Performance Partnership Agreements. Programs such as the Clinton administration's Partnership for the Next Generation of Vehicles (PNGV) envisioned the partnering of government and business. Besides the PNGV, which partnered government with the U.S. auto industry to develop alternative-fuel vehicles and alternative-transportation vehicles, these partnerships also include Great Britain's "Carbon Trust" program, which subsidizes business investments in low-carbon technologies for reducing greenhouse gases.[20]

Alternatively, de facto partnerships with business or among the states also play a role in reconnecting with citizens. These types of partnerships take a variety of forms. In some, a subset of state governments joins together to set stricter standards than national requirements impose in order to force industry to invest sooner in antipollution technologies or to build cleaner products. Comprising two-thirds of the existing market for diesel truck and bus engines, for example, thirteen states began the new millennium by agreeing to adopt strict California regulations to force manufacturers to use more stringent antipollution testing procedures on new vehicles. This agreement forced compliance two years sooner than a 1998 court consent decree required.[21]

In other forms of de facto partnerships, government effectively becomes a "market" for products that otherwise would be unprofitable for business to provide until larger markets develop. Initiatives conceived for these purposes in the United States include the 1992 Energy Policy Act quotas for government agencies to purchase alternative-fuel vehicles and

President Clinton's EO 13101 requiring the purchase of recycled paper and biologically based products ("Greening the Government through Leadership in Environmental Management"). Illustrative abroad is the effort by China's State Environmental Protection Administration to stimulate a mature market for businesses producing environmental protection products. Officials hope to use the Chinese government's 100 billion yuan investment in greening their state enterprises to leverage an additional 700 billion yuan investment by private corporations.[22]

In yet another form of de facto partnering, governments work on a bilateral basis with each other and with other stakeholders to develop areas of environmental cooperation ripe with business opportunities. Part and parcel of the "ecological modernization" movement in Europe and of "green capitalism" in the United States, such cooperation can have impressive results in opening up markets long closed to foreigners, in improving the environment, and in enhancing trade opportunities.[23] Germany and China, for example, held a forum in Nanjing in 2000 that was attended by more than 1,000 delegates, including government officials, industry representatives, research institutes, and NGOs.[24] Ultimately, China decided to take advantage of the advanced technology and environmental expertise that German businesses can offer in a variety of areas, including energy efficiency, sustainable energy development, urban environmental infrastructure, and air and solid waste pollution.

Finally, successful results-based environmental governance means more than government agencies or private organizations simply or grudgingly "reconnecting" with a disparate set of well-organized, disgruntled, and litigious stakeholders. Rather, it involves inspiring, arranging, coordinating, and monitoring community-based partnerships of public, private, and nongovernmental stakeholders who mutually define problems and coproduce consensus-based solutions with ENR agencies. The EPA and the National Park Service, for example, initiated the Colorado Plateau Ecosystem Partnership Project to help reconcile environmental values with prodevelopment uses (namely, ranching, mining, and oil and gas development).[25] Members of the partnership include representatives of other federal agencies, state governments, Native American tribes, universities, councils of government, and private businesses in western Colorado, southeastern and southern Utah, northern Arizona, and northwestern New Mexico.

Viewed worldwide as ways both to leverage scarce resources and to avoid litigation, ENR partnerships within, between, and among public, private, and nonprofit actors are increasing dramatically in number around the world.[26] Among them are results-oriented partnerships to reduce perfluorocompound emissions from the semiconductor industry,[27] to preserve local open space, to protect regional watersheds and ecosystems, to preserve the world's coral reefs,[28] and to promote "sustainable communities" in the United States.[29] Still other international cross-sectoral networks work toward increasing the transparency of business operations to the scrutiny of outsiders. The Coalition for Environmentally Responsible Economies (CERES), for instance, is a network of NGO environmentalists, investors, companies, and multinational corporations that has developed a standardized Corporate Environmental Responsibility reporting system so that progress and comparisons across businesses can be made. The Global Forest and Trade Network now operates worldwide and enrolls nearly 1,000 members in places as diverse as Australia, Belgium, Brazil, France, Germany, Great Britain, Hong Kong, Japan, the Netherlands, the Nordic countries, North America, and Spain.

Part and parcel of reconnecting with stakeholders in the United States in the hope of building a results-based sense of common purpose is yet another new governance idea that focuses more on communities: *civic environmentalism.*[30] Proffered less as a substitute for traditional regulatory approaches than as an important complement to them, civic environmentalism cuts traditional regulatory assumptions to the quick. First, proponents argue that states, communities, and neighborhoods are vitally interested in addressing any ENR problems that exist within their borders. Hence, they require decidedly less federal or even state prompting to act than typically is assumed to get desirable outcomes-based ENR results. Second, proponents argue that although top-down, federally driven regulation may be adequate and appropriate when pollution sources are readily identifiable, exhibit relatively uniform behavior, and are few in number, they are decidedly less effective and appropriate when the opposite conditions prevail. In these instances, nonregulatory approaches such as economic incentives, technical assistance, and public education are likely to be more appropriate and effective in coaxing better behavior from polluters. Finally, proponents contend that when these tools are used appropriately, a multisided bargaining process among stakeholders is likely to occur, one characterized more by collaboration than by confrontation.

The challenge of reconnecting with stakeholders is also premised on the idea that efficient, effective, equitable, and accountable environmental governance depends on more than technical, scientific, and economic rationality. Political, legal, and organizational sensitivity to advancing *environmental justice* must also be exhibited. ENR regimes specifically must address (if not redress) any inequalities in benefits and burdens that their decisions impose on different tribal, racial, ethnic, and economic groups. Nor is environmental justice deemed sufficiently advanced if equitable treatment prevails only within generations and only for historically disadvantaged or discriminated against groups. To realize environmental justice, ideas regarding intergenerational equity and *property rights involving regulatory takings* also must inform results-based ENR deliberations.

Good ENR stewardship, as such, means protecting public health and ecosystems in ways cognizant of the effects that today's economic, energy, *and* ENR decisions will have on the economic, physical, and ecological health and well-being of future generations. Yet good husbandry of the planet's ENR heritage also means balancing prudent regulation with an appropriate respect for the property rights of individuals currently living. Property owners have the right to develop the resources they own for profit and enjoyment. Yet they also must understand that part of the value of their properties often comes from public investments and that government has an interest in promoting development that ensures public health, safety, and environmental protection. As a consequence, owners must respect the government's duty to place limits on economic development and other land uses that diminish the collective well-being of present and future generations.

A final component of reconnecting with citizens in environmental governance, *environmental-conflict resolution* (ECR), is premised on the wisdom of diffusing conflict before it gets to court or sparks political backlashes such as the environmental justice and property rights movements. Unlike traditional litigation, in which a judge or jury makes a final determination or issues a judgment, ECR techniques use various forms of assisted negotiation to help the parties reach a mutually satisfactory agreement on their own terms. Legislation such as the Administrative Dispute Resolution Acts of 1990 and 1996 and the Negotiated Rule-making Acts of 1990 and 1996, as well as the growing awareness and acceptance of the potential benefits of ECR in resolving conflicts, have enabled different forms of this conflict resolution tool to become more regular and official parts of results-based environmental policymaking.

Redefining Administrative Rationality

A final emphasis for reformers in pursuing a results-based sense of common purpose in environmental governance is the need to redefine conventional notions of administrative rationality in the public, private, and nonprofit sectors. Central to this enterprise is persuading stakeholders that regula-tory rigidity is irrational administratively (less efficient and effective), politically (less likely to build support and more likely to invite attack), and environmentally (less likely to solve public problems). Eminently more rational amid the thrust to create risk-based, stakeholder-sensitive, and geographically focused ENR regulatory regimes, for example, is the idea of *devolution* of federal responsibilities to states and localities.

Of course, the idea of shifting responsibilities to subnational govern-ments was part of the downsizing, defunding, devolution, and deregulatory agenda animating governments worldwide by the end of the twentieth century. It also was a political strategy in many countries. In the United States, for instance, the Clinton administration pursued devolution as a means not only for reinventing government, but also for counteracting a full-bore assault on ENR programs after the Democratic Party lost its congressional majority in the 1994 elections. Yet devolution was also a practical recognition of the bureaucratic dysfunctions, intergovernmental conflicts, and functional labyrinths spawned over the decades by central-ization of responsibilities in Washington. Remote bureaucracies trying to implement first-generation regulatory regimes were also increasingly seen in many other countries as distinctly unsuitable to ENR challenges. They often lacked the resource capacity, acumen, and cultural tem-perament to address ENR problems that required tailoring to local circumstances, innovation, trade-offs among harms, and collaboration.

Devolution of responsibilities need not be an all-or-nothing proposition, nor need it involve only federal delegations of responsibility and authority to the states. Promoted as well is "differential oversight" (also known as "accountable devolution") of state activities. In this approach, the amount of responsibility and oversight accorded states varies across them based on their prior commitment to aggressive ENR regulation (for example, in terms of budgetary, personnel, and enforcement efforts). Likewise, differential oversight predicated on "good citizenship" is envisioned for businesses and other regulated entities, including other public agencies (for example, military bases or municipal wastewater treatment facilities). Those exhibiting behaviors related to advancing ENR protection receive more discretion in meeting overall standards. Behaviors in this category include evidence of a reduction in per capita waste generation rates, improved compliance rates, and higher rates of participation in and public reporting about voluntary pollution prevention programs.

Devolution of responsibilities without *flexibility*, however, is both a hoax and a hindrance to effective environmental governance.[31] As noted earlier, societies faced with problems of uncertain origins, ill-understood causes and remedies, cross-media impacts, and diverse and widely dispersed regulatory targets need to learn what to prefer and must grope their ways toward solutions. Reformers thus typically view flexibility as a central component of redefining administrative rationality. Perhaps the most renowned tools reformers offer for advancing flexibility are market and quasi-market incentives, although these incentives actually can decrease flexibility once markets have been established. Included among these types of market and quasi-market flexibility mechanisms are: pollution taxes; "cap and trade" emissions markets; land-oriented tradable permits (for example, wetlands mitigation banking and tradable development rights); reform of subsidies that encourage environmental degradation; promotion of subsidies that encourage ENR protection (for example, the U.S. Forestry Incentives Program, the U.S. Wildlife Habitat Incentive Program, and subsidies that encourage automakers to build alternative-fuel vehicles and gas-electric hybrids[32]); halon banks to avoid the production of virgin supplies;[33] voluntary systems of extended product liability by manufacturers throughout the entire lifecycle of products;

and free-market environmentalism proposals to advance ENR protection by creating property rights for individuals and groups.[34]

Another regulatory approach steeped in the idea of flexibility incorporates information-based strategies such as TRI reporting and integration of "environmental accounts" into national economic accounts (for example, the gross domestic product). Overall ENR policy goals are set, and progress toward them is reported publicly. Yet the means for attaining these results are left up to the regulated community to decide. Still other flexibility mechanisms include recognition (for example, the U.S. EPA's 33/50 Program), environmental dispute resolution, "naming and shaming" (for example, the European Commission's publication of a list of thirty-seven cities dumping raw sewage directly into rivers that flow into the North, Baltic, and Adriatic Seas), and ecological labeling (for example, the U.S. EPA's "green lights," Germany's "green dot," and France's "green disk" programs). To these, one also might add "private-sector stewardship" to the mix of voluntary information-sharing prescriptions. These prescriptions include such initiatives as the development of extensive networks of private organizations sharing ENR best practices[35] and private-sector partnerships such as those explored by Toyota Motor Company and Ford Motor Company to develop environmentally friendly cars (for example, gas-electric hybrids).[36]

A third results-based idea informing the challenge of redefining administrative rationality in environmental governance is that regulators and regulatees should eschew downstream end-of-pipe pollution control strategies in favor of upstream *pollution prevention* strategies. To the business community, proponents argue that pollution is, by definition, irrational: waste and inefficiency have bottom-line impacts on productivity and profits. To public agencies, proponents argue that end-of-pipe regulation is administratively irrational: having polluters prevent pollution before it happens by altering production processes is a more cost-effective approach to monitoring polluters' behavior. Among many other plans incorporating this notion internationally is an initiative by the UN Development Program to cut greenhouse-gas emissions by improving energy efficiency in buildings in West Africa. An integral part-and-parcel of these strategies is the ecological modernization movement: nations invest in more efficient and pollution-reducing technological advances.

Finally, redefining administrative rationality also incorporates the idea of using *third-party auditors* to hold EMSs accountable to green codes or self-certification standards set by industries and by national or international bodies. Included among these "regulation by revelation"[37] initiatives worldwide are certification programs such as those offered by the International Organization of Standardization (ISO 14000), the European Union's Habitats Directive, the Forest Sustainability Convention, the principles of CERES, and the World Commission on Dams (WCD).[38] Also included are purely voluntary domestic standardization efforts such as the U.S. EPA's Code of Environmental Management Principles. Each of these initiatives offers the promise of regulating on the basis of sound environmental and ecological judgments rather than administrative convenience. Moreover, by offering transregional or transnational standards, certification programs are designed to avoid the stymieing of regional or global trade by inflexible, multiple, and disparate national standards.[39]

Whither the Building of Common Purpose in the Twenty-First Century?

Perceptions of the need for building a results-based sense of common purpose through reconceptualizing regime values, reconnecting with stakeholders, and redefining administrative rationality have been resilient and roundly debated in recent years. The future of the elements of this reform agenda is thus anything but clear. In most countries, as Daniel Fiorino has noted elsewhere, the best that reformers have been able to accomplish to date is to graft various reforms onto "parts of [an] inflexible whole."[40] Moreover, as David Rosenbloom and Bernard Ross point out more generally, the dominant administrative theories of any era ultimately rest less on their logic, internal coherence, and empirical validity than they do on politics.[41]

Given the political, social, economic, and environmental uncertainties and stakes involved in the reforms discussed in this book, can anything less be expected? Certainly, proponents of the three pillars of environmental governance hope that they will last and argue vigorously that they should. Proponents of reform, to be sure, might disagree with or be agnostic about the effectiveness of any of the specific reform initiatives the authors discuss here. Yet all see the building of a results-based sense of common purpose as essential for realizing proactive, progressive, equitable, democratically informed, and cost-effective results-based environmental governance.

The chapters in this book will aid readers in drawing their own conclusions about how enduring the individual elements informing or complicating this results-based agenda will be *or* should be in the years ahead. Have we tried too long, as a frustrated and impatient Abraham Lincoln observed before relieving General McClellen of his command of the Union army, "to bore with an auger too dull to take hold" when it comes to the governance reforms discussed in this book? Or do they still have sufficient merit to warrant perseverance, comforted by the wisdom of Max Weber's observation that "politics is the art of patience"? We hope that these chapters help students discern the substance, logic, and coherence of the thirteen reforms for reconceptualizing purpose, reconnecting with citizens, and redefining administrative rationality. We also hope that they will appreciate the strategic challenges, choices, and opportunities proponents face in promoting reforms in the future. Likewise, we hope that researchers, practitioners, and reformers will garner insights into the strategic, tactical, and research agendas necessary to understand, apply, and evaluate these reforms as tools for building a results-based sense of common purpose in environmental governance in the twenty-first century.

Notes

The views expressed in this introduction and in all other portions of the book written or co-written by Daniel J. Fiorino are those of the author and not necessarily those of his employer, the U.S. Environmental Protection Agency.

1. Cited in Scott Lehigh, "As Joe Kennedy Steps Aside, the Governor's Race Begins," *Boston Globe,* March 14, 2001, www.boston.com/dailyglobe2/073/oped. Some, of course, lament this development, but it nonetheless represents a fundamental shift in value paradigms.

2. We use the term *regime* in this book to refer to a system of institutions, laws, rules, norms, and procedures for dealing with ENR issues. In the term *environmental governance,* we refer to the increasingly collaborative nature of ENR policy formulation and implementation. In this vein, a wide array of third parties

(for example, actors in the profit sector, the nonprofit sector, and civic society), in addition to government agencies, comprise nonhierarchical networks of actors wielding a variety of policy tools (for example, rules and regulations, subsidies, and information) to address diverse, complex, and evolving ENR problems. For an excellent review of the concept of governance in general, see Lester M. Salamon, "The New Governance and the Tools of Public Action: An Introduction," *Fordham Urban Law Journal* 28 (2001): 1611–1674.

3. The terms *results based* and *outcomes based* refer throughout this book to *positive* changes in environmental conditions, such as reductions of levels of air contaminants and water discharges. The terms also refer to changes in intermediate outcomes that affect environmental conditions and legal status, such as compliance levels and accident rates. Results-based management does not refer, however, to setting and managing goals and producing outputs unrelated to outcomes. If activity counts (such as the number of inspections) are not linked clearly to routinely measured outcomes, they may assure control within the organization, but without advancing environmental quality. In all cases, however, the alternative to "building a results-based sense of common purpose in environmental governance" (a phrase repeatedly used in this book to summarize reformers' aims) is a procedurally driven, bureaucratically inflexible, and command-and-control system of ENR protection.

4. Robert F. Durant, "The Political Economy of Results-Oriented Management in the 'Neoadministrative State': Lessons Learned from the MCDHHS Experience," *American Review of Public Administration* 29(4) (1999): 1–16.

5. Martin van Vliet, "Environmental Regulation of Business: Options and Constraints for Communicative Governance," in Jan Kooiman, ed., *Modern Governance: New Government-Society Interactions,* 105–118 (Thousand Oaks, Calif.: Sage, 1993).

6. The National Academy of Public Administration (NAPA), for example, reports that polluters are constrained in their ability to undertake new ideas under present ENR statutes. NAPA argues that present statutes discourage experimentation because of their ambiguity when it comes to the legal consequences for regulators and regulatees if experiments push legal limits. They also do so by not stretching those limits far enough (see NAPA, *Resolving the Paradox: EPA and the States Focus on Results* [Washington, D.C.: NAPA, 1997]). Likewise, because pollution prevention is inherently multimedia, the current single-media focus of most ENR statutes poses a basic impediment to implementing systematic prevention strategies (see, for example, California Unified Environmental Statute Commission Report, *Unifying Environmental Protection in California: Final Report* [Sacramento: Cooley Godward LLP, January 1997]).

7. Van Vliet, "Environmental Regulation of Business," p. 106.

8. See, for example, Peter Glasbergen, "Learning to Manage the Environment," in William M. Lafferty and James Meadowcroft, eds., *Democracy and the Environment: Problems and Prospects* (Cheltenham, England: Edward Elgar, 1996);

Paul A. Sabatier and Hank C. Jenkins-Smith, *Policy Change and Learning: An Advocacy Approach* (Boulder, Colo.: Westview, 1993).

9. For a summary of the implications of this realpolitik for ENR management, see Rosemary O'Leary, Robert F. Durant, Daniel Fiorino, and Paul S. Weiland, *Managing for the Environment: Understanding the Legal, Organizational, and Policy Challenges* (San Francisco: Jossey-Bass, 1999).

10. Hugh Heclo, *Modern Social Politics in Britain and Sweden: From Relief to Income Maintenance* (New Haven, Conn.: Yale University Press, 1994), p. 305.

11. Jan Kooiman, "Governance and Governability: Using Complexity, Dynamics, and Diversity," in Jan Kooiman, ed., *Modern Governance: New Government-Society Interactions,* 35–48 (Thousand Oaks, Calif.: Sage, 1993).

12. As quoted in Rene Dubos and Barbara Ward, *Only One Earth* (New York: Norton, 1972), p. 220.

13. Jane Lubchenco, "State of the Planet 2002: Science and Sustainability," paper presented at the Earth Institute, Columbia University, May 13, 2002, www.earth.columbia.edu/sop2002/sopagenda.html, accessed July 10, 2002.

14. Richard Leakey and Roger Lewin, *The Sixth Extinction: Patterns of Life and the Future of Humankind* (New York: Anchor, 1996). The first great extinction of species (defined loosely as the disappearance of half or more of all marine species in a short period of time) occurred around 450 million years ago. The second, around 350 million years ago, was followed by two mass extinctions in the Triassic period around 250 and 200 million years ago, respectively. The fifth mass extinction occurred around 65 million years ago, when the dinosaurs died off after a giant meteorite hit the Earth. Leakey and Lewin argue that unless reforms take place, 50 percent of all species presently existing will be extinct within 100 years—with logging, farming, and dam building being the major culprits in the process. Demonstrating precisely how inexact a science this is, however, estimates of the number of species existing today vary immensely (ranging from more than 100 million to 10 million or so), with 30 million an oft-cited figure (see Ed Stoddard, "Mass Extinction Looming for Planet," *Bangkok Post*, July 28, 2002, p. B4). Although most scientists agree that many estimates of species loss are wildly exaggerated, even such a noted skeptic as Bjørn Lomborg estimates a "nontrivial" loss of at least 0.7 percent of all species in the next 100 years (see Bjørn Lomborg, *The Skeptical Environmentalist: Measuring the Real State of the World* [Cambridge: Cambridge University Press, 2001]).

15. Gary P. Sampson, "The Environmental Paradox: The World Trade Organization's Challenges," *Harvard International Review* 23(4) (winter 2002), p. 60.

16. Friends of the Earth recently purchased $43,000 worth of shares in Balfour Beatty, a British construction company. It hoped to persuade shareholders at the company's 2001 board meeting to adopt guidelines for dam building issued by the World Commission on Dams. Their immediate target was the environmentally controversial Illisu Dam in Turkey. Similarly, the Free Tibet Campaign used the same strategy at British Petroleum's board meeting when it tried to get

the company to sell its stake in the PetroChina group (see Alan Beattie, "Dambusters Turn Against Builders," *London Financial Times,* March 21, 2001, www.ft.com).

17. Michael J. Sandel, *Democracy's Discontent: America in Search of a Public Philosophy* (Cambridge, Mass.: Belknap Press of Harvard University Press, 1996).

18. Reasoned debate focuses on "argument, statement, and proof" and avoids personal and unseemly attacks on the motives or integrity of opponents. Affective argument does precisely the opposite and often deteriorates in winner-take-all jeremiads where compromise, let alone consensus, is impossible.

19. Unlike in the United States, Canadian forests largely are publicly owned and valued according to a stumpage system. In this system, provincial governments compute the relative value of logging trees (that is, the stumpage rate), which then becomes the price that forest companies must pay per cubic meter to the government if they wish to harvest timber.

20. "Action on Climate Change–Carbon Trust Launched," *10 Downing Street,* March 20, 2001, http://www.number-10.gov.uk/news.asp?NewsId=1919& SectionId=30.

21. "States to Cut Diesel Emissions," *CBS News,* November 20, 2000, http://www.cbsnews.com.

22. "China Urges Enterprises to Engage in Environmental Protection," *People's Daily Online,* March 24, 2001, http://english.peopledaily.com.cn.

23. Although the term *ecological modernization* is not used much outside of Europe (where it began in Germany), it is akin to *green capitalism* in the United States. As John Dryzek and David Schlosberg define it, ecological modernization is seen by its proponents as "good for business, for it connotes happy and healthy workers, profits for companies developing conservation technologies or selling green products, high-quality material inputs into production (for example, clean air and water), and efficiency in materials usage" (see John Dryzek and David Schlosberg, eds., *Debating the Earth: The Environmental Politics Reader* [New York: Oxford University Press, 1998], p. 299).

24. "China, Germany Issue Joint Statement on Environmental Protection," *People's Daily Online,* December 14, 2000, http//www.english.peopledaily.online.

25. Colorado Plateau Ecosystem Partnership Project, 1995, http://www.epa.gov/ecoplaces/part1/site4.html, accessed April 8, 2003.

26. See, for example, Frans H. J. M. Coenen, Dave Huitema, and Laurence J. O'Toole Jr., eds., *Participation and the Quality of Environmental Decision Making* (Dordrecht: Kluwer Academic, 1998).

27. Perfluorocompounds are the most potent and persistent of all global-warming gases. They are used by the semiconductor industry to clean semiconductor manufacturing equipment. The Semiconductor Industry Association has signed a voluntary partnership agreement with the EPA to reduce these emissions 10 percent from 1995 levels by the end of 2010.

28. Nearly 60 percent of the world's coral reefs are at risk from dynamite fishing, overfishing, oil spills, overuse of fertilizers, and coastal development. The UN Environmental Program (UNEP) recently announced a four-year, $20 million initiative known as the International Coral Reef Action Network. Selected sites will be chosen in four regional seas—the wider Caribbean, East Africa, East Asia, and the South Pacific—and will be comanaged with local communities (see "UN Launches Multimillion Dollar Reef Project," *World News from Radio Australia,* March 19, 2001, www.abc.net.au/ra/newsdaily/s262581).

29. See, for example, Daniel A. Mazmanian and Michael Kraft, *Toward Sustainable Communities: Transition and Transformations in Environmental Policy* (Cambridge, Mass.: MIT Press, 1999).

30. DeWitt John, *Civic Environmentalism: Alternatives to Regulation in States and Communities* (Washington, D.C.: CQ, 1994).

31. The term *flexibility mechanisms,* although somewhat awkward, was first used to describe market- and information-based regulatory alternatives to command-and-control approaches by the Third Conference of Parties to the UN Framework Convention on Climate Change in 1997. The idea of flexibility, of course, centrally informs the challenges already discussed regarding reconceptualizing management regimes (integration) and reconnecting with stakeholders (for example, the U.S. EPA's Project XL and its Common Sense Initiative).

32. Both of these programs were enacted pursuant to the Food, Agriculture, Conservation, and Trade Act of 1990.

33. For example, UNEP's "Online Halon Trader" is a business-to-business web portal designed to help halon users in different countries avoid production of new supplies by redeploying halons from decommissioned systems or from nonessential applications to essential uses. Halons are fire extinguishants that are 3 to 10 times more detrimental in depleting the ozone layer than the chlorofluorocarbon refrigerants that the Montreal Protocol also addresses.

34. Manufacturers would be liable for any ENR problems that arise during design, production, supply, use, and disposal of their products.

35. This proposal is associated with a report issued by Enterprise for the Environment, which William Ruckelshaus, twice administrator of the EPA, organized and chaired. Analytic support for this group was provided by the Center for Strategic and International Studies and NAPA.

36. Mariko Ando, "Toyota, Ford in Talks on Hybrid Cars," *Financial Times Market Watch,* March 19, 2001, www.ftmarketwatch.com/news/story.asp.

37. Ann Florini, "Business and Global Governance," *Brookings Review* 21(2) (spring 2003): 4–8.

38. The WCD includes governments, international engineering and environmental experts, and the World Bank among its member. It offers stringent guidelines on the building of large dam projects.

39. That these programs may or may not attain either of these ideals in practice is an empirical research question covered in chapter 13.

40. Daniel J. Fiorino, "Rethinking Environmental Regulation: Perspectives on Law and Governance," *Harvard Environmental Law Review* 23 (1999), p. 442.

41. David H. Rosenbloom and Bernard H. Ross, "Administrative Theory, Political Power, and Government Reform," in Patricia W. Ingraham, Barbara S. Romzek, and associates, eds., *New Paradigms for Government: Issues for the Changing Public Service,* 145–167 (San Francisco: Jossey-Bass, 1994).

I

Reconceptualizing Purpose

Robert F. Durant

Policy analysts refer to some types of public policy issues as "wicked problems." These are issues where no accepted definition of the problem exists; where one problem is interrelated with others; and where the solutions proffered to address them are precarious, controversial, and difficult to implement. What is more, these types of problems pit those involved in trying to solve them against each other in jurisdictional conflict. Perhaps nowhere is this characterization more appropriate than for issues confronting environmental governance and dealing on an international scale with what Lynton Caldwell refers to as "the changing relationship of mankind's world to nature's Earth."[1] As he has written most recently, "the globe is not merely the ambience in which the transactions of international trade, investment and communications are carried on. . . . Environmental, holistic, and ecological, the 'Whole Earth' view sees the globe as a planet: a biogeochemical solar satellite, third from the Sun, the only planet on which life is known to exist today."[2] The battle is joined, of course, when humanity's activities threaten "ecosystem integrity and even the survival of the living properties of the Earth."[3]

Take, for example, global warming. Despite debate over the relative contribution of humanity to global warming, evidence of its existence and impact worldwide is beyond dispute. The number, severity, and spread, for example, of so-called extreme environmental incidents associated with higher global temperatures are apparent to scientists and insurance companies worldwide.[4] Increasingly common are damages from severe and frequent weather swings and events such as droughts and heavy rains. Increasingly prevalent as well are the revival and spread to new locations of infectious diseases long thought under control (for example, cholera). Moreover, a report published in 2001 by the Intergovernmental Panel on Climate Change (IPCC) concludes that the planet is undergoing warming at faster and higher rates than previously thought.[5] The IPCC projected temperature rises by the late twenty-first century of anywhere from 2.5 to 10.4 degrees Fahrenheit. Among other things, changes of that magnitude and pace will alter weather patterns, water resources, ecosystems, and the cycling of seasons. On top of these changes, demographers predict that food supplies worldwide will need to increase 50 percent by 2025 to meet the quantitative and nutritional needs of population growth. Yet they will have to be produced on less land, by fewer laborers, with less water, and with fewer pesticides.

Confronting these issues, sorting out the facts from the factoids, and coming to conclusions about what to do or not to do to attenuate these trends involves a series of difficult and strategic choices, challenges, and opportunities for environmental governance. Since the World Commission on Environment and Development published *Our Common Future* in 1987, critics have offered the concept of sustainable development as a useful, necessary, and effective metanarrative for reconciling economic development with environmental and natural resources (ENR) protection.[6] But sustainable development is a slippery concept, open to various interpretations and readily framed in policy debates as redistributive policy. Consequently, it is ripe either for conflict or for irrelevance. The United Nations Educational, Scientific, and Cultural Organization, for example, defines sustainable development as the imperative for every generation to leave the air, water, and soil resources "as pure and as unpolluted as when it came on earth."[7] Others, such as Noble Prize–winning economist Robert Solow, find leaving the world as each generation finds it precisely the wrong way to go. Solow defines sustainable development as every generation's having a responsibility "to leave open the option or the capacity to be as well-off" to future generations. This legacy, in practice, may entail leaving to future generations natural resources that are less robust than they were originally.

Others, such as Dan Esty of Yale University, argue that the concept of sustainable development is merely a buzzword that "slides over the difficult trade-offs between environment and development in the real world." Although the World Bank, for example, speaks of the "win-win" situations sustainable development can offer, critics argue that "environmental and economic policy goals are distinct, and the actions needed to achieve them are not the same." Yet even committed proponents of science- and evidentiary-based policymaking, such as the George W. Bush administration's John Graham, see value in the concept: "It's good therapy for the tunnel vision common in government ministries, as it forces integrated policy making": decision makers must clarify, weigh, and justify their decisions in terms of the economic trade-offs of environmental laws and the environmental consequences of economic development.

Our first two authors, Robert C. Paehlke and Gary C. Bryner, weigh directly into this debate over the capacity of sustainable development to help build a results-based sense of common purpose in environmental governance. Paehlke, after noting the multiple meanings attached to *sustainability*, argues in chapter 1 that it is really about one thing: learning as a species how to anticipate, avoid, or ameliorate the many risks we expose nature and ourselves to because of our economic, technological, and reproductive activities. In arguing for reconceptualizing present notions of the "bottom line" in business through the emerging science of contextual economics, he argues that the techniques of sustainability analysis can both clarify and advance the concept of sustainability worldwide and help us get beyond what he calls "cowboy economics." However, if sustainability analysis is to flourish in the twenty-first century as a means for building common purpose, proponents must think strategically about how to overcome formidable bureaucratic resistance, build institutional capacity, alter resource-costing structures, and attenuate North American predispositions toward unbridled consumerism.

In chapter 2, Bryner argues that over the past three decades positive, demonstrable, and meaningful progress has occurred in building international regimes for dealing with global issues. What has *not* progressed appreciably, however, is these regimes' capacity to advance sustainable development as a means for building a sense of common purpose as he defines it: preserving for future generations at least the same level of natural resources and environmental quality required for them to meet their needs and as enjoyed by the present generation. Progress, he argues, depends on the extent to which "ecological sustainability" becomes the basis for a new round of global accords and regimes. For that to happen, however, a sense of community—or as E. O. Wilson might put it, "a global land ethic"—will have to inform national and international actors' choices.[8] This is an animating purpose that has eluded them in the past, but for which he offers several suggestions for progress.

Regardless of how one defines sustainability or calculates the "triple bottom line" (namely, economic prosperity, social well-being, and environmental impacts) that its proponents seek to advance, judgments about the risks inherent in various activities, products, or technoscientific advances are central. As we note in our introduction, environmental governance typically has insisted that proponents of aggressive regulation prove that risks exist, are severe, and are unmanageable absent regulatory action. In contrast, the precautionary principle requires regulators to take aggressive regulatory steps *before* risks are proven if the magnitude of harm envisioned is potentially great. In chapter 3, Robert Durant, with Thanit Boodphetcharat, examines the promise versus the performance of this concept for building a results-based sense of common purpose in environmental governance. Their analytical focus is how the precautionary principle has contributed to ongoing and often strident debates worldwide over the testing, production, and marketing of genetically modified foods, feed, and fiber.

They argue, first, that these battles must be understood as contests over livelihood and cultural values, as much as over "good science." Second, and as a consequence, they contend that the precautionary principle both affects and is affected by today's tendency (encapsulated in the concept of sustainability) to morph ENR protective regulatory politics into the decidedly more conflictual realm of *redistributive* politics. Absent major adaptations in environmental governance perspectives, they conclude, precautionary politics may compromise rather than advance the building of common purpose. Moreover, these politics, misapplied or malapplied, can put at risk humanity's ability to explore empirically, democratically, and equitably the promise and pitfalls of major technoscientific advances that might help address pressing environmental governance challenges.

To be sure, many disagree over the definition, utility, and future of both sustainable development and the precautionary principle as normative animating purposes for environmental governance. Largely uncontested until recently, however, has been the idea that the tragedy of the commons both defiles the environment and militates against the building of a results-based sense of common purpose in environmental governance (locally, regionally, and internationally). In the final chapter of this section, however, Edella Schlager examines the claims of common-pool resource theorists that the tragedy of the commons itself needs fundamental rethinking in the twenty-first century. Contrary to Garrett Hardin's expectations, she argues, collaborative self-governing regimes of local stakeholders *have* emerged (largely in the developing world, but also in developed nations) and have applied successfully both sustainability and precautionary principles on both a local and regional basis. Such regimes have emerged usually in cases where a geographically based resource with which local stakeholders either identify or on which they depend for their livelihood is threatened ecologically. Knowing when and how to help maintain, catalyze, and nurture these types of self-governing institutions ought to become a central animating purpose of environmental governance. To demonstrate the kinds of strategic challenges, choices, and opportunities that await policymakers dealing with common-pool resource issues in the twenty-first century, Schlager reviews what the growing body of research on these arrangements indicates about the conditions under which results-based, collaborative, and self-governing regimes are more or less likely to arise, be effective, and endure.

Notes

1. Lynton Keith Caldwell, *Between Two Worlds: Science, the Environmental Movement, and Policy Choice* (Cambridge: Cambridge University Press, 1995), p. xiii.
2. Lynton Keith Caldwell, "Globalization," working paper available from author (2002), p. 1.
3. Ibid.
4. Sharon Reier, "Global Warming Makes Things Hot for Insurers," *International Herald Tribune*, March 17, 2001, www.iht.com/articles/13668.html.

5. "UNEP Chief Comments on U.S. Leadership and Climate Change," *Earth Vision Environmental News,* March 15, 2001, www.earthvision.net/ColdFusion/News_Page1.cfm?NewsID=15277.

6. World Commission on Environment and Development, *Our Common Future* (New York: Oxford University Press, 1987).

7. Quotations in this paragraph are from Vijay Vaitheeswaran, "Survey: The Global Environment," *The Economist,* July 4, 2002, www.economist.com/science/displayStory.cfm?storyid=1199867, accessed July 9, 2002.

8. Edward O. Wilson, *The Future of Life* (New York: Vintage, 2002), p. xxiii.

1

Sustainability

Robert C. Paehlke

Sustainability as a concept seems to have found a place within everyday discourse. One might ask, however, what it is that we wish to sustain. Reflection on this matter leads quickly to a conclusion that there is not yet a fully shared understanding of the meaning of sustainability. Conservation advocates often are most concerned with the sustainability of nature. For others, the meaning of sustainability is bound up with preserving human health and well-being, or—most broadly—"quality of life." For still others, sustainability is primarily about sustaining resources to fuel industrial society as we know it. Almost all individuals, meanwhile, are concerned about the sustainability of our collective (and, of course, thereby perhaps their own personal) prosperity.

What all these definitions have in common is a realization that any and all human activities, especially economic activities that depend on large-scale extractions from nature, carry costs that can and should be understood in terms of environmental sustainability. Nature is fragile, and we humans are a part of nature. Despite our considerable adaptive capabilities, we will not survive for long without breathable air, potable water, or food. Nor do we understand all of the ways in which we depend on the health of ecosystems and countless other species of plants and animals. Indeed, our capacity to affect negatively all those aspects of nature essential to our long-term prosperity and health is growing continuously as both human numbers expand and human technologies evolve.

Consequently, the growing concern worldwide with sustainability as an animating principle in building a results-based sense of common purpose is really a matter of learning as a species how to anticipate, avoid, or ameliorate many of the risks we continuously pose to ourselves and to nature. In the process, we must learn as well to judge and gauge our economic initiatives and efforts broadly rather than narrowly. Thus, analysts such as John Elkington indict societies' traditional focus on economic "bottom lines" as being decidedly too narrow (namely, economic development) for these purposes. They speak instead of the necessity of employing three bottom lines in order for sustainability to gain any traction in policy decisions: the social, the environmental, *and* the economic.[1]

To be sure, viewing economic initiatives more broadly within the context of this definition and operationalization of sustainable development is not without its perils. As Robert Durant with Thanit Boodphetcharat argues later in this volume (chapter 3), for example, traditional regulatory politics can morph readily into a highly conflictual redistributive politics of "livelihood" that effectively still allows economic bottom lines to trump environmental values. Likewise, the lessons drawn by various authors in this volume (especially Gary Bryner, Ken Geiser, James Meadowcroft, and Denise Scheberle) equally are applicable to operationalizing the concept of sustainability: in practice, it faces formidable methodological, bureaucratic, interorganizational, intergovernmental, political, and cultural obstacles. Thus, using sustainability as a basis for building a results-based sense of common purpose in environmental governance in the twenty-first century will not be easy.

Much as Amartya Sen argues within the context of development economics, however, the integrated analysis of economic, social, and environmental values that sustainability demands as a means for building common purpose is critical for humanity's future.[2] As such, the arguments of this chapter are fivefold. First, definitional differences aside, sustainability is fundamentally about relating economic purposes to limits imposed on them in the natural world and to the advancement of quality of life in the social world. Second, this "multiple-bottom-line" or "contextual economic" perspective is one that North Americans in particular must take to heart, given their decidedly disproportionate wealth and consumption patterns relative to the rest of the world. Third, embracing sustainability as a central animating concept of economic development means eschewing claims that economic progress automatically improves quality of life, using the evolving techniques of "sustainability analysis" to weigh such claims empirically, and then altering behavior accordingly. Fourth, informed by these social science techniques and aided by the natural sciences, humanity now has the capability to determine democratically the mix of expenditure allocations that will maximize public welfare. Finally, although the obstacles (especially among North Americans) to building a results-based sense of common purpose in this fashion are formidable, there is reason for guarded optimism.

The chapter begins by offering a synopsis of the logic and evolution of the concept of sustainability itself. It emphasizes how an ongoing tendency to distort the concept into a call for unconditional economic growth has occurred and explains that the best way to counter this call is to develop analytic methods that are neutral on this point. Next, and to this end, the chapter suggests how and why techniques of sustainability analysis can clarify and advance the concept of sustainability on a national, international, and global basis. Put most simply, sustainability analysis can model how societies and economies function in environmental and quality-of-life terms, rather than in economic terms alone. The chapter then concludes by reviewing the technical, political, and organizational challenges, choices, and opportunities facing reformers who strategically promote the use of sustainability analysis as a tool for building a results-based sense of common purpose in environmental governance in the future.

The Conceptual Foundations of Sustainability

Sustainability in its broadest terms is concerned with the optimization of human well-being, ever mindful of a simultaneous need to minimize ecological damage and resource depletion. Sustainability in this sense is at the heart of human existence: a perpetual development of economic and sociopolitical activities and institutions to better human lives individually and collectively in both the short and the long term.

The Malthusian Conundrum

The analytic consideration of environmental sustainability, broadly defined, goes back at least to the writings of Thomas Robert Malthus (1766–1834). Malthus was, of course, a rigid and gloomy moralist who concluded that human population inevitably would outstrip our ability to produce sufficient food. As he saw it, population increased geometrically (or exponentially), whereas production increased arithmetically (or incrementally).

Malthus was the ultimate naysayer to the boundless optimism of the ascendant liberal intellectual circles of his time. Within these circles, the intelligensia imagined that progress and increasing prosperity were natural characteristics of the human condition, not only in their time, but also for the foreseeable future. Whereas liberals believed in the perfectibility of humans through education, science, and democracy, Malthus was a pessimist who only hoped that human depravity and over-population could be checked sufficiently to avoid the worst of resource shortfalls and misery. He saw misery for the poor, however, as one of the necessary checks on excessive human population growth. In the spirit of some of today's extreme conservatives, he thus opposed the Poor Laws of his time as overly generous.

Few contemporary sustainability advocates are eager to embrace Malthus as an intellectual ancestor, nor are they enthusiastic about W. Stanley Jevons, who published *The Coal Question* in 1865. Jevons calculated a rise in coal consumption in Great Britain between 1854 and 1864 (at 3.5 percent annually) and concluded, given known domestic reserves, that the burgeoning nascent industrial society of his day was not likely to be long-lived. In his words, "We cannot long maintain our present rate of increase of consumption. . . . [W]e can never advance to the higher amounts of consumption supposed. . . . [T]he check on our progress must become perceptible within a century. . . . [T]he cost of fuel must rise, perhaps within a lifetime, to a rate injurious to our commercial and manufacturing supremacy; and the conclusion is inevitable, that our present happy condition is a thing of limited duration."[3] Jevons, of course, did not allow for the rise of an industrial economy based on other fossil fuels, traded globally and extracted even from the Arctic or from under the sea.

As off the mark as both Malthus and Jevons were, they *were* right that ultimately resources are available in only finite amounts. There *are* limits to the size of the human population that can be supported within nature's capacities, and resource limits *will* in some circumstances restrain economic development and social well-being. Where they were wrong, however, was in assuming that shortages in one particular resource, at one given level of technological development, always and significantly will limit human well-being for an extended period. Having not allowed for these possibilities, they naturally also failed to appreciate the implications of continuous and simultaneous growth in human population, resource extraction, *and* industrial production.

The greater danger, as it turns out, is not so much that the human population and total economic output cannot possibly continue to grow to levels unimaginable in Malthus's and Jevons's times. Rather, the danger is that they *can* do so and that ultimately a severe ecological price must be paid. This price can be reduced, of course, by technological innovation and technological selectivity. However, as we can now see, human numbers and human affluence are not boundless, even with optimal technologies. This more contemporary view of sustainability is accepted widely now (though decidedly not universally).

Toward Sustainability

Two other, more modern prophets of the contemporary sustainability debate are the twentieth-century American conservationists Fairfield Osborn and Samuel Ordway. Osborn spoke in 1953 of the goal of humanitarianism being "not the quantity, but the quality of living."[4] Population restraint and resource conservation in the name of a higher quality of life were central objectives for both Osborn and Ordway. Ordway, also writing in 1953, feared that without careful use "basic resources will come into such short supply that rising costs will make their use in additional production unprofitable, industrial production will cease, and we shall have reached the limit of growth. If this limit is reached *unexpectedly*, irreparable injury will have been done to the social order."[5] His solution: restraint and perhaps redirection of human material wants. In Osborn's words, we "must temper [our] demands and use and conserve the natural living resources of the earth."[6] Added Ordway with rhetorical flourish, "our needs can be supplied if our wants are bridled. . . . The false ideology which worships unlimited expansion must go."[7]

Osborn and Ordway's views were penned but not widely influential in the hyperexpansionist 1950s. At the time (as was almost as true in the 1990s, when we should have known better), each year's dominant new automobiles were larger and typically less fuel efficient.[8] These authors' sustainability-oriented views, as such, would have greater resonance when three strands of environmental thought—ecology, health, and sustainability—came together in an integrated way in the late 1960s. These concerns reached an even wider public following the 1972 publication of *The Limits to Growth* and especially in the wake of the 1973 and 1979 energy crises induced by the Organization of Petroleum Exporting Countries. Prior to these events, such concerns only rarely were taken to heart outside conservationist circles. However, in the 1970s and beyond, sustainability as a concept evolved rapidly from *Limits to Growth* to the 1987 publication of *Our Common Future* and on to sustainability indicators and sustainability analyses.[9]

Limits to Growth was read widely, in part because the research underpinning its findings utilized a then-novel tool: the computer. Technological novelty aside, however, it brought sustainability issues and concerns home to a significant segment of the public. The work was overstated, of course, in several aspects of its argument. For example, its authors (as had Malthus) underestimated potential increases in agricultural output and implied that reserves of nonrenewable resources (especially metals and minerals) were so limited that industrial society might experience shortfalls (in some cases within decades). Some readers, of course, quickly dismissed *Limits* as "Malthus with a computer."[10] Others raised doubts about its findings, arguing that it had not made sufficiently clear that global resource use is skewed radically in favor of a small number of wealthy nations. Consequently, these critics argued, "limiting growth" is altogether unwarranted in many contexts.

Incorporating these concerns, Mihajlo Mesarovic and Eduard Pestel soon updated *Limits* for the Club of Rome, the original sponsor. This second report, published in 1974, gave greater emphasis to the fundamentally uneven rates of resource use in the various regions of the world. As these authors put it, "Two gaps, steadily widening, appear to be at the heart of mankind's present crises: the gap between man and nature and the gap between 'North' and 'South,' rich and poor. Both gaps must be narrowed if world-shattering catastrophes are to be avoided."[11] Despite its flaws, this version of *Limits* did express effectively an intelligent discomfort with mindless opulence and thus joined its predecessor in advancing wider recognition that economic growth comes at a price. Moreover, in the context of the energy crisis of the 1970s and early 1980s, *Limits* informed wide discussions of steady-state economics and the impossibility of exponential growth.

Also notable in conveying an early sense of the normative and logical underpinnings of sustainability analysis was the Science Council of Canada's publication in 1976 of the report *Canada as a Conserver Society*. A conserver society was defined in part as a society that "promotes economy of design of all systems, that is, 'doing more with less'; favors re-use or recycling and, wherever possible, reduction at source; and questions the ever-growing per capita demand for consumer goods, artificially encouraged by modern marketing techniques."[12] The concept of a conserver society foreshadowed contemporary sustainability analysis in advocating materials- and energy-use efficiency, without necessarily excluding growth in gross domestic product (GDP). Yet the conserver society document (again in tune with contemporary analysis) also explicitly rejected a blanket endorsement of growth in all circumstances and by any means.

An additional aspect of the contemporary view of sustainability then arose out of *Our Common Future*, a work that made explicit many of the environmental costs associated with poverty. In the process, this report took the discussion of economic growth and sustainability toward a more balanced view. At the same time, however, it also risked lapsing contemporary debates back into a "growth-without-questions" mentality, especially whenever unbridled growth advocates distorted the meaning of the amorphous concept of sustainable development to advance their agendas.

The concept of sustainability thus has come to be informed by a perspective that is both complex and subtle. It rejects the view that the only societal and global goals of consequence are economic goals. Nonetheless, it allows that economic growth in some contexts can have net positive environmental, economic, and social effects, and that some forms of growth may impart only minimal environmental harm. The enormous challenge in this perspective, of course, is to sort out when, in what forms, and at what levels growth is or is not desirable. The ongoing risk remains that this view can be, and frequently is, distorted into something near to advocacy of unconditional economic growth. When this happens, "sustainable development" is understood as growth in marginally less-damaging forms. The best hope to avoid this lapse is to develop analytic methods such as sustainability analysis that are neutral on this point.

The Emerging Science of Sustainability Analysis

Sustainability analysis has been seen as, in essence, the study of the relationships among three corners of a triangle: economic factors (prosperity), social factors (well-being), and environmental factors (seen variously as a comprehensive array of indicators of environmental impact, as energy and material throughputs, or as "societal metabolism").[13] Each corner contributes to and may impose costs on the objectives embodied within each of the others. Thus, sustainability analysis depends fundamentally on the construction of valid, objective, and agreed-upon sustainability indicators. These indicators include measures not only of economic performance, but also of environmental inputs and impacts, as well as of social well-being. Sustainability analysis thus can be seen as a complement to economic analysis or even as a rebuttal to it. Indisputably, however, it is a means of systematically and rigorously integrating the findings of the natural and social sciences, including economics, into a comprehensive analytic model.

Consider, for example, what sustainability analysis can reveal to policymakers in the way of trade-offs. Environmental protection initiatives, for example, might contribute to economic prosperity by reducing health care costs, by making freshwater more available, or by helping to create pollution abatement and energy conservation technologies and industries. On the other hand, environmental protection might restrain some industries by imposing additional costs or by reducing the need for some products through technological selectivity or simply through the "imposition" of enhanced energy efficiency. Environmental protection also produces a variety of social benefits, of course, including improved health, recreational opportunities, or a greater subjective sense of well-being from knowing that biodiversity and wild nature will thrive into the future.

Looking from another angle, economic growth can benefit both society and the environment by enhancing a nation's capacity to spend on health, education, and environmental protection. But, alternatively, economic growth may be based on improved industrial competitiveness that in turn depends on slashing those very programs. This situation might occur in developed nations in an era of budget deficits or (as the editors of this volume suggest) in developing nations under pressure from the International Monetary Fund or World Bank to cut the size of public deficits as a condition for future loans.

As discussed later in this chapter, some analysts such as Aaron Wildavsky have argued that society is almost always better off in terms of net well-being if it opts for economic growth, even if that growth seems to carry an environmental risk. Wealth, they contend, produces health in a myriad of ways.[14] In contrast, others have argued that there may be a level of wealth per capita that is optimal or sufficient in terms of well-being outcomes; beyond this level, the environmental and social costs of wealth production may offset or even overwhelm the gains.[15] Even if this scenario is not true, larger gains in well-being may come from elevating societies to a level of basic food, education, health services, and shelter. Beyond that level, however, the gains are less dramatic per unit of GDP per capita.

To be sure, improved social well-being clearly involves improved health and education, which in turn make for a more effective economic workforce. Consider, for example, how the economies of many African nations are threatened today by hunger and the AIDS epidemic. In this same vein, indications are that rising levels of comfort associated with prosperity are also associated with increased attention to environmental protection, whereas economically challenging times tend to have the opposite effect.[16] Still, certain levels of social and environmental spending may reduce competitiveness. Indeed, this might even be the case were a pattern of social and environmental performance standards within trading blocs to be established, as the European Union has attempted. Overall, the point is clear: each dimension (the social, the environmental, and the economic) considered by sustainability analysis either can contribute to or impose on each of the other two.

The challenge to policymakers that sustainability analysis makes explicit, however, is how to achieve balance or, ideally, how to find policies and strategies that lead to win-win-win outcomes. Analysts John Robinson and Jon Tinker have explored this challenge in important ways in their work.[17] They note that "there is little consensus among experts in each discipline on how the ecological, economic, and social systems are related to one another."[18] Where John Elkington speaks of three bottom lines, Robinson and Tinker argue that "it is more fruitful to think in terms of three interacting, interconnected, and overlapping 'prime systems': *the biosphere* or ecological system; *the economy,* the market or economic system; and *human society,* the human social system. The third prime system includes the political system (governance), the social system (family, communities, and so on), and cultures."[19]

Each "system," according to these scholars, is understood to have its own value-laden imperative, and "sustainable development" is seen as an attempt to reconcile the three distinct imperatives. Again, in their words, "*The ecological imperative* is to remain within planetary biophysical carrying capacity. *The economic imperative* is to ensure and maintain adequate and equitable material standards of living for all people. *The social imperative* is to provide social structures, including systems of governance, that effectively propagate and sustain the values that people wish to live by."[20]

One important hesitation regarding the divisions Robinson and Tinker offer, however, is that the economic system as it actually functions today would not appear to be bound by such a set of imperatives. The social and ecological imperatives, in fact, might or might not have wide public support, especially were well-being gains to come at a cost to economic outcomes (as Wildavsky might suggest). The economic imperative within a capitalist economic system is quite clearly the maximization of total economic output (and of yield to the owners of capital). Thus, economic goals are sometimes compatible with each other, but less often incompatible with, and possibly contrary to, the equity-oriented imperative ascribed by Robinson and Tinker. Nevertheless, Robinson and Tinker *do* argue rightly that the three imperatives are interconnected, though each is independently important. Ignoring any of the imperatives, they say, is unacceptable because each of the three societal bottom lines is essential to human well-being. However, the attainment of "adequate material standards of living for all people" implies a significant political conflict with the owner-managers of the global economic system. Indeed, given the possibility of ecological and resource limits, there may even be three-way bottom-line conflicts.

It is arguably better, however, in terms of equity or environmental protection to have these complex tensions out in the open than simply to assume the existence of a beneficent economic system, as so many analysts presently do. With Wildavsky, many economists and almost all political conservatives argue that only what seems to be greed begets dynamic growth, and only dynamic growth will lead to adequate social and environmental outcomes. Whether or not this is the case is a matter sufficiently empirical in character that the interrelationship among the ecological, economic (in terms of growth), and social (in terms of broad human well-being) imperatives should be demonstrable through sustainability analysis. Moreover, no reason exists to think that a balanced outcome among the three imperatives could not be achieved were it to be attempted consciously and collectively.

In the end, Robinson and Tinker's principal policy objectives are important for this chapter because they adumbrate the role that sustainability analysis might play in building a results-based sense of common purpose in environmental governance. They advocate "uncoupling economic growth from environmental impact." That is, they seek ways whereby societies can achieve more economy per unit of environmental damage or per unit of energy and virgin raw materials used. In their words, "industrialized countries need to 'dematerialize' the economy by uncoupling human well-being from the throughput of matter and energy in our society." Such a process has been called *eco-efficiency* and is consonant with the basic premise of "industrial ecology."[21] One parallel measure of eco-efficiency, and inefficiency, is the size of a society's (or a city's or an industry's) "ecological footprint." This footprint is essentially a measure of sustainability where all factors are converted to the land area necessary to sustain human activities of a particular sort, or the sum total of activities within a given community or society.[22]

Consequently, Robinson and Tinker call for the development of "policy wedges" or policy tools (for example, changes in taxation) to accelerate gradually the separation of goods and services consumption from energy and materials usage. In their view, the economy gradually might "dematerialize": remain as large or larger in the dollar value of transactions, but become less materials and energy intensive. This dematerialization occurs whenever vehicles or light bulbs become more energy efficient, communications replace transportation (Internet use replacing trips to the library or bank), or appliances and other goods become lighter and more compact, but equally effective.

Robinson and Tinker identify two policy wedges and two forms of uncoupling as essential to moving toward sustainability as a central animating principle for building a results-based sense of common purpose in environmental governance. As noted, one form is the decoupling of economic output from energy and material throughputs, especially the extraction of raw resources from nature. The other is the partial decoupling of social well-being from GDP per capita (that is, improving quality of life faster than increases in wealth—or getting "more" well-being for the money expended). The former might be achieved through policy wedges such as increased energy taxation or, alternatively, by encouraging sustainable industrial design and process innovation. However, the policy basis for partially decoupling prosperity and well-being is both less obvious and almost certainly more politically controversial. It might be achieved, for example, through improved health services or income distribution, or even through reductions in work time. To many, such shifts may seem value laden and thereby controversial, but they are so only in contrast to the unquestioned assumption of contemporary economic policy that we need only to maximize total short-term prosperity in order for all that might be desired to come to pass.

Some of this potential "political heat" possibly can be converted to social scientific "light" through the use of sustainability indicators and sustainability analysis. This might be particularly true if the transition from social values to policy objectives can be made less value laden through polling and various public participation mechanisms (such as those James Meadowcroft discusses in greater detail in chapter 5). Indeed, in combination, communities themselves might help to select appropriate sustainability indicators.[23] Thus, although one should never underestimate the potential here for controversy, some aspects of well-being and environmental costs across jurisdictions and through time can be measured usefully (and even collaboratively).

Collaborative or not, a more fully developed sustainability analysis methodology holds great promise. It is capable of revealing the extent to which economic growth comes at an environmental price and the extent to which it leads to improved well-being for society. Perhaps even more important, sustainability analysis can be used to rank societal performances and thereby to challenge governments. It also can be used to identify production (goods and services) mixes and policy patterns that might help to minimize environmental costs and maximize well-being.

The Techniques of Sustainability Analysis: Implementation Lessons from the Field

In contrast to benefit-cost analysis that has the same broad objective, sustainability analysis does *not* attempt to reduce all values to monetary terms. For this reason, it might be called *nondollar economics* or (better yet) *embedded* or *contextual economics*. Regardless of what term is used, technical lessons are emerging already from implementation experiences related to the metrics, methods, and modeling that are necessary before sustainability analysis can become, at least technically, a key component of building a results-based sense of common purpose in environmental governance.

Alex Farrell and Maureen Hart define a *sustainability indicator* as a measure that "provides useful information about a physical, social, or economic system, usually in numerical terms." "Indicators," they go on to say, "can be used to describe the state of the system, to detect changes in it, and to show cause-and-effect relationships."[24] Everyday life is full of such indicators in other areas, from won-lost records in sports to blood pressure, temperature, and barometric pressure in the health and weather fields. Needless to say, economic indicators (including attitudinal indicators such as consumer confidence) are reported widely, understood, and acted upon. The challenge for proponents of sustainability is to make sustainability indicators just as widely understood.

To these ends, the organization *Sustainable Measures* identifies four characteristics of effective indicators that policymakers must ensure: relevance, ease of understanding, reliability and accessibility, and availability in sufficient time that action can be taken. Analogy is made to the gas gauge on a car: it provides the necessary information in a clear and reliable way and in sufficient time to remedy the potential problem. Likewise, during the Clinton administration, the White House Task Force on

Livable Communities offered the following list of what indicators should do: (1) reflect a trend, with a timeline appropriate to the topic; (2) be verifiable and reproducible; (3) be readily understandable; (4) reflect community circumstances and goals, as well as relationships to the region and the nation; (5) be supported by data; and (6) provide information for understanding the relationships among the economic, environmental, and social elements inherent in livable communities.

Overall, prior experience suggests that sustainability indicators should measure and communicate fundamental qualities of human societies, as well as the effects on the natural environment of the full range of their activities. It is crucial, as a consequence, that sustainability indicators be rooted in a larger theory of sustainability. As with outcome measures more generally, they should in the process be accurate, straightforward, powerfully communicative, and, when taken together, comprehensive. Sustainability indicators collectively must capture and convey a set of realities as important to society as are the vital signs (pulse, temperature, breathing rhythm) typically used as indices of human health. Indeed, some analysts see measures of environmental sustainability, the basic inputs and outputs of social economy, as measures of societal metabolism.[25]

In turn, the measures used must be meaningful in the sense that they measure what matters most to policymakers and to citizens. One way to achieve this goal is to involve the public in the process of selecting environmental and social indicators, much as Shelley Metzenbaum describes regarding the ongoing effort to clean up the Charles River in Boston, Massachusetts.[26] Similarly illustrative is how the 1990 Washington Global Tomorrow Conference in Seattle selected a set of forty indicators as bellwethers of sustainability. As Farrell and Hart put it, these indicators reflected "something basic and fundamental to the long-term cultural, economic, environmental, or social health of a community over generations" and were also "accepted by the community; attractive to local media; statistically measurable; and logically or scientifically defensible."[27]

To these ends, sustainability analysts have used different and varied measures as environmental indicators and as measures of well-being.[28] These differences notwithstanding, all of the environmental measures used to date imply a need for both demand-side and supply-side monitoring and management. Sustainability analyses, in general, thus have included both "input" (for example, energy and resource use) and "output" indicators (most basically, measures of pollutant releases or the degree of degradation of land areas or watercourses). The latter, in turn, tend to measure *unintended* outputs because the conscious goals of economic actors are personal income and wealth as well as general gains in societal income and wealth.

To date, sustainability analysts in a number of European or joint European–U.S. research initiatives have emphasized input variables as measures of environmental sustainability.[29] The most familiar and widely used of these variables has been total material requirement (TMR), essentially a measure that captures total energy and materials use within an economy. The overall efficiency of materials and energy use is then calculated as the ratio of TMR to GDP per capita, or material intensity per unit of "service." Units of service, in turn, are defined as nondollar substantive economic outputs, such as measures of transportation usage (passenger miles or ton miles), adequately lighted space, and calories in food produced. Presently, however, there is no commonly accepted combined measure on the unintended output side of this equation. Different analysts select different pollution indicators, usually on the basis of importance and data availability.

Prior experience suggests that the measures used, their precise nature aside, must operationalize a widely shared model of societal and economic functioning that goes beyond a traditional sense of economics to a more explicitly *contextual* sense. The model portrayed in figure 1.1—a variation on the models developed by Marina Fischer-Kowalski and Helmut Haberl, as well as by Robinson and Tinker—captures in broad strokes the logic of such a contextual perspective. This model portrays the economy as embedded in both the environment and society, and understands it as essentially a means by which to convert resources extracted from the environment into social well-being. In turn, the by-products of the processes comprising the economy are returned to the environment as a "sink."

The model significantly does not assume that economic output necessarily produces societal well-being. Or, put differently, it *does* assume that the efficiency by which this transformation takes place can be highly

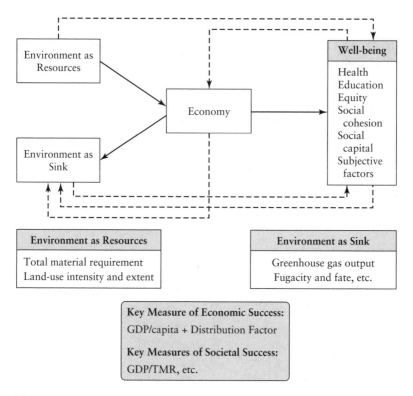

Figure 1.1
A sustainability analysis model.

variable. Especially important, the model implies, is studying the links among economic performance, environmental performance, and social performance in a systematic way. Granted, conditions and outcomes in each of the four boxes can be measured independently in their own terms. Yet the overall task of governance is understood to be three dimensional, rather than one dimensional: to minimize extractions and impositions on the environment as a sink, to maximize well-being, and to improve the efficient conversion of environmental capacities to social well-being. Economic output, as such, is optimized rather than maximized.

The well-being measures indicated in the upper right-hand box can be measured on an individual basis but are essentially based in, a part of, or a result of the effectiveness of social institutions. Conceptualized in this fashion, performance in relation to each of the four aspects of the embedded economic process can be measured independently. Whereas economic performance is measured traditionally in terms of GDP or GDP per capita, embedded economic performance is measured contextually in terms of the efficiency with which societal benefits are produced or with which environmental capacities are utilized.

Prior experience also suggests that "environment as resources," the upper left-hand box, can be measured in terms of such variables as the TMR or the extent and intensity of land use. TMR may be the best single comprehensive environmental indicator, given the proportion of environmental problems associated with materials and energy extraction (for example, mining, forestry, agriculture, fisheries, and energy production). However, other environment-as-source indicators might include land-use measures such as proportion of land degraded, proportion of all land designated as protected wilderness, rate of prime agricultural land urbanization, or the proportion of net primary production appropriated directly or indirectly for human needs.[30]

The extent of extraction required also has a significantly direct bearing on the impositions on the environment as a sink because extractive economic activities are especially waste intensive. Measures of utilization of the environment as a sink (see the lower right-hand box) are perhaps somewhat less standardized at this point but might include: (1) greenhouse gas emissions (especially carbon dioxide), (2) fugacity and fate measures and models,[31] (3) proportion of flux[32] of anthropogenic origin within basic natural chemical cycles, and (4) equilibrium lipid partitioning for organic pollutants in aquatic ecosystems.[33]

In addition, calculating both source and sink measures relative to GDP is animated by a conviction that improvements *per unit of GDP* should exceed the rate of GDP growth. Otherwise, prior experience suggests that overall environmental quality will not improve. Indeed, many of the sink measures typically taken today exceed acceptable levels. Thus, proposals such as President George W. Bush's alternative to the Kyoto Accords clearly are inadequate because they are premised on environmental gains as a proportion of GDP. *Current* emission levels, after all, are already warming the planet, and a good rate of economic growth would see, at best, overall U.S. emissions frozen at those levels.[34] More broadly, economic measures that incorporate embedded energy and material

throughputs (in effect measuring environmental as well as economic efficiency) are more valid measures of economic and societal success than
are more narrow economic measures such as GDP. Measures of a successful embedded economy might incorporate ratios of wealth per capita
to TMR, environmental outflows to carrying capacity, and level of
well-being relative to per capita GDP.

Sustainability: Challenges, Choices, and Opportunities

The preceding discussion has chronicled the development of sustainability as a concept for building a results-based sense of common purpose in
environmental governance and has suggested how and why sustainability
analysis might help clarify and advance this concept for policymakers.
Still, the question remains whether the triple bottom line that sustainability analysis offers policymakers can ever become a central animating
force in their decision making, let alone a tool for building common purpose among disparate interests in the twenty-first century. As Gary Bryner
and others in this volume attest, both of these aims are unrealized. Indeed, aside from the technical challenges of its implementation, and
implicit in the discussion in the previous section, a formidable set of
strategic challenges, choices, and opportunities faces proponents of
sustainability analysis in the years ahead. Not the least of these problems
involves societies making strategic choices to: (1) seize the opportunity to
use sustainability analysis to resolve ongoing policy debates empirically;
(2) overcome bureaucratic resistance to information sharing and invest in
the technical capacity building necessary to ensure that the information
culled from sustainability analyses can inform decision making; (3) create
a "race to the top" rather than one to the bottom in setting environmental standards; (4) shift cost structures to capture the true social costs of
development; and (5) rein in existing North American propensities
toward "cowboy capitalism."

Toward Empirically Informed Dispute Resolution?
Two of the most significant opportunities afforded by sustainability analysis are the promise it holds for clarifying what sustainability means and for
resolving long-standing debates over the relationship between economic

development and well-being. Consider, for example, Wildavsky's claim that wealth almost inevitably produces incremental improvements in health. As the upper right-hand box in figure 1.1 indicates, well-being is broader than human health, even though health might be the single most important measure. Nevertheless, comparative assessments of the health aspects of well-being relative to GDP per capita at the national level might help to determine the validity of Wildavsky's claim.

An initial look at this question suggests that the generalization includes many anomalies.[35] Some nations perform better than might be predicted by GDP per capita (for example, Belize, Cuba, and Sri Lanka), and some sharply less well (many Middle Eastern states). Moreover, the United States performs somewhat below expectations, despite having far and away the highest per capita health care expenditures in the world. The best explanation for this performance would seem to be relatively high rates of violent crime, less than universal access to health insurance, and very low incomes within the lowest income quintile (for example, compared to Canada, Japan, and many European nations).[36] Reasons aside, sustainability analysis offers to shed empirical light on this issue.

Relatedly, the comprehensive measures of environmental costs and well-being that sustainability analysis offers provide an opportunity to address another major set of issues that can be resolved only by using cross-national research designs. What is the relationship between a nation's level of economic development, its environmental quality, and its social well-being? How effective are public policies in different nations at converting wealth (as a means) into well-being (as an end)? To what extent and how can increases in GDP per capita be achieved with the least amount of resource demand (source data) and environmental damage (sink data)?

Some analysts, for example, have asserted that environmental damage is associated most strongly with the early and middle stages of economic development. That is, beyond some threshold of economic development, governments likely (almost automatically) will respond to increasing demands for pollution control. In trade policy circles, this tendency has been taken as a reason for concentrating on the possibilities of GDP growth among trading partners (for example, Mexico) rather than on the current effectiveness of their regulatory enforcement.

To be sure, Kenneth Arrow and his associates have responded effectively to these assertions. They argue, "The general proposition that economic growth is good for the environment has been justified by the claim that there exists an empirical relation between per capita income and some measures of environmental quality. It has been observed that as income goes up, there is increasing environmental degradation up to a point, after which environmental quality improves." They counter, however, that "it is important to be clear about the conclusions that can be drawn from these empirical findings. While [these findings] do indicate that economic growth may be associated with improvements in some environmental indicators, they imply neither that economic growth is sufficient to induce environmental improvement in general, nor that the environmental effects of growth can be ignored, nor, indeed, that the Earth's resource base is capable of supporting indefinite economic growth." [37]

Nor do Arrow and his associates deny the possibility of an inverted-U-shaped relationship between economic development and some forms of pollution. In this instance, a rise in early industrial stages might be followed by a stage where pollution is no longer "an acceptable side effect of economic growth." They *do* note, however, that this generalization is based on studies suggesting only that this pattern may hold for nitrous oxides, sulfur dioxide, suspended particulates, carbon monoxide, and basic sanitation (fecal chloroform). Moreover, they note five specific environmental impacts where prior experience suggests that the U-shaped pattern is *not* likely to apply, specifically when: (1) pollutants that have long-term and dispersed costs are involved (such as climate change); (2) accumulation of stocks of waste exist (emissions may tend to decline, but performance on ecological restoration is both less consistent and more expensive); (3) resource stocks are involved, especially soils, forests, and ecosystems (as nations get wealthier, they may reduce resource extraction per dollar of GDP, but none yet has done so absolutely); (4) opportunities for pollution export exist (nations may export as many of their environmental problems as they cure); and (5) environmental costs are borne by the poor, by future generations, or by those outside the jurisdiction within which they arise. Each of these propositions, however, remains controversial and ripe for testing with sustainability analysis.

Finally, the cross-jurisdictional aspect of the fifth proposition suggests that sustainability analyses might address fruitfully certain significant linkages between sustainability and trade policy. As chapter 3 chronicles in greater detail, this matter is highly contentious, at least in part because of the explicitly redistributive nature of the stakes involved. Indeed, redistribution has informed many recent protests in places such as Genoa, Quebec City, and Seattle. Still, time-series and comparative analyses of environmental and sustainability outcomes might clarify whether enhanced global economic integration helps or hinders environmental protection. One might compare, for example, high-trade and low-trade nations to determine if rising trade leads to rising wealth and if and when it also leads to increased environmental costs, to well-being gains, or to both.

Building a Will and a Way?

If taken seriously, sustainability analysis decidedly broadens the comprehensiveness of environmental governance well beyond the historic mandate of environmental and natural resources agencies. As such, it has the potential in the United States, for example, to elevate environmental and sustainability considerations to the level of the Treasury secretary, taxation policy, and the Office of Management and Budget. A useful beginning, however, will require policymakers' conscious choice to step up to this challenge by doing two things that have been the exception rather than the rule historically (as Denise Scheberle discusses in greater detail in chapter 10). First, they must choose to engage in greater coordination between natural-resources and environmental agencies, and, second, they must choose to pursue a wider mandate from legislators for the two types of agencies to act in concert. Ultimately, environmental agencies would play a greater and more institutionalized role in the sustainable demand-side management of scarce resources, especially water and energy, that historically have been handled largely by pro-development agencies.

Without question, a sustainability perspective appears to be critically dependent on the extent to which both information gathering and policies cut across traditional administrative distinctions at the federal government level (for example, among the Departments of Agriculture and the Interior, the Environmental Protection Agency [EPA], and even the various social agencies in the United States). Nor does this need end at the federal level or even among public agencies. States, localities, and private sectors or firms must make similar choices to cooperate and share information. Because sustainability analysis crosses quickly into the realm of economic analysis and equally quickly to all levels of government and to the private sector, all actors must ask: Are the most rapidly growing economic sectors more or less sustainable than older sectors of the economy? How and why are some firms within a sector more sustainable than others? How and why are some municipalities more or less sustainable than others? Are the key factors that account for these differences readily amenable to policy initiatives (or are they largely derivative of climate or topography)?

Also important is choosing to continue and deepen the shift within the EPA toward encouraging pollution prevention rather than end-of-pipe solutions. Pollution reduction can involve, of course, pollution abatement technologies. As Ken Geiser further elaborates in chapter 12, however, it is also part and parcel of any movement toward dematerialization. Resource extraction as well as energy production and use are responsible for the predominant share of all forms of environmental damage, including pollution. To the extent that policymakers encourage the adaptive modification and continuing reuse of existing buildings and urban infrastructure, for example, they promote dematerialization *and* pollution prevention.

This effort, of course, also would involve a parallel adaptation not only within the whole array of natural resources agencies (including the Department of Agriculture in the United States), but also within all other domestic and international agencies that affect development decisions. Historic and present practices have served as fundamental organizational, interorganizational, and cross-sectoral barriers to sustainability. Yet for the concept of sustainability to reach its full potential, U.S. departments such as Transportation and Housing and Urban Development will have to play a larger and unaccustomed role in resource management on both the supply and the demand side. Because the editors and other authors of this volume discuss these obstacles to organizational change in greater detail, it suffices here to note that the task of reframing administrative and political mindsets in this fashion is likely to be a long and arduous one.

Creating a Race to the Top?

Choosing to pursue sustainability initiatives in North America is vitally important to advancing sustainability in the world as a whole, most obviously because North Americans consume so much more of everything, especially on a per capita basis. Consumption patterns presently show that although North Americans constitute some 5 percent of the world's population, they are responsible for nearly 50 percent of its consumption. Indeed, some analysts plausibly assert that humans would require the resources of several Earths if the world as a whole lived a North American "lifestyle."[38] Perhaps just as important, however, is the potential for change inherent in this otherwise negative North American dominance in consumption in a global economy. More precisely, if North Americans (as well as the nations of the Organization for Economic Cooperation and Development [OECD]) choose to make sustainability a key component of international trade, they may create a positive "California effect" worldwide (like that *within* the United States, as described by Denise Scheberle in chapter 10).

According to David Vogel, the California effect arises whenever consuming jurisdictions adopt environmental standards that are significantly more stringent than the average standards within a trading region.[39] The effect, some claim, may be the opposite of a "race to the bottom" in terms of environmental standards (wherein jurisdictions seek to attract industries by *lowering* their environmental standards). In California's case, stringent air pollution standards for automobile emissions induced the redesign of automobiles. Moreover, they did so not only in all of North America, but even in jurisdictions worldwide, where the national standards for vehicle production were significantly less stringent than in the United States. Nearly everyone who produces automobiles, after all, wants to sell them in California, a state with a large market of wealthy consumers prone to use automobiles rather than public transportation.

Certain options short of choosing systematically to establish and enforce global environmental standards might expand the California effect worldwide. More precisely, policymakers might pursue an OECD-led initiative to set environmental (and perhaps social) minima for industries that produce primarily for export into OECD or other jurisdictions. Indeed, such an initiative might be effective were it applied *only* to

OECD-based firms and their suppliers, as Durant with Boodphetcharat's discussion of the impact of European Union regulations on the genetically modified food industry attests. Disallowed, thereby, would be competition between "our" firms on the basis of lesser environmental standards and intolerably low well-being outcomes for developing nations compared to "our own" or both.

Relatedly, opportunities to trade with North America or Europe or to become a full participant in the World Trade Organization (WTO) also might be available only to nations and corporations that meet tougher standards and who require that their suppliers meet certain standards of behavior. Lest a gigantic bureaucracy be created, such licenses need be reviewed only infrequently. Nevertheless, firms might be held to improving sustainability performance through whatever time period is chosen. In this way, the number of mandatory aspects of sustainability could be few (again to restrain the natural tendency to swell bureaucracies), but in each case significant. One aspect of such a regime might be rating the environmental performance of a nation in terms of existing international treaties, such as protection of biodiversity, climate change, and emissions of persistent organic pollutants.

In the present political climate, particularly in the United States, such a proposal might appear outlandish. It should be clear by now, however, that without linking environmental agreements to trade, they are often little more than a pretense. At the very least, sustainability analysis may show that trade policy and environmental policy should not be conceived as wholly detached administrative realms.

In this effort, one must distinguish such an approach to public policy from the increasingly widespread global movement to reject trade regimes (and global economic integration) altogether. The initiative offered here is a political middle ground between the unabated, unapologetic export of pollution and the rejection of the systematic expansion of global trade and global trade regimes. It asserts instead a limit to the export of environmental problems and a recognition that a global economy carries implications for all aspects of public policy within all nations.

Shifting Underlying Cost Structures?

Advancing sustainability as a central animating premise of environmental governance also would seem to require a fundamental and worldwide shift in natural resource costing structures. To be sure, consciously choosing this route flies in the face of both recent economic history and North American political culture, not to mention very powerful economic interests. But how else might societies accelerate the dematerialization of the economy, slowing growth in both source and sink environmental impacts while still achieving economic growth? Without detailed economic planning, which in all likelihood would fail abysmally, significant adjustments are difficult to imagine on the "source" side without a fundamental change in the price regime. This change, in turn, is difficult to imagine without a choice to change tax regimes fundamentally (albeit gradually) from income and property taxes to energy and raw materials taxes.[40]

Granted, a choice to use regulation as a policy tool might work within a limited range of sustainability objectives (such as fleet-average fuel efficiency standards or appliance efficiency standards). However, the myriad of shifts necessary to achieve sustainability—from product design to personal habits—requires changes in underlying cost structures. Moreover, for the necessary changes to occur in a nondisruptive manner, they must occur gradually. We design cities (and suburbs) now that will set transportation patterns for much of the twenty-first century. Energy costs in 2050 almost certainly will be very different, but the energy, materials, and environmental costs of altering, if not rebuilding, infrastructure and buildings will be no easier to meet than they are at present. It is arguably better to anticipate as best as possible the likely material conditions of the future through sustainability analysis and act gradually to shift cost structures for them with sustainability in mind.

Formidable obstacles stand in the way of policymakers making choices to shift the underlying cost structure of natural resources in this way. Natural resources agencies historically and currently have interpreted their mandates as maximizing, or at least optimizing, "resource outputs." To this end, they have engaged in all manner of direct and indirect production subsidies. Some of the cultural reasons for this approach are discussed in the concluding section of this chapter. The triumph of Pinchot's "gospel of efficiency" over preservation finally may have had its day, however. The negative externalities afforded, for example, by vast increases in the North American population, economic output, and personal consumption are known and lamented widely. And with this recognition has grown a politically active, influential, and networked postmaterialist movement concerned about the negative environmental consequences that these increases produce. If public subsidies exist, postmaterialists aver, they should favor end-use efficiency for key commodities such as energy, water, and nonmotorized travel (cycling and walking) or public transit. Consequently, a significant political opportunity may exist now for proponents of sustainability-based revisions in cost structures to advance their cause.[41]

Getting Beyond Cowboy Economics in a Globalizing Economy?

Meeting the sustainability challenge on a global scale means fundamentally that policymakers must choose to embrace the idea that certain energy, material, and land restraints to growth are not adequately taken into account today. Recognizing these constraints does not imply necessarily choices to limit overall economic growth. Indeed, *limit* and *restraint* may be the wrong terms here: it is better perhaps to speak of a growing need for energy-, materials-, and land-use efficiency. In the long term, sustainability is preferable not only socially and environmentally, but economically as well.

Attending to sustainability in this fashion, however, means challenging consistently the global economy and the subglobal economies and corporations within it to better their performance. This improvement must occur environmentally, socially, and economically. In an era of global economic integration, policymakers increasingly must choose to conceptualize their public policies on a global scale. Policies need not apply exactly equally to every nation or class of nations, but many of them must be adopted at the level of, and somehow enforced within, the global economic system.

The rub, of course, is that although sustainability *has* entered North American discourse, it is a very long way from being taken seriously at the political, policy, or administrative levels. The reasons for this neglect are to a considerable extent cultural. They thus represent a major challenge to those advocating sustainability as a central animating principle for building a results-based sense of common purpose in environmental governance. To be sure, economic interests (especially within the resource sector) also would be challenged were sustainability to be taken seriously.

But it is the cultural context that keeps North Americans from dealing with resources in terms of demand restraint (efficiency) rather than in terms of supply enhancement and "multiple use." The very limited effectiveness of the President's Council on Sustainable Development during the Clinton administration and its profound eclipse today indicate the level of challenge that lies ahead in the United States.[42]

The key cultural factors that have contributed historically to the inability of the United States to take sustainability seriously are fourfold: (1) the nation's frontier mentality; (2) its abiding faith in technological innovation; (3) its citizens' predisposition toward individualism and presumption against planning; and (4) the American Dream, understood in material terms as "getting rich." Some of the implications of the frontier for North American society and politics were identified and detailed in the mid-twentieth century by Frederick Turner and Louis Hartz, among others.[43] It suffices to note here that the frontier was an "escape valve" in the nation's culturally formative years, allowing waves of immigrants to seek their livelihoods and fortunes unbridled by competition for scarce resources in overcrowded and opportunity-deficient cities in the industrial East.

Much later Kenneth Boulding spoke of "cowboy" and "spaceship" economies resulting from this mentality. Indeed, even today, North Americans imagine wide-open spaces and vast tracts of "unsettled" and "undeveloped" land, especially in the West. This image occurs despite the fact that California and much of the mountain West have been overpopulated for decades, especially relative to sustainable supplies of water. As David Roodman argues, this lingering "frontier" perspective has led to a political and administrative unwillingness to rethink no-longer-warranted public subsidies to resource extraction.[44]

Inventiveness and innovation have been watchwords of the North American ethos for centuries and have served the nation well. Thomas Edison, Henry Ford, and the pioneers of the computer age, for example, rightly and widely are revered. These individuals and countless others have analyzed human needs and found new ways to meet them. As a consequence, however, U.S. citizens routinely presume that whatever needs might arise in the future similarly will be satisfied by innovation and technology. Indeed, such an article of faith is this that North

Americans travel only 0.3 of their passenger miles on fuel-efficient trains—despite the obvious limits of nuclear energy, the perils of Middle Eastern politics, and the imminent peaking of conventional oil supplies. Moreover, until very recently we have all but celebrated urban sprawl, and many still make possession of sport utility vehicles a middle-class suburban norm.

As Ken Burns, the noted producer of documentaries, was so right to assert, jazz music is quintessentially American music: it is inventive; it is individualistic; and it is unplanned. Jazz solos spring brilliantly from their creators' minds; they are unscripted. Similarly, Americans notoriously are disinclined to governmental "interference" except under the direst of circumstances. Detailed materials' inventories and calculations of GDP per ton of TMR might well strike captains of industry and assembly-line workers alike as pointless undertakings, if not akin to Soviet-style five-year plans. Many in the business community might argue, "If we can pay for it, we should be able to get it." They relatedly might argue that the (one-dimensional) balance sheet should define all limits and that governments should "stick to their business." Their plea, essentially, might be to let corporations handle problems spontaneously and creatively (as and when they arise), employing for redress the hard work and creative energy that the free market allows and requires.

Finally, the American Dream is in part about getting rich—or, rather, about hoping to get rich. A thousand enterprises are launched in that hope, despite a wide awareness that only a very few produce significant wealth. Consider, for example, how athletes spend endless hours playing basketball, knowing that only one in a million who play the game will be recruited into the National Basketball Association. The dream is, at once, about individual opportunity, crass materialism, and, as F. Scott Fitzgerald saw it in the 1920s, a redirection of the American frontier from the West toward the "green light" of wealth, east or west. Sustainability, in its recognition of the ultimate reality of resource limits, may well seem to challenge this deeply held, albeit improbable and possibly illusory hope of future comfort, prosperity, and wealth for all.

On the face of it, then, the United States is, in its own mind, still the land of Horatio Alger and accordingly an unlikely place for sustainability aspirations to take hold. They certainly would not have been a part of the mindset at Enron and other recent corporate failures. However, as Jan Mazurek points out in chapter 13 in this volume, many in the business community *are*, for various reasons, embracing environmental management systems. Likewise, as DeWitt John, James Meadowcroft, and other authors in the volume suggest, there *are* conditions under which public-private partnerships emerge at the grassroots to address environmental issues. At the same time, and as noted earlier in my discussion of postmaterialist values in American society, increasing numbers of Americans understand that their aspirations can be fulfilled in nonmaterial ways.

North Americans also must come to see that although free markets cannot be managed in detail, the inventiveness they allow and inspire perhaps can be harnessed to serve wider collective purposes. Indeed, Daniel Fiorino's chapter suggests a variety of ways that this already is occurring. Again, however, attaining sustainability requires both citizens and policymakers to make new and enduring fundamental choices. Merely producing sustainability analyses will not assure that they will change policymakers' behavior. For this change to occur, citizens and policymakers alike must understand more fully the ways in which nature is limited and thus how both the global economy and *our* particular economy are increasingly vulnerable in economic terms to the absence of effective sustainability initiatives.

In sum, environmental limits, in terms of both sources and sinks, imply choices that optimize the efficient creation of societal and personal well-being. Markets are not, in fact, "free" from nature because economies are embedded *in* nature. Moreover, markets are not ends in themselves, but tools at the service of human well-being—one of the greatest tools that human ingenuity has devised (with the possible exception of democratic governance). Humanity chose to invent markets. Similarly, it can opt to put them fully to use in service to collective social purposes, not to what some imagine are the "purposes" of the markets themselves. By means of democratic institutions and with the help of the social sciences, societies *can* choose to determine the mix of expenditure allocations that will maximize well-being outcomes. Policymakers also *can* determine, with the help of the natural sciences, source and sink limits and accelerate market-based sustainability initiatives through a small number of specific price, tax, and regulatory interventions.

In the end, sustainability is about choosing to see limits and purposes, while having the courage to view governance as a means for firmly and flexibly embedding our economy and society within that context. To date, as the editors suggest in their introduction, progress along this line and in other aspects of the reformers' agenda to build a results-based sense of common purpose has been halting, halfway, and patchworked. Unless both citizens and policymakers meet the challenges, make the choices, and seize the opportunities identified in this chapter, progress toward sustainable development will remain equally frustrated in the future.

Notes

1. John Elkington, *Cannibals with Forks: The Triple Bottom Line of 21st Century Business* (Stony Creek, Conn.: New Society, 1998). See also the excellent early discussion of sustainability analysis in B. J. Brown, M. E. Hanson, D. M. Livermore, and R. W. Meredith Jr., "Global Sustainability: Toward Definition," *Environmental Management* 11 (November 1987): 713–719, and the follow-up article by the same authors, "Global Sustainability," *Environmental Management* 12 (March 1988): 133–143.

2. Amartya Sen, *Development as Freedom* (New York: Random House, 1999).

3. W. Stanley Jevons, *The Coal Question* (New York: Augustus M. Kelley, 1965 reissue), p. 271.

4. Fairfield Osborn, *The Limits of the Earth* (Boston: Little, Brown, 1953), p. 226.

5. Samuel H. Ordway, *Resources and the American Dream* (New York: Ronald Press, 1953), p. 31.

6. Fairfield Osborn, *Our Plundered Planet* (Boston: Little, Brown, 1948), p. 201.

7. Ordway, *Resources and the American Dream,* p. 39.

8. "Automobiles" were becoming more fuel efficient, but only because sport utility vehicles (SUVs) were defined as trucks for purposes of calculating the fleet-average fuel efficiency of North American output, an ever-increasing proportion of which has been pickup trucks and SUVs.

9. Donella H. Meadows, Dennis L. Meadows, Jørgen Randers, and William W. Behrens III, *The Limits to Growth* (New York: Universe Books, 1972); World Commission on Environment and Development, *Our Common Future* (New York: Oxford University Press, 1987).

10. H. S. D. Cole, *Thinking about the Future* (London: Chatto and Windus, 1973), p. 5.

11. Mihajlo Mesarovic and Eduard Pestel, *Mankind at the Turning Point* (New York: Dutton, 1974), p. ix.

12. Science Council of Canada, *Canada as a Conserver Society* (Ottawa: Government of Canada, 1976), p. 14.

13. For a discussion of social metabolism, see Marina Fischer-Kowalski and Helmut Haberl, "Society's Metabolism," *Journal of Industrial Ecology* 2 (1 and 4): 61–78, 107–136.

14. Aaron Wildavsky, *Searching for Safety* (New Brunswick: Transaction, 1988).

15. Michael Carley and Philippe Spapens, *Sharing the World* (London: Earthscan, 1998).

16. Robert Paehlke, "Cycles of Closure in Environmental Politics and Policy," in Ben Minteer and Robert Pepperman Taylor, eds., *Democracy and the Claims of Nature*, 279–299 (Lanham, Md.: Rowman and Littlefield, 2002).

17. John Robinson and Jon Tinker, "Reconciling Ecological, Economic, and Social Imperatives: A New Conceptual Framework," in Ted Schrecker, ed., *Surviving Globalism: The Social and Environmental Challenges*, 71–94 (London: Macmillan, 1997).

18. Ibid., p. 73.

19. Ibid., p. 74, emphasis in original.

20. Ibid., p. 77.

21. Ibid., p. 80.

22. Mathis Wackernagel and William Rees, *Our Ecological Footprint* (Gabriola Island, British Columbia: New Society, 1996).

23. Alex Farrell and Maureen Hart, "What Does Sustainability Really Mean? The Search for Useful Indicators," *Environment* 40 (November 1998): 4–9, 26–31.

24. Ibid., p. 7.

25. Marina Fischer-Kowalski and Helmut Haberl, "Sustainable Development: Socio-economic Metabolism and Colonization of Nature," *International Social Science Journal* 158 (1998): 573–587.

26. Shelley H. Metzenbaum, "Measurement That Matters: Cleaning Up the Charles River," in Donald F. Kettl, ed., *Environmental Governance: A Report on the Next Generation of Environmental Policy*, 58–117 (Washington, D.C.: Brookings Institution Press, 2002).

27. Farrell and Hart, "What Does Sustainability Really Mean?" p. 28.

28. See Robert Paehlke, "Methods for Sustainability Analysis: Environmental Indicators," in Gertrude Hirsch Hadorn, ed., *Unity of Knowledge in Transdisciplinary Research for Sustainability, Encyclopedia of Life Support Systems*, 6.49.23, available at www.eolss.net.

29. See the studies cited in Carley and Spapens, *Sharing the World*, pp. 192–193; Ernst von Weizsäcker, Amory B. Lovins, and L. Hunter Lovins, *Factor Four: Doubling Wealth, Halving Resource Use* (London: Earthscan, 1998).

30. Helmut Haberl, "Human Appropriation of Net Primary Production as an Environmental Indicator: Implications for Sustainable Development," *Ambio* 26 (May 1997): 143–146. Proportion of land degraded is recommended as an indicator in Robert Prescott-Allen, *The Barometer of Sustainability* (Gland, Switzerland: IUCN website, 2001).

31. *Fate,* in this sense, is chemical behavior in the environment in terms of concentration, reactivity, and location in and movement between air, water, sediment, soils, and biota. *Fugacity* mathematically describes the rate at which chemicals diffuse, or are transported between, phases (as, for example, volatility from soil to air). Regarding the latter, see Donald Mackay, *Multimedia Environmental Models: The Fugacity Approach* (Boca Raton, Fla.: Lewis, 2001), p. 2 and elsewhere.

32. *Flux* is the transfer of material into or out of reservoirs; in total, all flux regarding a specific material is a *cycle* (such as the nitrogen cycle). These changes often are crucial environmentally, as with the flux of carbon from a solid state in biota or soil or coal to a gaseous state in the atmosphere, which underlies climate change. See, for example, James I. Drever, *The Geochemistry of Natural Waters* (Upper Saddle River, N.J.: Prentice Hall, 1997).

33. Equilibrium lipid partitioning has been proposed as a possible ecosystemwide (all media) synoptic indicator of trends in contaminant status. See Eva Webster, Donald Mackay, and Kang Qiang, "Equilibrium Lipid Partitioning Concentrations as a Multi-media Synoptic Indicator of Contamination Levels and Trends in Aquatic Ecosystems," *Journal of Great Lakes Research* 25(2) (1999): 318–329.

34. On this point, see the discussion in Paehlke, "Methods for Sustainability Analysis," and in Farrell and Hart, "What Does Sustainability Really Mean?" regarding critical limit and competing objective views of sustainability.

35. See Aaron Wildavsky, "The Secret of Safety Lies in Danger," *Society* 27 (November–December 1989): 4–5.

36. The tentative conclusions associated with these United Nations Development Program data are discussed more comprehensively in Robert Paehlke, *Democracy's Dilemma* (Cambridge, Mass.: MIT Press, 2003).

37. Kenneth Arrow, Bert Bolin, Robert Costanza, Partha Dasgupta, Carl Folke, C. S. Holling, Bengt-Owe Jansson, Simon Levin, Karl Göran Mäler, Charles Perrings, and David Pimental, "Economic Growth, Carrying Capacity, and the Environment," *Science* 268 (April 28, 1995): 20–21.

38. Wackernagel and Rees, *Our Ecological Footprint.*

39. David Vogel, *Trading Up: Consumer and Environmental Regulation in a Global Economy* (Cambridge, Mass.: Harvard University Press, 1995).

40. See, for example, Timothy O'Riordan, ed., *Ecotaxation* (London: Earthscan, 1997); Alan Thein Durning and Yoram Bauman, *Tax Shift* (Seattle: Northwest Environment Watch, 1998).

41. Samuel P. Hays, *Conservation and the Gospel of Efficiency* (Cambridge, Mass.: Harvard University Press, 1959).

42. The President's Council on Sustainable Development was an important initiative, but it saw little, if anything, through to legislation or policy implementation. Nonetheless, or indeed for this very reason, an analytic history of this organization should be written.

43. Frederick Jackson Turner, *The Frontier in American History* (New York: Holt, Rinehart and Winston, 1962); Louis Hartz, *The Liberal Tradition in America* (New York: Harcourt, Brace, 1955); Louis Hartz, *The Founding of New Societies* (New York: Harcourt, Brace and World, 1964).

44. Kenneth E. Boulding, "The Economics of the Coming Spaceship Earth," in Herman E. Daly, ed., *Toward a Steady-State Economy*, 121–132 (San Francisco: W. H. Freeman, 1973); David Malin Roodman, *Paying the Piper: Subsidies, Politics, and the Environment* (Washington, D.C.: Worldwatch Institute, 1996).

2

Global Interdependence

Gary C. Bryner

As the editors argue in the introduction to this book, each of the elements of the environmental reform agenda that has emerged over the past quarter century has been grafted on existing regulatory approaches, but none has replaced them. No more apt description can be applied to the concept of global interdependence. Given the limitations posed by a global political system firmly dedicated to recognizing national sovereignty and providing only limited support for the idea of global governance, however, the creation and development of international environmental and natural-resources (ENR) regimes predicated on building a results-based sense of common purpose in environmental governance are very significant.

This chapter argues that the creation of international ENR regimes *has* made a difference in fostering governments and nongovernmental actors' capacity to devise solutions to global environmental threats. Still, the existing network of global environmental regimes is woefully inadequate to meet global environmental challenges, particularly when the goals of sustainability (discussed by Robert Paehlke in chapter 1) are considered. Granted, when international ENR regimes are assessed in terms of how much progress has been made in global environmental institution building over the past three decades, a quite positive picture emerges and bodes cautious optimism for the future. Yet when these regimes are assessed from the more important perspective of their contributions to sustainable economic activity, a decidedly different picture emerges.

Still unproven is their capacity to help preserve for future generations at least the same level of ENR quality required for them to meet their needs as was enjoyed by the current generation. Equally suspect is their capacity to help secure a more equitable distribution of resources for the current generation. As such, the future development and performance of international environmental regimes will be driven and conditioned by the extent to which "ecological sustainability" becomes the conceptual basis for a new round of global environmental agreements. This, in turn, will depend on the extent to which a sense of community and steward-ship develops at the national and international levels, an ethic that has proven elusive thus far at anything but the community level.

To explore these arguments more fully, the chapter begins with an overview of the logic and protean dynamics driving the evolution of global interdependence in environmental governance over the past quarter century. It explores next the regimes that can produce (and in the past have produced) effective responses to global environmental problems. It then assesses the accomplishments of international environmental regimes to date in building a results-based sense of common purpose internationally, with a review of some of the most salient empirical literature on the topic. The chapter concludes by examining the strategic challenges, choices, and opportunities facing proponents of making ecological sustainability the central animating principle of results-based environmental regimes on local, national, and global scales.

Recognizing Global Interdependence

As Lynton Caldwell has long, wisely, and widely noted, ENR challenges increasingly have become global in scope. Some challenges, such as the threat to the stratospheric ozone layer, the global climate, the decline of oceanic fisheries, and the degradation of the oceans, center on the global commons—the ecosystems on which all life depends. Other challenges, such as acid rain, hazardous wastes, and river pollution are environmental problems that can cross national boundaries and require international cooperation or coordination for devising and implementing solutions. Still other global threats arise from the globalization of markets and trade that has increased greatly the interaction among countries. This interaction prompts in its wake international flows of pollution and wastes, chemicals, genetically modified organisms, and other products. Expanded industrialization and transportation—and the resultant air and water pollution, land use and degradation, and resource consumption—also can increase the severity of problems environmental regimes must solve and can complicate their task considerably. Similarly local in genesis but transboundary and even global in impact and funding solutions are the health effects of polluted air, water, and sanitation systems; the exhaustion of local nonrenewable resources; and damage to ecosystems that provide important environmental services (such as watersheds and wildlife habitat). Finally, the distribution of global resources requires collective efforts to ensure there is some fair distribution of access and use, as well as preservation for future generations.[1] All countries, for example, have a stake in preserving the Arctic, the Antarctic, and other unique areas that are part of the common heritage of humanity.

As ENR problems have become perceived widely as international challenges, the scope and interdependence of necessary responses have broadened commensurately.[2] Although developed countries' activities are responsible for disproportionate contributions to the threats to the global commons, for example, these countries cannot protect and restore the commons without the help of developing countries in implementing international laws, accords, and regimes. Economic growth in developing countries is and promises to continue contributing emissions that threaten the biosphere. Conversely, the developed world must be (and is) much less able to export its environmental pollution and problems to others because of a host of treaties and agreements aimed at managing international environmental relations. Meanwhile, local environmental problems in the developing world often overwhelm local resources and require technical and financial resources from elsewhere for timely and effective regulation, prevention, and remediation to occur. Indeed, most analysts now appreciate that poverty and environmental degradation in the developing world are intimately intertwined: the struggle for survival leads to unsustainable use of resources, while environmental decline threatens livelihoods tied closely to the health of the land and water.

Spawned by these realities, the idea of building and implementing global environmental regimes capable of dealing collaboratively with these problems has entered scholarly and practitioner parlance. Regimes are seen as important ways of conceptualizing both the nature of the global ENR challenges confronting humanity and the adequacy of the responses necessary to cope with these threats. As Oran Young defines them, regimes are "social institutions that consist of agreed upon principles, norms, rules, decision-making procedures, and programs that govern the interaction of actors in specific issue areas."[3]

Much of the focus on environmental regimes is on global institutions such as the United Nations (UN) and its many agencies (including, most notably, the UN Environmental Program [UNEP]), the World Bank, the International Monetary Fund, and the Global Environment Facility (GEF). Involved, as well, are the administrative bodies created expressly to manage the implementation of some major environmental treaties, bodies sometimes viewed as the center of environmental regimes. Also joining them as essential elements of environmental regimes are nongovernmental organizations (NGOs), including large, globally active environmental groups (such as Greenpeace, the World Wildlife Fund, and the World Conservation Union), as well as regional and even national and subnational advocacy groups (for example, the Sierra Club and BIOTHAI in Thailand).[4] Global corporations and multilateral efforts on corporate governance (for example, the UN Global Compact) are also essential components of regimes, a phenomenon that Jan Mazurek discusses in chapter 13. Before assessing the implementation challenges of building common purpose that have faced this disparate group of participants, however, it is important to place their efforts within a broader context of the diverse, sometimes divisive, and always politically constraining legal context within which they must function.

Diversity, Dissensus, and International Regime Management

International environmental law scholars have catalogued close to 200 international environmental agreements addressing a wide range of issues. Major treaties focus on pollution of the atmosphere; the protection of marine resources; imports and exports of hazardous substances; and protection of species, habitat, and biodiversity. The provisions contained in these treaties vary considerably in terms of their results-based orientations. Many of these agreements are in the form of framework conventions supplemented with protocols that establish specific goals and requirements. Other treaties take the form of "soft" law—principles proposed and tested before they become binding or "hard" law.[5] Variety aside, treaties typically either spawn the creation of secretariats or give authority to existing organizations. In this vein, although the UN, UNEP, and other UN special units have been given responsibility for many global accords, a more typical approach is to create a new body to manage the implementation of a treaty.[6] Whether new or established, however, they all are expected to formulate additional requirements, monitor implementation, and provide for resolution of disputes.

Unlike international trade, where one overarching regime exists—the World Trade Organization (WTO) and regional organizations that fit within the broader regime (such as the North American Free Trade Agreement and its implementing bodies)—there is no single global environmental regime. As a result, opponents of environmental regulation often use the dispute mechanisms of the WTO and regional trade regimes to reduce these rules' scope and impact on industry.[7] Realizing this strategy, environmentalists continue to press for representation of their values within these regimes.

These battles aside, the regimes surrounding each major environmental treaty vary widely in terms of the development of specific, binding rules; the resources given to the managing secretariat; the number of signatories; the level of commitment given to their goals; and other characteristics that help determine their effectiveness in averting, attenuating, or remedying environmental problems. Nor does agreement even exist over how many global environmental regimes have been created. A useful beginning point here is the Fridtjof Nansen Institute's description of major international environmental agreements. The institute lists four regimes dealing with the atmosphere; seven dealing with hazardous substances; eight global, five regional, and nine conventions within the UNEP Regional Seas Program; three agreements dealing with marine living resources; nine agreements on natural conservation and terrestrial living resources; four agreements dealing with nuclear safety; and one agreement on freshwater resources.[8]

In contrast, in their study of global environmental politics, Gareth Porter, Janet Brown, and Pamela Chasek identify nine major regimes:

1. Acid Rain: The Convention on Long-Range Transboundary Air Pollution, 1979;

2. Ozone Depletion: The Vienna Convention for the Protection of the Ozone Layer, 1985, including the Montreal Protocol on Substances that Deplete the Ozone Layer;

3. Whaling: The International Convention for the Regulation of Whaling, 1946;

4. African Ivory Trade: The Convention on International Trade in Endangered Species, 1973;

5. International Toxic Trade: The Convention on the Control of Transboundary Movements of Hazardous Wastes and Their Disposal, 1989;

6. The Antarctic: The Antarctic Treaty of 1959;

7. Climate Change: The United Nations Framework Convention on Climate Change, 1992, including the Kyoto Protocol;

8. Biodiversity Loss: The Convention on Biological Diversity, 1992; and

9. Desertification: The Convention to Combat Desertification, 1994.[9]

In sum, and regardless of which classificatory scheme is used, regimes vary tremendously across a wide set of variables and are difficult to compare and contrast. Some have received major attention, whereas others are largely unknown; some have been divisive, but others more consensus-driven; and some have major resources committed to them, whereas others are marginal undertakings.

Building Common Purpose? Assessing the Accomplishments of Global Environmental Regimes

Any analysis of the comparative effectiveness of international regimes in dealing with global interdependence largely is a subjective undertaking, especially as it relates to assessing the appropriateness and realization of the goals selected.[10] Further complicating this effort are a variety of factors that pose challenges to evaluators, including the wide variation across regimes noted in the previous section. Moreover, the relevant variables at each level of the regime(s) under investigation are either difficult to measure or limited in their explanatory power. What is more, because regimes are composed of a number of elements, even knowing which elements to examine is difficult. Their components, after all, are complex political phenomena that are difficult to compare precisely.[11]

Nor do problems cease if regime impacts are clear and positive. It remains difficult, for example, to know whether these benefits outweigh the costs of designing and implementing the regime. Often unclear as well is whether the benefits that occur exceed the costs that regulatory targets incur to comply with the regime's mandates. At the same time, measuring effectiveness also requires difficult assessments of what has been achieved versus what would have happened without the regime, or what the maximum impacts might have been in its absence. And were all this not challenging enough to evaluators, regimes may produce compliance with their goals and mandates without clearly improving environmental conditions. As Oran Young states in his book on the formation of regimes to protect the Arctic, although these regimes are "well into the stage of day-to-day operation," the "extent to which each . . . has contributed to solving the problems that motivated its members to create it in the first place is a complex issue."[12]

These caveats notwithstanding, researchers *have* attempted to assess international environmental regimes based on the extent to which treaties are implemented; compliance with the provisions implemented is achieved; the regime achieves the objectives laid out in the treaty; and the achievement of those objectives actually improves environmental quality and natural resources protection.[13] Researchers applying this analytical framework have made substantial progress in identifying in broad strokes the conditions under which regime effectiveness is more or less likely to occur. Here, four sets of factors appear especially noteworthy: variations in regime characteristics, pressures from civic society, difficulties in overcoming collective action problems, and levels of capacity in developing nations.

The Importance of Regime Characteristics

Research that has focused on how environmental regimes are formed and how well they promote policy implementation and compliance[14] typically conclude that regimes *have* made a difference in activities affecting environmental quality and natural resource protection.[15] Researchers vary, however, in their assessments of how much difference regimes have made. David Victor and Eugene Skolnikoff's study of the implementation and effectiveness of international environmental agreements, for example, found that although a high degree of compliance with these agreements exists, this compliance is largely owing to the modest requirements they have imposed on participating nations.[16] Edward Miles and his colleagues are more charitable in their study of the effectiveness of environmental regimes. They conclude that

1. most environmental regimes do succeed in changing actor behavior in the direction intended;

2. processes of regime formation and implementation can have a significant impact, even if they do not succeed in producing collective decisions;

3. governments, as well as societies, quite often make unilateral adjustments in response to new ideas and information or in anticipation of new regulations;

4. even strongly politically malignant (that is, politically risky) problems can be solved effectively (there are exceptions, but the overall progress made in coping with politically malignant problems is higher than expected);

5. most regimes tend to grow and become more effective as they develop beyond their initial stages;

6. knowledge can be improved through investment in research and be more effectively transformed into decision processes through the design of institutions and processes for dissemination and consensual interpretation.[17]

By the same token, however, these same researchers also offer several negative assessments of the effectiveness of environmental regimes:

1. the solutions achieved, by and large, leave substantial room for improvement;

2. some of the overall improvement observed seems attributable to fortunate circumstances for which the regime can claim little or no credit;

3. the most fundamental factor intervening is a general growth in public demand for and governmental supply of policies for environmental protection [so that] the success may be very hard to sustain in periods with declining public concern;

4. before rejoicing at instances of declining problem malignancy and increased political courage, we should realize that the shift is sometimes a consequence of the situation deteriorating to the point where there is not much left to fight over (see whaling);

5. ample evidence suggests that societies still have a long way to go and formidable obstacles to pass before ENR problems are effectively solved.[18]

Depth of impact aside, other researchers have begun compiling the conditions under which global environmental regimes have been more or less successful in promoting implementation and compliance. As Edella Schlager's review of common-pool resource theory in chapter 4 and DeWitt John's discussion of civic environmentalism in chapter 6 also show, successful regimes typically have (1) norms, rules, principles, and shared commitments about preservation of natural resources, protection of ecosystem health, and sustainability; (2) a broad cross-section of governmental and nongovernmental actors and institutions that come together for collective action; (3) binding obligations codified in formal agreements that specify what actions are prohibited and required; and (4) administrative and other mechanisms to monitor implementation, provide technical and financial support where needed, enforce obligations, and provide a forum for revisions to the agreements.[19] The more developed each of these characteristics is, the more likely the regime will have the capacity to engage with nation-states and other actors in the building of a results-based sense of common purpose and to encourage their implementation of and compliance with treaty provisions.

Other scholars studying the effectiveness of regimes have emphasized the importance of shared expectations and a common understanding of both the causes of problems and their remedies.[20] Regimes play a fundamentally important role in defining problems, identifying possible solutions, and articulating compelling rationales and reasons that provoke action. In fact, important scholarship emphasizes the role of "epistemic communities" in doing precisely these things for policymakers. The work of these communities of scientific and technical experts comes to the attention of influential policymakers and the general public and generates demands for actions to remedy the problems identified.[21]

Finally, because of the primacy of the principle of national sovereignty in global affairs, several variables associated with nation-states are important as well. Nations, after all, largely retain responsibility for the implementation of international laws within their borders. Therefore, what goes on in individual countries has tremendous implications for the success of any regime as a whole. Here, the capacity of nations to take effective regulatory action is especially critical (see below).[22] Prior research, in turn, suggests that the extent to which countries enact implementing legislation and effectively enforce provisions is a function of four factors: domestic political support for the international effort, the commitment of the government in power, its interest in global leadership, and the capacity of its regulatory agencies to monitor and enforce compliance.

The Critical Role of Civic Society

Still other assessments of the effectiveness of environmental regimes in dealing with global interdependence focus on the role of NGOs. Researchers argue that many of the issues on the international environmental agenda are there because of NGOs' efforts and that NGOs have played an indispensable role in designing and implementing effective environmental agreements. For example, national governments that otherwise are hesitant to impose strict requirements on domestic industries and other powerful interests may be compelled to act if environmental advocates create sufficient demand. Environmental NGOs also play a critical role in developing support for global agreements, for generating commitments from political leaders, and for generating domestic pressure to keep global commitments. Moreover, as Robert Durant with Thanit Boodphetcharat illustrate in chapter 3, NGOs that operate on a global scale are particularly important in helping to develop nascent movements in developing countries that can pressure their governments to take action.

No guarantee exists, however, that NGOs will decide to do any of these things. Victor and Skolnikoff warn, for example, that NGOs are rarely in a position to perform independent oversight of compliance efforts because they usually lack the resources to obtain the information required. Thus, they say, "the most successful efforts to engage stakeholders have been those that have altered the incentives for them to participate—for example, by making useful environmental data available so that public interest groups could participate on an equal footing with private firms and governments."[23] NGOs also are expected to play a major role in monitoring and enforcement, especially as regulatory regimes begin to embrace such market-based approaches to regulation as emissions trading. But governments need to have realistic expectations of what NGOs can and cannot do in contributing to the enforcement and, ultimately, the effectiveness of global environmental accords using these approaches.

In sum, the great diversity of environmental NGOs and the energy and dedication they bring to international negotiations, global consciousness-raising, and the monitoring of compliance with treaties and agreements are impressive. Their participation in international negotiations has had a major impact on the direction of talks and the agreements fashioned. They have provided strong voices to hold international institutions accountable for the environmental impacts of the projects they fund. They have played a critical role in putting a number of issues on the agenda (for example, persistent organic pollutants). They foster the sharing of information and the empowering of citizens worldwide, which can prove critical in building a sense of common purpose. They supply the political pressure to link global obligations with domestic laws and programs.

Nevertheless, they also are fragmented. As Durant with Boodphetcharat also note, major philosophical divisions exist between NGOs in the developed and developing worlds: they have different priorities; they struggle with different problems; they have greatly uneven resources; and they see risk through different cultural prisms. Some coalitions have formed, and some groups have broadened their vision to recognize that the interests of rich and poor are intertwined closely. Yet, as Philip Shabecoff has written, "it would take a great leap of faith to speak of a coherent global movement" among NGOs.[24]

Overcoming Collective Action Problems

The dynamics of international relations and the role of the international bodies created or charged to oversee implementation are additional factors conditioning the success of environmental regimes in coping with global interdependence. The problem of free riders pervades international relations: not signing agreements or signing but not implementing them offers nations some advantages. In both instances, nations can gain the benefits of international actions without bearing their costs. Thus, for results-based and collaborative environmental regimes to be effective, international agencies need to be able to compel the production of reports, to possess the technical capacity to assess the data provided and identify problems, and to create effective incentives and sanctions that promote compliance. They also need to be able to assess progress in remedying the problems the regime was created to address and to provide a forum for signatory states to revise agreements as circumstances require.[25]

Presently in place, however, is a complex set of global environmental institutions with varying capacities to address these factors. As noted earlier, these institutions include the traditional UN bodies, UNEP and other agencies, the GEF, various UN regional economic commissions, regional development banks, regional offices of major UN agencies, other regional organizations that are part of the UN structure for sustainable development and environmental protection, the World Bank, and other regional multilateral lending institutions.[26] Yet there is little coordination among these sometimes competing organizations, and no overarching body ensures that environmental concerns are given priority at the highest levels of policymaking. Also lacking are organizations for environmental talks comparable to those for arms talks and international trade, for example. And despite the success of the 1992 Earth Summit and the 2002 UN World Summit on Sustainable Development in drawing attention to environment and development issues, environmental concerns still tend to be marginalized in international relations.

A 1997 UNEP report argued that "significant progress" had been made during the previous decade "in the realm of institutional developments, international cooperation, public participation, and the emergence of private-sector action." In this regard, the report highlighted the spread of new environmental laws, environmental impact assessments, economic incentives, and other policy efforts, plus the development of cleaner, less polluting production processes and technologies. These innovations, its authors argued, resulted in several countries reporting "marked progress in curbing environmental pollution and slow[ing] the rate of resource degradation, as well as reducing the intensity of resource use."[27]

However, the report also concluded that "from a global perspective, the environment has continued to degrade during the past decade, and significant environmental problems remain deeply embedded in the socio-economic fabric of nations in all regions. Collective progress toward a global sustainable future is just too slow." The authors of the report also found that although technologies are available to remedy environmental problems, a "sense of urgency is lacking," as are the financial resources and the collective "political will" to reduce environmental degradation and to protect natural resources. There is, they said, a "general lack of sustained [collective] interest in global and long-term environmental issues," and global "governance structures and environmental solidarity remain too weak to make progress a world-wide reality." Consequently, the "gap between what has been done thus far and what is realistically needed is widening."[28]

This bleak assessment of collective action notwithstanding, one nonetheless finds innovative and important examples of progress in regime governance. Two very promising institutional developments, albeit not ones without problems,[29] are the Montreal Multilateral Fund (MMF) and the GEF. The MMF was created as part of the 1990 London amendments to the Montreal Protocol, wherein the industrialized countries agreed to pay developing countries' "incremental" costs of compliance with the Protocol. These costs are defined as the expenses for the development of alternatives to ozone-depleting substances beyond what developing countries would otherwise spend to modernize their economies.[30] A $240 million Interim Multilateral Fund was created for this purpose. The World Bank administers the trust fund; UNEP provides technical and scientific assistance in identifying and selecting projects, with help from an international scientific and technical advisory panel; and UNDP coordinates the financing and managing of technical assistance and preproject preparations.[31] In 1992, the parties to the Montreal Protocol made the MMF permanent.[32] Then, in 1999, they agreed to spend $440 million between 2000 and 2002 for a new round of projects to convert refrigerators, air conditioners, and other consumer goods and industrial processes in developing nations from halons and chlorofluorocarbons (CFCs). By 2000, the MMF had provided some $1 billion in aid to 100 countries.[33] Grants typically went to private sector parties for projects such as recycling of CFCs, monitoring greenhouse gas emission, and protecting biodiversity.[34] Still, project implementation has been slow, as has been progress in reducing emissions in developing countries.[35]

A parallel fund with a much broader agenda is the GEF. Created in 1991 by the World Bank and restructured in 1992 at the UN Conference on Environment and Development (UNCED), the GEF channels funds to developing countries to help them implement programs to reduce pressure on global ecosystems.[36] And not unlike the MMF, the GEF has had its share of both problems and progress. For example, both the UNCED climate change convention and biodiversity convention require that funding mechanisms be accountable to all parties and include an equitable and balanced system of representation and governance. One early study, however, found these requirements were not enough to ensure that projects funded address the developing world's environment and development priorities.[37] Researchers also found that the GEF generated widespread support initially because of strong commitment to the general idea of assisting developing countries. That consensus collapsed into conflict, however, when specific decisions regarding implementation were made.[38] As a result, during the pilot phase, the GEF failed to have an impact on developing countries' environmental policies.[39] This concern notwithstanding, since 1992 the GEF has disbursed $4.5 billion to 140 countries for some 1,300 projects.[40] As such, GEF projects today play a key role in ecologically sustainable development in particular areas around the globe.

Capacity Limitations on Sustainable Development in the Developing World

Effective national governing institutions, particularly in the developing world, are just as important as global institutions in building effective regimes for dealing with global interdependence. The World Bank's investments in building the institutional capacity of governments promise to have long-term benefits. They give recipient nations the tools to design and implement programs that will help them to meet international obligations and to ensure that economic activity is environmentally sustainable.[41] Unfortunately, these efforts face tremendous barriers to building a results-based sense of common purpose.[42] At best, many developing countries lack the government infrastructure to develop effective regulatory programs. Some, for example, do not have either the necessary scientific infrastructure to examine the problems they confront or a tradition and culture of compliance with regulatory requirements. At worst, before progress can be made, recipient nations must address such issues as "rapid population growth, corruption, inadequate technical and managerial standards of competence, extreme income disparities, and 'unrealistic' official rates of exchange."[43]

To be sure, World Bank and GEF projects that are aimed at reinforcing institutional capacity for environmental protection projects are important responses to these problems in developing nations. The level of funding provided, however, is insufficient to help build effective governing institutions. Furthermore, the political instability that has engulfed so many areas in the world that need this assistance continues to prevent progress in environmental protection and development and will do so even if spending were to increase. Wars and other forms of military activity, for example, pose tremendous environmental problems and program challenges, as do natural disasters.[44]

Into this breach as well in 1992 came Agenda 21, one of the major agreements to come out of the Rio Earth Summit. Creating an expectation of North-South partnership critical to the building of effective regimes, Agenda 21 as implemented over the past decade nevertheless calls into question whether the developed and the developing worlds have pursued their goals aggressively enough. In June 1997, for example, the UN General Assembly Special Session (UNGASS) to Review Implementation of Agenda 21 heard assessments of the progress made under the agreement from 197 heads of states, ministers, and UN representatives. To its credit, UNGASS made no attempt to "paper over the cracks in the celebrated 'global partnership' [of capacity building] for sustainable development and pretend that things are better than they are."[45]

Persistent and spiraling poverty since Rio had prevented many developing nations from participating in and benefiting from the global economy. This trend, in turn, further fueled the gap between the wealthy and poor countries, a gap that "ha[d] grown rapidly in recent years."[46] Some countries *had* reduced resource use, cut emissions of pollutants, and experienced declines in population growth rates since Rio. Yet not only had global environmental conditions worsened, but "significant environmental problems remain[ed] deeply embedded in the socio-economic fabric of countries in all regions."[47] Nor did it help that exorbitant levels of foreign debt remained in many developing countries, debt representing "a major [financial] constraint on achieving sustainable development."[48] In the process of inaction, a perverse vicious cycle ensued: "increasing levels of pollution . . . threaten[ed] to exceed the capacity of the global environment to absorb them [*sic*], increasing the potential obstacles to economic and social development in developing countries."[49]

UNGASS also outlined a number of capacity issues requiring urgent attention in order to implement Agenda 21. Most notable for this chapter, it urged that "international cooperation be reactivated and intensified" and promoted the "invigoration of a genuine new global partnership, taking into account the special needs and priorities of developing countries."[50] Within this general rubric, the list of capacity-related issues begging attention was (and remains) daunting. Among other things, UNGASS urged nations to

1. integrate economic, social, and environmental objectives in national policies;

2. foster a dynamic economy "favourable to all countries";

3. eradicate poverty and improve access to social services;

4. change unsustainable consumption and production patterns;

5. make trade and the environment "mutually supportive";

6. further promote the decline in population growth rates;

7. enable all people to "achieve a higher level of health and well-being";

8. improve living conditions throughout the world;[51]

9. increase private investment and foreign debt reduction in developing countries;

10. improve the transparency of subsidies; and

11. increase the transfer of environmentally sound technologies to developing countries.[52]

This clarion call to action notwithstanding, the 1997 UNGASS meeting did more to highlight than to address these capacity-building issues. It reminded global leaders of the idea of sustainable development but seemed to lack any ability to identify strategic plans, generate commitments to specific actions, or significantly improve funding for them. Also, although

UN documents dutifully cataloged the myriad of global environmental challenges, the meeting failed to take on the dominant forces in economic activity and development: international trade and private investment decisions. On the positive side, it propelled increasing discussion and monitoring of concrete indicators for such things as reproductive health care, consumption trends, and production patterns. Perhaps most troubling, however, was that 5 years after the launch of Agenda 21, the "question dominating debate at UNGASS," according to one observer, was, "Where to go from here?"[53]

The UN World Summit on Sustainable Development held in the late summer of 2002 in Johannesburg, South Africa, was the most recent round in this ongoing effort and is illustrative of both progress and continuing difficulties in building both capacity *and* common purpose on these issues. The summit organizers sought to renew the global dialogue over how to achieve the goals of reducing poverty and protecting natural systems and resources. In particular, they sought to produce concrete capacity-building action in five areas: water and sanitation, clean and affordable energy, agricultural productivity, biodiversity and ecosystem management, and public health.[54]

In the end, and quite positively, the South African summit produced a consensus that poverty, natural resources consumption, and environmental degradation are inextricably linked, and that economic development and environmental protection must be pursued in tandem.[55] In the process, it reaffirmed capacity-building goals enunciated previously. Among these goals were rich countries' donation of 0.7 percent of their national income to development assistance, the use of the precautionary principle to protect the environment in the face of uncertainties (as discussed in greater detail by Robert Durant with Thanit Boodphetcharat in chapter 3), and a recognition that all countries share common but differentiated responsibilities to protect the environment (for example, placing the burden for financing environmental protection investments primarily in the wealthy developed world).[56]

This consensus yet may help to shape future global policymaking. However, one widely shared concern is whether the South Africa summit generated sufficient commitment to ensure that significant progress in capacity building occurs. For example, part of the emergent consensus was the importance of partnerships among NGOs, businesses, and government in reducing the threat of climate change, protecting biodiversity, and developing clean energy technologies. Some summit participants even saw these partnerships as part of a promising new model of development.[57] Others, however, criticized them not only because they were voluntary, but also because they allowed corporations to control the substance, means, and pace of both compliance and capacity building.

A question about commitment also arose from the limited number of specific, measurable capacity-building and substantive targets produced in Johannesburg. Among the more specific and measurable targets produced were cutting by one-half the number of people without access to sanitation and clean water and restoring depleted ocean fish stocks by 2015. Yet most commitments were couched in general or ambiguous terms that did not provide clear benchmarks for assessing progress. Among the most illustrative of these commitments were:

• Producing chemicals by 2020 in ways that minimize harmful human and environmental impacts;

• Improving access to affordable energy and increasing the share of energy produced from renewable sources;

• Recognizing that access to health care should be consistent with basic human rights as well as with religious and cultural values;

• Reducing significantly by 2010 the rate at which threatened and endangered species are becoming extinct;

• Initiating strategies by 2005 to preserve resources for future generations.

It is, of course, too soon to assess the Johannesburg summit. Any evaluation awaits a determination not only of its success in meeting the specific commitments made, but also of whether it has reshaped and energized capacity-building efforts to promote sustainable development. As noted earlier, the 1992 Earth Summit similarly was touted as shifting the global environmental discourse, but there is little evidence that any transition in thinking and capacity building occurred or that environmental deterioration abated.[58] Nor are early reactions to Johannesburg encouraging. Adding to the specific concerns just noted, skeptics with larger philosophical concerns already have weighed in, ranging from free-market critics of environmental summits in general to those who demand faster and more nonincremental accomplishments in light of the ecological crises humanity currently faces. The former argue that global goals are achieved best through economic growth, expanded trade, and generation of wealth that can be invested in improved environmental quality.[59] The latter conclude that the seriousness and pervasiveness of human poverty and environmental threats dwarf the modest scope of issues addressed and the substantive and capacity-building commitments made at Johannesburg.[60] Others, of course, will say that Johannesburg at least kept alive the discussions about sustainability, about capacity building, and about the intersection of poverty and environmental protection. Definite commitments to these ends arguably may arise more readily, however, from meetings that focus on specific problems.

Global Interdependence, Institutional Regimes, and Ecological Sustainability: Challenges, Choices, and Opportunities

What does the future hold for international environmental regimes as tools for building a results-based sense of common purpose in a globally interdependent world? Some regimes are quite new, and it is not realistic to expect them to solve problems within a few short years. Causes are long term, and so are solutions. Moreover, some problems will never be solved, but only managed, and the expectations held for regimes dealing with those problems must reflect that reality.[61] These caveats notwithstanding, the research reviewed in this chapter suggests that proponents of regimes will have to grapple with a variety of strategic challenges, choices, and opportunities if their goals are to be realized in the years ahead.

These challenges, choices, and opportunities are understood best in terms of three primary and interrelated questions. First, to what extent will notions of ecological sustainability (defined in the next section) be given priority over traditional conceptualizations of sustainable development in future policy deliberations? Second, to what extent and how might notions of ecological sustainability become the conceptual basis for a new round of global environmental accords and regimes? Third, and informing the answers to the first two questions, to what extent will the sense of community that has been so critical to regime development at the local level be reproducible at the national, regional, and global level?

Toward Ecological Sustainability?

As Robert Paehlke so cogently summarized in chapter 1, the idea of sustainability has well-developed roots in ENR policy. Sustainability was most recently and prominently an essential underpinning of the 1992 Rio Earth Summit and the 2002 World Summit. The term *sustainability* was included in nearly half of the twenty-seven articles that made up the Rio Declaration, a statement of broad principles to guide economic development. Moreover, as noted, it was the basis for Agenda 21 and was featured in the title of the 2002 World Summit.[62] As Paehlke also noted, however, none of the Rio Summit documents or those of any of its predecessors ever provided a clear definition of *sustainable development*. According to one count, for example, there are some seventy competing definitions of the term.[63] Nor, despite efforts to broaden and strengthen the concept in Johannesburg in 2002, is agreement proving any easier to accomplish today.

The contested nature of the idea of sustainable development is rooted fundamentally in two disparate conceptions. The first concept is a weak or "thin" form of sustainable development that many proponents of sustainability in the United States embrace. They argue that economic and environmental concerns can and must be *balanced*. In the past, economic growth was given priority; now it must be refined and balanced by environmental sensitivity. What is not needed, advocates of this thin form argue, is a fundamental rethinking of contemporary business philosophy and practice: current technologies, patterns of production, and levels of consumption are acceptable as long as they are tempered by environmental and resource considerations. Put differently, we largely can continue to do what we did in the past as long as we are more "sensitive" to environmental conditions. Proponents of this view relatedly argue that the overall value of the natural and economic capital for future generations need not be undiminished by the current generation. The goal is to ensure the same level of resources, while permitting some substitution of natural resources for an equivalent amount of capital.

In contrast, a strong or "thick" form of sustainable development, what I call *ecological sustainability,* eschews balance in favor of making environmental preservation the paramount value. Proponents of thick forms of sustainability argue that ecological survival simply outweighs or trumps economic growth as the primary public priority.[64] Their reasoning is straightforward: because ecological conditions make all life (including economic activities) possible, preserving those conditions should be given priority. Balancing is not enough. Ecological values must come first and must define and limit what kinds and levels of economic activity are acceptable.

Proponents of this thick form of sustainability thus place a major constraint on economics; only economic activity that is consistent with the fundamental criterion of sustainability is acceptable. From this perspective, the current distribution of critical natural capital must be maintained in some form so that the ecosystem services it provides are maintained. In the process, what Paehlke (quoting others) terms *dematerialization* must occur: industrial activities, energy production, transportation, and consumption fundamentally must be transformed to avoid ecological disruptions and protect regenerative processes. Moreover, policy goals such as free trade and economic efficiency must be subordinated to the preservation of biodiversity, the protection of wild lands, and the reclamation of damaged areas.

Another important feature of this thick notion of development is its integration of ecological protection and economic activity with social equity and political empowerment. Sustainable development, proponents of this view argue, should give priority to reducing poverty and helping the poor gain some measure of self-sufficiency through a more equitable distribution of resources. Political participation, in turn, is a key ingredient in ensuring that decisions affecting economic and environmental conditions are made more inclusive, a position operationalized more fully later in James Meadowcroft's chapter on various forms of deliberative democracy.[65]

Prior to Johannesburg, the thin rather than the thick version of sustainability increasingly was finding its way into international environmental law. With Johannesburg, some movement toward the thicker version has occurred (for example, in more strongly giving priority to poverty and empowerment issues as a means of protecting the environment). But other major aspects of the thick version are still missing. Absent, for example, are specific, binding, and legally enforceable commitments that would require the revamping of production processes toward dematerialization, sustainability analysis (see chapter 1), and prioritization of environmental over market values. Moreover, mention of sustainable yields as goals in certain agreements reached at Johannesburg (for example, "to maintain or restore depleted fish stocks to levels that can produce the maximum sustainable yield") invoke the rhetoric of the thin form of sustainability.

Thus, a major strategic challenge for policymakers will be determining the extent to which thick forms of sustainability replace thin forms as the conceptual basis informing subsequent rounds of ENR laws, accords, and regimes. Ecological sustainability (or thick sustainability) is arguably a compelling framework for assessing environmentalism for several reasons. First, this widely discussed (and hence "softened") norm has already been the subject of international discussions and negotiations. Second, it calls for a comprehensive, integrated approach that includes social justice for the poor, transformation in economic aims and practices, and support for participatory democracy and empowerment of citizens. Third, it is a critically important notion in linking environmental problems in both the developed and the developing worlds. Both wealthy and poor countries, after all, share the strategic challenge of making their economies ecologically sustainable, reflective of the needs of the poor among them, and cognizant of the impact of their actions on future generations. The question remains, however, whether ecological sustainability is a politically feasible concept in the years ahead.

Ecological Sustainability, ENR Accords, and Institutional Regimes

Two arguments developed by scholars who write about sustainability are helpful in thinking about the pace, extent, and progress that might be made and measured toward establishing ecological sustainability as a central animating principle for building a results-based sense of common purpose in future international laws, accords, and treaties.[66] The first begs urgency in meeting the ecological sustainability challenge on the basis of the immediacy of a consumption crisis, whereas the second envisions a more incremental perspective and approach that sees the former ecological sustainability as a process or goal.

Those taking the former perspective argue that the problem of sustainability is rooted in the interaction of population, affluence, and technology, as shown in the following formula:

I (environmental or resource impacts)
= P (population) $\times$ A (affluence, usually per capita income)
$\times$ T (impacts per unit of income as determined by technology).[67]

On these grounds, they argue for an urgent, nonincremental shift toward ecological sustainability. World population trends are relatively well understood as multiplicative, resource intensive, and thus environmentally dysfunctional absent immediate actions (also see chapter 3). Granted, global population has grown in recent years by approximately 1.3 percent a year, down from a peak of 2.1 percent in the 1960s. The UN, however, projects that population growth will reach 8.9 billion in 2050, with growth primarily a result of death rates dropping more rapidly than birth rates.

There is, of course, a rather straightforward means of reducing population pressures in developing countries: increase the availability of contraceptives to prevent unwanted pregnancies; encourage smaller families by investing more in children, particularly in the education of girls; and encourage women to postpone childbearing by increasing educational opportunities for them.[68] But these projects take time to have impact and are controversial. Even more difficult to address is the growth of consumption. Although the Earth's population more than doubled between 1950 and 2000, agricultural output nearly tripled and energy use more than quadrupled. Energy efficiency has increased, and the amount of carbon used per unit of energy has declined. However, efficiency gains in both areas have been offset by growth in consumption. Consequently, solutions to consumption cannot wait and must include increasing efficiency; finding less environmentally damaging substitutes; fostering industrial ecology advances where industry learns from nature in redesigning production processes; and reducing, reusing, and recycling materials. That technological solutions will be sufficient, however, is far from established. Indeed, technology itself has been a major factor in driving the negative environmental impacts of consumption.

For those taking this perspective, nonetheless, part of the solution is a major behavioral shift by consumers as quickly as possible, with governments aiding these choices in part (albeit on the margins perhaps) by sending accurate market signals to them about the true social costs of their consumption decisions. Religious teachings that discourage material-ism and the simplicity movement's encouragement of less-consumptive practices also may reduce pressures. By whatever means, consumers in high-consumption societies must learn as quickly as possible to want and demand less so as to impose a smaller ecological footprint on the Earth.

It is presently difficult to imagine how such a perestroika in consumer and government thinking and action might occur, given the relentless em-phasis on growth that is the fundamental driving force of the global eco-nomic system. Wealth is generated by production and consumption. In turn, competitive pressures to keep up with the consumption of others help drive growth, and the great inequalities produced in the distribution of resources and wealth create tremendous demands for more growth. The wisdom and technical feasibility of ecological sustainability aside, its proponents nonetheless aim to break this vicious cycle. For them, the Western, industrialized, high-consumption way of living is not ecologi-cally feasible for all the planet's residents, or even for a majority of them. Indeed, notwithstanding marketing and advertising efforts to encourage this level of consumption worldwide, they argue that the impact of 6 bil-lion people living an American middle-class lifestyle would quickly over-whelm the ability of natural systems to sustain life.

Equally difficult is imagining how such a transformation in thinking might occur under current political, social, and cultural practices and in-stitutions. Consider, for example, the formidable technical, social, and political challenges implicit in Robert Kates's discussion of what such a behavioral shift entails:

To reduce the level of impacts per unit of consumption, it is necessary to separate out more damaging consumption and *shift* to less harmful forms, *shrink* the amounts of environmentally damaging energy and materials per unit of con-sumption, and *substitute* information for energy and materials. To reduce consumption per person or household, it is necessary to *satisfy* more with what is already had, *satiate* well-met consumption needs, and *sublimate* wants for a greater good. Finally, it is possible to *slow* population growth and then to *stabi-lize* population numbers.[69]

A second key idea from the literature on sustainability also speaks to how, when, and to what extent ecological sustainability might inform a new round of international laws, accords, and regimes. Viewed from the perspective of social movement theory, ecological sustainability is seen as a process or a goal against which to measure progress over the long term. From one such view, the importance of the concept is that various policies might be assessed in terms of whether they are consistent with or contrary to the elements of ecological sustainability. From another view, the real importance of the concept lies in its potential to reshape over time the terms of discourse about public policy in general and about production and consumption decisions in particular.

Thus, from the perspective of social movement theory, the debate over ecological sustainability eventually might produce a new paradigm to guide issues of production and consumption in the twenty-first century. Dennis Pirages, for example, argues that much as human survival and success are a result of "evolutionary mechanisms that have adapted the human body and human behavior to changing environmental constraints," sociocultural evolution is a similar process by which "survival-relevant information is passed from one generation to the next."[70] Hence, the strategic challenge for proponents of ecological sustainability is to identify and inculcate values and behaviors that will allow human society to function in ways consistent with ecological constraints.

This emphasis on ecological sustainability as social learning and evolution draws attention to sustainability as a long-term process that varies over time and across geographic areas and conditions. Creating a more sustainable world is thus, as Pirages puts it, a "dynamic, complex, and continuous process that will require decades of concerted effort."[71] Moreover, given the great diversity in human societies and ecological conditions, no single plan for ecological sustainability, no one international sustainability regime, will work everywhere. Still, to see if and how much ecological sustainability is becoming a central animating principle of results-based ENR laws, accords, and regimes, we need a way to measure progress in the processes necessary for realizing this end over time.

Table 2.1 summarizes the broad set of concepts operationalizing ecological sustainability that might inform ENR laws, accords, and regimes in the future. These variables can be present in varying levels of commitment. The weaker they are, the closer a community is to the weaker or thin form of sustainability or sustainable development. The stronger the commitments and their implementation, the closer the community has moved toward the stronger or thicker form of ecological sustainability.

Table 2.1
Elements of Sustainability

Ecological Integrity and Services
Maintain ecological integrity; protect key ecosystem services
Continue economic activity within ecological limits
Focus on intergenerational equity

Natural Capital
Sustainable yield of renewable resources
Preservation of natural capital base

• Allow substitutes among natural, human, economic, social, and cultural capital
• Allow some mixing of capital, but preserve key elements of natural capital
• Maintain each kind of capital: deplete oil but develop other forms of energy
• (Absolute preservation is the extreme but implausible form)

Regeneration of natural capital

Precautionary Principle
Uncertainty, irreversible impacts, cascading and synergistic effects, cliffs, exponential growth

True-Cost Prices: Internalize Environmental Costs in Market Exchanges
Pollution prevention: redesign of production; life-cycle management
Regulation: emission standards; integration across media and sectors
Property rights: prices reflect depletion; marketable rights: emissions trading
Taxes: pollution taxes, fees, and charges
Reduce subsidies that have harmful environmental consequences: water, energy
Legal liability, liability insurance
Economic valuation of natural resources: ecosystem functions

Economic Indicators and Measures
Reflect depletion of natural resources
Count pollution cleanup and illness treatment as costs
Include broader measures of social and economic factors: Genuine Progress Indicators

Wealth, Population, and Consumption
Intergenerational: nondeclining per capital wealth
Intragenerational: social, political, and economic equality and justice
Interaction of poverty and environmental degradation

Technology
Appropriate technology; efficiency and conservation; technology transfer to Southern Hemisphere

---

In sum, ecological sustainability in its strongest form involves the immediate development and implementation of a new paradigm for the interaction of humanity with its environment—a paradigm that champions ecological values. Some argue that this paradigm shift involves a transformation from an anthropocentric worldview to an ecocentric or biocentric paradigm, where humans are not the primary focus of attention, but instead where all forms of life are valued. Many find such a transformation inspiring, consistent with a commitment to a simpler, less selfish lifestyle that acknowledges the inherent value and sanctity of all forms of life and urges a strong commitment to ecological sustainability. Others find it utopian at best and misguided at worst. Everyone agrees, however, that it will be a very challenging transition to make.

A commitment to ecological sustainability, however, can also arise within the existing paradigm of self-interested humans. It is in our interest to preserve all forms of life and to help other species flourish because we all are elements of an intricate network of living things, and the health of each element of the system strengthens the entire biosphere and the life chances of its most intellectually advanced species. The factors summarized in table 2.1 can be useful in judging how far, fast, and meaningfully policymakers are choosing to make such a transition in international treaties, accords, and regimes. But, as the next section attests, progress on these factors ultimately will depend on how far, fast, and meaningfully societies choose to transfer their sense of community at the local level to national and international levels worldwide.

Building a Sense of Community?

Sustainability (either thin or thick) is largely a concept of community, and building a sense of community (or common purpose) represents a major strategic challenge to its becoming a central animating principle of global environmental politics. Without question, the most thriving examples of sustainability seem to be in the context of communities. Daniel Mazmanian and Michael Kraft, for example, even describe today's sustainable communities movement as a third epoch in the evolution of the environmental movement from an emphasis on reducing pollution to addressing the economic, environmental, psychological, and cultural well-being of communities.[72]

In these communities, sustainability is bound up with notions of strong democracy, participation, and community fostered through personal interaction. It is also bound up in a commitment to a land ethic. Sounding much like a proponent of sustainable communities, Aldo Leopold long ago defined a land ethic as follows: "An ethic, ecologically, is a limitation on freedom of action in the struggle for existence. . . . All ethics so far evolved rest upon a single premise: that the individual is a member of a community of interdependent parts. . . . The land ethic simply enlarges the boundaries of the community to include soils, water, plants, and animals, or collectively, the land."[73]

But can sustainability be extended beyond the community, to national and even international levels? Globalization, to an extent, weakens the power of individual national governments to implement the rules and regulations of environmental regimes because they are having increasing difficulty in regulating the growing power of the transnational corporations that are central drivers of globalization. Countries that fail to provide hospitable regulatory environments for business may lose out in global competition to attract jobs, investment, and industries. Given the tremendous pressures on governments to foster economic growth and the powerful global pressures to expand trade, it is difficult for nation-states to impose expensive regulations on industries in order to force them to internalize and reduce some of the costs of production, such as air and water pollution, rather than to externalize or impose pollution on others as a way to reduce costs.

Cities, nations, or regions also may find that their own community is sustainable, but only if they export the community's wastes or import unsustainable levels of resources. Likewise, they may find that their own community thrives, but others live lives mired in poverty. How does sustainability guide us in our policy, production, and consumption choices at a national and international scale under these circumstances? Michael Sandel suggests one way that it might. He argues that a commitment to a more engaged local environmental politics may contribute to the greater sense of global politics required to address problems affecting such commons issues as protecting the oceans, the stratospheric ozone layer, and the climate. "A more promising basis for democratic politics that reaches beyond nations," Sandel believes, "is a revitalized civic life nourished in the more particular communities we inhabit. . . . People will not pledge allegiance to vast and distant entities, whatever their importance, unless those institutions are somehow connected to political arrangements that reflect the identity of the participants."[74]

Sandel argues that the republican tradition of government, as articulated by Aristotle and subsequent theorists, is that self-government should be understood as "an activity rooted in a particular place, carried out by citizens loyal to that place and that way of life it embodies." However, self-government now requires "a politics that plays itself out in a multiplicity of settings, from neighborhoods to nations to the world as a whole. . . . The civic virtue distinctive to our time is the capacity to negotiate our way among the sometimes overlapping, sometimes conflicting obligations that claim us, and to live with the tension to which multiple loyalties give rise." Participation and engagement in local political problem solving may engender the kind of commitment and sense of responsibility that will spread to broader and eventually global issues.[75]

The prospects for ecological sustainability as a central animating principle of environmental governance and of international regimes that promote it thus are intertwined inextricably with the strategic challenge of promoting a much more vibrant and strong sense of global citizenship. And the roots of that citizenship may lie, paradoxically, in the kinds of locally based initiatives chronicled by Edella Schlager and DeWitt John in chapters 4 and 6 in this volume. To be sure, the forces standing in the way of developing this ethic are protean, profound, and politically challenging to accommodate. Blocking the building of this sense of community, for example, are legitimate and deep-felt economic, cultural, and political differences. Not the least of these strategic challenges today include U.S.–European differences over the precautionary principle as it applies to issues such as global warming and international trade (see chapter 3); differences between developed and developing nations over preserving national sovereignty while protecting global treasures such as the rain forests; and differences between developed and developing nations over international property rights as they apply to such things as bioprospecting for pharmaceuticals. Yet resolving or working around these differences is critical if the strong sense of global citizenship needed to advance ecological sustainability is ever to prevail as an animating principle of international regimes in a globally interdependent world.

Notes

1. The distribution of global resources requires collective efforts to ensure a fair distribution of access and use. The increasing globalization of markets and trade has contributed to increased aggregate wealth, but the gap between rich and poor across the planet and within individual countries has grown. The average income of residents of the twenty wealthiest countries is thirty-seven times that of people in the poorest twenty countries, and that ratio has doubled during the past forty years. Some countries continue to suffer negative growth rates, and the number of poor people in those countries has increased. The number of people living in extreme poverty in sub-Saharan Africa, for example, grew from 242 million in 1990 to 300 million by 2000. See, for example, World Bank, *World Development Report 2003* (Washington, D.C.: World Bank, 2003), p. 3; United Nations Development Program, *Human Development Report 2002* (New York: Oxford University Press, 2002), pp. 2, 10.

2. Most analysts now appreciate that poverty and environmental degradation in the developing world are intertwined. The struggle to survive may place severe pressure on natural resources, causing damage to or depletion of them. The need to survive causes poor people to "plunder their resources, pollute their environment, and overcrowd their habitats" (Jack M. Hollander, *The Real Environmental Crisis: Why Poverty, Not Affluence, Is the Environment's Number One Enemy* [Berkeley and Los Angeles: University of California Press, 2003], p. 2). Demand to expand arable lands so subsistence farmers can feed their families may overwhelm the goal of protecting the biodiversity of rain forests, for example, even though the fertility of such lands typically is depleted in only a relatively short time period. Conversely, high-consumption societies, even though they may possess the resources to reduce levels of air and water pollution, also produce serious threats to biodiversity and other measures of environmental quality through sprawl, chemical contamination, and emission of greenhouse gases. Degradation of environments and unsustainable consumption of resources occur both in the developing and developed countries, but the kinds of ecosystems and resources affected differ widely. For discussion of the unsustainability of consumption in the developed world, see Thomas Princen, Michael Maniates, and Ken Conca, eds., *Confronting Consumption* (Cambridge, Mass.: MIT Press, 2002); Paul Harrison, *The Third Revolution: Population, Environment, and a Sustainable World* (London: Penguin, 1992).

3. Oran Young, "Rights, Rules, and Resources in World Affairs," in Oran Young, ed., *Global Governance: Drawing Insights from the Environmental Experience* (Cambridge, Mass.: MIT Press, 1997), pp. 5–6. Oran Young's writings

are a necessary place to begin in exploring the idea of global environmental regimes. *Global Governance* contains chapters by Young and by other thoughtful scholars on this and related topics. See also Oran Young, *Creating Regimes: Arctic Accords and International Governance* (Ithaca, N.Y.: Cornell University Press, 1998). His work with other colleagues focuses on the role of institutions in international environmental policy making and is discussed in Young's *The Institutional Dimensions of Environmental Change: Fit, Interplay, and Scale* (Cambridge, Mass.: MIT Press, 2002).

4. Studies of the role these institutions have played in international environmental politics include Paul Wapner, *Environmental Activism and World Civic Politics* (Albany: State University of New York, 1996), and Margaret E. Keck and Kathryn Sikkink, *Activists Beyond Borders: Advocacy Networks in International Politics* (Ithaca, N.Y.: Cornell University Press, 1998).

5. See David Hunter, James Salzman, and Durwood Zaelke, *International Environmental Law and Policy,* 2d ed. (New York: Foundation, 2002), especially p. 349 for a discussion of soft law.

6. For a description of major environmental agreements and their managing secretariats, see Helge Ole Bergesen, Georg Parmann, and Oystein B. Thommessen, eds., *Yearbook of International Co-operation on Environment and Development* (London: Earthscan, 1998).

7. The literature on globalization is voluminous. For an introduction to the issues, see Council of Foreign Relations, *Globalization: Challenge and Opportunity* (New York: Foreign Affairs Magazine, 2002). For a discussion of the need for political power to match the power of transnational corporations and trade, see Theodore J. Lowi, Susan Rose-Ackerman, Sanford Lewis, Gerald E. Frug, Donald F. Kettl, Jerry L. Mashaw, Joel F. Handler, and Charles F. Sabel, "Think Globally, Lose Locally," *Boston Review* (April–May 1998): 4–22. For an assessment of the economics of globalization and trade and of the consequences for environmental regulation, see Joseph E. Stiglitz, *Globalization and Its Discontents* (New York: W. W. Norton, 2002).

8. Bergesen, Parmann, and Thommessen, *Yearbook of International Cooperation,* pp. 64–177.

9. Gareth Porter, Janet Welsh Brown, and Pamela S. Chasek, *Global Environmental Politics,* 3rd ed. (Boulder, Colo.: Westview, 2000), chap. 3.

10. By *regime effectiveness,* I mean here the commonsense notion of effectiveness as the extent to which a regime achieves the goals laid out for it by its creators and solves the problems that provoked its creation. In practice, assessing effectiveness can be a very complex undertaking because of different views about the object to be evaluated, what standard to use in evaluating the object, and how to go about comparing the object to the standard. The primary concern, of course, is whether the regime has produced a significant improvement in the environmental problem or condition it was created to ameliorate. Thus, one way to assess effectiveness is to examine the extent of (a) the regime's output, such as rules and regulations issued; (b) the regime's outcomes, including the implementation of rules and

regulations and the changed behavior of those at whom they are aimed; and (c) the impact of the regime on environmental conditions. Effectiveness inquiries alternatively can focus on assessing the impact produced with the resources invested and on making estimates about what might have occurred with more or fewer resources dedicated to the effort. But even these elements may be difficult to ascertain because there is no baseline to compare the problem before and after the regime began operating. Many environmental problems are so intractable and require such long-term intervention that progress is difficult to measure.

11. Edward L. Miles and his colleagues provide a very useful explanation of the problems involved in examining the effectiveness of environmental regimes. See Edward L. Miles, Arild Underdal, Steinar Andresen, John Bierger Skjaerseth, and Elaine M. Carlin, *Environmental Regime Effectiveness: Confronting Theory with Evidence* (Cambridge, Mass.: MIT Press, 2002), chap. 1.

12. Young, *Creating Regimes*, pp. 198–199.

13. See Harold K. Jacobson and Edith Brown Weiss, "A Framework for Analysis," in Edith Brown Weiss and Harold K. Jacobson, eds., *Engaging Countries: Strengthening Compliance with International Environmental Accords* (Cambridge, Mass.: MIT Press, 1998), p. 5.

14. For assessments of environmental regimes, see Robert O. Keohane and Marc A. Levy, eds., *Institutions for Environmental Aid* (Cambridge, Mass.: MIT Press, 1996); Peter M. Haas, Robert O. Keohane, and Marc A. Levy, *Institutions for the Earth: Sources of Effective Environmental Protection* (Cambridge, Mass.: MIT Press, 1993).

15. Oran Young, *Governance in World Affairs* (Ithaca, N.Y.: Cornell University Press, 1999), p. 249.

16. David G. Victor and Eugene B. Skolnikoff, "Translating Intent into Action: Implementing Environmental Commitments," *Environment* 41 (March 1999), p. 18.

17. Miles et al., *Environmental Regime Effectiveness*, pp. 456–457.

18. Miles et al., *Environmental Regime Effectiveness*, pp. 457–458.

19. Stephen D. Krasner's formulation of international regimes as "principles, norms, rules, and decision-making procedures around which actor expectations converge in a given issue-area" is cited widely as containing the core elements of regimes. See Stephen D. Krasner, ed., *International Regimes* (Ithaca, N.Y.: Cornell University Press, 1983), p. 1. Marvin Soroos similarly defines international environmental regimes as "the combination of international institutions, customary norms and principles, and formal treaty commitments that guide the behavior of states related to a specific subject, project, or region." See Marvin Soroos, "Global Institutions and the Environment," in Norman J. Vig and Regina S. Axelrod, eds., *The Global Environment: Institutions, Law, and Policy* (Washington, D.C.: CQ, 1998), p. 28.

20. See, for example, Nicholas Low and Brendan Gleeson, *Justice, Society, and Nature* (London: Routledge, 1998); David Orr, *Ecological Literacy: Education*

and the Transition to a Postmodern World (Albany: State University of New York Press, 1992). Other thoughtful books that do not expressly address the idea of regimes but emphasize the importance of shared understanding include Jim MacNeill, Pieter Winsenium, and Taizo Yakushiji, *Beyond Interdependence: The Meshing of the World's Economy and the Earth's Ecology* (New York: Oxford University Press, 1991); Lester W. Milbrath, *Envisioning a Sustainable Society: Learning Our Way Out* (Albany: State University of New York Press, 1989); Mary E. Clark, *Ariadne's Thread: The Search for New Modes of Thinking* (New York: St. Martin's, 1989).

21. Karen T. Litfin's study of the evolution of the scientific community surrounding the threat to the stratospheric ozone layer is an important contribution to the idea of epistemic communities and the understanding of the role of science in international environmental accords. See Karen T. Litfin, *Ozone Discourses: Science and Politics in Global Environmental Cooperation* (New York: Columbia University Press, 1994).

22. Karen T. Litfin and her colleagues explore the complexity of sovereignty, finding it sometimes consistent with efforts to protect the global environment and sometimes in opposition. See Karen T. Litfin, ed., *The Greening of Sovereignty in World Politics* (Cambridge, Mass.: MIT Press, 1998).

23. Victor and Skolnikoff, "Translating Intent into Action," p. 19. Renewable energy, environmental remediation, conservation, and other industries also can play key roles in generating support for implementing global agreements.

24. Philip Shabecoff, *A New Name for Peace: International Environmentalism, Sustainability Development, and Democracy* (Hanover, N.H.: University Press of New England, 1996), p. 73.

25. For a very helpful examination of a number of examples on how international bodies pursue this role in international environmental regimes, see David G. Victor, Kal Raustiala, and Eugene B. Skolnikoff, *The Implementation and Effectiveness of International Environmental Commitments: Theory and Practice* (Cambridge, Mass.: MIT Press, 1998), part 1.

26. World Resources Institute, *World Resources, 1994–95* (New York: Oxford University Press, 1994), p. 225.

27. United Nations Environment Program, *Global Environmental Outlook* (New York: Oxford University Press, 1997), p. 2.

28. Ibid., p. 3.

29. French, "Learning from the Ozone Experience."

30. Hilary F. French, "Learning from the Ozone Experience," in Lester R. Brown, Christopher Flavin, and Hilary French, eds., *State of the World 1997* (New York: W. W. Norton, 1997), pp. 162–163, 165.

31. Ibid., pp. 162–163; www.undp.org/seed/eap/montreal/rote.htm.

32. French, "Learning from the Ozone Experience," p. 163.

33. "Montreal Protocol Parties Reach Accord on Three-Year, $440 Million Package," *International Environment*, December 8, 1999, p. 978.

34. GEF, "The Restructured Global Environment Facility."

35. Ellizabeth DeSombre and Joanne Kauffman, "The Montreal Protocol Multilateral Fund: Partial Success Story," in Keohane and Levy, eds., *Institutions for Environmental Aid*, pp. 89–126.

36. Global Environment Facility (GEF), "The Restructured Global Environment Facility," http://www.worldbank.org/html/gef/intro/revqa.html, accessed November 5, 2002. The United States is the largest contributor to the GEF. In August 2002, the Bush administration pledged $500 million to the GEF over the next four years, and requested $70.3 million from Congress annually over the next three years to pay off U.S. pledges in arrears.

37. World Resources Institute, *World Resources 1994–95*, p. 230.

38. David Fairman, "The Global Environmental Facility: Haunted by the Shadow of the Future," in Robert O. Keohane and Marc A. Levy, eds., *Institutions for Environmental Aid* (Cambridge, Mass.: MIT Press, 1996), pp. 55–88.

39. Ibid.

40. Ibid.; www.gefweb.org/What_is_the_GEF/what_is_the_gef.html# Management.

41. *Editors' note:* For a competing perspective on the World Bank's contribution to sustainable development, see Bruce Rich, *Mortgaging the Earth: The World Bank, Environmental Impoverishment, and the Crisis of Development* (Boston: Beacon, 1994); David C. Korten, *When Corporations Rule the World* (West Hartford, Conn.: Kumarian, 1995); Joseph E. Stiglitz, *Globalization and Its Discontents* (New York: W. W. Norton, 2002).

42. For a more in-depth discussion of these issues, see Gary C. Bryner, *From Promises to Performance: Achieving Global Environmental Goals* (New York: W. W. Norton, 1998).

43. Morris Miller, *Debt and the Environment: Converging Crises* (New York: United Nations Publications, 1991), p. 46.

44. Jane Perlez, "African Dilemma: Food Aid May Prolong War and Famine," *New York Times*, May 12, 1991, p. A1.

45. *Earth Negotiations Bulletin* 5 (88) (June 30, 1997), http:\\www.iisd.ca/linkages/csd/enb0588e.html#1.

46. United Nations General Assembly, Nineteenth Special Session, agenda item 8, "Overall Review and Appraisal of the Implementation of Agenda 21," June 27, 1997, *Assessment of Progress Made Since the United Nations Conference on Environment and Development*, sect. 2, paragraphs 7–8, gopher://gopher.un.org:70/00/ga/docs/S-19/plenary/AS19–29.TXT, accessed November 5, 2002.

47. Ibid.

48. Ibid., paragraphs 17–20.

49. Ibid., paragraphs 9–10.

50. United Nations General Assembly, Nineteenth Special Session, agenda item 8, "Overall Review and Appraisal of the Implementation of Agenda 21," June 27, 1997, *Implementation in Areas Requiring Urgent Action,* sect. 3, paragraph 22, gopher://gopher.un.org:70/00/ga/docs/S-19/plenary/AS19-29.TXT, accessed November 5, 2002.

51. Ibid., paragraphs 23–32.

52. Ibid., paragraph 137.

53. *Earth Negotiations Bulletin* 5(88).

54. For a discussion of the goals animating the Johannesburg summit, see Kofi A. Annan, "Toward a Sustainable Future," *Environment* (September 2002): 10–15.

55. "Keeping Earth Fit for Development," *New York Times,* September 6, 2002, www.nytimes.com/2002/0906/opinion/06FR/html.

56. "Factbox: Key Points Agreed at Earth Summit Talks," *World Environment News,* September 5, 2002, www.planetark.irg/avantgo/dailynewsstory.cfm?newsid=17598.

57. Andrew C. Revkin, "Small World After All," *New York Times,* September 5, 2002, www.nytimes.com/2002/09/05/international/africa/05SUST.html.

58. For a recent review of global degradation, see James Gustave Speth, "A New Green Regime: Attacking the Root Causes of Global Environmental Deterioration," *Environment* (September 2002): 16–25.

59. Philip Stott, "Sustaining Environmentalists," *Wall Street Journal,* August 27, 2002, p. A12; James K. Glassman, "Johannesburg Summit: Moving on from 'Sustainability,'" American Enterprise Institute for Public Policy Research, www.aei.org/ra/raglas020812.htm, accessed September 16, 2002.

60. See, for example, Adil Najam, Janice M. Poling, Naoyuki Yamagishi, Daniel G. Straub, Jilian Sarno, Sara M. De Ritter, and Eonjeong Michelle Kim, "From Rio to Johannesburg: Progress and Prospects," *Environment* (September 2002): 26–38; Christopher Flavin, Hilary French, and Gary Gardner, *State of the World 2002* (Washington, D.C.: Worldwatch Institute, 2002).

61. In "Is Humanity Destined to Self-Destruct?" *Politics and the Life Sciences* 18(2) (1999): 3–14, Lynton Keith Caldwell argues that pollution, population, and exhausted resources are chronic concerns that are understood better as "climacterics," situations with which future generations are destined to grapple, rather than an environmental crisis that may one day be "solved."

62. For discussions of the Rio Summit, see Adam Rogers, *The Earth Summit* (Los Angeles: Global View Press, 1993); Daniel Sitarz, ed., *Agenda 21: The Earth Summit Strategy to Save Our Planet* (Boulder, Colo.: EarthPress, 1993).

63. John Kirby, Phil O'Keefe, and Lloyd Timberlake, *The Earthscan Reader in Sustainable Development* (London: Earthscan, 1995), p. 1.

64. For an exploration of these views from an economic perspective, see Todd Sandler, *Global Challenges* (Cambridge: Cambridge University Press, 1997); and for a broader ecological and political debate over sustainability, see Dennis C. Pirages, ed., *Building Sustainable Societies: A Blueprint for a Post-Industrial World* (Armonk, N.Y.: M. E. Sharpe, 1996).

65. Also see William Lafferty, "The Politics of Sustainable Development: Global Norms for National Implementation," *Environmental Politics* 5 (1996): 185–208.

66. Some readers might wonder why I give so much attention in this section to what appear to be domestic issues; my reason for doing so is straightforward. One essential element of international regimes is the support that member states give to them. The level of that support is in turn affected greatly by support for the regime found in domestic politics and by regime proponents' ability to create domestic political incentives for the national government to contribute to the regime's success. Governments can contribute both by implementing these provisions and incentives domestically and by endorsing a regime's efforts internationally and within other countries.

67. Robert W. Kates, "Population and Consumption: What We Know, What We Need to Know," *Environment* 42 (April 2000), p. 12.

68. Ibid., pp. 12–13.

69. Ibid., p. 18, emphasis in original.

70. Pirages, *Building Sustainable Societies*, pp. 4–5.

71. Ibid., p. 12.

72. Daniel A. Mazmanian and Michael E. Kraft, eds., *Toward Sustainable Communities: Transition and Transformations in Environmental Policy* (Cambridge, Mass.: MIT Press, 1999).

73. Aldo Leopold, *A Sand County Almanac* (New York: Ballantine, 1966), pp. 238–239.

74. Michael Sandel, *Democracy's Discontent* (Cambridge, Mass.: Harvard University Press, 1996), p. 46.

75. Ibid., p. 350.

3

The Precautionary Principle

Robert F. Durant
with Thanit Boodphetcharat

One of the most significant political fault lines hindering the worldwide building of a results-based sense of common purpose in environmental governance today involves debates over the so-called precautionary principle. The precautionary principle presumes "that in situations where there are threats of serious or irreversible damage, lack of full scientific certainty should not be used as reason for postponing measures to prevent environmental degradation."[1] In effect, activities and products are presumed harmful to public health or the environment until proven otherwise, if the magnitude of risk they possibly might afford is deemed too great (for example, mass extinction of species).

The precautionary principle, as such, is quite controversial. As an approach to regulating risk, it is the obverse of traditional regulatory approaches. The latter assume the safety of activities and products for commercial use unless they are proven scientifically or empirically harmful. But the precautionary principle shifts the burden of proof away from opponents to prove the harms that they speculate and toward proponents to prove that those speculative harms will not occur on the scale envisioned. Equally daunting for the building of common purpose on these issues is that risk perception and risk acceptability differ among individuals for cognitive, social, and cultural reasons.[2]

Nor does it help, as political ecology theorists argue, that debates over environmental risk can become surrogates for otherwise repressed debates over the distribution of power (economic, political, and social) and over the control of resources in and across societies.[3] Put most simply, marginalized people and their advocates use debates over risk to justify their otherwise overlooked or delegitimated claims for control over resources.[4] And were all this not trying enough, as governments, international treaties, and nongovernmental organizations (NGOs) in elaborate cross-national networks increasingly perceive and frame environmental issues as "livelihood" issues (for example, environmental degradation adversely affects the ability of farmers in the developing world to earn a living), the precautionary principle alternatively becomes a conflict-inducing tool for redistributing resources (for example, from developed to developing nations) and for protecting the resources one already has (for example, using environmental standards that disadvantage competitors as nontariff barriers to trade).

The precautionary principle typically is discussed in terms of stopping behaviors or activities that pose potentially great societal and ecological *harms* (for example, the need to reduce greenhouse gas emissions in order to combat global warming). But as the pace of breakthroughs in the sciences (and especially in the biological sciences) spirals, the precautionary principle now routinely is applied to transformative scientific and technical advances developed and patented by private corporations (rather than by public institutions) that may *improve* public health, safety, and the environment. Faced with this realpolitik, proponents of "techno-scientific" advances that might help attenuate some of humanity's most challenging problems (for example, fetal tissue research, toxicogenomics, pharmacogenomics, nutrigenomics, neutraceuticals, enzyme splicing, and xenotransplantation) increasingly find themselves on the defensive.[5] To regain the offense, they then try to reframe the debate by offering an alternative version of the precautionary principle: "When an activity has the potential to benefit human health or the environment, it should be implemented with due caution, knowing that some cause-and-effect relationships cannot fully be established scientifically. In this context the *opponent* of the activity, rather than the public, should bear the burden of proof."[6] Joined in this fashion, an often acerbic battle then begins over precisely what constitutes "due caution" in these matters.

This chapter examines this seldom explored aspect of the precautionary principle in terms of its implications for building a results-based sense of common purpose in environmental governance in the twenty-first century. The chapter argues, first, that battles over applying the precautionary principle to potentially promising technoscientific advances pursued largely by private corporations are a reality of environmental governance that is likely to endure in the years ahead. Second, these battles must be understood as contests over livelihood and cultural values, as much as over "good science." Third, and as a consequence, the precautionary principle both affects and is affected by today's tendency to morph environmental and natural-resources (ENR) regulatory politics into decidedly more conflictual *redistributive* politics.[7] Fourth, precautionary politics pose significant challenges, choices, and opportunities for building a results-based sense of common purpose in environmental governance, not the least of which require formidable institutional adaptations involving capacity building, transparency, and cultural sensitivity. Last, absent these adaptations, precautionary politics can put at risk humanity's ability to explore empirically, democratically, and equitably the promise and pitfalls of major technoscientific advances that might help address pressing environmental governance challenges.

In making these arguments, the chapter begins with a synopsis of the logic, evolution, and controversies informing contemporary battles over the precautionary principle. To illustrate these points, it turns next to the still roiling, acrimonious, and polarized redistributive politics of precaution that for a decade have framed policy debates over the use of bioengineered, or genetically modified (GM), food as a tool for meeting spiraling world hunger problems in environmentally sustainable ways. At the 1992 Rio Earth Summit, 178 nations agreed in the Convention on Biological Diversity and in the United Nation's (UN) Agenda 21 that biotechnology can improve food security, health care, and environmental protection, and they committed themselves to fostering its introduction.[8] Yet by 2001 the UN's Human Development Report found that "the opposition to yield-enhancing [biotech] crops in industrial countries with food surpluses could block the development and transfer of those crops to food-deficit countries."[9] The chapter concludes by reviewing more broadly how trust-building mechanisms such as capacity building, transparency, and cultural sensitivity will continue to be essential to creating a results-based sense of common purpose as the era of redistributive precautionary politics continues apace in the twenty-first century.

Risks, Rights, and Rationality: The Politics of Precaution in Analytical Perspective

Without question, technoscientific abilities to detect and model environmental risks have improved immensely since the launch of the contemporary environmental movement in the 1970s. Yet a paradox frequently accompanies these technoscientific advances: the greater the improvements in risk identification that these advances afford, the more heated is the political controversy surrounding their findings (for example, over global warming and loss of biodiversity). Similarly stimulating precautionary politics surround the methodologies used in determining risk.[10] Many NGOs, for example, condemn as too conservative the statistical standards of proof informing modern risk analysis (that is, the standards make it too difficult to prove adverse effects from epidemiology studies). They also assert that "clusters" of cancer outbreaks are sufficient to prompt regulatory relief. Proponents of deregulation in the United States and abroad conversely excoriate as too conservative the default standards that regulators use to ensure substantial margins of safety. Meanwhile, proponents of regulation worry about and opponents criticize the lack of understanding of true causal mechanisms in explaining the etiology of cancerous tumors, for example. Both, in turn, are uncomfortable making inferences from animal studies about health threats to human populations. Other participants in the debate want to see regulators shift their focus from "risk reduction" to "risk trade-offs."

Further fostering precautionary politics, those who want more aggressive environmental regulation complain that risk analysis focuses inordinately on the effects of single agents. They want legislation requiring regulators to focus more on the interactive (or synergistic) and cumulative effects of multiple agents over time. They also want regulators to consider more than the *direct* (or primary) effects of hazardous and toxic agents on the present generation. Deemphasized too facilely, they argue, are the *indirect* risks and costs both to present *and* future generations. Nor are these critics content with studies that focus on single rather than multiple pathways for agents to enter the body or when risk from low-level exposures is downplayed.

The stakes of these conflicts grow dearer and the level of passion and the political stalemates accompanying them grow more daunting when speculative risks with huge downside costs are involved. Those fearing global warming, for example, talk of coastal flooding, the spread of disease, mass species extinctions, weather-distorting desertification, and famines that will wreak unacceptable human, ecosystem, and global harm. In contrast, those fearing or wishing to avoid the economic costs of dealing aggressively with reducing greenhouse gases under treaties such as the Kyoto Protocol allege, among other things, shortcomings in the assumptions and mathematics on which the modeling supporting these claims of harm is based.

Science, of course, is an inherently iterative process, with controversy and uncertainty throughout history doggedly prodding advances in knowledge. For laypersons paying only fleeting attention to complex environmental governance issues, however, controversy over risks often inspires only confusion, skepticism, and polarization. Nor is this situation helped when science simply cannot discern the extent to which risk exists. This has occurred, for example, in the food safety arena, where animal studies cannot be applied to test the risks of whole foods because these foods are complex mixtures of compounds with wide variations in composition and nutritional values. To compensate, laypersons use a set of heuristics for weighing risk, which scientists find frustrating. Not only do these heuristics often produce fears wildly at odds with actual risk probabilities, but they are readily exploitable by the antagonists of technoscientific advances in precautionary debates. Especially trying for those promoting these advances is the tendency of laypersons (as well as of reporters unfamiliar with technoscientific issues) to overestimate the probability of risk when that risk is perceived as unfamiliar, unknown, or catastrophic.[11]

Even these heuristics, however, are complicated when proponents *and* opponents of aggressive environmental protection selectively use competing research findings to advance their disparate policy ends. Those touting deregulation, for example, frame disagreement and controversy in findings as signals to "go slow" lest polluters make unnecessary financial investments. Conversely, those touting more immediate and aggressive protection efforts frame disparate results as signals for applying the precautionary principle. Nor has this situation been helped by the rise of non-peer-reviewed "advocacy research" sponsored by the combatants in technoscientific debates, especially when it proffers sensationalized headlines for market-driven media outlets and is represented as objective, peer-reviewed research.[12] As Manual Castells so cogently argues, policy entrepreneurs in today's "network society" use such studies "to compete through the media to frame how issues are viewed."[13] Yet so dysfunctional has this practice become to deliberations over risk that the prestigious *New England Journal of Medicine* has called for "scientists, the media, legislators, and regulators to distinguish between scientific evidence and hypothesis, and not allow a 'paparazzi science' approach to [resolving] these problems."[14]

Were these emotion-provoking stimuli not challenging enough, assessments of socioeconomic, cultural, and ethical risks of technoscientific advances are ready fodder for incendiary precautionary politics. At one level, the end of the Cold War wrought not only the eclipse of the socialist world and a crisis in the neo-Marxist critique, but also the rise of environmentalism as a galvanizing force for opponents of capitalism and the state.[15] Indeed, "environmentalism [and the use of the precautionary principle as a driving force within it] has emerged as a powerful challenge [in general] to dominant industrial capitalism" and in particular to the so-called Washington consensus for attaining economic development in the developing world. That consensus touts development through fiscal austerity, privatization of state-owned enterprises, and trade and financial market liberalization.[16]

At another level, and as Robert Paehlke and Gary Bryner discuss in greater detail in chapters 1 and 2 of this volume, the logical link between environmental degradation and economic development made by proponents of sustainable development has helped morph environmental issues into livelihood issues. Although otherwise sensible, this morphing also means that the decidedly more conflictual nature of *redistributive* policies increasingly trumps the less politically charged politics of regulatory policy in both national and international ENR debates. Consider, for example, the intensity of conflict (others would call it a stalemate) that occurred in 2002 at the UN World Summit on Sustainable Development in Johannesburg, South Africa, when environmental degradation was linked so routinely to such livelihood issues as poverty, illiteracy, and infant mortality reduction. As one participant put it, "Even the negotiated text on biodiversity [had] a poverty focus. People ask if this summit is more about jobs or birds. It's jobs, so much more about jobs than the Rio meeting was ten years ago."[17]

At a third level, redistributive politics arise when evolving legal doctrine in U.S. courts (most notably, *Diamond v. Chakrabarty*, 447 U.S. 303, 1980) allows corporations to patent information, processes, and products (for example, microorganisms) that historically were treated as public-domain materials available to all to exploit for economic gain or social benefit. The Green Revolution in agriculture, for example, was overwhelmingly a public-sector initiative, thus obviating the need for patents that produced economic or nutritional winners and losers. In contrast, 80 percent of the crops produced by today's latest developments in agricultural biotechnology are produced by four multinational corporations (Monsanto, Syngenta, Dupont, and Aventis) with patents on their efforts. As a consequence, developing countries see these otherwise positive developments as major redistributive threats (that is, risks) from the developed world, not unlike their concerns about pharmaceutical companies "bioprospecting" in their countries without compensating them adequately.

Relatedly, as risks to the global commons spiral, perceptions of risks in developing nations are viewed through a very different prism than that used in the Western developed world. In developing nations, environmental issues have their "base in the livelihood struggles of the rural poor rather than in the aesthetics of emerging middle classes."[18] In comparison to Western environmentalism, for example, the Indian and Latin American environmentalists' critique and their attendant perceptions of risk are linked much more tautly to largely redistributive concerns about subsistence, poverty, and capitalist development.[19]

Likewise, in large segments of the developing world as opposed to the developed world, environmentalism (and perceptions of risk) is premised on successful non-Western principles of subsistence-oriented (rather than profit-oriented), small-scale (rather than large-scale), low-tech (rather than high-tech), and harmonizing (rather than dominating) uses of the environment.[20] Thus, although one errs in treating either category of nations as holding monolithic attitudes toward risk, one errs as well in assuming that Western environmentalism and its approaches to risk management are triumphant internationally. Rather, with regard to risk perceptions in Africa, Latin America, and Southeast Asia, a variety of indigenous, local, and traditional ideological bases for environmentalism (for example, Buddhist ideas about nature and economics, humanity's relationship to the natural world, and proper resource stewardship) exist and compete for ascendancy with Western rational and technical approaches.

Nor is the increasing morphing of environmental issues into redistributive livelihood issues confined to North-South relations. For example, much of the consternation presently existing among the European Union (EU) and the United States in environmental governance stems directly from conflicts over the precautionary principle and its effect on livelihood issues (for example, conflict over reduction of greenhouse gases, the EU ban of shipments of cattle injected with bovine growth hormones, and its 5-year moratorium on importing new GM products). Tensions likewise have arisen between developed and developing nations as the latter accuse the former of using national and international safety and quality standards less to protect their citizens than to protect their industries and markets from competition (for example, in the Sanitary and Phytosanitary Agreement).

Lessons from the Field: Precautionary Politics, Biotechnology, and Food Security

Most illustrative of how these dynamics can drive the politics of precaution in deliberatively dysfunctional ways is the now decade-long and still raging controversy worldwide over the research, production, and commercialization of GM food and fiber (for example, cotton). This transformative biotechnological advance is supported by six national academies of science, the Third World Academy of Sciences, twenty Nobel Prize winners, the World Bank, the World Health Organization (WHO), the Rockefeller and Ford Foundations, the American Medical Association, the American Dietetic Association, the American Society of Toxicologists, and the UN Development and Environment Programs (UNDP and UNEP). They see it as a means for helping nations meet spiraling problems of hunger, malnutrition, and economic development, while simultaneously protecting the environment.[21] Yet ten years after the 1992 Rio conference endorsed the potential of GM foods for fighting world hunger while protecting the environment, their future is precarious amid acrimonious, personalized, and polarized debate both within and outside the scientific community over how the precautionary principle applies to GM food research, production, and commercialization.[22]

Farming, Food Security, and Sustainable Agriculture

It took all of humanity's history for the Earth's population to reach a billion persons in 1800. It then took only one more century for the world's population to top 1.7 billion persons. And only 100 years after that, sweeping mortality declines caused by penicillin and other antibiotics catapulted the world's population past the 6 billion mark as the twenty-first century dawned.[23] Moreover, world population is expected to soar to 8 billion persons by 2025 and to 9.3 billion persons by 2050. In addition, 90 percent of global natural increase in population (the difference between births and deaths) is anticipated to occur in the world's poorest countries.

Demographers and scientists also see these population trends placing tremendous strains on food supplies and natural ecosystems over the next thirty years. The conundrum is that yields must soar to meet unprecedented demographic pressures at the same time that arable land, agricultural labor, and water supplies are diminishing.[24] As Jikun Huang, Carl Pray, and Scott Rozelle summarize the dilemma, "by 2020, increasingly wealthy and urbanized consumers and the 2 billion new [and overwhelmingly poorer] mouths will demand 40 percent more food."[25] Meeting these demands, moreover, will be all the more difficult in the developing world: "because of small holdings, the subsistence nature of farming, vagaries of the weather, limited water, poor land condition and stress factors such as drought, heat, and saline salt conditions . . . [m]uch of [today's] crop yield is lost due to disease, pests, and weeds while a considerable proportion of harvested fruits and vegetables are spoilt during transportation and storage."[26]

Were this not bad enough, the Green Revolution that helped to double global cereal production over the past four decades, saved millions from starvation, and spared natural ecosystems from conversion to agriculture "is showing signs of fatigue and farm productivity increases are now flattening."[27] Recent research, in fact, suggests that trying to meet projected food demands solely with Green Revolution technologies will require farmers to triple the rate of dumping environmentally noxious nitrogen and phosphorous into terrestrial ecosystems.[28] Some scientists argue that relying solely on present Green Revolution techniques to meet future world food needs will require the conversion of natural ecosystems covering an area larger than the size of the United States, including Alaska.[29] Others estimate that harvesting these lands will rival the effect that greenhouse gases have on global environmental change.[30]

The Case for Biotechnology

What fuels the exuberance of biotechnology supporters about its potential to attenuate these staggering food-security needs in environmentally sustainable ways? Genetic engineering of crops basically allows scientists using recombinant DNA technologies to gene-splice desirable traits into foods (such as corn, soybeans, canola, tomatoes, squash, papayas, and potatoes) in ways that conventional crop breeding simply cannot do. Three types of trait technology are presently under development that promise to increase crop yields at lower net costs to farmers, with greater health benefits to consumers, and in more environmentally benign ways. The first, *input trait technology,* promises to reduce substantially the use of environmentally harmful pesticides (for example, by introducing traits that give herbicide tolerance, disease resistance, and insect resistance). The second, *output trait technology,* promises to improve farm yields (both in general and on marginal lands in developing countries), nutritional content, quality, appearance, and shelf life. The third, *agronomic trait technology,* promises to afford protection against natural conditions and disasters that devastate the livelihood of farmers on marginal lands in developing countries (for example, by introducing traits that afford salt tolerance, drought tolerance, and water submergence tolerance).

Proponents, moreover, are buoyed by early research findings substantiating some of this promise. Researchers have found evidence, for example, of substantially increased crop yields (involving both food and fibers such as cotton) in a host of GM food studies. Findings in China and India show

GM crop yields that are two to three times greater than conventional crop yields; in Kenya, a ten-year experiment with genetically engineered African corn increased crop yields fourfold; and research by Denmark's National Environmental Research Institute indicates that GM crops might be better for the environment than conventional crops.[31] Equally promising in the United States in 1999 alone is the saving of 66 million bushels of corn from the corn borer. Many scientists also speak of research indicating that GM plants can become "microfactories" in the near future, producing "neutraceuticals" to deal with malnutrition in developing countries (for example, creating so-called golden rice by enriching rice with higher levels of iron and beta carotene—a precursor of vitamin A—to prevent premature births and blindness in children, respectively).

Proponents also cite research showing that GM food and fiber production can be more environmentally benign than conventional farm methods because of the higher yields produced by bioengineering; because GM crops can be bioengineered for drought tolerance, acidity tolerance, and pest resistance, and thus require fewer chemicals; and because crops can be bioengineered with delayed ripening genes to reduce spoilage. For example, in Mexico, research shows a reduction in pesticide costs of nearly $100 per hectare and a net profit advantage of nearly $600 per hectare because of the introduction of Bt cotton.[32] Thus, although GM seeds may cost more initially, research indicates that for small farmers using them in China and India, profit margins actually increased as overall production costs dropped. In the process, more biodiversity is preserved because bioengineered crops require less tilling of the soil (through no-till or conservation-till cultivation systems) and are less land intensive.

Finally, scientists supporting bioengineering tout its potential for reducing some of the developing world's most pressing health threats, including malaria and dengue fever, through the production of "edible vaccines." Scientists, for example, may be able to splice vaccines against malaria into bananas or other fruit, bio-reengineer mosquitoes and other disease carriers to render them innocuous, and splice vaccines against contagious diseases into animal feed. And were all this not enough, researchers have found evidence that plants may become "bioreactors" that can produce biofuels, biodegradable plastics, sturdier and more quickly replaced forests, and enhanced fish supplies.[33]

Biotechnology, Scientific Risk, and the Precautionary Principle

Notwithstanding the scientific eminence of the organizations making the case for these kinds of benefits from GM foods, critics of genetic modification (both within and outside the scientific community) hold, have seized upon, or have impressed upon others four analytically distinct yet interrelated categories of objections to GM foods. These include: (1) objections to speculative risk that are based on cultural belief systems, which make the objections nonfalsifiable and frame GM foods in terms of good versus evil; (2) objections to plausible risks that are more amenable to hypothesis testing, but over which claims and counterclaims by activists persist and grow more bitter, personalized, and demonizing; (3) objections that focusing on the promise of GM food diverts attention from more promising ways to address food security; and (4) objections premised more on livelihood issues than on "good science."

Belief and Cultural Systems   To some critics, the precautionary principle should be invoked because the bioengineering of food represents potentially disastrous meddling into natural processes best left to evolution. Those with this belief system label GM crops as "Frankenfoods" (with all the evocatively negative connotations of that word), perceiving and portraying them as much too dangerous. They charge that the bioengineering process goes far beyond conventional cross-breeding because it transfers genes across species and even across kingdoms (plants and animals). Proponents of bioengineering counter, among other things, that thousands of years of cross-breeding mean that there is no such thing as a "natural food" anymore and that conventional breeding is actually more dangerous because it is less precise. Genetic engineers know the specific trait and gene that they are splicing into a receptor (for example, rice) to acquire a desired trait (for example, drought resistance). In contrast, conventional breeders combine a host of genes with unknown traits into receptors with hosts of equally unknown genes. Moreover, genetic engineering produces positive results much more quickly than conventional breeding, speed that is urgent in light of the food crisis facing humanity. Against these claims, anti–GM food activists argue that bioengineering is not as precise as its proponents claim; bioengineers do not know precisely where spliced genes eventually will wind up within receptors because of "gene jumping" (a contention that most scientists strongly dispute as without empirical support and as highly unlikely to occur).

A second type of belief system that calls for applying the precautionary principle is religious, moral, or cultural in origin. Some traditions in Buddhism, for example, view plants and animals as part of the karmic cycle and thus fear anything that might intervene in or threaten the natural development of ecosystems. They are joined by indigenous tribal villagers in various parts of the world who are spiritualists or animists and who fear that GM crops will defile the spirit world. Others in this category fear the slippery slope of risks imposed by disrespecting life (for example, by patenting and thus commodifying life). Still others fear the risks of devaluing, if not marginalizing, the traditional knowledge and wisdom of indigenous peoples with a reductionist and exploitive Western model of science. Finally, other critics in this tradition worry on ethical grounds about widening wealth gaps that they speculate biotechnology will engender between the developed and the developing world, as well as within the latter.[34]

Proponents of bioengineering counter that GM foods need not compromise traditional values and actually may advance them (for example, by enhancing traditional values such as self-reliance and self-sufficiency). They also contend that traditional values frequently have harmed rather than advanced sustainable practices. Moreover, they argue that the attempt to meet food needs with traditional village wisdom is doomed to failure because it will require expanded use of greater and greater areas of extremely marginal lands. Finally, they argue that concerns about international inequities are real, but that groups such as the Consultative Group on International Agricultural Research (CGIAR), private philanthropists such as the Rockefeller Foundation, and the International Service for the Acquisition of Agri-Biotech Applications already have begun transferring these skills and technologies from the developed world to the developing world. Critics reply, however, that CGIAR has a budget of only $350 million divided among sixteen nations, with only approximately 20 percent going to training researchers in *all* agricultural areas (not just biotechnology). This amount, they argue, is a pittance compared to what corporations are investing in biotech research.[35]

A final type of cultural belief system animating calls for applying the precautionary principle to GM food issues is more anticorporate in nature. Opposition ranges from worry about the perverse incentives afforded to corporations by market pressures, to implacable distrust of corporations in particular, and on to strident philosophical opposition to globalization more generally. Risk perceptions within this belief system start with the inadvertent harms that normal market incentives might produce. For example, international inequities in food security may arise if companies do not invest in food crops that developing nations need because these crops are unprofitable. Anticorporate groups claim that this plausible risk has empirical support: corporations to date overwhelmingly have geared their research and development toward the highly profitable market needs of large-scale agribusiness for pest and herbicide control. Further exacerbating these concerns is the view that the corporate interests involved consider themselves more accountable to stockholders than to the general public and their elected representatives.

Proponents concede these worries. However, they argue that as controversy over GM foods has mounted, the extremely high costs of bioengineering investments and product development have compelled companies to concentrate on wealthy countries where agriculture is more profitable and intellectual property rights (IPRs) are more enforceable.[36] They also point to instances where companies now are working with foundations and international institutions to share their knowledge with poorer nations and to target more research toward food and nutritional needs (for example, Monsanto has donated its "working draft" of the sequencing of the rice genome to the International Rice Genome Sequencing Project for further development).[37] Anti–GM food activists portray these efforts as cynical public-relations ploys to gain support for GM foods and to "hook" poor farmers on company products.

Other GM food critics in this belief system cite even more malevolent intentions on the part of multinational and transnational corporations. They project, for example, that, past patent sharing aside, corporations yet will use IPRs law to patent life forms and become monopoly suppliers of foods worldwide.[38] As evidence, they point to corporations initially using so-called terminator genes that precluded farmers from saving seeds for use next season (as traditionally is done). Also indictable was corporate use of gene splicing to produce Bt cotton and Bt corn that would grow only if used with their own products (for example, with Monsanto's Roundup Ready pesticides). As such, these opponents see GM foods as part of a globalization of markets that boosts the power of rich nations and corporations to the detriment of poorer developing nations.

Proponents of GM foods respond that patenting is absolutely necessary. Because the financial costs of genetic research are frontloaded and the financial benefits are long deferred, companies who invest must be assured that they alone will capture these rewards over a significant period of time. Many proponents also urge corporations to share with or donate patents to developing nations. They point to the recent corporate donation of the IPRs for golden rice to the International Rice Research Institute, along with free-of-charge licensing to permit further study and breeding into local rice varieties.[39] Still others point out that terminator genes initially were designed to prevent harm to nearby species in adjacent ecosystems and to protect biodiversity. Many concede nonetheless that other ways now available can provide these same protections and that use of the term *terminator* was a public-relations disaster that played into the hands of anti–GM food activists. Finally, supporters of GM food research, production, and commercialization turn the moral argument around: "How, in all good conscience, can the well-fed of the world, by turning what should be a choice into a global dictate, opt out of the new technologies that could provide the opportunity for all the world's people to be well-fed?"[40]

Plausible Risks Subject to Hypothesis Testing   Opposition to bioengineered food also is proffered in empirically testable claims premised on a variety of unintended effects. The most prominent effects among those speculated are the disruption or silencing of existing genes, activation of silent genes, modification in the expression of existing genes, and the formation of new or altered patterns of metabolites. GM food critics in international networks tout a miscellany of plausible, yet testable, risk hypotheses as genetically engineered genes "drift" to nearby locations and cross-pollinate with wild relatives and compete with other species. For ecosystems, these hypotheses include (but are not limited to) the following very serious consequences: killing off otherwise useful natural pests and predators; introducing destructive alien species; enhancing the ecological fitness of GM plants at the expense of native species; creating "superweeds" that will damage crops; and inducing pathogen resistance in plants by using antibiotic resisters in gene splicing. Hypothesized effects for humans more directly are the creation of new allergies or harmful toxins for which the body is ill-prepared to deal, causing sickness and death among vulnerable populations. Anti–GM food activists also speculate that a rise in antibiotic resistance in humans may occur because of the use of antibiotic resisters in gene-splicing.

Although conceding the plausibility of some of these claims, GM food proponents in the scientific community vehemently argue that the more doomsday-oriented scenarios are scientifically flawed, wildly exaggerated, and deliberately designed for fear mongering. Especially galling to them is how anti–GM food activists such as Greenpeace frame complex technoscientific issues in simplistic and evocative slogans that stoke fear among laypersons (for example, "Hidden Ingredients Are in Your Baby's Food"; "Mommy, Please Stop Feeding Me GMOs"; and "The End of the World As We Know It"). Proponents of bioengineering argue that the same kinds of risks are present in conventional plant breeding, but that anti–GM food activists and the media seem uninterested in discussing them or in pointing out that these risks are extremely rare in both cases. They also argue that although drift can occur from GM plants, "so far there is no evidence that any GM crop plant is significantly more invasive than its conventional counterpart."[41] Moreover, they contend that existing research indicates that "gene flow from GE plants was neither significant nor a cause for concern."[42]

Critics invoking the precautionary principle use the "so far" qualifier, of course, to rally public opinion against GM food research. Framing debates less in terms of statistical probabilities and more in emotionally evocative ways, they say that "so far" means that scientists cannot definitively rule out the dire consequences they envision. To GM food proponents, anti–GM food activists use this scientifically nonfalsifiable argument merely as a political tactic. The latter know, they argue, that scientists can never prove with certainty that something will *not* happen, that they deal only in statistical probabilities of things occurring.

Moreover, if the discovery of any harm from any single GM food product justifies halting bioengineering (as some of the more strident anti–GM food activists claim), the same logic dictates the halting of conventional breeding as well (for example, corn and peanuts cause serious allergic reactions in some persons).

But, counter critics, GM food risks are so unknown and potentially devastating that the precautionary principle must trump traditional risk management approaches. To this argument, supporters of GM foods respond that scientists can never provide the answers to these questions as long as anti–GM food activists oppose (and often physically destroy) further field testing of GM crops. Again, supporters see this argument as consciously crafted to place them in a catch-22 situation: researchers must demonstrate the safety of GM crops before further field tests are allowed, but further field testing is the only way to demonstrate the safety of GM crops. Anti–GM food activists respond, however, that field tests can never be dispositive because they are both too risky and too flawed methodologically (for example, they typically look at only one growing season), a charge that scientists who support further research dismiss as inaccurate and insulting to their professionalism (for example, China has a stringent biosafety protocol requiring field testing for at least three cultivation seasons before certification).[43]

Anti–GM food activists who invoke the precautionary principle also dismiss claims that supporters make about the bioengineering process itself. They argue, for example, that GM food gene-splicing is not as precise as proponents purport; biologists cannot direct precisely where the new genetic material is placed in the DNA of the host or know where it winds up. To this argument, proponents respond that activists have the science only partially correct. Biologists cannot direct where the gene is placed in the DNA of a host, but they can place it more accurately than conventional breeders. Moreover, in contrast to traditional breeders, they know where the gene is located after it enters the host (thus mitigating risk). In assessing risk, it is more important to know what the characteristics of a transplanted gene are than to know its location; bioengineers have more of this knowledge than do conventional breeders.

Anti–GM food activists have responded vigorously to each of these arguments. They argue that although a variety of these claims and counterclaims can be tested empirically, a majority of studies testing them are flawed. Prior research, they say, typically lacks experimental data, reflects the authors' opinions rather than objective scientific testing, and appears mostly in non-peer-reviewed articles sponsored by corporations that have a direct financial interest in promoting GM foods. Scientists doing this research take great umbrage, of course, at this attack on their professionalism and integrity. In one meta-analysis of a subsample of GM food research, for example, plant geneticist C. S. Prakash cites 57 publications as evidence that activists' charges are unfounded and scurrilous. Supporters of GM products also argue that U.S. citizens have been consuming these products for more than a decade, and there has not been a single documented instance of harm reported. They then turn the tables, noting how prone anti–GM food activists are to sponsor or publicize non-peer-reviewed research whenever it suits their purposes.

To all this, anti–GM food activists respond that such arguments are disingenuous. As Sue Meyer, director of GeneWatch UK, puts it in precautionary principle terms, "No evidence of harm does not equal safety."[44] Not enough time has passed, critics argue, to see the impact of long-term use of GM products on U.S. citizens. Moreover, in cases of known harms of products for particular subsets of the population, the typical regulatory response is either to ban the products or to label them so that vulnerable consumers can avoid them. Yet, to date, pro–GM food activists and some major producer nations such as the United States have fought mandatory (as opposed to voluntary) labeling of GM products. To this argument, many (although not all) proponents of GM foods respond that mandatory labeling does several things that are both unfair and unwise.

For starters, mandatory labeling of foods as "GM free" implies that GM foods carry risks that other types of foods do not. Yet no scientific evidence exists that they are any more harmful than foods produced by conventional breeding. In addition, the intuitive appeal of labeling imposes on producers considerable costs that are not readily visible, but that they will have to pass on to consumers in higher food costs. More precisely, labeling to certify GM-free products requires that producers set up separate and distinct production lines to ensure that GM foods and conventional foods have no opportunity to interact from "farm to fork." Moreover, to ensure that crop segregation actually occurs, costly administrative procedures and processes for "tracing" separation are required (known as "traceability"). These precautions are not necessary, GM proponents argue, because existing regulatory regimes that certify the safety of all products are sufficient for protecting public health and safety.

Many (but by no means all) proponents are persuaded that mandatory labeling is merely a political strategy. Anti–GM food activists, they argue, try to use labeling to impose heavy costs on farmers and corporations that may cause them to shy away from GM foods altogether. Proponents prefer, instead, a system of voluntary labeling (as in the United States and Canada), with functional equivalents of the U.S. Food and Drug Administration (FDA) issuing guidelines to ensure truthfulness in advertising. In this fashion, they argue, the costs of segregating GM foods from conventional products will be borne by consumers who wish to pay a premium for GM-free crops.

Anti–GM food activists respond that labeling is a consumer protection issue, not a business protection issue. Consumers have a right to know what they are eating. Moreover, critics are especially skeptical of the will and wherewithal of existing regulatory regimes to certify GM products as safe. They begin by challenging as decidedly too risky the use of the regulatory standard used in the United States and most other countries: the "substantial equivalence" test. Under this standard, GM products are assumed safe for human consumption, in effect, if they do not exhibit characteristics known to be harmful in conventional foods. Ignored in the process, claim anti–GM food activists, is the circumstance that the assumption of equivalence is unsubstantiated empirically. They also argue that regulators use no defined protocol for what has to be measured in these biosafety tests and that they fail to look for unintended consequences. Citing studies by researchers at Johns Hopkins University in the United States and by the Royal Society in the United Kingdom, critics also argue that regulatory responsibilities regarding GM foods are scattered and uncoordinated among regulatory offices located in different departments. Moreover, these offices are dominated by pro-agribusiness cultures and constituencies, and they are inadequately budgeted and staffed.[45]

In response, pro–GM food activists argue that the substantial equivalence test is appropriate. Not only has no scientifically documented difference in risk been found between GM and conventionally bred products, but anti–GM food activists deliberately are confusing the public by implying that substantial equivalence is a scientific risk assessment process. The determination of substantial equivalence is made only *after* a product (for example, a GM tomato) is found by scientists to have the same composition and nutritional traits as a conventionally bred product (for example, a tomato) and to have no additional or new toxins or allergens. They hasten to point out as well that the FDA requires labeling on any product when these criteria are not met. And although conceding concerns about regulatory capacity, they argue that reforms are underway in many countries and that the absence of documented health problems indicates that biosafety procedures are working.

To all this, anti–GM food activists respond that they see little in the way of progress on cultural change or coordination among biosafety regulators. They also say that proponents of GM foods who aggressively stand behind the substantial equivalence doctrine do so more for the strategic advantage the doctrine can give GM producers in World Trade Organization (WTO) disputes than for its scientific value. Because the WTO has accepted substantial equivalence certification as a criterion for free trade, nations that refuse to open their markets to GM food imports or that ask for additional information on contents beyond these certifications impose unnecessary technical barriers to trade. Thus, when the UNDP published a substantial evidence-based report touting the safety of GM foods as a means for fighting world hunger, networked grassroots activists in fifty countries called the report "simplistic pandering to the GM industry."[46] In response, Klaus Leisenger of the Novartis Foundation described the opposition as "Luddites."

Genetic Engineering as a Distraction   Opposition to bioengineered food also is rooted in the belief that it only distracts attention from other more promising approaches to world hunger. According to these critics, GM food research diverts resources from promising conventional or alternative approaches to crop breeding where yield-demand gaps currently exist and might be closed. In addition to the lack of scientific evidence underpinning the productivity and safety of GM products, anti–GM food activists argue, claims of future nutritional gains are decidedly overblown, and GM food research distracts attention from what is actually a distribution problem occasioned by politics. As these critics see the issue, abundant food supplies exist, but they lie wasting in storage houses; are diverted for political gain, punishment, or warfare; or spoil in transit for want of adequate infrastructure.

To still others, third-world hunger is also the product of bad decisions foisted on these nations by international lenders and because of the food policies of the developed world. The citizens of many countries go hungry and suffer malnutrition at the same time that their governments are exporting cash crops to other nations (for example, coffee). In the process, major landowners seize large areas of properties to grow high-technology monoculture crops that in turn push previously employed subsistence farmers off the land and into cities where food costs are higher. Equally pernicious are the highly subsidized or tariff-protected food policies of developed nations such as the United States and the EU countries that give their farmers an unfair trade advantage over developing nations unable to offer the same level of protection to their farmers.[47]

Pro–GM food activists, of course, take issue with each of these claims. Just as they refute arguments about productivity and safety by noting existing research to the contrary, they counter anti–GM food claims about overblown promises by pointing to the development of golden rice and other neutraceuticals.[48] They also point to environmental and health benefits in countries such as China, where research indicates that the introduction of cotton with the Bt gene produced a 70 percent drop in pesticide use during the 1999 and 2000 growing seasons. Only 5 percent of Chinese farmers growing Bt cotton have reported health problems from it, compared with 22 percent of farmers using conventional techniques. Indeed, researchers estimate that in 2000 alone, total global reduction in pesticide use approximated 22.3 million kilograms as a result of herbicide-tolerant GM soybeans, cotton, corn, and rape seed, as well as a 14 percent reduction in insecticides.[49]

By citing the projections of experts to the contrary, pro–GM food scientists also vehemently challenge the idea that alternative approaches (for example, organic foods, conventional breeding, information technology, and microbiology) together can meet soaring world food needs in the future.[50] Moreover, while allowing that politics in a variety of forms produces distribution problems and economic distortions that result in hunger and malnutrition, they argue that biotechnology is even *more* important under these circumstances. To the extent that genetic engineering can allow local farmers who work marginal lands to become self-reliant, it reduces their dependence on expensive investments in transportation, on handouts from corrupt governments, on remote chances of land redistribution, and on the trade whims of foreign nations. In response to this point, international NGOs such as Oxfam and Greenpeace International, as well as 290 grassroots groups worldwide, stated recently that biotech companies "should stop exploiting the issues of malnutrition and hunger for their self-serving agenda."[51]

Risk, Livelihood Issues, and the Precautionary Principle   Informed by this sometimes virulent, demonizing, and polarizing debate, as well as by public-health regulatory failures that have shaken public confidence (for example, the BSE or "mad cow" disease scandal in Britain, the AIDS blood supply scandal in France, and the PCB in cattle feed scandal in Belgium), a variety of GM food regulatory responses have emerged worldwide. The most notable and far-reaching of these responses has been taken by the European Union (EU). Since 1997, for example, the EU has required mandatory labeling of GM foods. Moreover, as noted earlier, since 1998 a de facto EU moratorium has existed on the approval of new GM foods. Then, in June 2003, the European Parliament approved new regulations on GM food labeling and traceability that it argued paved the way for ending the five-year moratorium on approvals of new GM foods. These regulations are broader in their impact on exporting nations, covering previously excluded animal feeds and extending labeling laws to GM crops or seeds that do not have any GM DNA or protein in the final product. They also are stricter in the levels of GM materials in food and feed that trigger labeling (a 0.9 percent level, albeit one less stringent than the 0.5 level proposed by the EU Environment Committee), and they require complete (the U.S. argues "unfeasible") segregation of GM and non-GM products from farm to fork (that is, from farm, to processor, to manufacturer, to transporter, and on to the store). The EU's claims, of course, were disputed vehemently by the United States, Australia, and Canada as inaccurate, economically onerous to producing nations, and scientifically unjustified.

Meanwhile, countries like Australia, Japan, and New Zealand have passed or are considering legislation setting zero tolerance for imports containing unapproved GM products. Others, like Thailand, have reversed earlier policy and banned the field testing of GM crops (for example, Bt cotton and Bt corn).[52] Likewise, many of these same nations allow the importation of GM plants only for research, for animal feed, or in products where outright bans on imports would either hurt domestic industries or be nonimplementable (for example, corn and soy). In fact, more than two dozen nations (covering more than 30 percent of the world's population in nations as dispersed as China, India, Norway, Saudi Arabia, and Switzerland) presently use mandatory GM food labeling for various levels of GM food content (typically on a percentage basis ranging from 1 percent to 5 percent GM food content) across all or certain products.[53]

All this, of course, has significant implications for the livelihood of farmers, exporters, and importers worldwide. For example, the EU's five-year-old moratorium on biotechnology approvals alone has cost American farmers nearly $300 million annually in crop shipments.[54] Similarly costly to American and Argentinean cattle growers has been the EU's ban on the import of beef and dairy products produced from animals treated with bovine growth hormones. Although less costly in absolute dollar terms, GM food import restrictions can significantly affect key exports from developing nations. In 2000, for example, Egypt, Greece, the Netherlands, and Saudi Arabia blocked the import of Thailand's canned tuna.

Meanwhile, by 2003, nations such as Brazil were split between some farmers who want the government to allow them to plant and harvest GM soybean seeds and some who want more aggressive patrolling of the border to preclude GM soybean seeds from entering their country by way of Argentina. Similarly, in Australia, two of the nation's six states (New South Wales and South Australia) considered three-year bans on the commercialization of GM foods, and two others (Tasmania and Western Australia) considered declaring themselves GM-free areas for exports. Moreover, all this occurred as Australia's peak farm lobby (the National Farmers' Federation) strongly endorsed GM food crops and attacked state governments that proposed moratoria on them.

The rub, however, is finding accurate, objective, and independent research on the cumulative impacts of GM crops on the livelihood of farmers and industries in various nations. Instead, advocates on all sides of the GM food debate have used a plethora of non-peer-reviewed research to advance their disparate causes. For example, in mid-2002, the Soil Association of the United Kingdom released to the Scottish Parliament a non-peer-reviewed study by a GM food opponent that justified an immediate moratorium on field trials, characterizing GM food as "environmental dynamite." The study estimated that GM soya, oilseed rape, and corn "*could* have cost the U.S. economy over $12 billion in farm subsidies, lower crop prices, loss of major export orders, and product recalls" since 1999.[55] In response, GM food proponents in the parliamentary debate cited the non-peer-reviewed findings of a study by the National Center for Food and Agricultural Policy (NCFAP) in the United States. This report found that GM crops increased farm income by $973 million in 2001 alone. Left unreported, however, was that the Soil Association is the United Kingdom's leading campaigner and certifying body for organic food and farming and thus has a vested interest in diminishing the promise of GM foods. Unnoted, as well, was that NCFAP receives funding from various commodity groups, agribusiness, and agricultural chemical companies with vested interests in promoting GM foods.

Although the U.S. government recognizes legitimate concerns about health, ecological harm, and export market protection, it sees the EU moratorium (as well as recent import restriction initiatives by countries such as China and Russia) as an effort to use the precautionary principle as a protectionist nontariff trade barrier.[56] Depending on the nation involved, U.S. officials argue that with these restrictions, trade rivals are trying to protect domestic products and producers, to buy time for their own scientists to catch up with the United States in biotech research, or to impose such heavy costs on corporations that they either will slow down or abandon commercialization.[57] Nor is there any question in officials' minds that anti–GM food activists and governments concerned about livelihood as well as public-health threats are upping the costs of pursuing GM food research, production, and commercialization by making the precautionary principle the basis for international biosafety and trade regulations (for example, in the Cartagena Protocol on Biosafety, the Convention on Biological Diversity, the Sanitary and Phytosanitary Agreement, and the Codex Alimentarius standards).[58]

Through a Looking Glass Darkly

To be sure, postmortems for the biotech industry are premature. Contrary to the contention of extremists on either the pro- or the anti–GM food side of the debate, for example, recent opinion polls in the EU suggest that citizens are uncertain and persuadable.[59] Meanwhile, fearing economic dominance by their trade rivals, countries such as China, India, Malaysia, Singapore, and South Korea are pouring billions of dollars into biotech research. Indeed, although most of western Europe is hostile to GM crops, the United States and most of the developing world (with notable exceptions in Mozambique, Zambia, and Zimbabwe) "are embracing the technology enthusiastically."[60]

Still, GM food proponents in the research community worry aloud that "potential public and private investors [in GM food research] . . . may well decide that the only easy and logical solution [in the face of vocal hostility in some quarters, costly segregation, and traceability requirements] is to discount the use of genetic engineering technology in food production and focus exclusively on its use in human medicine."[61] Nor did they have to look far for evidence that this narrowing of focus already is occurring.

By mid-2002, for example, five of the seven leading agribusinesses originally involved in biotechnological research in Europe either had abandoned these efforts or had merged with other companies. Moreover, Europabio (the GM industry trade association in Europe) reported in 2003 an 80 percent drop in the number of GM food trials in Europe between 1997 (240 trials) and 2002 (40 trials), thus "virtually ending companies' abilit[ies] to develop any new GM crop varieties for the European market."[62] Meanwhile, one GM food corporation (Advanta), with almost all of its field trials in England and France destroyed by farmers and its permit applications for field tests stalled in the Netherlands, threatened to shut down its entire European operation. Moreover, Bolivia and Croatia put new limitations on GM food imports; Australia, the Czech Republic, and New Zealand ratcheted up existing mandatory labeling requirements; and Brazil, Hong Kong, Israel,

Mexico, and Thailand prepared to begin implementing mandatory labeling requirements.[63] And after the UK and Scottish governments announced eighteen sites in England and Scotland for three years of field trials for GM oilseed rape, they faced irate farmers who presented an anti–GM food petition with more than 5,000 signatures and pledged physically to destroy any further field trials in Scotland.[64]

All these controversies, in turn, place even food-sufficient developing nations in a difficult position. For example, although a variety of developing nations have rather well-developed biotechnology and genetic technology programs (for example, Brazil, India, Kenya, and Singapore), they have been slow to come up with products for use by farmers. Their fear is that export markets might collapse because of EU prohibitions. Moreover, if UNDP officials are correct, the results of these trends might be even more devastating for food-deficit nations. Criticizing European environmentalists for "scare mongering" about GM foods, Sakiko Fukuda-Parr, author of the 2001 UN *Human Development Report,* says, "The developing world badly needs these technologies as soon as possible and European countries and [international] campaigners are slowing everything up."[65] But as Britain's Department of Environment, Food, and Rural Affairs, along with the UK chief science advisor and the Food Standards Agency, prepared to launch a public debate in the United Kingdom about the implications of GM foods, its chief scientist put the matter bluntly for his country: "Hold on here, we're not going to do this [commercialize GM products] exactly in the same way as America. Let's take a more careful approach."[66]

Precautionary Politics: Challenges, Choices, and Opportunities

The preceding analysis of the still-evolving GM food issue worldwide has illustrated how battles involving precautionary politics are just as much livelihood and cultural issues as they are battles over "good science." As we have seen, and as Peter Drahos, an IPR specialist at the University of London, suggests more broadly, at issue in cases like these are principles with significant redistributive policy implications that policymakers must sort out: risk assessment, information exchange, substantial equivalence, nondiscrimination, private property, benefit sharing, and precaution.[67]

The GM food issue thus illustrates vividly how the precautionary principle both affects and is affected by the ongoing morphing of ENR regulatory politics into the decidedly more conflictual realm of redistributive politics. Under these circumstances, and with few signs that transformative technoscientific advances are abating, precautionary politics will endure and pose significant strategic challenges, choices, and opportunities for building a results-based sense of common purpose in environmental governance in the twenty-first century. Most critical for attenuating this tendency toward conflict, the GM food controversy suggests, are reform strategies geared toward building trust in all aspects of the technoscientific enterprise: through building capacity, ensuring transparency, and advancing cultural sensitivity. Without these adaptations, precautionary politics can put at risk humanity's ability to explore empirically, democratically, equitably, and with popular support the promise and pitfalls of major technoscientific advances that might help address pressing environmental governance challenges.

Trust Building Through Capacity Building

As Sir John Browne, chairman of British Petroleum, notes, "Globalization has certainly increased the scale and reach of companies. The twenty largest companies in the world have market capitalizations greater than the GDPs [gross domestic products] of all but twenty of the members of the UN General Assembly."[68] Moreover, precisely because of the financial size and power of multinationals relative to many governments, Browne argues that the corporate world has to "take on responsibilities formally in the hands of government" (for example, ENR protection). Although his comment was a plea for companies to become more socially responsible, many developing nations, greens, NGO activists, and ordinary citizens worry that growth trends in corporate size and power are precisely the problem, and they can be counted on to resist them (sometimes violently). Nor perhaps are these reactions more visible today and potentially dysfunctional tomorrow than when promising technoscientific advances are leveraged by private-sector rather than public-sector investments.

In the face of these realities, policymakers must choose to pursue any opportunity they have to invest in the research, oversight, and enforcement capabilities of regulatory agencies. This decision importantly involves more than investments in technoscientific research, although the GM food case suggests some of the untoward consequences of public-sector disinvestments by many countries over the past two decades. As Morven McLean and his associates counsel developing nations, and as the GM food case vividly illustrates, developing a national approach to biosafety regulation involves building the research capacity "to integrate political, social, ethical, health, economic, and environmental considerations into decisions regarding the safe and appropriate use of biotechnology methods and products."[69] Indeed, even many professionals in the technoscientific fields agree that to build common purpose, policymakers must choose to invest in social science research capacity as well.[70] What is more, in the face of "dueling" and non-peer-reviewed advocacy research over the impacts of technoscientific advances (such as those issued by the NCFAP and the UK Soil Association in the GM food case), the ability to offer credible, independent analyses will be critical to informed deliberation.

At the same time, multinational and transnational business leaders must recognize that capacity building in the public sector is in their interests as well. Otherwise, the profits that they hope to garner from technoscientific initiatives will be derailed by worldwide NGO networks plying public distrust of corporate motives. Consider, for example, the effect that the public-health scandals in Europe have had in destroying public faith that regulators are willing and able to protect them from GM food production hazards. Similarly, when the Global Conservation Trust tried to raise $260 million to ensure persistent funding of the world's germ plasm banks, anti–GM food groups concerned over the governance of the trust argued that it would only "open a wide vista for agribusinesses to serve their own purposes."[71] Indeed, polls in Europe indicate that a powerful factor in determining public attitudes toward risk is trust in the "behavior of institutions responsible for development and regulation of technological innovations and risks."[72]

Yet, with few exceptions, capacity-building trends in the developed world are not encouraging. Here, the biotech research arena in the United States is illustrative of general trends (excluding biomedical research in the wake of September 11, 2001, and the subsequent U.S. war on terrorism). For example, funding for primary and peer-reviewed research done or contracted out for GM food biosafety issues has been neither well funded by Congress nor well coordinated. Meanwhile, in the developing world, public investment in agricultural research generally (on average and with cross-regional differences) has decelerated during the 1990s. Indeed, in sub-Saharan Africa, where the food-security need is greatest, significant declines in research funding occurred during this period.[73] Most developing nations simply lack sufficient expertise and institutional capacity to develop and monitor their own biosafety regimes. Thus, recent initiatives such as the African Agricultural Technology Foundation are especially welcome and strategically savvy as means for building common purpose. In cases like these, private U.S. and European companies partner with local agricultural scientists to fight disease, drought, and insects by donating patent rights, laboratory capacity, and seed varieties.[74]

Trust Building Through Transparency

Whether or not capacity building is realizable immediately, policymakers also must choose to pursue strategic opportunities to build transparency into their decision-making processes for a results-based sense of common purpose to take root. With the morphing of environmental risk issues into livelihood and cultural issues, regulators (and the businesses they regulate) not only have to get the science right, but also must ensure that citizens *believe* that they have done so, while simultaneously considering the socioeconomic, cultural, and ethical consequences of what they are proposing. The paradox, as such, is this: the more difficult it is to explain complex, competing, and confusing technoscientific claims, the more important it is to ensure transparency in deliberative processes for policy-challenged laypersons and stakeholders.

Policymakers who understand this paradox must choose, however, to temper past tendencies toward public relations–based monologues and instead pursue opportunities for dialogue. Put most succinctly, they must listen as well as talk if they are to restore public confidence. Moreover, a critical element for advancing this dialogue is a broad-based multistakeholder participatory process involving governments, technocrats, NGOs, laypersons, and academics (including social scientists). Again, the precautionary politics of the GM food policy arena is instructive in this regard. As Nares Damrongchai laments, most GM crop information disseminated to the public in developing countries has been "left in the hands of companies' PR activities, comments from independent scientists, NGOs' propaganda, and mass media reporting" by inexperienced reporters.[75] As a result, "the debate [has] focused around international trade conflict and consumers' rights and has overshadowed the sound discussion of scientific facts on the real threat and benefit of GM crops."[76] Indeed, nations and businesses in the developed world have learned these lessons the hard way—for example, as Great Britain's public debate over GM products came only after its biotechnology industry was left reeling from public protests.

Choosing to embrace transparency through multistakeholder participation in decision making will be especially difficult for multinational corporations accustomed to getting their way in the past in low-income areas in both developed and developing nations. But in an increasingly internationally networked, sophisticated, and readily mobilizable world of potential NGO opponents, cutting deals on environmental issues with government leaders alone no longer will suffice (especially when these deals have significant livelihood implications). Arguably the only thing worse than failing to offer transparency through multistakeholder participation in technoscientific advances is failing to fulfill commitments to transparency and stakeholder involvement.

In 2000, for example, Monsanto's then-new president, Hendrik Verfaillie, admitted that the company had been "arrogant and secretive" in the past in dealing with the public in pressing its GM food agenda.[77] Heralding the "New Monsanto Pledge," he promised that the repositioned life sciences company henceforth would emphasize public dialogue, transparency, and technology sharing. Yet, by late 2002, this pledge seemed empty in developing nations such as Thailand, even among members of the technoscientific community, who are Monsanto's natural allies. Monsanto, they felt, had reneged on promises made three years earlier to involve the public in decision making after a technology-sharing, public-private partnership involving Thai village farmers had gone badly awry.[78] GM food opponents fully exploited these unfulfilled promises of transparency as but further evidence of the untrustworthiness of Monsanto's claims about GM foods more generally.

Similar and more recent examples of GM food, fiber, and pharmaceutical industry missteps include the StarLink and ProdiGene incidents in the United States. StarLink GM corn approved only for animal feed found its way into Kraft, Safeway, and Mission brand taco shells, prompting a defensive multi-million-dollar recall of these products. Similar recalls and significant fines were levied against ProdiGene when soybeans harvested in Iowa and Nebraska contained traces of GM corn engineered with chemicals and drugs (so-called biopharming).[79] This incident occurred after the GM corn was carelessly dumped into soybean storage bins, a development prompting the U.S. Department of Agriculture to issue more stringent regulations to keep pharmaceuticals grown in plants out of the food supply. This directive was accompanied in 2003 by legislative proposals mandating the FDA to conduct premarket reviews of GM foods and to test products already on the market for unapproved GM ingredients.

Trust Building Through Cultural Sensitivity
Building a results-based sense of common purpose in the wake of enduring precautionary politics also will require governments and corporations to choose to become more acutely attuned to the cultural prisms (that is, a society's or community's accumulated wisdom and practices) through which citizens filter their perceptions of risk, development, and corporate actions. Politically savvy, vocal, and internationally networked persons and NGOs, for example, perceive the discourses of globalization, capitalism, economic and scientific development, and Western models of scientific discovery as placing their very livelihoods and cultures at great risk. As a consequence, a "return to localism" discourse has sprouted among these activists in many developed and developing nations, a risk-based discourse that some scholars characterize as "a form of guerilla resistance to the peripheralization" of communities that activists see globalization promoting.[80] Thus, ripe for resistance-provoking exploitation by anti-globalization activists (principled or otherwise) are citizens who see or can be made to see links between speculative risks and assaults by global forces on the economic, religious, and cultural values that they cherish (for example, self-reliance, self-sufficiency, traditional knowledge and wisdom).

Also prominent in the developing world are memories of past and persistent exploitation of rural natural resources by foreign companies and urban interests with the aid of technoscientific advances unavailable to the local population (for example, in Indonesia, Malaysia, and Thailand).[81] Extant worldwide as well are perceptions of past promises of food productivity, economic development, and profits that did not materialize or were disastrous for communities or to cultural or natural resources (for example, promises in Thailand to increase productivity and profits by transferring land to higher-value crops and by logging timber, which has drastically depleted Thai forests).

We offer all this information less to counsel despair than to show how much grist for resistance is afforded when policymakers choose to ignore the cultural prism through which people filter technoscientific initiatives. Arriving at widely supported and science-based risk decisions that prudently balance risks with the benefits of progress clearly requires the capacity-building and transparency-building initiatives discussed earlier. But even these initiatives will fail if public- and private-sector policymakers are unwilling or unable to understand, strategically frame, and debate issues at stake in culturally sensitive ways. In this vein, recent survey research from Europe and Southeast Asia suggests that proponents of GM foods should emphasize consumer benefits (for example, better health rather than higher food productivity for farmers and consumers in these regions) or else risk opponents' success in keeping anti–GM food sentiments alive.[82] Policymakers who choose to ignore these realities do so not only at their own peril, but also at the peril of prudent, science-based, democratically informed, and popularly accepted ENR decision making in the twenty-first century.

Notes

The authors wish to thank the J. William Fulbright Scholarship Board of the Council for the International Exchange of Scholars, the Thai-U.S. Educational Foundation (Bangkok, Thailand), the John F. Kennedy Foundation of Thailand, and Payap University in Chiang Mai, Thailand, for their generous support of this research project.

1. Gary P. Sampson, "The Environmental Paradox: The World Trade Organization's Challenges," *Harvard International Review* 23(4) (winter 2002), p. 60.

2. See, for example, Paul Slovic, "Perceptions of Risk," *Science* 236 (1987): 280–285; Baruch Fischhoff, "Risk Perception and Risk Communication Unplugged: Twenty Years of Process," *Risk Analysis* 15 (1995): 137–145.

3. For an excellent application of this approach to ENR management, see Philip Hirsch, *Seeing Forests for Trees: Environment and Environmentalism in Thailand* (Chiang Mai, Thailand: Silkworm, 1996).

4. Ibid., p. 7.

5. *Toxicogenomics* involves the collection of data on gene and protein activity and their relationship to toxic substances in the environment. This knowledge might allow scientists, doctors, and regulators to tailor treatment and regulatory standards to persons at greatest risk of disease through exposure to environmental and toxic pollutants. *Nutrigenomics* proposes to tailor diets (so-called designer diets) to an individual's genetic makeup (once identified) in order to avoid illnesses such as diabetes, heart disease, and cancer. *Pharmacogenomics* holds the promise of creating "designer drugs" tailored toward genetic inheritance, thus avoiding negative side effects from broad-based applications of drugs. *Xenotransplantation* seeks to produce organs for transplant into humans by splicing human genes into animals.

6. Andrew Apel, "The Precautionary Principle," paper presented at the International Society of Regulatory Toxicology and Pharmacology Workshop on the Precautionary Principle, Arlington, Va., available at http://www.cei.org/gencon/027,03162.cfm, accessed August 15, 2002, emphasis in original.

7. Redistributive policies are those perceived to reallocate economic resources on the basis of social cleavages or classes in society. Put differently, the targets of these policies perceive permanent winners and losers. As such, they arouse much more opposition than do distributive (for example, farm subsidies) or traditional regulatory policies.

8. According to the Convention on Biological Diversity, biotechnology is "any technological application that uses biological systems, living organisms or derivatives thereof, to make or modify products or processes for specific use" (Article 2). These living organisms can be used to "create," modify, or improve animal or plant species, as well as to develop special microorganisms. Prior to the new biotechnologies, conventional breeding consisted of selections and hybridizations within the same species. In contrast, new biotechnologies have a transgenic element: to obtain new products, scientists transfer genes from one species to another.

9. Jan Bowman, "Pestering the Third World," July 29, 2002, www.agbioworld.com, accessed August 23, 2002.

10. For an excellent summary of the inherent uncertainties of risk analysis, see Howard Margolis, *Dealing with Risk: Why the Public and the Experts Disagree on Environmental Issues* (Chicago: University of Chicago Press, 1996).

11. For a summary of these heuristics, see Rosemary O'Leary, Robert F. Durant, Daniel Fiorino, and Paul S. Weiland, *Managing for the Environment: Understanding the Legal, Organizational, and Policy Challenges* (San Francisco: Jossey-Bass, 1999), p. 173.

12. Patrick J. Corcoran, counselor for public affairs, Embassy of the United States of America, Bangkok, Thailand, interviewed August 8, 2002. Even

reporters concede this point, attributing it as well to a lack of scientific training on their part, especially in developing countries (Pennapa Hongthong and Kamol Sukin, reporters for *The Nation,* Bangkok, Thailand, interviewed August 6, 2002).

13. Manuel Castells, *The Rise of the Network Society,* 2d ed. (Oxford: Blackwell, 2000).

14. S. H. Safe, "Xenoestrogens and Breast Cancer," *New England Journal of Medicine* 337 (1997): 1303–1304.

15. Robyn Eckersley, *Environmentalism and Political Theory: Toward an Eco-centric Approach* (London: University College Press, 1994).

16. Ibid., p. 5. For an excellent discussion of why this challenge to the Washington consensus occurs, see Joseph E. Stiglitz, *Globalization and Its Discontents* (New York: W. W. Norton, 2002).

17. Sharman Esarey, "Hunger Prevails Despite World's Rich Bounty," *Bangkok Post,* August 16, 2002, p. 11.

18. Hirsch, *Seeing Forests for Trees,* p. 5.

19. Ibid., p. 4.

20. Ibid., p. 2.

21. Esarey, "Hunger Prevails." Included among these organizations are the National Academy of Sciences in the United States and the Royal Society in Great Britain.

22. For example, when *Time* magazine honored anti–GM food Indian activist Vandana Shiva for "representing tradition's voice" and setting "an eco-friendly standard that agribusiness must show it can outperform" (namely, organic farming), one Indian farm rights group said, "Shiva would like all of us to grovel in poverty so that she could, in her jet setting ways, occasionally descend on us to preach about the virtues of poverty." Shiva responded that GM food supporters are typically part of "genocidal think tanks whose minds have been bought by money" from agribusinesses. See Marc Morano, "Green Activist Accused of Promoting Famine Wins *Time* Magazine Honor," www.CNSNews.com, September 17, 2002.

23. U.S. Census Bureau, *World Population Profile: 1998 Highlights,* March 19, 2001, http://www.census.gov/ipc/www/wp98001.html.

24. Jikun Huang, Carl Pray, and Scott Rozelle, "Enhancing the Crops to Feed the Poor," *Nature* 418 (August 8, 2002): 678–684.

25. Ibid., p. 678.

26. C. S. Prakash, "The Gene Revolution and Food Security," *Observer of Business and Politics,* March 2, 2000, www.agbioworld.org/biotech_info/topics/agbiotech/revolution.html.

27. Ibid.

28. David Tillman, Kenneth G. Cassman, Pamela A. Matson, Rosamond Naylor, and Stephen Polasky, "Agricultural Sustainability and Intensive Production Practices," *Nature* 418 (August 8, 2002): 671–677.

29. Ibid.

30. Ibid.

31. In the Danish study, insects and spiders flourished, allowing more foods for birds. See "Genetically Modified Crops Could Be Better for Environment, Danish Study Finds," Pew Initiative on Food and Biotechnology, March 13, 2003, www.pewagbiotech.org, accessed March 26, 2003.

32. Global Knowledge Center on Crop Biotechnology, "Documented Benefits of GM Crops," available from the International Service for the Acquisition of Agri-Biotech Applications (ISAAA), 2002.

33. Sutat Sriwatanapongse, "Biotechnology Development in Asia and Food Security," paper presented at the Export-Import Bank of India National Conference on Agricultural Product Export, January 21–22, 2002, Pune, India.

34. United Nations Development Program, *Human Development Report, 1997*, as cited in Sriwatanapongse, "Biotechnology Development in Asia," p. 9. For example, research staffing in Thailand has been estimated to be only about 0.2 scientists per 10,000 population, in contrast to 23 per 10,000 in Taiwan and 60 per 10,000 in Japan.

35. Per Pinstrup-Anderson and Ebbe Schioler, *Seeds of Contention: World Hunger and the Global Controversy over GM Crops* (Baltimore, Md.: Johns Hopkins University Press, 2000), p. 142.

36. See Anatole F. Krattiger, "Food Biotechnology: Promising Havoc or Hope for the Poor?" *Proteus: A Journal of New Ideas* 17(38) (2000), www.agbioworld. org/biotech_info/topics/agbiotech/havoc_hope.html, accessed July 26, 2002.

37. Sriwatanapongse, "Biotechnology Development in Asia," p. 3. Other companies (for example, Novartis and Syngenta) also have donated food biotech applications for the poor to the ISAAA for brokering to developing nations.

38. See Huang, Pray, and Rozelle, "Enhancing the Crops to Feed the Poor." As the result of a merger of the Novartis and Zeneca corporations, Syngenta holds more than half the world's patents on terminator and traitor technology. Syngenta, however, has long foresworn the use of terminator genes in favor of chemical-switching technologies and is working aggressively on developing this approach. The United States (70 percent) and Argentina (20 percent) produce 90 percent of all GM crops; Canada and China produce 9 percent; and South Africa and Australia produce the remainder. In 2001, 63 percent of the world's soybean crop and 24 percent of its corn crop were genetically engineered (Philip Brasher, "Farmers to Increase Biotech Crops," *Austin360.com*, March 29, 2001, http://www.austin360.com/shared/news/technology/ap_story.html/Sience/AP.V9155.AP-Biotech-Fo). In 2003 in the United States, 81 percent of all soybean acres planted, 40 percent of all corn acres planted, and 73 percent of all cotton acres planted were transgenic. In turn, food scientists estimate that approximately 70 percent of the food in grocery stores now contains bioengineered products (see Pew Initiative on Food and Biotechnology, *GM Crops in the United States* [Richmond, Va.: Pew Initiative, 2003]; and Daniel Charles, *Lords of the Harvest: Biotech, Big Money, and the Future of Food* [Cambridge, Mass.: Perseus, 2001]).

39. Gordon Conway, "The Rockefeller Foundation and Plant Biotechnology," June 24, 1999, www.biotech-info.net/gordon_conway.html, accessed July 15, 2002. Also see "Greenpeace: Golden Rice Over-Hyped," *Bangkok Post,* June 14, 2001, www.fadinap.org/news/news114.htm, accessed June 18, 2002. The companies involved in donating IPRs for golden rice were the companies involved in funding research for vitamin A deficiency–related diseases: Syngenta Seeds AG, Syngenta Ltd., Bayer AF, Monsanto Inc., Orynova BV, and Zeneca Mogen BV.

40. Pinstrup-Anderson and Schioler, *Seeds of Contention,* p. 146. These authors lament the opportunity that this situation offers GM critics in the wealthy developed world (especially in the EU) to dictate to the developing world that they will not accept the latter's exports if they contain genetically modified organisms (GMOs). Indeed, in 2002, fears of trade retaliation by the EU if developing countries accepted famine relief from the United States that included GM grains played a major role in Zimbabwe, Zambia, and Mozambique's refusal of food shipments even though millions of their citizens were facing starvation.

41. R. S. Hails, "Assessing the Risks Associated with New Agricultural Practices," *Nature* 418 (August 8, 2002), p. 685.

42. See "Pollen from GM Crops Spreads to Other Fields, But Effects are Minor, According to Study," Pew Initiative on Food and Biotechnology, www.pewagbiotch.org/newsroom/summaries/display.php3?NewsId=198.

43. Apisit Buranakanonda, "Bt Cotton Is Potential Economic Savior of Chinese Province," *Bangkok Post,* October 26, 1999, www.bangkokpost.com/issues/gmo/261099b.html, accessed August 31, 2002.

44. Sue Meyer, "Royal Society Endorses GeneWatch UK Concerns on Regulation of GM Foods," *GeneWatch UK Press Release,* February 6, 2002, www.genewatch.org/Pres%20Releases/pr22.htm, accessed July 3, 2002.

45. See, for example, Luca Bucchini and Lynn R. Goldman, "A Snapshot of Federal Research on Food Allergy: Implications for Genetically Modified Food," paper prepared for the Pew Initiative on Food and Biotechnology, 2002.

46. John Vidal and John Aglionby, "UN Agency Backs GM Food Crops," *The Guardian International,* July 11, 2001, www.guardian.co.uk/international/story/0,3604,519721,00.html, accessed August 22, 2002.

47. With the developed world spending approximately $350 billion a year to subsidize their own farmers, and only approximately $50 billion a year for development assistance to the developing world, farmers in the latter have no incentive to increase productivity.

48. "Greenpeace: Golden Rice Over-Hyped"; Vidal and Aglionby, "UN Agency Backs GM Food Crops." Greenpeace, for example, says the average adult would need to eat 12 times as much golden rice daily than she does today to get the vitamin A health benefits that GM proponents claim. Its developer, Ingo Potrykus, responds that the levels of vitamin A needed to prevent the most severe deficiency problems are much lower than Greenpeace calculated.

49. Global Knowledge Center on Crop Biotechnology, "GM Crops and the Environment," June 2002. Available upon request from ISAAA.

50. See, for example, Pinstrup-Anderson and Schioler, *Seeds of Contention.*

51. "Greenpeace: Golden Rice Over-Hyped."

52. Kultida Samabuddhi, "Farm Officials Plan GM Field Experiments," *Bangkok Post,* February 8, 2003, www.search.bangkokpost.co.th/bkkpost, accessed March 29, 2003.

53. As this volume goes to press, the EU, Australia, and New Zealand require labeling of foods or ingredients as "GMOs" if detectable DNA or protein in them exceeds 1 percent of total content. In contrast, Japan requires labeling of products as GMOs if any of the top three ingredients in them exceeds a 5 percent level, and Korea sets a 3 percent threshold for any one of the top five ingredients but does not allow any labeling of food as "non-GMO."

54. *Inside U.S. Trade,* January 11, 2002, p. 12.

55. "GM Crops Report 'Dynamite,'" *BBC World Report,* September 17, 2002, www.news.bbc.co.uk/2/hi/uk_news/scotland/2264497.stm, emphasis added.

56. During 2002 and 2003, China set new procedural rules that slowed down the approval process for GMOs and restricted its own trade in GMOs with countries such as the United States. Moreover, by mid-2003, it had approved the commercialization of only four GM crops (cotton, petunias, sweet peppers, and tomatoes), while simultaneously creating GM-free planting zones in the country.

57. Joseph Y. Yun, counselor, Economic Affairs, Embassy of the United States of America, Bangkok, Thailand, interviewed August 8, 2002; Sutat Sriwatanapongse, director, Thailand Biodiversity Center, Bangkok, Thailand, interviewed August 7, 2002. In fact, the WTO supported the U.S. contention that the EU's ban of bovine growth hormone was a discriminatory ban on trade because the EU failed to provide sufficient scientific evidence of harm to support this claim.

58. The Codex Alimentarius is a collection of common norms and standards for food quality and safety that has been adopted by 165 nations. Its purposes are, first, to protect the health and safety of consumers and, second, to give producers and the food industry guidelines for their products.

59. Michael Meacher, "Environment Minister Kick Starts Public Debate on GM," *The Guardian,* August 14, 2002, http://politics.guardian.co.uk/green/comment/0,9236,773988,00.html.

60. "The Grim Reaper," *The Economist* 364(8287) (August 24–30, 2002), p. 44.

61. Pinstrup-Anderson and Schioler, *Seeds of Contention,* p. 146.

62. Ibid.

63. Citing the significant costs to international trade, Hong Kong's Health, Welfare, and Food Bureau in 2003 proposed only a voluntary system of labeling GM products.

64. "Action Pledged by GM Protesters," *BBC News World Edition,* July 4, 2002, www.bbc.co.uk/2/hi/uk_news/Scotland/2149094.stm.

65. FuVuda-Parr quoted in Jan Bowman, "Pestering the Third World," July 29, 2002, www.agbioworld.com, accessed August 23, 2002.

66. Quoted in "Q&A: GM and Politics," *BBC News World Edition,* July 26, 2002, www.news.bbc.co.uk/2/hi/science/nature/215331.stm.

67. Peter Drahos, "Genetically Modified Organisms and Biosafety: The Global Regulatory Issues," paper presented at the Ninth International Conference of the Greening of Industry Network, Bangkok, Thailand, January 21–24, 2001, available at www.biotec.or.th.

68. Browne quoted in Jodie Ginsberg, "Business Takes a Keener Interest in Environment," *Bangkok Post,* August 20, 2002, p. 11.

69. Morven McLean, Robert Frederick, Patricia Traynor, Joel Cohen, and John Komen, "A Conceptual Framework for Implementing Biosafety: Linking Policy, Capacity, and Regulation," *IBS News Report,* August 2002, www.isb.vt.edu, accessed August 18, 2002.

70. For an excellent discussion of an innovative approach taken in Thailand, see Nares Damrongchai, "Stakeholder Dialogue in the GM Debate: A Stepwise Approach Toward Consensus," paper presented at the Tenth International Conference of the Greening of Industry Network, June 23–26, 2002, Göteborg, Sweden.

71. Cited in Alex Avery, "Science Gives False Credibility to Anti-Biotech Activists," www.agbioworld.com, accessed September 19, 2002.

72. Meacher, "Environment Minister Kick Starts Public Debate on GM." For a more recent work, see George Gaskell, Nick Allum, and Sally Stares, "Europeans and Biotechnology in 2002," report to the European Commission Directorate General for Research from the project, 'Life Sciences in European Society,' QLG7-CT-1999-00286 in *Eurobarometer 58.0,* 2d ed., March 21, 2003, pp. 1–69.

73. See Tilman et al., "Agricultural Sustainability."

74. Justin Gillis, "To Feed Hungry Africans, Firms Plant Seeds of Science," *Washington Post,* March 11, 2003, p. A1.

75. Damrongchai, "Stakeholder Dialogue in the GM Debate," p. 3.

76. Ibid.

77. "Genetically Modified Company: Sceptics Abound. Has Monsanto Learned Its Lesson Since Causing a Stir in the Late 1990s?" *The Economist* (August 15, 2002), www.agbioworld.com, accessed list serve August 18, 2002.

78. "Thai Ministry of Public Health Distances Itself from Monsanto in Response to Leaked Memo," *GeneWatch UK,* September 20, 2000, www.genewatch.org/press%20Releases/pr16.htm.

79. In the StarLink case, not a single instance of health problems was ever identified. However, when StarLink admitted that not all of its 2,000 farmers

growing the corn had signed agreements to follow procedures to keep the product from human consumption, critics of the existing "self-policing" regulatory system exploded. Likewise, in the ProdiGene case, soybeans never reached consumers, but the incident reinforced concerns about the capacity of the regulatory system to monitor this new technology for safety.

80. For an excellent discussion of the intellectual history of this dynamic, see Pasuk Phongpaichit and Chris Baker, *Thailand's Crisis* (Chiang Mai: Silkworm, 2002).

81. Chomchuan Boonrahong, director, Institute for a Sustainable Agriculture Community, Chiang Mai, Thailand, interviewed July 10, 2002; Anthony M. Zola, president, MIDAS Agronomics Co., Ltd., Bangkok, Thailand, interviewed August 7, 2002.

82. Gaskell, Allum, and Stares, "Europeans and Biotechnology in 2002," p. 5. This survey also offers tentative evidence that respondents were able to make distinctions between "red" biotechnologies (for example, those focusing on life science or public health) and "green" biotechnologies (for example, those with benefits to nature). They tend to favor the former over the latter. Also see Kultida Samabuddhi, "Thais Not Averse to Genetic Engineering," *Bangkok Post*, March 6, 2003, p. 1.

4

Common-Pool Resource Theory

Edella Schlager

An August 2000 article in the *New York Times Magazine* reported on "the ruined fisheries of the Northeast."[1] The cod, swordfish, and halibut fisheries no longer are economically viable. Only the lobster fishery remains productive, but it too is beginning to show signs of overharvesting. Fishers are using larger boats, spending more time at sea, setting more lobster traps, and harvesting increasingly smaller lobsters. Most lobsters harvested are just of legal minimum size, meaning that at most they have had one year in which to spawn and reproduce.[2] In the article a fisherman states, "I have no incentive to conserve the fishery, because any fish I leave is just going to be picked by the next guy."[3]

Many would not find the description of the New England lobster fishery surprising. After all, it mirrors the dynamic described by Garrett Hardin in his article "The Tragedy of the Commons."[4] The New England fishers, just like Hardin's herders, are locked in a deadly competition for resources, a competition from which they do not seem to be able to extricate themselves. As the fisherman quoted here noted, he faces few incentives to limit his harvest. Another will harvest whatever he conserves, and the fish stock will still be destroyed. The fishers collectively can limit their harvesting and preserve their fisheries, thus helping themselves in the process, yet that possibility appears remote because of the overwhelming temptations that each fisher faces to free-ride off of the others' efforts. The fishers seem doomed, short of forceful intervention by an external authority.

What may surprise many is the description of a different lobster fishery in the same newspaper article. On the southern coast of Australia, fishers make a generous living from the sea by limiting their catches and conserving the fish stocks.[5] Through a combination of community norms, rules, and enforcement plus government regulation, Australian fishers have extricated themselves from a tragedy of the commons. The lobstermen limit themselves to sixty traps each (substantially fewer than the 800 traps commonly used by New England lobstermen). Associated with each trap is a license that the Australian government allocated among working fishers in the 1960s.[6] The licenses are fully transferable, and, in fact, if an individual wants to enter the fishery, he must purchase licenses from working fishers willing to part with theirs. No longer do the lobstermen race to harvest as many lobsters as possible. They typically work eight-hour days up to 187 days per year (again, substantially fewer than the 240 days per year their American counterparts work).[7] Furthermore, the lobster stock remains healthy with larger, older lobsters still regularly harvested. As one fisherman is quoted as saying, "Why hurt the fishery? . . . It's my retirement fund. . . . If I rape and pillage the fishery now, in ten years my licenses won't be worth anything."[8]

The Australian fishers are not like Hardin's herders. They have avoided a tragedy of the commons. Why have Australian, but not New England, fishers figured a way out of their tragedy? Hardin's model cannot account for such success; it predicts failure. Until recently, if one turned to the very best scholarly work, one would find only explanations and predictions of failure. This chapter argues, however, that this attitude is beginning to change. Over the past fifteen years, scholars and practitioners have concluded that the tragedy of the commons is no longer the only model available to account for human use of common-pool resources. Furthermore, not only are appropriators able to extricate themselves from tragedies, but theoretically grounded and empirically tested explanations of the conditions under which they are likely to do so have been realized. As such, scholarship addressing common-pool resource dilemmas, done largely (but not exclusively) in the developing world, now offers a compass to practitioners and scholars for anticipating both failure and success in overcoming these dilemmas.[9]

Having developed more complete explanations of cooperation and of resource users' ability to coordinate and govern their behavior, however, is still a far cry from putting such insights into practice. The purpose of this chapter is thus threefold: (1) to review how and why local governance of common-pool resources has become an increasingly important approach to environmental management; (2) to review what we know about the conditions under which such governance is more likely to be adopted and to be successful when adopted; and (3) to assess the future strategic choices, challenges, and opportunities local governance poses for environmental management. In the process, the chapter demonstrates what contribution common-pool resource theory can make to the building of a results-based sense of common purpose in environmental governance.

Common-Pool Resources, Noncooperative Behavior, and the Tragedy of the Commons

Over the course of almost fifteen years, between 1954 and 1968, scholars developed a number of models of tragedy. H. Scott Gordon and Anthony Scott argued that open access conditions in fisheries lead to the economic destruction of fish stocks.[10] Individual fishers do not attend to the costs that they impose on other fishers who harvest from the same stock. They consequently continue to fish beyond the point of maximizing the revenue of the fishery and dissipate the fishery's rents.[11] In some instances, the fishery may be rendered biologically as well as economically nonviable. Gordon called for government intervention in fisheries to limit fishers' harvesting efforts. Scott demonstrated that such undesirable economic and biological outcomes might be avoided by imposing a single owner on the fishery.

At approximately the same time that Gordon and Scott published their fishery analyses, game theory was rapidly developing, and one of the most well-known and widely popularized games in game theory—the prisoners' dilemma—emerged.[12] The game pits individual rationality against collective rationality as each of the participants chooses his or her actions independently of one another. Narrowly self-interested behavior makes all participants worse off than if they acted cooperatively. Cooperative behavior with the other participants exposes oneself to terrible exploitation, but the choice and the outcome are incontrovertible: act narrowly self-interested and achieve an outcome in which all are made worse off. Like Hardin's herders and Gordon and Scott's fishers, the participants are trapped, unable to extricate themselves from the dilemma.

In 1965, Mancur Olson published a theory of collective action. Although substantially more nuanced than the preceding models—he explored conditions under which cooperation might emerge—the overall tenor of the work was less than positive.[13] Even if individuals share a common goal, he concluded, they are unlikely to cooperate voluntarily in achieving that goal. As he states, "unless the number of individuals in a group is quite small, or unless there is coercion or some other special device to make individuals act in their common interests, *rational, self-interested individuals will not act to achieve their common or group interests.*"[14] In almost every instance, free-riding behavior trumps cooperative behavior. Shortly thereafter, Hardin's tragedy of the commons popularized ideas that were becoming well established and accepted within the economics and political economy disciplines.

Such simple but powerful models made a convincing case that individuals left to their own devices would collectively destroy shared resources. Such a stark conclusion found its way into governments' and international aid organizations' policy prescriptions.[15] Swift and sure government intervention was needed to resolve and prevent commons tragedies. This policy prescription also dovetailed nicely with the goals and purposes of modern state building that was occurring in developing countries recently freed from the crush of colonialism. Only strong central states have the expertise and the resources to address the myriad problems of poverty, illiteracy, poor health, inadequate infrastructure, pollution, and natural-resource degradation.

Central governments acted forcefully. In the United States, for instance, the national government for the first time adopted strict laws establishing national standards for clean air and water.[16] Among other actions, the Canadian government created the Department of Fisheries and Oceans to establish national fishery regulation and enforcement as means of protecting and enhancing fish stocks and of improving fishers' welfare.[17] Developing countries, such as Honduras, India, Nepal, the Philippines, and Tanzania, nationalized resources that local communities once held in common. International aid organizations invested heavily in state capacity building so that governments would have the wherewithal to impose and enforce regulations. The dominant policy paradigm was state-centered control and regulation.

Over the past two decades, increasing dissatisfaction has emerged with the state-centered policy programs pursued. In many instances in which national governments and centralized bureaucratic agencies intervened, claimed ownership, built extensive infrastructure, or imposed management regimes, results have been disappointing. Most commercially valuable fish stocks are overharvested; government-owned or managed forests are degraded; many government-owned and operated irrigation projects are poorly maintained, and the health of many people the world over remains threatened by polluted air, unclean water, and exposure to toxic chemicals and wastes. In some instances, policymakers, analysts, and citizens came to realize that government-centered approaches, although successful in limiting and even reversing resource degradation, could not address single-handedly many environmental problems. In other instances, government-centered approaches failed and in their failure contributed to the worsening of environmental problems.

Furthermore, in the mid-1980s, policy scholars began questioning the general application of models patterned after the tragedy of the commons. Hundreds of cases were identified in which people managed to extricate themselves from environmental tragedies by cooperating and developing rules that carefully coordinated and limited their use of common-pool resources.[18] The case studies demonstrated that individuals are not always helplessly trapped in tragedies of their own creation. Rather, the interaction between humans and common-pool resources and the variety of institutional arrangements that individuals devise to mediate those interactions are much more complex and varied than suggested by the fishery, prisoners' dilemma, and collective action models.[19]

Still, certain questions needed answering if state-centered policies were going to be challenged, revised, and replaced: Under what conditions are appropriators likely to cooperate to devise self-governing institutions that allow them to address the multiple dilemmas they face? How well do such institutions perform, and how do they perform relative to government-centered institutions?

The Tragedy of the Commons Revisited

In 1985, the U.S. National Research Council convened a distinguished panel of scholars to investigate and report on self-governing institutional arrangements devised by appropriators to coordinate and limit their use of common-pool resources. That panel was the genesis of an international association of scholars and practitioners,[20] a newsletter,[21] several research institutes,[22] and numerous research programs. Out of that body of research has come a variety of findings that offer a more positive view of the chances of building common purpose in environmental governance when common-pool resources are involved.

One of the major research programs emerging from the National Research Council panel, and the one that is the primary focus of this chapter, is that of Elinor Ostrom.[23] Ostrom argues that in attempting to resolve common-pool resource dilemmas, appropriators must work through three closely related issues—supply, commitment, and monitoring.[24] Common-pool resource dilemmas emerge because individuals in interdependent situations do not coordinate their actions, which leads to outcomes in which all appropriators are made worse off. Better outcomes might be achieved if individuals devised and adopted sets of rules that coordinated their use of the common-pool resource. However, those rules are public goods. Once provided, the rules benefit all appropriators, whether or not all appropriators contributed to their creation. Consequently, when supplying institutional arrangements that may resolve common-pool resource dilemmas, appropriators are confronted with collective action problems: obtaining voluntary contributions of time and resources needed to identify and negotiate a set of rules acceptable to most of them.

Even if appropriators successfully supply a set of rules, they must follow those arrangements most of the time to make them credible and effective. In many instances, however, they will face temptations to disobey the rules. As Ostrom asks, "How does one appropriator credibly commit himself or herself to follow a rotation system when everyone knows that the temptation to break that commitment will be extremely strong in future time periods?"[25]

Monitoring to ensure that most appropriators are following the rules most of the time supports commitment to following the rules. Effective monitoring discourages rule breaking and assures rule followers that they are not being taken advantage of by rule breakers. Yet monitoring is itself a public good—it accrues to all appropriators' benefit, regardless of whether they all contributed to monitoring. But without monitoring, commitments to following the rules are not credible, and without credible commitments to the rules, no rules will be devised and adopted.[26] Thus, the process of devising, implementing, and sustaining institutional arrangements that resolve common-pool resource dilemmas is fraught with difficulty.

Ostrom's emerging theory of common-pool resources and related research programs present a convincing argument that appropriators are capable of resolving common-pool resource dilemmas.[27] Also, the institutional arrangements that appropriators participate in devising, revising, implementing, and enforcing outperform institutional arrangements that government officials devise, revise, implement, and enforce. Thus, the theory of common-pool resources represents a significant and promising approach for the governance of natural resources and the resolution of critical environmental problems. What is more, the empirical research generated by these related research programs affords both practitioners and theorists a robust contingency theory suitable for guiding practice and building theory. Among other things, the programs offer insights into the conditions under which self-governance regimes are more or less likely to arise and under which long-term cooperation within these regimes is more or less likely to occur.

The Emergence of Cooperative Behavior

Whereas Ostrom's initial work focused on explaining the conditions that support long-term cooperation and coordination among appropriators, her more recent work has focused on identifying the conditions under which appropriators are likely to cooperate to devise governing arrangements. The attributes of common-pool resources that are supportive of the emergence of cooperation are:

1. *Feasible improvement.* Resource conditions are not at such a point of deterioration that it is useless to organize, nor are they so underutilized that little advantage results from organizing;

2. *Indicators*. Reliable and valid indicators of the condition of the resource system frequently are available at a relatively low cost;

3. *Predictability*. The flow of resource units is relatively predictable;

4. *Spatial extent*. The resource system is sufficiently small, given the transportation and communication technology in use, that appropriators can develop accurate knowledge of external boundaries and internal microenvironments.[28]

Appropriator attributes that support the emergence of cooperation include:

1. *Salience*. Appropriators are dependent on the resource system for a major portion of their livelihood or other important activity;

2. *Common understanding*. Appropriators have a shared image of how the resource system operates . . . and how their actions affect each other and the resource system;

3. *Low discount rate*. Appropriators use a sufficiently low discount rate in relation to future benefits to be achieved from the resource;

4. *Trust and reciprocity*. Appropriators trust one another to keep promises and relate to one another with reciprocity;

5. *Autonomy*. Appropriators are able to determine access and harvesting rules without external authorities countermanding them;

6. *Prior organizational experience and local leadership*. Appropriators have learned at least minimal skills of organization and leadership through participating in other local associations or through studying ways that neighboring groups have organized.[29]

Characteristics of common-pool resources and characteristics of appropriators interact to affect the likelihood of appropriators engaging in the challenging and costly process of supplying rules. For instance, take the second appropriator condition—common understanding of the resource and how their actions affect it. How quickly and easily do appropriators arrive at such a conclusion? Arriving at a common understanding of the resource and of the effects of their actions on it will be more or less difficult to do depending on the number and types of reliable indicators of the resource condition available to them (resource characteristic two), the predictability of the resource (resource characteristic three), and the spatial extent of the resource (resource characteristic four). In relatively simple settings, appropriators are likely to assess their situation more quickly and accurately. In more complex settings, such as in the West Basin case in California, described more fully later in the chapter, it may take years for appropriators to understand the problems they face. In West Basin, signs of trouble began to emerge in 1912, but it was not until the early 1940s that some appropriators began alerting others and organizing for rule changes.

Even if appropriator characteristic two is met, appropriators still must decide whether it is worthwhile engaging in processes of changing rules to address the common-pool resource dilemmas that confront them. If appropriators highly value the common-pool resource (appropriator characteristic one) and would like for it to remain viable (appropriator characteristic three), if they share some social capital among themselves that they can use to begin working together (appropriator characteristic four), and if they believe that they will benefit from proposed rule changes, then they are likely to attempt to undertake a rule change. Whether such an attempt will be successful depends on appropriators' autonomy to change rules (appropriator characteristic five) and their leaders' skills and assets (appropriator characteristic six).

The attributes of common-pool resources and of appropriators should not be considered necessary or sufficient for appropriators to engage in collective action to create or change institutional arrangements. Rather, the attributes should be thought of as conditions positively related to the emergence of collective action. In a setting in which all attributes are met, appropriators are very likely to engage in collective action, whereas in a setting in which only one attribute is met, appropriators are much less likely to engage in collective action. Between these two extremes, many outcomes are possible, depending on the values of the ten attributes in relation to one another. Also, Ostrom argues that the attributes of a given common-pool resource situation are themselves conditioned and affected by the larger institutional setting.[30] Under different institutional settings, the values and therefore the significance of the ten attributes are likely to change. In other words, the theory is contingent (that is, context matters) and configurel (that is, the value of one variable depends on the values of the other variables). Thus, although the theory appears simple, at least on the surface, involving only ten variables, it is in fact quite complex.

Designing Long-Term Cooperation

According to Ostrom, appropriators are much more likely to commit themselves to and monitor institutional arrangements across many generations if the institutional arrangements are characterized by eight design principles. Ostrom was not willing to propose the principles as necessary conditions for long-term success; however, the principles do account for the success of institutional arrangements in sustaining common-pool resources and in gaining the compliance of generations of appropriators. The design principles are:

1. Individuals or households who have rights to withdraw resource units from the common-pool resource must be clearly defined, as must the boundaries of the common-pool resource itself. This is commonly referred to as the principle of exclusion.

2. Appropriation rules restricting time, place, technology, and/or quantity of resource units are related to local conditions and to provision rules requiring labor, material, and/or money.

3. Most individuals affected by the operational rules can participate in modifying them.

4. Monitors, who actively audit common-pool resource conditions and appropriator behavior, are accountable to the appropriators or are the appropriators.

5. Appropriators who violate operational rules are likely to be assessed graduated sanctions (depending on the seriousness and context of the offense) by other appropriators, by officials accountable to these appropriators, or by both.

6. Appropriators and their officials have rapid access to low-cost local arenas to resolve conflicts among appropriators or between appropriators and officials.

7. The rights of appropriators to devise their own institutions are not challenged by external governmental authorities.

8. Appropriation, provision, monitoring, enforcement, conflict resolution, and governance activities are organized in multiple layers of nested enterprises.[31]

Design principle one, exclusion, is critical if appropriators are to commit to following a set of institutional arrangements over time and to investing in modifying them as circumstances warrant. Appropriators must be assured that they will capture the benefits of their actions. Exclusion, although critical, is insufficient, however, to ensure long-term commitment to the rules. The rules themselves must make sense: they must be crafted to the exigencies of the situation, and as the situation changes, the appropriators must have the ability to modify them. Accountable monitors and graduated sanctioning maintain appropriators' commitment to institutional arrangements. In many instances, the rules support monitoring by appropriators while they are using the common-pool resource. Finally, conflict resolution mechanisms and at least a minimal recognition of the right to organize prevent institutional regimes from unraveling because of internal strife or invasion from external governmental authorities.

These eight principles have received considerable support from in-depth research conducted across several different types of common-pool resources. A study I conducted, for example, examined thirty case studies of coastal fisheries located around the world, involving forty-four groups of fishers.[32] The fishery cases demonstrate the importance of exclusion, carefully crafted rules designed by fishers, and monitoring.

Fishers commonly face several types of dilemmas, or conflicts, that require careful coordination if they are to be resolved. In addition to the overharvesting of fish, coastal fishers confront conflict over access to the most productive fishing grounds and over entanglement and destruction of incompatible types of gear.[33] In order to be resolved, these two types of dilemmas require fishers to exercise relatively high levels of control over access to their fishing grounds and to allocate themselves over the grounds. This must be done in such a way as to minimize destructive competition, whether for productive areas or among incompatible gear types. Of the forty-four subgroups of fishers in my study, thirty-three had adopted both access and harvesting rules.[34]

F. T. Christy, a highly regarded fisheries analyst, argues that for fishers to exercise real control over their fishing grounds, they must utilize more restrictive rules than simple residency in the village or region nearest the fishery.[35] Among the thirty-three subgroups of fishers in my study, all used a residency rule and at least one additional rule to control access to their fishing grounds. Fishers also used combinations of twelve different access rules. The most common rule combined with a residency rule was a fishing technology rule. Fishers specified that only particular types of fishing gear can be used in their fisheries. The next most common type of rule to combine with a residency rule was organization membership. In most cases, this rule required an individual to belong to the local fish cooperative. Other rules included owning a fishing license or participating in a lottery to allocate fishing spots. Among groups of fishers who exercised high levels of control over access, individuals not only had to be local residents, but they also had to meet additional qualifications before gaining entry to the fishery.

The thirty-three subgroups noted earlier also guided harvesting through the use of combinations of five different types of rules. Each subgroup adopted a rule of fishing at specific locations or spots. Fishers could not fish how and where they pleased; rather, rules allocated fishers across fishing grounds. In addition to a location rule, some subgroups adopted fish-size rules, others season rules, and yet others a taking-turns rule.

Although fishers from different fishing grounds located around the world adopted the same five general rules to guide their harvesting, the ways in which the rules were implemented or practiced varied substantially. The fishers crafted the specifics of their rules to fit the conditions of their grounds and their cultural norms and practices. Among coastal fishers along the Atlantic coast of Canada, lotteries commonly were used to allocate choice cod-fishing spots each year.[36] Coastal fishers from Alanya, Turkey, also used a lottery to allocate choice fishing spots. However, their lottery was used to make an initial allocation of spots, which the fishers then rotated through, switching spots each day until all fishers had fished all spots.[37]

Even though all groups of fishers did not utilize lotteries to allocate spots, all groups of fishers devised rules that separated potentially conflictual gear types by dividing fishing grounds among different types of technologies. For instance, the fishers of Fogo Island, Newfoundland, in addition to using a first-in-time, first-in-right rule to allocate choice cod spots, adopted rules regulating how close competing gears could be set to one another. They also banned particular types of technologies from specific areas; for example, baitless hooks, called jiggers, were forbidden on the fishing grounds farthest from shore.[38] In general, among the thirty-three subgroups, access and harvesting rules were used to limit entry, govern the use of space on the fishing grounds, control types of technologies, and mandate how those technologies were used.

My research also indicated that the rules selected made a difference. The groups of fishers who adopted more complete and varied sets of rules and who were able to exercise greater control over access were much more likely to experience fewer conflicts on their fishing grounds than fishers who devised limited sets of rules and who exercised less control over access. In any case, fishers who adopted rules were better off than fishers who had no rules governing access or harvesting.[39]

Like fishery studies, irrigation studies have confirmed the importance of exclusion and carefully crafted rules (design principles one and two), the importance of appropriators participating in devising and modifying rules (design principle three), and the importance of monitoring and enforcing the rules (design principles four and five).[40] Because irrigation systems are common-pool resources, irrigators experience dilemmas in the operation and maintenance of such systems. In many instances, water is insufficient to meet all irrigators' needs all of the time. Water allocation rules must be established to share water across irrigators. As water becomes increasingly scarce, and as water demands are not satisfied, irrigators face increasing temptation to cheat on the rules. Furthermore, irrigation structures must be built and maintained, and rules must be established governing irrigator contributions. Again, irrigators face temptations to shirk or avoid their contributions because it is difficult to prevent them from enjoying the benefits of a system, even if they did not contribute to it.[41]

Y. S. Tang studied forty-three irrigation systems: twenty-nine farmer-owned and farmer-governed systems, and fourteen government-owned systems.[42] He used three performance measures to capture the extent to which governing systems mitigated the multiple dilemmas experienced by irrigators—system maintenance, adequacy of water supply, and rule-following behavior.[43] High-performing cases were ranked positively on both rule conformance and maintenance, whereas low-performing cases were ranked negatively on rule conformance or maintenance or both. Among the fourteen government-owned systems, six performed highly and eight did not. Among the twenty-nine farmer-owned irrigation systems, only twenty-five had sufficient information concerning the three performance measures. Of those twenty-five, eighteen performed highly and seven did not.

What accounts for the differences between high-performing and low-performing irrigation systems? Tang argues that among irrigation systems that perform well, rules that govern water allocation and maintenance activities are better crafted to the specific conditions of each irrigation system.[44] High-performing systems were associated with multiple rules that adequately limited access to the system and that fairly allocated water among the irrigators. Low-performing irrigation systems were characterized by a single simple rule set or by no rules at all. Access to the irrigation systems was not regulated adequately, and water allocation rules often did not work well.[45]

Although low-performing irrigation systems have rules of access and allocation that are similar to those of high-performing systems, they are much more likely to be government owned rather than farmer owned. Because government officials are not directly subject to the irrigation rules that they devise, they face few incentives to design rules that ensure the effective operation of irrigation systems. Instead, they face incentives to devise rules that increase their political support and that lighten their administrative burdens. Conversely, because farmers directly experience the consequences of their rule-making decisions, they confront incentives to craft carefully the rules to their particular situations.[46]

Monitoring and enforcement systems also differ between irrigator-owned systems and government-owned systems in some surprising and unusual ways. Government-owned systems appear to have ideal monitoring systems in place—full-time, paid guards. Farmer-owned systems appear to have questionable monitoring systems in place—part-time guards who are not paid.[47] However, guards in farmer-owned systems are much more likely to impose sanctions on rule breakers than are guards in government-owned systems. Furthermore, rule-following behavior is much more common in farmer-owned systems than in government-owned systems, whether guards are present or not.[48] Farmers who participate in devising their own irrigation rules are much more likely to follow, monitor actively, and enforce their rules.

The evidence from irrigation systems should not be interpreted to suggest that governments have no role to play in addressing common-pool resource dilemmas. That would be as great an error as suggesting that only governments can resolve common-pool resource dilemmas. The issue is not whether governments should be involved; rather, it is *how* governments should be involved in addressing such dilemmas. Tang's evidence suggests that, in general, appropriators are better than government agencies at crafting governance structures that fit well to specific situations. Research by William Blomquist on the governance of groundwater basins in California suggests that governments can be of greatest benefit to appropriators by providing a supportive environment that encourages appropriators to devise their own solutions to the dilemmas that they face (that is, design principles six, seven, and eight).[49] Southern California is one of the most populated, rapidly growing regions of the United States. For instance, the population of Los Angeles County quintupled from 2,208,492 in 1930 to 8,863,164 in 1990.[50] During this same time, much of the county's land was transformed from farms to cities and suburbs. Southern California is also one of the driest regions of the United States. Subject to periods of extended drought, it receives from fifteen to twenty inches of rainfall per year.[51]

Fortunately, the area is blessed with a series of interconnected, relatively deep, and highly productive groundwater basins. The basins provide an important source of water and a relatively inexpensive but critical source of water storage. For instance, West Basin, located beneath the coastal area of Los Angeles County, is estimated to hold 6.5 million acre-feet of water.[52]

West Basin provides an excellent example of the complex dilemmas that can besiege pumpers if access, use, and maintenance of a groundwater basin are not attended to appropriately. West Basin is relatively vulnerable. Because one of its boundaries adjoins the ocean, saltwater can pour into the basin if water levels along that boundary drop below sea level, contaminating the freshwater of the basin as well as its storage capacity. The basin itself is covered by clay soils that are relatively impermeable, preventing basin recharge through rainfall seeping into the ground or through constructed recharge ponds. Instead, it is recharged primarily through water discharges from Central Basin, the groundwater basin directly upstream of it.[53]

West Basin began to experience degradation problems in 1912. By the end of the 1950s, "with water levels down 200 feet in some places, an accumulated over-draft of more than 800,000 acre-feet, and a half-million acre-feet of salt-water underlying thousands of acres of land and advancing on two fronts, the groundwater supply in West Basin was threatened with destruction."[54] The West Basin appropriators had created a tragedy for themselves. Could they extricate themselves from it?

In 1943, appropriators created the West Basin Water Users Association. One of its first actions was to issue a report on the state of the West Basin based on federal, state, and county investigations. This report alerted everyone in the basin to the substantial dilemmas emerging. Next, it assisted its members in forming the West Basin Municipal Water District, which would contract with other water providers to import water into the basin. While cities sought to import water into the basin, three major water providers filed suit against all other basin pumpers to adjudicate groundwater rights and to limit pumping. The court subsequently defined all relevant participants and provided a forum for which agreements could be negotiated and actions taken to benefit the basin as a whole.[55]

The judge asked the California Division of Water Resources to act as fact finder and to report on the physical condition of the basin. In 1952, a report was issued suggesting that pumping be limited to 30,000 acre-feet annually. Most major water producers in the basin were alarmed by the possibility of having to reduce their pumping by two-thirds. After substantial negotiations and conflict, in 1961, the court accepted the settlement offered by the parties: "It gave ninety-nine parties transferable 'adjudicated rights' totaling 64,064.09 acre-feet."[56]

Although basin appropriators took steps to import additional water and to limit pumping, pumping still exceeded replenishment by 100 percent. The West Basin Water Users Association decided to explore the possibility of increasing the recharge to the basin, to align pumping more nearly with replenishment. Because the basin was recharged by flows from Central Basin, water users in Central Basin would have to cooperate. The West Basin Water Users Association worked with the Los Angeles County Flood Control District, which operated recharge projects in Central Basin, and with the Central Basin Water Users Association to create a stable, long-term replenishment program that would benefit both basins.

In 1960, the Central and West Basin Water Replenishment District was created and was financed by a pump tax. The district purchases imported replenishment water from the Central Basin Municipal Water District. The Municipal Water District conveys the water to the recharge sites, which the Los Angeles County Flood Control District operates. In addition to replenishment activities, the Replenishment District worked with the Flood Control District to create a freshwater barrier along the coast to mitigate the intrusion of seawater into West Basin.[57] West Basin is no longer in critical overdraft.

Through a complex series of steps over the course of two and one-half decades, the appropriators of West Basin had confronted and addressed a series of dilemmas that had brought the basin to the edge of destruction. The appropriators had formed their own organization, worked cooperatively with other organizations, and called on high-level decision makers such as the state courts and the state legislature to devise solutions.

In sum, Ostrom's eight design principles are given strong support from the research on fisheries, irrigation systems, and groundwater basins. In the instances in which appropriators have designed well-performing governing arrangements in both fisheries and irrigation systems, the rules match the setting, whether the process involves carefully allocating portions of a fishing ground to a particular type of fishing gear or allocating water by farmers taking turns.[58] Indeed, even among the seven southern California groundwater basins that had governing arrangements, appropriators from each basin designed different types of rules. In the case of fisheries, mutual monitoring occurred as fishers ensured that no one invaded their allocated spot or that someone was not using banned gear that might become entangled with their own.[59] In irrigation systems, mutual monitoring was supplemented by appropriators who employed fellow irrigators to monitor rule-following behavior, and those monitors actively sanctioned rule violators.[60] West Basin appropriators relied on the court-appointed special water master to monitor their pumping activities. If the master identified a violation, however, it was up to the appropriators to pursue sanctions against the offending party.[61]

In the case of West Basin, the state of California provided a supportive institutional environment (design principles seven and eight). It provided courts that acted as low-cost conflict resolution mechanisms for the appropriators. Furthermore, it provided monitors and vital information about the condition of the basin, and as a home-rule state, it recognized and supported appropriators in their search for solutions to their groundwater basin problems.

Common-Pool Resource Theory: Challenges, Choices, and Opportunities

As the preceding discussion illustrates, there is reason for optimism that a major animating principle of environmental governance (namely, the tragedy of the commons) is more contingent and conditional than it was previously thought to be. Moreover, empirical research is suggesting the conditions under which common-pool resource management is likely to produce a results-based sense of common purpose for protecting these types of threatened resources. A central animating purpose for environmental governance when common-pool resources are involved is knowing when and how to help catalyze, maintain, and nurture these types of self-governing institutions. Still, a variety of strategic challenges, choices, and opportunities exist that render the future application of the concept difficult to discern. Most notable are those associated with (1) appreciating its wider applicability, (2) coming to terms with its contextual and configurel nature, (3) defining community, and (4) catalyzing a results-based sense of common purpose.

Toward Wider Applicability?
Opportunities to extend local governance models to a broader range of settings than originally envisioned clearly exist. This did not always seem to be the case. Because most empirical evidence informing and testing common-pool resource theory was drawn initially from cases involving relatively small numbers of mostly homogeneous appropriators, even those who saw the promise of local-level, self-governance models questioned their wider applicability. Many inferred that such an approach likely was viable only in relatively small, simple, and isolated settings.[62]

A second generation of empirical work belies such a claim, however. Research has failed to find a significant relationship between the likelihood of collective action and the numbers and heterogeneity of appropriators. Tang and Lam, for instance, find that size of group does not affect the likelihood of collective action in irrigation systems.[63] Similarly,

Varughese and Ostrom, in a study of eighteen forest user groups in Nepal, did not find a significant relationship between numbers of appropriators and the emergence of collective action.[64] Agrawal, in a study of five community forests in India, however, found that size may matter, but in a somewhat different way.[65] Size of user group did not affect appropriators' ability to engage in collective action, but it did affect the performance of the institutional arrangements devised by the appropriators. Very small forest communities struggled to collect the resources needed to engage in effective monitoring and sanctioning of locally designed rules. Moderate-size communities were able to tap into a larger resource base and engage in more effective monitoring and sanctioning of forest access and use.

Many researchers also incorrectly assumed that differences among appropriators (for example, in terms of skill at harvesting, technologies used, income, social status) would interact with area size and location to inhibit their ability to engage in collective action. In other words, individuals would find it much more difficult to agree on a set of institutional arrangements because their interests would differ significantly from one another.[66] Yet empirical findings thus far concerning area size, location, and heterogeneity suggest that appropriators of common-pool resources are capable of engaging in collective action under a wide and varied set of circumstances.

Varughese and Ostrom, for example, examined the effects of locational differences, wealth disparities, and sociocultural differences on the likelihood and success of collective action.[67] They found that differences in distance from forests, wealth, and sociocultural composition did not affect significantly levels of collective action.[68] Rather, the success of collective action was related significantly to the specifics of the self-governing regime created. The forests used by persons who had both devised *and* enforced rules of access and use were in much better condition than those used by persons who had devised rules but did not enforce them. They also were in better condition than those used by persons operating without rules. Lam, too, found that differences in income did not affect significantly the performance of irrigation organizations.[69]

Thus even in relatively large and complex social settings, appropriators may devise and adopt governing arrangements. Collective action is not restricted just to relatively small, simple, and isolated settings.[70] Recognition of this situation, in turn, brings a legitimate opportunity for policymakers to choose to extend self-governing models to a broader range of environmental and natural resources (ENR) management settings than previously appreciated.

Understanding Contextuality

A much more difficult challenge for incorporating theoretical insights into ENR governance is the contingent and configurel nature of the theory, which places a premium on local knowledge and context if policymakers are to choose appropriate and workable policies. As this chapter has demonstrated, a robust list of contingency factors exist, depend on how they interact with others, and depend for their success on policymakers accurately matching them (singly or in combination) to appropriate implementation contexts. An example of the contingent nature of the theory is provided by recent work on conjunctive water management.

Blomquist, Heikkila, and I examined and compared the conjunctive water management activities of local jurisdictions among three states—Arizona, California, and Colorado.[71] Conjunctive water management refers to the coordinated use of surface water and groundwater as a means of developing additional water supplies and limiting the waste of existing supplies. The coordination of the two water sources typically occurs through recharge projects. Surplus surface water is stored, or recharged, in an underground basin for use at a later time.

Water appropriators who contemplate investing in recharge projects must have assurances that the water they store underground will be available to them at a later time. In other words, they must be able to exclude from access to the stored water those who did not contribute to their project. Thus, attribute four of Ostrom's common-pool resource theory—spatial extent—appears to be critical in building a sense of common purpose. The spatial extent of a basin must be such that water appropriators can gain control over the basin and exercise exclusion if they are to cooperate in conjunctive water management.

But consider the contingent and configurel nature of these conjunctive water management initiatives. In California, conjunctive water management activities occur *only* in basins in which appropriators have organized themselves and have developed a set of institutional arrangements whereby they control access to and use of the basins.[72] Yet, even though appropriators in Arizona and Colorado do not control access to and use of groundwater basins, they too actively and successfully engage in conjunctive water management. Why? The governments of Arizona and Colorado, unlike the government of California, have devised and allocated private-property rights in surface water, in groundwater, and in stored, or recharged, groundwater. Appropriators in Arizona and Colorado, because of their state-granted private-property rights in water, are assured that if they store water underground, they will be able to retrieve it at a later date because of their property rights in that water. They do not first have to gain control over a groundwater basin. Appropriators in California, on the other hand, must first gain control over their basin and define property rights in it (see the earlier discussion of the West Basin case) before they are sufficiently secure to invest in conjunctive water management projects.

Defining Community

Of course, the local knowledge and contextual information critical for designing workable rules and policies for common-pool resources is centered among appropriators. Thus, workable rules and policies require that appropriators choose to participate actively in governance. By the same token, however, empowering appropriators is fraught with its own strategic challenges, choices, and opportunities—many of them encapsulated within the concept of *community*. Providing aid and assistance to local communities to bolster their conservation activities is hardly a straightforward process. As noted, communities are not necessarily homogeneous political, social, and economic groupings that can be treated as single units. External interventions, if not carefully crafted to this reality, may result in tragic unintended consequences.

For instance, Lam, in his study of Nepal irrigation systems, noted instances in which the government of Nepal replaced crude mud-and-stick diversion works with permanent concrete diversion structures as a means of lessening irrigators' labor demands. The cooperative, self-governing institutional arrangements irrigators had devised promptly fell apart. Why? One of the major schisms within irrigation communities is between irrigators at the head end of the canal who have first access to water and irrigators at the end of the canal who are at the mercy of those ahead of them for water.

One means policymakers have of addressing head-ender/tail-ender conflicts is choosing to develop multiple ties between the two groups. In the Nepalese irrigation systems prior to the change in diversion structures, head-enders had cooperated with tail-enders in developing fair water allocation methods. Similarly, tail-enders had cooperated with head-enders in rebuilding and maintaining the crude stick-and-mud diversion works. Once permanent diversion works were installed, however, head-enders, who no longer needed the labor of the tail-enders, stopped cooperating in allocating water.

Intracommunity divisions and inequities may also be exacerbated if policymakers decide to provide financial, technical, or legal aid to communities without considering who should receive the resources. Already powerful members of communities may gain control over those resources and use them in ways unintended by the donors.[73] Likewise, even understandable attempts to re-create "community" where it is believed once to have existed can have perverse effects. Re-creating community aims to help persons who rely on severely degraded resources to reclaim their livelihoods from those resources. The problem with such an approach is that no such community may have ever existed. The people subject to such interventions consequently may not be capable of taking advantage of the resources provided, or the resources may be inadequate or inappropriate for the task.

The government of the Philippines, for instance, adopted legislation granting Certificates of Ancestral Domain to communities. These certificates allowed communities greater autonomy in managing their resources. To qualify, communities had to demonstrate that they had lived continuously in communally bounded and defined territories, that they were governed by traditional leaders, and that they managed their natural resources in a sustainable manner.[74] Although no such communities existed on Palawan Island, one certificate was granted to two loosely grouped ethnic communities there. Little changed for these two communities after they received a certificate, however. They did not gain greater control over the resources they depend on for their livelihoods. As one researcher concludes, the legislation creating the certificates only assumed community capacity and therefore failed to provide resources to create it.[75] "'Capacity' means nothing if there is no means or discretion with which to exercise it."[76]

Thus, as Agrawal and Gibson conclude, one key to implementing the insights of common-pool resource theory is for policymakers to avoid making heroic or romanticized assumptions about communities and their capacities. Most important, they should not assume that communities are small spatial units whose members are economically, politically, and socially homogeneous, and who share norms and beliefs that encourage resource conservation.[77] Developing and implementing policy based on those assumptions is sure to lead to failure and disillusionment. Agrawal and Gibson argue that implementation should be based instead on a careful understanding of the multiple actors and their diverse interests in using common-pool resources, the processes by which they interact with one another, and the institutional arrangements that structure their interaction.[78]

Catalyzing Common Purpose?

The challenges of contingencies aside, scholars and policymakers *have* discovered the potential of local-level actors for governing and conserving natural resources. What remains, however, is determining how to unleash this potential appropriately for building a results-based sense of common purpose. This task, in turn, requires a fundamental choice involving how public managers and elected officials conceptualize the means and ends of environmental governance. For self-regulatory governance structures to succeed, officials will have to work with and encourage appropriators to govern themselves and solve their own common-pool resource dilemmas.

Numerous scholars and analysts have noted, however, that public managers, trained as experts, come to view themselves as active problem solvers and to view citizens, at best, as incapable of helping themselves and, at worst, as active and purposeful problem creators.[79] Furthermore, numerous legislative mandates direct and constrain managers. They also are expected dutifully to achieve multiple and often conflicting mandates in an administratively competent manner. In so doing, they often lose sight of the goals that they and their programs were intended to achieve.[80]

As Mark Moore summarizes the dilemma, public managers adopt the mindsets of bureaucrats and administrators and not of facilitators and leaders.[81]

If the insights of common-pool resource theory are to be realized, ENR managers must reconceptualize their sense of role and purpose, both in their own and in legislators' minds. As Robert Reich proposes more generally, ENR managers must learn to facilitate public education and deliberation about public problems in a process of "civic discovery."[82] Deliberation, in these instances, focuses on mutually identifying and defining problems with citizens, on considering alternative and coproduced solutions to these problems, and on discussing with citizens how solutions can be realized. Meanwhile, legislators must follow Moore's suggestion that they enable public managers to become "explorers who, with others, seek to discover, define, and produce public value."[83]

Undertaking this reorientation is critical for common-pool resource management to succeed. No longer must public managers see resource appropriators as individuals who are trapped hopelessly in tragedies of the commons, but rather as individuals who are and must be active problem solvers. As this chapter has discussed, ENR managers must see appropriator participation as vital for two reasons. First, they must appreciate that appropriators possess critical time and place knowledge— about resources, about their own social norms, about the rules and practices that they follow. This knowledge, in turn, must be taken into account in formulating ENR policies in order to make them workable. Second, managers and legislators must understand that monitoring and enforcing policies will be less problematic if appropriators embrace those policies. Rule—following is likely to be high in that case, and appropriators are likely to engage in self-monitoring and enforcement.

To these ends, common-pool resource theory requires both flexibility and varied approaches to inclusivity. It points to numerous activities in which governments can engage, such as lowering the information and enforcement costs confronting appropriators and providing appropriators with fair conflict resolution mechanisms. In turn, while the activities that governments can engage in are many and varied, policymakers must invest in appropriators' governing capacities rather than in command-and-control policy prescriptions. Indeed, the theory points to the centrality of allowing appropriators to devise their own solutions or at least to participate actively in problem solving, with managers facilitating rather than controlling the process.

The difficulty of realizing this fundamental perestroika in thinking cannot be overestimated. Reorienting public managers, for example, will require more than changing graduate schools' curricula; it also will require changing the context in which public managers act. The current context of multiple and highly constraining mandates and procedures described by Denise Scheberle and others in their chapters in this volume focuses managers' attention on control. These procedures will have to be redesigned to focus managers' attention on facilitation and problem solving in partnership with citizens. The conditions under which legislatures will be willing to loosen their control over public managers by relaxing strict mandates is, no doubt, dependent on circumstances. But try they must if the insights of common-pool resource theory are to be realized.

Granted, common-pool resource theory does not predict that appropriators always will be successful. Instead, success or failure is conditioned on the specific circumstances in which appropriators and policymakers find themselves. Moreover, as noted, significant organizational, political, and analytical obstacles exist to complicate success. Nevertheless, developing more complete explanations of cooperation and resource users' ability to coordinate and govern their behavior in pursuit of building a results-based sense of common purpose is a significant contribution to environmental governance in the twenty-first century. Given the relative infancy of the theory and its testing, this is no small accomplishment.

Whether policymakers choose to take advantage of these insights in order to help build common purpose when common-pool resources are at risk remains an unanswered yet important question as the twenty-first century unfolds. What is *not* in question, however, is the need for humanity to find ways to address collaboratively the risks to common-pool resources that are so vital to livelihoods worldwide. Nor is it debatable that developing the common understanding, trust, and reciprocity essential for collaboration to occur is often the product of regular interpersonal interactions and participation in decision-making processes. It is to the topic of reconnecting citizens and stakeholders with environmental governance that this volume turns next.

Notes

1. J. Tierney, "A Tale of Two Fisheries," *New York Times Magazine,* August 27, 2000, pp. 38–43.

2. Ibid., p. 40.

3. Ibid., p. 38.

4. Garrett Hardin, "The Tragedy of the Commons," *Science* 162 (1968): 1243–1248.

5. Tierney, "A Tale of Two Fisheries," p. 41.

6. Ibid.

7. Ibid.

8. Ibid.

9. For an excellent review of the emerging evidence from nonenvironmental areas concerning cooperation and the conditions under which prisoners' dilemma problems are addressed effectively, see Mark Van Vugt, Mark Snyder, Tom R. Tyler, and Anders Biel, eds., *Cooperation in Modern Society: Promoting the Welfare of Communities, Organizations, and States* (London: Routledge, 2000).

10. H. Scott Gordon, "The Economic Theory of a Common Property Resource: The Fishery," *Journal of Political Economy* 62 (1954): 124–142; Anthony Scott, "The Fishery: The Objectives of Sole Ownership," *Journal of Political Economy* 63 (1955): 116–124.

11. "By ignoring the negative impact of an individual's appropriation on others' returns, the appropriator creates a negative externality. The presence of the externality leads to overinvestment of resources into the appropriation process" (E. Ostrom, R. Gardner, and J. Walker, eds., *Rules, Games, and Common-Pool Resources* [Ann Arbor: University of Michigan Press, 1994], p. 11).

12. According to Davis and Holt, Tucker was the first to articulate the prisoners' dilemma (D. Davis and C. Holt, *Experimental Economics* [Princeton, N.J.: Princeton University Press, 1993]; See A. W. Tucker, "A Two Person Dilemma," working paper, Stanford University, 1950).

13. Mancur Olson, *The Logic of Collective Action: Public Goods and the Theory of Groups* (Cambridge, Mass.: Harvard University Press, 1965). See Russell Hardin, *Collective Action* (Baltimore, Md.: Johns Hopkins University Press, 1982), for a careful explication and examination of the conditions under which cooperation can emerge under Olson's theory.

14. Olson, *The Logic of Collective Action,* p. 2, italics in the original.

15. As late as the 1980s, the Canadian minister of fisheries publicly was comparing Atlantic fisheries to the tragedy of the commons (D. R. Matthews, *Controlling Common Property: Regulating Canada's East Coast Fishery* [Toronto: University of Toronto Press, 1993]).

16. Marc Landy, Marc Roberts, and Stephen Thomas, *The Environmental Protection Agency* (New York: Oxford University Press, 1994).

17. Consolidated Statutes and Regulations, Department of Fisheries and Oceans Act, Canada, 1978, http://laws.justice.gc.ca/en/F-15/44268.html.

18. National Research Council, *Proceedings of the Conference on Common Property Resource Management* (Washington, D.C.: National Academy Press, 1986); B. McCay and J. Acheson, *The Question of the Commons: The Culture and Ecology of Communal Resources* (Tucson: University of Arizona Press, 1987); F. Berkes, ed., *Common Property Resources: Ecology and Community-Based Sustainable Development* (London: Belhaven, 1989); F. Martin, *Common Pool Resources and Collective Action: A Bibliography,* vol. 1 (Bloomington: Indiana University, Workshop in Political Theory and Policy Analysis, 1989).

19. Such models are not incorrect; they simply have been used incorrectly—applied to many situations and circumstances whose essential features they fail to capture (Elinor Ostrom, *Governing the Commons: The Evolution of Institutions for Collective Action* [Cambridge: Cambridge University Press, 1990]).

20. The International Association for the Study of Common Property, www.indiana.edu/~iascp/.

21. The *Common Property Resource Digest,* published three to four times per year, www.indiana.edu/~iascp/aboutcpr/html.

22. For instance, the Center for the Study of Institutions, Population, and Environmental Change, www.indiana.edu/~cipec/.

23. Ostrom, *Governing the Commons;* Elinor Ostrom, "Institutional Rational Choice: An Assessment of the Institutional Analysis and Development Framework," in Paul Sabatier, ed., *Theories of the Policy Process,* 35–71 (Boulder, Colo.: Westview, 1999); Elinor Ostrom, "The Danger of Self-Evident Truths," *PS: Political Science and Politics* 33(1) (2000): 33–44.

24. Ostrom, *Governing the Commons.*

25. Ibid., p. 44.

26. Ibid., p. 45.

27. Ostrom, Gardner, and Walker, *Rules, Games, and Common-Pool Resources;* F. Berkes, *Sacred Ecology: Traditional Ecological Knowledge and Resource Management* (Philadelphia, Pa.: Taylor and Francis, 1999); B. McCay, "Emergence of Institutions for the Commons: Contexts, Situations, and Events," in Elinor Ostrom, Thomas Dietz, Nives Dolsak, Paul C. Stern, Susan Stonich, and Elke U. Weber, eds., *The Drama of the Commons,* 361–402 (Washington, DC: National Academy Press, 2002).

28. Ostrom, "The Danger of Self-Evident Truths," p. 40.

29. Ibid., p. 40.

30. Ibid.

31. Ostrom, *Governing the Commons,* p. 90.

32. Edella Schlager, "Model Specification and Policy Analysis: The Governance of Coastal Fisheries," Ph.D. diss., Indiana University, 1990; Edella Schlager, "Fishers' Institutional Responses to Common-Pool Resource Dilemmas," in E. Ostrom, R. Gardner, and J. Walker, eds., *Rules, Games, and Common-Pool Resources,* 247–266 (Ann Arbor: University of Michigan Press, 1994).

33. The fishery analysis focuses only on conflict over space and not on overharvesting. Accurately measuring overharvesting is difficult, and no such measures were reported in any of the case studies included in the analysis. See Schlager, "Fishers' Institutional Responses," p. 260, for a more extensive discussion.

34. Ibid.

35. F. T. Christy, *Territorial Use Rights in Marine Fisheries: Definitions and Conditions,* FAO Fisheries Technical Paper no. 227 (Rome: Food and Agricultural Organization of the United Nations, 1982).

36. K. O. Martin, "'The Law in St. John's Says . . .': Space Division and Resource Allocation in the Newfoundland Fishing Community of Fermeuse," master's thesis, Memorial University of Newfoundland, 1973.

37. F. Berkes, "Local Level Management and the Commons Problem: A Comparative Study of Turkish Coastal Fisheries," *Marine Policy* 10 (July 1986): 215–229.

38. B. McCay, "Community Based and Cooperative Fisheries: Solutions to Fishermen's Problems," in J. Burger, E. Ostrom, R. Norgaard, D. Policansky, and B. Goldstein, eds., *Protecting the Commons* (Washington, D.C.: Island, 2001), p. 183.

39. Schlager, "Model Specification and Policy Analysis"; Edella Schlager and Elinor Ostrom, "Property Rights Regimes and Coastal Fisheries: An Empirical Analysis," in T. L. Anderson and R. T. Simmons, eds., *The Political Economy of Customs and Culture: Informal Solutions to the Commons Problem,* 13–42 (Lanham, Md.: Rowman and Littlefield, 1993).

40. Y. S. Tang, "Institutions and Collective Action in Irrigation Systems," Ph.D. diss., Indiana University, 1989; Y. S. Tang, *Institutions and Collective Action: Self-Governance in Irrigation* (San Francisco: ICS, 1992); Y. S. Tang, "Institutions and Performance in Irrigation Systems," in Ostrom, Gardner, and Walker, eds., *Rules, Games, and Common-Pool Resources,* 225–246; W. F. Lam, *Governing Irrigation Systems in Nepal: Institutions, Infrastructure and Collective Action* (San Francisco: ICS, 1998).

41. Tang, "Institutions and Collective Action"; Tang, "Institutions and Performance in Irrigation Systems."

42. Tang, "Institutions and Collective Action"; Tang, *Institutions and Collective Action;* Tang, "Institutions and Performance in Irrigation Systems."

43. The level of maintenance of an irrigation system is tied directly to how well farmers' contributions to construction and maintenance are elicited and coordinated. It measures the extent to which provision dilemmas have been mitigated.

The adequacy of water supply depends on the rules used to allocate water and the level of maintenance. Both water allocation and system maintenance depend on how well-crafted the rules governing each are and the extent to which irrigators follow those rules.

44. Tang, "Institutions and Performance in Irrigation Systems."

45. The type of water allocation rule found among poorly performing systems was a fixed-time-slot rule. The irrigator was allowed to take water for a fixed period of time at set intervals. Although fixed-time-slot rules are relatively easy to define and enforce (presumably irrigators will protect their time slots or risk losing their water), they are fraught with uncertainty. A fixed time slot only guarantees a farmer a certain amount of time, not a certain amount of water. If the fixed time slots are not carefully coordinated with water availability, or if water availability is unpredictable, a fixed time slot will have little value.

46. Tang, *Institutions and Collective Action*. W. F. Lam analyzes extensive data on 150 Nepalese irrigation systems in *Governing Irrigation Systems in Nepal;* see also W. F. Lam, M. Lee, and E. Ostrom, "An Institutional Analysis Approach: Findings from the NIIS on Irrigation Performance," in J. Sowerwine, G. Shivakoti, U. Pradhan, A. Shukla, and E. Ostrom, eds., *From Farmers' Fields to Data Fields and Back: A Synthesis of Participatory Information Systems for Irrigation and Other Resources,* pp. 69–93 (Colombo, Sri Lanka: International Irrigation Management Institute; and Rampur, Nepal: Institute of Agriculture and Animal Science, 1994). Like Tang (*Institutions and Collective Action;* "Institutions and Performance in Irrigation Systems"), Lam found that farmer-managed irrigation systems perform significantly better than do government-managed irrigation systems. Irrigators in farmer-managed systems exhibit significantly higher levels of entrepreneurial activities in attempting to coordinate irrigation activities, information and understanding of the irrigation system, and mutual trust (*Governing Irrigation Systems in Nepal,* pp. 26–133). Irrigators in farmer-managed systems also use more varied and complex sets of rules for governing their activities. In addition, irrigators in farmer-managed systems are significantly more likely to be monitored and sanctioned for rule violations than are irrigators in government-managed systems. Rule-following behavior is significantly higher in farmer-managed systems (Lam, *Governing Irrigation Systems in Nepal,* p. 131).

47. Among the farmer-owned systems examined by Tang ("Institutions and Performance in Irrigation Systems," p. 241), 41 percent did not use any guards.

48. Ibid., p. 241.

49. W. Blomquist, *Dividing the Waters: Governing Groundwater in Southern California* (San Francisco: ICS, 1992).

50. Ibid., p. 51.

51. Ibid., p. 32.

52. Ibid., p. 33.

53. Ibid.

54. Ibid., p. 102.

55. Ibid., pp. 104, 106, 76.

56. Ibid., pp. 106, 109.

57. Ibid., p. 116.

58. Ibid.; Tang, *Institutions and Collective Action.*

59. Schlager, "Model Specification and Policy Analysis."

60. Tang, "Institutions and Performance in Irrigation Systems."

61. Blomquist, *Dividing the Waters.*

62. R. Q. Grafton, D. Squires, and J. E. Kirkley, "Private Property Rights and Crises in World Fisheries: Turning the Tide?" *Contemporary Economic Policy* 14 (1996): 90–99.

63. Tang, *Institutions and Collective Action;* Lam, *Governing Irrigation Systems in Nepal.*

64. G. Varughese and E. Ostrom, *The Contested Role of Heterogeneity,* working paper no. 32 (Bloomington: Workshop in Political Theory and Policy Analysis, Indiana University, 1998).

65. A. Agrawal, "Group Size and Successful Collective Action: A Case Study of Forest Management Institutions in the Indian Himalayas," in G. Clark, M. McKean, and E. Ostrom, eds., *Forest Resources and Institutions,* 49–74, Forests, Trees, and People: Programme Working Paper no. 3 (Rome: FAO, 1998).

66. Steven Hackett, Edella Schlager, and James Walker, "The Role of Communication in Resolving Commons Dilemmas: Experimental Evidence with Heterogeneous Appropriators," *Journal of Environmental Economics and Management* 27 (1994): 99–126; M. Taylor and S. Singleton, "The Communal Resource: Transaction Costs and the Solution of Collective Action Problems," *Politics and Society* 21(2) (1993): 195–214; Varughese and Ostrom, "The Contested Role of Heterogeneity."

67. Varughese and Ostrom, "The Contested Role of Heterogeneity," p. 29.

68. Ibid.

69. Lam, *Governing Irrigation Systems in Nepal.*

70. Grafton, Squires, and Kirkley, "Private Property Rights and Crises in World Fisheries."

71. B. Blomquist, T. Heikkila, and E. Schlager, "Institutions and Conjunctive Water Management among Three Western States," *Natural Resources Journal* 41(3) (2001): 653–683.

72. T. Heikkila, "Managing Common Pool Resources in a Public Service Industry: The Case of Conjunctive Water Management," Ph.D. diss., School of Public Administration and Policy, University of Arizona, 2001; Blomquist, Heikkila, and Schlager, "Institutions and Conjunctive Water Management."

73. J. Ensminger, "Culture and Property Rights," in S. Hanna, C. Folke, and K. Maler, eds., *Rights to Nature,* 179–204 (Washington, D.C.: Island, 1997);

R. Meinzen-Dick and M. Zwarteveen, "Gender Dimensions of Community Resource Management: The Case of Water Users' Associations in South Asia," in A. Agrawal and C. Gibson, eds., *Communities and the Environment: Ethnicity, Gender, and the State in Community-Based Conservation*, 63–88 (New Brunswick, N.J.: Rutgers University Press, 2001).

74. M. H. McDermott, "Invoking Community: Indigenous People and Ancestral Domain in Palawan, the Philippines," in Agrawal and Gibson, eds., *Communities and the Environment*, 32–62, specifically pp. 46–50.

75. Ibid., p. 58.

76. Ibid.

77. A. Agrawal and C. Gibson, "The Role of Community in Natural Resource Conservation," in Agrawal and Gibson, *Communities and the Environment*, 1–31.

78. Ibid., pp. 12–13.

79. James Q. Wilson, *Bureaucracy* (New York: Free Press, 1989); R. Reich, *Public Management in a Democratic Society* (Englewood Cliffs, N.J.: Prentice-Hall, 1990); M. Moore, *Creating Public Value* (Cambridge, Mass.: Harvard University Press, 1995); F. Fischer, *Citizens, Experts, and the Environment* (Durham, N.C.: Duke University Press, 2000).

80. Wilson, *Bureaucracy;* Moore, *Creating Public Value.*

81. Moore, *Creating Public Value,* p. 17.

82. Reich, *Public Management in a Democratic Society.*

83. Moore, *Creating Public Value,* p. 20.

II

Reconnecting with Stakeholders

Robert F. Durant

During most of the twentieth century, the positive-state philosophy informed the growth of Western governments and the expansion of their responsibilities worldwide, particularly in the United States. Under this philosophy, governments were viewed as the ultimate promoter, provider, and guarantor of essential goods, services, and opportunities to their citizens. To these ends, the first seven decades of the century witnessed the rise of economic regulation and then a burst of what William Lilly and James Miller initially called the "new social regulation." The latter dealt with public health and safety, consumer protection, occupational safety, affirmative action, and environmental protection.[1]

Social regulation—as reflected in the environmental and natural-resources (ENR) focus of this book—was decidedly different from economic regulation in focus, process, and (consequently) the scope and intensity of the conflict it engendered. Economic regulation tended to focus on single industries, on both regulating *and* promoting various industries, and on changing or modifying the behavior of the private sector. In contrast, social regulation in the ENR protection arena was solely about regulating industries rather than promoting their interests, cutting across industries to focus on regulating their production processes, and counting both private- and public-sector actors among its regulatory targets.

As Denise Scheberle describes in chapter 10, a spate of ENR legislation followed during the remainder of the twentieth century that focused sequentially on one problem at a time (for example, the Clean Air Act, the Federal Water Pollution Control Act, and the Resource Conservation and Recovery Act). This single-media focus then was institutionalized within the organizational structures of the agencies charged with implementing these laws, which, in turn, created a perverse incentive structure within each agency that members of Congress and various interest groups were loath to change because of the access, influence, and power the structure afforded them. Within each agency, units and subunits were fragmented by purpose (for example, separate air, water, and land divisions), were rewarded budgetarily for focusing exclusively on that purpose, and then developed rules and regulations solely for programs within their responsibility. They also developed decision-making procedures that were focused similarly; that centralized decision-making authority in Washington; and that grew increasingly more expertise based (legal and technical), administratively fragmented and complex, legally adversarial, and difficult for ordinary citizens to understand and participate in as time passed.

All this made cross-program, cross-agency, interorganizational, and intergovernmental cooperation at the grassroots level in the United States extremely difficult, thus further marginalizing citizens and communities in the environmental governance process. To be sure, environmental statutes long had incorporated community participation requirements within them. But unenthusiastic program managers routinely finessed these requirements. Some mandates were so vague that they left it to managers to decide what degree of participation was needed, when and how it would occur, and what impact it would have on final decisions. Consequently, the only redress that citizens and communities had when marginalized or excluded either intentionally or inadvertently from ENR agency deliberations was court suits. But these suits only spawned the further fragmentation and judicialization of rule making and adjudicatory processes by lawmakers and defensive agencies, consequently marginalizing average citizens from environmental governance even more.

Grassroots organizations roundly criticized this "procedural republic" for marginalizing citizens from the deliberative processes of government, for engendering adversarial legalism among participants, and for strewing often insuperable obstacles in the path of multimedia, community-based, and collaborative governance. Thus, as the twenty-first century dawned, public agencies at all levels of environmental governance were urged persistently on both instrumental and normative grounds to tap into citizen and community insights early and repeatedly in agency deliberative processes, to coproduce with them both the definition of and responses to ENR problems, and to involve stakeholders in meaningful ways in the oversight of the governance decisions that are produced. The epoxy for building a sense of common purpose among these disparate actors was a sense for results-based environmental governance.

In chapter 5, James Meadowcroft argues that a vigorous extension of the concept of deliberative democracy within environmental governance might enhance significantly society's capacity to manage environment-related problems in this fashion in the coming decades. Doing so, however, will require a major shift in emphasis that is rife with political, organizational, and legal conflict. Although general calls for increased public "participation" for individuals and groups in subsystem decision making remain important, he contends, they are inadequate for dealing with the kinds of problems that environmental governance is likely to face in the first half of the twenty-first century. Policymakers will need to take into account a variety of dynamic, uncertain, and protean natural-resource, market, and social conditions. Thus, in order to succeed, solutions to these types of problems will require broad support, equity in impact, and a capability to advance societal learning as policymakers find their way toward knowing what policies they ought to prefer. The key strategic element in achieving these requirements, argues Meadowcroft, will be the extension of group-based collaborative and deliberative interactions that draw together stakeholders from government, business, and civil society. His review of various participatory approaches used in the environmental field reveals that no single approach to establishing deliberative democracy is likely to build a results-based sense of common purpose satisfactorily. Rather, Meadowcroft argues that if applied carefully and in appropriate circumstances, a combination of these mechanisms and others offers significant opportunities to raise the deliberative content and results of environmental governance in the United States and abroad.

Perhaps nowhere has Meadowcroft's emphasis on cross-sector collaborative governance been operationalized more fully as a tool for reconnecting with citizens, building a results-based sense of common purpose, and improving deliberative processes in the United States than in the concept of *civic environmentalism*. Known variously as "community-based environmental protection," "bottom-up" or "place-based" approaches, "collaborative natural-resources management," or "ecosystem management," civic environmentalism involves efforts to tailor responses to local conditions, overcome bureaucratic fragmentation, and bring democracy directly into environmental decisions. Energized by a strong civic impulse to address ENR problems, civic environmentalism has produced a rising tide of watershed councils, river keepers, land trusts, voluntary monitoring programs, and plans for creating sustainable communities across the United States.

In chapter 6, DeWitt John argues that despite its accomplishments, civic environmentalism must be a *supplement* not a replacement to conventional regulation and does not work everywhere. After placing civic environmentalism within the broader context of four theoretical traditions of governance, he illustrates why all four traditions in combination—and not any one alone—have the requisite strengths for affording effective results-based environmental governance. In the process, John offers a set of propositions for policymakers and researchers to consider and test about the conditions under which civic environmentalism is more or less likely to produce desirable results. The future of civic environmentalism also depends, he avers, on whose version of civic environmentalism is used to define the concept (the right, the left, or the radical center), on which version (if any) prevails politically, and on how well proponents of each version can confront and resolve internal contradictions in its vision of civic environmentalism.

Evan Ringquist and Charles Wise then survey what can happen when ENR agencies fail to "connect" with key community stakeholders in the decisions they make and why they must make an effort to do so in the future. In chapter 7, on the concept of environmental justice, Ringquist explores and finds empirical support for arguments that the health, safety, and environmental burdens of public policy decisions in the United States fall disproportionately on low-income communities and persons of color. He chronicles how a vocal, sustained, and aggressive effort over the past two decades has sought to make public agencies minimize the negative results that their decisions can have on historically disadvantaged communities. He concludes, however, that the efforts to build a results-based sense of common purpose that incorporates the concept of environmental justice have beached routinely on the shoals of a formidable mix of scientific, political, organizational, and financial obstacles. Concluding that calls for reform are unlikely to go away, Ringquist argues that policymakers have essentially three ways to advance the cause of environmental justice as a unifying principle in environmental governance: creating new legislation, adapting civil rights laws, and adapting existing environmental statutes. The future prospects for success, however, are not encouraging. Both the legislative and civil rights avenues are effectively closed for the foreseeable future because of current political realities and recent Supreme Court decisions, respectively. And although adapting existing environmental statutes is a more promising approach, it has formidable technical, legal, and organizational resistance to overcome.

Charles Wise then explores in chapter 8 how evolving case law and legislation dealing with regulatory "takings" claims in property rights cases in the United States not only diminish a sense of common purpose in the country, but also mean that regulators *must* adapt their behavior in the face of serious legal and political threats to ENR regulation as a whole. The formidable constraints that these developments in case law have imposed on regulators also afford, to some, yet another reason for moving away from command-and-control and procedure-based regulation. Although takings claims of the form seen in the United States are not yet issues in other nations, property rights generally are becoming especially salient in the newly emerging (formerly Soviet) states in Europe and in other parts of the world. As such, regulatory takings issues abroad may grow in importance as the twenty-first century progresses. In these types of cases, plaintiffs argue that regulatory actions have reduced unconstitutionally the economic value of properties that they own, work on, or invest in and that the state has not compensated them adequately for their losses.

Premised on these realities and on the likelihood that they will continue in the future regardless of changes on the U.S. Supreme Court, Wise argues that regulators must become more proactive rather than reactive. They must "reconnect" with citizens by anticipating how property owners will react to their rulings, how judges will respond to their "takings" arguments, and how they themselves both might head off and compensate for negative court rulings. Absent these actions, Wise contends that regulators will continue to face costly battles in the courts, add fuel to extreme antienvironmental fires, and thus jeopardize rather than build a results-based sense of common purpose in environmental governance in the United States. In calling for these actions, however, he does not downplay the substantial legal, organizational, and political obstacles to making them a reality. Although the federal courts have clarified some of the constitutional issues that regulators need to take into consideration in their decisions, determining precisely what "going too far" means in all the various takings situations that regulators face has proven difficult and is likely to remain so in the future.

Whereas both Ringquist and Wise take stock of and assess the consequences and future of two environmental movements spawned *because of* "disconnects" between stakeholders and environmental governance, proponents of environmental conflict resolution (ECR) seek to "reconnect" the two *before* conflict spills into the courts or provokes political backlashes. In the final chapter in this section, Rosemary O'Leary, Tina Nabatchi, and Lisa Bingham warn that ECR can be oversold as a means for building a results-based sense of common purpose in environmental governance. After reviewing the range of approaches involved in ECR, they cull lessons from the still sparse empirically grounded literature on the topic. Taking research on conflict resolution more generally as a model, they conclude that the future of ECR as a tool for building common purpose depends on scholars and practitioners confronting and empirically assessing its true nature, processes, and purposes. Most notably, scholars and practitioners must evaluate more rigorously ECR interventions as targeted at aggregate rather than dyadic relationships, as embedded in even larger complex systems, as time-extended phenomena, and as linked to substantive environmental outcomes. Conceding that the data collection and methodological challenges to doing all this are profound, these authors argue that they are not insurmountable. Moreover, absent these efforts, ECR will remain hostage in the future to the same political, organizational, and professional barriers to its application that have restricted it in the past.

Note

1. William Lilly and James C. Miller, "The New Social Regulation," *The Public Interest* 47 (spring 1977): 28–36.

5

Deliberative Democracy

James Meadowcroft

Over the past decade and a half, the notion of deliberative democracy has become increasingly visible in discussions of democratic governance. This chapter argues that a vigorous extension of deliberative democratic practice within the environmental and natural resources (ENR) policy domain can enhance significantly society's capacity to manage environment-related problems in the coming decades. It advocates a shift in emphasis from general calls for increased public "participation" in environmental policymaking to more focused efforts to extend deliberative democratic engagement. It suggests that although the involvement of both individual citizens and organized groups in the policy subsystem is important, the extension of group-based deliberative interactions—which draw together actors from government, business, and civil society to address specific problems—has the greatest potential. This is especially true given the new and more challenging forms in which environmental problems will present themselves in the first half of the new century.

After a brief examination of the general character of deliberative democracy, the chapter moves on to consider its relevance for the building of a results-based sense of common purpose in environmental governance, particularly at the "meso-level" of political interaction involving organizations drawn from the state, the economy, and civil society. A discussion of participatory and interactive mechanisms already employed in the environmental policy realm serves to clarify the requirements of deliberative democracy and to establish the significance of group-based processes. Emphasized is how the types of problems facing environmental governance in the future will force policymakers to take into account a variety of dynamic, uncertain, and protean natural resource, market, and social conditions. This recognition, in turn, is a process best realized through group-based deliberative forums. The argument then moves on to consider reservations about group-based deliberative forums and the strategic challenges, choices, and opportunities facing those trying to advance the concept of deliberative democracy in the twenty-first century. This final discussion looks at how this major shift in emphasis toward building a results-based sense of common purpose will be rife with political, organizational, and legal conflict.

The Ideal of Deliberative Democracy

Deliberative democracy typically is defined in contradistinction to "aggregative" visions of the democratic process, which emphasize voting as a mechanism for counting preferences and selecting preferred outcomes. This contrast can be understood in two ways. First, deliberative democrats argue that it is not the act of casting a ballot that represents the core of democratic decision making, but the reasoned argument and public reflection that should proceed voting. Thus, deliberation eclipses voting as the paradigmatic democratic activity. Second, deliberative democrats insist that the public interest cannot emerge merely by summing preexisting preferences, but can come to the fore only through a deliberative process, which generates new insights and transforms initial perspectives. In other words, deliberative interaction allows the democratic constituency to construct a collective path forward. As two recent commentators explain, "broadly defined, deliberative democracy refers to the idea that legitimate lawmaking issues from the public deliberation of citizens."[1]

Central to this understanding of democratic deliberation are the ideas of reasoned debate, public justification, and political equality.[2] Collective choices are to be made through *reasoned discussion* rather than by blind acceptance of the views of established authorities, by deals concluded among vested interests, or by recourse to intimidation. As participants deliberate, they advance arguments and listen to counterarguments; they employ critical reason to weigh alternatives and make judgments. Although some theorists interpret the ascendancy of reason as excluding appeal to the emotions, others acknowledge a legitimate place for a wide range of communicative approaches provided they are directed toward the reasoned resolution of collective problems. All agree that coercion, threats, and manipulation are to be excluded.

Deliberative democracy implies the *public justification* of proposals and outcomes. To advocate publicly a particular course of action as appropriate for the collectivity implies establishing a link to some notion of the public interest or the collective good. It is not enough to say "this alternative will benefit me," for the logic of the deliberative context is oriented toward determining what is right and good for the community. Participants legitimately may insist that their perspectives and interests should be admitted to the deliberative exchange, but they must acknowledge that the final outcome will depend also on others' perspectives and interests. Although some theorists impose rather demanding tests on the sorts of arguments that should be admitted for consideration (that is, what are to count as valid exercises of "public reason"), others are willing to leave adjudication to the deliberative process itself.

Finally, if deliberation is to be democratic, it must depend on substantive *political equality:* all concerned interests should have access to the process, and each participant should enjoy an equal opportunity to present perspectives, hear contributions, and take part in debates and decisions. Needless to say, every individual cannot be involved personally in each deliberative context; representative mechanisms are essential for the working of modern democracy. But the overall structure of decision-making processes must be fair for all, lest a results-based sense of common purpose be squandered. In particular, inequalities of wealth and status should not corrupt deliberative interaction, and systemic bias on the basis of class, race, religion, gender, and so on must be precluded.

Advocates of deliberative norms present varied justifications for this approach.[3] They argue that the *process* itself is a fair and reasonable method of collective decision making. Deliberation can enhance the *quality* of political decisions because they will be substantively fairer, more adequately reflect collectively and rationally determined goals, or more successfully deploy appropriate means to secure these goals. Proponents also claim that citizens will more likely regard decisions as *legitimate*, thus improving chances of implementing these decisions successfully while simultaneously enhancing the perceived legitimacy of the system as a whole.

Moreover, deliberation can *educate* citizens, thus allowing them to appreciate others' interests and to gain insight into the moral and practical complexity of political judgment. This, in turn, raises the quality of deliberation and of decisions taken in the future. Deliberative democracy can be presented as a necessary dimension of the *good life* for moral agents, as an essential feature of a society that encourages human *flourishing*, or as the fundamental basis for *political obligation*. Different versions of the theory integrate these sorts of arguments and establish linkages with other values (such as freedom, justice, autonomy, and welfare) in characteristic ways.

Sometimes the idea of deliberative democracy is invoked to demonstrate the significance and explain the workings of actually existing democracies—to make intelligible those practices that already operate. But if emphasis is placed on the extent to which the political system departs from the normative ideal, deliberative democracy also can ground a powerful critique of contemporary institutions. Manipulation by moneyed interests, unprincipled bargaining among politicians, media infatuation with personalities instead of policies, the systematic exclusion of disadvantaged groups—all are among the routinely cited failings of modern democracy. To rectify such ills, as we shall see, deliberative democrats have proposed a range of reforms to current practices.[4]

The deliberative ideal is certainly not new. The deliberative potential of representative bodies—such as parliament, Congress, and the U.S. electoral college—long has been central to the defense of these institutions (consider Burke's speech to the electors of Bristol or the arguments at the time of the founding of the United States). And public debate was important to reform-oriented democrats such as J. S. Mill, L. T. Hobhouse, and John Dewey. The more focused modern preoccupation with deliberative democracy is linked to current controversies within liberal political philosophy. These controversies involve debates over the basis of political association, the nature of community, and the limits of diversity. Within them, two prominent concerns exist. One is with trumping the social choice critique that voting paradoxes render popular democracy an incoherent ideal, and the other is with reinterpreting the participatory approaches of the 1970s. Overall, however, the modern preoccupation with deliberative democracy reflects a broader "communicative turn" in political theory and the social sciences. In this respect, the influence of Jürgen Habermas is significant, in particular his concepts of "communicative rationality" and "the ideal speech situation."[5]

Deliberative Democracy and Environmental Governance

To this point, the discussion has provided a brief overview of the claims of deliberative democracy. I now turn to its salience for building a results-based sense of common purpose in environmental governance. Overall, green theorists have been sympathetic to the idea of deliberative democracy, suggesting that it provides a context in which citizens can reflect more deeply on the value of natural systems and processes and make decisions that more adequately acknowledge the needs of future generations and of the nonhuman natural world.[6] But how can such potential actually be realized? One way to approach this question is to distinguish three forms of deliberative interaction that can be described as operative on the "politico-constitutional," "societal," and "meso" levels. Much of the theoretical literature on deliberative democracy is concerned with the first alternative. It focuses on core political institutions (for example, the legislature, the executive, and the courts) and on constitution-making and amending bodies. At issue is the deliberative democratic character of these bodies and how this character can be enhanced. Yet changes in the rules governing core political institutions are notoriously difficult to achieve, and although such systemic reforms can be of great consequence to a polity, it is not clear that much can be said about their *specific* impact on environmental policy.

The second (societal) level relates to public debate in the widest sense: to the enhancement of democratic deliberation in the media, within associations of all types, and among the citizenry at large. One concern is to improve the overall quality of public-opinion formation (for example, in reducing distortions generated by moneyed interests) so as to ground better subsequent phases of deliberation by professional politicians and administrators. Another concern is to improve the selection of candidates for public office. Habermas talks of open deliberation in civil society orientating formal decision-making processes within the political-legal sphere.[7] Analysts who are especially skeptical of official structures emphasize civil society as an autonomous and dynamic deliberative domain that can check the instrumental and bureaucratic rationality characteristic of the administrative state.[8] An improvement in the general quality of public debate and a reduction in the influence of entrenched economic lobbies presumably would strengthen the position of those advocating environmental protection (provided, of course, their arguments were appropriate and well reasoned). But this being said, more specific implications for ENR management are difficult to discern.

Finally, there is the third ("meso") level involving deliberative interactions at the interface between state and society, where the personnel and structures of the state meet individuals and groups rooted in civil and commercial life. It is in relation to this zone, where state and society overlap and interpenetrate, that it makes sense to consider the implications of deliberative democracy for a specific policy sector such as environmental decision making. And it is with this level of interaction for building a results-based sense of common purpose that the remainder of this chapter is concerned.[9]

The claim is that in many contexts where decisions about ENR policy are to be made, an appropriate extension of deliberative democratic mechanisms at the interface between state and society can enhance social outcomes. Inputs from a wider cross-section of actors, the more judicious discussion of alternatives and consideration of expert advice, and the focus on the construction of common perspectives, agreed solutions, and collaborative implementation—associated with deliberative democratic interaction—can generate policy outputs that are more likely to take account of natural and social conditions, realize desired objectives, achieve equity, and be viewed as legitimate. Furthermore, such practices can enhance societal learning in the ENR policy domain.

What does such an extension of deliberative mechanisms for building common purpose at the interface between state and society actually entail? It requires *the development of an array of venues and processes concerned with specific ENR issues, which draw interested actors from the public and private spheres into closer deliberative democratic interaction.* Such forums and processes should be accessible to a range of affected social interests; provide the opportunity for collective exchange, reflection, and decision; and be focused on addressing concrete problems.

It is here that the discussion of deliberative democracy ties in with exist-ing theoretical and practical concerns with *"participation,"* and with governments' recent interest in cooperative problem solving and social partnerships such as those discussed in chapters 6, 9, and 13 in this volume.

Public participation has been a recurrent theme in environmental pol-icy since the establishment of the institutions of modern environmental governance in the late 1960s and early 1970s. For environmental move-ments, the participatory ideals of citizen activism and local empower-ment long have stood in opposition to bureaucratic control by big government and big business. Furthermore, over the past decade, governments themselves have come to emphasize the involvement of "stakeholders" and the general public in making and implementing envi-ronmental policy. They also have experimented with mechanisms for testing public opinion, building consensus, and extending social cooper-ation on issues related to the environment, natural resources, and sustainability. Governments have been led in this direction for many rea-sons, including an ideological climate unfavorable to a new wave of command-and-control regulation, a desire to escape policy deadlock, and a perception that the public is disenchanted with politics and the policy process. Above all, they have realized that more traditional—closed, cen-tralized, and rule-based—approaches are unlikely to work in the face of emergent problems associated with sustainable development.[10]

Yet despite the renewed talk about participation, publics and govern-ments remain cautious. Citizens have seen official enthusiasm for partic-ipation wax and wane (a high point in the 1970s, a low point in the 1980s). Their experience is that consultation often takes place when plans are already far advanced and there is little room for change, when citizens suspect politicians' and bureaucrats' motives, and when the vast majority resist attempts to draw them into closer involvement with envi-ronmental policymaking. Officials may experience participation as a frustrating delay or as a tiresome routine. Their concern often is to mini-mize the impact of ill-informed publics and special-interest pleading on their agencies' and political masters' projects.

The ideal of deliberative democracy sets the substantial body of participatory theory and practical experiences with participation in environmental decision making in a new context. It suggests that one kind of participation—*participation in a deliberative democratic process*—is especially valuable for building common purpose. In logical terms, this form of participation stands in contrast to participation which is nondeliberative, nondemocratic, or both. In practice, of course, it is more a question of degree—of how adequately a given process embodies deliberative democratic norms. The deliberative ideal also provides a perspective from which to assess governmental support for social partnerships and cooperative management. It implies that the kinds of partnerships and comanagement to be encouraged are those that contribute to deliberative democratic practice, rather than those that undermine authentic deliberation and democratic control.

Evaluating Participatory and Interactive Mechanisms

Public enquiries, referendums, citizen juries, environmental mediation, covenants, and stakeholder roundtables are among the mechanisms deployed to encourage participation, dialogue, and consensus in environmental decision making. Singly or in combination, they have been applied to a vast array of environmental problems, including those related to facility siting, large infrastructure projects, land-use planning, agriculture and fisheries management, habitat protection, climate change, and Local Agenda 21. In addition to the chapters by John, Schlager, and Bryner in this volume, a substantial literature deals with the operation of such practices and their impact on the quality of environmental decision making.[11] Research also exists that assesses such techniques in terms of participative and communicative ideals.[12] One recent volume, for instance, evaluated eight participatory decision processes in terms of their "fairness" and "competence" in relation to four discursive types (explicative, theoretical, practical, and therapeutic discourses) analyzed by Habermas.[13] Adding "transparency" and "accountability" to "fairness" and "competence," the author of another recent study (of local waste management strategies in the United Kingdom) suggested ten questions that should be used to appraise participatory processes.[14]

Here I invoke a more direct approach that weighs the deliberative democratic content of specific participatory or interactive mechanisms across four dimensions: *representation, deliberation, decision,* and *execution.* The first element concerns the representation of affected interests. Do all interested parties have an equal opportunity to express their views and influence proceedings? Who actually participates in the deliberative interaction? Is the process open to scrutiny by affected interests who cannot take part directly? The second relates to the quality of deliberation. Is the encounter structured to facilitate reasoned analysis, to give careful attention to expert opinions, or to encourage the emergence of shared understandings and new solutions? The third element refers to the decisional character of the exercise. What is the character of the collective output? How is it linked to any broader decisional process? How significant are the substantive issues on which decisions are being taken? The fourth element deals with collective implementation, monitoring, and review. To what extent are participants involved in implementing any decision? Do they have opportunities to monitor progress or to revisit issues at a later point? Is the deliberative exercise a one-shot affair or an ongoing process?

Each dimension engages with core elements of the deliberative democratic ideal: *representation* with the claim to fairness and equality; *deliberation* with the notion of communicative exchange where reasoned debate (not force or deception) leads to shared understandings; and *decision* with the democratic requirement for closure, collective determination, and authentic influence. The fourth element, *execution,* is usually neglected in discussions of deliberative democracy, but it, too, is important, for democracy is not just about discussion and decision, but also about responsibility and action. Those who make decisions should have some role in carrying them out and assessing their consequences.

How do the sorts of techniques employed in the environmental policy sphere to bridge the gap between political decision makers and society perform on these four criteria? I briefly consider seven devices: the public inquiry, the referendum, the citizen advisory panel, the citizen jury, mediation, environmental covenants, and negotiated regulation. This list is not exhaustive, and many related mechanisms (such as deliberative opinion polls, citizen working groups, the popular initiative, and various roundtable processes) might be added. However, it is sufficiently diverse for illustrative purposes.[15] For the reader's convenience, table 5.1 summarizes some of the characteristics of these seven participatory devices.

Table 5.1
Characteristics of Some Participatory Techniques Used in Environmental Governance

	Modes of Interest Representation	Participants in Deliberation	Character of Output	Role in Execution
Public Inquiry	Presentations to impartial judge or panel	Inquiry panel	Detailed report and recommendations to sponsoring agency	None
Referendum	Public campaign by concerned groups and individuals	The public	Reject or approve one or more options (decisional or consultative)	None
Citizen Advisory Panel	Views submitted to or solicited by the panel; "representative" composition (selected)	Lay panel members	Advice to sponsoring agency	None
Citizen Jury	Views submitted to panel; "representative" composition (stratified sample)	Lay jury members	Verdict and explanation: recommendation to sponsoring agency	None
Environmental Covenant	Direct input from participating groups	Agency and industry representatives	Environmental agreement	Sell agreement to constituencies; perform mandated actions
Negotiated Regulation	Direct input from participating groups	Concerned group representatives	Draft regulatory rule	Sell agreement to constituencies
Mediation	Direct input from participating groups	Concerned group representatives	Mediated agreement	Sell agreement to constituencies; perform mandated actions

The most traditional of the seven mechanisms are the public inquiry and the referendum. A *public inquiry* involves appointment of a senior official or officials (often from a legal background) to investigate an issue of public concern. Public inquiries often adopt a quasi-judicial form, with legal representation of interested parties and formal cross-examination of witnesses. They have been employed widely in the United Kingdom and other countries in relation to planning decisions, sites for nuclear and waste treatment facilities, and the design of large infrastructure projects. Within the terms of reference established by the sponsoring authority, representation of the views of affected interests may be relatively broad, although well-financed and well-organized parties will be able to make better use of the formal, legal, and protracted character of proceedings. Deliberation does not occur directly among the interested parties, but within the officiating panel (assuming it has more than one member). The exercise is decisional to the extent that it produces an official report, but the sponsoring authority reserves the right to decide how to act on the findings. Such an inquiry generally has no role in execution.

A *referendum* allows voters at the local, regional, or national level to choose directly among a small range of policy alternatives. Referenda have been used in many countries to decide local environmental issues,[16] but they also have been conducted on the national level—the Swedish referendum on nuclear power, for example. Participation is open to the enfranchised population of the relevant jurisdiction, but effective representation of interests may be skewed by factors similar to those affecting mass electoral competition. Voters may lack the time or inclination to examine the issues, and the context for consideration of expert inputs is poor. Discussion typically is polarized, and alternatives are confined to those presented in the initial question. This gives considerable power to the question framers and precludes the development of new solutions as the debate advances. The referendum produces a clear decisional output, and even when the exercise is merely consultative (rather than legally binding), there is powerful pressure on political authorities to accept the popular verdict. Participants have no direct role in implementation or review, although another referendum on a similar topic at some point in the future remains a possibility.

A *citizen advisory panel,* composed of individuals chosen to reflect different segments of the community, provides recommendations to the sponsoring authority on issues defined in its enabling brief. Participants do not act as formal representatives of groups or interests, but as lay assessors reflecting a cross-section of the community. Such panels have been used in the United States and elsewhere to examine contentious environmental issues. Representation of a range of interests can be secured through the composition of the panel and through decisional inputs provided by the sponsoring authority or solicited by the group. Deliberation takes place among panel members, with relatively favorable conditions for the consideration of expert advice and the emergence of new alternatives—subject, of course, to the panel members' capacities and the time constraints under which the group operates. Although the panel agrees on a recommendation, the choice of action remains the sponsoring authority's prerogative. Most citizen advisory groups report and then pass out of existence, but it is possible for them to continue follow-up activities.

The *citizen jury* is a small group of citizens, selected through stratified random sampling to ensure representative balance (for example, region, gender, race), which is asked to pronounce judgment on a contentious issue facing public authorities. The jury is presented with a small number of alternatives, and over the course of several days it considers the arguments of advocates and the testimony of expert witnesses before pronouncing its opinion on the initial charge. Representation depends on the appropriateness of the sampling categories and on the range of options and arguments the organizers present to the jury. Deliberation takes place among the jurors, who can debate expert advice and contrast alternatives. On the other hand, the initial options put to the lay assessors must be reasonably straightforward; moreover, participants have no opportunity to formulate alternative propositions and only limited time to acquire detailed technical knowledge. The jury decides how to respond to the charge, but any decision to act rests with the sponsoring authority. Citizen juries are one-shot affairs. Should there be a need to reconsider or to examine a related issue, a new panel has to be convened.

Environmental mediation (as Rosemary O'Leary, Tina Nabatchi, and Lisa Bingham discuss in greater detail in chapter 9) depends on bringing together parties to a dispute in a flexibly structured encounter to bridge differences and construct an agreed solution. The exercise typically is led by a trained mediator, who may take a more or less active role in designing and leading the parties to accept a consensual solution. Mediation has been applied extensively in the United States, where the litigious nature of the environmental policy process makes it appealing to parties who are trying to avoid the time, costs, and winner-take-all risks of a court-imposed solution. In contrast, Europe has relatively little experience with this technique. In terms of representation, mediation provides a forum for the organized parties to a conflict, generally those who would otherwise have had recourse to the courts. Conditions favorable to deliberation are provided by the participants' agreement to an attempt to negotiate a solution and by the presence of an independent mediator. Although groups inevitably approach the exercise with the idea of bargaining, they can be led to explore the reasoning behind their initial positions, to redefine their interests, and to discover win-win alternatives. On the other hand, mediation kicks in only when disputes are well established and when relations between the parties may have become acrimonious. The problem parameters, therefore, can be redefined only to a certain extent. Moreover, the device is reactive rather than proactive: it does not give policymakers a mechanism to draw organizations together before conflict erupts. If the parties do come to a mutually acceptable solution, the mechanism is directly decisional, and each partner typically will have some role to play in implementation. Because mediation is dispute focused, it ends with (or without) an accord, but contacts among the parties occasionally spill over into more long-term cooperation.

Environmental covenants are formal agreements regulating environmental conduct concluded between governmental and private actors. Companies or industrial associations accept certain results-based environmental performance criteria but are left substantial freedom to organize the way they meet those targets. Governments typically make an implicit or explicit commitment not to introduce additional regulation in the implicated sector, and they commit to continued consultation with their industrial partners. Covenants have been incorporated formally into the system of environmental governance in the Netherlands, but experiments with similar sorts of agreement are ongoing in many European countries. Covenant negotiation is conducted between government and industry, but other interests typically are not represented. Participants have both good knowledge of the specific field and the time for detailed discussion. New perspectives may emerge from the encounters, but the narrow range of participants may hamper new perspectives, the critical analysis of received scientific wisdom, and the building of a broader sense of common purpose. Participants directly decide whether or not to conclude an agreement, and each partner has some obligation to ensure implementation.

Negotiated regulation is sponsored by an administrative agency and involves meetings with interested parties (representatives from industry, other public bodies, and environmental groups) to consider the content of a regulatory rule. In the United States, the approach has been employed by the Environmental Protection Agency. Representation of organized interests may be wide, but unorganized publics have no direct access to proceedings. Participants have the time and knowledge to consider difficult technical issues and the opportunity to challenge each other's perspectives, and they can suggest innovative approaches. On the other hand, because the focus of the activity is a regulatory rule, non-rule-based solutions may be precluded. The negotiating panel can recommend a draft, but the decision to adopt the negotiated ordinance rests with the regulatory agency. All parties may assume some role in implementation (at least in selling the agreement to their constituencies), but the primary responsibility lies with the sponsor. In principle, such forums might remain active to monitor subsequent developments, but in practice this is not usually the case.

Two points must be made initially in relation to this brief presentation of some of the participatory and interactive mechanisms employed in environmental decision making. First, although the discussion has suggested the potentialities and limitations of each device, the particular way in which it is applied in a concrete situation determines how these factors are operative. Such factors as the rules governing the admission of evidence to a public inquiry, the manner in which panel members are selected for a citizen advisory committee, and the framing of the issue for consideration by a citizen jury influence the extent to which deliberative democratic norms are realized. In other words, the details of the procedures matter.

Second, as deployed in practice, each mechanism also will be embedded in a broader policymaking process and will have a definite relation to established institutions for democratic decision making. It is only in relation to the process as a whole and to the formal structures of democratic government that a conclusive judgment about the deliberative democratic character of an exercise is possible. For example, a government may ignore completely the recommendations of a citizen advisory panel that is judged (on internal grounds alone) to have operated in a reasonably fair and competent manner. Thus, although use of the panel reflected deliberative democratic norms, the wider processes in which it was embedded apparently did not, and the authenticity of the mechanism was compromised.

Even worse, the sponsoring agency might have set up the panel after already having decided its course of action. In this case, the participatory exercise was not just irrelevant, but rather a conscious deception. Again, the context of the wider process partially overrides any assessment of the detailed mechanism. On the other hand, an authority might have good democratic grounds to ignore an output from a consultative body (even an output generated by an apparently fair deliberative process). Perhaps it possessed information unavailable to the panel, or conditions changed before implementation was practical, or the government had an electoral mandate that precluded enactment of the panel's recommendation. The point is that only by considering the relationship to the larger democratic decision-making context can judgments be made about the broader significance of a particular collaborative mechanism.

This said, it is clear that none of the mechanisms presented earlier appears to be a particularly pure expression of deliberative democratic norms, at least as this ideal has been interpreted here. Rather, each device has stronger and weaker points. Thus, although a public inquiry can admit inputs from many concerned parties, its format usually encourages confrontation rather than deliberation; indeed, many analysts scarcely consider it a participatory mechanism at all. The referendum, in some ways the most open and the most decisive mechanism from a decisional perspective, also provides relatively poor conditions for deliberation. Negotiating an environmental covenant allows detailed discussion between government and business, but other actors are excluded and the private character of proceedings may encourage bargaining over interests rather than creative deliberation. Because a citizen jury includes a representative cross-section of the community collectively weighing evidence, it encourages impartial deliberation, but the experience is shared directly by only a small group that lacks any systematic linkage to the wider society. Nor can the group play any role in implementation and follow-up.

This uneven performance reflects a real difficulty in actualizing the ideal. Deliberative democracy that aims at building a results-based sense of common purpose requires equal access and representation, profound discussion and reflection, and a collective movement to decision and execution. In practice, however, the requirements of representation, deliberation, decision, and execution *can pull in different ways.* A small group that is well placed to deliberate cannot represent fully a complex whole, and lay participants who bring the perspective of ordinary citizens to decision making cannot be expected to remain active for implementation and follow-up. Deliberative democracy is most clear conceptually in the context of a group that collectively deliberates, decides, and acts—a group that constructs a common perspective and is free to carry through an agreed endeavor. But modern societies are characterized by large-scale political and economic units and by complex interdependencies among individuals, groups, and systems. Moreover, the potential of any group to deliberate, decide, and execute is hemmed in by interactions with other societal complexes.

From Participatory Mechanisms to Deliberative Processes in Environmental Governance?

Given this reality, can deliberative democracy contribute positively to the building of a results-based sense of common purpose in environmental governance? The deliberative democratic features of participatory processes at the interface between state and society, such as those discussed earlier, are significant, even if they do fall short of the ideal. Moreover, as pointed out, the details of the procedure matter. By getting these details right, the substantive results of the deliberation can be improved and the democratic legitimacy of the procedure enhanced. Thus, despite the difficulties I have noted, there *are* substantial grounds for optimism.

First, prior research suggests that success is more likely whenever the mechanisms of deliberative democracy are matched deftly (in single units and in combination) to the specific contexts. Second, a group-based subset of deliberative mechanisms performs consistently better on average than conventional participatory approaches across all four evaluative criteria noted earlier. Third, group-based deliberative approaches are distinctly well suited to the complexities of decision making characteristic of environmental governance in the twenty-first century.

Matching Deliberative Mechanisms with Contexts

Because different deliberative mechanisms have different characteristics, they are better suited to different contexts. Thus, by strategically deploying them under appropriate circumstances, their positive features can be enhanced and the impact of shortcomings curtailed. For example, the organization of a referendum to select one site from several alternatives for a hazardous-waste facility easily can become a mechanism by which a majority can transfer the burden to a disfavored community, rather than an exercise of deliberative democracy. Thus, when strategically selecting mechanisms, participants in a deliberative process should consider at least three sorts of factors: the nature of the environmental problem, the geopolitical scale on which it is to be managed, and the phase of the process to which the technique is to be applied.

Ortwin Renn, Thomas Webler, and Peter Wiedemann suggest that environmental policy problems can be distinguished by their degree of complexity and by the intensity of the associated conflict; they argue that different participatory mechanisms become appropriate as problems vary across these two dimensions. Thus, for example, regulatory negotiation is more suited to problems of high complexity but low conflict intensity (because it allows detailed discussion of technical issues between specialist parties). In contrast, mediation is more suited to issues of lower complexity that generate greater conflict (because it emphasizes building trust among a more open range of parties). Nor are all mechanisms appropriate to every scale. Thus, regulatory negotiation and environmental covenants are more applicable on the national level. In contrast, the referendum can be adjusted more easily to differently scaled jurisdictions. Daniel Fiorino emphasizes that opportunities for participation vary at different stages of the policy process—setting an agenda, developing frameworks for policy choice, and making the choices themselves.[17] Again, a mechanism that might be appropriate for defining policy priorities (a citizen advisory panel, for example) might be less suited to channeling public inputs for a final decision.

Finally, because what counts is the quality of the overall process (rather than the results of any given phase), it is possible to combine several mechanisms to raise the deliberative democratic content of the whole. By strategically combining mechanisms with different mixes of representative, deliberative, decisional, and executive features, participants can construct a more balanced decision procedure. For example, a more open deliberative mechanism such as a citizen advisory panel might play a part in establishing social priorities with respect to environmental risk, whereas regulatory negotiation might be used to establish the content of the rule targeting a priority hazard. Or a referendum might be held to accept or reject a program of environmental measures drawn up after earlier rounds of consultation involving more intensive deliberative engagement.

In practice, many contentious decisions in the ENR policy realm now involve multiple and overlapping participatory processes, with citizen forums, public inquiries, and various types of stakeholder interactions being combined. This combined approach is particularly appropriate with respect to schemes for urban development and large infrastructure projects that link a national or regional dimension (because of their strategic economic importance) with local salience (because they have to be built somewhere). But it is also appropriate in all sorts of other areas, including habitat protection, the operation of national parks, strategic responses on biodiversity and climate change, and Local Agenda 21 initiatives.[18]

Consonance with Deliberative Criteria

Another reason to be confident of the potential contribution deliberative democracy can make to the building of a results-based sense of common purpose in environmental governance is that one subset of the approaches canvassed previously performs consistently better than other participatory approaches across all four evaluative categories applied earlier. By privileging such an approach and its subsets, and by placing them at the heart of compound processes, it is possible to achieve the deliberative democratic ideal more fully. This point brings us to the fundamental distinction between citizen-based and group-based participatory practices.[19]

The referendum, citizen jury, and citizen advisory panel are *citizen-based mechanisms*. Individuals take part as members of society, in their capacity as citizens; they have no formal obligation to "represent" anyone but themselves; and to the extent that their judgments are valued, it is precisely because ordinary citizens make them. In contrast, negotiated regulation, mediation, and environmental covenants are *group-based processes*. The seats at the table are allocated to groups (companies, trade associations, nongovernmental organizations [NGOs], and governmental organizations); individuals take part as representatives of groups; and what makes the mechanism valuable is that organized interests are involved directly. Strictly speaking, the public inquiry falls into neither category, for although both individual citizens and groups can make representations to the inquiry, the deliberation and decision are the prerogative of specialist assessors.[20]

The strengths of group-based processes are most evident in terms of the third and forth criteria—*decision* and *execution*—where (with the exception of the decisional credentials of the referendum) citizen-based approaches generally perform weakly. Because group-based processes involve the parties directly concerned with a problem, it is feasible to devolve to them more of the responsibility for actually making a decision. Parties know their own circumstances, and in devising an agreed solution, they become involved in a form of problem-related "self-government." Moreover, because participating groups have a structural connection to the issue, they are more likely to be able to participate in implementing an agreed solution. They also have a standing concern with the issue and an organizational life beyond that of any individual delegate, so they can assume a longer-term follow-up role.

In contrast, the individuals who participate in a citizen-based process that uses a group of electors as a microcosm for society as a whole cannot be entrusted with a final decision. After all, no formal lines of accountability tie them to any wider constituency, and when they bind themselves to an agreed solution, they can make no claim (whether practical or moral) to bind a broader group to this solution. The result of their deliberation still has to be sold to the affected interests; and though the solution arguably is a reasoned product of citizen deliberation, it is also produced by individuals one step removed from the parties most directly involved. Moreover, as we have seen, citizen-based processes are ill-equipped for a role in implementing, monitoring, or revisiting an agreed solution.

Group-based processes also have *representational* and *deliberative* advantages. In a group-based process, representatives of organizations linked to affected interests are involved directly in the deliberative encounter. Each participant interacts with others and in so doing encounters new dimensions of the problem. Advances in understanding and proposals for action can be communicated back to participating organizations and transferred to their broader constituencies. In other words, the representation of interests is more direct. In contrast, in a citizen microcosm, environmental interests are in the main represented indirectly—through witnesses, advocates, and reports. In one sense, this indirect representation can be seen as an advantage because it insulates the deliberators from bias, but, in another sense, it is a handicap because it also separates them from direct experience. Of course, the panel or jury arguably is "representative" of the larger community from which it is drawn, but the categories used to compose the body (through selection for the panel or sampling for the jury) are not necessarily the categories most salient for the specific environmental problem. With respect to the deliberative process itself, the advantages of the group-based approach relate primarily to the specialist knowledge that participants bring to the process at the outset, their capacity to absorb technical issues more readily, and the time they can invest in the process.

Consonance with ENR Policy Context

The potential of group-based deliberative processes for building a results-based sense of common purpose can be appreciated further if one considers that they are well placed to address some of the most challenging characteristics of contemporary environmental problems. Included among these characteristics are the variety of implicated interests, the substantial uncertainties and technical complexities involved, the protracted timeframes over which issues evolve, and the need to learn through practice how best to manage socioecological issues. Group processes can *engage complex interests within a constructive framework, provide a context to explore contradictory scientific claims and to reconcile different forms of knowledge, favor long-term interaction,* and *encourage learning among organizations and broader social constituencies.* These advantages are particularly important in a context where environmental policy is no longer to be understood simply in terms of pollution abatement, resource management, and nature conservation, but increasingly is being called on to address broader issues such as integrated ecosystem management, movement toward a postcarbon energy system, the greening of patterns of production and consumption, and the achievement of ecologically sustainable development.

In practice, group-based processes have developed rapidly over the past decade and a half. The particular variants discussed here—regulatory negotiation, environmental covenants, and mediation—are well-defined models. Yet a vast array of processes exists that involve interaction among a more or less extensive range of social partners to address specific environmental issues. More precisely, encounter groups, multistakeholder forums, roundtables, cooperative management bodies, and environmental partnerships of all kinds have come into being. Such bodies may play a variety of roles, from advising established institutions to taking charge of the direct management of resource systems. The proliferation of multistakeholder processes has been encouraged by international events such as the 1992 Rio Earth Summit and the 2002 Johannesburg World Summit on Sustainable Development, as well as by international bodies such as the United Nations Commission on Sustainable Development and the Organization for Economic Cooperation and Development.[21] But the main impetus has come from domestic environmental policy actors—governments, businesses, and environmental groups—who seek to break the policy deadlock and find new ways of approaching environmental governance.

The Dutch Ministry of Transport and Public Works, for example, established a collaborative initiative to draw up environmental guidelines for Schiphol airport, one of the country's main transport hubs. The body included representatives from the airport authority, three airlines, environmental groups, municipal and provincial authorities, trade unions and employers, and local residents' associations. After six months of dialogue, the working group failed to agree on a comprehensive recommendation, remaining divided on fundamental points relating to noise and safety assessment. Nevertheless, the discussion generated agreement on many specific issues and clarified areas for further investigation. Moreover, the participants were satisfied with the consultative process, believing it had advanced mutual understanding and clarified problem areas for sponsoring bodies and the political arena to address further.[22] The Schiphol process now is seen as part of the more general emergence of a "Green Polder Model" in the Netherlands, where government formally is committed to consulting key societal actors—including environmental organizations—when taking major initiatives relating to sustainability and to spatial and infrastructure planning.[23]

The development and implementation of local biodiversity action plans in the United Kingdom (following publication of the 1994 national biodiversity "Action Plan") involved complex collaboration among scientific and conservation organizations, government agencies, and private businesses. Stephen Young, for example, cites implementation of the Red Squirrel Action Plan on the Lancashire coast as involving the participation of "public and private sector landowners . . . Sefton Council, the Forestry Commission, the National Trust, English Nature, the Territorial Army, the Mersey Forest, and a golf club." Involving a "top-down" stimulus from central government, an up-swell of initiatives from other social actors, and the emergence of "partnerships" at all levels, this process had resulted by the end of 1998 in "costed action plans for 400 species and thirty-nine habitat types."[24]

Meanwhile, in the United States, Habitat Conservation Plans (HCPs) prepared under the framework of the Endangered Species Act sometimes involve complex, multipartite deliberative interactions. Interests wishing to undertake activities that threaten the habitat of a protected species are obliged to prepare an HCP to secure an "incidental take permit" from the U.S. Fish and Wildlife Service. Although many HCPs are submitted by individual landowners, others result from complex interorganizational negotiating processes that draw together government and private partners, environmental organizations, and civic groups. The plans outline a framework to reconcile conservation with economic development, and their preparation provides a context within which concerned parties can interact. In these instances, the pressure to complete an acceptable HCP and the threat of legal action serve as stimuli toward constructive engagement.[25]

Cooperative mechanisms such as these adopt many different forms, but—unless they are mere deceptions—they all entail a mutual recognition among the parties that each is a legitimate interlocutor and has a shared commitment to the common enterprise. They vary in the extent to which they embody deliberative democratic ideals, but they do have the potential to perform across the four criteria I invoked earlier to advance the building of a results-based sense of common purpose among stakeholders. Moreover, they can be flexible, problem specific, practically focused, and long running.

Worries about Group-Based Deliberative Processes

Many enthusiasts of deliberative democracy frankly would be horrified by the case for group-based processes outlined here. Of those concerned with extending deliberative democracy at the interface between state and society (rather than within existing representative institutions or across society generally), most are skeptical of an approach that depends on interaction among established interests and leaves too little place for citizen involvement. Indeed, such arrangements sometimes have been referred to (semi-pejoratively) as "environmental corporatism" because of parallels with corporatist modes of governance that rely on a compact between representatives of business, labor, and the state. Discussing the weaknesses of group-based processes, one recent commentator worried that "deliberation is mediated by representation" and noted questions concerning the representative and democratic character of associations, as well as the capacity of their delegates "to be open to the possibility of transformation."[26]

The emphasis on group interaction in environmental governance *does* resemble corporatism, but here we are dealing not with three-way peak agreements, but with an array of problem-specific forums in the environmental policy field involving the different constellations of groups. In this sense, group-based deliberative forums are just as much a form of "environmental pluralism." As we have seen, group-based deliberative processes do depend on representation. But citizen-based mechanisms (with the exception of the referendum) also are mediated by representation, although of a different type. The rationale for these devices rests on a small group's being taken as representative of the larger community from which it is drawn; and this, in turn, depends on the very loose sense in which individual members can be understood to "represent" segments of a population whose characteristics they share. The question, however, is which form of representation is more appropriate for the building of a results-based sense of common purpose in environmental governance. Here I have argued that, in the context of contemporary environmental decision making, group-based representation is often more appropriate.[27]

Nevertheless, this point does not lay to rest the worries about reliance on group-based deliberative interaction. First, there is suspicion about the groups themselves—private companies and business organizations, environmental movements, and government agencies. Or, to put it less charitably: profit makers, troublemakers, and bureaucrats. Why should citizens place their confidence in interaction among representatives of organizations of this kind? Who do these groups really represent? And how can they serve democracy when internally they do not function on democratic lines? Second, there is concern about the authenticity of deliberation in group-based forums. Will such encounters degenerate into bargaining among special interests? What will prevent groups from colluding for mutual benefit, while ignoring the true public interest? Do we not risk a tyranny of the organized? Third, there is the issue of the room remaining for citizen-based participation. Will a proliferation of group-based processes leave any room at all for citizen participation in deliberation?

These concerns are significant, and I only can hope to sketch out some answers here. The starting place for such a response must be to emphasize the importance of organizations as social actors. Our world is dense with organizations, created for all sorts of purposes, interacting in many different ways. Government itself is not a single monolith, but a tissue of organizations that have resources, knowledge, experience, and histories. Environmental problems are entwined with organizational life; if their action generates environmental impacts, it is only when organized forces take up an issue that it becomes fully constituted as a social problem. Considering that organizations help define environmental problems, why not involve them directly in deriving solutions? And considering that no single organization has the full picture, why not bring all of them together in interactive, problem-focused processes?

From this perspective, the internal working of an organization is secondary so long as it reflects adequately the preoccupations of the wider social forces it claims to represent. Of course, if the chemical producers' association is so inefficient or if an environmental NGO is so out of touch with its base that their respective constituencies ignore them, then neither body will be a fruitful partner for deliberative engagement. This said, the absence of democratic structures within firms or NGOs does not prevent them from making a meaningful contribution to a deliberative democratic practice. True, it can be argued that a further democratization of corporations and voluntary associations is desirable. In the meantime, however, their not being fully democratized does not preclude their functioning as legitimate social partners in deliberative exercises. Much evidence also suggests that group representatives can act in a creative way to solve environmental problems. Needless to say, conditions must be right: there must be a collective perception that a problem needs to be addressed, a willingness to accept others as viable partners, and an acknowledgement that other avenues (such as regulation and litigation) are less attractive.

Another answer, of course, to concerns about the possibility of collusion among concerned interests and of subversion of the social good is that governmental participants in such processes have a responsibility to look to the public interest. The state, after all, does oblige corporations and voluntary organizations to conform to certain norms if they are to receive legal recognition. Yet another answer is that elected political authorities can lay down clear policy guidance and exercise oversight functions to ensure that collaborative governance mechanisms work in the public interest. Perhaps the crucial guarantee, however, lies in the *openness* of the process. The greater the range of interests represented, the less likely it is that the forum will be captured by sectional interests. And if a particular mechanism does not easily admit direct participation from all social sectors (environmental covenants, for example), then at least the results of the negotiation should be open to legislative and public scrutiny.

Nor does a strategic emphasis on stakeholder-based processes preclude an extension of citizen-based deliberative approaches. Mechanisms involving a citizen microcosm are suited in particular to identifying the values, policies, and alternatives that citizens find compelling—after careful consideration. These mechanisms can function as a useful decision aid to authorities formally charged with making an environmental policy decision and as a valuable input to more general deliberative processes in society. The referendum also has potential to give citizens a decisive say on a socially divisive issue, once all the arguments have been aired and when some alternative must be selected. Moreover, it can serve as the culmination of a compound decision process involving other deliberative forms or in combination with the initiative as a device to drive forward the policy agenda beyond that envisaged by dominant governmental and economic actors.[28]

Nevertheless, citizen-based deliberative processes cannot be expected to bear the main burden of the increasingly complex, diverse, and knowledge-intensive management decisions required in the environmental sector. The extension of citizen juries throughout the environmental domain or the proliferation of referenda on every imaginable question (perhaps through weekly e-democracy polls) will not lead to better environmental governance. There *are* limits to the capacity both of citizens to handle such a crush of technically demanding issues and of the political system to manage such frenetic participation. As such, an extension of group-based deliberative processes is potentially more feasible and more productive.

Deliberative Democracy and Environmental Governance: Challenges, Choices, and Opportunities

This chapter has explored the idea of deliberative democracy and considered its relevance for ENR policymaking in the coming decades. It has argued that an extension of deliberative democratic practices at the boundary between state and society offers policymakers an opportunity to enhance the capacity of the environmental governance system to generate sound and acceptable decisions. Wider participation in environmental policymaking, in turn, can augment the informational basis on which decisions are made and raise public confidence in decisions and decision-making processes. Invoking an understanding of deliberative democracy that places comparatively greater emphasis than is the norm on the phases of collective decision and execution, the discussion reviewed a selection of participatory processes employed in the environmental field. No single approach was found to be satisfactory, yet it was suggested that if applied carefully and in appropriate circumstances, a combination of these mechanisms and others offers significant strategic opportunities to raise the deliberative democratic content of decision processes. Finally, group-based collaborative interactions were identified as *the key strategic element* for decisively increasing the deliberative democratic content of the environmental policy system.

What, then, are the major strategic challenges, choices, and opportunities facing those who wish to see to an extension of such group-based interactive modes of environmental governance as a means for building a results-based sense of common purpose? Perhaps the greatest strategic challenge remains the attitude of government itself, for although such processes devolve responsibility outward to a vast array of specialized management bodies, they also require significant support from government at all levels. On the one hand, public agencies and departments must be prepared to act as responsible partners in an array of initiatives and projects. On the other hand, they must coordinate the policy response across the ENR policy domain, ensure that the public interest and general political priorities are respected, and take initiatives to facilitate the operation of the emergent processes. To put this another way, the wide-scale development of such an approach requires political authorities committed *both* to substantive environmental policy goals and to the encouragement of group-based deliberative mechanisms.

The interactive policy processes described here typically depend on a clear impulse from government that identifies an issue as important, signals that the time for action has arrived, and provides the general context within which the issue is to be addressed. Once the political commitment to a particular project or goal is clear (for example, phasing out the use of certain substances, preparing a biodiversity conservation plan, improving economic efficiency and environmental performance in the pulp-and-paper sector, expanding the proportion of electricity generated from renewables), then an opportunity exists to draw actors into an interactive policy matrix. Without such a commitment, however, organizations (not just business and civil society organizations, but also organizations from other branches and levels of government) are unlikely to engage seriously. In fact, a more or less explicit threat is often an essential background stimulus to initiating constructive multigroup engagement— namely, the threat that issue-related actors' failure to participate in a cooperative response may oblige government to act unilaterally (through regulation or possibly taxation).

Thus, the expansion of group-based deliberative democratic processes in the environmental policy field remains at least in part a hostage to broader trends within the political system. Not the least of these trends involves the strategic choices political leaders make. If, for example, the national political leadership has resolved not to act on climate change, and the political context does not force their hand, then the growth of meso-level, group-based deliberative democratic initiatives is hampered (at least on this specific issue) for the time being at the national level. On the other hand, and as DeWitt John documents in chapter 6, a great advantage of group-based interactive processes is that they can be implemented piecemeal: blockage on one issue or at one administrative level does not necessarily preclude movement on other issues or in other jurisdictions. Thus, to pursue the climate change example, political sponsors for collaborative engagement on climate change might be found in subnational governments or in quasi-public bodies and agencies. Therefore, even in the absence of a central commitment, strategic opportunities might exist for local processes to get underway.

Yet the systematic extension of group-based deliberative processes requires something more from governments in the way of strategic choices. It demands that politicians and administrators refrain from "oversteering." They must resist the lure of attempting to micromanage environmental policy. If legislation fixes everything or administrative ordinance proscribes all action, then the room for creative interaction among group actors is squeezed out before the collaborative process even gets underway. If deliberative democratic forums for managing environmental burdens are to work, they must be given the latitude to make significant decisions about how problems are to be dealt with—subject to the general policy guidance established by political authorities and to appropriate monitoring and review. In other words, governments will have to change the way they conduct environmental policy. Thus, a consistent and comprehensive application of a group-based deliberative approach will require, in the long term, substantial amendments to existing environmental legislation and reforms to provide more robust legal underpinning for the expanding web of group-based management processes.

Of course, politicians are not the only ones who have difficulty adjusting to new ways of doing things. Much as Gary Bryner and Edella Schlager note in their respective chapters on global interdependence and common-pool resource management, public administrators also have significant strategic choices to make for deliberative democracy to work effectively. Habituated to drafting and applying fixed rules and to operating with closed policy networks, ENR managers will find the task of management through group-based deliberative interaction a real challenge. So, too, will environmental organizations and businesses face striking strategic choices. Raised on protest, lobbying, and litigation, environmental groups will have to alter their operating modes (and their relationships with rank-and-file members and financial contributors) if they are to manage a portfolio of partnerships with business and government. Businesses, too, will have to adjust. Although they will appreciate a move away from the compliance treadmill, the management demands placed on them by deliberative group processes will not be trivial. Nevertheless, business and environmental group obstacles appear less formidable than those posed by established practices of government and thus offer strategic opportunities for proponents of group-based deliberative processes to exploit.

In this context, one further issue deserves mention: the ideological and cultural dispositions of national political systems. Polities with traditions of consensual or corporatist policymaking, which employ flexible regulatory strategies and have little hesitation about turning to government to take the lead in resolving societal problems, are likely to choose and embrace the approach discussed here more readily. Experience from the

Netherlands and the Nordic countries seems to support such a hypothesis.[29] In contrast, the adversarial political culture, legalistic regulatory approach, litigious proclivity, and deep suspicion of government found in the United States may represent insuperable barriers to the growth of this mode of environmental governance (also see the chapters by Robert Paehlke and Ken Geiser for similar points).

Yet the trend toward group-based deliberative democratic interaction in the environmental realm is evident in North America also, as DeWitt John's chapter in particular attests. This trend presumably reflects how these approaches in part bridge the gap between corporatism and pluralism. Thus, the strong pluralist dimensions of American political life can create partial opportunities for such arrangements, whereas the rigidities of the regulatory system and the tendency toward political stalemate (encouraged by the constitutional separation of powers) create pressure for alternative approaches. Moreover, federalism requires constant interorganizational coordination and negotiation, which also may dispose the system toward movement in the direction discussed here. As we have seen, however, group-based deliberative democratic initiatives require not just bargaining among established interests, but constructive engagement to manage common problems within the parameters of a substantive policy framework set by government. It is here that the environmental policy community in the American republic may confront a more serious challenge.[30]

Finally, two caveats are in order. Raising the deliberative democratic character of decision making cannot be public officials' only concern when they confront a major environmental issue. At times, it is more important to act quickly (even if there is a strong likelihood that mistakes will be made) than to engage in lengthy consultations and deliberative processes. At the other extreme, potential gains from increasing deliberation in many routine decisions would be trivial—although one must be careful here. What appears to be a routine decision from the summit of a bureaucracy nevertheless can affect significantly the lives of individuals and communities at ground level. Moreover, even in the case of important social decisions, promoting deliberative democracy is only one consideration. All participatory processes incur costs and require copious inputs of money, time, and managerial attention. "Stakeholder" fatigue can set in rapidly, especially if the same few faces are sitting around the table in every forum. So public officials and other social partners must make strategic choices about what sorts of decisions and contexts really offer worthwhile opportunities for investing their time and effort.

One also has to acknowledge that there are many decision contexts where meso-level deliberative democratic approaches are of limited help. This is the case where an issue is highly polarized and framed in terms of a difference of principle that admits little compromise: for example, whether genetically modified foods, logging in old-growth forests, mining in national parks, or fox hunting are to be banned or permitted. Even here, however, citizen-based deliberative forums can be used to explore the range of public feeling on an issue and provide informed advice to decision makers.

Organizations rooted on different sides of these disputes, nevertheless, will be unlikely to reach a working consensus. An authoritative decision from established representative (or perhaps judicial) mechanisms is essential to resolve such issues (at least for the time being). This resolution, of course, inevitably leaves a dissatisfied minority who, however much it might accept the legitimacy of the process whereby the decision was reached, will still believe the outcome constituted a grave mistake, an injustice, or both. Once such an authoritative judgment is in place, however, an opportunity to pursue a group-based management solution (that includes representatives of the dissenters) might arise. Yet there is no getting away from the fact that environmental politics include sharp differences of interest and value. Only after such a decisive decision in favor of one alternative might it be possible to consider an interactive group-based process to manage change within the imposed framework.

This said, group-based deliberative democratic processes offer an exciting opportunity to build a results-based sense of common purpose in environmental governance. This is particularly true where one can envisage the establishment of long-term partnerships among governmental, economic, and societal organizations that are focused on a particular dimension of the dynamic interaction between social and ecological processes. Such interactive forums are really all about managing change. Provided they allow for the due representation of concerned interests, encourage deliberative engagement, draw together decision making about environment and development, and remain focused on the practical resolution of particular problems, they can encourage collective learning and help ensure that this change will be in a direction society regards as desirable.

Notes

1. James Bohman and William Rehg, eds., *Deliberative Democracy: Essays on Reason and Politics* (Cambridge, Mass.: MIT Press, 1997), p. ix.

2. For a more elaborate discussion relating to these points, see James Bohman, *Public Deliberation* (Cambridge, Mass.: MIT Press, 1996).

3. Insight into theoretical debates surrounding deliberative democracy can be found in Bohman and Rehg, *Deliberative Democracy*; Jon Elster, ed., *Deliberative Democracy* (Cambridge: Cambridge University Press, 1998); Stephen Macedo, ed., *Deliberative Politics: Essays on Democracy and Disagreement* (Oxford: Oxford University Press, 1999).

4. The surprise is just how modest most of these proposals are. Suggestions include using deliberative panels as part of the U.S. primary process, tightening rules on campaign financing, and increasing government support for education. Some more adventurous deliberative democrats argue for a substantial redistribution of wealth to make political equality real.

5. For Habermas, "communicative rationality" implies communicative interaction directed at noncoerced understanding and agreement. He considers this normative standard to be implicit in the very existence of language, which is predicated on the search for mutual understanding. The "ideal speech situation" is an imagined context in which communication is undistorted by any consideration of power. For a discussion, see Martin Leet, "Jürgen Habermas and Deliberative Democracy," in April Carter and Geoffrey Stokes, eds., *Liberal Democracy and Its Critics*, 77–97 (Cambridge: Polity, 1998).

6. Consider, for example, Robert Goodin, "Enfranchising the Earth and Its Alternatives," *Political Studies* 44(4) (1996): 835–845; Adolf Gunderson, *The Environmental Promise of Democratic Deliberation* (Madison: University of Wisconsin Press, 1995); Andrew Dobson, "Democratising Green Theory: Preconditions and Principles," in Brian Doherty and Marius de Geus, eds., *Democracy and Green Political Thought*, 132–150 (London: Routledge, 1996); John Barry, *Rethinking Green Politics* (London: Sage, 1999).

7. Jürgen Habermas, *Between Facts and Norms: Contributions to a Discourse Theory of Law and Democracy* (Cambridge, Mass.: MIT Press, 1996).

8. See, for example, Douglas Torgerson, *The Promise of Green Politics* (Chapel Hill, N. C.: Duke University Press, 1999); John Dryzek, *Deliberative Democracy and Beyond* (Oxford: Oxford University Press, 2000).

9. For an enthusiastic presentation of the general potential of local and problem-centered deliberative democratic management bodies to improve ordinary citizens' lives, see Archon Fung and Erik Olin Wright, "Deepening Democracy: Innovations in Empowered Participatory Governance," *Politics and Society* 29 (2001): 5–41. The authors' defense of what they describe as "empowered deliberative democracy" parallels some of the arguments developed in this chapter, although they place somewhat more faith in local, bottom-up, and citizen-based initiatives than I do here.

10. William Lafferty and James Meadowcroft, "Concluding Perspectives," in William Lafferty and James Meadowcroft, eds., *Implementing Sustainable Development: Strategies and Initiatives in High Consumption Societies,* 422–459 (Oxford: Oxford University Press, 2000).

11. For example, Greg Hampton, "Environmental Equity and Public Participation," *Policy Sciences* 32 (1999): 163–199.

12. See Daniel Fiorino, "Environmental Risk and Democratic Process: A Critical Review," *Columbia Journal of Environmental Law* 14(2) (1989): 501–547; Ortwin Renn, Thomas Webler, and Peter Wiedemann, eds., *Fairness and Competence in Citizen Participation: Evaluating Models for Environmental Discourse,* Technology, Risk, and Society series, no. 10 (Dordrecht: Kluwer Academic, 1995); Graham Smith, "Institutional Design and Green Politics," *Environmental Politics* 10(3) (2001): 72–93.

13. The volume was Renn, Webler, and Wiedemann, *Fairness and Competence in Citizen Participation*. Thomas Webler elaborated on the approach in chapter 3, "'Right' Discourse in Citizen Participation: An Evaluative Yardstick," pp. 35–86.

14. Judith Petts, "Evaluating the Effectiveness of Deliberative Processes: Waste Management Case-Studies," *Journal of Environmental Planning and Management* 44(2) (2001): 207–226.

15. Voluminous literatures on many of these mechanisms explore their strengths and weaknesses in much more detail than is possible here. As a starting point, on the referendum, see Ian Budge, *The New Challenge of Direct Democracy* (Cambridge: Polity, 1996); on citizen advisory panels, see Frances Lynn and G. Busenberg, "Citizen Advisory Committees and Environmental Policy: What We Know, What's Left to Discover," *Risk Analysis* 15(2) (1995): 147–162; on citizen juries, see Ned Crosby, "Citizen Juries: One Solution for Difficult Environmental Questions," in Renn, Webler, and Wiedemann, *Fairness and Competence in Citizen Participation,* 157–174; on mediation, see Walton Blackburn and William Bruce, eds., *Mediating Environmental Conflicts: Theory and Practice* (Westport, Conn.: Quorum, 1995); on environmental covenants, see Pieter Glasbergen, "Modern Environmental Agreements: A Policy Instrument Becomes a Management Strategy," *Journal of Environmental Planning and Management* 41(6) (1998): 693–707; and on regulatory negotiation, see Daniel Fiorino, "Regulatory Negotiation as a Form of Public Participation," in Renn, Webler, and Wiedemann, *Fairness and Competence in Citizen Participation,* 223–238.

16. For examples of practical experiences with the referendum, see Jane Mansbridge, *Beyond Adversary Democracy* (Chicago: University of Chicago Press, 1994); Jeffrey M. Berry, Kent E. Portney, and Ken Thomson, *The Rebirth of Urban Democracy* (Washington, D.C.: Brookings Institution Press, 1993).

17. Daniel Fiorino, "Environmental Policy and the Participation Gap," in William Lafferty and James Meadowcroft, eds., *Democracy and the Environment: Problems and Prospects,* 192–212 (Cheltenham, England: Edward Elgar, 1996).

18. There is a rapidly growing literature on practical experiences with deliberative processes. See, for example, Bruce Williams and Albert Matheny, *Democracy, Dialogue, and Environmental Disputes* (New Haven, Conn.: Yale University Press, 1995); Paul Seiman and Jane Parker, "Citizenship, Civicness, and Social Capital in Local Agenda 21," *Local Environment* 2(2) (1997): 171–187; and Michael Mason, "Participative Capacity Building in Environmental Policy: Fish Protection and Parks Management in British Columbia, Canada," *Policy Studies* 21 (2000): 79–98.

19. This distinction does not exactly coincide with the distinction between *elite* and *citizen* participation (Fiorino, "Environmental Policy and the Participation Gap") because elite processes are not necessarily group based. On the other hand, the group-based mechanisms discussed here are clearly elite processes.

20. An advisory or oversight body composed of prominent individuals with well-known links to established organizations is also neither a genuinely citizen-based nor a group-based mechanism. Those who deliberate and decide are not there as ordinary citizens (but rather as public personalities), nor do they actually represent the groups of which they are members.

21. James Meadowcroft, "The Politics of Sustainable Development: Emergent Arenas and the Challenge for Political Science," *International Political Science Review* 20 (1999): 219–237.

22. Peter Glasbergen, "Fallible Ecological Modernisation," unpublished working paper, Utrecht, 2002.

23. Peter Driessen and Peter Glasbergen, *Greening Society: The Paradigm Shift in Dutch Environmental Politics* (Dordrecht: Kluwer Academic Publishers, 2002).

24. Stephen Young, "The United Kingdom: From Political Containment to Integrated Thinking?" in Lafferty and Meadowcroft, eds., *Implementing Sustainable Development* 263–264.

25. For an interesting assessment of the deliberative democratic content of U.S. HCPs, see Craig Thomas, "Habitat Conservation Planning: Certainly Empowered, Somewhat Deliberative, Questionably Democratic," *Politics and Society* 29 (2001): 105–130.

26. Smith, "Institutional Design and Green Politics," p. 81.

27. For a discussion of interorganizational collaboration and the challenge of sustainable development, see James Meadowcroft, "Co-operative Management

Regimes: Collaborative Problem Solving to Implement Sustainable Development," *International Negotiation* 4(2) (1999): 225–254.

28. See Smith, "Institutional Design and Green Politics."

29. Michael Andersen and Duncan Liefferink, eds., *European Environmental Policy: The Pioneers* (Manchester: Manchester University Press, 1997).

30. Michael Sandel, *Democracy's Discontent* (Cambridge, Mass.: Harvard University Press, 1996).

6

Civic Environmentalism

DeWitt John

Civic environmentalism is the process of custom designing answers to local environmental problems.[1] It takes place when a critical mass of community leaders, local activists, and businesspersons work with frontline staff of federal and state agencies and perhaps with others to address local issues that they care about deeply. Civic environmentalism cannot succeed without some participation and support by government agencies, but it is essentially a bottom-up process that epitomizes reformers' aims to build a results-based sense of common purpose in environmental governance. And not unlike what the editors of this volume describe more generally, civic environmentalism in practice remains an effort to graft flexibility onto an otherwise inflexible regulatory whole.

In the 1970s, environmentalists rallied to the call to "think global, act local," but, for the most part, the system of environmental governance created by Congress in the 1970s was not civic. The statutes developed then dramatically centralized power in Washington and lodged authority in a maze of narrowly focused agencies and programs. Each had highly technical, nationwide regulations and complex bureaucratic procedures that impeded meaningful local problem solving, as Denise Scheberle explains in detail in chapter 10 in this volume. Rules do provide opportunities for public participation, but lawyers and technical experts for national environmental groups and their adversaries have been able to use these opportunities far more effectively than have ordinary citizens. As Michael Sandel explains, this disconnection between citizens and government is a systemwide problem in America's "procedural republic."[2]

Sometimes the feeling of loss of control or disconnection sparks backlash against environmentalism, as Charles Wise explains in his chapter on property rights. In other situations, citizens and activists demand environmental justice, seeing business and government in league to ignore environmental burdens on poor minority communities, as Evan Ringquist's chapter describes. In a growing number of communities of all kinds, however, grassroots leaders and professionals are finding civic ways to make decisions tailored to local conditions, overcoming bureaucratic fragmentation, and bringing democracy directly into policymaking. This civic impulse has resulted in a rising tide of watershed councils, river keepers, land trusts, voluntary monitoring programs, and plans for creating sustainable communities. The bottom line for the environment: an uncounted but promising number of conservation easements, restoration projects, investment funds, public-education efforts, and local regulatory changes that protect the environment while achieving other goals as well.[3]

Civic environmentalism is not the only way to reconnect citizens to environmental and natural resources (ENR) governance to help advance a results-based sense of common purpose. It is similar to comanagement of common-pool resources by local communities, where resource users overcome the tragedy of the commons by acting on their shared interest in subordinating narrow, short-term gains in order to stem pollution and overuse of those resources. As Edella Schlager explains in chapter 4, comanagement works best if users of a common-pool resource are in direct contact with each other. If not, "nested" decision-making processes must occur from the local level up to broader geographic areas, with requisite information, rules, and participation at each level. But far from being neatly nested, American federalism is shot through with political tensions, economic cleavages, and constitutional ambiguities. Moreover, many environmental problems cross boundaries. Mercury from coal-fired power plants drifts across oceans, and fertilizers from Iowa farms float down the Mississippi to create a "dead zone" in the Gulf of Mexico.

Thus, the concept of civic environmentalism is an attempt to explain when and how humanity can overcome fragmented institutions, limited information, and uncertain regulation to build a results-based sense of common purpose. It is also similar to the deliberative democracy James Meadowcroft advocates in chapter 5. Some agencies have experimented with the techniques that Meadowcroft describes—such as referenda, citizen juries, advisory panels, and covenants—and civic environmentalism often involves mediation. Unlike many of the models that Meadowcroft discusses, however, civic environmentalism is a decidedly *bottom-up* response to bureaucratic failure or gridlock, rather than an agency-led response to bureaucratic failure.[4]

This chapter argues that civic environmentalism has limits that one ignores at one's peril if relying on it alone to build a results-based sense of common purpose in environmental governance. It is a *supplement,* not a replacement for regulation. It does not work everywhere. Thus, although civic environmentalism will be an indispensable part of environmental governance in the twenty-first century, it cannot become the primary way of protecting environmental quality. To marshal evidence for this argument, this chapter addresses three questions. First, what are the theoretical underpinnings of civic environmentalism? Second, when does civic environmentalism work well? Finally, what are the strategic challenges, choices, and opportunities facing civic environmentalism as a tool for building common purpose in environmental governance in the future?

The chapter begins by placing civic environmentalism in the broader context of American political theory, as one of four competing models of governance. Each of the four is indispensable; the trick is how to deploy them simultaneously. Next, from case studies the chapter culls lessons about how civic environmentalism works and when it works best. The chapter concludes by examining the future of civic environmentalism as seen by conservatives, progressives, and the radical center, and it explains why the strengths afforded by each of the four models are needed for effectively building a results-based sense of common purpose in environmental governance.

The Theoretical Underpinnings of Civic Environmentalism: An Analytical Perspective

Civic environmentalism engages a wide spectrum of stakeholders in a place—a community, region, ecosystem, or state—in discussions about the full array of substantive issues in that place. Table 6.1 shows broadly how civic environmentalism differs from the fragmented system of nationwide federal programs and adds two other approaches to governance: comprehensive policies that operate nationally and narrow issues

Table 6.1
Four Approaches to Environmental Governance

	Substantive Focus	
Geographic Locus	Disparate, Symptom by Symptom	Systemic, Holistic
National	1. Interest-group governance/environmentalism: the backbone of environmental policy Regulatory statutes (Clean Air Act, Clean Water Act, etc.) Administrative Procedures Act Land management agencies (National Park Service, Forest Service, Fish and Wildlife Service, etc.) Federal grants or incentives Environment vs. economy National campaigns Lobbying, legislation Policy entrepreneurs Expert bureaucracies	2. Rational governance/environmentalism: the eyes of environmental policy Comprehensive planning National commissions (e.g., President's Council on Sustainable Development) National Environmental Policy Act Broad consensus Ringing declarations of purpose Far-seeing visionaries Theoreticians
Place by place, situation by situation	3. Populist governance/environmentalism: the conscience of environmental policy "Not-in-my-backyard" protests (Love Canal, etc.) Local cleanups and recycling Local land trusts Protests or local do-good projects Common law; class-action lawsuits Charismatic local leaders	4. Civic governance/environmentalism: the muscle of environmental policy Ecosystem restoration Sustainable communities Watershed protection Shared goals; implemented projects Contract law; site-specific legislation Shadow communities of experts Local "sparkplug" leaders High-placed sponsors

that are addressed locally. These four approaches represent different ways of understanding the world and taking action, each corresponding to a distinct tradition in American political thought.

Interest-Group Governance

Interest-group governance, as shown in the upper-left cell of table 6.1, is the "backbone" of environmental governance and the dominant tradition in American politics. Its intellectual father is James Madison, who saw politics as a struggle between different interests, each focused on its own advantage and its own conception of the common good. Madison favored the separation of powers at the federal level to ensure that no one interest group would dominate nationally, and he saw the federal government as a check on the tyranny of local elites. When Congress added the modern welfare state to the Madisonian structure and followed this addition by enacting the public-health, safety, and environmental statutes known as the "new social regulation" in the 1970s, the result was a fragmented array of agencies, statutes, regulatory systems, and grant programs.

For each public purpose—public health, workforce development, economic improvement, agricultural development, and the environment—there are dozens of loosely related programs. The U.S. Environmental Protection Agency (EPA), for example, has many separate programs for different forms of pollution: air, water, waste, and toxics. Each program takes its own approach to setting standards, regulating emissions, enforcing rules, and monitoring results. Federal natural-resource agencies are also fragmented spatially. Lands managed by the U.S. Forest Service, the Bureau of Land Management, the Fish and Wildlife Service, and the National Parks Service often lie side by side with each other and with private lands. But each agency has a different mission, procedures, and culture, which frustrate effective land management.[5] Fragmentation also reaches beyond the federal government to states and often to local governments, which have agencies organized along the same lines. Accompanying all these agencies are professional associations and advocacy groups that typically organize themselves on the same topical lines.

Running the programs, of course, are complex, functionally specialized ENR bureaucracies, staffed by professionals with expertise in history, lore, and substantive issues. In turn, their discretion is constrained by statutes, regulations, written guidance, and the rules of administrative law. In many cases, these regulations and rules define program operations in great detail. This area is the quadrant of categorical grants, command-and-control regulation, and unfunded mandates. The politics of these programs center in Washington, D.C., in a power game of eternal struggle among rival interests. The style of conflict varies: long-term ideological battles or holy wars between black-hat polluters and white-hat environmentalists, as well as less-visible logrolling—"I'll support your proposals if you support mine."[6]

Rational Governance

While interest-group governance is the backbone of our system, *rational governance* is its "eyes." Rational governance, as shown in the upper-right cell of table 6.1, is intellectually and politically more ambitious. It contains statutes and programs that frame issues broadly, considering the full gamut from specific threats to the environment, to economics, and on to social values. An effort to develop national policy for sustainability or pollution prevention (as depicted, for example, in the chapters by Robert Paehlke, Gary Bryner, and Ken Geiser) would fit neatly into this approach.

There is a lively political tradition in the United States for approaching public issues in this comprehensive way. One of its early exponents was Alexander Hamilton, our first secretary of the Treasury and a firm believer in a powerful federal government and a strong president. He created the federally supported Bank of the United States, which financed diverse investments in industries, infrastructure, and commerce, seeking to bind the young nation into a well-integrated national economy and thus ensure its independence. Madisonians detested the bank and refused to renew its charter. Today, many environmental scientists gravitate to the rational approach because ecology is about understanding the web of connections among disparate species, chemicals, and ecosystems. A comprehensive approach seems the only logical way to organize humanity's efforts to protect this web of life.

As described earlier, however, American politics is not a fertile soil for rational governance. The constitutional basis for holistic action is weak in our system of divided powers. In wartime, American politics is capable of dramatic, comprehensive, federally driven actions, but coherent domestic programs for sweeping change are less common and typically less successful. During the Great Depression of the 1930s, the federal government did experiment with centralized natural resource planning, and Congress created the powerful Tennessee Valley Authority to write and implement a comprehensive plan for economic, social, and resource development. But other regional authorities made little progress beyond planning. For the most part, the New Deal and the Great Society turned out as agglomerations of dozens of narrow Madisonian programs. President Reagan's later efforts to eliminate or rationalize these programs slowed their growth but failed to end or consolidate many of them.

Nevertheless, programs occupying the cell of rational governance make an important contribution to environmental governance by envisioning possibilities and tracking progress toward desirable futures. They typically stop, however, with fine-sounding, vague declarations of purpose, open-ended mandates to coordinate, and authorizations for planning and review, like those in the National Environmental Policy Act. In addition, they impose procedural requirements that push agencies to work out disagreements, but they also lead to lawsuits and delay. In Washington, rational governance takes the form of presidential commissions and high-sounding policy pronouncements with little follow-up. At the local level, this cell is the home for comprehensive land-use plans, which are amended regularly to accommodate proposals for new developments. Rational environmentalists, in short, see the future but lack the power to get us there.

Populist Governance

Populist governance, as shown in the lower-left cell of table 6.1, represents the "conscience" of the American political system. It reflects a rather narrow view of the scope of politics and governance. Populists distrust central authority and are motivated to action by specific threats or opportunities. They often are concerned about how some national powers—such as the federal government, Wall Street, or big corporations—are taking actions that cause serious local distress. This is the cell of "not-in-my-backyard" protests or, in its proactive form, of efforts to build a local park or to recycle, without worrying too much about underlying causes.

Common law is the channel that our legal system has provided to populists (and others) for challenging polluters and corporate miscreants.[7] In recent years, lawyers have pushed the borders of common law to bring class-action suits on behalf of injured parties against deep-pocket corporate polluters in tobacco, asbestos, and other industries. More often, however, populists who see the larger picture decide that "there ought to be a law," and they take their cause to Washington to establish new programs or regulations. Andrew Jackson in the 1830s, Rosa Parks in the 1960s, and Lois Gibbs since 1980 were populists who shifted operations from the populist cell into the cell of interest-group governance to shape national policies to address specific outrages. Gibbs, for instance, organized the protests against toxic wastes at Love Canal, which sparked the creation of the Superfund program. However, since moving to Washington, D.C., Gibbs also has kept her localist populism very much alive by helping activists in other communities organize protests against toxic-waste dumps. The Sierra Club and some other national environmental organizations also have active local chapters that operate according to populist governance, and its national office competes in national interest-group politics. Theda Skocpol calls these national groups "widespread federated interests."[8] Regardless of labels, however, populist uprisings long have provided much of the dynamism of American interest-group governance, serving as the conscience of environmental governance at home and abroad.

Civic Governance

Civic governance, as shown in the lower-right cell of table 6.1, is the "muscle" of the American political system. Jefferson is one of the patron saints of civic governance, with his philosophical preference for the egalitarian culture of rural communities. But Alexis de Tocqueville, a French nobleman who wrote *Democracy in America* based on his visits in the 1820s, is identified even more closely with civic governance. In his view, the key to American politics and society was Americans' readiness to organize themselves spontaneously and informally to tackle local problems. Tocqueville's intellectual descendents celebrate the modern version of locally organized, mutual self-help, community development, and social service.

In a system where interest-group governance is dominant, civic environmentalism involves reaching across the boundaries that fragment agencies and that divide the citizens and leaders of local communities. It is about custom designing both process and substance to fit local circumstances. Thus, not only does inherent tension exist between civic efforts and interest-group governance; if we took a snapshot of civic environmentalism in action, we would see that it differs in every case. Civic environmentalism is emergent behavior; that is, its substantive purpose, organizational form, and management tools depend on random local factors. Included among these are individual personalities, the sequence of events, details of local issues, the history of earlier efforts to address local problems, and peculiarities of local social and political institutions.

Although the structure and substance of civic environmentalism varies widely, underlying principles explain how it works. In brief, civic environmentalism generates local social capacity and mobilizes latent capacity; it attracts specific kinds of outside support; and it works through certain collaborative processes. Where this capacity and support are strong, and where participants follow the rules of collaborative problem solving, civic environmentalism can be effective in addressing many kinds of environmental problems. It provides the muscle to resolve local problems where it most matters—at the operational level.

What constitutes this muscle? For those of us used to thinking in terms of national problems and programs, the best way to grasp civic environmentalism is to watch it up close, or at least to read vivid case studies. A rich literature of case studies on civic environmentalism initiatives fortunately exists from which we can begin to understand both the movement's accomplishments and its limitations.[9] The next section of this chapter turns to that literature to describe how civic environmentalism works on the ground.

Civic Environmentalism: Lessons from the Grassroots

Consider the following vignettes:

When three freighters ran aground on coral reefs off the Florida Keys in December 1989, local residents rallied behind a proposal to create a National Marine Sanctuary to provide federal protection. Congress created the sanctuary and directed the National Oceanic and Atmospheric Administration (NOAA) to write a plan for managing the area and to create an advisory committee. National environmental groups had field staff in the area and, like NOAA, were eager to see a strong sanctuary that would take on a broad range of issues. When NOAA indicated it was prepared to shut some waters to commercial fishing and to regulate divers searching for sunken Spanish galleons filled with gold, local opposition developed. NOAA's planning team met in Maryland and wrote a draft plan that suggested that NOAA might even regulate commercial flights over the Keys and force the county to restrict land use to reduce polluted runoff. A crowd hanged the sanctuary manager in effigy. Then the advisory committee stepped forward. Encouraged by the sanctuary manager, who was a long-time local resident with friends in all camps, the council organized dozens of small meetings to listen to both sides. The council drafted extensive revisions for the final plan and regulations, and NOAA accepted the revisions. Members of the advisory committee then persuaded state officials to approve the plan, approval required because the sanctuary includes state waters. Most local fishermen now accept bans on fishing in some areas, including a spawning zone for a popular commercial species. Volunteers enforce sanctuary regulations as members of Team Ocean. They ride federal boats, hand out leaflets to violators, and ask for compliance.[10]

Noisy, smoggy freeways run through Fruitvale, a poor Latino neighborhood in Oakland, California. In 1991, the Bay Area Transit Authority (BART) proposed building a massive parking garage next to a transit station. Neighborhood protests killed the proposal, but then students at the nearby University of California in Berkeley suggested that the proposal be redesigned to beautify and revitalize Fruitvale. The university worked with neighborhood groups to develop a plan and organized a nonprofit entity to work with the city to obtain federal funding. The funds supported the first transit-oriented development in a poor neighborhood in the United States. The results: more transit use, less air pollution, more jobs in Fruitvale, new businesses and offices, affordable housing, and a safer, prettier neighborhood.[11]

After years of local disputes about logging on national forests near the small town of Quincy, California, someone shot through the window of a local environmentalist's office and others vandalized timber roads and equipment. The environmentalist, the manager of the local timber mill, and a county supervisor called an informal meeting in the library. It was neutral ground where they could talk quietly about how to protect the forests without shutting down logging, the biggest employer in town. They kept meeting, consulted with university experts, and two years later agreed on a plan. It proposed not only reduced logging in sensitive areas, but also the cutting of old stands susceptible to wildfire. Statewide and national environmental groups objected to any logging, however, and the Forest Service refused to implement a plan that it had not prepared. Despite this opposition, the Quincy Library Group won passage of a federal law that forced the Forest Service to approve the plan and begin implementing it. But then the Forest Service adopted another plan for all national forests in the state, allowing less logging. After nine years, the Quincy Library Group stopped its monthly meetings, saying that the statewide plan made it impossible to implement their local plan. Industry is fighting to overturn the statewide plan.[12]

Water flows slowly from central Florida through a large area of sugarcane farms, into a massive system of pumps and canals built by the U.S. Army Corps of Engineers and eventually through vast state-owned water retention areas and into Everglades National Park. As the water leaves the cane fields, it is contaminated by natural nutrients and fertilizers. A small group of frontline state and federal agency staff and professional environment advocates became increasingly concerned. In 1988, they helped a free-wheeling U.S. attorney from Miami, the equally independent superintendent of the park, and the superintendent of a national wildlife refuge prepare a lawsuit against the state of Florida for allowing polluted water to flow into the park. "This is like a cancer, and the cancer is spreading south," said the park superintendent. None of the three had informed their supervisors about the impending litigation, but because a presidential election campaign was in progress, federal agencies were unwilling to disavow the suit. The state of Florida and its regional water management district spent more than $6 million fighting the suit for two years. Then Lawton Chiles was elected governor, in part on the promise to settle the lawsuit. He was unable to do so until he went into federal court and told the judge that he wanted to "surrender. . . . I have brought my sword; I want to find out who I can give my sword to." Thus, he forced the process out of courtrooms and into the hands of agency scientists and environmentalists, including several who had helped design the lawsuit. They developed a plan satisfactory to the judge, but the sugar industry refused to sign off and continued litigation. When Bruce Babbitt became U.S. interior secretary, he agreed with Chiles to cosponsor the process and pressured the sugar industry to open another round of negotiations. This round included most of the same scientists, plus experts hired by the sugar industry. An outside mediator helped negotiate an agreement that industry endorsed and the state legislature and Congress approved. Wrought from the process was a signed commitment to spend $8 billion to restore flows to something like original patterns. Runoff from the cane fields is cleaner; implementation of the plan is beginning; and there is substantial cash in hand to increase the size of the park and protect other lands. However, pressures from local real estate developers and local governments have forced changes in the plan, which some environmentalists object to strongly.

These four stories illustrate the dynamics of civic environmentalism, ecosystem management, and collaborative natural resource management. In each case, there were and still are serious local economic and environmental problems—threats to coral reefs, smog, poverty, overharvesting, and unemployment—as in other communities throughout the nation. The usual tensions also exist between economic self-interest and environmental quality. In 2003, for example, sugar growers sponsored a bill in the Florida legislature to reset phosphorus standards for the Everglades at biologically unacceptable levels of 15 parts per billion and to postpone compliance deadlines by 20 years. The factors that set civic environmentalism apart from other ways of addressing environmental issues, however, are the distinctive way it mobilizes social capacity, builds collaborative processes, garners outside support, and gets its plans implemented. For the reader's convenience, table 6.2 summarizes these factors, their key components, and the key contextual variables.

Social Capacity: Shadow Communities, Core Groups, and Sparkplugs

Many analysts in recent years have commented on how influential nongovernmental public-purpose institutions, cultural norms of cooperation and public-spirited behavior, a web of interpersonal ties, and a history of effective local cooperation provide a context in which formal leaders can address public issues effectively.[13] In cases involving environmental issues, civic initiatives get off the ground when a network of frontline environmental professionals joins forces with business and community leaders, including a respected leader who invests his or her personal reputation in resolving a local environmental problem.

The leadership in each of the four stories told here came initially from a few individuals and then from a larger group of twenty to thirty people. In communities with many public and nonprofit organizations interested in the environment, there is often an informal network or "shadow community" of professionals who are interested in overlapping problems and who know each other personally. A civic process gets going when this shadow community develops a shared understanding of a complex local environmental (or social or economic or political) problem. This vision or purpose is broader than the mandates of individual agencies, the desires of interest groups, or the convictions about necessary changes. As the members of the shadow community come to understand their *shared* views, they jell into a core group of colleagues committed to setting things right.

Shadow communities and core groups include several kinds of people. Almost always, there are environmental professionals who have worked with each other for years. The best frontline staffers in agencies and

Table 6.2
Factors Affecting the Success of Civic Environmentalism Initiatives

Factors	Success is more likely when local civic environmentalism includes:	Success is more likely when external factors are favorable.
Social capacity	A "shadow community": a network of frontline professionals who share a common understanding of a local environmental problem A shadow community as a "core group": participants develop a shared vision that is broader than the mandates of individual agencies; local business and civic leaders who understand the problem and the vision join the core group and dedicate themselves to taking action Members of the core group with strong personal and professional commitments to the "place" Members of the core group with a high level of commitment to professional principles and to serving the public interest Many members of the core group who are smart, tough, and politically astute A highly respected, neutral "sparkplug" who steps forward to drive the process	Environmental professionals have worked with each other before and have won some victories. There is substantial public interest in the environmental problem and recognition of the need to do something. The environmental issue covers an area small enough (perhaps 100 square miles) so key leaders can drive to evening meetings. Some participants in the core group have strong personal ties to influential political officials. A local power elite exists that can help win support for the core group but is not so strong that it will try to exclude local environmentalists, minority groups, or others who might veto action. Other local collaborative, boundary-spanning efforts have been successful.

Table 6.2
(continued)

Factors	Success is more likely when local civic environmentalism includes:	Success is more likely when external factors are favorable.
Collaborative processes	A situation in crisis, where everyone may lose something important A process that starts with informal meetings among the shadow community of frontline agency staff plus local business and environmental leaders Group expansion to include representatives of potential veto points and marginalized groups Personal relationships that are established among the broader group Participants who enjoy the learning that comes with collaboration A focus of collaboration that begins with common goals rather than disagreements Group agreement on criteria for accepting proposals, then on proposals Core group members who stay in touch with peers and win their support	There is a tough regulatory environment so that regulated entities cannot hope to evade or postpone compliance. Participation in the core group will create opportunities for career advancement for frontline professionals. A professional mediator is available when needed. Funding is available for meetings, communications, professional mediation, and scientific studies to clarify key questions and explore "out-of-the box" ideas, but not so much money that participants want to keep the process going for its own sake.

Table 6.2
(continued)

Factors	Success is more likely when local civic environmentalism includes:	Success is more likely when external factors are favorable.
Outside support	Sponsors who protect frontline employees from middle managers and local environmentalists from their national peers Data about local environmental conditions Moderate levels of funds planning, research on local issues, and implementation	Sponsors have links to local leaders and take an interest in local affairs. Middle managers and agency staff are familiar with collaborative processes and will tolerate frontline independence. Funds are available for implementation of costly civic plans. Agencies and legislatures will earmark funds for projects. Data systems track local conditions accurately.
Implementation	Court consent decrees that legitimize agreement Legislators who pass site-specific statutes or earmark funds to implement agreements Quasi-public or nonprofit organizations that implement or monitor agreements Contracts that can be negotiated to give force of law to agreements	Sponsors remain present and supportive. Civic proposals turn out to be effective.

environmental groups have deep experience with local environmental problems and are committed personally and professionally to fixing them. In the Florida Keys, the decision by several national environmental groups to hire local field staff helped build this shadow community of frontline professionals.

Local business people are another element of the core group. These business people usually lack skills as environmental professionals, though they may have become familiar with environmental issues by serving on advisory boards and fighting earlier environmental battles. Their interest in environmental matters may arise from personal interests—for example, in fishing or other forms of recreation—or from an understanding that the future of the local economy depends on reconciling economic and environmental goals. The most effective business people within the core group may have personal ties to key politicians. For example, when the advisory committee in the Keys took the leading role in resolving the disputes about NOAA's plan, its chair was a former Wall Street broker who retired early to become a fishing guide for people such as former president George H. W. Bush. In the Everglades, a local real estate developer became a leading campaigner for ending sugar industry pollution.

Ordinary citizens and community leaders with no special environmental skills also can be key members of the core group. Indeed, at the center of many civic environmental enterprises is a person who represents no particular interest, is respected for integrity and intelligence, and is committed fully to making the process work. This person is the sparkplug that keeps participants fired up through long months of dialogue and negotiation. Participants alternatively sometimes hire a professional mediator who may win enough respect to become the neutral sparkplug. One of the participants who represents a particular agency or interest group occasionally may try to be the neutral sparkplug, but it is difficult to be fully neutral while also being a representative of a particular agency or interest group. Consequently, the sparkplug is often someone new to public life (a teacher, an owner of a small business, a housewife) or someone who has won respect as a general-purpose civic leader (perhaps a newspaper editor or highly respected, retired elected official).

The Collaborative Process

Civic environmentalism often begins in protest against gridlock or against actions by outside agencies that threaten local environmental and economic values. In the Keys, NOAA bungled a planning process and threatened to preempt local autonomy. In Fruitvale, California, BART bungled plans for the garage. In Quincy, there was bitter conflict about Forest Service plans, so local leaders created another process to try to resolve conflict. As the civic process gets organized and gains strength, the emphasis shifts from the crisis to the opportunity for a fresh start in addressing deeper problems. For example, in the Everglades, the issue broadened from polluted runoff from cane fields to the timing, volume, and direction of the flow of water through southern Florida. As the focus of civic environmentalism deepens, the participants gain a powerful self-confidence and sense of hope. As a member of the Applegate partnership (a group that stepped forward to resolve disputes about logging on federal lands in southwest Oregon) explained, "It was desperation and gridlock that brought us together, but it is trust and respect that keep us going."[14]

How does this trust build? The participants in a core group go through a collaborative process that has been described extensively in many books and articles. Indeed, as Rosemary O'Leary, Tina Nabatchi, and Lisa Bingham discuss in greater detail in chapter 9, the process has turned into a profession—that of environmental dispute mediation. This is not to say that a professional mediator must guide civic environmentalism at every step. Many environmental professionals have a working knowledge of how mediation works and can manage a collaborative process well enough, at least for a time, without professional guidance.

Collaborative processes ("getting to yes," as the title of a seminal book puts it)[15] are successful when people with different interests can set aside their current positions on a controversial issue, discover shared values and aspirations, find fresh ways of achieving shared goals, and agree on a strategy to implement this fresh approach. For example, in Fruitvale, neighborhood leaders and BART discovered that they could agree on the goals of enriching, beautifying, and improving access to the neighborhood, and they were able to develop a specific design and a funding strategy to build the facilities.

Turning a shadow community into a core group and then into an effective collaborative decision-making group involves several steps. The group can start by meeting informally. It must decide which interested parties need to be at the table. The rule of thumb is that any group that can veto implementation of an agreement should be represented, including poor people, minorities, tribes, and others who often are left out of decision making. Then the group has to recruit specific individuals to represent the interested parties. The bosses and peers of these individuals must agree, at least implicitly, that the individuals are their representatives.

Discussions usually start by sharing information about the issues and building good interpersonal relationships. Field trips often help. As the discussion gets going, it moves from making statements about what different parties want, to deciding underlying purposes and goals, and on to drafting shared goals. The process then moves on to identifying fresh ideas about how to achieve these goals and to criteria for deciding what specific proposals to make. When the group has agreed on a proposal, it may think its work is over, but this is never so. The really hard work is fleshing out the details, convincing people who did not participate directly in the negotiations, and getting formal approval and resources to implement the proposal. If the process works, the group often proposes the creation of a permanent partnership or a new nonprofit organization to manage or monitor implementation.

These processes take a great deal of time, usually more time than anyone except the professional mediator imagines. They require hard work by all participants, not just in expressing their views and defending their interests, but also in listening carefully to others' positions, assimilating extensive technical information, and struggling to find new words to express agreement. Many meetings often take place outside work hours. The transaction costs of collaboration can be very high. Although data are sketchy, there seem to be more examples of civic environmentalism with regard to comparatively small watersheds (small enough so the core group is within an hour's drive and can attend evening meetings), national forests (which are about the same size as such watersheds), and low-income neighborhoods. However, as Schlager describes in chapter 4, if different core groups are talking the same language and addressing similar issues, agencies may be able to help build a nested hierarchy of core groups, with participants in local groups working in parallel with their counterparts in a larger watershed or ecosystem. For example, in the Chesapeake Bay region, collaborative efforts in the Maryland portion of the bay's watershed are strengthened by and lend power to teams working at the levels of individual tributaries.

Why are people willing to invest so much of their energy and time in a collaborative process? Personal factors are important. In each of the four vignettes told earlier, the leaders of the core group were entrepreneurial, courageous people. Making the transition from "desperation and grid-lock" to "trust and respect" is not a job for the meek, the impatient, or the politically naive. Planning students in Oakland, the manager of the sanctuary, the chair of the sanctuary advisory committee, the U.S. attorney and park superintendent in the Everglades, and many in the shadow community not mentioned here took intelligent risks to make these processes work.

In addition to effective leaders, civic environmentalism also depends on perceptions about career advancement and professional satisfaction. Some of the motivations of practicing civic environmentalists have been hinted at already. At first, participation may flow easily out of the day-to-day contact among the members of the shadow community and their shared professional commitment to doing things right. Many participants enjoy the learning that comes with collaboration. As action nears, some participants may see opportunities to advance their careers. If the collaborative process focuses on hot political issues, politicians and top agency officials may pay attention, and the participants may get to know them personally. If the process succeeds, the participants may become local heroes. For example, in the Everglades case, the park superintendent who helped file the suit against the state of Florida went on to run Yosemite National Park and then Yellowstone National Park before becoming head of a large foundation. Another key Park Service staffer quit the agency but came back to a top position in its headquarters.

But often something deeper is at work. Focusing one's work on protecting environmental values in a particular place can help meet a fundamental human need for meaning. Many participants have a deep affection for the place where they live and work. They may find deep personal satisfaction in focusing on this place, trying to understand how it works and how the community functions in relationship to the physical environment, and finding practical ways to nurture and heal both the place and the human community. Indeed, at its best, the spirit of civic environmentalism is not a concern about local insults to the environment or national outrages, but a deep, shared commitment to a physical place and to the community of people who live there. This commitment provides participants a sense of shared spiritual direction.

Be clear, however. The spirit of civic environmentalism may sustain the participants, but it does not resolve local conflicts. Proponents of civic action sometimes lapse into a vague optimism that affection for a place will melt away differences if everyone will just join hands and sing "Kumbaya." This optimism is enough to make partisans of rational governance, Madisonians, and populists jump up in righteous protest. Furthermore, as both populists and Madisonians would argue, there is a whiff of elitism in civic environmentalism—perhaps even a dark side. They might ask, "Isn't there something undemocratic about a 'shadow community' of experts meeting informally in the evening and on field trips? What is their authority to decide how to balance economic and environmental interests? Can even well-motivated shadow communities stand up to pressures from powerful local businesses or even from ideological anti-environmentalists? Might citizens be overwhelmed by the high-priced technical consultants that the business can bring to bear on the issue?"

These questions *are* realistic concerns. Letting self-designated people in a place make decisions can lead to ignoring the interests and values of those who live elsewhere or are excluded from the process for other reasons—hence, the need for ensuring inclusivity of representation noted earlier. However, the chances that local business interests will dominate civic environmentalism are less now than they were thirty years ago. "Power elites" in many cities and towns are smaller, less cohesive, and less concerned about local issues than they were thirty years ago. Deregulation, the rise of regional banks, and the centralization of information and power in corporations have eliminated many local bigwigs. Often the top executive in town is a midlevel manager who stays for only a few years before moving on. It is therefore easier today for agency officials, citizens, local environmentalists, and others to have a voice in local debates and decisions.

Outside Support: Backbones, Information, Cash, and Sponsors

Tough outside regulators can provide powerful support to local civic processes. If regulators are not tough, polluters will have less reason to sit down with citizens and frontline agency staff to work out local problems. It is true that rigid outside regulation is often the target of the dissatisfaction that galvanizes a local civic process. Yet without this target, civic energies may lie dormant.

Information and financial support are also critically important to civic environmentalism. Scientific studies may help bring a shadow community together if they reveal unexpected local problems or interactions among species or pollutants that fragmented regulations and programs do not address. As core groups develop agendas for action, they often need expensive research studies and new kinds of data to assess the severity of local problems and to measure progress in implementing a custom-designed response.

The collaborative process itself is also a costly activity. Evening meetings, field trips, and professional mediators do not come cheap and are not affordable within many agency budgets. What is more, civic environmentalism almost always leads to expensive proposals. Civic leaders inevitably have to look to the federal government for a deep pocket. For example, half of the funds for the Everglades restoration and at least half of the funds for Everglades planning came from federal agencies. Likewise, much of the money in Fruitvale, and all of the funds for the Florida Keys and for implementation of the Quincy Library Project's plan, came from federal agencies, with Congress earmarking appropriations for the Keys, Quincy, and the Everglades.

As such, an outside sponsor is just as important as backbones, information, and cash in civic environmentalism. The sponsor is usually an elected official or a top agency manager. Moreover, state legislatures on a very few occasions have explicitly authorized civic efforts to resolve local ENR disputes.[16] The sponsor has two roles. One is to help obtain funding and information to support the collaborative process and to implement the settlement. The second is to protect frontline government employees from conflicts with middle managers in their agencies and sometimes to protect local environmentalists from their national peers.

Such protection is essential. The first responsibilities of frontline agency staff are to pursue the mission, uphold the authority, and implement the programs of their agency. The first responsibility of an environmental advocate is to advocate. Civic processes usually challenge established advocacy positions and ways of doing business, however, so civic environmentalists who get too far out of line with their employer may risk their jobs and reputations. As civic debate gets down to the details, the members of the core group come under strong pressures from their organizations' middle managers and from lawyers who are worried about setting precedents. Frontline agency staff must find a path that transcends their job descriptions, taking as their guiding star an understanding of how their agency's mission fits into a larger vision of the public good. An elected official or top agency official is in a better position to understand this broad perspective and may provide some level of protection to the frontline worker.

For example, Governor Chiles's intervention allowed the shadow community to design the settlement of the Everglades lawsuit. Later on, both Chiles and Interior Secretary Babbitt provided critical support to the core group by forcing state agencies and the sugar industry into negotiations. In contrast, the Quincy Library Group tried to operate without either a reliable outside sponsor or a neutral sparkplug. There is no impartial published account of the inner dynamics of the group, but press reports suggest that the three leaders who called the first meeting were themselves the sparkplugs. When the local Forest Service office rejected the group's plan, the group asked the new chief of the Forest Service to impose it. The chief initially ordered that the plan be adopted, but for whatever reason his staff failed to go along. The group then approached the two senators and other members of Congress from California. They forced the Forest Service to accept the plan but were too preoccupied with other issues to be effective day-to-day sponsors. State and national environmentalists were particularly unhappy with the role that the local environmentalists played. The Congressmen were pushing for a bigger prize—more aggressive reductions in logging on all Forest Service lands. Lacking a neutral sparkplug and a sponsor, the Quincy Library Group ultimately lacked staying power.

Implementing the Results of Collaboration

As events in Quincy show, the work is not over when local collaborative processes result in plans for action. Civic environmentalists must next go back to the fragmented, federally driven system to get the authority and resources for implementation. Agencies can and sometimes will implement the plan. However, because the purpose of local collaboration is often to "think outside the box," civic plans often require agencies to behave differently and to spend more. For example, the core group in the Everglades followed the logic of science to raise an issue that was not part of the original lawsuit—the size and timing of flows into the park. Their plan ended up costing billions.

Local collaborators sometimes ask Congress or a state legislature to appropriate funds or pass a site-specific statute to implement an agreement. Or, if the civic process came as an effort to short-circuit litigation, the sponsor may ask a court to write the plan into a legal settlement. Local participants alternatively might ask agencies and relevant businesses to enter into a contract to give the force of law to the substantive and procedural agreements that they negotiate. Indeed, contracts are being used more often today to solidify agreements that go beyond the - requirements of law. For example, several corporations seeking public support and regulatory flexibility have written contracts with agencies, environmental groups, communities, or other organizations. In these contracts, they promise to adopt environmental management practices that go "beyond compliance" to a higher level of protection than statutes and regulations require.[17] This approach can be used in civic environmentalism as well.

When civic environmentalists ask for a site-specific statute, appropriation, or contract, they put agencies in a difficult position. The agencies may have the authority and willingness to adopt the civic recommendations nationwide (for example, to fund similar recommendations, rewrite regulations, and follow similar procedures across the country). But if the agency decides to apply the recommendations locally only, not nationally, the result of civic environmentalism is essentially a more complex and more fragmented governmental system. It is unlikely that anyone—civic environmentalists, agency staff, or sponsors—has this result in mind.

For this reason, civic environmentalists may have difficulty getting their recommendations to stick when sponsors, sparkplugs, and key members of the core group move on. Jim Webb—a Wilderness Society attorney who was the strategist behind the Everglades lawsuit, the settlement, and the alliance between Babbitt and Chiles—fretted until the end of his days about this problem. He hoped to institutionalize the alliances that supported restoration of the Everglades, perhaps by creating some kind of nonprofit foundation or research organization that would outlast Chiles and Babbitt. Chiles created the Governor's Committee for a Sustainable South Florida, and Babbitt created a federal interagency working group on the Everglades restoration. Their successors, however, disbanded both, leaving the Army Corps of Engineers and a regional water management agency in southern Florida to manage the restoration. Critics argue that the Corps and the regional agency have modified the program to use costly and risky new engineering techniques that provide water to sprawling new real estate developments rather than to the Everglades.[18]

The Future of Civic Environmentalism: Challenges, Choices, and Opportunities

What, then, is the future of civic environmentalism? Will it inevitably remain an interesting and positive part of the picture of building a results-based sense of common purpose in environmental governance, but only at the margins? As civic efforts to address environmental issues spread in the 1990s, the federal government took notice. Officials recognized the shortcomings of the fragmentation, grew frustrated by gridlock in Washington, became intrigued by the concept of ecosystem management, and watched enviously as frontline staff became involved in collaborative processes. Eager to respond to influential "sponsors" who were frustrated with the local workings of federal programs, many officials inside the EPA, the Forest Service, and other agencies looked for ways to embrace civic environmentalism as a more effective way of doing business. President Clinton's Council on Sustainable Development blessed these efforts by endorsing "civic engagement" and "sustainable communities." The latter were to be achieved by agency efforts that "[would foster] collaboration in problem solving and planning among companies, agencies, and citizens to achieve mutually beneficial results."[19]

The EPA's Chesapeake Bay Program, Great Lakes Program, and National Estuary Program—all launched in the 1980s—were the earliest and best known of the federal efforts to tap civic energies. They are financed mostly by the EPA (often with earmarked appropriations), but they give a central role to state governments. Moreover, they have had some success in engaging frontline staff, local officials, citizens, and diverse interests in ways that break through gridlock and overcome fragmentation. The Chesapeake Bay Program built impressive political momentum, public support, and norms of cooperation that have enabled it to survive political shifts in states and local areas.[20] Water quality has improved significantly in the bay, and some fisheries have rebounded—in part because of traditional federal regulations and subsidies, but in part also because of new measures fostered by the program. The National Estuary and Great Lakes Programs also have had their successes. For example, the Tampa Bay estuary project negotiated an interlocal agreement to restore thousands of acres of wetlands.[21]

Yet other efforts have been more disappointing, wherein months of talk with little agreement embittered people and made working relationships worse.[22] One despondent participant in such an effort reported, "Sometimes I think I spent five years of my life on that thing and all we got was a little more support for what we were all going to do anyway. . . . Other days, I think working it did help by creating dialogues between people who weren't on speaking terms and helping them communicate on important issues later."[23] This effort sounds like a partial success in nurturing a shadow community, but other ingredients of civic environmentalism—a sparkplug, an effective collaborative process, and meaningful outside support—were apparently missing.

By the same token, some federal efforts to encourage civic approaches clearly have failed. The EPA disbanded its Office of Community-Based Environmental Protection, moving many of its staff to the Office of Water, which long has encouraged collaborative watershed efforts. In June 2001, the Office of Water reported that "not all watershed protection and restoration efforts are effective. Watershed stakeholders often do not fully implement solutions. . . . Partnerships can break down, priorities can change, and funding can cease."[24]

Nevertheless, civic efforts are still widespread, and many federal officials are still trying to figure out how to work with them. The strategic question for reformers is how to reconcile civic environmentalism with interest-group governance, which seems likely to continue as the dominant style of governance in the United States for years to come. Writers on civic environmentalism fall into three schools of thought—right, left, and centrist—each with very different answers to the strategic question. As a result, the future of civic environmentalism depends not only on variations in the political climate, but also on how proponents resolve a variety of unresolved strategic challenges, choices, and opportunities facing them in the twenty-first century.

The Conservative Perspective on Civic Environmentalism

Skeptical of federal regulation, many conservatives find civic environmentalism appealing. Steven Hayward of the Pacific Research Institute writes that

The next wave of environmental improvement is going to take place on the local level through actions stemming from a sense of civic responsibility, in much the same manner as we have come to think about our obligations and opportunities to fight crime and improve our local schools. This won't be much fun for the crisis-mongers in Washington, but the environment will be the winner.[25]

Some conservatives seem to see civic environmentalism as a way around the need for governmental regulation. For example, the National Environmental Policy Institute, a small Washington nonprofit led by a former Republican member of Congress, favors a civic environmentalism act to "begin the privatization of decisions regarding environmental problems." It would begin shifting money away from "punitive" enforcement toward support for technical assistance to "help local farmers and business owners reduce environmental impacts."[26] This certainly sounds like a reduction in the level of environmental protection rather than a better way to improve it.

However, other conservative environmentalists recognize the need for a continuing regulatory regime. Lynn Scarlett, who led the libertarian Reason Public Policy Institute before becoming assistant secretary for policy, management, and budget in the Interior Department, calls for a "new environmentalism" where citizens will "have the incentives and ability to act as private stewards for the environment. While punishment is necessary for those who callously flout environmental law, a balance should be struck between punishment and incentives that encourage environmental innovation."[27]

Meanwhile, free-market environmentalists see private ownership of natural resources as the best way of coping with the tragedy of the commons. Where some kind of government action is necessary, they look to local communities rather than to the federal government. Terry Anderson and Donald Leal, for example, cite Elinor Ostrom's work (as Schlager discusses thoroughly in chapter 4) with approval in touting their brand of "market environmentalism." They encourage local communities to purchase control over natural resources (for example, game parks in Africa) or to obtain the authority to regulate themselves.[28]

As noted earlier, however, private ownership and community self-regulation do not work under all circumstances. They work most easily for resources that are valuable, measurable, and concentrated. Trading systems for emissions and for the rights to harvest resources also can make rights-based governance work in larger areas. In large, complex ecosystems and when there is pervasive uncertainty, however, some governmental authority must set the rules, help gather data, and decide if the results constitute an adequate level of protection overall and for particular places and subgroups.

Conservatives, therefore, do provide part of the answer. Community ownership will turn some decisions over to civic environmentalists, and trading systems will make the fragmented regulatory system more efficient and flexible. But the conservatives have not laid out a detailed roadmap for how civic processes will fit into local, state, and federal structures. It will be revealing to see how far conservatives will go to replace federally driven ENR governance with market forces and community ownership, and when they will use civic environmentalism simply as a reason to reduce regulatory protection of the environment.

Regardless of how these issues are sorted out in the future, the conservative vision of civic environmentalism faces another formidable set of challenges. It presently fails both to lay out a coherent and concrete program for incorporating the rational environmentalism that serves as the eyes of environmental governance and to establish strategies for coping with the interest-group environmentalism that is its backbone. By not confronting these types of governance challenges, and showing how their approach will cope with them, conservatives avoid strategic challenges and choices that risk marginalizing their movement in both the long run and the short run in the United States.

Civic Environmentalism, the Left, and the Politics of Conscience

To the left of the political spectrum, William Shutkin, Carmen Sirianni, and Lewis Friedland use the term *civic environmentalism* to describe how citizens can take power into their own hands to improve the places where they live. Shutkin sees environmental quality as one dimension of social justice—in particular, as a good way to organize citizens because "the physical and emotional space we inhabit . . . inspires civic action."[29] He celebrates residents of poor inner-city neighborhoods who defend their neighborhoods from pollution, create economic opportunity, and ensure environmental justice. He also emphasizes how citizens and locally controlled nonprofits, such as foundation-funded community development corporations, can drive social change. His book *The Land That Could Be* is an eloquent appeal to environmentalists, foundations, and liberals that environmentalism should evolve "from an essentially elitist movement accompanied by a complex systems of laws and policies . . . to a more democratic call for healthy, sustainable communities across geographic, economic and cultural lines."[30] But it contains few recommendations for states or federal agencies.

Sirianni and Friedland are concerned more about civic engagement than about social justice. They admire efforts to improve environmental conditions in poor neighborhoods for the same reasons as Shutkin—in particular because such efforts can "catalyze a range of civic innovations."[31] But they are not enthusiastic about the environmental justice movement, saying that focusing narrowly on toxic pollution has "limited and distorted civic capacity building." Or, one might say, they see the environmental justice community as narrow-minded populists stuck firmly in the lower-left cell of table 6.1.

Sirianni and Friedland care most about "civic renewal": providing more direct involvement in democracy, building new institutions to mobilize and direct citizen involvement, and restoring a sense of optimism that democracy can cope with serious problems. They feel that fragmentation and rigidity are problems not just for environmental governance, but also for most social issues. They consequently support a national movement for civic renewal, currently led by three nonprofit organizations: the National Civic League, the Kettering Foundation, and the Center for Democracy and Citizenship at the University of Minnesota.

Despite their differences, these liberal proponents of civic environmentalism see the driving force for civic environmentalism as being outside government: in communities, foundations, and nonprofit organizations. They say little, however, about how to reconcile these civic efforts with the imperatives of interest-group governance. Thus, their "politics of conscience" brings readily to mind a set of strategic challenges and choices that they have not yet resolved. Most significant, liberal proponents tend to give short shrift to the contributions made to environmental governance by the rational and interest-group models of environmental governance. Their politics lacks an explanation of how their version of civic environmentalism will compensate for or engage strategically these essential components of building a results-based sense of common purpose in environmental governance in the future.

Civic Environmentalism and the Radical Center

Among proponents of civic environmentalism, those in the radical center have more faith in traditional regulation than do conservatives or liberals, as well as more interest in how to reconcile interest-group governance with civic environmentalism. They insist that traditional regulation is still important, but they ask for dramatic change in federal statutes and operations to accommodate the civic impulse. For example, Marc Landy, Megan Sussman, and Debra Knopman, writing for the Progressive Policy Institute (an affiliate of the Democratic Leadership Council), endorse civic environmentalism as "a cornerstone of a second generation of environmental leadership" that "strikes a new balance between national standards and local solutions."[32] They want strong federal regulation and enforcement; "regulatory agencies must not shed enforcement responsibilities."[33]

Although these analysts believe that "civic environmentalism is quintessentially a local activity,"[34] they believe that agencies can nurture it by providing financial and technical assistance to local efforts. Agencies also should create "regional ombudsmen to provide one-stop shopping for regulatory guidance." Knopman and Landy would have EPA regional offices reorganize to focus on states and other high-priority places, rather than around air, water, and waste media programs. And they applaud interagency, intergovernmental planning that leads to new formal mechanisms to implement jointly designed programs of environmental restoration.[35]

The scrupulously nonpartisan National Academy of Public Administration (NAPA) has laid out a similar agenda in more detail.[36] It argues that the current system is "broken"; it fails to take full advantage of the technical capabilities and moral support that states, communities, the public, and some elements of the business community can lend to environmental protection. To engage these forces in environmental governance and to give them more flexibility in setting goals and deciding how best to meet them, NAPA has proposed shifting the EPA's emphasis from process (permits, inspections, fines, hearings, paperwork) to environmental results. To ensure accountability, the EPA would invest heavily in gathering and making public extensive data and analysis about environmental conditions. NAPA also calls for the EPA to begin reorganizing to reduce its internal fragmentation and for Congress to write a crosscutting statutory mission for the agency. Congress also would explicitly authorize emission trading systems and encourage negotiations between the EPA and states about how to custom design local processes to set goals, develop strategies, and implement plans.

In short, the radical centrists propose to continue interest-group ENR governance but to moderate its excesses by reducing fragmentation, refocusing rules from process to results, and allowing more state flexibility in designing low-level processes for setting goals and making plans. Nevertheless, a fundamental tension remains between civic environmentalism and interest-group environmental governance, with three important dimensions: agency structure, consistency, and the role of technical expertise. Civic environmentalism defines issues in ways that cut across fragmented interest-group governance and break out of programmatic categories. To be successful, civic initiatives also must be custom de-signed, whereas interest-group governance stresses consistency and equity, especially in legal and procedural matters. Further frustrating communication, the environmental agencies of traditional interest-group governance are staffed, in the finest traditions of rational environmental-ism, by experts in science, engineering, and law, and they use the languages of these professions to frame and make decisions. Finally, the radical center is, of necessity, in the business of making trade-offs with corporate interests, trade-offs that populist environmentalists find unac-ceptable. Finding, choosing, and faithfully implementing ways to address these challenges to building a results-based sense of common purpose will be important components of success in the years ahead.

Toward Synergy? Reconciling Civic and Interest-Group Governance

Although these conceptual challenges and choices are real and notewor-thy, the overall fate of civic environmentalism may depend less on them than on the continued failure of the present system. If leaders in Washington do not choose to mobilize themselves to update the prescrip-tive and excessively fragmented first-generation regulatory regime established in the 1970s and 1980s, civic environmentalism is likely to spread as a stronger, more disruptive, but usually more positive alterna-tive for environmental governance. It may even become a check on the Madisonian state.

For example, when local ENR crises and conditions are right, civic outbreaks are likely to continue to occur. But because civic environmen-talism runs against the grain of environmental law, transaction costs will remain high, and civic energies may flag after a while. There will be breakthroughs, some additional flexibility and improvements in environ-mental conditions, and perhaps some erosion. Yet when the fragmented first-generation system yet again fails to deliver on some hot new issue, another new shadow community, sparkplug, or sponsor is likely to emerge (under the right conditions), and the cycle will start again. More-over, as more civic efforts win victories (no matter how transient), the habit of turning to them for redress may grow. Should these initial efforts be successful, they may set the stage for ever more successful applications in the future. One of the most common findings of research about civic efforts is that as communities take successful action, they build the capacity for future efforts.

To the extent that local civic environmentalist leaders and radical centrists can persuade Congress and agencies to abandon out-of-date structures and focus on results, they will find it easier to custom design local strategies. Moreover, to the extent that market mechanisms and local management are workable, as conservatives argue, policymakers can choose to make federal rules simpler and more flexible. And to the extent that liberal civic environmentalists choose to persuade activists and foundations to participate in civic efforts, these local efforts will advance social justice and make democracy more open and vibrant. Paradoxically, however, repairing and updating interest-group environmentalism also may make it less necessary to organize civic efforts.

In short, the best way to reconcile interest-group environmentalism with civic environmentalism in order to build a results-based sense of common purpose is to update traditional laws and structures. To the extent that civic environmentalism turns out to prompt such a response, it may serve more as a driver for **reform** of interest-group environmentalism than as an impetus for local successes. However, governance in the United States probably always will be centered on interest-group governance. Thus, we always will experience some degree of frustration with fragmented, one-size-fits-all rules and procedures. Consequently, frontline professionals, civic leaders, and state and local governments always will push to custom design responses to local environmental problems.

In the long run, however, neither civic environmentalism nor interest-group environmentalism can or should become *the* primary way of protecting environmental quality. Effective policy requires that the eyes, conscience, muscle, and backbone of environmental governance—that is, all four of its models—work synergistically to advance the public interest. Each represents a very different way of dealing with the world, and each makes substantial contributions that environmental governance can ill afford to lose. Interest-group environmentalism—currently the backbone of environmental policy in the American political system—has provided the structure for American politics and political representation since the beginning. It will, and probably should, do so for environmental policy in the future. Rational environmentalism, as the eyes of environmental policy, provides the vision of where environmental policy might go next. Populist environmentalism, in turn, is the conscience that makes us aware of shortcomings and motivates us to act. Finally, civic environmentalism is the muscle. It provides the heft to address the environmental problems of the future, which are more complex than simply forcing others to stop polluting, and which require everyone to rethink how they live and produce goods and services. As environmental governance becomes mature, public administrators surely can, and must, learn to operate effectively according to each of these four models for any hope of a results-based sense of common purpose to materialize.

Notes

1. DeWitt John, *Civic Environmentalism: Alternatives to Regulation in States and Communities* (Washington, D.C.: CQ, 1994).

2. Michael J. Sandel, *Democracy's Discontent: America in Search of a Public Philosophy* (Cambridge, Mass.: Belknap, Harvard University Press, 1996).

3. See, for example, Natural Resources Law Center, *The New Watershed Source Book: A Directory and Review of Watershed Initiatives in the Western United States* (Boulder: University of Colorado, 2000); William A. Shutkin, *The Land That Could Be: Environmentalism and Democracy in the Twenty-First Century* (Cambridge, Mass.: MIT Press, 2000); Julia M. Wondoleck and Steven L. Yaffee, *Making Collaboration Work: Lessons from Innovation in Natural Resource Management* (Washington, D.C.: Island, 2000); Carmen Sirianni and Lewis Friedland, *Civic Innovation in America* (Berkeley: University of California Press, 2001); Philip Brick, Donald Snow, and Van de Wetering, *Across the Great Divide: Explorations in Collaborative Conservation in the American West* (Washington, D.C.: Island, 2001); John, *Civic Environmentalism*.

4. Meadowcroft (in chapter 5) sees deliberation as a style that governments should use to elevate debate and enrich democracy at all levels. Thus, deliberative democracy can work within national political institutions such as Congress or in forums where designated representatives of national interest groups meet with officials for reasoned discussions of policy. It is also suitable for what he calls the "meso-level," where frontline staff meet with local civic leaders.

5. Robert F. Durant, *The Administrative Presidency Revisited: Public Lands, the BLM, and the Reagan Revolution* (Albany: State University of New York Press, 1992).

6. A voluminous literature debates the strengths and shortcomings of interest-group governance. This type of governance has been the primary vehicle for protecting the environment, as described in the opening section of this chapter, but the price has been a disconnect between citizens and their government, as well as

policies and programs that are fragmented and difficult to modernize. For an overview of the pros and cons of interest-group influence in policymaking in general, see Ronald J. Hrebenar, *Interest Group Politics in America*, 3rd ed. (Armonk, N.Y.: M. E. Sharpe, 1997). For a somewhat different view, see Jeffrey M. Berry, *The New Liberalism: The Rising Power of Citizen Groups* (Washington, D.C., Brookings Institute Press, 1999). Berry argues that interest-group liberalism has been transformed by the rise of a new kind of interest group. The latter type of group focuses on postmaterialist, quality-of-life values such as environmental quality rather than on economics and equality. His "citizen groups" are professionally staffed organizations based in Washington, D.C., and focused on federal legislation, regulation, and policy. He argues that these groups exert great influence at the federal level and that liberal groups were far more influential than conservative groups, at least through the early 1990s. Civic environmentalism is the local face of postmaterialism—the face that tries to apply value orientations to specific places and cases. It seeks to balance environmental and economic values and does a better job of this than fragmented federal policies. For a thought-provoking analysis of the state of interest-group theory and how best to advance it, see Frank Baumgartner and Beth Leech, *Interest Groups* (Princeton, N.J.: Princeton University Press, 2000).

7. Some conservatives argue that common law operated efficiently to control pollution.

8. Theda Skocpol, *Protecting Soldiers and Mothers* (Cambridge Mass.: Harvard University Press, 1992), especially pp. 54–57.

9. See, for example, John, *Civic Environmentalism*; Wondoleck and Yaffee, *Making Collaboration Work*; Sirianni and Friedland, *Civic Innovation in America*; Shutkin, *The Land That Could Be*; Natural Resources Law Center, *The New Watershed Source Book*.

10. DeWitt John, *Protecting Our National Marine Sanctuaries* (Washington, D.C.: National Academy of Public Administration, 1999), pp. 25–26, 72–79. Available as a .pdf file at www.napawash.org.

11. Shutkin, *The Land That Could Be*, pp. 167–187.

12. Jon Margolis, "How a Foe Saved Quincy Library Group's Bacon," *High Country News*, September 29, 1997, http://www.hcn.org; Ed Marston, "The Timber Wars Evolve into a Divisive Attempt at Peace," *High Country News*, September 29, 1997, http://www.hcn.org; Jane Braxton Little, "A Quiet Victory in Quincy," *High Country News*, November 9, 1998, http://www.hcn.org; Wondoleck and Yaffee, *Making Collaboration Work*, pp. 71–73; "Quincy Library Group Bars Outsiders," *High Country News*, April 26, 1999, http://www.hcn.org; "Frustrated, Quincy Forest Coalition to Regroup," *Sacramento Bee*, November 28, 2001, p. B3; "Quincy Group to Redirect Efforts," *Sacramento Bee*, November 28, 2001, p. B1.

13. See, for example, Robert Putnam, *Bowling Alone: The Collapse and Revival of American Community* (New York: Simon and Schuster, 2000); Skocpol, *Protecting Soldiers and Mothers*; Sandel, *Democracy's Discontent*.

14. Quoted in Wondoleck and Yaffee, *Making Collaboration Work*, p. 9.

15. Roger Fisher and William Ury, *Getting to Yes* (New York: Penguin, 1991).

16. The only example I am familiar with is an act by the Montana legislature that suspended certain provisions of state water law for two years to allow a collaborative effort funded by the Ford Foundation to resolve disputes in the Upper Clark Fork Valley. See National Academy of Public Administration (NAPA), *Resolving the Paradox of Environmental Protection: An Agenda for Congress, EPA, and the States* (Washington, D.C.: NAPA, 1997), pp. 107–126.

17. Eric W. Orts and Kurt R. Deketelaere, eds., *Environmental Contracts: Comparative Approaches to Regulatory Innovation in the United States and Europe* (The Hague, Netherlands: Kluwer Law International, 2000).

18. Michael Grunwald, "A Rescue Plan, Bold and Uncertain," *Washington Post*, June 23, 2002, p. A1.

19. President's Council on Sustainable Development, *Towards a Sustainable America: Advancing Prosperity, Opportunity, and an Healthy Environment for the 21st Century* (Washington, D.C.: Government Printing Office, May 1999), p. 77.

20. Jon Cannon, "Choices and Institutions in Watershed Management," *William and Mary Environmental Law and Policy Review* 25(2) (winter 2000): 379–428.

21. Mark T. Imperial and Timothy Hennessey, "Environmental Governance in Watersheds: The Importance of Collaboration to Institutional Performance," in *environment.gov: Transforming Environmental Protection for the 21st Century*, NAPA, vol. 2 (Washington, D.C.: NAPA, 2000), pp. 8, 42–43.

22. Ibid., pp. 8, 34–38.

23. Quoted in DeWitt John and Marian Mlay, "Community-Based Environmental Protection: How Federal and State Agencies Can Encourage Civic Environmentalism," in Ken Sexton, Alfred A. Marcus, K. William Easter, and Timothy Burkhardt, eds., *Better Environmental Decisions: Strategies for Governments, Businesses, and Communities* (Washington, D.C.: Island, 1998), p. 363.

24. U.S. EPA Office of Water, *Protecting and Restoring America's Watersheds: Status, Trends, and Initiatives in Watershed Management* (Washington, D.C.: EPA, June 2001), p. 4, also available at http://www.epa.gov/owow/protecting.

25. Steven Hayward, "Think Globally, Act Locally—Rightly Understood," *Capital Ideas: Intellectual Capital from the Nation's Capital* 6(11) (March 23, 2001), http://www.pacificresearch.org/pub/cap/2001/01-03-23.html.

26. National Environmental Policy Institute, "Civic Environmentalism" (2000). (No longer on the Web at www.nepi.org.)

27. Lynn Scarlett, "New Environmentalism," National Center for Policy Analysis, Dallas, Texas, n.d., www.ncpa.org/studies/s201/s201h.html.

28. Terry L. Anderson and Donald R. Leal, *Free Market Environmentalism*, rev. ed. (New York: Palgrave, 1999), pp. 143–158.

29. Shutkin, *The Land That Could Be*, p. 240.

30. Ibid., p. xiv.

31. Sirianni and Friedland, *Civic Innovation in America*, p. 128.

32. Marc Landy, Megan Sussman, and Debra Knopman, *Civic Environmentalism in Action: A Field Guide to Regional and Local Initiatives* (Washington, D.C.: Progressive Policy Institute, 1999), p. 3.

33. Debra S. Knopman and Marc K. Landy, "A New Model of Governance," *DLC Blueprint Magazine*, September 1, 2000, http://www.ndol.org/ndol_ci.cfm?contentid=2125&kaid=116&subid=151.

34. Landy, Sussman, and Knopman, *Civic Environmentalism in Action*, p. 3.

35. Knopman and Landy, "A New Model of Governance," p. 3.

36. I was the project director for all three reports, and Richard Minard was associate project director. Panels of academy fellows and other experts guided staff work and signed each of the reports. Marc Landy was on the panel for the first NAPA report about the EPA. See NAPA, *Setting Priorities, Getting Results: A New Direction for EPA* (Washington, D.C.: NAPA, 1995); NAPA, *Resolving the Paradox of Environmental Protection*; NAPA, *environment.gov: Transforming Environmental Protection for the 21st Century*.

7

Environmental Justice

Evan J. Ringquist

As many of the other authors in this volume have documented, the scope of the conflict surrounding environmental governance worldwide expanded dramatically over the last three decades of the twentieth century. Yet despite the broadening of participants and participatory opportunities that these new governance models offer, both friends and foes of aggressive environmental and natural-resources (ENR) policies remain dissatisfied. The reasons for their discontent are multiple: these dynamics have not broadened sufficiently the range of who participates in environmental governance networks (see, for example, chapters 4 and 5); the ways in which the ENR "audience" participates in environmental governance (see chapters 5, 6, and 8); the terms upon which the debate is premised (see chapters 1, 2, 10, and 12); or how one determines success or failure (see chapter 13). Consequently, as the editors argue, a fundamental challenge bequeathed to environmental governance in the twenty-first century is finding ways to "reconnect" citizens to the process in new, creative, and effective ways (for example, see chapters 4, 9, and 11).

Among the most vocal, sustained, and persistent of these ENR governance critics in the late twentieth century were members of the environmental justice movement in the United States. As an alternative, they articulated a wide-ranging political agenda for "reconnecting" with poor and minority communities, many aspects of which challenge traditional approaches to environmental management. First, they argued that the pursuit of environmental justice requires greater and more meaningful participation for people of color and the poor in the policy-making process. Second, they wanted policymakers and administrators at the federal, state, and local level to make greater efforts to address and redress inequities in the distribution of noxious facilities, pollution, environmental risk, and the health consequences stemming from these risks. Finally, environmental justice proponents sought to expand the public role in the private market. They proposed that such expansion be accomplished by allowing community representatives to participate in industrial decisions regarding facility location and operation, and by broadening the definition of environmental policy to address the multiple factors contributing to lower quality of life in poor and/or minority communities (for example, health care, public amenities, and employment opportunities).[1]

Faced with these pressures from environmental justice advocates wielding reports documenting environmental risk concentrated in poor neighborhoods and communities of color, policymakers at all levels of government responded. During the Clinton administration, for example, a concerted focus on environmental justice issues arose within the federal government and especially within the Environmental Protection Agency (EPA), where Administrator Carol Browner consistently listed it as a top priority of her agency. The most visible manifestations of this effort across the federal government included the creation in 1992 of the Office of Environmental Justice within the EPA and the issuance of an executive order in 1994 ("Federal Actions to Address Environmental Justice in Minority Populations and Low-Income Populations," henceforth known as EO 12898). The latter imposed research, data collection, and public participation requirements on all federal agencies. In the process, they were charged with making environmental justice an integral part of their respective missions and to address any disproportionate environmental justice impacts resulting from their policies, programs, or activities.

Subsequently, in 1995, the EPA issued its Environmental Justice Strategy, a sweeping proclamation that "no segment of the population, regardless of race, color, national origin or income" should "suffer disproportionately from adverse human health or environmental effects" as the result of the EPA's actions.[2] To these ends, policymakers both inside and outside the EPA either pursued or proposed a thorough scouring of their discretionary authority under existing environmental laws to find ways to advance environmental justice goals across all federal agencies. Then, in August 2001, Browner's successor in the George W. Bush administration, Christine Todd Whitman, issued an agencywide memorandum proclaiming that "environmental justice is the goal to be achieved for all communities and persons across this Nation."[3]

While all this was transpiring at the federal level, many state and local governments struck out on their own to address the issues raised by environmental justice advocates. For example, of the forty-four states responding to a national survey in 1999, twenty-seven had taken some action to study potential problems of environmental inequity, but only three had changed state statutes to remedy environmental injustices.[4] Several municipalities also took steps to promote environmental justice. The contemporary model for local efforts to ensure environmental justice is New York City's "fair share" policy, whereby policymakers must take into account the extent to which the addition of polluting facilities in a neighborhood will change its character. Borough presidents and community residents then have at least two years to comment on these plans.[5]

By all accounts, however, these ambitious goals and initiatives have beached routinely on the shoals of a formidable mix of scientific, political, organizational, and financial obstacles. Addressing these inequities, after all, necessarily abandons a remarkable political strength of the environmental movement historically. Unlike most political advocates, environmental groups pursue government action that will benefit all citizens, not just their members (that is, they pursue "public goods"). By calling attention to the possibility that environmental risks may be concentrated among certain groups (that is, racial and ethnic minorities, the poor), environmental justice advocates call into question the public-good nature of environmental quality. In effect, as Durant with Boodphetcharat chronicle in chapter 3, protective regulatory policy morphs into decidedly more conflictual redistributive policy. Were this not difficult enough, while implementing this redistributive agenda, environmental policy professionals must make decisions in the face of significant scientific uncertainty regarding causes and effects. Moreover, they must do so in a political climate largely hostile to expanded governmental efforts to protect environmental quality and to pursue social justice.

What does all this mean for the future of environmental justice in the United States? This chapter argues that environmental justice concerns are likely to be enduring in the United States for the foreseeable future, posing in the process a substantial obstacle to the building of a results-based sense of common purpose in environmental governance. Perceptions that environmental justice remedies are inherently redistributive must be addressed. Moreover, policymakers essentially have three avenues for advancing their cause: new legislation, adapting civil rights laws, and adapting existing environmental statutes. Yet each of these options faces formidable strategic challenges, choices, and opportunities. Both the legislative and civil rights avenues effectively are closed to them. Moreover, while the adaptation of existing environmental statutes is a more promising approach for eliminating environmental injustice, proponents of environmental justice have formidable technical, legal, and cultural obstacles to overcome in building common purpose.

To support this argument, the chapter begins with a brief synopsis of the political economy that has marginalized the salience of legislative efforts to advance environmental justice agendas. Next, it turns to the implementation dilemmas faced when the EPA and other agencies have tried to use their discretionary authority under other laws to advance more aggressive environmental justice policies. A statute-by-statute review is, of course, beyond the scope of this chapter. However, to illustrate its points, this section analyzes in broad strokes the two major components of the EPA's Environmental Justice Strategy: using the discretionary authority available to the agency under other environmental statutes and under Title VI of the Civil Rights Act of 1964 to advance environmental justice goals. In light of this discussion, the chapter concludes by discussing the strategic challenges, choices, and opportunities that environmental justice advocates face in crafting and implementing policies capable of advancing a results-based sense of common purpose in the future.

The Political Economy of Environmental Justice in the United States: Assessing the Prospects for New Legislation

As public policy scholars have long appreciated, several major factors condition the adoption and success of innovations of the magnitude promoted by the environmental justice movement. Absent these characteristics, policy innovation is unlikely to occur in the United States. Most notable in this regard are a mobilized public; a favorable political climate; a supportive and powerful policy subsystem; and a clearly defined set of policy problems, causes, and solutions.[6] Any clear-eyed assessment of the extent to which environmental justice issues meet these necessary conditions cannot help but reach pessimistic conclusions regarding the prospects for major new initiatives in the future.

A Mobilized Public

Thirty-two years ago, Anthony Downs posited that environmental concern among the public would fall prey to the "issue-attention cycle" and wane appreciably as public attention shifted to other problems.[7] Public-opinion research, however, clearly shows that overall citizen support for environmental protection has not followed the pattern that Downs predicted. Since the early 1970s, solid majorities of survey respondents have supported greater governmental efforts to protect and improve environmental quality, and public support for environmental protection may be higher today than at the beginning of the modern environmental era.[8]

Downs's hypothesis has fared better with regard to support for specific elements of environmental policy. Public concern about abandoned hazardous-waste sites, indoor radon levels, acid rain, and a host of other environmental problems has followed the pattern he suggested. Moreover, there is some evidence that public interest for environmental justice policy is beginning to show signs of the issue-attention cycle. For example, the mainstream media published far fewer articles with an environmental justice storyline in 2000–2001 than in the mid-1990s.[9] Nevertheless, focusing events like those that catalyzed the environmental justice movement in the United States in the 1980s still get media attention (for example, efforts by the EPA and a hazardous-waste management company to site a hazardous-waste dump in Warren County, North Carolina; the release of a 1983 U.S. General Accounting Office study expressing concern about inequities in the siting of these facilities;[10] and the first People of Color Leadership Summit on the Environment, held in Washington, D.C., in 1991).

What is more, by 1992, events like these had led to the creation of nearly 200 local groups active in opposing facility siting and basing their opposition on civil rights grounds.[11] Many of these groups subsequently banded together into national networks of organizations that continue to press for redress today (for example, the Environmental Justice Action Group, Southwest Network for Environmental and Economic Justice, and the EcoJustice Network). The diminution of media coverage, however, reduces the size of the public audience that pays attention to this issue, thus rendering it difficult to expand political coalitions beyond these networks of interest groups.

A Favorable Political Climate

The political climate of the early 1990s clearly favored the adoption of environmental justice policy. In 1992, the nation elected Bill Clinton (a Democratic president committed to improving race relations), Al Gore (the most forceful advocate of environmental protection ever to hold the position of vice president), and Democratic majorities in both houses of Congress. Indeed, in that year, Al Gore, as senator, had cosponsored with John Lewis (D-Ga.) the first major piece of environmental justice legislation, the Environmental Justice Act (EJA). The EJA required the EPA to identify 100 areas of the country most polluted by toxic chemicals and to designate them as "environmental high-impact areas." For each of these areas, the bill required the EPA to impose a moratorium on siting new sources of toxic pollution if the agency found evidence of adverse health effects.

This bill and others, such as the Environmental Equal Rights Act (preventing the siting of new hazardous-waste facilities in poor or minority communities), as well as amendments to the Resource Conservation and Recovery Act (RCRA, requiring demographic information about surrounding communities when sites were proposed), were never enacted. Undaunted, however, a flurry of administration-introduced or backed environmental justice bills soon followed, punctuated by Clinton's environmental justice EO 12898, noted earlier. Indeed, during the 1993–94 congressional session alone, six pieces of legislation were introduced. Despite this favorable political climate, these bills met the same fate as their predecessors.

After these defeats, moreover, things only got worse for environmental justice proponents. In 1994, Republican leadership far less supportive of environmental protection in general—and of environmental justice in particular—took control of the House and the Senate. Not surprisingly under these circumstances, not a single piece of environmental justice legislation was introduced for three years. Moreover, only five environmental justice bills have been introduced since 1998, and none have passed. Meanwhile, the EPA's appropriations bills for fiscal years 1999–2001 prevented the agency from spending any money to implement or administer environmental justice programs under Title VI of the Civil Rights Act. And, for good measure, Congress went so far as to prevent the EPA from pursuing environmental justice policy through the courts. Thus, absent a sea change in the margins of partisan control of the Congress, it is extraordinarily unlikely that Capitol Hill will actively pursue environmental justice legislation in the near future.

A Powerful and Supportive Policy Subsystem

Many scholars see policy subsystems as creating a "structurally induced equilibrium" in the policymaking process that produces stability and predictability,[12] perhaps at the cost of public access and democratic accountability.[13] Such is certainly the view held by environmental justice advocates, who see themselves decidedly marginalized in the environmental justice policy subsystem. Several obstacles to their participation are noteworthy. The first hurdle is gaining entry to the subsystem through interest groups. Early in the modern environmental era (when the environmental policy subsystem was being created), environmental groups sought to keep the environmental movement separate from broader social justice concerns, fearing that an association with these causes might dilute their effectiveness. For their part, civil rights and social justice groups had a vague distrust of environmentalists, seeing them as more attuned to the preservationist concerns of the affluent than to the problems of the urban environment most relevant to their membership. This situation has changed somewhat in the past decade, with environmental groups appointing people of color to leadership positions, forging working relationships with local and national social justice groups, and reaching out to minority communities for members.[14] Nevertheless, representation within these more powerful groups remains inadequate to reach a critical mass for change.

A second hurdle is that potential environmental justice advocates have not been well represented among the governmental members of the environmental policy subsystem. For example, although the congressional black caucus routinely has the strongest average environmental voting scores among organized legislative groups, African American legislators rarely are found on key environmental committees and have never attained leadership positions on these committees. To a lesser extent, the same is true of Latino representatives. African Americans and Latinos also have been underrepresented among upper-level management within the EPA, compared to their representation at similar levels in other governmental agencies.

Third, the entry of environmental justice advocates into the environmental policy subsystem has the potential to redefine certain elements of environmental protection in the public mind. Recognizing the important distributional concerns raised by environmental justice advocates might mean that environmentalists will have to abandon, at least in part, their construction of environmental protection as a "public good." Evidence from the states, in fact, suggests that policies to address environmental inequities are defined more accurately as redistributive than as regulatory.[15] The beneficiaries of redistributive policy generally have less political power and a more negative public image than do the beneficiaries of regulatory policy,[16] and policy success is more difficult in this area.[17] Consequently, some members of the environmental policy subsystem may be reluctant to open the subsystem to environmental justice advocates.

Clearly Defined Problems, Causes, and Solutions

In demanding social empowerment, pollution prevention, direct access to environmental decision making, attention to community preferences in environmental priorities, and the redistribution of power, the environmental justice movement is "almost boundary-less, covering all races and classes, and all manners of perceived environmental slights."[18] Asking it to do less, however, also presents problems because of formidable disagreements about whether disparities actually exist and, hence, what the true scope of the problem is. In trying to answer these questions, an explosion of research investigating potential environmental inequities within poor communities and communities of color has ensued over the past decade. For definitive answers to these questions to emerge, however, two things need to happen. First, more research needs to examine the distribution of pollution emissions, pollutant levels, and sources of pollution other than hazardous-waste facilities.[19] Second, this research needs to be conducted using various spatial definitions of "community" (for example, census tracts, postal codes, and units defined by global information systems) to make sure that the results are not a function of aggregation bias. Until then, as the following brief review of findings suggests, disagreements over the scope of the problem, its causes, and its solutions will continue.

Inequities in the Location of Polluting Facilities   The first study to analyze systematically possible connections between race, class, and the location of noxious facilities on a national scale was completed by the United Church of Christ's Commission on Racial Justice (CRJ) in 1987. The CRJ gathered data on the location of every commercial hazardous-waste handler in the country and created a statistical model showing that as the percentage of poor and minority residents of a neighborhood increased, the likelihood that the neighborhood contained a hazardous-waste site increased as well, even when controlling for other factors.[20] An update to the CRJ report found that these same relationships existed in the 1990s.[21] More recent research has found that poor and minority neighborhoods are more likely to contain commercial hazardous-waste facilities,[22] hazardous-waste handlers of any sort,[23] sources of toxic pollutants,[24] and sources of air and water pollution.[25] Although other researchers have found no racial or class inequities in the distribution of noxious facilities,[26] the majority of research in this area finds empirical support for the proposition that noxious facilities are concentrated among poor and minority communities.

Inequities in Pollutant Levels   Simply because a person lives close to a polluting facility does not mean he or she is exposed to higher levels of pollution. If regulated facilities and their pollution control equipment are operating properly, and if environmental regulations are enforced diligently, the level of exposure near these facilities should be minimal. Far fewer researchers have examined environmental inequities with respect to pollutant levels, but their work consistently finds that poor and minority communities are exposed to higher levels of pollution. For example, toxic chemical releases are significantly greater in areas with large minority populations.[27] In addition, air and water pollution levels are higher in areas with high concentrations of poor and minority residents.[28] Finally, a recent meta-analysis finds even stronger evidence for racial and class inequities in the distribution of pollution than in the distribution of polluting facilities themselves.[29]

Inequities in the Implementation of Environmental Policies   Because government policy decisions play a large role in the location of noxious facilities (and in the pollution these facilities emit), these decisions may contribute to the inequities noted here. Government officials, specifically, may be more likely to approve permits for noxious facilities in poor and minority communities; they may be less diligent in enforcing regulations in poor and minority communities; and the punishments they levy for violating environmental standards may be more lenient in these communities. Indeed, one oft-cited study provided evidence that civil penalties for violating environmental regulations are systematically lower in poor and minority communities, and that the cleanup of abandoned hazardous-waste sites was far slower in poor and minority communities.[30] Upon closer examination, however, the first claim cannot be substantiated.[31] John Hird, nonetheless, does produce evidence suggesting that officials in charge of administering the federal Superfund program are more responsive to the concerns of wealthier communities than to those of poorer communities.[32] Finally, at least one study finds evidence that the EPA may be more likely to approve permit applications for hazardous-waste facilities in minority communities.[33]

Causality of Environmental Justice Problems   Even if one restricts attention to a single core environmental justice problem such as the inequitable distribution of sources of environmental risk, there is no commonly accepted cause of these environmental inequities. Without a clear causal link between public problems and proposed solutions, policy innovation is both less likely to occur[34] and less likely to be effective if it does occur.[35] Elsewhere I have culled from the literature four possible explanations for the current distribution of noxious facilities, other than intentional discrimination.[36] The first is *scientific rationality*. According to most experts, the siting of polluting facilities, especially landfills and hazardous-waste facilities, is driven by technical criteria. When attempts are made to site a hazardous-waste landfill, for example, what matters are the geological characteristics of the site. If polluting facilities are concentrated in poor and minority areas, the scientific rationality explanation posits that this concentration is owing to random chance.

The second explanation for disparities is *market rationality*. According to proponents of the market rationality explanation, economic factors drive decisions regarding the location of noxious facilities. For companies, the most important economic factors in deciding where to locate are cheap land, available labor, access to transportation infrastructure, and access to raw materials. Ignoring these factors in order to target poor and minority communities for polluting facilities would be economically irrational. Thus, although firms may locate facilities in poor communities, economics rather than discrimination drive this decision.

A third explanation is *political power*. Although the right to vote is distributed equally, political power is not. Political power is a function of wealth, education, group organizational skills, frequent participation in the political process, and so forth. Certain citizens, in particular members of minority groups and the poor, have fewer of these resources. Because rational actors will attempt to site polluting facilities where they will face the least amount of political resistance, political rationality, rather than outright discrimination, may explain best why these facilities tend to be located in poor and minority neighborhoods.

A final explanation for disparities is *neighborhood transition*. Any attempt to evaluate the extent of environmental inequities faces an important "chicken-and-egg" question. The neighborhood transition explanation paints the following scenario. Many polluting facilities were originally located in urban, working-class areas for many of the reasons cited by the market rationality explanation. Over time, those residents with the resources to move away did so. Because these facilities had reduced the value of the surrounding property, the departing residents were replaced by people who were poor or members of minority groups or both. Thus, although the present-day risks from these facilities may be distributed inequitably, the initial process of siting these facilities was not discriminatory.

Not surprisingly, most of the causal stories posited here receive at least some empirical support. My own work shows that hazardous-waste facilities are less likely to be located (and permits for hazardous-waste facilities are less likely to be approved) where the surrounding population relies on underground sources of drinking water.[37] Researchers have demonstrated that the political power of area residents also is associated with decisions to build, expand, and permit hazardous-waste facilities.[38] Although extant research finds little evidence to support the neighborhood transition thesis, the scarcity of this research makes such a conclusion premature.[39]

Perhaps the greatest degree of empirical evidence supports the economic rationality hypothesis, as nearly every environmental equity study to date finds that property values, the availability of skilled labor, raw materials, and a well-developed transportation infrastructure help to predict the location of polluting facilities.[40] The intentional discrimination hypothesis is the most difficult to test because it requires proprietary information regarding confidential deliberations within private firms. But, alas, all this only means that the intentional discrimination hypothesis—the centerpiece of environmental justice movement concerns—is by far the most difficult to prove.

From Movement Politics to Policy Change? The Realpolitik of the Litigation Adaptation Strategy

Given the low probability of new presidential or legislative policies with respect to environmental justice beginning in 1994, a host of incremental administrative adaptations have been attempted or proposed over the past decade. The EPA, for example, has pursued several sets of strategies aimed at producing better environmental justice outcomes, including reorganization, research, education, and outreach. In terms of reorganization, the EPA created the Office of Environmental Justice, currently located within the Office of Enforcement and Compliance Assurance. In addition, the EPA now houses (1) an environmental justice steering committee composed of senior managers from all EPA offices and regions and responsible for strategic planning; (2) an environmental justice policy working group composed of high-level policy staff and responsible for the design of cross-media environmental justice policies; (3) the Office of Civil Rights, located within the office of the administrator; and (4) environmental justice coordinators within each headquarters office and within each region and responsible for implementing environmental justice policies. In addition, the agency helped to create the National Environmental Justice Advisory Council, composed of governmental and nongovernmental stakeholders, which helps local communities pursue remedies for instances of environmental discrimination.

The EPA's strategic plan for environmental justice, in turn, focused agency resources on five elements: (1) improving public participation, partnerships, and outreach to stakeholders; (2) increasing research regarding the public-health and environmental impacts of pollution; (3) improving data collection, data analysis, and stakeholder access to agency data; (4) protecting Native Americans and other indigenous groups; and (5) incorporating environmental justice into enforcement, compliance assurance, and regulatory reviews.[41] Over the past decade, the EPA also has required each regional office to conduct research on elements of environmental justice that are particularly relevant in its region; has created an Environmental Justice Small Grants Program, which provides funding for community-based projects to remedy environmental justice problems; and has held environmental justice seminars for EPA personnel and for business and community groups across the country. Lastly, it has embarked on an ambitious program to devise measures of cumulative risk from exposures to multiple environmental hazards.

As noted earlier, however, perhaps the EPA's most ambitious effort to address environmental justice concerns is what might be called the agency's "litigation adaptation" strategy. Catalyzed by EO 12898 and President Clinton's Memorandum on Environmental Justice, the agency has tried, proposed, or considered proposals by others to interpret both traditional ENR statutes and existing antidiscrimination statutes in ways that advance the environmental justice agenda. Yet, as the following section illustrates, while careful analysis suggests that each of these adaptation strategies has its limitations, the most viable avenue for reform may be the adaptation of ENR laws to accommodate environmental justice goals.

Pursuing Environmental Justice Through Civil Rights Law

One commonly offered incremental innovation in the environmental justice area is to prosecute the actors responsible for environmental inequities by using existing antidiscrimination statutes. Title VI of the 1964 Civil Rights Act prohibits recipients of federal funds from using these funds in a discriminatory fashion. Because the EPA provides federal grant money to all state environmental agencies and to many nongovernmental actors, many legal experts see Title VI as "the most viable option for minority plaintiffs in their search for environmental justice."[42]

Although the EPA first adopted implementing regulations for the Civil Right Acts in the early 1970s, these regulations were silent on the topic of how to handle disparate impacts of environmental programs within communities of color. Nor did much change in this area until the late 1990s. For example, in 1993, the EPA's Office of Civil Rights began an investigation into the process by which permits were granted to operate polluting facilities in Louisiana's "cancer alley." This investigation bore fruit in 1994 when the EPA sued Borden Chemicals and Plastics for illegally storing and disposing of large quantities of hazardous chemicals that eventually contaminated the groundwater in nearby poor and minority communities. *Borden* was the first case in which the EPA raised the issue of environmental justice, and its successors quickly revealed that the EPA had no clearly developed plan for pursuing environmental justice through the courts.

Consequently, in 1998, the EPA revised these regulations and formalized policy in this area by issuing interim guidelines for investigating Title VI complaints and for challenging permits under Title VI. Under these guidelines, state or local agencies can be sued for issuing permits to noxious facilities that place a disproportionate burden on poor or minority communities. Facility owners themselves also might be subject to these suits. Moreover, Title VI suits can be filed even if the facility in question poses a relatively small risk but contributes to an unacceptable overall risk in the area in question. Finally, the EPA reserved the right to file suit against states and localities under Title VI even if these states and localities followed EPA guidelines (see below), but their decisions were later shown to contribute to a disproportionate impact on communities of color.

As of August 2001, 107 Title VI complaints had been filed with the EPA, and twenty-three of them had been accepted by the agency under its guidelines and sent on to the Department of Justice for further investigation. A sober assessment of Title VI and of the EPA's experience in pursuing this strategy, however, suggests that it will have limited utility as a tool for combating environmental injustice. The strategy most notably faces formidable legal and political obstacles. Nor does evolving case law in this area make one optimistic about its chances as a tool for reconnecting poor and minority communities with decisions affecting their health, safety, and environment.

Statutory Hurdles   Any large-scale effort to use Title VI in the pursuit of environmental justice must address successfully three sources of complexity in the act: the source of the legal authority for pursuing discrimination claims, the definition of *discrimination* itself, and the extent to which a "private right of action" is available to the victims of environmental discrimination. Thus, not unlike the interpretative ambiguities that Charles Wise describes in his chapter as plaguing ENR regulatory agencies that try to anticipate property rights takings claims, daunting statutory ambiguities challenge regulators in the environmental justice area as well.

In terms of legal authority under Title VI, most assessments have focused on Section 601 of the statute. This section states that no person shall "on the ground of race, color, or national origin, be excluded from participation in, be denied the benefits of, or be subjected to discrimination under any program or activity" of the federal government. Although Section 601 clearly outlaws discrimination in federal programs, it does not offer guidelines for assessing discrimination. Nor does this section give any guidance to federal grant recipients as to how they might avoid running afoul of Title VI in the implementation of federally funded programs. Such directions are provided for in Section 602, which authorizes federal agencies "to effectuate the provisions of [Section 601] . . . by issuing rules, regulations, or orders of general applicability." Under Section 602, then, federal agencies find themselves in the familiar position of designing regulations to implement an act of Congress. More important, recipients of federal funds can be charged with violating the tenets of the

Civil Rights Act itself (that is, Section 601) or with violating agency rules that implement this act (Section 602). As we shall see, however, this seemingly trivial legal distinction has enormous implications for how Title VI might be used in the pursuit of environmental justice.

Similar problems are encountered in trying to define *discrimination*. A common (though simplistic) way of categorizing discriminatory actions is to define the effects of these actions as intentional or unintentional. Intentional discrimination occurs when actors make a conscious effort to deny protected groups participation in or the benefits of federally funded programs. Unintentional discrimination, on the other hand, typically is defined using a disparate impact standard: actions that concentrate the benefits or costs of a federal program to the detriment of protected groups are discriminatory, regardless of whether the actions leading to these disparate impacts were motivated by discriminatory intent. Applicable definitions of discrimination also vary across areas of federal law. Therein, one common understanding of this distinction is that the Fourteenth Amendment to the Constitution forbids only intentional discrimination, whereas Title VI of the Civil Rights Act outlaws both intentional and unintentional discrimination. As discussed more fully later, however, this understanding must be reevaluated in light of recent Supreme Court decisions.

Finally, hurdles also must be overcome in terms of defining who may sue whom. Almost any action taken by the federal government is potentially actionable under Title VI. Moreover, given that state governments make an overwhelming majority of permit decisions and enforcement actions that might concentrate environmental risks in communities of color,[43] the actions of these governments and of their municipal agents are subject to the provisions of Title VI as well. The federal government can also bring suits to enforce Title VI against a federal agency, state governments, local governments, or private actors who receive federal program funds. More important for our discussion, private actors may be able to sue the federal and state governments under Title VI.

The extent to which private actors can *enforce* the antidiscrimination requirements of Title VI, however, depends solely on the existence of a private right of action in Sections 601 and 602. Moreover, private suits against state governments under Title VI face an additional obstacle.

Over the past several years, the Supreme Court has "rediscovered" the Eleventh Amendment's protection of state governments through sovereign immunity. In part, these decisions have established that private actors have no right to compel state governments to comply, among other things, with federal patent laws, federal antidiscrimination laws, and federal fair labor standards.[44] Consequently, citizens seeking to compel state governments to abide by the provisions of Title VI must first demonstrate a private right of action under Title VI. They then must convince the court that the state is not protected from such citizen suits by virtue of sovereign immunity.

Intergovernmental Obstacles to Using Title VI   Although the EPA, state governments, and local governments have acted independently to address environmental justice concerns, federal-state relations in this area increasingly are "coming apart and [becoming] contentious," as Denise Scheberle puts it.[45] A prime example of this contentiousness is the withering and almost unanimous opposition from state and local governments to EPA draft guidelines for implementing Section 602 of Title VI. In response to the draft guidelines, the Environmental Council of the States adopted a resolution stating that "EPA's interim guidance is not workable in its current form and should be withdrawn until States have resolved outstanding issues with U.S. EPA."[46] The U.S. Conference of Mayors urged "the U.S. EPA to suspend its current interim guidance with respect to Title VI administrative complaints."[47] The National Association of Counties also registered complaints with the EPA, stating that association members were "strongly opposed to the new 'Interim Guidance for Investigating Title VI Administrative Complaints Challenging Permits.'"[48] Similar objections came from the Western Governors' Association and the National Association of Black County Officials.[49]

State and local opposition to the EPA's proposed policy for handling Title VI cases stems from five sources. First, as recipients of federal grant money and as the parties responsible for more than 90 percent of all permit decisions and inspections, state and local agencies will most likely be the targets of lawsuits for issuing permits to facilities that allegedly violate environmental justice criteria. Second, the criteria for identifying "disparate impacts" to a community (the triggering mechanism for a

Title VI complaint) are quite vague. Third, the EPA's second-guessing of facility permitting decisions is seen as an unwarranted infringement on traditional state and local authority regarding land-use decisions. Fourth, the EPA's Title VI guidance documents were developed without consulting the state and local officials who would be subject to the requirements of the policy—a situation all too common for those familiar with federal-state relations in environmental protection. Finally, the threat of Title VI lawsuits might interfere with state and local efforts to revitalize urban areas through industrial development. This opposition from important stakeholder groups, coupled with congressional hostility to Title VI enforcement, further leaves the EPA little choice but to deemphasize Title VI suits as a management tool in environmental justice.

Evolving Case Law   Although the EPA may have to reduce its reliance on Title VI in addressing environmental justice concerns, private actors still may press these claims. Private efforts to make states comply with the Title VI regulations issued by federal agencies, however, face three obstacles: courts may find no private right of action under Section 602; courts may disallow Section 602 suits against states on the grounds of sovereign immunity; and courts may outlaw disparate impact regulations under Section 602. These obstacles notwithstanding, a reasonable reading of precedent gave environmental justice advocates some hope that the courts would be receptive to private claims of discrimination under Title VI. However, the recent Supreme Court decision in *Alexander v. Sandoval* may all but end the utility of Title VI as a tool in the pursuit of environmental justice.[50]

Reason for optimism began in 1979 when the Supreme Court clearly found an implied right of private action under Section 601.[51] Next, a majority of the Court concluded in 1983 that agencies can adopt Section 602 regulations proscribing activities that have a disparate impact on racial groups.[52] Finally, in 1986 Congress passed the Rehabilitation Act Amendments of 1986. In doing so, it expressly overruled the states' sovereign immunity against Title VI suits under Section 601. At this point, it was not unreasonable to assume, therefore, that the EPA might adopt disparate impact regulations under Section 602 and that the Court would find a private right of action for enforcing these regulations.

Environmental justice advocates seemed to have the perfect case for testing this interpretation of precedent in *Seif v. Chester Residents Concerned for Quality Living*.[53] Chester, Pennsylvania, is a small town outside of Philadelphia that contains a remarkably large number of hazardous-waste facilities capable of handling more than 2 million tons of hazardous waste each year. In 1996, the Pennsylvania Department of Environmental Protection issued a permit for yet another hazardous-waste facility in Chester, prompting the Chester Residents Concerned for Quality Living to file a Title VI lawsuit. A district court judge initially dismissed the case, finding (1) no intent to discriminate on the part of the Pennsylvania Department of Environmental Protection and (2) no private right of action under Title VI. In December 1997, however, the Third Circuit Court of Appeals overturned the district court decision.

The Third Circuit found that Title VI does not require discriminatory intent, only disproportionate impact, and that there was an implied right of private action under Section 602 of Title VI. Pennsylvania appealed this decision, and the case was placed on the U.S. Supreme Court's docket in 1998. However, before the high court could rule on the case, the state agency revoked the permit for the commercial transportation, storage, and disposal facility in accordance with the facility owner's wishes.[54] Hope soared again, however, in 2001. A federal district court judge ruled in *South Camden Citizens in Action v. New Jersey Department of Environmental Protection* that the department violated the civil rights of citizens in Camden when it approved a permit for a cement plant in an area that already contained several other noxious facilities.[55]

Despite the optimism generated in the environmental justice movement by the *Camden* and *Chester* cases, however, *Alexander v. Sandoval* dramatically undermines the utility of pursuing environmental justice through Title VI claims. In fact, although the case has nothing to do with environmental policy, it may eliminate this legal avenue altogether. At a minimum, *Alexander v. Sandoval* should alter fundamentally the extent to which environmental justice can be pursued through Title VI claims. With Justice Antonine Scalia writing for the five-member majority, the Court concluded a number of things. First, and most important, it found no private right of action—implied or otherwise—in Section 602 of the Civil Rights Act. Although such a right exists under

Section 601, this right, first assumed by the Court, later was established by an act of Congress. No act of Congress has established such a right under Section 602. Second, the opinion reiterates that Section 601 prohibits only intentional discrimination. Third, in addition to finding no private right of action under Section 602, the Court majority was sympathetic to the notion of disallowing disparate impact regulations under this section as well. Finally, the Court's opinion makes it reasonable to conclude that this five-justice majority might find in the future that states have sovereign immunity from regulations promulgated under Section 602, regardless of congressional abrogation of this immunity under Section 601.

Pursuing Environmental Justice through Traditional Environmental Regulation

With this bleak assessment of adapting a Title VI litigation strategy, does the EPA's strategy of adapting existing environmental regulations offer more promise as a vehicle for advancing environmental justice goals? The answer is a qualified "yes," although the obstacles to doing so suggest cautious optimism. To understand how and why, it is useful to investigate the four primary areas where existing environmental regulations may be amended: establishing public-participation requirements; setting environmental quality standards; issuing permits for noxious facilities; and assessing penalties for violating participation requirements, environmental standards, and permit terms.

Public Participation Requirements   One common complaint by environmental justice advocates is that members of disproportionately affected communities rarely participate in the siting of noxious facilities. Environmental managers may be able to address this complaint through two tactics. First, they may increase opportunities for public participation in permit decisions. Second, they may require entities who seek to locate noxious facilities in residential areas to invest in the host community's capacity to participate in the decision and to oversee facility operation and compliance. In this instance, these entities may provide funding for legal representation, expert consultants, or access to proprietary information regarding manufacturing inputs and processes.

There is little doubt that the EPA has the authority to require additional public outreach and public participation prior to granting a permit in a disproportionately affected area. Moreover, there is some evidence that dramatically increasing the participation of local communities in environmental decision making is successful at both reducing community opposition to noxious facilities and extracting community capacity-building concessions.[56] For example, Texas has adopted such a policy, requiring public notice at the point where facility owners express their intention to seek a facility permit, and public input into these decisions has increased nearly fourfold as a result.[57]

Some scholars have advocated going beyond increasing opportunities for public participation in facility siting. They suggest that the entities proposing such facilities should be responsible for ensuring that their opponents have the resources to participate effectively.[58] Nothing in the Administrative Procedures Act empowers the EPA to force these types of concessions, however, and the major pieces of environmental legislation are silent on this issue as well. The one possible caveat to this conclusion is that many environmental statutes provide citizen-suit provisions. To make proper use of these citizen-suit provisions, communities still need a level of technical and administrative capacity not often found among the victims of environmental inequities. Consequently, it may be possible for the EPA to attach certain conditions to environmental permits granted in disproportionately affected areas. Technical assistance, on-site monitoring by community representatives, the provision of a facility ombudsman, and other capacity-building features might be justified by claiming they are necessary to ensure that citizen-suit provisions can be used effectively.[59]

Environmental Standards   The EPA and empowered state agencies employ two types of environmental standards. First, the Clean Air Act (CAA) and Clean Water Act (CWA) require the EPA and state environmental agencies to adopt ambient environmental quality standards (for example, the National Ambient Air Quality Standards [NAAQSs] under the CAA and water quality standards promulgated by the states under the CWA). Second, environmental agencies also adopt a host of more place-based standards that are specific to particular facilities or areas (for example,

New Source Performance Standards under the CAA) and are set with an eye toward meeting the ambient environmental standards. Some scholars have suggested setting more stringent standards in communities where the cumulative risk posed by numerous polluting facilities is particularly large.[60] It is arguably unreasonable, however, to assume that ambient environmental standards will be changed to suit the needs of residents of disproportionately affected communities (for example, the NAAQSs are for all intents and purposes national standards). A more realistic approach might be for environmental agencies to adopt place-based standards of varying stringency, depending on the distribution of existing environmental risks (see below).

In addition to amending existing air and water quality standards in the face of environmental justice concerns, the EPA might adopt new environmental standards based on estimates of cumulative risk. As noted earlier, when the EPA (or the agency's authorized agent) considers a permit application under the CWA or the RCRA, it evaluates only the risks posed by the facility in question. It does not consider background risks posed by existing facilities in the immediate area. Nor, for example, do CAA permits consider environmental risks from other media. Considering cumulative risks in permit decisions is not prohibited, however. Indeed, the CWA and the RCRA require responsible agencies to consider the consequences facilities may have on human and ecosystem health when making permit decisions. A strong argument can clearly be made, then, for formally mandating consideration of cumulative risk.

Permit Decisions   Environmental managers also may be able to address environmental justice concerns by placing additional permit requirements on firms that seek to site facilities in disproportionately affected communities (for example, higher environmental standards, more frequent inspections, the use of a citizen oversight board). More restrictive still, environmental justice concerns might serve as justification for denying a permit in an area that already contains additional noxious facilities. I address each of these possibilities in turn.

According to the EPA's Office of General Counsel, the agency can use environmental justice concerns to attach conditions to environmental permits if the agency can show that the facility poses a threat to public health.[61] Little or no case law exists that tests this statutory interpretation, and the major pieces of environmental legislation are silent on this issue as well. To assess the likely boundaries of agency discretion in this area, we must look to the decisions of the Environmental Appeals Board within the EPA. When stakeholders with standing take issue with the decision regarding a permit application or the conditions attached to that decision, their final administrative remedy is to appeal the decision with the Environmental Appeals Board.

At least initially, EO 12898 did little to influence Appeals Board decisions in this area. When considering an environmental justice challenge to a landfill permit granted by the EPA Region V office, for example, the board held that EO 12898 "does not have the effect of changing the substantive requirements for issuance of a permit under RCRA . . . if a permit applicant meets the requirements of RCRA and its implementing regulations, the Agency must issue a permit, regardless of the racial or socioeconomic composition of the surrounding community."[62] On the other hand, the Appeals Board did recognize that traditional assessments of the threat to human health required under RCRA might miss greater than average threats faced by certain communities and subgroups of the population. Thus, the board concluded that the EPA had the authority to take "a more refined look at its health and environmental impacts assessment" in the face of environmental justice objections. It also intimated that the agency should maximize opportunities for public participation when these objections were present.[63]

Over the ensuing several years, the Appeals Board has become disposed more favorably to considering environmental justice claims as relevant to permit conditions. In AES Puerto Rico, L.P.,[64] the board "expressly endorses EPA's discretionary authority to include permit conditions designed to address environmental justice concerns raised by the affected community."[65] Although it ultimately denied the environmental justice objections in this case, it did so based on technical merits, rather than on a blanket rejection of the relevance of environmental justice claims in the permitting process.

Nevertheless, the prospects for using the permitting process to prevent the concentration of noxious facilities in poor and minority neighborhoods *independent* of the cumulative risks posed by these facilities seem especially bleak. Nothing in the major pieces of environmental legislation suggests that facility clustering alone can serve as a justification for denying a permit application. Thus, the courts almost certainly will strike down any EPA effort to do so as inconsistent with legislative intent. Indeed, the Appeals Board repeatedly has stressed that authorities may consider only whether the proposed facility meets statutory requirements, regardless of the distributional consequences.[66]

Assessing Penalties for Noncompliance   Finally, the CAA and CWA (but not the RCRA) allow the EPA to consider "such other factors as justice may require" when determining civil penalties for regulatory violations.[67] These "other factors" historically have included items such as the profits accruing to regulated entities through noncompliance and whether the firm in question is a repeat offender. However, the agency may be able to include environmental justice considerations when making penalty determinations. Indeed, as noted, some observers have charged that the EPA and the federal courts took such factors into consideration by levying *smaller* penalties on firms that violated environmental standards in poor and minority communities.[68] Subsequent analyses, however, demonstrated that civil penalty severity in environmental protection is in fact unrelated to the demographic characteristics of the surrounding area.[69] Still, the EPA hypothetically might be able to assess higher penalties for regulatory violations in disproportionately affected communities, "as justice may require."

Environmental Justice, Environmental Governance, and Building Common Purpose: Challenges, Choices, and Opportunities

The preceding discussion has argued that policymakers have three potential tools they might rely on when seeking to incorporate environmental justice concerns into environmental governance: new environmental justice legislation, the adaptation of civil rights laws, and the adaptation of existing environmental statutes. The previous discussions illustrate that the first two avenues effectively are closed off now, leaving only the third as a potentially viable strategy for eliminating perceptions of environmental justice as barriers to building a results-based sense of common purpose in the future. But the effectiveness of this strategy depends greatly on the extent to which the EPA and other environmental agencies can overcome the technical, legal, and cultural challenges such a strategy entails.

Technical Challenges

Effectively addressing environmental justice problems presupposes the ability to identify and prioritize instances of environmental inequity. The EPA currently has the tools to do neither, which means that problem identification and resource allocation in environmental justice are driven by political concerns (for example, lawsuits filed by interest groups and political pressure from members of Congress or governors). To its credit, the EPA has been working hard to meet these challenges. With respect to identifying instances of environmental inequity, the agency is integrating its numerous pollution and facility location databases with an eye toward developing a protocol to identify communities exposed to disproportionate concentrations of pollutants and noxious facilities. Based on the Environmental Justice Query Mapper, this effort will offer significant opportunities to identify environmental justice problem areas better by creating a uniform, national approach for using global information systems to conduct environmental justice assessments. Once areas of environmental justice concern have been identified, the environmental and health risks present in these areas must be measured, and those areas that need priority attention must be chosen. For nearly five years, the EPA has been developing a method of cumulative risk assessment that may enable it to complete just this type of measurement and prioritization. So far, however, it has made only limited progress in this area.[70]

Legal Challenges

Although both the Office of General Counsel and the Environmental Appeals Board have taken the position that existing ENR statutes offer opportunities to address environmental justice concerns, these opinions are predicated on the assumption that administrators can demonstrate inequities in exposure to cumulative environmental risk. Until this technical challenge is solved, however, any action beyond requiring additional opportunities for public participation—among others, more stringent place-based environmental standards, more stringent permit requirements, more severe penalties for violating environmental regulations, agency regulations that implement Title VI of the Civil Rights Act—must rest on the disparate impact standard. To be sure, the National Academy of Public Administration (NAPA) suggests that in the absence of a complete cumulative risk assessment, the agency might base these actions on the calculation of the "environmental load" placed on a community by multiple sources of pollution. Yet the questionable scientific validity of such "environmental loads" makes it unlikely that this strategy will withstand legal challenge. The EPA thus has no choice but to improve further its cumulative impact technology to avoid further setbacks in the courts.

Cultural Challenges

One of the biggest challenges to the creation of effective environmental justice policy is the organizational culture of the EPA and other ENR regulatory authorities. The first cultural challenge for the agency is redefining the place and purpose of public participation in administrative decision making. Decision making at the agency has long been described as a battle between the scientific and legal cultures represented within it.[71] Neither culture, however, places much value on public participation in decision making; scientists are leery of input from nonexperts and attorneys seek to limit this input by channeling it through formal legal administrative procedures.[72]

Over the past decade, the EPA and others in the ENR regulatory community have undertaken a number of initiatives aimed at incorporating a wider range of stakeholders into agency decision making. In addition to those initiatives discussed earlier and in chapters 5, 6, and 9 of this volume, the EPA in particular has chosen to provide financial assistance to communities in the form of technical assistance grants and technical assistance through the Technical Outreach Services for Communities program. At the same time, EPA regional agency personnel receive training in community involvement, facilitation, and cross-cultural collaboration through the Community Involvement University, established by the EPA's Office of Solid Waste and Emergency Response.[73] Observers note that the EPA nevertheless must choose to devote more resources to public participation efforts, involve the public earlier in the regulatory process, and provide more assistance to stakeholders unfamiliar with the process.

The second cultural challenge for the EPA is incorporating the goals of environmental justice into the core mission of the agency. NAPA found that despite the high priority that the EPA leadership places on environmental justice, few environmental managers treat environmental justice as central to the agency's mission.[74] Part of the explanation for this lack of integration is simple bureaucratic inertia. Yet, as NAPA avers, part of the problem is structural. Thus, for progress to be made in redressing this cultural shortcoming, the EPA must choose to pursue two major reforms. First, agency leaders have to communicate to line managers more clearly their expectations regarding environmental justice outcomes. Second, they must institute an accountability process that measures progress toward environmental justice goals.[75] With no clear expectations regarding how to manage for environmental justice and no incentives for pursuing environmental justice goals, it is not surprising that administrators overwhelmed with other demands give less attention to environmental justice.

The final cultural challenge to successful environmental justice is the agency's relationship with state governments. Truth be told, if tomorrow the EPA successfully adopted all of the adaptations of existing environmental statutes discussed here, these actions would have little effect because the agency makes fewer than 5 percent of all decisions on environmental permit applications. State environmental agencies make the remainder. The states also set the majority of environmental standards (for example, all water quality standards under the CWA; most existing source performance standards and many new source performance standards under the CAA; and many hazardous-waste disposal standards under RCRA). Moreover, land-use decisions and industrial facility permitting historically have been state responsibilities. State governments clearly must play a central role in addressing environmental justice issues, but the EPA initially tried to craft an environmental justice policy without the input of the states. On the other hand, because state authority to issue permits and set standards emanates from federal legislation, leaders in Washington, D.C., cannot leave the task of addressing environmental justice to the states alone. Thus, for progress to be made, the EPA must choose to step back from its typical leadership role in environmental policy and work more collaboratively with the states in crafting acceptable environmental justice policy initiatives.

Political Challenges

The final challenges facing the successful management of environmental justice issues are political. In large part, these difficulties stem from the fact that the main participants in the environmental justice debate have different definitions of a "successful" environmental justice policy. For environmental justice advocates, a successful policy is one that does the following: guarantees the effective participation of affected communities in environmental policy decisions (both public and private); reduces or halts altogether the siting of noxious facilities in disproportionately affected communities; promotes the future redistribution of environmental risk; and establishes compensation for the victims of environmental inequities. In contrast, the regulated community defines an effective environmental justice policy as one that produces a predictable permitting process with few delays, lawsuits, and protests. It also is one that allows firms to retain control over decisions regarding the use of private property, industrial processes, and the like. Environmental managers, for their part, prefer an environmental justice policy that allows for the siting of technically sound facilities that pose minimal environmental risk, that produces few legal challenges, and that enhances public support for the agency. The political challenge for environmental managers is to pursue these goals in a productive way while at the same time creating and seizing opportunities to serve as the arbiters of the sometimes contradictory goals of environmental justice advocates and the regulated community.

Notes

1. See Christopher Foreman, *The Promise and Peril of Environmental Justice* (Washington, D.C.: Brookings Institution Press, 1998).

2. Carol Browner, "EPA's Environmental Justice Strategy," Internal Agency Memorandum, April 3, 1995, www.epa.gov/compliance/resources/policies/ej/ej_strategy_1995.pdf, accessed May 9, 2002.

3. Christine Todd Whitman, "EPA's Commitment to Environmental Justice," Internal Agency Memorandum, August 9, 2001, http://www.epa.gov, accessed October 1, 2001.

4. Evan J. Ringquist and David Clark, "Local Risks, State's Rights, and Federal Mandates: Remedying Environmental Inequities in a Federalist System," *Publius* 29(2) (1999): 73–94.

5. Vicki Been, "What's Fairness Got to Do with It? Environmental Justice and the Siting of Locally Undesirable Land Uses," *Cornell Law Review* 78 (1993): 1001–1085.

6. See, for example, John Kingdon, *Agendas, Alternatives, and Public Policies* (Boston: Little, Brown, 1985); Paul Sabatier, ed., *Theories of the Policy Process* (Boulder, Colo.: Westview, 1999).

7. Anthony Downs, "Up and Down with Ecology: The 'Issue-Attention' Cycle," *Public Interest* 28 (1972): 38–50.

8. Riley Dunlap, Chengyang Xiao, and Aaron McCright, "Politics and Environment in America: Partisan and Ideological Cleavages in Public Support for Environmentalism," *Environmental Politics* 10(4) (2001): 23–48.

9. Evan J. Ringquist, "Environmental Justice: Normative Concerns, Empirical Evidence, and Governmental Action," in Norman J. Vig and Michael E. Kraft, eds., *Environmental Policy,* 5th ed., 249–274 (Washington, D.C.: Congressional Quarterly, 2003).

10. U.S. General Accounting Office, *Siting of Hazardous Waste Landfills and Their Correlation with Racial and Economic Status of Surrounding Communities* (Washington, D.C.: U.S. Government Printing Office, 1983).

11. Robert Bullard, ed., *Confronting Environmental Racism: Voices from the Grassroots* (Boston: South End, 1993).

12. Frank Baumgartner and Bryan Jones, *Agendas and Instabilities in American Politics* (Chicago: University of Chicago Press, 1993).

13. Theodore Lowi, *The End of Liberalism* (New York: W. W. Norton, 1979).

14. Evan J. Ringquist, "Environmental Justice: Normative Concerns and Empirical Evidence," in Norman J. Vig and Michael E. Kraft, eds., *Environmental Policy,* 4th ed., 232–256 (Washington, D.C.: Congressional Quarterly, 2000).

15. Evan J. Ringquist and David Clark, "Issue Definition and the Politics of State Environmental Justice Policy Adoption," *International Journal of Public Administration* 25(2–3) (2002): 351–389.

16. Anne Schneider and Helen Ingram, "Social Construction of Target Populations: Implications for Politics and Policy," *American Political Science Review* 87(2) (1993): 334–347.

17. Randall Ripley and Grace Franklin, *Congress, the Bureaucracy, and Public Policy* (Pacific Grove, Calif.: Brooks/Cole, 1991).

18. Foreman, *The Promise and Peril of Environmental Justice,* p. 12.

19. Although emissions and ambient pollution levels are not direct indicators of actual exposure, they clearly are superior to facility location as proxies for risk.

20. Commission for Racial Justice, *Toxic Wastes and Race in the United States* (New York: United Church of Christ, 1987).

21. Benjamin Goldman and Laura Fitton, *Toxic Wastes and Race Revisited* (Washington, D.C.: Center for Policy Alternatives, 1994).

22. Vicki Been, "Analyzing Evidence of Environmental Justice," *Journal of Land Use and Environmental Law* 11 (fall 1995): 1–36; Vicki Been, "Coming to the Nuisance or Going to the Barrios? A Longitudinal Analysis of Environmental Justice Claims," *Ecology Law Quarterly* 24(1) (1997): 1–56.

23. Evan J. Ringquist, "Race, Class, and the Politics of Environmental Risk," Department of Political Science, Florida State University, 1998, unpublished article.

24. John Hird and Michael Reese, "The Distribution of Environmental Quality," *Social Science Quarterly* 79 (1998): 693–716; James Lester, David Allen, and Kelly Hill, *Environmental Injustice in the United States* (Boulder, Colo.: Westview, 2001); Evan J. Ringquist, "Equity and the Distribution of Environmental Risk: The Case of TRI Facilities," *Social Science Quarterly* 78 (1997): 811–829.

25. Hird and Reese, "The Distribution of Environmental Quality"; Lester, Allen, and Hill, *Environmental Injustice in the United States*.

26. Douglas Anderton, Andy Anderson, John Michael Oakes, and Michael Fraser, "Environmental Equity: The Demographics of Dumping," *Demography* 31 (1994): 229–248; Pamela Davidson and Douglas Anderton, "Demographics of Dumping II: A National Environmental Equity Survey and the Distribution of Hazardous Materials Handlers," *Demography* 37 (2000): 461–466; Andrew Holmes, Barrett Slade, and Larry Cowart, "Are Minority Neighborhoods Exposed to More Environmental Hazards? Allegations of Environmental Racism," *Real Estate Review* 30(2) (2000): 50–57.

27. Laura Burke, "Race and Environmental Equity: A Geographic Analysis in Los Angeles," *Geo Info Systems* (October 1994): 44–50; Glynis Daniels and Samantha Friedman, "Spatial Inequality and the Distribution of Industrial Toxic Releases: Evidence from the 1990 TRI," *Social Science Quarterly* 80(2) (1999): 244–257; Rachel Morello-Frosch, Manuel Pastor, and James Sadd, "Environmental Justice and Southern California's 'Riskscape,'" *Urban Affairs Review* 36(4) (2001): 551–578; Susan R. Perlin, Woodrow Setzer, John Creason, and Ken Sexton, "Distribution of Industrial Air Emissions by Income and Race in the United States," *Environmental Science and Technology* 29 (1995): 69–80; Philip Pollock and M. Elliot Vittas, "Who Bears the Burdens of Environmental Pollution? Race, Ethnicity, and Environmental Equity in Florida," *Social Science Quarterly* 76 (1995): 294–310; Ringquist, "Equity and the Distribution of Environmental Risk"; James Sadd, Manuel Pastor, J. Boer, and L. Snyder, "Every Breath You Take: The Demographics of Toxic Releases in Southern California," *Economic Development Quarterly* 13(2) (1999): 103–123; Paul Stretesky and Michael Lynch, "Environmental Justice and the Predictions of Distance to Accidental Chemical Releases in Hillsborough County, Florida," *Social Science Quarterly* 80(4) (1999): 830–846.

28. Peter Asch and Joseph Seneca, "Some Evidence on the Distribution of Air Quality," *Land Economics* 54 (1978): 278–297; Leonard Gianessi and Henry Peskin, "The Distribution of Federal Water Pollution Control Policy in the U.S.,"

Land Economics 56 (1980): 85–102; Hird and Reese, "The Distribution of Environmental Quality"; Julian McCaull, "Discriminatory Air Pollution: If Poor, Don't Breathe," *Environment* 18 (1976): 26–31; K. Sexton, H. Gong, J. Bailar, J. Ford, D. Gold, W. Lambert, and M. Utell, "Air Pollution Health Effects: Do Race and Class Matter?" *Toxicology and Industrial Health* 9(5) (1993): 843–879.

29. Evan J. Ringquist and Joohyun Kang, "Assessing the Evidence Regarding Environmental Inequities: A Meta-analysis," paper presented at the annual meeting of the Midwest Political Science Association, Chicago, April 25–28, 2002.

30. Marianne Lavelle and Marcia Coyle, "Unequal Protection: The Racial Divide on Environmental Law," *National Law Journal,* September 21, 1992, p. S1.

31. Evan J. Ringquist, "A Question of Justice: Equity in Environmental Litigation, 1974–91," *Journal of Politics* 60 (4) (1998): 1148–1165.

32. John Hird, *Superfund: The Political Economy of Environmental Risk* (Baltimore: Johns Hopkins University Press, 1994).

33. Ringquist, "Race, Class, and the Politics of Environmental Risk."

34. R. Douglas Arnold, *The Logic of Congressional Action* (New Haven, Conn.: Yale University Press, 1990).

35. Dan Mazmanian and Paul Sabatier, *Implementation and Public Policy* (Lanham, Md.: University Press of America, 1989).

36. Ringquist, "Environmental Justice: Normative Concerns and Empirical Evidence."

37. Ringquist, "Race, Class, and the Politics of Environmental Risk."

38. Ibid.; James Hamilton, "Testing for Environmental Racism: Prejudice, Profits, Political Power?" *Journal of Policy Analysis and Management* 95 (1995): 107–132.

39. Been, "Coming to the Nuisance or Going to the Barrios?"; John Oates, Douglas Anderton, and Andy Anderson, "A Longitudinal Analysis of Environmental Equity in Communities with Hazardous Waste Facilities," *Social Science Research* 25 (1996): 125–148; Manuel Pastor, James Sadd, and John Hipp, "Which Came First? Toxic Facilities, Minority Move In, and Environmental Justice," *Journal of Urban Affairs* 23(1) (2001): 1–21.

40. Anderton et al., "Environmental Equity"; Been, "Analyzing Evidence of Environmental Justice"; Been, "Coming to the Nuisance or Going to the Barrios?"; Commission for Racial Justice, *Toxic Wastes and Race in the United States;* Davidson and Anderton, "Demographics of Dumping II"; Goldman and Fitton, *Toxic Wastes and Race Revisited;* Lester, Allen, and Hill, *Environmental Injustice in the United States;* Pollock and Vittas, "Who Bears the Burdens of Environmental Pollution?"; Ringquist, "Equity and the Distribution of Environmental Risk"; Ringquist, "Race, Class, and the Politics of Environmental Risk."

41. National Academy of Public Administration (NAPA), *Environmental Justice in EPA Permitting* (Washington, D.C.: NAPA, 2001).

42. Natalie Hammer, "Title VI as a Means of Achieving Environmental Justice," *Northern Illinois University Law Review* 16 (1996), p. 693; see also Luke Cole, "Remedies for Environmental Racism: A View from the Field," *Michigan Law Review* 90 (1991): 1991–1997; Rachel Godsil, "Remedying Environmental Racism," *Michigan Law Review* 90 (1991): 394–427; Barry Hill, "Chester, Pennsylvania—Was It a Classic Example of Environmental Injustice?" *Vermont Law Review* 23 (1999): 479–528.

43. Evan J. Ringquist, *Environmental Protection at the State Level: Politics and Progress in Controlling Pollution* (Armonk, N.Y.: M. E. Sharpe, 1993).

44. Charles Wise, "Judicial Federalism: The Resurgence of the Supreme Court's Role in the Protection of State Sovereignty," *Public Administration Review* 58(2) (1998): 95–98; Charles Wise, "The Supreme Court's New Constitutional Federalism: Implications for Public Administration," *Public Administration Review* 61(3) (2001): 343–358.

45. Denise Scheberle, *Federalism and Environmental Policy* (Washington, D.C.: Georgetown University Press, 1997), p. 18.

46. Environmental Council of the States (ECOS), *Environmental Protection Agency's Interim Guidance for Investigating Environmental Permit Challenges*, ECOS Resolution 98–2 (Washington, D.C.: ECOS, 1998), p. 2.

47. U.S. Conference of Mayors, *U.S. EPA's Interim Guidance for Investigating Title VI Administrative Complaints*, Resolution no. 32, 1998, www.ecos.org, accessed January 23, 2002.

48. National Association of Counties, "National Association of Counties Title VI Guidance Letter to EPA," 1999, www.ecos.org, accessed January 23, 2002.

49. Environmental Council of the States, "Environmental Justice and the States," 2002, www.ecos.org, accessed January 23, 2002.

50. *Alexander v. Sandoval*, 532 U.S., 2001.

51. *Cannon v. University of Chicago*, 441 U.S., 1979.

52. *Guardians Association v. Civil Service Commission of New York City*, 463 U.S., 1983.

53. *Seif v. Chester Residents Concerned for Quality Living*, 66 U.S.L.W. 3777, 1998.

54. Hill, "Chester, Pennsylvania—Was It a Classic Example of Environmental Injustice?"

55. For *South Camden Citizens in Action v. New Jersey Department of Environmental Protection*, see Kara Sissell, "Federal Ruling Redraws Environmental Justice Debate," *Chemical Week* 163 (2001), pp. 22, 48.

56. Michael O'Hare, Lawrence Bascow, and Debra Sanderson, *Facility Siting and Public Opposition* (New York: Van Nostrand Reinhold, 1983); Barry Rabe,

Beyond NIMBY: Hazardous Waste Siting in Canada and the United States (Washington, D.C.: Brookings Institution Press, 1994).

57. NAPA, *Environmental Justice in EPA Permitting.*

58. Richard Lazarus and Stephanie Tai, "Integrating Environmental Justice into EPA Permitting Authority," *Ecology Law Quarterly* 26 (1999): 617–678.

59. Ibid.

60. Ibid.

61. NAPA, *Environmental Justice in EPA Permitting.*

62. U.S. Environmental Appeals Board, WL 395962, EPA, June 29, 1995.

63. Lazarus and Tai, "Integrating Environmental Justice."

64. U.S. Environmental Appeals Board, WL 345288, EPA, May 27, 1999.

65. Lazarus and Tai, "Integrating Environmental Justice."

66. U.S. Environmental Appeals Board, WL 484880, EPA, September 8, 1993; U.S. Environmental Appeals Board, WL 395962, EPA, June 29, 1995.

67. Lazarus and Tai, "Integrating Environmental Justice."

68. Lavelle and Coyle, "Unequal Protection."

69. Ringquist, "A Question of Justice."

70. NAPA, *Environmental Justice in EPA Permitting.*

71. Alfred Marcus, *Promise and Performance: Choosing and Implementing an Environmental Policy* (Westport, Conn.: Greenwood, 1980).

72. Cornelius Kerwin, *Rulemaking: How Government Agencies Write Law and Make Policy* (Washington, D.C.: Congressional Quarterly, 1994).

73. NAPA, *Environmental Justice in EPA Permitting.*

74. Ibid.

75. Ibid.

8

Property Rights and Regulatory Takings

Charles R. Wise

Perhaps at no time over the past quarter century have the strategic challenges, choices, and opportunities involved with reconnecting with citizens in the United States been more visible, conflictual, and litigious than when citizens feel that environmental and natural resources (ENR) regulations have reduced the economic value of properties that they own, work on, or invest in. Perceived initially by environmentalists as an antigovernment and antienvironment movement led and funded by conservative interests and foundations in the western states, citizen resistance to burgeoning ENR regulations based on claims of property rights now is viewed often as a legitimate and permanent ENR tension.

The first widely documented manifestation of this tension came packaged in the Sagebrush Rebellion of the late 1970s. Grounding their argument in both states' rights and property rights, lawmakers in western states where the federal government owned very large tracts of property (for example, Nevada and New Mexico) that were leased for grazing, energy, mining, and forestry purposes attacked agencies such as the U.S. Bureau of Land Management, the U.S. Forest Service, and the U.S. Fish and Wildlife Service. They claimed that these agencies were applying rules and regulations to landowners' operations in ways that made their properties less profitable.

Similar sentiments subsequently followed in the Wise Use and County Rights movements of the 1980s and 1990s, respectively. Environmentalists widely assailed the former, again based largely in western states, as a ploy by conservative foundations and resource development industries to undermine statutes such as the Endangered Species Act and the National

Environmental Policy Act. Wise Use proponents alleged that too aggressive implementation of these statutes imposed an unfair and unwise economic toll on property owners by limiting development on these lands. Later, the County Rights movement would revive the Sagebrush Rebellion cudgel against ENR incursions, only this time with a focus on federal and state preemption of the regulatory discretion of counties. Like the Sagebrush Rebellion and Wise Use movement, the County Rights movement was limited to the West (albeit in smaller pockets). And not unlike the Sagebrush Rebellion, it sometimes made use of physical threats and violent behavior (for example, destruction of BLM offices) in its efforts to intimidate regulators.

But another battleground of the property rights movement during these decades attracted considerably less media attention. Here, skirmishes occurred on a case-by-case basis in various federal and state courts across the nation. Facilitated in the past fifteen years by pronouncements from the U.S. Supreme Court as well as by changes in federal and state laws, spiraling numbers of lawsuits premised on the "takings clause" of the U.S. Constitution have quietly "reconnected" government ENR regulators and their governance decisions to citizens in ways that many would have preferred to avoid. Indeed, in their implications for environmental governance, these takings clause lawsuits today collectively dwarf the more reported on "rebellions" occurring alongside them.

This rise in the number of property rights lawsuits is attributable to several factors. One is the proliferation of environmental laws at federal and state levels that impose increased obligations on property owners and constrain the uses to which they may put their properties. In addition, many federal environmental statutes have forced and continue to force environmental protection mandates to move from the federal level to state and local levels. In contrast to earlier decades, the federal environmental objectives are not pursued by means of federal financial grants to states and localities, but rather through mandatory regulatory activities that impose obligations on private-property owners.

The courts have responded as they have in other areas to provide redress for individuals for actions by the administrative state that impinge on constitutional rights.[1] Success in the courts then led to successes in state legislatures: property rights groups have been able to expand the avenues and criteria for redress available to them by means of expanded state legislation.[2] This expanded regulatory taking doctrine, in turn, has put regulators at all levels of government on notice that their actions are subject to an unprecedented degree of detailed review in state courts, federal courts, or both.

Of course, some courts are more deferential to regulators than others, but on balance a greater degree of judicialization of property regulation can be said to exist now than just two decades ago. In particular, regulators today may be obliged to pay monetary damages to property owners when the latter can prove that a taking has occurred. Such monetary awards pose significant penalties to environmental regulators for errors in understanding what the law requires if they impose inordinate regulatory burdens on private-property owners. This trend also may chill significantly the predisposition and ability of environmental managers to implement environmental regulations, in the process persuading some that a move away from command-and-control regulation is a necessity.

The advent of regulatory takings jurisprudence consequently has significant implications for environmental policy in numerous venues. Those drafting environmental laws must take care to ensure that such new laws, whether federal or state, can survive facial challenges alleging that they will cause property rights automatically to be taken. Regulators also are on notice that implementation of environmental laws can cause the government to incur liability for enforcement decisions that are judged to take property rights. Too great a fear of such litigation can cause underregulation, which will undermine the purpose of environmental laws. Too little regard for the risks of takings litigation can cause suits that result in new judicial prescriptions. These, in turn, can lead to less regulatory discretion and thus increase the complexity of the regulatory process. Moreover, losses in regulatory takings litigation also can result in the assessment of substantial financial damage awards against the regulating authority, thereby reducing the resources available for other environmental programs.

This chapter argues that an important issue facing the building of a results-based sense of common purpose in environmental governance in the twenty-first century in the United States is the challenge of gaining an understanding of the conditions under which a court is likely to assess liability against a regulatory agency for what is known as a "regulatory taking." Another issue is how to understand the ambiguities and the associated risks in the regulatory takings doctrine and how they are likely to unfold in the future. But sorely complicating both of these issues is the reality that the development of takings doctrine continues to unfold and is thus subject to disparate interpretations by the courts. Although the federal courts have clarified some of the doctrinal issues that regulators need to take into consideration in their regulatory decisions with regard to federal constitutional law, other issues are still fraught with ambiguity. For example, the logic of compensating a property owner when the application of an environmental regulation goes "too far" in exacting a contribution from the individual is inherent in our constitutional structure and comports with ordinary notions of fairness and justice. Yet federal courts provide few clear rules for regulators to use in guiding their actions. As a result, determining precisely what "too far" means in all the various concrete situations that environmental regulators face has proven difficult and is likely to remain so in the future.

In making these arguments, the chapter begins by discussing the history and logic behind the doctrine of regulatory takings and the forces encouraging the property rights movement to expand it. Next, it analyzes the implementation of the regulatory takings doctrine by the courts, highlighting the issues that have been resolved and those that remain unresolved to hinder the building of a results-based sense of common purpose in environmental governance. The chapter concludes by discussing the strategic challenges, choices, and opportunities facing environmental regulators in the context of the development of regulatory takings doctrine. Chronicled are the ways that courts and legislatures have tried inconsistently and ambiguously to balance communities' needs to protect public health, safety, and the environment with the rights of citizens to be secure in their property rights.

History and Logic of the Doctrine of Regulatory Takings

The prohibition on government's taking of private property is expressed explicitly in the U.S. Constitution's Fifth Amendment provision: "nor shall private property be taken for public use without just compensation."

Its application to government action takes place in two significant arenas. The first, not relevant to the topic of regulatory takings and hence not treated further in this chapter, occurs in the context of condemnation proceedings. In these instances, a government invokes its power of eminent domain and secures legal title to property in private ownership for a public purpose.[3]

The second arena is catalyzed when government applies a regulation to property in private ownership and the owner believes the application constitutes an encroachment that effectively "takes" his property. The owner files a suit for the taking and demands compensation. The primary logic of "taking" is based on the premise that the use of private property is a basic right. Although it long has been recognized in U.S. law that the government cannot take title to a person's private property without providing the individual with adequate compensation, only recently has it been recognized that government actions may so severely *restrict* an individual's use of property that its use effectively is denied. The logic behind the regulatory takings doctrine is that if government by regulation, in essence, denies property owners the use of their land, the government must compensate them the same as if it had taken physical possession of it.

In the 1922 case *Pennsylvania Coal v. Mahon*, the U.S. Supreme Court made the key interpretation that a government regulation could cause a taking that violated the Constitution.[4] The opinion authored by Justice Holmes specified, "the general rule at least is, that while property may be regulated to a certain extent, if regulation goes too far it will be recognized as a taking."[5] However, for decades after the *Pennsylvania Coal* decision, the Supreme Court did not specify any rules for the determination of a regulatory taking. Neither did it specify what actually constitutes "too far" or what compensation is due a property owner once "too far" has been crossed by the government issuing the regulation. For the most part, the Supreme Court was content to leave such interpretive matters to the state courts, where governments were overwhelmingly successful in defending themselves against regulatory taking challenges.

The Supreme Court's quiescence began to change in the late 1970s. In the 1978 case *Penn Central Transportation v. New York City*, the Court specified three factors as having particular significance in determining a regulatory taking: (1) the economic impact of the regulation on the property owner; (2) the extent to which the regulation interfered with distinct investment-backed expectations; and (3) the character of the governmental action.[6] The Court said that these three factors must be weighed and balanced with the public purpose underlying the regulation. Just a year later it declared that the methodology to be employed in weighing these factors consisted of "engaging in essentially ad hoc, factual inquiries."[7]

However, this decision provided no clear standard to the lower courts for weighing these factors. In *Ruckelshaus v. Monsanto* (1984), the Supreme Court indicated that the relative significance of the factors would vary from case to case.[8] Still, the Court did opine in a subsequent case that a taking could be found if an "ordinance does not substantially advance legitimate state interests . . . or denies an owner economically viable use of his land."[9] It also confirmed that it meant to stay with its preferred methodology, again citing the "'essentially ad hoc factual inquiry' involved in taking analysis."[10] Nonetheless, the Supreme Court was making these pronouncements largely in the context of cases that it decided in favor of the challenged governments.

In 1987, all this began to change. The Supreme Court handed down a trilogy of regulatory takings cases that substantially began to transform the legal landscape surrounding regulatory takings analysis. In the first case, *Keystone Bituminous Coal Association v. DeBenedictus,* the government won again, and no regulatory taking was determined to have been caused by the regulation. In a footnote, however, the Court directed the lower courts to examine how agencies operationalized regulatory statutes to assess substantial advancement of "legitimate state interests."[11] This direction to scrutinize how regulations were applied clearly portended potential for further challenges to government regulations.

In *Nolan v. California Coastal Commission* (1987), the Supreme Court acknowledged a gap in its jurisprudence involving takings when the majority opinion stated, "Our cases have not elaborated on the standards for determining what constitutes a 'legitimate state interest' or what type of connection between the regulation and the state interest satisfies the requirement that the former 'substantially advance' the latter."[12] The Court did not fill the gap but significantly began the process of addressing it, if only in part in this case. The case involved an application of a

California state law that authorized the Coastal commission to issue building permits along the coast. In this instance, the commission conditioned the granting of a building permit to the Nolans on the deeding of an access easement laterally between two public beaches, one on either side of the Nolan's property. The Nolan's beach was in back of their house. The commission said the large house would impede visual and psychological public access to the beach from the road that was on the front side of the house. The Supreme Court, however, could not find a logical connection between the access that was perpendicular from the road and the demanded easement that was lateral along the beach. In finding "the lack of nexus between the condition and the original purpose of the building restriction,"[13] the Court specified that an "essential nexus" must exist between the "end advanced" and the "condition imposed" by a regulation. If it does not, the regulation "is not a valid regulation of land use but 'an out-and-out plan of extortion.'"[14]

As indicated, this pronouncement of the requirement for an essential nexus only began to address the interpretive gap because the Court specified no definite method for ascertaining when the essential nexus was absent. The Court as much as admitted that this method would have to be developed later: "whatever may be the outer limits of 'legitimate state interests' in the takings and land use context, this is not one of them."[15] The Court did acknowledge, however, that although previous decisions had not set standards for "legitimate state interests," they "made clear that a broad range of governmental purposes and regulations satisfy those requirements."[16] Thus, it signaled that it was not circumscribing what governments might attempt to accomplish with their regulations, but that it was going to scrutinize the connection between governments' claims of purpose in particular applications and the effect of the regulations.

The third case in the trilogy, *First English Evangelical Lutheran Church of Glendale v. County of Los Angeles* (1987), dealt with the question of what was the appropriate remedy for a regulation that had denied a landowner use of his property temporarily. The question specifically was whether a regulator would be liable to pay compensation for the time the regulation was in effect or whether invalidation of the regulatory action would be the only remedy available to plaintiff property owners. The Supreme Court held that "[w]here the government's activities have already worked a taking for all use of property, no subsequent action by government can relieve it of its duty to provide compensation for the period during which the taking was effective."[17] Thus, temporary takings would require governments to pay compensation just the same as permanent ones. The Court also provided that the application of this payment requirement under the Just Compensation Clause of the Constitution applies to federal as well as to state and local government regulatory actions.[18] It did not answer the question, however, of how long the regulation would have to be in effect even to constitute a temporary taking.

As noted earlier, the Supreme Court directed the lower courts to use an "ad hoc balancing" methodology to weigh several factors in deciding on whether or not the application of a particular regulation constituted a taking. However, in *Lucas v. South Carolina Coastal Council* (1992), the Court set out one category of cases where the lower courts were to set aside this method and automatically find that a taking had occurred. It specified that regulators have to provide compensation when the regulation denies "all economic viable use" of the property.[19] For regulations in this category, government regulators cannot argue that the impact of the regulation on the property owner is mitigated by a legitimate regulatory purpose. In addition, the Court specified that the regulation "cannot be newly legislated or decreed [without compensation], but must inhere in the title itself, in the restrictions that background principles already place upon land ownership."[20] As a result, any new laws that impose new regulations denying all economic viable use of a property will be judged a taking, unless they can be interpreted as already restricting property ownership. If newly legislated restrictions extend far enough from this base, then the courts can require compensation.

After the *Nolan* decision, many regulators wondered what they needed to do to demonstrate that an essential nexus exists between the end advanced and the condition imposed by a regulation. In a subsequent case, the Supreme Court said more about this in the context of required exactions (or stipulations) that a city planning commission placed on a hardware store owner trying to secure a building permit. In *Dolan v. Tigard* (1994), the Court sought to determine in its analysis whether the exactions demanded in the commission's permit conditions bore the requisite relationship to the projected impact of the store owner's proposed development. It held that the test to be met would be its own enunciated test of "rough proportionality." As the justices stated, "No precise mathematical calculation is required, but the city must make some sort of individualized determination that the required dedication is related both in nature and extent to the impact of the proposed development."[21]

In this instance, the Court did not accept the city's general findings that the proposed larger store would generate more traffic, necessitating dedication of property to a pedestrian and bicycle pathway, nor that a larger parking lot necessitated a dedication of land to a floodplain. It stated that the city must make some effort to quantify its findings, demonstrating the store's contribution to the asserted problems and the relationship of the dedications to offsetting that contribution. In short, an individualized determination of the store's impact on the problem and of the impact of required exactions on both the property and the problem would be required. This decision placed more responsibility on regulators to provide more detailed analysis to support their determinations and applications of regulations on property owners.

In the case *City of Monterey v. Del Monte Dunes* (1999), however, the Supreme Court clarified that the Dolan proportionality test was not relevant to cases that did not involve exactions.[22] Yet numerous courts have given the concept of exactions a very broad meaning and have applied a higher level of scrutiny. Not only in cases involving the dedication of land for public use has this occurred, but also in cases involving a variety of types of exactions and restrictions, including impact fees, the financing of onsite or offsite improvements, the reservation of open space, setback requirements, restrictions on occupancy, and even hours of operation.[23] The Supreme Court in *Del Monte Dunes* also held, however, that a jury can decide if a city's decision to deny a development proposal is reasonably related to a city's proffered justifications.[24]

Implementation of the Regulatory Takings Doctrine by the Courts: Issues Resolved and Unresolved

In implementing the Supreme Court's regulatory takings doctrine, the federal courts have had to address several key components and subcomponents in takings analysis. The key components include the definition of *property*, the determination of the effect of the regulation on the property, and the effect of timing factors. At this stage of development of the regulatory takings doctrine, some issues involved in applying these components and their associated subcomponents have been resolved, but others have not. These numerous unresolved issues, in turn, pose risks for environmental regulators. The following discussion of the major components and subcomponents addresses both the resolved and unresolved issues associated with each and points out the risks and problems they occasion for building a results-based sense of common purpose in environmental governance in the twenty-first century.

The Definition of Property in Takings Analysis

The first task of the property owner in stating a claim for a taking is to specify a property interest that has been violated according to federal or state constitutional takings clauses. For purposes of takings analysis, *property* is not a physical thing such as the land or the coal under the land owned by an individual. Rather, *property* refers to the "group of rights inhering in the citizen's relation to the physical thing, as the right to possess, use, and dispose of it."[25] The logic of this rights-based definition is consistent with the foundational theory of regulatory takings in that a regulation does not take the physical thing, but instead takes rights from the property owner, which therefore interferes with the owner's use of the property.[26]

Notice that there is not one particular "right in property" at issue in regulatory takings cases. Rather, the Supreme Court uses a "bundle of sticks" approach in which various rights in property are treated as "sticks" making up the "bundle" that constitutes all the rights associated with a property. It is thus possible for a government regulation to "take" the whole bundle or one or more sticks that constitute the bundle. These property interests, or sticks, are not enumerated in the U.S. Constitution itself, but their dimensions are defined by existing rules or understandings that stem from sources such as state law.[27]

When we normally think of property, real estate or commodities associated with real estate (such as minerals found on or under the land) come to mind. However, the courts have taken a wider view by considering property that is not associated with real estate, but that is affected by regulations that limit economic activity or require payments, in the context of takings analysis.[28] Whether dealing with real property or not, however, the courts must resolve two major and challenging issues in any takings analysis. First, what constitutes the unit of property involved in the taking? Second, because different criteria are applied to different types of takings, what type of regulatory taking is involved?

Defining the Unit of Property That Is the Subject of Takings Analysis
Defining what unit of property is involved in a takings controversy has two major aspects. The first involves the court's determining exactly which parcel of real estate is to be the subject of takings analysis. Consider the case, for example, of a property owner who owns acreage, some of which is a lowland wetland and some of which is dry upland. If the regulator refuses to allow the filling in of the wetland for development to prevent damage to the wider waters of which the wetland is a part, the court must decide if the relevant parcel is just the lowland wetland or both the lowland-wetland parcel and the upland parcel. In turn, the second aspect of defining units of property occurs in the context of cases where one or more property interests, such as water rights or the right to exclude others, is claimed to have been taken. The issue for the court involves the significance of these particular sticks in the bundle of sticks that constitute the property rights.

Establishing the relevant parcel of land is a critical point in takings analysis because that determination can affect significantly whether the court holds that a taking has or has not occurred. If a regulation denies the use of part of a parcel of property, but the remaining property is unaffected, the chances of compensation being awarded are reduced. Thus, landowners try to have the court declare the piece affected as the relevant parcel, and regulators attempt to have the entire property declared as the relevant parcel.[29] The Supreme Court has not issued definitive guidance for making this determination but rather has said seemingly contradictory things. In *Penn Central Transportation v. City of New York* (1978), for example, the Court inveighed against dividing a single parcel into discrete segments,[30] but in *Concrete Pipe & Products of California v. Construction Laborers Pension Trust* (1993), it seemed to endorse the idea that only a portion could be "taken."[31] Although it has referred to this dilemma in subsequent cases, it has said nothing to resolve the ambiguity, apparently leaving it to the lower courts to try various approaches to resolving it.[32]

Defining What Type of Taking Is Involved   The Supreme Court does not necessarily treat all types of regulatory takings uniformly, but tends to apply somewhat different criteria to each of three major types: physical, title or exaction, and economic. Allegations of a physical taking involve some physical invasion, occupation, or destruction of the property by a government entity. If the application of a regulation by a government entity involves any of these actions, a taking is much more likely to be found. The Supreme Court has stated that any regulation, regardless of the government interest, that involves a permanent physical invasion of a property will be found to be a taking.[33] A district court found, for example, that a state-authorized underground injection of wastewater on a company's property resulted in a subsurface migration of wastewater on a plaintiff landowner's property. This, the court argued, could constitute a permanent physical occupation, thus creating a per se taking.[34] The occupation does not necessarily have to preclude other uses to be judged a taking. Moreover, even if the occupation is done pursuant to a legitimate purpose, a court can require compensation. Also, neither the extent of the diminution of the property value nor the duration of the taking make a difference when a physical invasion is involved.[35] The Federal Circuit has specified that a taking can be for a limited term, so even limited or episodic physical invasions require compensation.[36]

In contrast, allegations of a title or exaction taking involve the government's acquiring ownership or title to a property or an exaction in lieu of the dedication of land.[37] For example, in *Nolan,* the regulatory commission required the property owners to covey an easement to their beach property. Because the Supreme Court held that the right to exclude others was an "essential stick" in the bundle of property rights, it employed a heightened level of scrutiny to the application of the regulation. The justices specifically required an essential nexus between the legitimate state interest and the regulatory conditions applied to the property. In addition, in *Dolan,* the Court employed a two-prong test, the first prong consisting of the essential nexus test and the second requiring that the exaction demanded by the regulator must be roughly proportional to the projected impact of the proposed development.[38] With regard to this second prong, the burden of proof is on the regulator to demonstrate that the required dedication or exaction is roughly proportional to the impact of the owner's proposed project.[39]

The regulator's burden requires an "individualized determination" of project impact. In *Goss v. City of Little Rock* (1998), the city argued that it did not have to prepare a site-specific study. The Eighth Circuit disagreed and held that the city's requirement of street improvements constituted a taking because the ordinance that required improvements was based only on the fact that the street abutted the proposed subdivision. It did not depend on proof that the subdivision would cause additional use of the street. The court found that the exaction did not meet the test of rough proportionality.[40] The city also claimed that it did not have to meet that test because it was demanding a fee rather than a dedication of land. The Eighth Circuit, however, stated that the essential nexus test is designed to prevent government from imposing conditions on landowners, requiring either land or money, and that the lack of the requisite connection between the demand and the public impact of the project constituted a taking.[41] The rough proportionality test also has been applied to dedications and exactions involving subdivision approvals,[42] rezoning,[43] annexation,[44] and housing preservation.[45] Courts have varied significantly in their disposition to defer to local planning analyses and findings. Some have deferred provided there is evidence of individualized findings,[46] whereas others have subjected local analyses to intense scrutiny.[47]

Last, allegations of economic takings represent most of the regulatory takings cases heard by the courts. For these, the general rule, as stated by the Supreme Court in *Agins v. Tiburon* (1980), is that a regulation does not constitute a taking if it "substantially advances legitimate state interests" and does not "deny an owner economically viable use of his land."[48] As stated in *Lucas v. South Carolina Coastal Commission*, a per se taking will be found to have occurred if the regulation denies 100 percent of the economically viable use of the property, unless the regulation is preventing an established common law nuisance.[49] For cases where 100 percent is not taken, courts must engage in the ad hoc balancing test described earlier.

The Effect of a Regulation on Property

Another major component of takings analysis by the courts involves determining the effect of a regulation on the property as defined. In this area, the courts have recognized that regulations must be allowed to affect property rights to some extent without triggering government liability for takings. Nonetheless, the Supreme Court has set out some markers for trial courts to use in assessing the nature of the effects in order to determine if liability is triggered. Here, three tests are relevant: whether a legitimate state interest is involved, whether a viable economic interest exists, and what investment-based expectations are realistic.

Is a Legitimate State Interest Involved?   The Supreme Court has made it clear that trial courts engaging in "ad hoc balancing" will assess the asserted public purpose of the regulation in question. In *Nolan,* the Court explicitly affirmed that a broad range of governmental purposes and regulations can be considered "legitimate state purposes."[50] Nonetheless, a court's inquiry does not stop with the finding that there is some asserted public purpose. The court will assess the degree to which the application of the regulation on the specific property "substantially advances" the asserted public purpose and will weigh that assessment against the burden on the property owner.

In weighing the public benefit versus the private burden, the court may make a distinction between public purposes. It may weigh more heavily in the regulator's favor when the regulation is found to prevent a public harm, but more heavily in the property owner's favor when the regulation is found to maintain a public benefit. The balance is most likely to fall in the regulator's favor when the public purpose falls under the nuisance exception. The nuisance principle, which the courts have long recognized, simply means that individuals may not make a "noxious use of their property to inflict injury upon the community."[51] The nuisance exception can apply even when significant diminution in property value results from the application of the regulation.[52] However, the

Supreme Court has made it clear that the nuisance exception is not coterminous with the police power itself,[53] so that regulators cannot claim that every public harm they seek to prevent can be classified as a nuisance. The Court has stated that if this were not the case, then the Just Compensation Clause would become a nullity, always subordinate to the police power.[54]

The trial court is required to find the actual relationship of the regulation to a real public harm and not to accept general assertions. The Supreme Court has held that it is appropriate for a federal court to submit to a jury the predominantly factual question of whether a landowner has been denied all economically viable use of his property, and the question of whether a city's development denial bears a reasonable relationship to the justifications offered by the regulator.[55] Thus, not only will juries have a significant role in assessing the presence of legitimate state interests, but the question is raised regarding how courts will draw the line between what is a matter of constitutional law for the court and what is a factual matter for the jury.[56] Further complicating matters for regulators, the level of judicial scrutiny of governments' asserted public purposes has not been consistent among various courts.[57]

What Constitutes Economic Viability?   In order to determine economic viability, the court compares the value of the property before the regulation with the value remaining after application of the regulation. The Supreme Court has stated often that "mere diminution" of property value is not enough for the regulation to be judged to effect a taking.[58] However, the Court also has said, "One fact for consideration in determining such limits is the extent of diminution. When it reaches a certain magnitude, in most if not all cases there must be an exercise of eminent domain and compensation to sustain the act."[59] Nonetheless, it has not provided a figure or percentage of how much diminution in value signifies that this "certain magnitude" has been reached.

Also complicating this determination is the consideration that the economically viable use of a property is not limited to immediate uses, but also can include future uses of the property.[60] This does not mean that the regulator may assert hypothetical alternative future uses of the property in order to escape the requirement to provide compensation. As the U.S.

Court of Claims explained, "The court sitting as a finder of fact must discount proposed uses that do not meet the showing of reasonable probability that the land is both physically adaptable for such use and that there is a demand for such use in the reasonable near future."[61]

Although the Supreme Court has said that "mere diminution" of property value is not enough, it also has carved out a special category of per se taking when all economically viable use has been taken. If the value taken is less than 100 percent, trial courts are directed to use the ad hoc balancing methodology. Therefore, the court must be expecting that this stipulation is directed at cases where some percentage in value is taken, but less than 100 percent. That is the way the Federal Circuit interpreted it: "Nothing in the language of the Fifth Amendment compels a court to find a taking *only* when the Government divests the total ownership of the property; The Fifth Amendment prohibits the uncompensated taking of private property without reference to the owner's remaining property interests."[62] In deciding that a 73 percent diminution in value justifies a finding of a taking, for example, the U.S. Court of Claims opined:

The notion that the government can take two thirds of your property and not compensate you but must compensate you if it takes 100% has a ring of irrationality, if not unfairness about it. If the law said that those injured by tortuous conduct could only have their estates compensated if they were killed, but not themselves if they could still breathe, no matter how seriously injured, we would certainly think it odd, if not barbaric. Yet in takings trials, we have the government trying to prove that the patient has a few breaths left, while the plaintiffs seek to prove, often at great expense, that the patient is dead. This all-or-nothing approach seems to ignore the point of the Takings Clause.[63]

What Constitutes a Reasonable "Investment-Backed Expectation"?
Recall from the Supreme Court's decision in the *Penn Central* case that one of the three factors trial courts are supposed to weigh in assessing whether a regulation causes a taking is interference of the regulation with "distinct investment-backed expectations." With respect to determining the parameters of this factor, however, confusion exists. Although the courts have employed it in decisions, "at no point has the concept of 'investment-backed expectations' been defined or its implications fully explored," as one commentator put it.[64]

One of the issues for the courts is how to take profits into consideration of what constitutes investment-backed expectations. In *Andrus v. Allard*

(1979), the Supreme Court refused to consider lost profits from sales as a criterion.[65] Yet in *Williamson Planning Commission v. Hamilton Bank* (1985), the Supreme Court actually *added* profit to the investment factor, referring to it as "investment-backed profit expectations."[66] Lower courts also have treated profits in various ways. The Federal Circuit in one case denied a property owner's expectation of immediate profit-making use as a criterion in determining investment-backed expectations. It did state, however, that profits from future possible development under the regulation should be a criterion. The Court of Appeals of New York invalidated a city regulation and pointed to the fact that the property owner had purchased the properties solely to turn them into profitable investments, concluding that these development rights "standing alone" constituted valuable components of the "bundle of rights" making up their fee interests.[67]

Another issue is what must factor into an owner's "expectation." In *Good v. United States* (1999), the Federal Circuit denied a developer's appeal of a Corps of Engineers' denial of a renewal application for a permit to develop his land in the Florida Keys. The developer had an approved permit, but it expired because of numerous delays and court battles in his attempts to obtain state authorization. The Corps refused the renewal application on the basis of the Endangered Species Act, which had been passed after the developer had acquired his land. The developer argued that at the time of his purchase, he could not have expected a denial based on an act that had yet to be enacted. The court acknowledged that his position was not unreasonable. Yet in view of the "regulatory climate" that existed when he purchased his property, the developer could not have had a reasonable expectation that he would obtain approval to fill ten acres of wetlands so that he could develop the land.[68]

Issues Involved with Timing

The final set of issues with both resolved and unresolved aspects that regulators must struggle with in takings analyses involves timing. Here, the courts deal with three questions that have significant effects on the resolution of the controversy: When can a takings appeal be filed? When did the taking actually occur? What is the duration of the taking?

When Can a Takings Appeal Be Filed?   Federal courts are not necessarily going to grant a full trial on the merits when a suit for a regulatory taking is filed. A court first will decide if the case is ready for federal court review. Key issues involved in the determination are whether a facial challenge is permissible, whether the case meets the standards for ripeness, or both. Facial challenges occur when property owner plaintiffs file their allegations of a regulatory taking at the point that a regulator issues a regulation and before application to a specific property. In such cases, the plaintiff attempts to prove that the regulation amounts to a taking on its face. As noted earlier, however, the Supreme Court's preferred method for judges deciding regulatory takings is an "as applied basis." Nonetheless, some courts have allowed facial challenges to proceed. For instance, a facial challenge to a New York City ordinance establishing a five-year moratorium on conversion, alteration, or demolition of single-room occupancy housing was successful,[69] as was a challenge to the Surface Mining Control Act.[70]

If a property owner challenges a regulation on its face rather than as applied, there is little, if any, debate as to whether the claim is ripe for adjudication. Ripeness is not a component of a facial challenge in that the property owner is alleging that the regulation constitutes a taking not only of his or her property, but of all property subject to the regulation.[71] In contrast, if the challenge is classified as applied, it immediately necessitates application of judicial ripeness doctrine. In these vastly more common types of takings challenges, the Supreme Court has made it clear that "[a]ny analysis in an as-applied regulatory taking claim must start with the threshold question of ripeness: Has there been a final decision from the appropriate governmental entity as to the nature and extent of the development that will be permitted?"[72] In these cases, the Court has emphasized the inherent relationship between the land-use taking question and the ripeness issue.[73] It has suggested that the final decision requirement is not satisfied when a developer submits and a land-use authority denies a grandiose development proposal, leaving open the possibility that lesser uses of the property might be permitted.[74] Nonetheless, the Court also has specified that a landowner does not need to resubmit revised plans repeatedly. It has said, "while a landowner must give a land-use authority an opportunity to exercise its discretion, once it becomes clear that the agency lacks the discretion to permit any development, or the permissible uses of the property are known to a reasonable degree of certainty, a takings claim is likely to have ripened."[75]

The significance of the use of ripeness doctrine should not be underestimated. It has constituted a powerful defense for local governments facing takings challenges, often forcing claims out of the courts and back into the local administrative process.[76] It also can serve to keep takings claims out of federal courts. Federal courts, for example, often grant motions to dismiss takings claims made by state and local regulators because the property owner failed to pursue state court remedies. This decision can be made under the Supreme Court's pronouncement in *Williamson County* that a "property owner has not suffered a violation of the Just Compensation Clause until the owner has unsuccessfully attempted to obtain just compensation through the procedures provided by the State."[77] Again, however, ambiguity faces ENR regulators because courts have been inconsistent in their holdings.[78]

When Did the Taking Actually Occur?   The issue of when a taking occurs is significant for several reasons. First, the date on which the taking cause of action is found to be ripe determines who may maintain the action and collect compensation. Only those with ownership interests as of the date of the taking qualify for compensation. Second, the date of the taking starts the running of the statute of limitations. Third, the taking date defines how much money the property owner gets. The amount of compensation owed is the market value of the property at the time the taking occurs. Also, the taking date begins the period during which interest on the award accumulates.[79]

Despite the apparent straightforwardness of these determinations, the courts have had to resolve issues relevant to them. The Supreme Court, for instance, recently stated that some legislative enactments affecting the time at which a property holder is declared to be an owner for purposes of a taking determination may be held to be unreasonable. In *Palazzolo v. Rhode Island* (2001), the precursor decision by the Rhode Island Supreme Court held that the owner had no right to challenge regulations predating 1978, when he succeeded to legal ownership of the property from a partnership in which he was involved. The U.S. Supreme Court rejected the Rhode Island decision and stated:

Just as a prospective enactment, such as a new zoning ordinance, can limit the value of land without effecting a taking because it can be understood as reasonable by all concerned, other enactments are unreasonable and do not become less so through the passage of time or title. Were we to accept the State's rule, the postenactment transfer of title would absolve the State of its obligation to defend any action restricting land use, no matter how extreme or unreasonable. A State would be allowed, in effect, to put an expiration date on the Takings Clause. This ought not to be the rule. Future generations, too, have a right to challenge unreasonable limitations on the use and value of land.[80]

Thus, the Supreme Court is saying that the states' ability to create and extinguish property rights, including who has the right to exercise them, is limited to a criteria of reasonableness.[81]

Does the Duration of the Taking Make a Difference?   Another timing issue concerns the requirement for compensation for regulations that are in effect temporarily. As discussed earlier, in *First English,* the Supreme Court held that when a regulation was found to have caused a taking, even if it was in effect for a temporary period and was subsequently changed, the owner was still owed compensation. Nonetheless, the Court did not specify what constituted a temporary taking in that case. It merely limited its holding "to the facts presented" and said that it recognized "the quite different questions that would arise in the case of normal delays in obtaining building permits, changes in zoning ordinances, variances and the like which are not before us."[82]

Since then, however, the Supreme Court has not said much about what constitutes "normal" or "abnormal" delays, or about the process or criteria for assessing them. In the case *Tahoe Sierra Preservation Council v. Tahoe Regional Planning Agency* (2002),[83] the Court did provide some direction. At issue in this case was whether a moratorium on development imposed during the process of devising a comprehensive plan constituted a per se taking of property requiring compensation under the Constitution's Takings Clause. The Tahoe Regional Planning Agency had ordered two moratoria on development to maintain the status quo while studying the impact of development on Lake Tahoe and designing a strategy for environmentally sound growth. The moratoria prohibited any development over a thirty-two-month period. An organization representing property owners, joined by individual property owners, sued, alleging a temporary taking and demanding compensation. They contended that the mere enactment of a temporary regulation that, while in effect, denies a property owner all viable use of his or her land gives rise to an unqualified constitutional obligation to compensate him or her for the value of its use during that period.[84]

The Court found in favor of the Tahoe Regional Planning Agency and concluded that the moratoria did not require compensation. In doing so, it refused to adopt a categorical criterion for how long rules such as the moratorium can preclude development. Instead, it directed the lower courts to engage in its preferred method of ad hoc balancing in which the time period prohibiting development would constitute only one of the factors for consideration.[85] The Court stated that in rejecting the owner's per se rule, it did not hold that the temporary nature of a land-use restriction precludes finding that the temporary restriction effects a taking; it simply recognizes that the temporary nature of the restriction should not be given exclusive significance one way or the other.[86] The Court did say, however, that any moratorium that lasts for more than one year should be viewed with special skepticism. Yet it also pointed out that the District Court had found the thirty-two months required by the agency to formulate a regional plan not unreasonable, so it was not going to conclude that every delay more than one year was constitutionally unacceptable.[87]

Thus, regulators should not expect any categorical rule for calculating duration in a temporary takings claim. Instead, the courts will assess the reasonableness of the duration of the impact of a regulation with other factors in their ad hoc analysis. Moreover, in the process of upholding the reasonableness of the Tahoe moratorium, the Supreme Court justices made several observations that seem to provide some support for regulations involving actions such as moratoria. Most significant, they pointed out that "At least with a moratorium there is a clear 'reciprocity of advantage,' because it protects the interests of all affected landowners against immediate construction that might be inconsistent with the provisions of the plan that is ultimately adopted."[88]

Reprise

In sum, the unresolved issues discussed here do portend continuing risks for environmental regulators, as well as continuing barriers to building a sense of common purpose among stakeholders if agencies do not attend to them. Becoming aware of such areas of ambiguity and the resultant risks is the first step in preparing for such risks, minimizing them, and moving toward a results-based sense of common purpose in environmental governance. Some risks are clearer than others. Administration of regulations that require a physical occupation, such as positioning test equipment on private property, carries with it a high risk of liability. In these cases, regulators can seek to obtain the owner's permission, offer compensation in advance, or select an alternative method.

Implementation of regulations that result in demands for exaction from property owners also carries risks. Regulators who can document carefully the link between an increased burden posed by a proposed use of property and an exaction requirement to mitigate it will reduce the risk of liability. The remaining ambiguity is in the extensiveness of analysis a court may require. Application of regulations that remove all economically viable use of a property is most likely to result in liability. Regulators who can demonstrate that the impacted property retains alternative uses can reduce the risk of liability, but the projected uses must be realistic.

Whether diminution in value of a property below 100 percent will result in liability is also uncertain, although small diminutions are unlikely to pose significant risks. The method for determining the relevant parcel still is not resolved and thus poses a risk for regulators. Consistent documentation that an affected portion of a whole parcel has been considered legally as a part of the whole can help minimize risk but not entirely eliminate it. The determination of whether a final regulatory decision has been made and thus whether a regulatory action is ripe for court review is also somewhat ambiguous. Consequently, regulators who can adopt procedures and criteria to clarify the issue of final determination may reduce risk in this area.

Future Challenges, Choices, and Opportunities for Environmental Governance

The ambiguities in the federal regulatory takings doctrine chronicled in this chapter reflect the difficulties in coming to grips with some very nettlesome issues and pose real obstacles for building a results-based sense of common purpose in environmental governance in the future. Drawing from this review and from ongoing legislative developments regarding takings issues at the federal, state, and local government levels, a formidable set of strategic challenges, choices, and opportunities is involved in doing so. Most prominent among those facing regulators are monitoring and adapting to evolving takings doctrines in the courts, doing the same when it comes to new responsibilities imposed on them by statutory changes, and building the administrative capacity to both respond to and shape these evolving legislative and judicial interpretations.

Adapting to Evolving Judicial Takings Doctrines

As the preceding material has chronicled, monitoring and adapting to evolving judicial doctrine on takings issues are not easy tasks. The standard for "economic viability" and the extent of diminution an environmental regulation can cause to that viability without being declared as effecting a taking reflect the difficulty in resolving competing values in the takings calculus. On the one hand, there is no recognized principle that any amount of loss to an individual requires compensation. We all have responsibilities as citizens to the general welfare, and the constitutional scheme recognizes our responsibility to give up some individual advantages so that the overall community can be maintained. Thus, the Supreme Court has made it clear that even if an individual property owner suffers a net loss after the application of a regulation (note: this loss is implied), compensation is not necessarily owed. It does not have to balance out. On the other hand, and less laudably, the government has a perverse incentive to foist the costs of environmental improvements for the community onto the fewest individuals possible. If allowed to do so, the courts have a responsibility to step in to prevent, for example, threats to the economic viability of affected persons' properties. In the process of adjudication, of course, the building of a results-based sense of common purpose suffers immensely.

The difficulty for regulators comes in identifying all the contributing factors and finding a balance point. That can be difficult even when a single property is involved, but the challenge becomes all the more difficult when several or even hundreds of properties are affected by enforcement of a regulation. Differential impacts are most likely to be the rule, and they are difficult to anticipate, let alone mediate. In one sense, the developing regulatory takings doctrine serves as a positive impetus to encourage environmental regulators to assess the impacts of their contemplated regulatory actions and to assure equitable treatment of property owners. The danger is that the risks of liability will chill environmental regulators' legitimate activities in pursuit of environmental values that they have legal responsibilities to protect aggressively.

The federal courts have made it clear that a very broad array of legitimate state purposes can be pursued by regulation, and if the application of a legitimate regulation is proportionate, then no liability will be attached. Thus, regulators who clearly can demonstrate a linkage between their implementation of a regulation and the demands placed on a property owner are advantaged in a court proceeding concerning liability for a regulatory taking. Regulators thus are encouraged in choosing among regulatory applications to emphasize those for which a clear linkage can be demonstrated.

Monitoring State and Federal Legislation

Areas of growing present and future strategic challenges, choices, and opportunities for regulators also may be found in state constitutions, state statutes, and federal statutes. With regard to state constitutions, it should be recognized that forty-seven of fifty state constitutions contain a "takings clause," with Kansas, New Hampshire, and North Carolina the exceptions. Thus, property owners can file suits in state courts pursuant to their state constitutional takings provisions to challenge state or local regulations. Some states' taking clauses have a slightly different textual reference, with several requiring compensation for property that is "taken or damaged." Some state courts attribute no meaning to the "or damaged" term beyond what the federal and state courts have determined as takings.

Nonetheless, others have concluded that the "or damaged" term constitutes a higher level of constitutional protection.[89] Thus, it should be understood that federal Fifth Amendment doctrine constitutes a floor of property rights protection and not a ceiling, with individual states thus able to create a higher constitutional standard for property rights protection on "independent state grounds."[90]

In recent years, various state legislatures have passed statutes creating new responsibilities for state and local agencies with respect to regulatory takings, as well as some new state causes of action for them on which property owners can seek relief in state courts. These statutory enactments encompass four basic approaches to property rights legislation: preliminary measures, procedural changes, assessment provisions, and compensation measures. Preliminary measures create no procedural or substantive changes to the regulatory process, but they include symbolic declarations or create study commissions to examine the matter. Procedural modifications include a range of changes to existing administrative procedures that either incorporate consideration of private-property rights within their purview or provide specific rule-making provisions to limit state liability under specific conditions. An example of a procedural modification is Idaho's amendment to its local land-use planning act so that it includes analysis of private-property protection as an element in the comprehensive planning process.

Assessment provisions included in state laws generally represent one of two types. The first type gives an official outside the regulatory agency, usually the state attorney general, responsibility for reviewing rules and regulations proposed by state agencies. This review, in turn, is based on criteria involving property rights included in the statute. This type of statute alternatively can require the attorney general to issue guidelines for the agencies to use as they incorporate the criteria into the law. The second approach to assessment provisions gives the state agencies the responsibility for reviewing their proposed regulations, although in some instances they must use criteria that the statute directs the attorney general to develop. The Idaho statute, for example, requires the attorney general to develop a checklist for state agencies to use in assessing their regulatory actions, prior to taking any action with takings implications.

Compensation measures, in contrast to the *ex ante* assessment measures just discussed, provide post hoc remedies for reductions in property value owing to governmental action. They create new causes of action above and beyond those previously available to property owners through judicial avenues. The intent is to provide a line that, when crossed by a state or local regulatory action, defines the occurrence of a regulatory taking and the requirement of compensation to the property owner. For example, the Texas Private Real Property Protection Act waives government entities' sovereign immunity to suit and liability in actions to determine if a taking has occurred. Property owners alleging a taking have 180 days after the regulatory action to file a judicial action or to seek an administrative proceeding to determine if a taking has occurred. A judgment in their favor may order rescission of the action, or the government defendant may elect to pay compensation to the property owner. In the Texas statute, governmental actions by the state or political subdivisions that diminish property value by as little as 25 percent may be compensable. In Mississippi, the amended Forestry and Agricultural Activity Law creates a private right of action to seek compensation for certain governmental actions that reduce the value of agricultural and forestry lands by 40 percent or more.

The new state laws raise numerous policy and administrative questions that affect environmental governance and further challenge the acumen of environmental regulators. In assigning a responsibility to either the state attorney general or administrative agencies, some assessment measures transport much of the ambiguity surrounding regulatory takings into the administrative process. Difficult matters of interpretation of what constitutes a taking impact must be resolved because they can hamper the regulatory process and potentially may cause risk-averse regulatory behavior. Likewise, statutory measures that define criteria for takings create greater liability for state regulators. Meanwhile, compensation measures clearly expand the liability of state regulators beyond that declared in extant Supreme Court doctrine and by doing so allow less latitude than the federal courts have allowed to state regulators.[91]

In recent years, numerous attempts have been made to enact new federal statutes that in many ways parallel the types of assessment and compensation requirements enacted at the state level. An example of an assessment approach is found in S.1412, introduced in the 107th Congress. This bill would require each federal agency to complete an impact analysis before any agency action is begun (including the promulgation of a regulation) that is likely to result in a taking of private property. With specified exemptions, agencies would have to consider alternatives fully and to alter their action(s) to avoid or minimize the taking of private property. Likewise, an example of a compensation approach is found in H.R. 1403. That bill sought to amend the Endangered Species Act to prohibit a federal agency from taking an action affecting privately owned property by an amount equal to or greater than half of the value of the portion of the property, unless compensation is offered. The bill also directs the agency to buy that portion of the property at fair market value, at the owner's option.

Another compensation bill, H.R. 472, would amend the Endangered Species Act by directing that no agency may take an action affecting private property that results in a diminishment of the value of any portion of that property by an amount equal to or greater than 25 percent of the value of that portion, unless compensation is offered. It would also provide that if the owner and the agency have not reached agreement on compensation within 180 days after a written request is made, the owner may elect binding arbitration or seek compensation through civil action. If enacted, such amendments to federal law will constitute even greater challenges for environmental regulators than they face presently.

Building Administrative Capacity
Given all this, effective environmental governance makes it incumbent on regulators to establish mechanisms within their administrative operations to track the outcomes of the application of various regulations. These outcomes must be tracked in terms of the degree to which they do in fact trigger liability for regulatory takings, which decidedly undermines opportunities for building common purpose among stakeholders. This information is potentially useful not only for planning regulatory initiatives to avoid takings judgments, but also to provide feedback to courts and legislatures concerning the real effects of regulatory takings statutes. Environmental regulators, after all, are in a key position to document and assess the real impacts of regulatory takings judgments and

statutes in terms of environmental protection. In order to achieve needed modifications in statutory policies in particular, environmental regulators will have to demonstrate the effects of these regulatory takings policies in operation.

Nor are the needs for these data likely to attenuate soon. Environmental regulators will be administering their regulatory programs in a context where regulatory takings doctrine will be a factor for the foreseeable future. Justices may modify the U.S. Supreme Court's previous pronouncements, but it is highly unlikely that they will eliminate those earlier decisions. In addition, the premises of the takings doctrine have found their way into numerous statutory enactments at the state level, further spreading the reach of property protection. Environmental regulators, as a consequence, will need to anticipate how the application of their regulations can trigger takings liability and engage in contingency planning for implementing their regulations.

To be sure, opportunities for dispute resolution, deliberative democracy, and self-regulative common-pool resource management, like those discussed in chapters 4, 5, and 9, may inform environmental governance more frequently in the future. Yet, as each of these chapters also recounts, these more collaborative approaches to building a results-based sense of common purpose in environmental governance face contingencies of their own; each has conditions under which it is more or less likely to succeed. Although proponents of the new resource economics correctly point out how important a role property rights can play under certain circumstances in fostering more effective ENR protection, the flip side of property rights discussed in this chapter also says much about the future of building a results-based sense of common purpose in environmental governance in the United States. Regulators who fail to anticipate how, when, and why their decisions can be interpreted as regulatory takings do so not only at their own peril, but also at the risk of putting environmental governance on a continuing litigious treadmill that is decidedly ill-suited to the building of common purpose in the twenty-first century.

Notes

1. David H. Rosenbloom and Rosemary O'Leary, *Public Administration and Law,* 2d ed. (New York: Marcel Dekker, 1996).

2. Kirk Emerson and Charles R. Wise, "Statutory Approaches to Regulatory Takings," *Public Administration Review* 57 (1997): 411–422.

3. In a condemnation proceeding, most of the judicial focus is on what amount will be determined to constitute "just compensation" to recompense the owner for the value of the property taken, although there has been some litigation over what constitutes a legitimate public purpose for which government can condemn property. See *Hawaii Housing Authority v. Midkiff*, 467 U.S. 229, 1984; *Oakland v. Oakland Raiders*, 32 Cal. 3d 60, 646 P.2d 835, 183 Cal. Rptr. 673, 1982.

4. *Pennsylvania Coal v. Mahon*, 260 U.S. 393, 1922.

5. Ibid., 415.

6. *Penn Central Transportation v. New York City*, 438 U.S. 104/124, 1978.

7. *Kaiser Aetna v. United States*, 444 U.S. 175, 1979.

8. *Ruckelshaus v. Monsanto Co.*, 467 U.S. 986, 1984.

9. *Agins v. City of Tiburon*, 447 U.S. 255/260, 1980.

10. *Pennell v. City of San Jose*, 108 S.Ct. 849/856, 1988.

11. *Keystone Bituminous Coal Association v. DeBenedictus*, 480 U.S. 470/487, 1987.

12. *Nolan v. California Coastal Commission*, 483 U.S. 825/834, 1987.

13. Ibid., 825/837.

14. Ibid.

15. Ibid.

16. Ibid., 825/835.

17. *First English Evangelical Lutheran Church of Glendale v. County of Los Angeles*, 482 U.S. 304/321, 1987.

18. Ibid., 304/316 n.9.

19. *Lucas v. South Carolina Coastal Council*, 112 S.Ct. 2886, 1992.

20. Ibid., 2886/2900.

21. *Dolan v. Tigard*, 114 S.Ct. 2322, 1994.

22. *City of Monterey v. Del Monte Dunes*, 526 U.S. 687, 1999.

23. Edward H. Ziegler, "Development Exactions and Permit Decisions: The Supreme Court's *Nolan, Dolan,* and *Del Monte Dunes* Decisions," *The Urban Lawyer* 34 (2002), p. 162.

24. *City of Monterey v. Del Monte Dunes*, 526 U.S., at 706.

25. *Ruckelshaus v. Monsanto Co.*, 1003.

26. See Robert Meltz, Dwight Merriam, and Richard Frank, *The Takings Issue* (Washington, D.C.: Island, 1999), p. 27.

27. *Webb's Fabulous Pharmacies v. Beckwith*, 449 U.S. 155/161, 1980.

28. See *Andrus v. Allard*, 444 U.S. 51, 1979; *Eastern Enterprises v. Apfel*, 524 U.S. 498, 1998.

29. Imagine, for example, that an owner has a property bordering a lake that includes ten acres of uplands and five acres of lowlands. The owner asks the regulator to allow development on the five acres but is denied and is told that he cannot build anything there. The owner will claim that 100 percent of his five acres has been "taken." However, the regulator will say that the owner still has two-thirds of his property that he can develop; therefore, all economically viable use has not been taken, and the state owes him no compensation.

30. "Takings jurisprudence does not divide a single parcel into discrete segments and attempt to determine whether rights in a particular segment have been entirely abrogated. In deciding whether a particular governmental action has effected a taking, this Court focuses rather on both the character of the action and on the nature and extent of interference with rights in the parcel as a whole" (*Penn Central Transportation v. City of New York*, 104/130-131).

31. "To the extent that any portion of the property is taken, that portion is always taken in its entirety: the relevant question, however, is whether the property taken is all, or only a portion of the parcel in question" (*Concrete Pipe & Products of California v. Construction Laborers Pension Trust*, 508 U.S. 602/644, 1993).

32. *Palazzolo v. Rhode Island*, 121 S.Ct. 2448/2465, 2001. For examples of the various approaches utilized by the courts, see *Ciampitti v. U.S.*, 22 Cl. Ct. 310/319, 1991; *Deltona Corp. v. United States*, 657 F.2d. 1184/1192, Ct. Cl., 1981, *cert. denied*, 455 U.S. 1017, 1982; *Loveladies Harbor v. United States*, 15 Cl. Ct. 381/391–393, 1988; *Hodel v. Irving*, 481 U.S. 704/716, 1987; *Dolan v. City of Tigard*, 512 U.S. 374, 1994; *Babbit v. Youpee*, 519 U.S. 1232, 1997; *Florida Rock Industries v. United States*, 18 F.3d 1560/1572, Fed. Cir., 1994; *Clajon Production Corp. v. Petera*, 70 F.3d 1566/1577, 10th Cir., 1995.

33. *Loretto v. Teleprompter Manhattan CATV Corp.*, 458n U.S. 419/426, 1982.

34. *Mongrue v. Monsanto*, No. 98-2531, 199 U.S. Dist., LEXIS 5543, E.D. La. April 9, 1999.

35. *Kaiser Aetna v. United States*, 444 U.S. 164/175-176, 1979.

36. "[T]he concept of permanent physical occupation does not require that the occupation be exclusive, or continuous and uninterrupted" (*Hendler v. United States*, 952 F.2d 1364, 1991).

37. Robert H. Freilich and Elizabeth A. Garvin, "Takings after Lucas: Growth Management, Planning, and Regulatory Implementation Will Work Better Than Before," *Stetson Law Review* 22 (spring 1993), p. 414.

38. *Dolan v. City of Tigard*, 512 U.S. 374/391.

39. Ibid.

40. *Goss v. City of Little Rock*, 151 F.3d 861/863, 8th Cir., 1998.

41. Ibid., 861/864.

42. *Art Piculell Group v. Clackamas County*, 922 P.2d. 1227, Or. App., 1996; *Sparks v. Douglas County*, 904 P.2d 738/746, Wash., 1995; *Hoepker v. City of Madison Plan Commission*, 563 N.W.2d 145, Wis. 1997.

43. *Goss v. City of Little Rock*, 90 F.3d. 306, 8th Cir., 1996; *Amoco Oil Co. v. Village of Schaumberg*, 661 N.E.2d 380, Ill. App., 1995.

44. *Hoepker v. City of Madison Plan Commission*, 145/151.

45. *Lambert v. City and County of San Francisco*, 67 Cal. Rptr. 2d 562, Cal. App., 1997.

46. See *F & W Associates v. County of Somerset*, 648 A.2d 482/487, N.J. Super. Ct. Div., 1994; *Grogan v. Zoning Board of Appeals*, 633 N.Y.S.2d 809/810, N.y. App. Div., 1995.

47. *Amoco Oil Co. v. Village of Schaumberg*, 661 N.E.2d 380/392, Ill. App., 1995; *Art Piculell Group v. Clackamas County*, 1227/1234.

48. *Agins v. City of Tiburon*.

49. *Lucas v. South Carolina Coastal Commission*, 505 U.S. 1003/1029, 1992.

50. *Nolan v. California Coastal Commission*, 835.

51. *Mugler v. Kansas*, 123 U.S. 623/669, 1887.

52. *Miller v. Schoene*, 276 U.S. 272, 1928.

53. *Keystone Bituminous Coal Association v. DeBenedictus*, 491 n.20.

54. *Lucas v. South Carolina Coastal Council*, 112 S.Ct. 2886/2889.

55. *City of Monterey v. Del Monte Dunes at Monterey Ltd.*, 119 S.Ct. 1624/1644, 1999.

56. See Robert H. Freilich and Jason M. Divelbiss, "The Public Interest Is Vindicated: City of Monterey v. Del Monte Dunes," in Patricia E. Salkin and Robert Freilich, eds., *Hot Topics in Land Use Law* (Chicago: American Bar Association, 2000), p. 25.

57. Ronald H. Rosenberg and Nancy Stroud, "When *Lochner* Met *Dolan*: The Attempted Transformation of American Land-Use Law by Constitutional Interpretation," *The Urban Lawyer* 33 (2001), p. 663. See, for example, *Bonnie Briar Syndicate Inc. v. Town of Mamaroneck*, 94 N.Y. 2d 96/108, Ct. App., 1999; *Tandy Corporation v. City of Livonia*, 81 F. Supp. 2d 800/812, E.D. Mich., 1999.

58. See *Concrete Pipe and Products v. Construction Pension Laborers Trust*, 508 U.S. 602, 1993.

59. *Williamson County Regional Planning Commission v. Hamilton Bank*, 473 U.S. 172/199, 1985.

60. *Florida Rock v. United States*, 791 F.2d 893, Fed. Cir., 1986.

61. *Loveladies Harbor, Inc. v. United States*, 21 Cl. Ct. 153/158, 1990.

62. *Florida Rock Industries v. United States*, 18 F.3d 1560, Fed. Cir., 1994, emphasis in original.

63. *Florida Rock Industries, Inc. v. United States*, 1999 W.L. 692836, Fed. Cl., Aug. 31, 1999.

64. Steven J. Eagle, "The Rise and Rise of 'Investment-Backed Expectations,'" *The Urban Lawyer*, 32 (2000), p. 437.

65. *Andrus v. Allard.*

66. *Williamson County Regional Planning Commission v. Hamilton Bank*, 473 U.S. 200, 1985.

67. *Seawall Associates v. City of New York*, 542 N.E. 2d 1067, N.Y., 1989.

68. *Good v. United States*, 189 F.3d 1361-1362, Fed. Cir., 1999.

69. *Seawall Associates v. City of New York*, 1059.

70. *Whitney Benefits, Inc. v. United States*, 926 F. 2d 1169, Fed. Cir., 1991.

71. Michael K. Whitman, "The Ripeness Doctrine in the Land Use Context: The Municipality's Ally and the Landowner's Nemesis," *The Urban Lawyer* 29 (1997), p. 24.

72. *Williamson County Regional Planning Commission v. Hamilton Bank*, 170/186–194.

73. See, for example, *Palazzolo v. Rhode Island*, 2448/2458; *MacDonald, Sommer, and Frates v. Yolo County*, 477 U.S. 340, 1986.

74. *MacDonald, Sommer, and Frates v. Yolo County*, 353 n.9.

75. *Palazzolo v. Rhode Island*, 2448/2458.

76. Douglas Kendall, Timothy Dowling, and Andrew Schwartz, "Choice of Forum and Finality Ripeness: The Unappreciated Hot Topics of Regulatory Takings Cases," *The Urban Lawyer* 33 (2001), p. 407.

77. *Williamson County Regional Planning Commission v. Hamilton Bank*, 170/195.

78. See, for example, *Levald v. City of Palm Desert*, 998 F.2d, 680/689, 9th Cir., 1993; *Schnuck v. City of Santa Monica*, 935 F.2d, 171/174, 9th Cir., 1991; *MacDonald, Sommer, and Frates v. Yolo County*, 350; *City of Monterey v. Del Monte Dunes at Monterey Ltd.*, 119 S.Ct. 1624; *Palazzolo v. Rhode Island*, 2448.

79. Meltz, Merriam, and Frank, *The Takings Issue*, pp. 164–165.

80. *Palazzolo v. Rhode Island*, 2448/2463.

81. Ibid., 2448/2462.

82. *First English Evangelical Lutheran Church of Glendale v. County of Los Angeles*, 321.

83. *Tahoe Sierra Preservation Council v. Tahoe Regional Planning Agency*, 122 S.Ct. 1465, 2002.

84. Ibid., 1477.

85. Ibid., 1489.

86. Ibid., 1486.

87. Ibid., 1489.

88. Ibid.

89. For example, the Illinois Supreme Court, citing the Illinois Constitution, struck down a municipal transportation impact fee by finding that the fees were not "specifically and uniquely attributable" to the affected development. It did so even though the federal standard as enunciated in the U.S. Supreme Court's decision in *Dolan v. Tigard* did not require such a precise constitutional fit.

90. Meltz, Merriam, and Frank, *The Takings Issue*, p. 21.

91. For more discussion of policy implications, see Kirk Emerson and Charles Wise, "Statutory Approaches to Regulatory Takings: State Property Rights Legislation Issues and Implications for Public Administration," *Public Administration Review* 57 (1997), p. 411.

9

Environmental Conflict Resolution

Rosemary O'Leary, Tina Nabatchi, and Lisa B. Bingham

Unease with the adversarial process engrained in many countries' legal systems is part and parcel of the assault on conventional bureaucratic thinking worldwide and of the push to reconnect with citizens in the administrative state. As the preceding chapter by Charles Wise illustrates particularly well, the increasingly high stakes of administrative rule making can increase conflicts, produce decision making predicated on an "us-versus-them" mentality, and ultimately propel these conflicts into courts for judges to resolve. The consequences of these dynamics are profound for public agencies. Among other things (some of which are quite positive), the fear of and actual verdicts rendered by court decisions can disrupt agency planning, shift resources from higher- to lower-priority items, increase risk aversion among employees, and fortify bureaucratic rigidity.[1] In the process, as James Meadowcroft argues in his chapter, the deliberative and representational processes so vital to democracy may suffer appreciably as reasoned discussion, public justification of positions, and political equality are marginalized at times.

The idea of building a results-based sense of common purpose under these circumstances may seem ludicrous to some. Yet over the past fifteen years, a sea change has occurred in how people and their institutions view and handle conflict in the United States and abroad. As Meadowcroft and DeWitt John discuss in greater detail in their chapters, focus groups, multistakeholder forums, roundtables, cooperative management bodies, and environmental partnerships of all kinds, at all levels of government, and in confederated arrangements have come into being. As these authors note, this proliferation of multistakeholder processes has been encouraged by international events such as the Rio Earth Summit and by international bodies such as the United Nations Commission on Sustainable Development and the Organization for Economic Cooperation and Development.[2] But the main impetus has come from domestic environmental policy actors—governments, businesses, and environmental groups—who seek to break the policy deadlock and find new ways of approaching environmental and natural resources (ENR) governance. As Edella Schlager notes in chapter 4, these stakeholders also have come to appreciate how "conflict resolution mechanisms and at least a minimal recognition of the right to organize prevent institutional regimes from unraveling because of internal strife or invasion from external governmental authorities."

The stakeholders who participate in these new deliberative mechanisms play a variety of roles in ENR governance, from advising established institutions to taking charge of the direct management of resource systems. And a vast array of conflict resolution processes exists to aid a more or less extensive range of social partners to address specific environmental issues. Thus, for example, in the United States, the alternative dispute resolution (ADR) movement has grown from a handful of mediators working in community mediation centers to institutionalized programs in courts, public agencies, nonprofit organizations, and corporations.

Without question, then, interest has grown dramatically in consensus building, facilitation, mediation, and other forms of resolving ENR conflict through assisted negotiation and voluntary settlement. Some analysts, such as Daniel Fiorino in chapter 11, even speculate that we are seeing a generational shift from command and control to less authoritarian forms of human organization and decision making. The magnitude of this shift aside, however, there is no question that a framework supporting public-agency ADR exists in federal statutes and in a growing number of state statutes. Moreover, in no field has the application of ADR been more pronounced than in the emergence of environmental conflict resolution (ECR) as a tool for building common purpose. The terms *environmental conflict resolution* and *environmental dispute resolution* (EDR) refer to the various ADR techniques, overviewed later in this chapter, that can be applied to environmental conflicts.

But how effective is ADR as a tool for building a results-based sense of common purpose in environmental governance? After all, although the use of ADR in labor and community disputes has a long and well-established history, its application to environmental conflicts is relatively recent. The first documented instance of using mediation in an environmental conflict dates back to 1974,[3] but before the late 1980s and early 1990s, ECR efforts were largely infrequent and impromptu interactions that occurred only when the disputing parties expressed interest in the approach.[4] More recent legislation such as the Administrative Dispute Resolution Acts of 1990 and 1996 and the Negotiated Rulemaking Acts of 1990 and 1996, as well as the growing awareness and acceptance of the potential benefits of ADR in resolving conflicts, have enabled different forms of ECR to become more regular and official parts of environmental policymaking.

After reviewing the logic and basics of ECR, this chapter analyzes the praise for and criticisms of this tool of environmental governance. It acknowledges the initial successes in the 1970s and 1980s that led to a major period of expansion for ECR,[5] which continues today. However, the chapter also argues that ECR must do a better job of proving itself if it is to remain an effective tool for building common purpose. That is, proponents must conduct more rigorous assessments of its utility under different conditions and invest in data collection that goes far beyond present efforts. The chapter concludes by reviewing the strategic challenges, choices, and opportunities facing ECR as a tool for building common purpose in environmental governance in the twenty-first century. Singled out for attention is the need for scholars and practitioners to understand ECR interventions as procedures targeted at aggregate rather than dyadic relationships; as complex systems embedded in even larger complex systems; as time-extended phenomena; and as elements ripe for evaluation of their impact on substantive environmental outcomes.

ECR: Scope, Techniques, Processes, and Roles

Given the hyperpluralism rife in environmental governance, perhaps no field is more ripe for using the tools of ADR as means for building a results-based sense of common purpose.[6] Environmental conflicts are fundamental and ongoing differences among parties concerning values and behavior as they relate to the environment.[7] More specifically, environmental conflicts are actual or potential disputes involving issues regarding the environment, natural resources, public lands, or all of these things.[8] They usually involve multiple parties who are engaged in a decision-making process and disagree about one or more issues traceable to an action or policy with potential environmental impacts.[9] Thus, before coming to terms with the contribution that ECR can make to environmental governance, one needs to appreciate three things: the scope or kinds of conflicts that ECR faces, the logic that proponents use to promote it as a tool for addressing these types of conflicts, and the varieties of consensus-based and quasi-adjudicatory approaches ECR applies to building common purpose.

Types of Applicable Conflicts

Environmental disputes can be classified as *upstream* (those involving planning or policymaking) or *downstream* (those involving compliance and enforcement). For example, upstream environmental conflicts can involve the creation and implementation of governmental policy at the national, regional, state, or local level. Downstream environmental conflicts can involve the ways that lands are used, the allocation or distribution of natural resources, the siting of industrial or other large facilities, and the granting of environmental permits, among other issues. Environmental conflicts also can involve the prevention, cleanup, and consequences of water, air, or soil pollution. They also can be categorized generally by the scope of the dispute. For example, policy-level disputes pertain more generally to classes of resources, locations, or situations, whereas site-specific disputes involve particular natural resources, locations, or situations.[10] A policy-level dispute is normally an upstream dispute, whereas a site-specific dispute is usually a downstream dispute.

Thus, the context of an environmental dispute is determined by whether it is upstream or downstream, at the policy level or site specific. However, the dispute itself really emerges from differences in values and worldviews, conflicting interests, and the uncertainty that surrounds environmental courses of action.[11] In addition, popular attitudes and political culture, technology, laws, political interests, economics, and religion (especially as related to Native American culture and to the often disparate cultures of developing countries and the developed world) can trigger environmental conflicts.[12]

Given this breadth of contextual issues and potential philosophical differences, many possible government, public, and private interests have a stake in an environmental conflict. Elected and appointed government officials at the local, county, state, and federal levels in the United States usually are involved in environmental conflicts because many of these conflicts arise from the formation or implementation of legislation and policies. These government officials often represent different agencies (for example, the Department of Interior and the Environmental Protection Agency [EPA]), different departments or subdivisions within an agency (for example, the Bureau of Land Management and the Fish and Wildlife Service within the Department of Interior), or even different branches of government (for example, officials in Congress and officials from an administrative agency such as the Department of Agriculture). Meanwhile, at the level of international disputes discussed by Gary Bryner in chapter 2, conflict arises within governments (for example, between ministers who hold economic versus environmental portfolios over issues such as greenhouse gas emissions, farm subsidies, and genetically modified foods); between developed and developing nations over issues such as state sovereignty and biodiversity preservation; and between Europe and the United States over risk management versus the precautionary principle.

The numerous public interests represented in environmental conflicts include community residents, interest groups, and public interest law firms. At the same time, of course, private interests also play a large role. Industry, commercial, and other interests in the business community often become combatants in environmental conflicts such as those that involve siting facilities, establishing pollution abatement policy, or granting various permits. These various government, public, and private interests also frequently need and use the services of scientific, research, and technical consultants, thus adding to the number of stakeholders involved in the conflict.

In Praise of ECR

ECR processes clearly are derived from the philosophy of the ADR move-ment, which stands in contrast to traditional adversarial methods of dis-pute resolution, especially litigation. Unlike traditional litigation, in which a judge or jury makes a final determination or issues a judgment, ECR techniques use various forms of assisted negotiation to help the parties reach a mutually satisfactory agreement on their own terms. Advocates of ECR generally find fault with traditional modes of environmental policymaking and dispute resolution, specifically pointing to failures in legislative and administrative arenas and to the drawbacks of litigation.[13]

Advocates of ECR suggest several problems that subvert the handling of environmental conflicts at the legislative level. First, it is difficult for all of the interests affected by environmental decisions to be heard. Many environmental and other interest groups cannot participate effectively in the legislative arena because they lack adequate financial resources or staff to engage in lobbying. Second, even without the many voices in the process, most environmental issues that legislatures deal with are inher-ently controversial. The innate controversy surrounding environmental policies often precludes a viable consensus among legislators, which results in vague and ambiguous legislation.

The legislative arena's failure effectively to address conflicts, in turn, sets the stage for conflicts to reemerge in the administrative arena. As the agencies try to interpret and implement vague policies, controver-sies about specific actions or projects flare up. As in the legislative arena, it is very difficult for groups to become involved in decision-making processes in the administrative arena. Some parties are ignored deliber-ately or left out of processes, and some parties, even if invited to the table, lack the financial or human resources necessary to participate effectively.[14] Of course, most agencies, at least at the federal level, must receive public comments or hold hearings where concerned parties can voice their preferences. But critics suggest that these procedures give only the appearance of participation, and that comments and testimony actually are not considered in policy implementation.[15]

The legislative and administrative arenas' failure to address envi-ronmental conflicts effectively often means that litigation will ensue. However, advocates of ECR produce two primary criticisms of litigation as a dispute resolution process for these conflicts.[16] First, litigation usually does not allow for adequate public participation in important environmental decisions. The costs of litigation are often prohibitive to interest groups, especially to those groups that are small or that represent local interests. The process of litigation is also extremely time-consuming, often taking months for cases to come to trial. After accounting for appeals time, the entire litigation process can take years. These time delays are costly to all of the parties involved. Second, litigation is often ineffective for actually resolving the issues at stake in environmental disputes. Court decisions frequently fail to resolve the basic issues in dispute between the parties. For example, when the courts are limited in their ability to address the substantive dimensions of environmental conflicts, they render decisions only on procedural grounds.[17] Many of the underlying controversies therefore remain unresolved, and, hence, more lawsuits often emerge in the future.[18]

In contrast, advocates of ECR suggest that its informal negotiation techniques have several advantages,[19] including: (1) less risk for the parties than those associated with the uncertainty of win-all or lose-all litigation; (2) a reduction in court costs, legal fees, inflationary delays, and other conflict-related expenses, as well as a reduction of time spent on the dispute; (3) an increase in the efficiency of the outcome, such that all disputants or stakeholders prefer it over all other feasible outcomes; and (4) an increased likelihood of achieving a stable agreement (one that all parties honor for at least several years).[20]

Advocates also identify benefits derived from the participatory nature of ECR processes. They suggest that full participation by all of the interested parties promotes effective negotiation and is a key element in producing better and more equitable environmental decisions. When all parties are at the table, they have a better chance of raising all the relevant issues and of situating themselves better to make efficient trades, produce more stable and efficient outcomes, and reach decisions that effectively address the substantive nature of the dispute.[21]

The participatory nature of ECR techniques and processes typically also promotes a sense of procedural justice. Procedural justice is a commonly used framework in ADR research. It suggests that participants' satisfaction with an ADR process, in addition to being a function of the outcome of the dispute, is a function of their opportunities to control and participate in the process, present views, and receive fair treatment from the mediator.[22] When participants sense that they have received procedural justice, their perception of the legitimacy of the decision and outcome increases, reducing the likelihood that the outcome will be challenged in the future.[23] Finally, the participatory nature of ECR compensates for the lack of public access to negotiation sessions in the legislative, administrative, and judicial systems. Promoted in the process is the idea of citizen participation in policymaking and decision making, a strongly heralded value in this era of administrative reform (as Meadowcroft discusses in greater detail in chapter 5).

ECR Processes

Precisely how is ECR supposed to fashion these outcomes? ECR consists of assorted techniques, processes, and roles that enable parties in a dispute to reach agreement. This is usually done with the help of one or more third-party neutrals, as discussed in more detail later. Despite the variance in ECR techniques and processes, however, researchers have identified five characteristics[24] shared by all forms of ECR (except binding arbitration):

1. participation must be voluntary for all participants;

2. the parties or their representatives must be able to participate directly in the process;

3. any and all participants must have the option to withdraw from the ECR process and to seek a resolution through a more formal process, such as litigation;

4. the third-party neutral must not have independent, formal authority to impose an outcome, but rather should help the parties reach their own agreement;

5. the parties must agree to the outcome or resolution of the dispute (the purpose of the process is to help parties reach their own solutions, which requires their consent to the decision or recommendation).[25]

It is possible to arrange ECR processes along a continuum from less formal, interest-based negotiation techniques or consensus-based techniques, to more formal, adjudicatory arrangements. Consensus-based techniques require that everyone, not just a majority, agree with the outcome or decision. However, the Negotiated Rulemaking Acts of 1990 and 1996 allow for consensus to be redefined as a majority decision if all the parties agree to that redefinition. In consensus-based processes, disputing parties work together to develop an agreement that is mutually acceptable. Moving along the continuum toward quasi-adjudicatory processes, as the goal of the processes shifts to making a determination about the issues in controversy, the nature of the techniques used also changes. Consensus-based techniques generally are used for upstream disputes, whereas quasi-adjudicatory processes generally are used for downstream disputes.

All ECR processes, perhaps with the exception of binding arbitration, are based on the idea of negotiation. Negotiation is simply bargaining— a process of discussion and give-and-take among disputants who want to find a solution to a common problem. It can be relatively cooperative, as it is when both sides seek a solution that is mutually beneficial (commonly called *interest-based* or *principled negotiation*). Alternatively, it can be confrontational (commonly called *win-lose* or *adversarial negotiation*), where each side seeks to prevail over the other.[26] Some of the more common ECR techniques, categorized as consensus-based or quasi-adjudicatory processes, follows.[27]

Consensus-Based Processes   Consensus-based or consensus-building processes include a number of collaborative decision-making techniques in which a third-party neutral such as a facilitator or mediator assists diverse or competing interest groups in reaching an agreement on a site-specific or policy-level environmental conflict.[28] Consensus-building processes typically are used to foster dialogue, clarify areas of agreement and disagreement, improve the information on which a decision is based, and resolve controversial issues in ways that are acceptable to all interests. Usually used for upstream disputes, consensus building typically involves informal, structured, face-to-face interaction among representatives of different stakeholder groups who hold different viewpoints. The goals are to promote early participation by the affected stakeholders, to produce sensible and stable policies or decisions that have a strong and wide base of support, and to reduce the likelihood of subsequent disagreements or legal challenges. The most common consensus-based processes used in environmental conflicts are conflict assessment (or convening), facilitation, mediation, conciliation, negotiated rule making, and policy dialogues.

Conflict assessment, also known as convening, is valuable as a first step in ECR processes.[29] Its goal is to help identify the issues in controversy, the affected stakeholders, and the appropriate form(s) of ECR for handling the conflict. The assessment process typically involves multiple steps, beginning with a conference among potential stakeholders to evaluate the causes of the conflict and to identify the entities and individuals who would be affected substantively by the conflict's outcome. The next steps are to assess the stakeholders' interests and needs, identify a preliminary set of relevant issues to be discussed, and evaluate the feasibility of using consensus building or other collaborative processes to address the issues in dispute. Other prospective stakeholders then are informed and educated about the possible consensus-building ECR processes so that they can determine whether they should or want to participate. The final step of the conflict assessment process is to select and structure the ECR technique most appropriate for the conflict. In this step, often called process design, a neutral recommends or assists in developing an appropriate process for addressing a particular controversy or dispute.

Facilitation is a collaborative process in which a neutral party assists a group of stakeholders in constructively discussing the issues in controversy. The facilitator typically works with participants before and during these discussions to assure that the appropriate persons are at the table, to help the parties set and enforce ground rules and agendas, to assist parties in communicating effectively, and to help the participants keep on track in working toward their goals. Although facilitation bears many similarities to mediation, the neutral party or facilitator usually plays a less active role than a mediator and, unlike a mediator, often does not see "resolution" as a goal of his or her work.

Mediation is a form of facilitated negotiation where a skilled, impartial third party with neither decision-making authority nor the power to impose a settlement assists the parties in reaching a voluntary, mutually agreeable resolution to all or some of the disputed issues.[30] Mediation is one of the oldest forms of conflict resolution and one of the most common forms of ECR. A mediator works with the disputing parties to help them to improve communication and analysis of the conflict, to identify interests, and to explore possibilities for a mutually agreeable resolution that meets all of their interests or needs.

The mediator lacks power to impose any solution, but rather must assist the process in ways acceptable to the parties and help the disputants themselves design a solution. This assistance typically involves supervising the bargaining, helping the disputants to find areas of common ground and to understand their alternatives, offering possible solutions, and helping parties draft a final settlement agreement. Mediation usually occurs in the context of a specific dispute involving a limited number of parties. It is also employed, however, to develop broad policies or regulatory mandates and may involve dozens of participants who represent a variety of interests. It is most often a voluntary process, but court orders or statutes mandate its use in some jurisdictions.

In most ECR cases, a mediator will use a facilitative, directive, or evaluative mediation style. In *facilitative mediation,* mediators are less likely to provide direct advice, propose solutions, or predict outcomes. They are also more likely to assist the parties in identifying and merging their interests by establishing an atmosphere that allows parties to communicate more effectively about their interests, options, and realistic alternatives.[31] Conversely, in *directive mediation,* the mediator diagnoses the problem and tries to persuade the parties to accept a reasonable solution.[32] In *evaluative mediation,* the mediator gives the parties an expert opinion on the merits of the dispute to help them understand the strengths and weaknesses of their cases,[33] provides guidance about the likely outcome in court, and suggests appropriate grounds for settling.

In contrast, *conciliation* involves efforts by a third party to improve the relationship between two or more disputants. The third party generally works with the disputants to correct misunderstandings, reduce their fear and distrust, and improve communication between them. Conciliation is not a common ECR technique; however, when used, it generally prepares the disputants for a future ECR process.

Negotiated rule making, also known as regulatory negotiation or regneg, is another form of ECR that involves efforts by regulatory agencies to design environmental regulations by first negotiating with interested stakeholders.[34] It is a multiparty, consensus-building process in which a balanced negotiating committee, comprised of the rule-making agency and other stakeholders that might be affected by or have an interest in the new rule, tries to negotiate the substance of that proposed agency rule, policy, or standard. The purpose and intent of negotiated rule making is to avoid litigation that may arise to challenge the new rule; it instead generates agreement among the affected interests so that they abide by the decision and its implementation. Federal law requires both a thorough conflict assessment before the use of reg-neg, and the involvement and assistance of a skilled, neutral mediator or facilitator.[35]

Policy dialogues are a relatively new form of ECR that generally are used to address complex environmental conflicts or public policy disputes. In the policy dialogue process, representatives of groups with divergent views or interests are assembled to generate discussion and improve communication and mutual understanding. The goal is to explore the issues in controversy to see if general recommendations can be developed and to try to reach agreement on the policy standard or guidelines the government will propose. Unlike the other consensus-based ECR processes, policy dialogues usually do not seek to achieve a full, specific agreement that binds all participating interests. Rather, participants in a policy dialogue may seek to assess the potential for developing a full consensus resolution at some later time or may put forward general, nonbinding recommendations or broad policy preferences for an agency (or other governmental entity) to consider in its subsequent decision making.

Quasi-adjudicatory Processes   In contrast to consensus-based processes, quasi-adjudicatory processes supply the disputing parties with an expert opinion about the merits of their case, furnish more information about their best alternative to a negotiated agreement, and provide the disputants with an avenue or loop back to negotiation. In theory, this loop-back function can allow the parties to engage more effectively in a new round of settlement negotiations with the additional information gained in these processes. Some of the most common quasi-adjudicatory processes used in environmental conflicts are early neutral evaluation, minitrials, summary jury trials, settlement judges, fact finding, and arbitration.

Early neutral evaluation is a quasi-adjudicatory process in which a third-party neutral—often someone with specifically relevant legal, substantive, or technical expertise—hears informal evidence and arguments from all of the parties involved in the dispute and issues a nonbinding report advising them about the strengths and weaknesses of their cases.[36] The report also may evaluate the likely reaction of a judge or jury if settlement is not reached, provide guidance about an appropriate range of outcomes, and assist the parties in narrowing the areas of disagreement or in identifying information that may enhance the chances of settlement.

Minitrials and *summary jury trials* commonly are used to resolve litigation over complex environmental issues. In a minitrial, parties generally are represented by counsel and by an agent with the authority to agree to a settlement or decision, for example a company's chief executive officer or an agency official. Abbreviated versions of the evidence and arguments are presented, after which the decision-making representatives attempt to negotiate a settlement.[37] In a summary jury trial, the disputing parties impanel a jury and present short versions of the evidence and arguments. The jury deliberates and makes findings of fact and liability when appropriate, which the judge then releases.[38] The parties are not bound by the jury's findings, but rather use the information to assist with settlement negotiations. Minitrials and summary jury trials are alike in that they both serve as a loop back to future negotiations.

A *settlement judge* process is similar to minitrials and summary jury trials, but it is used for litigation that already has reached administrative adjudication. In a settlement judge process, a judge who is different from the presiding judge in the case acts as a mediator or neutral evaluator and meets both separately and jointly with the parties.[39] If the settlement judge's efforts do not produce full agreement, the case returns to the presiding judge. A settlement judge often plays a more authoritative role than a private mediator by sometimes providing parties with specific legal or substantive information and recommendations.

Fact finding is an ECR process that is related closely to nonbinding arbitration. In this process, a neutral (called a fact finder) receives information about the dispute and listens to the disputants' arguments. The fact finder may conduct additional research to investigate the issues in dispute, but he or she eventually evaluates the evidence and submits a report that contains findings of fact and sometimes recommendations based on those findings.[40] The fact-finding process is typically informal, and the recommendations are nonbinding. Disputants occasionally use this process to define literally the facts of a case so that all parties can use them in subsequent negotiations. In such cases, the disputed facts usually involve highly technical scientific or engineering issues and require the fact finder to have subject matter expertise.

Finally, *arbitration* is a quasi-adjudicatory process in which the disputants present their case to an impartial third party, who then issues an opinion. An arbitration decision can be binding or nonbinding. In binding arbitration, the opinion is final and subject to very limited judicial review. In nonbinding arbitration, the opinion is advisory and can be rejected; however, it also can serve as a loop back to negotiation.

ECR in Practice: Emerging Lessons from the Field

Considering the potential scope, logic, and variety of consensus-based and quasi-adjudicatory approaches to ECR, the obvious question is how well ECR fulfills proponents' promises about it. Systematic and empirical research using rigorous research designs are unfortunately the exception rather than the rule in assessing ECR to date.[41] Yet Lawrence Susskind has combined the results of empirical studies with his own experiences and with mediators' and participants' views to predict when ECR is most helpful. Box 9.1 summarizes some of these predictions.

Case studies reveal that ECR techniques have been used successfully in both site-specific and policy-level disputes involving a wide variety of issues.[42] For example, ECR has been used for land-use disputes involving commercial development, housing, facility siting, and transportation; natural resource use or management issues involving fisheries, timber, and mining; water resources issues such as water quality, flood protection, and water use; air quality issues such as odor, acid rain, and air pollution; and issues related to toxics, such as chemical regulation, asbestos removal, and waste cleanup policies.[43] Equally significant, however, certain characteristics of environmental conflicts clearly add to their

Box 9.1
When ECR Is Most Helpful

ECR Is Most Helpful When:
• Each participant views the outcome as very important.
• The issues are relatively clear.
• The relevant laws are flexible enough to permit a negotiated settlement.
• ECR is started at an early stage of conflict, before going to public hearings.
• The actual decision makers are willing to participate or to designate representatives.
• There is no inherent danger to the participants' safety.

ECR Should Not Be Used When:
• Public health or safety requires that action be taken immediately.
• Precedent setting is important.
• Participants do not recognize the other side's rights.
• The party providing financial support insists on complete control over the process.
• The process is being used as a means to delay real action or to create an illusion that something is being done.

Source: Adapted from Lawrence Susskind, Ole Amundsen, Masahiro Matsuura, Marshall Kaplan, and David Lampe, "Recommendations on the Use of Mediation," in Lawrence Susskind et al., *Using Assisted Negotiation to Settle Land Use Disputes* (Cambridge, Mass.: Lincoln Institute of Land Policy, 1999), p. 23.

complexity, making the application of ECR techniques more difficult in these circumstances. Some of these characteristics include: multiple forums for decision making; interorganizational, as opposed to interpersonal, conflicts; multiple parties; multiple issues; technical complexity and scientific uncertainty; unequal power and resources; and both public and political arenas for problem solving.[44]

Critics of ECR, however, challenge it on many fronts, including the following general charges:[45]

1. The image of ECR is an exaggerated one. Negotiation sessions are not all "hearts and flowers," simple and easy processes; rather, they can be as adversarial and as combative as litigation.

2. Comparing ECR with litigation in terms of time to address a dispute is misguided and perhaps ludicrous because most disputes never make it to court.

3. Even if ECR works more quickly than litigation, there is no proof that faster is necessarily better in terms of the quality of decision making.

4. Depending on the case, ECR can be just as expensive as going to court.

5. So-called neutrals might not be truly neutral, nor is the process truly neutral.

6. As mediators "reframe" issues for disputants, they may distort issues.

7. It is naive to assume that these types of negotiations routinely can resolve festering political problems. Those who advocate ECR do not understand that much of politics is about power struggles, and that ECR can be no fairer than the larger political context in which it takes place.

One of the most successful attacks on ECR comes from environmental groups charging that ECR is a form of political control that exploits weaker political groups who are seduced into thinking they are being treated fairly.[46] The face-to-face nature of the interaction not only encourages trust, they say, but invites abuse of that trust. Mediators may disarm participants of their legitimate feelings and serve as catalysts for compromises that are not always reasonable or are not always in the participants' best interests. In fact, many in the EDR arena already see signs that the George W. Bush administration may be promoting ECR in an effort to calm and seduce environmentalists.[47]

In a similar vein, both scholars and environmental activists have attacked negotiated rule making, arguing that claims concerning its benefits are overblown and undersubstantiated.[48] They maintain that negotiated rule-making processes are so infrequent that comparing them with traditional rule-making processes is meaningless. In addition, agency staff are not supportive of negotiated rule-making processes. Further, analyses of the time expended in negotiated rule making show that it is impossible to conclude that this approach successfully has increased the speed of the regulatory process.[49] Lastly, critics argue that there is no evidence to conclude that negotiated rule making actually reduces litigation.[50]

Finally, a spate of individual studies has analyzed institutional barriers to the acceptance of ECR. A two-year examination of the EPA's ECR program, for example, concluded that although ECR participants generally were satisfied with the process and outcome, challenges to the program nevertheless persist.[51] The most significant problem is that despite official EPA pronouncements that it is agency policy to use ECR techniques where appropriate, ECR is not part of the agency's day-to-day business. Rather, it is the exception to the rule. The EPA seems to have a split personality: proponents argue for using ECR, but many agency attorneys are reluctant to use it. As a result, the decision to use ECR is based more on an individual attorney's familiarity with the ECR process than on the needs of a particular case.[52]

Another recent study found that acceptance of ECR among environmental attorneys, although growing, still faces challenges.[53] The most frequent reasons cited by environmental attorneys as to why they are reluctant to participate in ECR are the fear of losing control of the process and the view that their strength lies in their training in the adversarial process. They also mentioned a general lack of familiarity with ECR skills and processes as an impediment to their greater acceptance of ECR. Other attorneys expressed the view that the ECR process might sacrifice justice in an effort to reach a compromise. In addition, some said that they felt unable to represent adequately their clients' interests through ECR. "If I can win, why use ECR?" they ask. Still other attorneys noted their perception that ECR is less financially lucrative than litigation, that clients will perceive the lawyer as compromising their interests, and that ECR may give the other party damaging information. Almost as frequently noted were the sense that attornies cannot represent their clients zealously in ECR and a fear that clients will become second in importance to reaching an agreement or consensus.

Long-Term Prospects for ECR: Challenges, Choices, and Opportunities

Imagine you are the administrator of the EPA, and you have just approved a $41 million program to contract out for facilitators, conveners, and mediators to assist in the resolution of environmental disputes (as did EPA administrator Carol Browner in 1999). Advocates of ECR say that it saves money and time, that participants in ECR processes generally are satisfied with outcomes, and that ECR can serve as a catalyst for individual empowerment, personal transformation, and positive relationships among disputing parties.

But how will you *really* know whether your $41 million investment is a success? Congress has passed the Government Performance and Results Act, which mandates that you demonstrate accountability in your annual performance reports. How will you do this? Further, what will you have to show taxpayers who are interested in seeing public funds spent as judiciously as possible? How will you respond to critics of ECR? You are in favor of more transparency in government, but how can that transparency be implemented with ECR when it requires discretion and sometimes confidentiality? Is there any proof for claims both for and against ECR? And what about the environment: Does ECR enhance environmental protection?

This scenario is a brief glimpse into the window of strategic challenges, choices, and opportunities facing ECR in the future. In the long term, the most compelling challenge facing the adroit application of ECR as a tool for building a results-based sense of common purpose is the lack of empirical evidence to support its use. As the discussion in the previous section illustrates, much of the political, organizational, and professional resistance to ECR is rooted in fears directly related to questions for which proponents have few ready answers. Indeed, despite the plethora of literature touting the advantages of ECR (and, at times, the disadvantages), the empirical foundations for most of the conclusions are quite weak. Thus, proponents often cannot convince stakeholders that ECR is a valuable set of tools to use to meet environmental governance challenges, choices, and opportunities.

To be sure, some strong conceptual works concerning ECR *do* exist. Yet few scholars have studied ECR through one or more of the standard empirical methods: theoretically informed case studies, comparative case analyses, surveys, interviews, and statistical analyses of quantitative data.[54] Furthermore, the research that does exist on ECR has tended to base its judgments concerning effectiveness on two narrow questions: whether a settlement occurred and whether the parties to the ECR effort were satisfied with and derived personal value from their participation in ECR.

The field of ECR, however, must move beyond settlement and satisfaction as the principal measures of effectiveness. These measures only begin to get at the kinds of information that stakeholders need in deciding whether or not to use ECR in particular circumstances. Moreover, in making this move, ECR will join the rest of the ADR field. Across subject matter contexts, researchers and evaluators are working on contingency theories to broaden and deepen both scholarly and practitioner understanding of what these resolution processes can and cannot deliver in the way of building common purpose under varying circumstances.

Consequently, the future of ECR as a tool for building a results-based sense of common purpose in environmental governance depends on researchers coming to grips with four major sets of research challenges. First, researchers must move from studies on negotiating dyads to field research on aggregate relationships. Second, they must look at ECR from a systemic perspective. More precisely, they must look not only at individual ECR cases, but also at the ECR process as a system and at ECR cases within the larger system. Third, they must adapt their methods to capture the time-extended nature of ECR. Finally, and most appropriately when results-based environmental governance is the aim, they must examine ECR in terms of its environmental impacts.

From the Dyad to the Aggregate

Much of the current research on ECR examines the interpersonal dyad: two people involved in a dispute. It also tends to examine negotiated decisions that are binary: agree or disagree, cooperate or defect. This is true of both experimental social psychology research on negotiation and game theoretic research from the disciplines of economics and political science.[55] Although important, this type of research has some drawbacks for those scholars and practitioners who are trying to understand when ECR is more or less likely to be effective in building common purpose. First, interpersonal relationships do not exist in a vacuum. Researchers increasingly recognize that the dyad must be seen and studied within its organizational, cultural, and historical contexts.[56] Second, and perhaps more important, ECR processes consistently involve groups of people, not dyads. Researchers, fortunately, have begun to model the aggregate— that is, they are examining group cooperative behavior.[57] Finally, the outcomes of ECR are not binary decisions; they are complex, multifaceted agreements that address many issues. These agreements do not cover a simple purchase and sale between parties who will not have future dealings; they instead provide a framework for carrying out a plan of action extended in time that affects the environment and thus members of the general public not at the table.

All of these factors contribute to making ECR difficult to research in ways that scholars and practitioners can quantify. Yet for ECR research to inform practice better, researchers must look at the aggregate. Such a refocusing means that they must not ask simply whether a given party was satisfied with and derived personal value from participating in an ECR process. They should instead attempt to measure how that party, by virtue of the ECR experience, does or does not behave differently in handling conflict with others. Do people who have experienced consensus-based processes form more cooperative groups? Do they participate more in future policymaking either as individuals or as part of a group? Are they empowered or exhausted by their experience with consensus processes?

Research from political science especially is valuable for addressing these questions. For example, in iterated prisoner dilemma games using genetic algorithm modeling, game theory research suggests that cooperators will conquer a population of competitors.[58] In addition, researchers are examining the Truth and Reconciliation Commission in South Africa and the genocide trials in Rwanda to determine the effectiveness of conflict resolution institutions for healing the wounds of large-scale racial and ethnic conflict.[59] They are looking for evidence that those who witnessed testimonials to truth and scenes of reconciliation have different beliefs about the racial divide in their society. They also are looking for evidence that these institutions are effective means to promote reconciliation. These examples show only a few of the many research initiatives in other ADR subfields that may prove to be valuable to scholars and practitioners as they try to understand the full promise and performance of ECR as a tool for building common purpose in environmental governance.

Understanding ECR as Complex Systems

A second set of strategic challenges, choices, and opportunities for researchers and practitioners to grapple with if ECR is to become a major tool for building a results-based sense of common purpose in environmental governance is understanding its systemic properties and dynamics. To date, however, relatively little empirical work on ECR examines this systemic level.[60] Complexity theory is influencing research across many disciplines and provides insight on how researchers and practitioners alike might understand ECR both as a complex system in itself and as a system operating within a larger societal system for managing conflict. Complexity theory suggests that individual actors behaving in accordance with simple decision rules may give rise, through the aggregation of their individual acts, to a self-organizing complex system.[61]

One area that might provide a model worthwhile for ECR researchers to emulate is studies done at the systemic level of labor and employment dispute resolution processes. These include studies of grievance procedures and voice mechanisms in organizations in the fields of industrial relations, human resource management, and organizational behavior.[62] Researchers in these disciplines attempt to measure the impact of aggregate participation on productivity and efficiency in the dispute resolution process. As they do so, they examine the function of dispute resolution programs and compare different dispute system designs.

The U.S. Postal Service (USPS), for example, has worked with the Indiana Conflict Resolution Institute since the inception of its mediation program for employment disputes in order to collect comprehensive, national data on the system using a number of different variables and indicators. This collection of data permitted a controlled comparison of two different dispute system designs, one using inside neutral USPS employee mediators and the other using outside independent contractor mediators. Although the inside neutral program included selection bias intended to send the easier cases to mediation, and although almost all cases were permitted in the subsequent outside neutral program, the outside neutral program produced superior results.[63] A subsequent study examined the impact of the program on national patterns of formal discrimination complaints. It found a statistically significant drop in formal complaints correlated with implementation of the mediation program.[64]

These studies were possible only because the organization maintained comprehensive, aggregate data not simply on rates of settlement in the mediation cases, but also on other aspects of the system for handling various kinds of conflict within the organization. This data collection allowed researchers to examine what happened to the immediate disputants involved in ADR and to look at the pattern of outcomes produced by all the disputants' uses of various dispute-processing mechanisms.

This type of aggregate research is sorely needed in the ECR field if researchers and practitioners are ever going to be able to assess confidently its promise as a tool for building common purpose in environmental governance. Such an effort, however, requires baseline data on environmental disputes that simply are not available at present. Moreover, it is more difficult to do ECR research analogous to the organizational-level literature. The ECR cases are fewer and bigger, and they involve more time and many more participants than is typical in an ADR case. They also generally occur outside of any single organizational context and often involve participants who are appearing as representatives of organizations or unincorporated associations of stakeholders with shared interests.

Another possibility worthy of exploration is for researchers and practitioners to view a single ECR case as a system in itself. One reason this construct might assist in analysis is that ECR processes often involve multiple interim determinations and agreements (for example, in response to ongoing monitoring for levels of a contaminant in water or air). These cases might be viewed as individual types of disputes, wherein the ECR process functions over time as a system for resolving them. Thus, instead of treating the case as the unit of measurement, researchers might take measurements of diverse indicators across participants, at multiple points in time, both before and after a supposed settlement or agreement. This would permit them to develop much better descriptions of how the ECR case as system develops over time, descriptions that might improve practitioners' understandings of the dynamics of the ECR process. Even if researchers and practitioners think of the ECR case as a dispute system, however, there remains the question of context. If ECR is not a case, but a system, what is the organization for which it constitutes the dispute system design? In turn, how will researchers capture data to evaluate ECR as a system within that context?

Other systemic-level research approaches from other branches of ADR may prove useful in addressing these problems, as well as for informing practice and theory building on ECR more generally. For example, one scholar has proposed a systemic approach to identity-based conflicts.[65] In identity-based conflicts, the argument begins with an individual actor operating to reduce anxiety by identifying with beliefs and values. Researchers then examine social identity and its attendant stereotyping, fully understanding that "in-groups" tend to institutionalize status differences between themselves and "out-groups." In doing so, they render *institutions* the carriers of beliefs that may include biases.

Institutions, in turn, may become elements of the dispute if they are part of the mechanisms that society uses to create or enforce fairness through access to opportunities or resources. The involvement of institutions in disputes also may occur if they are mechanisms for society to manage conflict (such as through the justice system). When institutions become the focus of disputes, social identity may deepen and tempt outgroups toward violence. When in-groups respond with repression, a feedback loop is created, and the system comes into existence. This systemic approach to examining racial or ethnic conflict also may apply to other identity-based conflicts, such as water resource allocation disputes involving multiple cultural and economic groups (such as those discussed in chapters 3 and 4).

Other scholars recently have begun to examine how individual litigants and lawyers organize into the more complex systems of class action and large-scale litigation.[66] This work focuses on mass tort claims and has relevance to mass environmental tort litigation. Researchers find a complex mix of multiple actors, perceptions of information, calculations of costs and benefits, and political judgments that interact and give rise to this relatively small but growing subset of litigation. Researchers and practitioners can understand this phenomenon best from a systemic perspective. What is more, they must understand that systemic level analysis is as important in this downstream use of ECR in litigation as it is in the midstream use involving disputes over allocation of resources.

Understanding ECR as a Time-Extended Phenomenon

A third set of strategic challenges, choices, and opportunities for researchers and practitioners to grapple with in the future occurs because of the tendency for ECR to take place over protracted periods of time. Practitioners have observed that disputants often think ADR ends with the settlement agreement, as if settlement were a fixed point at the end of a linear process. Instead, as one mediator argues, settlement is part of a wavelike form.[67] The settlement occurs after the peak point of tension, just past the crest in a diminishing sine wave. After settlement, the level of tension falls to a low point as the parties agree on a structure for handling future conflict. But conflict *does* recur, and tensions increase, prompting the wave to crest again. Nevertheless, the earlier agreement means that when conflict does recur, the parties will handle it differently, and tension will not rise to the previous level of intensity.

Appreciating ECR interventions as time-extended phenomena means that researchers and practitioners must view, examine, and weigh their benefits and costs in these terms. They must test the hypothesis that people who participate in ECR processes think or behave differently over time from those who do not. Such a research agenda fortunately has been somewhat advanced in areas related to ECR. For example, some negotiation researchers have proposed a method for evaluating how collaborative negotiation training affects individuals and groups.[68] They emphasize the need to examine participants for evidence of change not just in perceptions immediately after training, but also in behavior over time. Others argue that consensus building and other collaborative-planning processes must be examined in light of how members of the group and subgroups learn to work together over time, after the process concludes. There may be, after all, intangible products in the nature of social, intellectual, and political capital that are outcomes of value for evaluation to test.[69] Finally, as theorists have asserted in the policy sciences more generally, going through the process can clarify policy values and options to achieve maximum human dignity.[70]

One possibility for future ECR research is to build on these differing disciplinary traditions to find ways of measuring whether ECR does enhance these less-tangible forms of capital and contribute to maximizing human dignity.[71] Studying ECR in this fashion as time-extended phenomena poses several difficulties, of course. One of the most immediate challenges, some might say, is that researchers will find it difficult to complete a study of an environmental dispute on a timescale commensurate with incentives for productivity in academia. However, this difficulty and others simply mean that researchers must adapt their research methods to the phenomenon in order to learn from it (for example, employing ARIMA time-series analyses where data already exist).

Outcomes for the Environment

A final set of strategic challenges, choices, and opportunities regarding the future of ECR as a tool for building a results-based sense of common purpose in environmental governance ironically concerns measuring its own impact on environmental outcomes. Researchers and practitioners are reluctant to impose on ECR the burden of proving itself effective in advancing substantive environmental policy. This is not the case in other conflict resolution contexts, where researchers attempt to relate participation in an ADR program to objective indicators of impact. For example, work on employment conflict resolution goes beyond the impact of the process on participants. It also looks to such organizational impacts as the rate of complaints filed throughout grievance or dispute appeals processes, and ADR's correlates with productivity, morale, or retention of employees. Likewise, court ADR evaluators have examined overall case processing and docket times, looking for differences in negotiated, mediated, arbitrated, and adjudicated cases. Some of these researchers examine a variable (often named *outcome*) defined as the percentage of the claimant's original demand that she or he ultimately settles on through mediation or arbitration of the dispute.[72]

Despite their reluctance, ECR researchers and practitioners must begin to consider outcomes in terms of protecting the environment. It is important as a matter of public policy and management to determine whether ADR methods are effective tools for implementing national environmental policy. After all, other policy implementation tools must withstand substantive scrutiny in an era of results-based management. Why, then, should ECR evaluators limit their analysis to whether a given set of participants reached agreement and were satisfied with the process and the outcome?

Taking ECR outcomes seriously, of course, requires information not only about ECR, but also about the consequences of using traditional mechanisms for policy development and enforcement. Researchers and practitioners must begin asking questions that go to the heart of the claims of ECR proponents. For example, in the area of environmental enforcement, what does on-the-ground, in-the-water, or in-the-air testing reveal about the state of the environment and its ecosystems in environmental conflicts before and after ECR activities, or in cases with and without ECR interventions? Does remediation happen more quickly? How do cleanup activities conducted at sites that use ECR compare with those at sites that do not? What is the success of permitting under ECR as compared to permitting under traditional processes? At what rate do different groups of permits generate litigation or enforcement conflict?

Questions such as these provide formidable challenges for ECR advocates. Answering them persuasively means that they must collect and analyze ECR data on indicators that go beyond the process and its immediate outcome. They also must collect the best available scientific and technical information about the state of the environmental media, resource, ecosystem, or species that is the subject of the environmental conflict. As Durant with Boodphetcharat note in chapter 3, research necessary to inform practice in this regard requires interdisciplinary cooperation among social scientists and biophysical scientists to collect and analyze their implications astutely.[73]

Researchers may not be able to draw meaningful conclusions about outcomes for the environment with data from a single case or site. By consistently collecting data at multiple points in time for a number of cases or sites, however, they can aggregate results and begin to look for patterns. This search for patterns is especially important and challenging because ECR cases differ widely. Unlike small claims cases, they are often sui generis. However, it might be possible to examine them for patterns in the proportion of improvement in various scientific indicators over time. By what percentage does a given contaminant decline in the water or soil? By what proportion of the ultimate goal does the environment improve or a species population recover? Are these proportions similar over a given period of time for cases where ECR is and is not used?

Thus, as with each of the other sets of strategic challenges, choices, and opportunities noted in this section, the future of ECR as a tool for building common purpose in environmental governance will depend in part on the extent to which scholars and practitioners can amass data for answering these types of questions. The rub, of course, is that these data are difficult to collect, a challenge compounded by the massive amounts of data required. Nevertheless, these challenges are not insurmountable if scholars and practitioners choose to pursue serious and consistent efforts to institutionalize the collection of both environmental and ECR data. Granted, Congress has created a new federal agency, the U.S. Institute for

Environmental Conflict Resolution, to address the complex intergovernmental relationships in the myriad of disputes involving the environment. Yet that action is not enough. To assess ECR approaches to environmental governance in empirically informed ways, a bureau for environmental (and public policy) conflict resolution processes and programs, equivalent to the Bureau of Labor Statistics, is needed. Moreover, as ECR programs themselves become institutionalized and funding sources develop higher expectations regarding demonstrated performance, the field needs to build an infrastructure that will support the next generation of research and evaluation. This, in turn, will require comprehensive, electronic, routine, decentralized, and longitudinal data collection.

Such approaches optimally will meld data collection and scholarly analysis with an information system that gives environmental and natural resources managers something they need and can routinely use on their own. As a consequence, intense collaboration among agency top managers, records administrators, computer systems technicians, and researchers is key to attaining a well-designed, integrated, and implemented system. Hopefully in the future, with such standardized data collection and analysis, researchers and practitioners alike will be able to step back, look at the system as a whole, and ask whether ECR really does produce better environmental policies, fairer processes, and a results-based sense of common purpose among stakeholders.

Notes

1. Rosemary O'Leary, *Environmental Change: Federal Courts and the EPA* (Philadelphia: Temple University Press, 1993).

2. James Meadowcroft, "The Politics of Sustainable Development: Emergent Arenas and the Challenge for Political Science," *International Political Science Review* 20 (1999): 219–237.

3. Ibid.

4. Douglas J. Amy, *The Politics of Environmental Mediation* (New York: Columbia University Press, 1987), p. 6.

5. Gail Bingham, *Resolving Environmental Disputes: A Decade of Experience* (Washington, D.C.: Conservation Foundation, 1986).

6. For an extended discussion of hyperpluralism in environmental governance, see Robert F. Durant, Young-Pyoung Chun, Byungseob Kim, and Seongjong Lee,

"Toward a New Governance Paradigm for Environmental Management in the 21st Century?" *Administration and Society* 35(6) (2004): 643–682.

7. Alissa J. Stern and Tim Hicks, *The Process of Business/Environmental Collaborations: Partnering for Sustainability* (Westport, Conn.: Quorum, 2000), p. 196.

8. U.S. Institute for Environmental Conflict Resolution, http://www.ecr.gov.

9. J. Walton Blackburn and Willa Marie Bruce, *Mediating Environmental Conflicts: Theory and Practice* (Westport, Conn.: Quorum, 1995), pp. 1–2.

10. Bingham, *Resolving Environmental Disputes;* Rosemary O'Leary, Robert F. Durant, Daniel J. Fiorino, and Paul S. Weiland, *Managing for the Environment: Understanding the Legal, Organizational, and Policy Challenges* (San Francisco: Jossey-Bass, 1999), p. 203.

11. O'Leary et al., *Managing for the Environment,* p. 197.

12. Scott Mernitz, *Mediation of Environmental Disputes: A Sourcebook* (New York: Praeger, 1980).

13. For a more detailed discussion, see Amy, *The Politics of Environmental Mediation.*

14. Ibid.

15. Ibid.

16. Ibid.

17. Laura M. Lake, "Judicial Review: From Procedure to Substance," in Laura M. Lake, ed., *Environmental Mediation,* 32–57 (Boulder, Colo.: Westview, 1980).

18. O'Leary, *Environmental Change.*

19. O'Leary et al., *Managing for the Environment,* p. 198; Jay Folberg and Alison Taylor, *Mediation: A Comprehensive Guide to Resolving Conflicts Without Litigation* (San Francisco: Jossey-Bass, 1984).

20. Lawrence Susskind, Lawrence Bacow, and Michael Wheeler, *Resolving Environmental Regulatory Disputes* (Cambridge, Mass.: Schenkman, 1983), p. 2.

21. Lawrence S. Bacow and Michael Wheeler, *Environmental Dispute Resolution* (New York: Plenum, 1984), p. 360.

22. E. Allan Lind and Tom R. Tyler, *The Social Psychology of Procedural Justice* (New York: Plenum, 1988).

23. Amy, *The Politics of Environmental Mediation,* pp. 37–38.

24. O'Leary et al., *Managing for the Environment.*

25. Ibid.

26. Conflict Resolution Information Sources, http://www.crinfo.org.

27. Definition of terms can be found at the U.S. Institute for Environmental Conflict Resolution website, http://www.ecr.gov, and at the Conflict Resolution Information Sources website.

28. For more information on consensus building, see Barbara Gray, *Collaborating* (San Francisco: Jossey-Bass, 1987); Lawrence Susskind and Jeffrey Cruikshank, *Breaking the Impasse: Consensual Approaches to Resolving Public Disputes* (New York: Basic, 1987); Judith E. Innes, "Evaluating Consensus Building," in Lawrence Susskind, Sarah McKearnan, and Jennifer Thomas-Larmer, eds., *The Consensus Building Handbook: A Comprehensive Guide to Reaching Agreement*, 631–675 (Thousand Oaks, Calif.: Sage, 1999); Cary Coglianese, "Is Consensus an Appropriate Basis for Regulatory Policy?" in Eric Orts and Kurt Deketelaere, eds., *Environmental Contracts: Comparative Approaches to Regulatory Innovation in the United States and Europe*, 93–113 (New York: Kluwer Academic, 2001). See also the Policy Consensus Initiative, http://www.policyconsensus.org.

29. See, generally, Gerald W. Cormick, "Strategic Issues in Structuring Multiparty Public Policy Negotiations," *Negotiation Journal* 5 (April 1989): 125–132; Gerald W. Cormick, "The Theory and Practice of Environmental Mediation," *The Environmental Professional* 2 (1980): 24–33; Gerald W. Cormick and L. K. Patton, "Environmental Mediation: Defining the Process Through Experience," in L. M. Lake, ed., *Environmental Mediation: The Search for Consensus*, 79–97 (Boulder, Colo.: Westview Press, 1990); Lawrence Susskind and Jennifer Thomas-Larmer, "Conducting a Conflict Assessment," in Susskind, McKearnan, and Thomas-Larmer, eds., *The Consensus Building Handbook*, 99–136.

30. See, generally, Christopher W. Moore, *The Mediation Process*, 2d ed. (San Francisco: Jossey-Bass, 1996); James A. Wall and Ann Lynn, "Mediation: A Current Review," *Journal of Conflict Resolution* 37 (1993): 160–194; James A. Wall, John B. Stark, and Rhetta H. Standifer, "Mediation: A Current Review and Theory Development," *Journal of Conflict Resolution* 45(3) (2001): 370–391.

31. Roger Fisher, William Ury, and Bruce Patton, *Getting to Yes*, 2d ed. (New York: Penguin, 1991); Ellen A. Waldman, "Identifying the Role of Social Norms in Mediation: A Multiple Model Approach," *Hastings Law Journal* 48(4) (1997): 703–769; Ellen A. Waldman, "The Evaluative-Facilitative Debate in Mediation: Applying the Lens of Therapeutic Jurisprudence," *Marquette Law Review* 82(1) (1998): 155–170.

32. Adrienne E. Eaton and Jeffrey H. Keefe, eds., *Employment Dispute Resolution and Worker Rights in the Changing Workplace* (Champaign, Ill.: Industrial Relations Research Association, 1999).

33. Waldman, "The Evaluative-Facilitative Debate in Mediation."

34. See, generally, Cornelius M. Kerwin, *Rulemaking: How Government Agencies Write Law and Make Policy* (Washington, D.C.: Congressional Quarterly, 1994); Cornelius M. Kerwin, "Negotiated Rulemaking," in Phillip J. Cooper and Chester A. Newland, eds., *Handbook of Public Law and Administration*, 225–236 (San Francisco: Jossey-Bass, 1997); Cornelius M. Kerwin and Laura Langbein, *An Evaluation of Negotiated Rulemaking at the Environmental Protection Agency, Phase I* (Washington, D.C.: Administrative Conference of the United States, 1995); Laura Langbein and Cornelius M. Kerwin, "Regulatory

Negotiation Versus Conventional Rule Making: Claims, Counterclaims, and Empirical Evidence," *Journal of Public Administration Research and Theory* 10 (2000): 599–632; Cary Coglianese, "Assessing Consensus: The Promise and Performance of Negotiated Rulemaking," *Duke Law Journal* 46 (1997): 1255–1349; Phillip J. Harter, "Negotiating Regulations: A Cure for Malaise," *Georgetown Law Journal* 71(1) (1982): 100–118; Phillip J. Harter, "Assessing the Assessors: The Actual Performance of Negotiated Rulemaking," *New York University Environmental Law Journal* 9 (2000): 32–59; Lawrence Susskind and Gerard McMahon, "The Theory and Practice of Negotiated Rulemaking," *Yale Journal of Regulation* 3 (1985): 133–165.

35. Kerwin, "Negotiated Rulemaking."

36. Lisa B. Bingham, "Alternative Dispute Resolution in Public Administration," in Cooper and Newland, eds., *Handbook of Public Law and Administration*, 546–566.

37. Ibid.

38. Ibid.

39. Ibid.

40. Ibid.

41. Rosemary O'Leary and Lisa Bingham, eds., *The Promise of Environmental Conflict Resolution* (Washington, D.C.: Resources for the Future, 2003).

42. O'Leary et al., *Managing for the Environment*, p. 193.

43. Bingham, *Resolving Environmental Disputes*.

44. J. Walton Blackburn and Willa Marie Bruce, eds., *Mediating Environmental Conflicts: Theory and Practice* (Westport, Conn.: Quorum, 1995), pp. 18–19.

45. Amy, *The Politics of Environmental Mediation*.

46. Ibid.

47. O'Leary and Bingham, *The Promise of Environmental Conflict Resolution*.

48. Coglianese, "Assessing Consensus"; Harter, "Assessing the Assessors."

49. Ibid.

50. Ibid.

51. Rosemary O'Leary and Susan Raines, "Lessons Learned from Two Decades of Alternative Dispute Resolution Programs and Processes at the U.S. Environmental Protection Agency," *Public Administration Review* 61(6) (2001): 682–692.

52. Ibid.

53. Rosemary O'Leary and Maja Husar, "What Environmental Attorneys Really Think about ADR," *Natural Resources and Environment* 16(4) (spring 2002): 262–264.

54. Rosemary O'Leary, "Environmental Mediation: What Do We Know and How Do We Know It?" in Blackburn and Bruce, *Mediating Environmental Conflicts*, 17–35.

55. Morton Deutsch and Peter T. Coleman, eds., *The Handbook of Conflict Resolution* (San Francisco: Jossey-Bass, 2000).

56. Michael Alan Sacks, Karaleah S. Reichart, and W. Trexler Proffitt Jr., "Broadening the Evaluation of Dispute Resolution: Context and Relationships over Time," *Negotiation Journal* 15(4) (1999): 339–345.

57. For example, Ann. E. Tenbrunsel and David M. Messick, "Sanctioning Systems, Decision Frames, and Cooperation," *Administration Science Quarterly* 44(4), (1999): 684–707.

58. Robert Axelrod, *The Evolution of Cooperation* (New York: Basic, 1984).

59. See, for example, Catherine Honeyman, *Gacaca Jurisdictions: Interim Report of Observations,* draft report of Rwanda observation project supervised by Dr. Jens Meierhenrich, lecturer in the Departments of Government and Social Studies, Harvard University, Cambridge, Mass., August 20, 2002 (on file with editors).

60. For an example of the systems approach applied to natural resources management initiatives, see Jennifer A. Bellamy, Daniel H. Walker, Geoffrey T. McDonald, and Geoffrey J. Syme, "A Systems Approach to the Evaluation of Natural Resource Management Initiatives," *Journal of Environmental Management* 63 (2000): 407–423.

61. Judith E. Innes and David E. Booher, "Consensus Building and Complex Adaptive Systems: A Framework for Evaluating Collaborative Planning," *Journal of the American Planning Association* 65(4) (1999): 412–423; Innes, "Evaluating Consensus Building."

62. Eaton and Keefe, *Employment Dispute Resolution and Worker Rights in the Changing Workplace.*

63. Lisa B. Bingham, Gregory Chesmore, Yuseok Moon, and Lisa Marie Napoli, "Mediating Employment Disputes at the United States Postal Service: A Comparison of In-House and Outside Neutral Mediators," *Review of Public Personnel Administration* 20(1) (2000): 5–19.

64. Lisa B. Bingham and Mikaela Cristina Novac, "Mediation's Impact on Formal Discrimination Complaint Filing: Before and After the REDRESS® Program at the United States Postal Service," *Review of Public Personnel Administration* 21(4) (2001): 308–331.

65. Leo F. Smyth, "Identity-Based Conflicts: A Systemic Approach," *Negotiation Journal* 18(1) (2002): 147–161.

66. Deborah R. Hensler, "Revisiting the Monster: New Myths and Realities of Class Action and Other Large Scale Litigation," *Duke Journal of Comparative and International Law* 11 (2001): 179–213.

67. Christopher Honeyman, "The Wrong Mental Image of Settlement," *Negotiation Journal* 17(1) (2001): 25–32.

68. Peter T. Coleman and Ying Ying Joanne Lim, "Research Report: A Systematic Approach to Evaluating the Effects of Collaborative Negotiation Training on Individuals and Groups," *Negotiation Journal* 17(4) (2001): 363–392.

69. Innes and Booher, "Consensus Building and Complex Adaptive Systems," pp. 412, 423.

70. Udaya Wagle, "The Policy Science of Democracy: The Issues of Methodology and Citizen Participation," *Policy Sciences* 33 (2000): 207–223.

71. William Ascher, "Resolving the Hidden Differences among Perspectives on Sustainable Development," *Policy Sciences* 32 (1999): 351–377.

72. There is an ongoing debate about whether this ratio ought to be equal for arbitrated and litigated outcomes. For example, if a hypothetical set of disputants in arbitration recovers on average 20 percent of what they claim, but a different hypothetical set of disputants in litigation recovers 60 percent on average, does this mean that arbitration is flawed or somehow unjust? Does it simply mean there is selection bias because some disputants opt for arbitration, whereas others opt to litigate? Does it mean that the two sets of disputants and their claims differ? Are the disputants different in terms of personality characteristics? In some evaluations of court-annexed arbitration, the fact that the outcome ratio is the same for arbitrated and litigated cases is cited as evidence that the program is effective. All of these efforts relate participation in ADR to some outside, more objective measure of impact. For examples of this analysis and a review of some of the literature about employment arbitration, see Lisa B. Bingham, "On Repeat Players, Adhesive Contracts, and the Use of Statistics in Judicial Review of Arbitration Awards," *McGeorge Law Review* 29(2) (1998): 223–260.

73. For an interesting discussion of the difficulties in merging the policy sciences with ecological sciences, see Ascher, "Resolving the Hidden Differences among Perspectives on Sustainable Development."

III

Redefining Administrative Rationality

Robert F. Durant

In the early twentieth century in the United States, the progressive reform movement embraced the principles of administration as a partial antidote to the diseconomies, inefficiencies, ineffectiveness, and sordidness of existing regulatory regimes in the nation. The administrative rationality that progressive reformers borrowed from Europe and embraced enthusiastically as a reform agenda for building common purpose was premised on the presumed superiority of apolitical, expertise-based organizations; structured on the basis of functional problems and the division of labor; and coordinated by hierarchy, rules, and regulations. Living amid existing and often corrupt regimes that favored special or particularized interests in public policy over the common good, these reformers placed their fate in technocratic solutions to resolving public problems in democratically accountable ways. Highly competent professionals, working in politically insulated public agencies run on the principles of administration, would apply their public interest–oriented expertise on behalf of the public good in effective, efficient, and accountable ways.

Thus, in the environmental and natural resources (ENR) policy area, experts in functionally based administrative agencies such as the Department of Interior, the U.S. Forest Service, and the U.S. Public Health Service were envisioned as acting to countervail the negative externalities of markets on public health, safety, and the environment. Forests on public lands in the United States, for example, would be regulated according to scientific principles of conservation (for example, multiple use and sustained yield) imported from Germany. In turn, these experts would be held accountable to the public interest through hierarchical process controls (for example, rules and regulations).

At its best, this administrative orthodoxy lived up to the expectations of the progressive reformers. Relatively unbridled, mission-driven agency professionalism wrought a triumph of competence, political insularity, and public interest–oriented expertise in a variety of ENR areas. At its worst, however, the administrative state also exhibited a spate of dysfunctions that are as much a product of their political environments as any inherent bureaucratic pathology. Indeed, as noted in the preface, many pathologies associated with public agencies are readily traceable to external agency political factors beyond their control (for example, funding deficiencies; structural and programmatic fragmentation; court suits; and political appointees with varying levels of commitment, skill, or political savvy when it comes to ENR protection).

These dysfunctions were (and typically remain) real, formidable, and stubbornly resistant to change. Among others, they included agency allegiance to professional or organizational norms rather than responsiveness to changing conditions and needs; tunnel vision on the part of narrowly and functionally organized experts; and bureaucratic pluralism that pitted subunits and agencies against each other in zero-sum competition for resources, influence, and advantage. Lost, too often, was an operational and evaluative focus on the results that an agency produced rather than on the inputs of resources it sought.

Thus, by the end of the twentieth century, many critics worldwide saw the administrative orthodoxy of the progressive era as producing individual rationality (that is, the pursuit of individual self-interest), but collective irrationality (that is, loss of a sense of common purpose). The chapters in this part reflect how frustration with these significant downsides of the administrative orthodoxy has led many ENR reformers to conclude that administrative rationality must be redefined. Otherwise, they argue, we stand little chance of building the results-based sense of common purpose that is vital to efficient, effective, equitable, and accountable environmental governance in the twenty-first century. What is more, redefining administrative rationality in this way means simultaneously reinventing the expectations and foci of the elected officials who oversee ENR agencies—a task that will require patience, persistence, and aplomb.

As noted in the introduction to this volume, variations on the theme of increasing the discretion given to both regulators and the regulated community lie at the heart of the ENR reformers' assault on administrative rationality. In chapter 10, Denise Scheberle focuses on one dimension of this effort: the devolution of the responsibilities for environmental governance from Washington to subnational actors. She uses the still-evolving experience of the U.S. Environmental Protection Agency (EPA) to take stock of the logic, choices, and challenges of pursuing such a strategy in the United States. Because the evidence about the success of EPA devolution efforts over the past decade is decidedly mixed, Scheberle argues that debates over whether or not to continue devolving responsibilities for environmental governance will continue apace. She also contends that simplistic debates over centralization versus decentralization in many ways have been overtaken by events on the ground in intergovernmental relations. Thus, future debates must be informed by a contingency-based perspective on devolution that fully captures the variety of intergovernmental management models currently animating environmental governance. Even then, however, the ultimate fate of devolution as an approach to building a results-based sense of common purpose in environmental governance will hinge on changes in political and economic climates, as well as on a variety of organizational, network, and capacity challenges, choices, and opportunities at all levels of our Madisonian system.

Regardless of who ultimately carries out these responsibilities, however, reformers seek to give greater discretion to regulatory targets. Their logic is straightforward and turns what was once seen as a vice into a virtue: flexibility as a way to meet regulatory standards will result in more efficient, effective, and collaborative compliance rather than noncompliance from polluters. In chapter 11, Daniel Fiorino argues that reformers must answer a fundamental question if the concept of flexibility is to be an enduring one: How can we design more flexibility into regulation and still keep pressure on industry to improve? He argues not only that this question *can* be answered by proponents and suggests ways to do so, but also that it *must* be answered compellingly. Otherwise, distrust will stymie any hope for building a results-based sense of common purpose in environmental governance. According to Fiorino, existing administrative rationality is premised on outmoded ideas about the state's role and capacities, the nature of environmental problems, and industry motivations that pose barriers to environmental problem solving. Decidedly more appropriate than this existing strategy based on *rules and deterrence* is one based on *information, incentives, and cooperation* geared toward positive ENR results.

Perhaps nowhere are discretion and flexibility needed to work more profoundly in building a results-based sense of common purpose than in moving environmental governance away from administratively irrational end-of-pipe regulatory approaches and toward more rational "upstream" pollution prevention regimes. And nowhere has gaining this flexibility to break with rule- and deterrence-based strategies proven to be more difficult. To most observers, the problem lies in pollution prevention aims being too ambitious. In chapter 12, however, Ken Geiser argues to the contrary: pollution prevention strategies have not realized their full potential largely because over the years they have lost early proponents' visionary precepts. As a consequence, they are not ambitious, inspirational, or strategically savvy enough to occasion broader, results-based political support and impact. Using the cleaner production and preventive medicine experiences abroad to illustrate his points, he argues that bolder approaches not only must be as inspiring and visionary as they can be, but also must be well grounded in market incentives and opportunities that regulatory targets understand. Acknowledging how administrative rationality, among other aspects of the American political and economic system, has watered down a bolder pollution prevention agenda, he nonetheless suggests how a well-articulated, inspirational, and transformative national commitment to a cleaner production agenda might yet occur in the United States.

In the final chapter in this part, Jan Mazurek examines the logic, historical experience, and future of a decidedly different mode of results-based assessment: certification standards for environmental management systems (EMSs). This approach is predicated in part on the argument that present regulatory regimes are based on outdated assumptions about the motives of industry, undermine ENR problem solving, and unnecessarily dissipate opportunities for business-government collaboration.

Proponents thus see EMSs generally as a way to attenuate these problems, and many see certification of EMS compliance as one means for ensuring that the accountability aspects of the new covenant do not get lost in the process. In contrast to outcomes-based accountability tools, however, EMSs not only focus on compliance accountability, but also depend on industries themselves to set the standards.

Mazurek argues that the controversy over using third-party certification of EMSs as a public policy tool for building a results-based sense of common purpose is a function of different expectations among various stakeholders. These expectations, in turn, are a function of confusing certification with other types of auditing. In the process, third-party certification suffers from "guilt by association": stakeholders associate it with auditing problems in general. Thus, in her judgment, EMSs as politically viable, effective, and credible tools of environmental governance face a decidedly uphill battle in the future. Their durability and acceptance as public policy tools depend on the extent to which proponents can eliminate confusion over the means and ends of certification, while simultaneously rebuilding public trust in business more generally after the embarrassing and sobering spate of accounting-related scandals in recent years.

10

Devolution

Denise Scheberle

When Congress passed a series of environmental laws three decades ago, lawmakers envisioned federalism and intergovernmental relations in environmental governance changing in dramatic and permanent ways.[1] Yet so profound were these changes in practice that questions about the constitutionally proper role of the federal government vis-à-vis state governments soon escalated as state and local governments faced a host of costly environmental requirements. Tensions mounted as state governments saw little evidence of intergovernmental cooperation in a policy area rhetorically embracing "cooperative federalism."[2] Equally distressing, as well as most ironic to the states, was that the federal gorilla in the closet in the form of command-and-control, preemptive federal law actually was growing significantly during a period when presidential administrations from Nixon's to Clinton's were persistently pledging allegiance to a "new" federalism that devolved power to the states.

These tensions notwithstanding, substantial progress *was* made in cleaning up the nation's air, water, and land. As the editors of this volume allude to in their introduction, for example, national airborne levels of lead, carbon monoxide, nitrogen dioxide, and ozone decreased between 1980 and 1999, sometimes significantly: 94 percent, 57 percent, 25 percent, and 20 percent, respectively.[3] Approximately 30 percent less hazardous waste was generated and sent to treatment facilities,[4] and roughly 60 percent of assessed U.S. streams, lakes, and estuaries could support their designated uses, such as fishing and swimming.[5]

Nevertheless, as the editors also note, efforts to protect the environment using these first-generation approaches to environmental and natural resources (ENR) protection have been criticized roundly over the years from all quarters, leading to calls for the broader reform agenda discussed in this volume. Though national levels of airborne pollutants have declined, air pollution is still an issue in many U.S. cities. Meanwhile, nearly all (96 percent) of the assessed shoreline around the Great Lakes remains impaired, and approximately 100,000 acres of wetlands is being lost annually in the contiguous United States.[6] Conversions of land from rural to urban uses also threaten habitats and consequently imperil biodiversity. Moreover, very little has been done to control runoff from agriculture or municipal storm sewers, and beach closings and drinking water alerts are still part of the American experience.

From dilemmas like these, two major questions with important implications for federalism and for the building of common purpose emerged in the 1990s. The first was a *how* question: Could greater environmental protection be achieved through continued reliance on traditional techniques, notably "end-of-pipe" controls on industrial polluters, or was a more innovative approach giving more flexibility to subnational actors necessary to make substantial progress? As others in this volume chronicle in greater detail, animating this question was the recognition that the law of diminishing returns applied to command-and-control regulatory requirements. Continuing to ratchet down industrial emissions of pollutants would be costly and yield relatively little in return. Tighter controls on industry could not address thornier "second-generation" environmental concerns that included controlling pollution from nonpoint sources. America's impaired rivers and lakes—most of which are polluted by siltation, pathogens (bacteria), and nutrients—offered a stark example of the need to find new answers to how the environment could be protected.

A second emerging issue with implications for federalism and the building of common purpose was a *who* question: Should the federal government continue to be the major player in environmental protection, or had the time come for state and local governments to assume greater levels of responsibility? In response to the *who* question, advocates for moving or devolving power out of Washington argued that state and local governments were positioned best to respond to the needs of their constituents. Many environmental issues involved development of land,

and land-use control was the province of subnational governments. Effective land-use controls and other local activities could protect wetlands and biodiversity in a way that the federal government could not. More important, and as DeWitt John describes in chapter 6, civic engagement was emerging as an important tool to protect or restore sensitive ecological areas, or both. Moreover, citizens were said to interact most often with the government closest to them—local and state government. But opponents of devolution argued that it would undercut federal laws, ultimately prompting states to "race to the bottom" in an effort to have a more attractive climate for business operations than that found in neighboring states.

Answers to the *how* and *who* questions today remain both controversial and fundamental to building a results-based sense of common purpose. Moreover, they are likely to remain so for the foreseeable future. These answers depend in large part, however, on the political ideologies of actors involved in devolution. Decentralizing power is a political calculation made by conservatives and liberals, Democrats and Republicans, based on the likelihood that the chosen governmental venue (national, state, or local) will be favorably disposed to their political view. Conservatives historically advocated devolution because they believed that local and state governments were less likely to compel businesses to comply with environmental demands, thus minimizing the costs of regulation. Liberals, on the other hand, believed that a strong national role in environmental protection was desirable because state and local governments would be unwilling to regulate local industry.

Though the trend has been toward devolving authority out of Washington, it is not clear how far this trend will or should go. While the George W. Bush administration has stated clearly its willingness to let states take on a greater role, it is highly unlikely that Congress will eliminate anytime soon the current array of federal environmental laws, or that ENR agencies such as the U.S. Environmental Protection Agency (EPA) will move away from stringent regulatory requirements. Equally implausible is that state or local governments will lose interest in environmental protection, grow less frustrated or indignant about costly federal requirements, or be held less accountable by their citizens for environmental quality.

With this realpolitik in mind, and using the experience of the EPA as an analytical focus, the arguments of this chapter are fourfold. First, more than three decades of experience suggest both definite limits on the ability of prescriptive top-down approaches to meet second-generation environmental governance challenges and the importance of collaborative, place-based approaches to building a results-based sense of common purpose in environmental governance. Second, these observations notwithstanding, the answers to questions about who will lead efforts to protect the environment and how environmental protection will occur in the twenty-first century likely will be found in compromise positions involving all levels of government. Thus, the "halting, halfway, and patchworked" nature of environmental governance that the editors describe as today's legacy of reform is likely to continue unabated in the twenty-first century.

Third, future debates will benefit from an empirically based understanding of the conditions under which devolution is more or less likely to be effective in building common purpose in environmental governance. Yet such a contingency-based perspective on devolution is lacking today, especially one that fully captures the variety of intergovernmental management models that currently animate environmental governance. Finally, with or without this research, the extent and nature of the compromises crafted to sort out federal, state, and local environmental responsibilities in the future will hinge on changes in political and economic climates, as well as on changes in the organizational, interorganizational, and cross-sectoral capacities of government at all levels of the Madisonian system.

To provide historical context, the chapter begins by exploring the logic, tensions, and patterns of politics accompanying the ebb and flow of the devolution of environmental governance responsibilities among federal, state, and local governments over the past three decades. Revealed in the process is how the legacy of the 1990s is both disappointing and promising for advocates of devolution as a tool for building common purpose in environmental governance. Next, the chapter reviews the arguments for and against continuing to devolve environmental governance responsibilities to the states. It documents how uncertain we presently are about the success of devolution and why arguments over its efficacy are not going to be resolved anytime soon. In light of these findings, the chapter concludes by reviewing three of the most pressing sets of challenges, choices, and opportunities facing proponents of continuing devolution in the years ahead: ensuring resource capacity, developing performance measurement for place-based and networked approaches to environmental governance, and promoting role-based cultural change in ENR agencies.

The Anatomy of a Devolutionary Agenda

As political scientist Edward Corwin once famously observed, "The Constitution is an invitation to struggle."[7] Perhaps nowhere has this invitation been accepted more persistently than in what John Donahue calls "America's endless argument" over the appropriate scope and division of power, responsibilities, and authority among the federal, state, and local government in the Madisonian system.[8] And perhaps nowhere are the political, economic, and social stakes of sorting out the answers to these questions greater for building common purpose than in the arena of environmental governance.

National and State Environmental Law

In the past thirty years, environmental protection has become a major public policy area, with an array of laws and regulations that rivals the tax code in its complexity. Beginning with the Clean Air Act of 1970, Congress used the Commerce Clause in the U.S. Constitution to pass major pollution control legislation for cleaner air, water, and land. The prevailing legislative pattern was to write strong statutory language that relied on command-and-control regulatory schemes and initial preemption of state laws, then to permit devolution of responsibility back to state and local governments.[9]

Under this legislative strategy, Congress requires the federal oversight agency (usually the EPA) to set national environmental quality standards. It envisions that states will act as the workhorses in implementing environmental laws and allows the EPA to grant states primacy upon a showing that they have adopted regulations at least as stringent as those at the national level. A state with primacy has full authority to implement both the programmatic aspects of the law (such as providing information or conducting inspections) and the enforcement of the law (such as issuing a notice of violation). Primacy preserves a state's right to pass requirements that are more stringent than those found under national law and regulations. However, even in states with approved programs, the federal agency still maintains oversight authority over state regulators and enforcement authority over regulated industries.

Though most states have pursued delegated authority, they sometimes decide it is not in their best interests to pursue primacy. As of 1998, 71 percent of all environmental programs were delegated to the states, up from 41 percent in 1993.[10] Complicating primacy further, states may have authority for one section of the law but not for other sections. For example, only two states (Michigan and New Jersey) have approval for operating the federal wetlands permitting program under Section 404 of the Clean Water Act. However, forty-four states are authorized to run the National Pollutant Discharge Elimination System permitting program for point-source dischargers under Section 402 of the Clean Water Act, the most important component of that law (the exceptions are Alaska, Arizona, Idaho, Massachusetts, New Hampshire, and New Mexico).[11] Meanwhile, forty-two states have primacy for the Resource Conservation and Recovery Act, the nation's hazardous-waste law.[12] In the absence of state authority, the federal government runs the program.

Thus, federalism is at the heart of this tangle of media-specific environmental laws. States no longer are free to dictate the level of environmental controls (or absence thereof) on industry. From constitutional and legal perspectives, and often whether states like it or not, national environmental law legitimately can intrude on what previously has been exclusively state domain. This intrusion has occurred with the blessing of the Supreme Court, which seldom finds any such national legislative encroachments unconstitutional.[13]

Cooperative and Coercive Federalism

When Congress decided to change the rules about who would protect the environment and how such protection would be done, Senator Muskie and other congressional architects employed the language of cooperative federalism.[14] Cooperative federalism meant that national and state governments shared a desire to accomplish social goals. In this case, the goal was pollution control. Cooperative federalism also implied federal financial assistance. Because as a practical matter the federal government effectively could not run pollution control programs on the ground (hence the need for a system of delegated authority), it would provide grants-in-aid to facilitate implementation of these new rules by state and local governments.

As the costs of environmental protection escalated, and as the EPA promulgated stringent regulations, critics quickly began to argue that federal-state relationships were less cooperative than coercive. Coercive federalism means reducing the federal government's reliance on fiscal tools while simultaneously increasing its reliance on regulatory tools to achieve national policy goals.[15] Like the old Nike ads, state and local governments were instructed to "just do it." During the 1970s and 1980s, federal assertion into previous state policy territory reached its zenith, with preemptions more than doubling after 1969. Indeed, more than 50 percent of the preemption statutes enacted since 1789 were passed in the 1970s and 1980s, and many of these preemptions dealt with environmental protection.[16]

Since then, the states' share of the costs of implementing environmental regulatory programs has grown appreciably. In 2000, states budgeted more than $13.5 billion for environmental and natural resources. This amount was nearly twice the EPA budget of $7.4 billion and an increase of nearly 65 percent since 1986. Meanwhile, the federal contribution to state budgets increased less than 5 percent over the same period. In 1986, as well, roughly 40 percent of funding for state environmental programs came from EPA grants. However, by 2000, EPA funding accounted for less than one-fourth of state budgets for environmental protection.[17] Thus, coercive federalism—mandates without sufficient funds—became an apt description of environmental federalism.

Federal Oversight and Federal-State Working Relationships

Underneath the macrolevel discussions of federal-state arrangements under national environmental law is a more practical and logistical component: working relationships among federal, state, and local managers charged with implementing these environmental programs. Scholars long have noted the challenges of organizing public managers and getting them to cooperate in running federal programs.[18] New national environmental laws meant that state bureaucracies would have to change their approach to industries, sometimes significantly, while at the same time the federal government would be adding regulatory staff. The new situation raised certain questions: How would state, local, and EPA officials get along? Would these relationships be cooperative, with federal and state officials partnering to accomplish environmental goals? Or would intergovernmental interactions between staff in the various federal, state, and local agencies be confrontational?

The answers soon were clear: state politicians resented national laws that preempted state laws with too little federal financial assistance, and state agency officials resented the EPA and other federal officials for prescribing what they should do in the field. Federal-state animosities also increased because state officials resented the *way* federal oversight was conducted.[19] EPA and other federal oversight agencies needed to "prove" to Congress that environmental programs delegated to state agencies were working. However, measuring positive environmental outcomes (for example, a cleaner river) was considerably more difficult than measuring state activities (for example, the number of inspections of industrial facilities conducted by state inspectors). Thus, the EPA relied on agency outputs—such as number of permits issued, inspections made, or enforcement actions taken—to judge state performance.

To many state officials, this approach only meant that federal bureaucrats were micromanaging their programs and were acting more like drill sergeants than partners. They also argued that federal oversight staff ignored the essential question: Was the environment actually better than in the past? As one state inspector noted, "They [federal officials] seem more interested in bean counting than in the big environmental picture."[20]

In sum, when Congress passed a host of major environmental laws three decades ago, it envisioned a cooperative kind of federalism wherein state and federal governments shared the goal of protecting the environment. However, from the state and local governments' perspective, environmental federalism on the eve of the 1990s had a dark side as the number of regulatory requirements and unfunded or underfunded mandates grew. Even when states assumed primacy for environmental programs, federal funding was increasingly insufficient to implement environmental programs. Moreover, a "one-size-fits-all" regulatory program reduced regulatory flexibility, and intergovernmental relationships deteriorated owing to the nature of federal agency oversight. In response, the rhetoric of devolution would crescendo by the mid-1990s, leading to major new laws and attempts to improve federal-state working relationships in the years ahead.

The Devolution Revolution of the 1990s

The 1990s was an intriguing decade for policy devolution in general. Criticism of the performance of the national government came from members of Congress and the Clinton administration, as well as from state and local governmental organizations. The Republican-controlled Congress led the charge to devolve power out of Washington, especially in the areas of welfare, environmental protection, and transportation.[21] Indeed, dismantling "big government" programs became a rallying cry during the 1994 elections and was part of the Contract with America that catapulted the control of the U.S. House of Representatives into Republican Party hands after the party's forty years in the wilderness.

Not to be outdone, the Democrats were quick to indicate their support of state and local governments. President Clinton declared that the "era of big government is over" in his 1994 State of the Union Address. He saw the devolution of authority as both a political strategy and a tool for reinventing the federal government.[22] In terms of the latter, he wanted to reform the federal bureaucracy to make it less top-heavy, more decentralized, and more committed to serving "customer" interests. With state and local governments now to be seen as customers of the federal government, the first report of the National Performance Review recommended enhancing intergovernmental relationships and building federal-state partnerships.[23]

By the same token, the Unfunded Mandates Reform Act (UMRA), signed by President Clinton on March 22, 1995, signaled that Congress fully and finally had recognized subnational governments' concern about increasing national mandates. Senator Dirk Kempthorne (R-Idaho), a sponsor of the unfunded mandates legislation, epitomized the devolution rhetoric that accompanied the new law: "You'll get better decisions, because they [state officials] are closer to the problem. Washington, D.C., does not corner the market on wisdom."[24] UMRA requires Congress and the administration to gauge the potential effects of unfunded mandates before imposing them on states or businesses. Under the law, the Congressional Budget Office reviews bills for the presence of federal mandates on state and local governments that will cost more than $50 million annually. Once an unfunded mandate is identified, Congress must approve it in a separate vote, a process that creates both a political and legislative hurdle for imposing the mandate.

As movements toward devolution and reducing unfunded mandates were afoot in the political arena, they also were very much a part of federal, state, and local agency activities. Here, however, the most salient issues for devolving environmental responsibilities to state and local governments included more than just the adequacy of federal financial assistance. They again included the extent of federal micromanagement of state programs and the degree to which states were given flexibility to set policy priorities that would reflect problems of local importance.[25]

In its April 1995 report, *EPA and the States: Environmental Challenges Require a Better Working Relationship,* the U.S. General Accounting Office (GAO) confirmed that lack of sufficient resources was a major impediment to environmental policy implementation. However, the report also noted that intergovernmental relationships were less than stellar, resulting in significant obstacles to environmental protection efforts.[26] As other authors in this volume have noted, the National Academy of Public Administration (NAPA) also suggested a new direction for the EPA—a direction toward devolution. Noting states' increased capabilities to run environmental programs, the academy called on the EPA and Congress to hand more responsibility and decision-making authority to the states: "A new partnership needs to be formed, one based on 'accountable devolution' of national programs and on a reduction in EPA oversight when it is not needed."[27]

By the middle of the 1990s, the EPA and other federal oversight agencies responded by beginning to shift oversight policies in the hope of developing more positive intergovernmental working relationships.[28] The agency established the State/EPA Capacity Steering Committee in

1993 to lead a federal-state dialogue on creating and maintaining an environmental partnership between state and federal officials. Then, in 1994, state officials—unhappy with the pace of changing federal-state relationships and what they saw as the heavy-handedness of the EPA—formed the Environmental Council of the States (ECOS) to lobby for greater flexibility. Explained Mary Gade, director of the Illinois Environmental Protection Agency, "State environmental leaders could no longer stand by and let EPA take the lead. States were quite simply, 'Fed up.'"[29]

As a result, on May 17, 1995, EPA administrator Carol Browner and several state officials signed the Joint Commitment to Reform Oversight and created the National Environmental Performance Partnership System (NEPPS), which was to embrace new approaches to assessing state environmental programs. States now could enter into environmental performance agreements that potentially would focus federal oversight on measures of environmental outcomes rather than on agency conduct. Most important, NEPPS became the vehicle for performance partnership grants that allowed states to consolidate environmental categorical grants.

Proclaimed EPA deputy administrator Fred Hansen in recognizing the first six states to enter into performance partnership agreements with the agency in 1996, "We have entered a new era in state-EPA relations."[30] Based on rates of state participation in the program during the decade, his exuberance might seem warranted. State participation grew from six states in NEPPS's initial year (1996) to forty-five states by the end of 1998.[31] Thirty-one states had both performance partnership agreements and performance partnership grants; twelve states had only grants; two states had only performance partnership agreements. Of the $745 million in state environmental program grants available in 1998, $217 million were consolidated into performance partnership grants, an increase of 28 percent from the previous year.[32]

However, changing oversight in intergovernmental relations is no easy task. On paper, federal-state relationships were changing, but in its review, the GAO noted several barriers to attempts to promote innovation in the federal-state relationship.[33] It observed that the EPA struggled to get buy-in from its rank and file, many of whom had grown accustomed to the regulatory structure. Disagreements over EPA and state roles continued to center on issues of state flexibility and the extent to which external stakeholders should be part of negotiations. Federal-state dis-agreements then came to a head in February 1997 when the EPA with-drew from discussions of an EPA/ECOS joint proposal to promote and implement regulatory reinvention efforts.[34] Though the agency eventu-ally came back to the table with ECOS, it would take more than a year before EPA officials signed the agreement.[35]

Nor has NEPPS yet fulfilled the promise of programmatic flexibility or the ability to address the most pressing environmental priorities, as the states perceive them. GAO and NAPA studies found that most state offi-cials believed participation in NEPPS had not brought significant reduc-tions in EPA staff reporting and other oversight activities.[36] Researchers pointed to bureaucratic norms and agency culture as obstacles, a conclu-sion with which at least some EPA officials agreed. According to EPA regional officials, many regional managers and staff were more comfort-able with preexisting ways of doing business and were unsure how they could accomplish their work in the context of the partnership approach under NEPPS. In fairness, of course, their comfort no doubt stemmed in part from their *discomfort* with court suits that challenged perceived failures in procedural compliance. The EPA can be sued, and has been sued, for failure to perform nondiscretionary duties under U.S. pollution control laws. And the movement toward performance partnership agree-ments in no way absolved the EPA of these obligations.

Fair or not, however, the GAO's critique did not end there. It also in-dicted the EPA's multilevel organizational structure of headquarters and regional offices, an arrangement that made it difficult to "get the word out" to all frontline regional staff.[37] In 2001, EPA officials themselves ob-served in the agency's strategic report that "some EPA oversight practices resulted in duplication of effort, burdensome reporting and unproductive relationships."[38] By the same token, however, EPA officials also identified ongoing compliance problems in state programs, which necessitated greater oversight. EPA regulators were reluctant to reduce oversight without measures in place to ensure that environmental quality would not be compromised.

The difficulty in resolving disagreements over the extent to which states could exercise regulatory flexibility was clearly a setback for the fledgling NEPPS. After all, the new federal-state partnership was built on increased levels of trust and diminished levels of federal prescription. Yet state officials listed burdensome federal requirements and a resistant culture at the EPA as the two largest obstacles to moving beyond traditional command-and-control regulatory approaches.[39] Indeed, they perceived that elements of the intergovernmental working relationship were larger impediments to innovative environmental programs than were lack of resources, statutory constraints, state political factors, workload constraints, and environmental group opposition.

Networking in the Shadow of Hierarchy?

As the preceding discussion suggests, the legacy of devolution efforts as tools for building a results-based sense of common purpose during the 1990s is both disappointing and promising for advocates of devolution. On the one hand, it is yet unclear how successful the paradigm shift away from close federal oversight and toward intergovernmental partnerships and flexibility has been or is likely to be in the future, given the patch-worked nature of that shift. On the other hand, UMRA made it more difficult for Congress to enact burdensome requirements on state or local governments. Moreover, the 1990s saw the beginning of a dialogue over intergovernmental cooperation, something that took tangible form in the NEPPS program. Not everyone, of course, agrees that devolution should proceed, but proceed it has, in ways typical of American pragmatism. In the process, the existence of new models of environmental governance have in some ways overtaken these debates and cry out for a contingency approach that can identify the conditions under which devolution is more or less likely to be appropriate for building a sense of common purpose.

The Case Against Devolution

Five major themes emerge from the chorus of voices that oppose devolving more authority from the federal government to state and local governments: minimum protection, the race to the bottom, equity, transboundary migration, and innovation. In many senses, these themes echo the reasons why the federal government became involved in protecting the environment in the first place, and why many think that it must stay engaged and dominant in the future.

Those who employ the minimum-protection argument contend that federal regulations establish a minimum threshold, or floor, for environmental programs, ensuring that citizens in all states enjoy at least some minimal level of protection. Before federal command-and-control laws were enacted, states had freedom to set their own environmental regulations, yet most failed to do so. Indeed, the primary impetus for federal environmental laws was the states' inability to protect environmental quality effectively. Even today there is evidence supporting the need for a national floor. For example, twenty states have laws prohibiting their environmental agencies from adopting requirements more stringent than those established under at least one federal program. Two states (Kentucky and South Dakota) have statutes that broadly prohibit adoption of regulatory requirements more stringent than the baseline for all federal programs.[40]

Moreover, as previously discussed, the partial-preemption arrangement of federal environmental laws provides an important check on state activities. This is the case because the EPA or another federal agency first must approve and then monitor state environmental programs for consistency with minimum federal requirements designed to implement national laws. What is more, most national environmental laws give citizens (often acting through environmental groups) the right to sue federal agencies for failure to perform these types of nondiscretionary duties.

Consider, for example, section 303(d) of the Clean Water Act. For years, states were reluctant to establish total maximum daily load (TMDL) allocations that potentially would restrict nonpoint sources of pollution in impaired waters. A TMDL specifies the maximum amount of a pollutant that a water body can receive and still meet water quality standards, and it allocates pollutant loadings among point and nonpoint pollutant sources. Only after citizen organizations began bringing legal actions did EPA take states to task to develop TMDLs. As of 2002, legal actions have occurred in thirty-eight states, and in many states, the EPA is under court order to ensure that TMDL allocations are established.[41] Thus, national laws with strict requirements provide an important threshold for environmental protection. As one advocate of strong federal programs noted, "Transforming the state-federal partnership by substantially limiting the federal role and placing in its stead greater reliance on states to protect environmental quality presupposes that states can fill the federal void. . . . [S]tate and federal roles under the major environmental statutes are complementary, not fungible."[42]

Opponents of further devolution also invoke the race-to-the-bottom argument: states may be reluctant to act because environmental protection comes with an economic cost that local industry must bear. Companies, for example, naturally resist increased costs of doing business and will shop around to locate in states with the least burdensome environmental requirements. And because states are often in a fierce competition for industries that will promote economic growth, they are likely to engage in a race with their neighbors to lower regulatory burdens. Opponents also point to research showing that some states *are* more vulnerable than others to interests that traditionally have lobbied for relaxing regulatory requirements.[43] The central conclusion of these studies is that absent strong federal oversight and funding, some states will join a race to the bottom.

A third argument leveled by opponents—the equity argument—is premised on the idea that devolution will reveal the worst of local political and social realities. Here, states are not laboratories of democracy, but stalwarts of existing prejudicial treatment of disadvantaged groups. The federal government may be more protective of environmental justice for minority and low-income groups, as it was in offering civil rights protections in the 1960s. As Evan Ringquist discusses in greater detail in chapter 7, some studies of environmental justice suggest that state and local governments traditionally seem to be more willing to locate hazardous-waste facilities in poor and minority neighborhoods than in wealthy ones. Recent studies of the devolution of welfare also suggest that states may engage in discriminatory practices.[44]

Opponents of devolution also note the transboundary nature of many pressing environmental problems. Absent federal laws that address the transboundary migration of pollution, they argue, state governments will be forced to look at common-law remedies or at provisions in other statutes to find relief from interstate pollution. Indeed, the problem of dealing with interstate pollution was a key reason why Congress passed environmental laws. Few analysts would suggest that the array of national pollution control laws has solved adequately the interstate transport of pollution. Most would agree, however, that without a federal presence, states would be hard pressed to protect their citizens downwind or downstream from polluters in neighboring states.

Finally, advocates of strong federal roles in environmental policy strongly reject concerns that the heavy hand of the federal government will stifle innovation. Both Gregory Amacher and William Lowry, for example, have found that national forests are more protected than state forests because state governments historically have responded to their own revenue needs and constituents when setting policy.[45] Likewise, Barry Rabe's comparative study of Canadian provinces with four U.S. states found that the latter were more likely to devise innovative approaches to environmental protection, more likely to move to outcome measures, and more likely to integrate multimedia permitting processes.[46] He notes, "the absence of any significant federal role in Canada has failed to foster a comparable, much less superior level of innovation. . . . Policy options such as decentralization and delegation must be examined carefully rather than merely asserted as enduring virtues."[47] Finally, and more broadly, Frank Baumgartner and Bryan Jones see opportunity for federal and state governments to coalesce and mutually encourage stronger reforms than otherwise might be possible by either acting alone.[48]

The Case for Continued Devolution
Supporters for continued devolution counter the opposing positions with many reasons for returning control to state and local governments. Three of these best capture the essence of their enduring enthusiasm for the process: state innovation, local wisdom, and distorted policy priorities. They argue, first, that it is foolish to assume that the federal government is always more dedicated to protecting the environment and natural resources than are state and local governments. The race to the bottom, if it ever applied, is no longer an apt description of state environmental protection efforts.[49] State agencies are more capable of effective environmental protection than they were thirty years ago. Instead of racing to the bottom, states recently have moved ahead of the federal government.

One needs only to look at global warming to find confirmation of this argument. For decades, Congress has failed legislatively to mandate cuts in greenhouse gas emissions decisively. Moreover, early signs in this first decade of the twenty-first century suggest that the national government will continue to stumble around this issue. The 107th Congress refused once again, for example, to raise fuel efficiency requirements on automobiles, and the George W. Bush administration has withdrawn support for the Kyoto Protocol, the international treaty on global warming. Yet states such as California (see below), Massachusetts, New Jersey, New York, and Oregon have stepped up to fill the regulatory void.[50] Nor are state abilities to transcend federal environmental requirements limited to air pollution. Winston Porter, a former EPA official in the Superfund program and former head of the Waste Policy Center, observed similarly superior state initiatives in cleaning up hazardous-waste sites. He reported that California, New York, and Wisconsin each remediated 200 hazardous-waste sites, which means that these three states cleaned up approximately as many sites as were cleaned up under the entire federal program.[51]

Consider, as well, the leadership role in environmental governance played by California in recent years. In July 2002, California governor Gray Davis signed the first legislation in the nation aimed at combating global warming. The law requires automakers to cut carbon dioxide emissions by the 2009 model year. The *New York Times* called this law the "most significant step ever taken to control heat-trapping gases in the United States" and quoted Fred Kropp, president of Environmental Defense, as saying, "Finally, somewhere in our governmental system, one state has taken action."[52]

What makes California's action to curb greenhouse gases more impressive is that it comes in addition to the state's new zero-emission standard for automobiles, a requirement that Daimler-Chrysler and General Motors challenged in federal court on the grounds that only the federal government has the right to set fuel efficiency standards.[53] The California Air Resources Board originally had stipulated that 10 percent of all new cars offered for sale in 2003 would have no emissions of pollutants.[54] But because California's air quality regulations predate the federal Clean Air Act, Congress recognized the state's ability to set its own emission rules for mobile sources—effectively establishing two emission standards (California's and the federal government's). Meanwhile, Massachusetts, New York, and Vermont have plans to adopt similar versions of California's zero-emission requirement. Together, these states represent nearly 20 percent of the U.S. auto market and eventually could change the way automakers do business.[55]

Advocates of devolution also offer a second rationale premised on perceptions that many of the second-generation problems facing environmental governance are more amenable to local rather than national solutions. This "local wisdom" argument contends, first, that the national "gorilla in the closet" is really more like a slow-moving sloth. Solutions are best found closest to the problem at hand, and a centralized regulatory structure cannot address problems that are largely local and regional. Proponents of devolution also dismiss monolithic approaches to environmental protection as anachronistic. The one-size-fits-all regulatory model, they argue, easily can become a size that fits nobody, a challenge that the EPA's own Science Advisory Board has recognized. In 1998, for example, the board concluded that most remaining environmental problems are "site specific . . . requiring tailored controls at the regional, state or local level for effective mitigation."[56]

The EPA's recent efforts to advance place-based ecosystem and watershed management, as well as its creation of local government advisory committees, attest to its desire to move toward more holistic, site-specific, and collaborative approaches. Many of these approaches are discussed in greater depth elsewhere in this book, most especially in DeWitt John's chapter on civic environmentalism (for example, the Chesapeake Bay Program, the Great Lakes Program, and the Florida Everglades project) and in Edella Schlager's chapter on common-pool resource management. Jonathan Adler, a supporter of environmental policy devolution, puts it this way:

The local and regional nature of many environmental problems means that local knowledge and expertise is necessary to develop proper solutions. Such localized knowledge is inevitably beyond the reach of even the most intrepid federal regulators. For example, the most effective and equitable strategy for controlling ozone precursors will vary from city to city depending upon the local mix of stationary and mobile sources. . . . Federal regulators never have been and never will be able to acquire and assimilate the enormous amount of information necessary to make optimal regulatory judgments that reflect the technical requirements of particular locations and pollution sources."[57]

Finally, proponents of continuing devolution of environmental responsibilities and authorities see it as an antidote to prescriptive national approaches that distort local policy priorities. National policies and regulations, they argue, become de facto local priorities and regulations. Overly prescriptive federal requirements make it difficult or impossible for subnational governments to shift priorities to meet more pressing local needs.[58] Examples abound. Public water supply systems must test for contaminants never previously found in drinking water supplies. Older communities with homes built before 1978 (when lead was banned from residential paint) may have critical needs to test homes and monitor blood lead levels in children. Yet federal funding virtually has been absent in protecting children from this environmental contaminant. This problem may be rectified in part by the performance partnership grants and agreements under NEPPS, but research to date suggests relatively little shifting of funding or priorities. In short, local and state initiatives have long been linked inexorably to national, rather than their own, priorities.

The Case Gone Missing

The arguments and perspectives addressed in the previous sections are certainly not going to be resolved any time soon, if ever. Legal, political, economic, and bureaucratic forces virtually guarantee that the federal government will always play a preeminent role in environmental policy, especially because of the typically cross-boundary migration of pollution. However, environmental policy *has* turned a corner toward greater decentralization, and it is likely (especially under the current George W. Bush administration) that state and local governments will play increasingly larger roles in environmental policy implementation.

Under these circumstances, one may hope that a rich, empirically grounded research base will inform these debates, especially one suggesting the conditions under which devolution of environmental responsibilities is more or less likely to succeed. Our understanding of these conditions is presently impressionistic at best, however. Fortunately, the chapters by Edella Schlager and DeWitt John in this volume *indirectly* advance this enterprise in thoughtful and useful ways. They do so by offering empirically grounded propositional inventories that cry out for further testing, refinement, and elaboration by scholars who study and practitioners who work on devolution issues in environmental governance. But much remains to be done *directly* for a contingency theory of devolution to emerge.

To be sure, traditional public-finance theory proffered largely by economists asserts that government's stabilization and distribution functions should be handled at the federal government level. They alternatively posit that its allocation functions should rest at subnational levels of government, where differing local preferences for goods and services are accommodated best.[59] As Alice Rivlin notes, however, economists have been long on theory and prescription, but short on descriptive realism, missing the complex, multilevel interrelationships driving intergovernmental relations today. Nor have political scientists been silent on this issue. As John Donahue summarizes, devolution is said to be wise whenever "states vary greatly in circumstances or goals, where external impacts are minor or manageable, where the payoff from innovation exceeds the advantages of uniformity, and where competition boosts efficiency instead of inspiring destructive stratagems."[60] But these "lessons learned" are quite thin and subject to myriad interpretations of both fact and application in concrete circumstances.

Further compounding this dilemma, devolution debates focus inordinately on only two models of management presently regnant in American federalism in general and in environmental governance in particular. As Robert Agranoff and Michael McGuire describe, the *top-down* model is consonant with coercive federalism.[61] It envisions the federal government managing its policy preferences and programs through state and local managers, with the latter serving as mere extensions of the former. Here, subnational actors spend a great deal of time on "transactions relating to meeting [federal] program intent and expectation—that is, trying to fit [their own] programs into [federal] standards, rules, and regulations."[62]

In contrast, the *donor-recipient* model is most consonant with cooperative federalism. It envisions federal, state, and local relationships as premised on mutual dependence, wherein negotiation rather than prescription takes place premised on adaptation to local circumstances or goals. For example, in the case of safe drinking water in the United States, cities negotiate with the EPA to gain exemptions from costly testing requirements for chemicals that are highly unlikely to affect their water sources, or they propose writing their own water quality standards that give priority to important local risks.

Yet, as these scholars also note, two additional models of management inform contemporary federalism, models that simplistic coercive-versus-cooperative normative debates over devolution fail to consider. The *jurisdiction-based* model is especially relevant to place-based models of environmental governance and to civic environmentalism initiatives. In this model, local managers pursue the goals of a *subnational* jurisdiction that is in a superior position to other actors by virtue of its public authority. They then proceed to attain those subnational goals by identifying and mobilizing actors from *all* levels of government and sectors (public, private, and nonprofit) who possess the place-based resources necessary for success (for example, financial, expertise, organizational, informational, and legal authorities). The *network* model of intergovernmental management is reminiscent of the jurisdiction-based model but is decidedly less hierarchical. More specifically, networks are patterns of structured interdependence in which various actors act strategically to pursue goals collectively that none would be able to accomplish on its own. In contrast to the other models, however, "no central actor [that is, no federal, state, or local government agency], no ruler-defined relationships, and no pre-established goals of a single actor . . . provide guidance and control."[63]

Thus, although political debates over devolution have been framed over the past decade as normative disputes over centralization versus decentralization of federal authority, they have been overtaken in some ways by events on the ground (namely, by jurisdiction-based and network models of environmental federalism). Not only has the devolution debate been focused too narrowly on the top-down and donor-recipient models of federalism, but it also has offered few empirically grounded prescriptions for guiding devolution debates in the future across all four models of federal management. A reframing of the debate to attenuate these shortcomings by advancing a contingency-based theory of devolution is arguably long overdue.

Devolution: Challenges, Choices, and Opportunities

This chapter has explored the evolution of federal-state relationships since the 1970s, when Congress decided that pollution control was a major national issue. Over the next thirty years, state and local governments built capacity to run environmental programs, though with increasing resentment regarding the nature of federal oversight and escalating costs of compliance. The environment would be cleaner, but not totally clean, and new concerns about the limits of command-and-control regulations would emerge. This point returns us to the two questions posed at the beginning of the chapter: Who should be responsible for environmental protection efforts, and how should further environmental protection be accomplished? In part, the answers to these questions were found in cries for devolving authority out of Washington, with the idea that a results-based sense of common purpose might be advanced more readily in that arena. Increasing intergovernmental partnerships helped to answer both questions: the *who* more often would be state and local governments; the *how* would include innovative approaches sensitive to local concerns.

The rhetoric of devolution of responsibility to subnational governments is still used in nearly every arena: the George W. Bush administration, executive agencies at all levels of government, Congress, state and local governmental associations, and various research institutions. What is more, devolution likely will continue in the foreseeable future, though slowly and at the margins. As mentioned earlier, devolving power is most successful when all intergovernmental actors support it. Even the strongest advocates of devolution are reluctant, however, to see a roll-back of national environmental laws. Moreover, the current system of national environmental laws holds the EPA ultimately responsible for implementation and empowers citizens to sue the agency for nonperformance. As long as the EPA (not state or local governments) is held legally responsible for effective implementation of pollution control laws such as the Clean Air and Clean Water Acts, the agency *must* monitor state performance.

But if bureaucratic patterns and national environmental laws are not likely to change quickly, what *is* emerging more rapidly is a recognition of the importance of place-based environmental management in answering the *how* question. As the chapters in the second part of this book attest to more broadly, stakeholder involvement is essential if local and state governments are to work collaboratively to protect watersheds, wetlands, and sensitive ecosystems effectively. Thirty plus years of watching national environmental laws unfold make it clear that prescriptive top-down approaches have their limits. Many future environmental problems will be solved best at the local level using collaborative approaches.

As a consequence, the relationship between federal, state, and local governments in environmental policy continues to shift, as policymakers look beyond command-and-control regulations in an effort to address ongoing and more localized environmental problems. State governments always have been key players in implementing national environmental laws, and efforts to shift more programmatic and funding flexibility out of Washington continue. It remains to be seen, however, how successful these efforts will be in the complex fabric of environmental policy, but three things are clear. First, the landscape of environmental protection will continue to change with shifts in political and economic climates and organizational capacities at all levels of government. Second, and as noted in the previous section, a more robust understanding is essential of the conditions under which devolution is more or less likely to ensure the building of common purpose. Finally, all of this means that major strategic challenges, choices, and opportunities lie ahead for proponents of the continued devolution of environmental responsibilities to state and local entities. The most pressing challenges will be those related to ensuring resource capacity, developing jurisdiction-based and network-based performance measurement, and establishing role-based cultural change in ENR agencies.

Resource Capacity

One legacy of the 1990s devolution revolution has been mounting compliance costs for local and state governments. Nowhere is the need for funding as striking as in the provision of safe drinking water under the Safe Drinking Water Act and sewage treatment under the Clean Water Act. Over the years, public water supply systems and publicly owned treatment facilities increasingly have faced costly compliance requirements. Two notable examples with regard to drinking water are the new radionuclides rule, effective in 2003, and the arsenic rule, effective in 2006. Both of these regulations have estimated compliance costs for public water supply systems of more than $75 million.[64]

Even more troubling than complying with new testing and monitoring requirements is dealing with aging infrastructure. In 1995, the

Association of Metropolitan Sewer Agencies' survey of 108 large metropolitan areas estimated that municipalities would have to raise more than $22 billion for mandated capital improvements, of which the federal government would provide less than 10 percent.[65] This year, however, even more budgetary shortfalls are predicted. Moreover, by 2016, the EPA estimates that more than half of the country's sewer systems will be in poor or very poor condition. These predictions led former EPA administrator Christine Todd Whitman to observe that threats to water quality and quantity—owing in large part to antiquated and deteriorating water supply and treatment systems—pose the greatest environmental challenge in the United States.[66]

The Drinking Water Infrastructure Survey—a joint effort of the states, public water utilities, and the EPA—has equally dire predictions for the drinking water system infrastructure. Observing that the nation's 55,000 community water systems must make "significant investments to install, upgrade or replace infrastructure," the survey indicated that $138 billion was needed between 2000 and 2019, with nearly $77 billion needed before 2014 to protect human health.[67] The Congressional Budget Office, in turn, has made its own estimate of costs of maintaining drinking water and wastewater infrastructure over the same time period (2000–2019).[68] Its analysis provides a range of between $11.6 billion and $20.1 billion per year needed for drinking water systems, and between $13 billion and $20.9 billion per year needed for wastewater systems. These estimates do not include operation and maintenance of these systems or any allowance for future growth.

The writing is on the wall. Regardless of which cost forecast one chooses, getting the U.S. water supply infrastructure in shape will require a great deal of money. Moreover, when efforts to establish homeland security are realized finally, it is likely that the costs of guaranteeing the safety of the nation's drinking water supplies will increase even more. In addition, passing these costs completely on to ratepayers is difficult. Approximately 46,500 of the nation's 55,000 water systems (approximately 84 percent) are small systems that serve less than 3,300 people.[69] Small communities that do not enjoy the economies of scale that large cities enjoy will be hard pressed to pay for infrastructure needs on their own.

What is the outlook for additional federal requirements that will continue to pressure state and local finances? To date, UMRA appears to have limited *congressional* inclinations toward more coercive federalism. However, the law has not been as successful in limiting *federal agencies* from promulgating underfunded or unfunded regulatory requirements. The Office of Management and Budget reports that since 1995 between thirteen and seventeen unfunded mandates were created through federal regulations each year, with the EPA promulgating more rules than all other federal agencies combined.[70]

The bottom line is that environmental protection is an expensive proposition for state and local governments. Given projected federal and state budget deficits, the war on terrorism, and still-recovering economies in many states, deciding which government (or which combination of governments and regulatory targets) will pay for various aspects of environmental protection will remain a persistent and enormous challenge well into the next decade. Absent efforts to address these resource issues, proponents of continued devolution of environmental governance responsibilities to states and localities as a mechanism for building a results-based sense of common purpose will find their efforts persistently challenged in legislatures and courts across the country.

Toward Place-Based Performance Measurement?

Devolving authority for environmental programs implies that a new kind of oversight will occur. As mentioned, the EPA traditionally engaged in a typical oversight pattern of bean counting state agency outputs (for example, counting the number of inspections conducted or number of permits issued). Long arguing that the statistics derived from such an approach may bear no relationship to on-the-ground environmental outcomes, the states eventually made outcomes part of NEPPS and the performance partnership agreements.

NAPA agreed and recommended that the EPA stop relying on activities data to evaluate the effectiveness of environmental protection programs: "Collecting data limited solely to enforcement and compliance activities provides little insight into how these activities contribute to actual improvements in environmental conditions."[71] Instead, NAPA argued, states and the EPA should implement results-focused, multimedia systems for managing their agencies. It also suggested that EPA regions negotiate *location-specific* outcome goals with states through NEPPS and include information about these goals as part of the agency's compliance with the Government Performance and Results Act.

Evaluating state programs based on improvements in environmental conditions, however, is wonderful in theory, but difficult in practice. Two important choices face policymakers in this regard. First, current single-medium EPA and state data systems are flawed and not easily manipulated, and they provide an inaccurate baseline from which to judge ongoing performance. Movements toward environmental management systems (like those discussed by Jan Mazurek in chapter 13) and the creation of the National Environmental Information Exchange Network are promising steps. Policymakers, however, still must seize upon opportunities to resolve issues of data insufficiency and incomparability if any meaningful progress is to be made on this front.

The second choice involves the formidable challenge of creating environmental indicators that measure on-the-ground results, something states have begun to do under performance partnership agreements. Here, the challenge for proponents of continued devolution is to create indicators that are acceptable to the public as well as to the EPA, and that are free from the data problems noted earlier. Location-specific outcomes have the advantage of scale, but they also may prove challenging if needed data are not being collected currently. Once identified, these performance indicators also must be made amenable to tracking—a daunting task, especially if successful environmental outcomes may not be known for years. As such, much additional work needs to be done on this front in the years to come.

Role-Based Cultural Change

As nearly all of the authors in this volume attest, one of the most significant challenges to building a results-based sense of common purpose in environmental governance in the twenty-first century is finding ways to change existing cultures in ENR agencies. Proponents of devolution are similarly challenged. Indeed, a not-so-subtle and essential challenge in devolving responsibility from federal to state and local governments is convincing agency staff—and their congressional overseers—that it is the right thing to do. Intergovernmental actors' role orientations can affect working relationships and implementation patterns. As noted, much has been written on how vigorously federal overseers "lean" on their state counterparts in order to secure compliance with federal goals and on how much state staff resents it when they do.[72]

Perhaps nowhere is the clash of role orientation between state and federal personnel more apparent than in environmental enforcement. The EPA and states have long held different visions of how pollution control laws should be enforced. The EPA favors deterrence, where the essential task is to make penalties high enough and detection likely enough that it becomes irrational for regulated industries not to comply.[73] In contrast, state enforcement personnel are more likely to favor cooperation-based enforcement, where emphasis is placed on securing compliance through consultation with regulated companies.[74]

Not surprisingly, these predispositions have created tensions. Many state officials, for example, argue that EPA enforcement actions usurp their own efforts at securing compliance. EPA staff, in turn, view state enforcement efforts as no effort at all. Cooperation-based enforcement to some officials on both sides is simply a euphemism for looking the other way. Of course, not all states embrace a cooperative model, nor do all EPA enforcement personnel steadfastly reject compromise and negotiation. Nevertheless, the challenge of reconciling agency cultures and role orientations at all levels of government looms large should devolution continue.

Nor is this challenge limited to federal-state relations. Chapters 3, 4, and 6 illustrate that as efforts to protect natural resources and the environment devolve into watershed and regional approaches, local governments and networks of nongovernmental actors will play increasingly important roles. Thus, another dimension of devolution is how successful states will be in avoiding the same mistakes when dealing with localities and stakeholders that they have accused the federal government of making.[75] One major test will come in the extent to which state governments will seize opportunities to assist county and local governments in funding environmental protection efforts. Another will depend on the extent to which states choose to partner with these governments to develop strategies for dealing with complex issues such as polluted runoff, storm water management, and smart growth. A repetition of "fend-for-yourself federalism" in state-local relations will be as disruptive and dysfunctional to the building of a results-based sense of common purpose in this arena as it has proved to be in federal-state relations.

Notes

1. As defined by the noted intergovernmental relations scholar Thomas Anton, *federalism* is "the system of rules for the division of public policy responsibilities" among national and state governments (Thomas Anton, *American Federalism and Public Policy: How the System Works* [Philadelphia: Temple University Press, 1988], p. 3).

2. Leon G. Billings, "The Founder: Why Edmund Muskie Mattered," *The Environmental Forum* 13(3) (May–June 1996): 23–27.

3. U.S. Environmental Protection Agency (EPA), Office of Air Quality, *National Air Quality and Emissions Trends Report 1999*, EPA 454/R-01-004 (Washington, D.C.: EPA, March 2001), www.epa.gov/oar/aqtrnd99/chapter1.pdf.

4. U.S. EPA, Office of Solid Waste and Emergency Response, *Executive Summary: The National Biennial RCRA Hazardous Waste Report*, EPA 530-S-01-001 (Washington, D.C.: EPA, June 2001).

5. U.S. EPA, Office of Water, *Water Quality Conditions in the United States: A Profile from the National Water Quality Inventory*, EPA 841-F-00-006 (Washington, D.C.: EPA, June 2000).

6. Ibid.

7. Edward S. Corwin, *The President: Office and Powers* (New York: New York University Press, 1957), p. 171.

8. John D. Donahue, *Disunited States* (New York: Basic, 1997).

9. Patricia McGee Crotty, "The New Federalism Game: Primacy Implementation of Environmental Policy," *Publius: The Journal of Federalism* 17(2) (1987): 53–67.

10. Environmental Council of the States (ECOS), *States Protect the Environment* (Washington, D.C.: ECOS, April 2000), http://www.ecos.org/, accessed July 21, 2002.

11. U.S. EPA, Wetlands, Oceans, and Watersheds, *State or Tribal Assumption of the Section 404 Permit Program*, www.epa.gov/owow/wetlands/facts/fact23.html, accessed July 20, 2002.

12. U.S. EPA, Office of Wastewater Management, *National Pollutant Discharge Elimination System*, http://cfpub.epa.gov/npdes/statestribes/astatus.cfm, accessed July 20, 2002.

13. However, the Court recently signaled some willingness to limit Congress's use of the Commerce Clause. In its 2001 decision in *Solid Waste Agency of*

Northern Cook County v. U.S. Army Corps of Engineers, the Supreme Court limited the use of the Commerce Clause to regulate environmental protection. In this case, brought by a coalition of twenty-three local governments, the Court found that the Corps had gone too far in regulating isolated intrastate wetlands that were not contiguous to waters of the United States. See William Funk, "The Court, the Clean Water Act, and the Constitution: SWANNC and Beyond," *Environmental Law Reporter* 31 (July 2001): 10741–10772.

14. Billings, "The Founder."

15. John Kincaid, "From Cooperative to Coercive Federalism," *Annals of the American Academy of Political and Social Science* 509 (May 1990): 139–152.

16. Ibid., p. 148.

17. R. Stephen Brown, *States Put Their Money Where Their Environment Is* (Washington, D.C.: ECOS, 2002), http://www.sso.org/ecos/publications.htm, accessed July 21, 2002.

18. Martha Derthick, *New Towns In-Town* (Washington, D.C.: Urban Institute, 1972); Jeffrey L. Pressman and Aaron Wildavsky, *Implementation* (Berkeley: University of California Press, 1973).

19. See, for example, Robert F. Durant, "Hazardous Waste, Regulatory Reform, and the Reagan Revolution: The Ironies of an Activist Approach to Deactivating Bureaucracy," *Public Administration Review* 53(6) (1993): 550–560.

20. Quoted in Denise Scheberle, "Scratching the Surface: State Implementation of the Surface Mining Control and Reclamation Act," Ph.D. diss., Colorado State University, 1991, p. 180.

21. Peter Eisinger, "Cities in the New Federal Order: Effects of Devolution," *LaFollette Policy Report* 8(1) (1997): 1–7; David Hosansky, "Federalism," *Congressional Quarterly Weekly Report* 54(40) (October 5, 1996): 2824–2825.

22. Paul C. Light, *The True Size of Government* (Washington, D.C.: Brookings Institution Press, 1999); Robert F. Durant, "Agenda Setting, the 'Third Wave,' and the Administrative State," *Administration and Society* 30(3) (1998): 211–247; Robert F. Durant and Adam Warber, "Networking in the Shadow of Hierarchy: Public Policy, the Administrative Presidency, and the Neoadministrative State," *Presidential Studies Quarterly* 31(2) (2001): 221–244.

23. National Performance Review, *From Red Tape to Results: Creating a Government That Works Better and Costs Less* (Washington, D.C.: Government Printing Office, 1993).

24. Quoted in Hosansky, "Federalism," p. 2825.

25. Michael E. Kraft and Denise Scheberle, "Environmental Federalism at Decade's End: New Approaches and Strategies," *Publius: The Journal of Federalism* 28(1) (winter 1998): 131–146.

26. U.S. General Accounting Office (GAO), *EPA and the States: Environmental Challenges Require a Better Working Relationship,* GAO/RCED-95-64 (Washington, D.C.: U.S. GAO, April 1995).

27. National Academy of Public Administration (NAPA), *Setting Priorities, Getting Results: A New Direction for the Environmental Protection Agency* (Washington, D.C.: NAPA, 1995), p. 2.

28. Denise Scheberle, *Trust and the Politics of Implementation: Federalism and Environmental Policy* (Washington, D.C.: Georgetown University Press, 1997).

29. Jonathan H. Adler, "A New Environmental Federalism," *Forum for Applied Research and Public Policy* 13(4) (winter 1998), p. 55; Mary A. Gade, "When the States Come Marching In," *Natural Resources and Environment* 10 (winter 1996), p. 5.

30. U.S. EPA, Office of Regional Operations and State/Local Relations, Memorandum from Fred Hansen, deputy administrator, dated July 15, 1996.

31. U.S. EPA, *EPA Strategic Plan: New Ways of Achieving Our Overall Mission: Key Cross-Agency Programs* (Washington, D.C.: EPA, 2001), pp. 82–83.

32. U.S. GAO, *Environmental Protection: Collaborative EPA-State Effort Needed to Improve New Performance Partnership System*, GAO/RCED-99-171 (Washington, D.C.: U.S. GAO, June 1999).

33. U.S. GAO, *Environmental Protection: EPA's and States' Efforts to "Reinvent" Environmental Regulation*, GAO/T-RCED-98-33 (Washington, D.C.: U.S. GAO, November 1997).

34. Ibid., p. 3.

35. U.S. EPA, "Joint EPA/State Agreement to Pursue Regulatory Innovation," *Federal Register* 63(86) (May 5, 1998): 24784–24796.

36. U.S. GAO, *Environmental Protection: Collaborative EPA-State Effort*; Jeanne Herb, Jennifer Sullivan, Mark Stoughton, and Allen White, *The National Environmental Performance Partnership System: Making Good on Its Promise? Learning from Innovations in Environmental Protection*, NAPA Research Paper no. 12 (Washington, D.C.: NAPA, June 2000).

37. U.S. GAO, *Environmental Protection: Collaborative EPA-State Effort.*

38. U.S. EPA, *EPA Strategic Plan*, p. 82.

39. U.S. GAO, *Environmental Protection: Overcoming Obstacles to Innovative State Regulatory Programs*, GAO-02-268 (Washington, D.C.: U.S. GAO, January 2002).

40. Vickie L. Patton, "A Balanced Partnership," *The Environmental Forum* 13(3) (May–June 1996): 16–22.

41. U.S. EPA, Office of Water, *Overview of Current Total Maximum Daily Load—TMDL—Program and Regulations* http://www.epa.gov/owow/tmdl/overviewfs.html, accessed September 15, 2002.

42. Patton, "A Balanced Partnership," p. 17.

43. William R. Lowry, *The Dimensions of Federalism: State Governments and Pollution Control Policies* (Durham, N.C.: Duke University Press, 1992); Evan J. Ringquist, "Does Regulation Matter? Evaluating the Effects of State Air

Pollution Control Programs," *Journal of Politics* 55(4) (1993): 1022–1045; David Hedge, Donald C. Menzel, and George Williams, "Regulatory Attitudes and Behavior: The Case of Surface Mining Regulation," *Western Political Quarterly* 41 (1990): 323–340; James P. Lester, "A New Federalism? Environmental Policy in the States," in Norman J. Vig and Michael E. Kraft, eds., *Environmental Policy in the 1990s: Toward a New Agenda*, 59–79 (Washington, D.C.: Congressional Quarterly, 1990).

44. Joe Soss, Sanford F. Schram, Thomas P. Vartanian, and Erin O'Brien, "Setting the Term of Relief: Explaining State Policy Choices in the Devolution Revolution," *American Journal of Political Science* 45(2) (April 2001): 378–395.

45. Gregory Amacher, "Forest Policies and Many Governments," *Forest Science* 48(1) (2002): 146–155; William Lowry, "State Parks Found to Be Source of Innovation," *Public Administration Times* 19(10) (1996), pp. 1, 12–13.

46. Barry G. Rabe, "Federalism and Entrepreneurship: Explaining American and Canadian Innovation in Pollution Prevention and Regulatory Integration," *Policy Studies Journal* 27(2) (1999): 288–307.

47. Ibid., p. 307.

48. Frank R. Baumgartner and Bryan D. Jones, *Agenda and Instability in American Politics* (Chicago: University of Chicago Press, 1993).

49. Scott P. Hays, Michael Elser, and Carol F. Hays, "Environmental Commitment among the States: Integrating Alternative Approaches to State Environmental Policy," *Publius: The Journal of Federalism* 26(2) (1996): 41–58; Matthew Potoski, "Clean Air Federalism: Do States Race to the Bottom?" *Public Administration Review* 61(3) (May–June 2001): 335–342.

50. Barry G. Rabe, "Statehouse and Greenhouse: The States Are Taking the Lead on Climate Change," *Brookings Review* 20(2) (spring 2002): 11–13.

51. Adler, "A New Environmental Federalism"; J. Winston Porter, *Cleaning Up Superfund: The Case for State Environmental Leadership*, Reason Foundation Policy Study no. 195 (Los Angeles: Reason Foundation, 1995).

52. John H. Cushman, "California Lawmakers Vote to Lower Auto Emissions," *New York Times on the Web*, July 2, 2002, p. 1, www.nytimes.com/2002/07/02/national/02POLL.html, accessed July 2, 2002.

53. As of this writing, implementation of the zero-emission standard continues to be delayed by a court injunction.

54. Charles J. Murray, "California Mandates Electric Cars by 2003," *Electronic Engineering Times* 1152 (February 5, 2001): 1–3.

55. Danny Hakim, "In California, Clean Air Rules Force Changes in Autos," *New York Times on the Web*, July 22, 2002, www.nytimes.com/2002/07/22/business/22ZERO.html, accessed July 25, 2002.

56. Quoted in Adler, "A New Environmental Federalism," p. 55.

57. Ibid., p. 57.

58. David Schoenbrod, "Putting the 'Law' Back into Environmental Law," *Regulation* 22(1) (winter 1999): 17–23.

59. Alice M. Rivlin, "A New Vision of American Federalism," *Public Administration Review* 52(4) (1992): 315–320.

60. Donahue, *Disunited States,* p. 165.

61. Robert Agranoff and Michael McGuire, "American Federalism and the Search for Models of Management," *Public Administration Review* 61(6) (2001): 671–681.

62. Ibid., p. 673.

63. Ibid., p. 676.

64. "EPA Publishes New Radionuclides Rule," *Water World* (January 2001), pp. 1, 18.

65. Michael Pompili, "Environmental Mandates: The Impact on Local Government," *Journal of Environmental Health* 57(6) (January–February 1995): 6–12.

66. James Laughlin, "Water Funding Concerns Float to the Top," *Water World* (May 2002), p. 3.

67. U.S. EPA, *Drinking Water Infrastructure Needs Survey: A Report to Congress* (Washington, D.C.: EPA, February 2001).

68. Congressional Budget Office, *Future Investment in Drinking Water and Wastewater Infrastructure* (Washington, D.C.: Government Printing Office, May 2002).

69. U.S. EPA, *Drinking Water Infrastructure Needs Survey.*

70. J. L. Laws, "OMB Official Pledges Strict Adherence to Unfunded Mandates Law," *E&E Daily,* May 25, 2001, www.eenews.net/EEDaily.

71. NAPA, *Evaluating Environmental Progress: How EPA and the States Can Improve the Quality of Enforcement and Compliance Information* (Washington, D.C.: NAPA, June 2001), p. 2.

72. Scheberle, *Trust and the Politics of Implementation;* William Gormley, "Food Fights: Regulatory Enforcement in a Federal System," *Public Administration Review* 52(3) (1992): 271–280; Eugene Bardach and Robert A. Kagan, *Going by the Book: The Problem of Regulatory Unreasonableness* (Philadelphia: Temple University Press, 1982).

73. Clifford Rechtschaffen, "Competing Visions: EPA and the States Battle for the Future of Environmental Enforcement," *Environmental Law Reporter* 30(10) (October 2000): 10803–10828.

74. Ibid.

75. Steven D. Gold, "Devolution: Stage II. How States Treat Cities and Counties Will Make or Break the Devolution Revolution," excerpt of an article in *State Legislatures* (April 1996), www.naco.org/pubs/cnews/96-05-13/27devolu.htm, accessed June 24, 2002.

11

Flexibility

Daniel J. Fiorino

Like many applications of bureaucratic rationality in the late twentieth century, environmental governance in general and environmental and natural resources (ENR) regulation in particular have drawn a great deal of criticism for their inflexibility. This criticism falls into two streams. The first, as old as ENR regulation and leveled largely by those wary of or philosophically opposed to aggressive regulation, contends that it is inefficient and too costly. Critics mounting this *traditionalist* critique call for more use of economic and risk analysis (such as cost-benefit analysis) in regulatory decision making, as well as market-based incentives such as pollution fees or emissions trading, to complement or replace conventional regulation.

The second, more recent stream of criticism is reflected in many of the chapters in this book. ENR regulation as practiced in the United States and abroad, critics argue, will not deliver the results needed to achieve an environmentally sustainable future. Counting many strong supporters of environmental values in its ranks, this *revisionist* critique recognizes the inefficiencies of regulation and agrees with at least some of the traditionalists' proposals for improving the analytical basis for decisions. But as Denise Scheberle in particular describes in greater detail in chapter 10, revisionists have raised more fundamental issues about the effectiveness of regulation because of the inflexibilities inherent in its single-media, end-of-pipe, process-centered, and command-and-control bureaucratic design. Thus, focusing less on economic effects, revisionists worry most about the ineffectiveness of ENR regulation because its traditional structures and relationships are ill-suited to an increasingly dynamic and interdependent world.

The emergence of this second, revisionist stream of criticism is significant. To argue that regulation is costly, chases too many small risks, or delivers too few benefits reflects a traditional concern with regulatory efficiency. These issues, mounted largely by members of the regulated community, have defined the regulatory debate for decades. What is new and noteworthy, as we editors point out in our introduction to this volume, is that many of the architects of environmental regulation in the United States have concluded that the system is not up to the task of protecting the environment because it is not flexible, adaptable, and responsive.

Should environmental regulation be more flexible, adaptable, and responsive? Would such a system deliver better results, with more accountability? Or is there a risk, as many regulators and activists assert, that industry will face less pressure for results if greater flexibility is given? Should flexibility, then, be seen as a virtue rather than a vice? This chapter argues that the lack of flexibility in the current regulatory system in the United States poses a barrier to environmental problem solving. With outmoded ideas about the roles and capacities of the state, the nature of environmental problems, and the motivations of industry, the system relies on a strategy based on *rules and deterrence* when one based on *information, incentives, and cooperation* would be more appropriate. In the process of shifting strategies, greater flexibility will advance the building of a results-based sense of common purpose in environmental governance.

The discussion in this chapter begins with the idea of flexibility in environmental management. What today is valued as part of a revisionist critique of environmental policy was seen as a defect not so long ago. This was especially the case in the United States, where fears of industry "capture" led policymakers to adopt a legalistic, adversarial, process-driven regulatory system that allowed little flexibility. Over time, the limits of this approach in (among other things) helping to build a results-based sense of common purpose became more apparent. Policymakers struggled with the challenge of building greater flexibility and adaptability into the regulatory system, while still protecting society against a real or perceived capture by industry influence. The chapter then turns to a discussion of five alternative policy instruments—marketable permits, emission fees, mandatory information disclosures, challenge programs, and management systems—and to a discussion of their role in designing a more flexible, accountable, and results-based environmental regulatory system. It assesses each instrument individually and comparatively across six criteria deemed critical for creating an information-driven, incentive-based, and cooperative system of environmental governance. The chapter concludes with a discussion of the strategic challenges, choices, and opportunities facing proponents of more regulatory flexibility in the future. It offers ways to address the quintessential question that reformers must answer or risk becoming marginalized: How can we design more flexibility into regulation and still keep pressure on industry to improve?

The Idea of Flexibility in Environmental Management

Flexibility in public policy may be seen as the capacity of both regulators and regulated entities to adapt their behavior in response to new information and opportunities. It is particularly important in regulatory policy, where government acts to constrain the behavior of actors in society in order to achieve a social goal.[1] By definition, a constraint on behavior implies a degree of inflexibility. The question for designers of regulatory institutions and laws has been how much flexibility, or inflexibility, to allow. If, on the one hand, regulated entities are allowed too much scope, they are in a position to subvert the public good. This possibility is reflected in regulatory scholars' traditional concern over vague standards and lenient oversight. If, on the other hand, these entities have too little scope for adapting their behavior, there is the prospect of unreasonableness and inefficiency, both of which critics commonly cite as among the principal weaknesses of environmental regulation.

Probably the most common complaint about environmental regulation in the United States is that it is inflexible because it does not allow actors to adapt their behavior in response to new information or opportunities. This inflexibility has several dimensions. One is that laws and regulations are highly *prescriptive*. Because legislatures and agencies assume that entities want to avoid regulation when possible, they tend to adopt detailed, specific rules that allow little discretion. When industry seeks to preserve discretion by finding loopholes, government responds with even more detailed rules to close them, "in a progression toward more costly, detailed, and intrusive forms of regulation."[2]

Another dimension to this inflexibility is what Eugene Bardach and Robert Kagan call *regulatory unreasonableness:* the "imposition of uniform regulatory requirements in situations where they do not make sense."[3] Centralized, top-down regulation requires a degree of standardization. With the current approach, regulators typically cannot tailor strategies or rules to the circumstances of each firm or situation, so they set uniform rules for broad classes of firms. Yet the real world is fluid, diverse, and unpredictable, where uniform rules may not make sense when applied to diverse circumstances. Any environmental manager in industry has a story about some expensive requirement that had to be met simply because "that is how the rule is written," even though regulators admitted that no environmental benefit would result.

Yet a third dimension to inflexibility in environmental governance is the attitude of *coercion* that permeates regulation and that sorely complicates the building of a results-based sense of common purpose.[4] Relationships between regulators and industry in such countries as Canada, Great Britain, the Netherlands, and Sweden routinely are described as more cooperative and collegial than those in the United States.[5] There is greater sharing of information, more respect for mutual competence, and greater trust.[6] It is accepted in these countries that regulators should have discretion to accommodate diversity among sources. Such discretion is accepted far less in the United States, as illustrated by the Environmental Protection Agency's (EPA) experience in the 1990s with reinvention projects (for example, Project XL). From its perspective, the regulated industry complains of regulators' near obsession with compliance rather than with environmental performance and of the near impossibility of maintaining compliance in such a complex regulatory system. There now are so many rules, with so many checkpoints, that even enforcement officials have conceded that full compliance is impossible.

Critics attribute several problems to this lack of flexibility. One is the lack of incentive to improve environmental performance beyond legal requirements. With so much emphasis placed on achieving and documenting compliance, and with no regulatory benefits for doing more, the objective for most firms is to meet the regulations but not to exceed them.[7] Another problem is barriers to technology innovation. When the rules are highly prescriptive and focus on technology rather than on performance goals, firms are reluctant to take risks with innovative approaches that regulators have not endorsed. Regulations tend to "lock in" technologies for use and discourage a search for better alternatives.[8] Another product of this inflexibility that militates against the building of common purpose is a lack of trust and communication between government and industry, which also impedes the learning that must occur if a newer generation of environmental problems is to be tackled. Indeed, a regulatory system that is low on trust and dialogue but high on transaction costs is likely to embody a high degree of inflexibility.

Is flexibility a good thing in regulation? The main virtue of flexibility in policymaking may seem obvious: the capacity to adapt to information and opportunities. Of course, people and institutions should be able to adapt. One of the advantages of the application of systems theory to public policy is the notion of feedback loops. Organizations and larger policy systems adapt their behavior in response to feedback from the larger environment. In environmental regulation, however, many people see flexibility as more vice than virtue—as an excuse for special treatment of private over public interests. It is for this reason that inflexibility deliberately was built into the regulatory system created in the late 1960s and early 1970s. The idea of flexibility as vice more than virtue is illustrated in the notion of regulatory "capture," which influenced the design of health and safety laws and institutions in the 1960s and 1970s.[9] Backed by analyses of economic regulatory agencies such as the Interstate Commerce Commission and the Civil Aeronautics Board, activists argued that agencies usually ended up being controlled, or "captured," by the very industries they were created to regulate.

Fears of the capture of health and safety regulators led to the adoption of a formal, legalistic model of environmental regulation in the United States. In this model, interactions among industry and government are highly structured. Government specifies the rules that industry is expected to meet. The model often is described as a deterrence-based approach because the typical strategies for changing behavior rely on sticks (sanctions for nonconformance) rather than carrots (incentives for conforming or doing better). Signs of regulator collaboration with industry are suspect. Each side has a role to play. Government's role is to squeeze out as much environmental improvement as is feasible, both economically and politically. Industry's role is to resist while regulations are being developed, then to find loopholes once they are issued.

This model of regulation reflects several assumptions. The most important is that the private, economic interests of industry inevitably conflict with the public, environmental interests of society. At a macrolevel, economic and environmental goals present a steady stream of zero-sum choices. At a microlevel, firms are seen as narrow profit seekers who always assert their self-interests over those of society. Indeed, to an enforcement official, every firm is a likely violator, and only the blunt hand of regulation is effective in changing industry behavior. At a macrolevel, the model sees environmental protection as in almost inevitable conflict with economic growth and competitiveness. This assumption of an inevitable zero sum accounts for much of the political conflict that has characterized environmental regulation in the United States.

Another assumption is that government has the cognitive capacity to determine not only what society's environmental goals should be, but how they should be achieved. Consider, as examples, New Source Performance Standards under the Clean Air Act or Effluent Guidelines under the Clean Water Act, which establish emission and discharge limits for specific categories of industrial facilities. The EPA is directed to set emission and discharge limits that incorporate the best available technology for each industry category and that are feasible economically, then to update the limits every four years. Although the EPA has developed mechanisms for consulting with industry experts, the agency remains the outsider telling those who manage the business what to do, a system that imposes high cognitive demands on government. There also is the problem of regulatory lag: by the time agencies complete the rule-making process, prescribed technologies are already out of date.

Evidence now demonstrates that the first assumption, if not invalid, is greatly overstated. Regulation is only one of many factors that affect firms' environmental behavior. A growing body of case studies and surveys suggests that operating efficiencies, community pressures, investor evaluations, market pressures, and customer demands combine with the effects of government regulation to induce firms to behave in environmentally responsible ways.[10] Many firms now use the environmental soundness of their processes and products as a source of competitive advantage in the marketplace. Although environmental and economic goals are not always complementary, to be sure, they often coincide. The assumption of an inevitable zero sum is outmoded, as is the notion that all of industry is made up of "amoral profit maximizers" for whom detailed commands and threats of legal sanctions are the only appropriate governmental response.[11] In fact, for a variety of reasons, firms often deliver environmental goods to society that legally are not required.

Likewise, the assumption that government has the cognitive capacities to determine the best technologies for a range of industry categories is unrealistic. This point is not meant as a criticism of legislators and regulators, but as an appreciation for the complexity of the task and the limits of the notion of the "omniscient regulator." Like a professor who cannot know all the answers but creates conditions under which students search for truth, so must the regulator now engage industry in a search for the technologies, processes, and products that will lead to improvement. In a dynamic and increasingly interdependent world, the old model in which government issues commands and industry responds in a repeated cycle is antiquated.

This lack of flexibility and the need to make regulation more flexible and adaptable have been at the center of the revisionist critique of environmental policy. In the United States, three sets of recommendations illustrate the key themes in this critique. The first, formed in 1994 with representatives of a wide range of interests but having a pro-environmental slant, is the President's Council on Sustainable Development. The council called for changes to make regulation more flexible. A second set of recommendations is the advice of the Enterprise for the Environment initiative, organized in 1996 by former EPA administrator William Ruckelshaus. A major influence on the evolution of U.S. environmental policy in the 1970s, Ruckelshaus was one of many people who argued by the 1990s that changes were needed. A third call for flexibility is that of the National Academy of Public Administration (NAPA). In a set of three reports Congress requested in the 1990s, NAPA recommended several steps that were aimed at weaving flexibility and adaptability more effectively into the regulatory fabric.

These criticisms of flexibility are reflected in the literature on comparative regulation as well. An example is David Wallace's comparison of environmental regulation and its effects on innovation in six countries. He argues that two dimensions of the regulatory system are important: the *quality of dialogue* among government, industry, and other actors; and the *independence of government* from industry influence. The first describes the capacity for productive interaction and collaborative problem solving, which are based on trust and respect for mutual competence among actors. The second describes the degree to which government is able to maintain pressure on industry for improved performance. Policy regimes that promote innovation, Wallace concludes, are characterized by "a high quality, honest dialogue that nevertheless does not compromise the independence of environmental policy making from industry's special interests."[12]

In a similar vein, some theorists call for "reflexivity" and "communicative governance" in policymaking.[13] The concept of reflexive law describes a recent stage in the evolution of modern legal systems. Like traditional regulatory or substantive law, its purpose is to change behavior to achieve societal goals such as environmental protection. Unlike substantive law, however, reflexive law does not prescribe action directly. "Under a regime of reflexive law, the legal control of social action is indirect and abstract, for the legal system only determines the organizational and procedural premises of action."[14] The role of government is not to issue commands, but to create incentives and procedures that induce actors to behave in socially desired ways.

Likewise, the concept of communicative governance suggests new ways of coping with "the growing complexity, dynamics, and diversity" of postmodern societies.[15] Its proponents argue that a bureaucratic, hierarchical, state-centered approach to governing is outmoded. A new approach would involve the sharing of responsibility among state and private actors, cooperative (horizontal) rather than adversarial (vertical) relationships, and adaptive learning approaches. Communicative governance suggests a model for changing environmental regulation: governing is more a learning process geared to results and the building of common purpose than one of social control. Distinctions between public and private actors are blurred. High trust and flexible policy instruments allow for adaptation.[16]

In sum, the traditional reliance in the United States on direct regulatory controls—along with intrusive oversight, negative sanctions, and technology-forcing rules—has produced a regulatory system that is low in flexibility. At a time when environmental problems are more complex and interdependent, economic relationships are global and dynamic, and patterns of governance are changing, this inflexibility poses a significant barrier to environmental progress. But what policy instruments are available to policymakers for pursuing a more flexible regulatory regime geared more toward results rather than toward procedural compliance? What are the strengths and weaknesses associated with each for advancing ENR values efficiently, effectively, and equitably? Are some better able than others to advance these values?

Flexibility in Policy Instruments: A Comparative Perspective

We already have many ways of incorporating flexibility into the regulatory institutions and policies of environmental governance, some of which other authors in this volume discuss in great detail. The present discussion focuses on one of the principal ways of achieving results-inducing flexibility as a means for building common purpose: policy instruments that government can use to influence behavior by actors in society. Experience and prior research, however, suggest that some instruments are more likely than others to allow for and encourage adaptation in response to new opportunities or information.

To consider the relationships between policy instruments and flexibility, this section assesses five alternatives to conventional regulation: marketable permits, emission fees, mandatory information disclosures, voluntary challenge programs, and management systems.[17] These instruments first are described and evaluated in terms of six critical criteria identified in the policy literature. The aim is not to evaluate each instrument comprehensively, but to assess its relevance to advancing a more flexible and results-based (rather than procedure-driven) regulatory regime. Next, the instruments are rated in terms of their relative or comparative ability to advance the flexibility aims of today's revisionists. The six criteria are:

1. *Adaptability:* Does the policy instrument allow for changes in behavior in response to new information or opportunities?

2. *Reflexive potential:* Does it promote self-critical behavior and continuous improvement?

3. *Knowledge about effects:* What do we know about the consequences of its use?

4. *Certainty:* How much confidence may we have in the expected results of the instrument?

5. *Complexity:* How difficult is it to design and administer?

6. *Acceptance:* Is the political climate likely to support the use of the instrument?

The first two criteria refer to the degree of flexibility that typically may be expected with use of an instrument. Adaptability describes the extent to which entities are able to change their behavior in response to new information and opportunities; it is more likely in a system based on communicative governance. Reflexive potential describes the extent to which entities are induced to evaluate and improve their behavior. The purpose of reflexive law is to promote self-critical analysis and environmentally desirable behavior.

The third and fourth criteria assess the likelihood that actors (including regulators) may be held accountable when each class of instrument is used. To take an example, environmental management systems, such as those described by Jan Mazurek in chapter 13, encourage adaptation and self-critical assessment of performance by actors. At the same time, without measurable goals, there may be little pressure for results and thus minimal accountability. From government's perspective, as well, emission fees offer an incentive for achieving results in cost-effective ways, but they may be unreliable when it is important to achieve specific environmental goals. There are many trade-offs between flexibility and accountability, which make it necessary to use several instruments in combination.

The last two criteria evaluate each instrument in terms of its feasibility. What looks to be ideal on paper may be administratively impractical or politically unacceptable. Indeed, the primary constraint on the use of technology-based regulation in the 1990s was the political conflict over traditional regulation. For issues such as climate change, where there is not a political consensus in the United States over the need for action, government has developed a number of voluntary challenge programs that do not require legislative authority. The complexity criterion allows one to assess the feasibility of using an instrument in different conditions. For example, in developing nations that lack the infrastructure, emissions trading may not work.

Marketable Permits

As noted, standard regulatory strategy entails a determination of what technologies are available for a problem and then requires their use by firms in defined categories. Regulators typically make technology requirements as uniform as possible. Although rules may be written to specify results rather than to prescribe technologies, most regulated entities take a low-risk approach by using a technology that the regulator has determined will achieve the necessary results. As also noted, however, this approach is not without its problems, among them the higher than necessary costs and lack of incentive for innovating beyond the technology standard. Addressing these concerns, marketable permits (also known as tradable emission or discharge rights) have emerged over the past two decades as an alternative tool of environmental governance. In this approach, the regulator sets a target for total releases, then allocates allowable shares among sources. Sources then are free to buy, sell, or trade permits, as circumstances dictate. This system allows those with the higher marginal control costs to buy emission permits from those with lower marginal costs; the latter therefore are induced to reduce emissions below allowable levels, thus generating an asset.[18]

In a pure economic approach, emission rights would be allocated through an auction. In practice, however, the United States has adopted a hybrid approach that combines direct regulation and trading. In the sulfur oxides allowance-trading program established in the 1990 Clean Air Act, for example, emission rights were allocated on the basis of previous emission levels and the characteristics of the source. Allowance trading in the United States is a hybrid of direct regulation and trading because it combines a core set of standards that all sources must meet with a system for trading permits that allows sources to emit above or below the prescribed levels.

The United States has used marketable permits extensively. Beginning with the emission offsets in the 1980s, and continuing with emissions trading and banking in the 1980s and acid rain allowance trading in the 1990s, marketable permits became an integral part of air quality programs. The George W. Bush administration currently intends further to incorporate trading approaches into water programs as well. Of particular appeal for water quality is allowing trading among point and nonpoint sources. Industrial dischargers and sewage treatment works, both already highly regulated, can arrange for cost-effective reductions by nonpoint sources (such as agricultural operations) as a way to offset additional, more expensive controls on point-source discharges.

Marketable permits offer several advantages in their adaptability and reflexive potential, although these advantages are limited somewhat by the many restrictions in current designs. In theory, they are the best example of an approach that focuses on ends over means. At a macrolevel, policymakers set a goal, allocate responsibilities for achieving it among actors, then allow them to determine how best to meet the goal. The goal drives the behavior of actors, who then search for ways to reduce emissions to required levels (for example, with technology improvements, changes in production processes, different raw materials, and even new product designs). Depending on the results of this search and the costs of the relative options, sources may create an asset either by reducing emissions beyond what is prescribed and trading or selling the excess, or by achieving less than required reductions and meeting obligations by purchasing allowances in the market.

Marketable permits similarly offer reflexive potential. Rather than specify a solution, the role of the state is to define a goal and enable the source to find a solution. Government does not specify what action must be taken, only the result that must be achieved. This encourages sources to evaluate a range of options for compliance, including pollution prevention, rather than just requiring them to use particular technologies. Trading not only promotes cost-effective solutions, but also induces firms to search for the best way of achieving or exceeding the goal (if they decide to create an asset in the form of credits that may be sold). An incentive thus exists for sources continuously to improve their environmental performance beyond the mandated goal.

A particular advantage of marketable permits is the certainty of the result that will be achieved. Assuming there is the capacity to track releases from covered sources, permits define a maximum in the total emissions. The overall targets drive the system. However, trading systems are not easily designed and administered. They require a capacity to allocate initial permits fairly, monitor releases, and document changes in allowances—a capacity that not all nations have. In the United States, both capacity and our knowledge about the effects of marketable permits are relatively high. Thus, not only are marketable permits effective in meeting policy goals, but they are far more cost-effective than a conventional approach.

One survey of studies, for example, found that "traditional air quality regulation may be, on average, about three or four times more expensive than the most cost-effective approach."[19] The same survey estimated that emissions trading and other approaches designed to lower the marginal costs of control overall might have reduced air pollution costs by $11 billion in 1990 alone. One area of uncertainty with respect to marketable permits, however, is that they may redistribute pollution and create "hot spots." Environmental justice groups especially are concerned that pollution might shift to minority or low-income areas (but see Evan Ringquist's chapter on environmental justice). To be equitable as well as efficient, trading would need to be designed to avoid such a redistribution of risks.

In sum, marketable permits should rank high as an instrument for achieving flexibility. They address many of the deficiencies of the conventional regulatory approach, principally the lack of incentive for continuous improvement and technology innovation, the few opportunities to reduce marginal control costs, and the "one-size-fits-all" approach that leads to unreasonable outcomes. Their gradual but steady incorporation into U.S. air quality programs and their likely expansion into water quality programs also suggest that they will play a prominent role in the design of a more flexible system. Because they require an advanced regulatory infrastructure, however, their use in developing countries may prove to be problematic.

Fees and Charges

Fees, as Robert Paehlke and others in this volume attest, are an economically elegant way of influencing behavior because they directly make actors internalize the costs of the externalities they impose on society. Fees may be applied to both inputs and outputs. An example of an input fee is Denmark's carbon tax, in which actors are assessed a fee based on the carbon content of fuels that they use.[20] A fee applied to an air emission, water discharge, or waste generated is an output fee. Examples are fees applied to air emissions on a per pound or ton basis or to waste generated, as in "pay-by-the-bag" systems for municipal waste that have been adopted in several cities.

Except for municipal waste collection and a few other specialized applications, fees have been used rarely in the United States. One reason is that a fee is viewed as the equivalent of a tax, and the political environment for new taxes has been unfavorable in recent years. Indeed, the laudable efforts from economists to distinguish taxes on a social "evil" such as pollution from taxes on a social "good" such as income have drawn little interest politically. Neither have the efforts to present fees as revenue neutral, where income to government from fees would be used to offset other tax sources.

Another reason that fees, particularly on outputs, have drawn little support is the complexity and uncertainty associated with their use. Output fees require a well-developed capacity for monitoring and measuring pollution releases. If actors are paying on a per unit basis, they will want reliable information so as to be assessed fairly. The capacity for such measurement may be expensive in developed countries and may not exist at all in developing countries. There is also the analytical question of where to set the fee. In theory, the fee for each unit of emissions should reflect the marginal costs to society. In practice, this level of precision is difficult to achieve. Moreover, the consequences of getting it wrong are not trivial: if the fee is too low, pollution may be unreasonably high; if the fee is too high, there could be serious economic effects and dislocations for society.

Fees also involve considerable uncertainty regarding results. Unlike marketable permits, which specify a target and allocate responsibilities within the framework of that target, fees specify a means that policy-makers only *hope* will achieve a target. Whether or not they achieve that target depends on the quality of the information and the analytic skills of those setting the fee. The level of the fee constitutes government's best guess, which it may have to modify with experience. The fact that policy-makers may have to modify the fee, however, undermines its effectiveness because modification creates uncertainty. If sources do not know from year to year what the penalty will be, they cannot plan. If they cannot plan, they cannot make investment decisions with any degree of confidence. Yet if government cannot revise the fees based on experience about their effects, they risk too much pollution. These uncertainties have posed a barrier to the broader use of fees.

Pollution fees do offer a kind of reflexive potential, however. They make firms account directly for the costs of the damages they impose on society. How they account for them—by lowering releases or paying a fee—is left to them. Fees encourage reflexivity, but within a narrow range of choice, covering a specific kind of release, substance, or activity. If a fee system can be designed to cover a broader range of releases or sub-stances, based perhaps on an index of environmental damages, it might encourage a broader kind of reflexivity. The analytical and political obstacles to designing such a composite environmental fee would be for-midable, however, and implementing such a program would be complex administratively.

Most fees applied to outputs, such as pollution releases, do not fare well in their certainty and complexity. As noted earlier, it is difficult to get the fee right. Consequently, relying on a fee alone to achieve an environ-mental goal might be risky. Fees make more sense when the goal is to in-duce people to behave in certain ways, but a specific level of performance is not essential. An example is a volume-based fee to reduce the genera-tion of nonhazardous waste. The policy goal would be to reduce the vol-ume of waste steadily over time, rather than to protect against specific health or environmental risks from toxic releases.

Fees in inputs—such as a carbon tax, a fee on lead mined, or a gasoline tax applied at the pump—are more feasible administratively. Govern-ment may assess the fee for these substances at any of several points in the production and distribution process. There is also somewhat more room for uncertainty in results than with an output fee, where government is setting targets for pollution levels. If the policy goal is to discourage the use of virgin lead, for example, a fee on lead production might be combined with other instruments to control lead exposures in specific ways. The input fee would be only one element in a larger policy strategy.

Thus, as a class of instruments, fees and charges offer reflexive potential. Government does not tell firms directly what to do; it creates incentives for them to decide how best to achieve a goal. Depending on their design, fees also may allow firms to adapt to new information or opportunities. Under the other criteria, it makes sense to distinguish output from input fees. Output fees require high administrative and monitoring capacities, to the extent that even developed countries with advanced regulatory capacities rarely use them. Input fees, like a charge on the carbon content of fuels, are more feasible administratively. Although their association with government taxation has discouraged their use in the United States, their adaptability and reflexive potential make them worth considering in the design of a more flexible regulation.

Information Disclosure
A core tenet of postmodern thinking is that this is the information age. The value of information in environmental policy has been recognized increasingly in recent years. For a time, information was seen as a means for government to communicate to the public about how to reduce risks, through product warnings and risk communication. These uses of information still matter, and government has become more sophisticated about their use. Since the late 1980s, however, information has taken on another dimension in environmental policy. In addition to providing risk information to the public to influence behavior and to help build a results-based sense of common purpose, government now requires firms to release information about their environmental practices and performance. The theory of an information disclosure strategy is that making information publicly available will induce firms to evaluate their behavior and improve it because of the effects of disclosure on their reputation.

In the 1960s and 1970s, information disclosure was not appreciated fully as an instrument for affecting environmental performance. One reason was that neither government nor industry knew how to measure releases with any precision. A more significant reason was that polluting was not necessarily seen as an activity that warranted social disapproval. Until the National Environmental Policy Act of 1969, the federal government had not clearly taken a position in favor of environmental protection. Similarly, until the passage of the Clean Air Act of 1970 and the Federal Water Pollution Control Act of 1972, Congress had not clearly established that air and water releases were harmful and should be reduced or eliminated. Industry had no legal obligation to dispose of hazardous wastes safely until the Superfund law assigned liability in 1980 and the EPA issued hazardous-waste management regulations in the early 1980s. Indeed, a major contribution of environmental law has been to establish this ethical principle to support environmental values.

A defining event in the use of information disclosure globally was the creation of the Toxics Release Inventory (TRI) in the United States and the Pollutant Transfer and Release Registries elsewhere in the world during the late 1980s and early 1990s. The initial stimulus for these laws was the principle that people have a "right to know" about the use, storage, and release of harmful chemicals in their communities. Yet once the laws were adopted, evidence began to accumulate as to their effects on industrial facilities that had to report. Many firms reacted to the adverse publicity about chemical releases by ordering immediate efforts to lower them. Studies have shown an immediate drop in the stock valuations of companies that report bad news in the TRI, although the long-term effects are unclear. The lesson was that even though these releases violated no laws, industry fears of social disapproval induced them to improve their environmental performance and present a more positive image.[21]

Information disclosure also may have significant advantages in developing countries. The World Bank has promoted strongly an information disclosure program developed with the Indonesian government.[22] In the Program for Pollution Control Evaluation and Rating (PROPER), the government placed water dischargers in one of six categories based on their pollution control and monitoring efforts. These categories ranged from "Gold" for world-class facilities to "Black" for those making no efforts at all. Facility ratings were revealed in stages, from best to worst, and all had an opportunity to improve before the ratings were released to the public.

An evaluation of the program demonstrated significant increases in compliance with discharge standards. The World Bank concluded that "public disclosure can play a powerful role in developing countries where conventional regulation is weak."[23]

The World Bank makes an interesting case with PROPER: the strength of this approach lies in its simplicity. For developing countries with a limited administrative infrastructure, for example, an information strategy is more feasible than technology-based regulation. Unlike a fee, it does not require precise information. The goal, after all, is to place sources in categories, not to charge them for each unit of pollution. Government makes the information publicly available, then lets sources deal with the consequences. An information strategy also does not require that government specify technologies or best practices, which even in a developed economy is a difficult undertaking. Rather, the theory of information disclosure is that public exposure of poor performance will induce firms to improve. Market forces and community pressures will achieve what regulation has done elsewhere.

Information disclosure aptly illustrates the concept of using reflexive law to advance a results-based sense of common purpose in environmental governance. Government does not tell firms what to do, as in substantive law. It creates the conditions that will lead firms to search for ways to make their behavior more acceptable socially and politically. If designed properly, information disclosure should cause firms to engage in a process of "critical self-assessment" that will induce them to make steady improvements in environmental performance. Information disclosure also rates high in terms of adaptability. It does not specify the means for achieving environmental results, but instead uses government's authority indirectly to pressure firms. It unfortunately does *not* specify ends though. This is a limitation. Rather, it applies pressure that leads some, but not all, firms to perform better. Granted, many firms may not respond at all, and those that do may not aim for any particular result. Information disclosure nevertheless can be effective, especially (again) when used in combination with other instruments.

In terms of acceptance and complexity, information disclosure offers important advantages. As political support for regulation declined in recent decades, policymakers and advocates turned to community right-to-know approaches as less controversial alternatives. They were less intrusive and corresponded to the sense that people should have access to information about risks around them. In addition to the TRI, which was expanded in the 1990s, the United States adopted disclosure rules for drinking water, emergency planning, and other areas. The political climate for continued use of information disclosure generally is positive. This political acceptance and the relative simplicity of its use recommend information disclosure as a core instrument in a more flexible regulatory system.

Voluntary Challenge Programs

One aspect in which old-style regulation has not been very adaptable is in dealing with problems that do not fit the conventional model of industrial, point-source pollution. As noted in the introduction to this volume, students of environmental policy write of the second-generation problems that increasingly have come to occupy the agenda—climate change, nonpoint-source pollution, or releases from small sources (such as dry cleaners).[24] In addition, contemporary definitions of ENR problems are much broader than they were in the early years of the environmental movement, encompassing not only pollution releases but energy, water, and materials use as well. Given the recent political hostility to expanding centralized regulation, these new problems and the need to respond to them have stimulated interest in voluntary programs.

Voluntary programs offer several benefits to environmental agencies. They usually do not require legislative authority because they impose no binding obligations; industry participates by choice. They offer a way for regulators to build positive relations with industry, a respite from typically negative interactions that complicate the building of common purpose. They also allow regulators to claim measurable benefits for the environment at what are alleged to be virtually no costs to society. Indeed, the designers of EPA voluntary programs have not been required to conduct the economic or cost-benefit analyses expected for new regulatory programs. The rationale is that voluntary programs are "free" because firms take them on willingly and may withdraw at any time. That participation in such programs involves opportunity costs for both industry and society appears not to have occurred to policymakers.

In voluntary challenge programs, government asks firms to commit to reducing environmental impacts, usually in measurable terms, or to adopt practices or behaviors that lead to such reductions. In addition to committing to the reductions, firms agree to report publicly on their progress. At times, as in the 33/50 Program, government sets targets. At other times, as with the Waste Wise and Climate Wise Programs of the 1990s, firms set their own targets. The failure to meet the target involves no formal sanctions, although firms do bear the public-relations burden of not meeting a commitment made publicly. Even this burden may not matter much. Because proponents want to maintain high levels of participation (at least in the United States) in order to justify continuation of their programs, they generally have not held participants to their commitments. In the EPA's Waste Wise Program, for example, it was found that fewer than 20 percent of the firms even filed their annual report.

A strength of challenge programs is their adaptability. Freed from the normal constraints of statutory authorization and administrative procedures, these programs are created and modified relatively easily. It is worth noting that although the EPA has elaborate internal and public processes for developing regulations, it has no internal review or approval process for voluntary programs. Because participation is voluntary, requirements are less than rigorous, and the rewards usually are limited to recognition, agencies have wide discretion to create, modify, and end these programs. In the 1990s, when Congress often was deadlocked and the climate for new regulation inhospitable, challenge programs offered a way for agencies to respond to emerging issues.

Along with their adaptability, challenge programs offer simplicity and political acceptance. Because participation does not involve any legal exceptions or benefits (such as reduced reporting) for firms, conditions for participation are loose. Participating firms usually are on the honor system; they claim results with no verification by government or other third parties. Firms decide whether or not to join these programs and are free to withdraw when they fail to see value in them. The programs thus have drawn little political criticism. However, the lack of tangible benefits beyond government has drawn criticism from industry and others, who say that their continued involvement or broader participation is becoming increasingly questionable.[25]

The most serious questions about challenge programs concern their effectiveness. Even if we accept that recognition induces firms to reduce waste, conserve water, or improve energy efficiency beyond what they otherwise would do, this inducement applies to only a small fraction of participants in the EPA's voluntary programs. Proponents' tendency to claim more credit than is probably reasonable adds to the doubts about the programs' effects.[26] In the context of the overall economy, then, the gains from challenge programs are negligible.

This is not to say that establishing challenge programs is not worth doing. On a cost-benefit basis, the resources needed to create and run programs such as Waste Wise or Energy Star well may be justified by the modest gains in environmental performance. Moreover, society realizes longer-term benefits when government and business work cooperatively to achieve shared goals. Many firms clearly are performing well beyond their legal obligations, and they are eager for validation by government. Challenge programs also demonstrate that cooperative relationships *are* possible and that business will commit to doing more than legally required. These lessons may spill over to other firms and issues.

In sum, challenge programs offer reflexive potential. They induce firms to evaluate their behavior in the specific areas covered by the program and to determine how to improve it. They offer an avenue for developing a sense of shared responsibility (and perhaps a results-based sense of common purpose) among government, business, and others. Formal, public validation of the voluntary efforts by "change agents" in firms to improve performance also strengthens their hands internally. However, the fact that challenge programs are voluntary and appeal only to a small subset of firms—those especially sensitive to reputation—makes them useful only in combination with other instruments. Thus, voluntary challenge programs do not offer an alternative to other instruments so much as they offer a potentially useful complement to them.

Environmental Management Systems

As Jan Mazurek discusses more thoroughly in chapter 13, many organizations began adopting environmental management systems (EMSs) in the 1990s. This trend increased after the issuance of the International Organization of Standardization (ISO) 14001 series in 1996. EMSs have been developed and promoted largely by industry, for industry, rather than by government as a public policy instrument. Mazurek offers a thorough review of the variety of formidable challenges and choices faced by proponents of third-party auditing of EMSs as a progeny of the business community, but the issue in this chapter is whether or not the EMS can and should play a more prominent role in the design of a more flexible system for ENR regulation.

Of course, for as long as firms have had to comply with regulations, they have had to use management systems of a sort. If they were to stay out of legal trouble, they needed to identify rules that applied to them, respond at least minimally, and document their compliance. But as Mazurek's chapter illustrates, a full EMS is something more comprehensive and dynamic than just managing compliance: it is "a formal set of policies and procedures that define how an organization will manage its potential impacts on the environment and on the health and welfare of the people who depend on it."[27] And an EMS most definitely is capable of fostering adaptability and reflexivity in those organizations that live scrupulously by its tenets. One need only look to the Eco-Management and Audit Scheme used in the European Union and in the EPA's National Environmental Performance Track Program in the United States to see how self-critical reflection and continuous improvement can be the keystones of these systems. Both voluntary programs elegantly illustrate Gunther Teubner's concept of reflexive law: they are efforts to influence the behavior of firms by "shaping both their procedures of internal discourse and their methods of coordination with other social systems."[28]

Nevertheless, and although the particulars vary, another keystone of the EMS is complexity. Consider, for example, what Mazurek describes as the typical process of designing and administering an EMS: organizations adopt a written environmental policy; identify aspects of their activities, products, and services that affect the environment; set objectives and targets for improving their environmental performance; assign responsibility for taking actions that are necessary for implementing the EMS (such as training and corrective action); and evaluate and refine the EMS to improve performance over time. Not only does this process require the kind of rational-comprehensive decision making in organizations that most theorists find the exception to the rule, but it can require expensive investments in data-processing capabilities, in combating bureaucratic turf battles, and in reforming central administrative units bent on control rather than adaptability.[29]

These obstacles notwithstanding, what is most intriguing here for adaptability and reflexivity is the process of identifying the "significant environmental aspects" of activities and setting "targets and objectives" for improving them. Studies of EMS implementation suggest that this planning process may stimulate a systematic search within the organization for environmental impacts that fall totally outside of current regulations. Among these impacts are opportunities that may lead to bottom-line cost savings (for example, eliminating the use of a solvent or switching to a less-toxic substitute, lowering disposal costs) or to "top-line" benefits (for example, increasing sales by designing a greener product). This may be a way of achieving, at a practical level, the theoretical win-win that motivates continuous environmental improvement.

Great uncertainty still exists, however, about the effects an EMS has on environmental performance. Simply having an EMS, even one certified by a third party, offers no guarantee about the results that will be achieved. An EMS may be many things—a sign of commitment, an engine for improvement, a tool for compliance—but it is not evidence of a result. Although a body of empirical research suggests that organizations that adopt and implement an EMS are likely to do better than those that do not, other research suggests that such improvement does not occur in all cases. It depends on where the organizations start, how committed they are to using the EMS, and what external pressures are driving them to improve.[30] Indeed, the EMS itself is only one of many factors influencing performance. It is unclear even if the EMS should be seen as the dependent or independent variable: Should it be seen as the result of a commitment by a firm to improve or as an engine for continued progress? As such, it is difficult to defend the EMS as a self-standing substitute for regulation.

Finally, political controversy of the kind outlined by Mazurek in her chapter has plagued EMS regulatory approaches persistently. Perhaps most significant, and as she chronicles, public trust in the corporate sector will not soon rebound after recent disclosures of widespread corporate accounting misfeasance and malfeasance (for example, at Enron, Vivendi, WorldCom, Xerox, and Merck). Even before these scandals, however, EMS was plagued by disagreement over its appropriate role in environmental governance. Some people argued that having a well-documented EMS with third-party certification eventually might substitute for regulation and the oversight associated with it. Others viewed EMS as complementary; facilities might earn reduced oversight and reporting, but they should remain subject to most regulation. Still others argued that an EMS deserves no formal recognition in the regulatory system because it is an internal tool that does not guarantee a particular result and has no public policy relevance. Finally, although the ISO 14001 series has become the generally accepted standard, others have their own advocates.

In sum, the EMS has impressive reflexive potential. Where there is an organizational commitment to using one, the likelihood of improved environmental performance exists, especially when economic and financial opportunities coincide. Although these benefits are only suggested and not yet proved, the EMS also may provide a discipline and protocol for allowing the organization to adapt its actions to changes in its economic and social environments as well as in its physical environment. Still, the lack of normative standards and lack of certainty about environmental results require that the EMS be used in combination with other instruments. The EMS is all about means and not much about ends. Thus, whether and how to integrate the EMS into regulation are controversial, given the newness of the tool and limited knowledge about its effects. However, in combination with a system of normative performance standards, it might play a role in more flexible regulation.

Relative Rankings on Flexibility

As the preceding discussion of alternative policy instruments illustrates, policymakers may design flexibility into ENR regulation in many ways. The way that different policy instruments are designed and used determines in large part how well actors may adapt to new information and opportunities. For the reader's convenience, table 11.1 gives a summary of the instruments under the criteria proposed here. Each is categorized

Table 11.1
Evaluation of Policy Instruments under Six Criteria

	Adaptability	Reflexive Potential	Knowledge of Effects	Certainty	Complexity	Acceptance
Marketable permits	High	Medium	High	High	High	High
Emission fees	High	High	Medium	Low	High	Low
Information disclosures	High	High	Medium	Low	Low	High
Challenge programs	High	Medium	Medium	Low	Low	High
Management systems	High	High	Low	Low	Medium	High

as ranking high, medium, or low under each criterion in comparison to conventional regulation.

These assessments are subjective, to be sure, and are offered only as a starting point for considering the role of each instrument in a more flexible regulation. They also should be seen as general and only indicative. We need to be able, after all, to evaluate how an instrument is designed and applied to determine the specific consequences of its use. For example, incorporating a highly specific set of EMS requirements with a series of process checkpoints is unlikely to deliver much in the way of flexibility. It consequently is best to see these rankings as assessments of the *capacity* of each instrument to increase flexibility. The categorizations of high, medium, or low for each instrument under the criteria reflect my assessment of each instrument's capacity when compared to conventional, technology-based environmental regulation.

All five instruments rank high in their capacity for allowing both government and regulated entities to adapt as they get more information or learn of new opportunities. This high ranking reflects selection bias because the aim of this chapter has been to consider how to use different classes of instruments to achieve greater flexibility. All but one of the instruments (voluntary challenge programs) rank high in their reflexive potential as well. Indeed, the gradual shift by government toward use of marketable permits, information disclosures, and EMSs implies a greater appreciation of the concept of reflexive law and of the limits of regulation based on substantive law. The reflexive potential of voluntary challenge programs is ranked medium rather than high. This is because at this point the evidence suggests that such programs are used more as platforms for firms to claim credit for actions they already have or would have taken, rather than as inducements for the critical self-assessment that leads to continuous environmental improvement. However, if voluntary programs were designed to ensure greater accountability and offer more tangible rewards to participants, they may have higher reflexive potential.

The instruments rank relatively low (that is, in comparison to conventional regulation) in the knowledge about and certainty of their effects on environmental quality. The notable exception is marketable permits, which offer policymakers a high degree of confidence about environmental outcomes. Indeed, the steady growth in marketable permit and trading programs in the United States over the past 30 years reflects an appreciation of a policy instrument that takes an environmental target as its starting point and allows entities some flexibility in deciding how to achieve it. For the other instruments, it is difficult to have any confidence in the likely outcome. For information disclosures, voluntary programs, and EMSs in particular, it may be said that entities are headed in the right direction, but without any guarantee as to their destination.

My evaluations of the instruments under the last two criteria present a mixed bag. Marketable permits and fees demand a relatively high level of administrative and legal capacity, although it is fair to say that the conventional regulatory system does as well. The others require relatively less administrative and legal capacity, especially information disclosures and voluntary programs. Fairly basic "shaming" programs and voluntary challenges may be created with little legal authority and limited institutional capacity. The instruments also vary in their political acceptability. Fees are probably the most difficult to sell because they create clear winners and losers, and the latter will mobilize to oppose them. Fees also are difficult to sell politically because they assign obvious costs to parties rather than hidden ones, which are more typical of the other instruments and of conventional regulation. The public tolerates high compliance costs for industrial "polluters" because it does not recognize that consumers (that is, the public) eventually bear these costs in the prices of goods and services. Fees and taxes may make this consumer burden explicit.

What is the Future of Flexibility in Environmental Policy? Challenges, Choices, and Opportunities

The growing appreciation of flexibility as a potential virtue rather than a definite vice in helping to build a results-based sense of common purpose has been gradual but perceptible in both the public and private sectors. Dissatisfaction with the current system—with its formal, legalistic relationships, legacy of distrust, and high transaction costs, for example—has led to calls for change. At the heart of these calls for change have been criticisms of the rigidity of regulation and perceptions of a need for greater flexibility and adaptability in how government regulates others.

If, however, flexibility has become more of a virtue, it is not without risks. The original design of regulation in the United States reflected two things. First, as Gary Bryner and others in this volume suggest, there exists no widespread acceptance in the United States of a strong state role in economic planning, such as that seen in the Netherlands or Sweden. Second, unlike in nations with corporatist traditions, there exists widespread suspicion in the United States about the political power and motives of industry. As such, policymakers believed that only a legalistic, adversarial, and deterrence-based approach could enable agencies to offset industry influence and capture.

Thus, perhaps the fundamental strategic challenge facing revisionists touting flexibility as a means for building a results-based sense of common purpose is answering two questions to the satisfaction of skeptical citizens. First, how can we design more flexibility into regulation and still keep pressure on industry to improve? Second, how can we ensure that the cooperation and communication that revisionist critics call for among government, business, and activists do not lead to collusion and capture? In turn, getting the correct answers to these questions means making a series of policy and program choices in the design and application of policy instruments that advance rather than retard these purposes. Among the most important of these strategic choices are:

1. *Preferring instruments that allow for adaptation and have reflexive potential.* The purpose of the comparisons presented in this chapter is to describe the different capacities for incorporating flexibility. Some instruments are more flexible than others. The trade-off, of course, is that instruments that are high in their reflexive potential, such as information disclosures or EMSs, do not provide on their own any particular level of certainty regarding what results are achieved. Combined with other instruments and with a system of measurable targets, they can be effective. These instruments should be seen as part of a larger strategy. Indeed, a recurring theme in policy debates should be that policy instruments such as those described here should be used in combination.

2. *Using third parties to leverage government's influence.* A common feature of instruments that compare well in adaptability and reflexive potential is that they use nongovernmental actors to influence behavior. Instruments based on mandatory disclosure, for example, provide information to third parties (for example communities or investors) whose reactions matter to those making the disclosures. Recognition from challenge programs also helps to establish a firm as a good performer and solid member of the community, which may matter to consumers and shareholders. The government role becomes one of creating "the necessary preconditions for second or third parties to assume a greater share of the regulatory burden, rather than engaging in direct intervention."[31] Reminiscent of the government role that DeWitt John presents in his chapter on civic environmentalism, in this case government does not use its limited capacities to try and control the behavior of large numbers of actors in society. Rather, it creates conditions that encourage desired behavior.

3. *Relying on measurable and transparent goals.* A key element in flexibility is to determine what results are needed and to assign accountability for achieving them. As the chapters in this book exemplify, the need for a greater emphasis on performance and results is now standard fare in policy discussions. Advisory groups and regulatory agencies' recurring emphasis on incentives that promote "beyond compliance" suggest that compliance as a goal increasingly is outmoded and may tell us little about actual performance. Flexibility in means requires clear accountability for results, which is why the Netherlands' approach has drawn attention.

4. *Using alternative regulatory tracks, based on performance.* The symptoms of inflexibility in current regulation—high transaction costs, overly prescriptive rules, adversarial relationships, and reliance on coercion—reflect the effects of a system designed to deal with the worst actors. Yet, as most enforcement officials will admit and as Jan Mazurek illustrates in chapter 13, regulated entities possess varying degrees of ability and willingness to meet their legal obligations. The EPA itself has depicted industry as representing a theoretical bell-shaped curve, with a high number of generally compliant entities in the middle, and very poor and very strong ones at the two tails. For the most part, however, regulated entities on the

right end of the curve are treated the same as those on the left end. Flexibility is more justified when it is allowed for high performers, who require less oversight. Alternative tracks that differentiate based on past and likely future behavior offer a rational basis for allowing more flexibility to some entities than others. The EPA's Performance Track Program and similar state programs are steps in this direction.

Can an enduring policy bias in favor of this revisionist agenda take root in the twenty-first century to build a results-based sense of common purpose better than it did during the last three decades of the twentieth century? Past history, as well as the ongoing imbroglio of corporate scandals, do not augur well for this outcome. An alternative scenario, however, is that an unprecedented opportunity exists today for strategically advancing the concept of flexibility as a predicate for results. Environmental governance worldwide specifically is facing the kinds of discontinuities in elite attitudes that scholars suggest can lead to quantum or nonincremental shifts in programs.[32] This chapter has argued that many architects of the conventional model of regulation have come to realize that this model is inappropriate for the demands of a new, postmodern era in environmental governance. Previously seen as a vice in the early design of regulatory regimes, flexibility is seen now more as a virtue. The time thus may be right for a system based on controls and deterrence to evolve into one that is more adaptable, reflexive, results based, and collaborative in the twenty-first century.

Notes

1. On defining regulation, see Barry M. Mitnick, *The Political Economy of Regulation* (New York: Columbia University Press, 1980).

2. Eugene Bardach and Robert Kagan, *Going by the Book: The Problem of Regulatory Unreasonableness* (Philadelphia: Temple University Press, 1982), p. 20.

3. Ibid., p. 58.

4. The term *coercion* is used here to refer to "the extent to which external parties or instruments place negative pressure on a firm to improve its performance" (Neil Gunningham and Peter Grabosky, *Smart Regulation: Designing Environmental Policy* [Oxford: Clarendon, 1998], p. 391).

5. See, for example, Lennart J. Lundqvist, *The Hare and the Tortoise: Clean Air Policies in the United States and Sweden* (Ann Arbor: University of Michigan Press, 1980); Ronald Brickman, Sheila Jasanoff, and Thomas Ilgen, *Controlling*

Chemicals: The Politics of Regulation in Europe and the United States (Ithaca, N.Y.: Cornell University Press, 1985); David Vogel, *National Styles of Regulation: Environmental Policy in Great Britain and the United States* (Ithaca, N.Y.: Cornell University Press, 1986).

6. David Wallace, *Environmental Policy and Industrial Innovation: Strategies in Europe, the U.S. and Japan* (London: Earthscan, 1995).

7. A point that the EPA itself has recognized (see EPA, *Aiming for Excellence: Actions to Encourage Stewardship and Accelerate Environmental Progress* [Washington, D.C.: EPA, 1999], pp. 13–15).

8. Environmental Law Institute (ELI), *Barriers to Environmental Technology and Use* (Washington, D.C.: ELI, 1998).

9. Marver Bernstein, *Regulating Business by Independent Commission* (Princeton, N.J.: Princeton University Press, 1955).

10. The writing on the "greening of industry" is a large and rapidly growing literature. See, for example, Kurt Fischer and Johan Schot, *Environmental Strategies for Industry: International Perspectives on Research Needs and Policy Implications* (Washington, D.C.: Island, 1993); Nigel Roome, ed., *Sustainability Strategies for Industry: The Future of Corporate Practice* (Washington, D.C.: Island, 1998); Daniel Press and Daniel A. Mazmanian, "Understanding the Transition to a Sustainable Economy," in Norman J. Vig and Michael E. Kraft, eds., *Environmental Policy*, 257–280 (Washington, D.C.: CQ, 2000).

11. On the deterrence model of regulation, see Robert A. Kagan and John T. Scholz, "The 'Criminology of the Corporation' and Regulatory Enforcement Strategies," in Keith Hawkins and John M. Thomas, eds., *Enforcement Regulation*, 67–95 (Boston: Kluwer, 1984).

12. Wallace, *Environmental Policy and Industrial Innovation*, p. xviii.

13. These writers and their relevance for U.S. environmental policy are discussed further in Daniel J. Fiorino, "Rethinking Environmental Regulation: Perspectives on Law and Governance," *Harvard Environmental Law Review* 23 (1999): 441–469.

14. Gunther Teubner, "Substantive and Reflexive Elements in Modern Law," *Law and Society Review* 17 (1983), p. 255. Eric Orts applied the concept of reflexive law to environmental law (Eric Orts, "Reflexive Environmental Law," *Northwestern University Law Review* 89 [1995]: 1227–1340).

15. An excellent resource on this literature is the collection in Jan Kooiman, ed., *Modern Governance: New Government-Society Interactions* (London: Sage, 1993), p. 1.

16. Martijn Van Vliet, "Environmental Regulation of Business: Options and Constraints for Communicative Governance," in Kooiman, ed., *Modern Governance*, 105–118.

17. For a sample of the many differing ways to classify policy instruments, see Daniel J. Fiorino, *Making Environmental Policy* (Berkeley: University of California Press, 1995), pp. 167–188; U.S. Congress, Office of Technology

Assessment, *Environmental Policy Tools: A User's Guide* (Washington, D.C.: Office of Technology Assessment, 1995); Rosemary O'Leary, Robert F. Durant, Daniel J. Fiorino, and Paul Weiland, *Managing for the Environment: Understanding the Legal, Organizational, and Policy Challenges* (San Francisco: Jossey-Bass, 1999), pp. 307–336.

18. On economic incentives, see Robert N. Stavins, "Market-Based Environmental Policy," in Paul R. Portney and Robert N. Stavins, eds., *Public Policies for Environmental Protection,* 2d ed., 31–76 (Washington, D.C.: Resources for the Future, 2000).

19. Paul R. Portney, "Air Pollution Policy," in Portney and Stavins, eds., *Public Policies for Environmental Protection,* p. 114.

20. On the Danish carbon tax, see Arther Mol, Volkmar Lauber, and Duncan Lieffernink, eds., *The Voluntary Approach to Environmental Policy: Joint Environmental Policy-Making in Europe* (Oxford: Oxford University Press, 2000), pp. 62–103.

21. Shameek Konar and Mark A. Cohen, "Information as Regulation: The Effect of Community Right to Know Laws on Toxic Emissions," *Journal of Environmental Economics and Management* 32 (1997): 109–124; James T. Hamilton, "Pollution as News: Media and Stock Market Reactions to the Toxics Release Inventory Data," *Journal of Environmental Economics and Management* 28 (1995): 98–113.

22. David Shaman and David Wheeler, "Controlling Industrial Pollution in the Developing World," *Environmental Quality Management* 69 (1998): 69–75.

23. Ibid., p. 70.

24. For a discussion of environmental policy from this perspective, see Mary Graham, *The Morning after Earth Day: Practical Environmental Politics* (Washington, D.C.: Brookings Institution Press, 1999).

25. A conclusion reached in Terry Davies and Jan Mazurek, *Industry Incentives for Environmental Improvement: An Evaluation of U.S. Federal Initiatives* (Washington, D.C.: Resources for the Future, 1996).

26. Jan Mazurek, *The Use of Voluntary Agreements in the United States: An Initial Survey* (Paris: Organization for Economic Cooperation and Development, 1998).

27. Richard N. L. Andrews, Nicole Darnall, Deborah Rigling Gallagher, Suellen Terrill Keiner, Eric Feldman, Matthew L. Mitchell, Deborah Amaral, and Jessica D. Jacoby, "Environmental Management Systems: History, Theory, and Implementation Research," in Cary Coglianese and Jennifer Nash, eds., *Regulating from the Inside: Can Environmental Management Systems Achieve Policy Goals?* (Washington, D.C.: Resources for the Future, 2001), p. 32.

28. Teubner, "Substantive and Reflexive Elements in Modern Law," p. 255.

29. O'Leary et al., *Managing for the Environment,* especially chap. 9.

30. For an excellent resource on EMS research, see Coglianese and Nash, *Regulating from the Inside*.

31. Gunningham and Grabosky, *Smart Regulation,* p. 411.

32. John W. Kingdon, *Agendas, Alternatives, and Public Policies,* 2d ed. (New York: Longman, 1997); Frank R. Baumgartner and Bryan D. Jones, *Agendas and Instability in American Politics* (Chicago: University of Chicago Press, 1993); Paul A. Sabatier and Hank C. Jenkins-Smith, *Policy Change and Learning: An Advocacy Coalition Approach* (Boulder, Colo.: Westview, 1993); Robert F. Durant and Paul F. Diehl, "Agendas, Alternatives, and Public Policy: Lessons from the U.S. Foreign Policy Arena," *Journal of Public Policy* 9(2) (1989): 179–205.

12

Pollution Prevention

Ken Geiser

The prevention of harm is an underlying theme in many environmental policies. Federal policies in the United States permit government interventions in the market where necessary to prevent harm to human health and ecological systems. Thus, the public ownership of special lands is defended as necessary to prevent the desecration of significant ecological, aesthetic, or cultural sites. Legal prohibitions and licenses are instituted to prevent overhunting, overfishing, and overexploiting natural resources. Standard-based regulations and facility-operating permits are developed to prevent hazardous wastes and emissions from overwhelming the assimilative capacities of natural systems.

The bold state and national environmental laws enacted in the United States during the 1970s were likewise intended to prevent environmental damage by protecting the environment from the hazards of human economic activities. For instance, the regulations promulgated under the federal Clean Air Act and the Clean Water Act focused on controlling and managing industrial pollution at the point where contaminants were released from a regulated facility into the environment. Thus, clean air regulations focused on the installation of air filtering and scrubbing technologies for controlling gaseous emissions before they could be released from facility stacks and chimneys. Similarly, national water pollution control standards required the application of wastewater treatment technologies before wastewater could be discharged to receiving waters.

Still, as DeWitt John and Denise Scheberle (in particular) recount in greater detail in chapters 6 and 10 in this volume, each of these statutes was focused on "end-of-pipe" reductions in pollutants; pollution was seen as a negative but inevitable by-product of industrial processes. Scant thought was given to reducing pollution "upstream" by altering production inputs, processes, and procedures before they entered the environment. Moreover, because these statutes were single medium (that is, air or water or hazardous waste) in focus, any reductions that did occur in one medium tended merely to shift pollution problems to another medium. Not until a spate of state pollution prevention laws were enacted during the 1980s and 1990s, along with the federal Pollution Prevention Act, did policymakers pursue the most direct, cross-media, and consciously focused effort to exploit the concept of upstream rather than end-of-pipe pollution reduction in the United States.

What have these efforts wrought in the United States? Despite the intuitive appeal of pollution prevention, its promise as an approach to environmental protection has not been matched by its accomplishments. Success can be documented, but widespread adoption of pollution prevention in the United States has remained elusive, as has its potential for building a results-based sense of common purpose in environmental governance. Since the passage of the early pollution control statutes, the release of some pollutants has been reduced dramatically. This is certainly true for lead, phosphorous, polychlorinated biphenyls, and chlorofluorocarbons, as well as for the air emissions of sulfur dioxide, carbon monoxide, volatile organic compounds, and dust particulates. Trends in the environmental release of more than 600 toxic chemicals tracked by the U.S. Environmental Protection Agency (EPA) over a twelve-year period also show an aggregate decrease of more than 40 percent.

However, the ambient condition of much of the environment remains fairly polluted. Nearly all urban areas exceed safe levels of atmospheric ozone at least part of the year, and a significant number of areas exceed safe levels of carbon monoxide and sulfur dioxide as well. Of the surface waters in lakes assessed by the states in 1994, nearly half could not support their intended uses, and the overall quality of drinking water has remained unchanged for the past two decades. In other words, the success of these environmental regulatory laws has been mixed at best.[1]

In light of this record, we have to ask: Are conventional pollution prevention approaches capable of satisfactorily protecting human health and the environment in the United States? Recognizing that a large amount of money and effort has been expended on these prevention strategies, why have they not had better outcomes in terms of environmental quality? Indeed, recognizing the limited success of these programs, should we continue to focus on prevention as a central strategy for building a results-based sense of common purpose in the future? With these questions in mind, this chapter is organized around four objectives: (1) to examine the logic of the pollution prevention approach and assess its implementation in the United States; (2) to consider the political and economic factors that have constrained its adoption; (3) to consider international approaches that have responded to these and similar prevention shortcomings by taking a broader and bolder approach to it; and (4) to cull lessons from these experiences about what it will take to make pollution prevention more effective in the United States as a tool for fostering a results-based sense of common purpose in environmental governance.

Conventional wisdom in the United States is that pollution prevention efforts have not realized their full potential because the approach is too ambitious. This chapter argues, to the contrary, that the limits of pollution prevention effectiveness occur largely because the vision has not been ambitious enough. To support this argument, the chapter begins with a brief history of the U.S. experience with pollution prevention and an analysis of the political economy that has diminished its widespread acceptance and impact. An analysis then follows of the evolution of the international cleaner production and health promotion movements as parallel, yet bolder, prevention efforts. These ambitious initiatives illustrate that resistance to prevention is deeply rooted; that traditional approaches to prevention are too reactive and require bolder visions of the future to become politically inspiring; and that bolder approaches not only must be inspiring, but also must be well grounded in market incentives and opportunities that regulatory targets understand. Arguing that a focus on cleaner production incorporates better the more visionary precepts that originally informed the pollution prevention movement in the United States, the chapter concludes by summarizing the major strategic challenges, choices, and opportunities facing advocates of this approach in the years ahead.

Pollution Prevention: A Boat Without a Rudder?

The early environmental statutes directed at air and water quality were intended to prevent pollution by seeking to control and manage industrial emissions. The media-specific boundaries of these early regulations tended to reduce pollution in one medium, such as air, only to end up increasing pollution in other ways, such as contaminated rinse waters and filter residues. Coupled with the growing costs of pollution control technologies and their management, this problem led to increasing criticism during the 1980s. Indeed, the overall ineffectiveness of these policies was lamented alike by business interests, environmental professionals and advocates. Some recommended that pollution might be prevented more effectively by shifting the focus of policy from the point of environmental release (the end of the pipe) to the point of pollution generation (the source of the pollution within a facility's production processes). By reducing pollution at the *source* of generation, this new policy approach conveniently was called *source reduction* by some, while the broader movement adopted the term *pollution prevention* because the approach focused on eliminating rather than controlling pollution.

Early leaders in the movement for pollution prevention spoke in terms of a revolution in policy that would lead to a shift in the conventional way of thinking, or the paradigm, under which pollution management policy had been carried out. For its early promoters, pollution prevention included several critical policy innovations. First, pollution prevention was to shift the policy focus from waste treatment and end-of-pipe technologies to production processes. Second, it was to shift the conventional regulatory approach that focused on singular environmental media to a multimedia approach that was more comprehensively and holistically to reduce damage to all environmental media. Third, the pollution prevention approach was to replace the traditional adversarial "command-and-control" approach of regulatory compliance with a new performance-based, win-win approach that would improve a facility's environmental and economic performance at the same time. This new approach would not be compliance driven, but it instead would rely on the ingenuity of industrial plant managers who would be encouraged to improve production efficiencies so as to prevent the generation of pollutants.[2]

In 1986, the congressional Office of Technology Assessment (OTA) issued a landmark report that helped to clarify the language and the shift in policy focus. Entitled *Serious Reduction of Hazardous Waste: For Pollution Prevention and Industrial Efficiency,* the report was useful at documenting in-plant technologies and processes for reducing hazardous waste. Yet the most significant contribution of the report was the clarity with which it sketched out the new pollution prevention approach under which industrial production facilities would be encouraged, assisted, and pressed to reduce the generation of hazardous wastes and pollutants. This new pollution prevention approach involved several different techniques for redesigning the processes of production: substituting benign materials for hazardous materials, optimizing and modernizing production technologies, conserving raw materials and energy, improving operations and maintenance, redesigning the products of production, and closing conventional production process lines to form loops that recycled and reused materials. Cost reductions, it was argued, would result from reduced expenditures for raw materials and energy; reduced costs for government compliance and the purchase of pollution control technologies; avoided waste treatment services; reduced liability costs; and improved efficiencies in operating systems.[3]

These financial incentives *were* a significant attraction for business leaders, and many progressive business managers were among the earliest proponents of the pollution prevention approach. Industry professionals from firms such as AT&T, Dupont, Digital, Dow, Kodak, Shell Oil, Texas Instruments, Hewlett Packard, and Polaroid emerged as spokespersons. They did so because they could document environmental benefits and cost savings and because they believed that pollution prevention offered a way to avoid future regulations. Indeed, the Minneapolis-based 3M Corporation championed its corporatewide "Pollution Prevention Pays ('3P') Program" because its managers could document how preventing pollution saved the firm money by reducing waste management and regulatory compliance costs.[4]

Enthusiastic advocacy for pollution prevention quickly blossomed, with the states particularly active. In 1985, a group of state environmental professionals established the National Roundtable of State Waste Reduction Programs (later renamed the National Pollution Prevention

Roundtable), which a decade later was hosting an annual conference of more than 500 participants. Although only one state law included any reference to pollution prevention in 1985, by 1989 thirty-four states had set up new waste reduction technical assistance units or added new functions to existing units to encourage hazardous-waste reduction. In turn, between 1988 and 1991, twenty-eight states passed some kind of pollution prevention or waste reduction law.

The federal government moved more cautiously, but in 1990 Congress enacted the Pollution Prevention Act. Although this pivotal act was long on policy statements and short on program, it did formally define pollution prevention as source reduction and declared "it to be the national policy of the United States that pollution should be prevented or reduced at the source whenever feasible."[5] In turn, by 1993 the EPA established a special pollution prevention office and released a national strategy statement that defined pollution prevention as "the use of materials, processes, or practices that reduce or eliminate the creation of pollutants or wastes at the source." During the next several years, the agency also established various programs to promote pollution prevention. Included among these programs were the special Source Reduction Review Project to identify opportunities for promoting pollution prevention within the traditional regulatory programs, the 33/50 Program to encourage industrial firms voluntarily to reduce their release of toxic pollutants, and the Design for the Environment Program to encourage firms to incorporate environmental considerations into the earliest stages of product and process design. Meanwhile, a 1993 executive order from President Bill Clinton required that all federal agencies prepare pollution prevention plans.[6]

Yet by 1996 a noticeable slackening of enthusiasm and progress in pollution prevention was palpable. The special pollution prevention office at the EPA had been merged into the conventional institutional structure of the agency. Funding for pollution prevention programs at the federal and state levels was stagnant and in some cases declining. No new federal or state statutes were being considered. Industry professionals continued to present compelling case studies of pollution prevention successes, but they also acknowledged a certain level of frustration in their efforts to convince the upper management of their firms that pollution prevention investments should be a priority.

Several of the early promoters began offering retrospective reviews of a movement they saw in recession. Joel Hirschhorn, the author of the 1986 OTA report, saw the EPA and state government staff as drawing the pollution prevention concept away from its more visionary mission and reducing it to incremental reforms. For Hirschhorn, the pollution prevention vision was broad and ambitious, "encompassing changes in manufacturing technologies and practices, chemicals and other raw materials, and even products and packaging. It also covered resource and energy conservation."[7] But, according to Hirschhorn, this bolder vision was eaten away by agency incrementalists who feared "a systematic assault against chemicals." Thus, he believed that government bureaucrats had betrayed the revolutionary spirit of the pollution prevention paradigm.[8]

Warren Muir, a respected environmental policy researcher, concurred by arguing that the accumulated effects of the many pollution prevention programs had not affected seriously the aggregate amount of toxic chemical use or hazardous-waste generation in the country. He noted that the volume of hazardous-waste generation had continued to increase over the 1990s, while the total number of source reduction activities had declined each year. Muir observed, "We've learned how to talk pollution prevention, but are a long way from putting it into action nationally"[9] Similarly, writing about the history of the pollution prevention movement, Robert Gottlieb observed that "pollution prevention had become a concept without a home, a set of policies without direction or even a set of tangible goals to be accomplished. A stepchild of the environmental policy system, pollution prevention remained in regulatory limbo, a revolution still seeking to find its champions and unable to change the existing rules of the game."[10]

The Political Economy of Pollution Prevention in the United States

Preventing pollution was an obvious and potent idea. The experience is historically rich with lessons about hazardous-waste reduction, energy conservation, and cost savings for industry. It is full of inspiring stories about zealous and committed individuals and scores of examples of new solution-oriented collaborations between government and industry. Nevertheless, today the pollution prevention movement is a less compelling movement than it once was. Indeed, some researchers and practitioners argue that it only skimmed off the easier and cheaper achievements, leaving many highly wasteful processes untouched. Hazardous-waste generation has continued to increase, after all, and there remains plenty of pollution in need of attention.

Why was the drive for prevention so difficult to maintain, and what does it teach us about future efforts to shift our way of thinking about environmental protection? Hirschhorn's review of the betrayal of the pollution prevention movement is a good starting point. In his analysis, Hirschhorn identifies four contributing factors: the transfer of leadership from the original visionaries to more incremental technicians, the resistance of the pollution control technologies industry, the co-optation of regulators by the pollution generators, and the weak support provided by government agencies. Unfortunately, there is evidence to support each of these claims.[11] For example, although the early promoters were visionary, most were not well prepared for the detailed, technical work of redesigning industrial processes. Instead, more pragmatic practitioners carried out much of the daily work of program implementation. Many of these practitioners were trained as engineers, business managers, or scientists and were not prone to speculative, big-picture advocacy. The early promoters did not stick with the project over the years, and no significant charismatic leadership emerged. Indeed, leaders in the environmental advocacy movement displayed a tepid reaction toward pollution prevention. Here, the leadership of the mainstream national organizations focused heavily on defending the older pollution control statutes, and the leadership of grassroots and environmental justice organizations were occupied largely with site cleanup and facility siting controversies.

Nor did the pollution control industry simply fold its camp when confronted with pollution prevention advocacy. Most of the large engineering consulting firms and equipment manufacturers added new language or services directed at preventing pollution. However, they mostly went on recommending and selling technologies that were known to achieve basic regulatory compliance within the existing laws. Meanwhile, pollution prevention proponents did not try to rewrite the pollution control laws that continued to mandate specific control technologies. Convinced that regulations were adversarial and not conducive to win-win solutions, they made little attempt to mandate pollution prevention techniques in statutes so as to level the playing field with the conventional "best available control technologies."

At the same time, the large pollution generators embraced pollution prevention more symbolically than functionally. The largest stationary sources of hazardous wastes in the country are the production facilities in the chemical, petroleum, and energy industries. There is little market incentive for these firms to control pollution, reduce the sales of toxic chemicals, or encourage others to reduce wastes. Cautious about overtly opposing pollution prevention, representatives of these industries resorted to various co-opting and undercutting initiatives that watered down the bold vision and washed out the clear definition of pollution prevention. For instance, the Chemical Manufacturers Association continued to maintain that hazardous-waste treatment was a form of pollution prevention, and the association's much publicized "Responsible Care" Program permitted "recycling/reuse or treatment" to remain in its definition of pollution prevention.

Finally, state and federal environmental agencies tended to stay within their statutory mandates, and the federal Pollution Prevention Act of 1990 and many of the state statutes required little more than voluntary and awareness-raising gestures. The federal government, for example, never created a major focal point, such as a presidential commission or a national task force, on pollution prevention. Meanwhile, government efforts to integrate pollution prevention into existing regulatory programs proceeded slowly and often were resisted by traditional, single-media regulatory staff. Nor were federal and state funding for pollution prevention ever adequate. During much of the 1990s, for instance, the EPA's targeted funding for state pollution prevention programs remained far less than what the states actually received from the agency to implement their delegated pollution control regulatory programs.[12]

These four factors certainly played a large part in restraining the ultimate triumph of the pollution prevention approach, but they do not adequately account for at least three fundamental challenges that the prevention approach had to address in order to realize its full potential as a tool of environmental governance: (1) its relationship to conventional regulations, (2) its relationship to conventional production management, and (3) its relationship to the market economy.

In using a paradigm shift metaphor, for example, the early promoters of pollution prevention naively argued that the cooperative, preventive approach could replace the old regulatory command-and-control approach that they routinely denigrated as ineffective. They were less forthcoming, however, about the need for a stringent pollution control regulatory system to exist in order to make prevention successes possible. Indeed, it was because tough regulatory controls were in place that hazardous-waste treatment costs were high, that regulatory compliance procedures were burdensome, that insurance premiums were costly, and that waste generators simply could not dispose of their wastes responsibly. It is these artificially created costs that provide the motivation for reducing pollution, whereas the various pollution prevention techniques serve more as means than as motivators. Thus, pollution prevention cannot replace the conventional pollution control regulatory structure; its success depends on strong regulatory compliance and enforcement programs as policy drivers.[13]

For their part, industrial managers typically have seen environmental issues as secondary to the primary mission of industrial production. The promotion of pollution control equipment and services has tended to respect that orientation. Control technologies typically are ancillary to the basic production processes of a firm and thus of little interest to production managers. Many facilities traditionally complied with emission and discharge regulations by buying equipment that could be installed without affecting basic production processes; indeed, that is a virtue of an end-of-pipe solution. Such initiatives may add to overall corporate costs, but such costs typically are written off against taxes or passed on to consumers. However, preventing pollution at the source often requires a much more invasive intervention. It may involve redesigning process technologies, changing product specifications, or changing management practices in the basic production processes. These changes are likely to necessitate more penetrating incursions into the fundamental production processes of the firm, requiring interruptions in production schedules and potentially significant risks to product quality. Therefore, resistance by production managers has been more likely, and the attitudes of senior management often have been chilly.

Neither did it help that pollution prevention posed a fundamental challenge to the market economy. Granted, the early pollution prevention advocates were forceful in calling pollution prevention a new environmental management policy approach. They shied away, however, from acknowledging that promoting prevention does not reflect easily the commodity sales objectives of a market economy. A market economy is built around selling goods and services. Pollution control regulations fit this economy well. The regulations create markets for selling pollution control goods and services, and they therefore encourage a robust, commercial interest. The waste treatment and pollution control equipment industries are understandably among the strongest proponents of certain pollution regulations.

In contrast, successes in pollution prevention more often involve changes in management practices than the purchase of new technologies. Thus, pollution prevention projects are less likely to increase the sales of goods and services. Without the potential for equipment or service sales, there is less external commercial interest. Indeed, pollution prevention is promoted as a way to save, not spend, money. These cost savings can be passed on to consumers, but they more likely are eaten up by increased internal investments, so they do not appear of much benefit to corporate managers. Preventing costs that are artificial to begin with simply does not offer the same economic motivations as increasing markets for new products and services.

Thus, although the early proponents of pollution prevention may have overused revolutionary rhetoric, true success for the concept of pollution prevention *does* require fundamental (some might say, "revolutionary") shifts in conventional approaches to corporate management and government functions. The movement may have stalled because the vision was limited, the resistance was high, and the support was meager, but in hindsight the transformations required to assure the primacy of prevention *are* formidable. A true prevention approach requires fairly broad changes not only in the management and technologies of production, but also in the way firms consider what they do and how they integrate environmental values into business decision making.

Pollution Prevention and Environmental Governance: Too Bold or Not Bold Enough?

Is pollution prevention too ambitious a goal, given the formidability of the political economy that so sorely has compromised its impact in the United States? To the contrary, and perhaps counterintuitively, the current barriers to the effective adoption of pollution prevention have occurred precisely because its aims are not ambitious enough. Moreover, if the aims of pollution prevention were bolder—in particular, if policymakers were to embrace what other nations call the "cleaner production" approach to prevention—the perceptions of self-interest that have attenuated the impact of traditional approaches to pollution prevention might be reordered. This approach, in turn, might permit a more protean and effective political economy of business, political, and social interests to develop in support of more robust and comprehensive pollution prevention strategies. To appreciate the logic of this argument, it is helpful to review parallel developments in the "cleaner production" and "health promotion" movements internationally.

From Pollution Prevention to Cleaner Production

The term *pollution prevention* has had particular currency in the United States (and Canada), but in international settings similar approaches have had different names. In 1989, the United Nations Environment Program (UNEP) adopted the term *cleaner production,* a term now widely accepted in international forums. In adopting the term, UNEP offered an ambitious definition:

Cleaner production means the continuous application of an integrated preventive environmental strategy to processes and products to reduce risks to humans and the environment. For production processes, cleaner production includes conserving raw materials and energy, eliminating toxic raw materials, and reducing the quantity and toxicity of all emissions and wastes before they leave a process. For products, the strategy focuses on reducing impacts along the entire life cycle of the product, from raw material extraction to ultimate disposal of the product. Cleaner production is achieved by applying know-how, by improving technologies, and by changing attitudes.[14]

Government-sponsored cleaner production programs have been established in most European countries, and the United Nations has assisted in developing national cleaner production centers in many industrializing countries. Although these programs are quite diverse functionally, most offer business-oriented workshops, on-site professional technical assistance, and in-plant demonstrations to raise awareness of cleaner production processes. Some also offer financial incentives and government awards to encourage firms to adopt new, cleaner technologies. Thus, as part of the European-based ecological modernization movement, the cleaner production movement shares the belief that environmental protection is good for business. As John Dryzek and David Schlosberg summarize, pollution prevention "connotes happy and healthy workers, profits for companies developing conservation technologies or selling green products, high-quality material inputs into production (for example, clean air and water), and efficiency in materials usage."[15]

The international cleaner production movement grew in parallel with and as rapidly as the U.S. pollution prevention movement. Today, regional roundtables on cleaner production are held throughout the world. Although the similarities between pollution prevention and cleaner production have permitted the two terms to be used interchangeably, there are differences between the two approaches. Prevention, as a concept, focuses on the avoidance of negatively valued outcomes (pollution). It conceptually is *reactive* and *corrective*. Indeed, many government pollution prevention programs in the United States measure their impacts by noting reductions in the generation of hazardous wastes or the pollutants that firms annually report under the federal Toxics Release Inventory, an inventory that compiles data on waste transfers and pollution releases from more than 60,000 domestic facilities.

The cleaner production concept, by definition, also is focused on preventing negatives, but conceptually the term hints at a more forward-looking enterprise. In seeking to achieve cleaner processes and products, the concept of *cleaner* has a positive value—something to achieve in the future. By focusing on materials and energy conservation as well as on toxic chemical reduction, and by focusing on the full lifecycle of products as well as on pollution and wastes, cleaner production is broader, more positive, and better directed toward the international goals of sustainable development. Indeed, the United Nations promotes cleaner production as a staging platform for future work linking "cleaner production" and "sustainable consumption."[16]

By focusing on both processes and products, cleaner production approaches come to address the full lifecycle of products quite naturally, to promote design for the environment, and to integrate the post-consumption issues of product management directly within the reconsideration of production processes. "End-of-life" recycling and materials "loop-closing" initiatives (such as product stewardship, product take-back, and extended producer responsibility) are integrated easily into cleaner production programs. Thus, cleaner production is more ambitious than pollution prevention and better directed at changes in national economies, not just changes in industrial production. Greater ambition and usefulness, in turn, have meant that more attention has been paid to the role that cleaner production can play in helping countries achieve their commitments under multilateral environmental agreements such as the Basel Convention on the Trans-Boundary Movement of Hazardous Waste, the UNEP Regional Seas Program, and the Stockholm Convention on Persistent Organic Pollutants.[17]

Most significant for this chapter, promoters of cleaner production generally have avoided the serious dilemmas that have limited the success of pollution prevention in the United States. For instance, cleaner production seldom is promoted with rhetoric about "revolutions" or paradigm shifts. Instead, it is advocated as simply the next step in industrial development and not as an alternative to mandatory environmental regulations. European advocacy for cleaner production has recognized the role of a sound regulatory infrastructure and built cleaner production programs as companions to regulatory programs. In some industrializing countries with lax enforcement regimes, cleaner production has even been promoted as a means of meeting regulatory standards. The benefits of cleaner production are advocated in these cases as means to achieve production efficiencies, lower costs, and environmental protection.[18]

The conscious attention of cleaner production to new environmental technologies and to developing markets and financial incentives to facilitate their adoption has meant that these technologies have been supported by commercial ventures interested in product and services sales. Indeed, because cleaner production has been promoted as a means of *modernizing* existing production systems, it has been marketed successfully as a "best available" process technology capable of "lean and clean production." Thus, environmental benefits aside, cleaner production tends to be attractive, or at least appropriate, to the conventional interests of production managers. This comfort level also extends to upper-level managers, who tend to be interested primarily in financial performance.[19]

In turn, the development of new low- and no-waste process technologies has been viewed, particularly in Europe, as an investment in "cleaner technologies" that governments ought to support with various taxes, procurement, and subsidies. These investments can help create and penetrate lucrative markets and expand exports. Governments in industrializing countries also have funded and run technology transfer and "locally developed technology" programs to promote the adoption of cleaner technologies. Recognizing that cleaner production investments are likely to generate economic growth, international organizations have established new investment programs, revolving loan funds, and credit line programs. For example, the World Bank, Asian Development Bank, Nordic Environment Finance Corporation, and the Inter-American Development Bank have pursued such initiatives to provide for investments in cleaner production projects.[20]

Like the movement for pollution prevention, the advocates for cleaner production can point to many programs and cite hundreds of specific case studies. Both show similarities in implementation, and both can demonstrate many successes. But in more generalized terms, it is difficult to compare the effects of the two approaches because no international data track either of the initiatives. What is clear, however, is that although there has been a recognized slowing of progress in pollution prevention efforts in the United States, no one currently is arguing that cleaner production efforts are slowing.

Nor is it necessary for the purposes of this chapter to compare the effectiveness of the two approaches. Rather, the point here is that cleaner production is simply a broader, more encompassing, and more forward-oriented conceptual framework than the pollution prevention approach. Moreover, by moderating their rhetoric, stressing the commercial opportunities that cleaner production offers, and linking rather than decoupling their movement to existing regulatory approaches, proponents of cleaner production (and of ecological modernization more generally) have created an incentive system more consonant with market values and more attractive to business interests.

From Preventive Medicine to Health Promotion?

Not unlike in environmental governance, the history of public health also is full of discourse on prevention—the prevention of injury and disease. In a seminal report to the city of Boston in 1850 on the "promotion of public and personal health," for example, one of the early leaders in public health, Lemuel Shattuck, was critical of physicians' narrow focus on treating "sickness, debility and injury." Instead, Shattuck argued, "the advice of the physician should be sought for and paid for while in health, to keep the patient well; and not . . . as now, while in sickness, to cure disease . . . which might . . . have been prevented."[21]

Over the next 80 years, remarkable initiatives took place in municipal sanitation, public hygiene, infant care, and the control of infectious pathogens. In each of these areas of advancement, the concept of prevention played a key role. By improving public sanitation, controlling vectors, and instituting immunization programs, governments prevented communicable diseases such as malaria, cholera, influenza, and polio. Maternal education programs and family services were developed to prevent infant disease and death. Campaigns to control tobacco use and the abuse of alcohol were organized to reduce the incidence of cancer and alcoholism.

These preventative campaigns began to affect traditional medical practice as well, and by the 1940s a new medical specialty called "preventive medicine" championed annual health exams to promote early disease detection. Within a decade, this new discipline was developing "prevention guidelines" for rationalizing disease prevention practices by participating physicians. By the 1980s, the U.S. Public Health Service had launched a special Preventive Services Task Force to develop a comprehensive set of clinical preventive services. Today, *Guide to Clinical Preventive Services,* now in its second edition, addresses some 200 potential interventions in some 70 areas of medical attention.[22]

Much of this early-prevention orientation focused on preventing the onset of chronic disease. The practice came to be classified into two types. *Primary prevention* focuses on identifying and controlling the classic risk factors of disease such as smoking, obesity, physical inactivity, alcohol and drug abuse, and poor diet. *Secondary prevention*, in contrast, focuses on surveillance and early intervention to stop the progress of chronic disease. In secondary prevention, clinicians typically focus on periodic physical exams, screening tests such as blood and urine chemistry panels, chest radiograms, electrocardiograms, mammograms, and various preventive therapies.[23]

Primary prevention, like pollution prevention, tends toward interventions designed to preclude negatively valued outcomes. It seeks to take measures to avoid or eliminate the possibility of disease, and, like pollution prevention, it has as much to do with changes in practices and behaviors as it does with the marketing of products and services. Many primary preventive strategies, for example, rely on educating patients through professional counseling on subjects that range from drug abuse to diet. Traditionally trained clinicians tend to see these topics as tasks outside their expertise and as incompatible with the conventional doctor-patient relationship. To the degree that addressing these outcomes (for example, curing diseases) tends not to provide a justification for conventional medical practice, the traditional medical profession has been hesitant about fully embracing preventive medicine. Moreover, although abstaining from smoking or reducing drug use may lead to better health, they do not generate sales. As a consequence, they are less likely to have market value and therefore are less likely to generate a strong commercial interest.

In contrast, and not unlike the cleaner production strategy in environmental governance, secondary prevention tends to fit more comfortably into the traditional dynamics of medical practice and economics. Annual health checkups, laboratory tests, and the pharmaceuticals used to treat disease in its early stages all fit the general routines of doctor-patient relationships. All also have market implications, with money to be made on the sales of products and services. Not surprisingly then, preventive medicine—in particular primary prevention practices—has remained constrained within the conventional boundaries of medical practice. Instead, secondary prevention has been emphasized, even though it is often acknowledged that environmental or social factors, in particular those related to occupational health hazards, can play a significant role in determining disease outcomes. Seeing more profit in secondary prevention, the preventive medicine clinician has focused largely on immunizations, screening exams (mammograms and blood pressure and cholesterol testing), behavioral counseling, and various preventive therapies.

This limited reactive and defensive approach has led to an element of professional discontent within the health field, a discontent parallel to that expressed by some pollution prevention professionals who seek a more comprehensive and proactive approach that addresses the root causes of pollution. For instance, in its conclusions, the most recent edition of *Guide to Clinical Preventive Services* notes:

For some health problems, community-level interventions may be more effective than clinical preventive services. Important health problems that are likely to require broader-based interventions than can be offered in the clinical setting alone include youth and family violence, initiation of tobacco use, unintended pregnancy in adolescents, and certain unintentional injuries. Other types of interventions, such as school-based curricula, community programs, and regulatory and legislative initiatives, might prove more effective for preventing morbidity and mortality from these conditions than will preventive services delivered in the clinical setting.[24]

Thus, for some in the public health services, this realization has provoked an international dialogue about what is most commonly termed *health promotion*. Rather than focusing narrowly on preventing disease, proponents of health promotion have focused on encouraging those practices that will promote good health, including not only good nutrition, personal hygiene, and physical exercise, but also psychological well-being, economic security, social support, and other "social determinants of health."

The World Health Organization (WHO) has become a champion of this new and more ambitious health promotion approach. In 1985, it convened a meeting in Ottawa, Canada, to draft a formal charter for defining and encouraging the adoption of health promotion as a principle goal for health authorities around the world. The Ottawa Charter, as it is known, called for changes in medicine that would place a far greater emphasis on patient empowerment; on the development of health literacy among patients, families, and communities; on holistic care; and on new social organizations that can promote social and psychological well-being. Indeed, the charter's ambitious commitment is reflected best in its definition of *health promotion:*

Health promotion is the process of enabling people to increase control over, and to improve, their health. To reach a state of complete physical, mental and social well-being, an individual or group must be able to identify and to realize aspirations, to satisfy needs, and to change or cope with the environment. . . . Health is a positive concept emphasizing social and personal resources, as well as physical capacities.[25]

Thus, like cleaner production, the concept of health promotion has a distinctive, forward perspective. The approach accepts health as a norm and, rather than focusing on the prevention of health deterioration, encourages professional practices that will maintain and enhance health quality. It enables people to take action to protect their own health. Social participation and the empowerment of individuals and communities are valued parts of a health promotion orientation, as are social and economic security, poverty eradication, and the elimination of social and economic discrimination. Here, individuals act to change their lifestyle habits and conditions, and communities act to change social, economic, and environmental conditions that lead to poor health outcomes. In the process, ameliorating these conditions affords business opportunities. Finally, because health promotion is promoted in a broad international context, the focus is on flexible, performance-based solutions that are culturally, politically, and economically sensitive to the different conditions in which individuals, communities, and nations exist. Health promotion is about achievements and results rather than about prescribed programs and harmonized policies. It focuses attention on health literacy at the individual level, social mobilization at the community level, and public policy and organizational practice at the national level.[26]

As ambitious and transformative as these broad-based concepts of health promotion are, and despite their challenges to conventional medical practice and to economic incentives, evidence abounds of their increasing influence throughout the world. In 2001, for example, the U.S. Institute of Medicine Committee on Quality of Health Care in America released a call for a new health system for the twenty-first century that stresses many health promotion concepts. Meanwhile, in Great Britain, the national Expert Patients Task Force called for a new patient-led, self-managed approach to health care, and the WHO Global Strategy for Prevention and Control of Non-communicable Diseases recommended national implementation plans that encourage patient participation, social empowerment, and community action.[27]

Finally, and not unlike proponents of cleaner production, advocates of health promotion eschew talk of revolutions or paradigm shifts. Although they draw a distinction between primary and secondary prevention, they are sympathetic to the role each plays in advancing public health. Granted, they argue that improving the quality of health requires moving beyond the "static" model of disease prevention focused on modifying the classical risk factors to a model that recognizes the interactive and cumulative impact of social, economic, and biological factors in determining health outcomes. But, as a recent editorial by Colin Central argues, they see a role for both models: "Health promotion, and disease prevention and control, are not one and the same, and attempts to reduce the former to the latter should be resisted. . . . But if common ground can be found between health promotion and chronic disease prevention, health development would sit on firmer terrain."[28]

A Future for Pollution Prevention? Challenges, Choices, and Opportunities

As the preceding discussion shows, the concept of prevention has played an important role in both environmental and human health protection. This quick review of the experiences of the cleaner production and disease prevention movements internationally demonstrates not only the ongoing push for more ambitious prevention approaches in each area, but also the strategic challenges, choices, and opportunities facing advocates of broader and bolder agendas. For example, similarities have been noted in the way in which advocates of pollution prevention, cleaner production, and health promotion have labored under acute disadvantages relative to conventional prevention practices based on treatment and control. In medicine, as in environmental protection, market incentives have favored treatment and control practices. This occurs because these techniques promote technological solutions for which there are significant commercial opportunities and interests. Perhaps as important, treatment and control techniques interfere least with professional norms in these fields and with the social and economic factors that generate pollution and disease. Therefore, they do not require individuals to confront fundamental issues about the design of industrial production systems or the organization of domestic lifestyles and consumption patterns.

Even where preventive techniques have been accepted in conventional medical practice, the benefits often have been defined narrowly in terms of improvements in the efficiency of achieving health outcomes. Likewise, improving productive efficiency also has been a central justification for promoting pollution prevention. However, efficiency improvements focus on means rather than ends. Consequently, efficiency improvements alone will not lead to the quality of health or environmental outcome that will satisfy public expectations. By the same token, if the cleaner production movement is a guide, reformers ignore market incentives and existing understandings of professionals' traditional roles at their peril. A daunting set of challenges thus faces reformers seeking to transform conventional pollution prevention approaches into more comprehensive "cleaner production" approaches in the United States. Not only must they link their initiatives to existing regulatory, professional, and business operations and worldviews, but they also must make their initiatives financially attractive to business managers and industrial leaders.

These challenges presume that U.S. policymakers will choose to pursue the bolder cleaner production agenda, rather than merely continue current conventional and underperforming pollution prevention approaches. They must decide that cleaner production—and its vision of a future that is more environmentally benign and healthier—is a more politically compelling agenda, one that presents greater electoral opportunities and less business opposition for them than traditional pollution prevention strategies. To date, neither pollution prevention nor preventive medicine has been able to convey such a vision of the future. Although both forms of prevention practice have struggled to break with the treatment-and-control conventions of the past, both have remained focused largely on correcting and reversing undesirable outcomes, rather than on affirmatively seeking desirable ones.

Of course, broad generalizations about either field tend to hide the pioneering efforts of those engaged in prevention who *do* draw the linkage between prevention and a positive strategy that recognizes the need for fundamental changes in the social and economic context. Nevertheless, it is safe to conclude that for a large percentage of those who promote a prevention approach, success is counted by what has been avoided, not by what might be gained in the future. The former emphasis is arguably a less politically, economically, and socially attractive vision than the latter for constructing the coalitions necessary for prevention to realize its full potential in the United States.

All this is not to denigrate the role that pollution prevention strategies have played in the past. Aside from the pollution reductions that these strategies have helped achieve, the struggle to promote a prevention approach has provided a sound platform for launching a promising movement for cleaner production and for a sustainable economy. The effort to prevent human poisoning and ecological deterioration by promulgating and enforcing media-specific environmental regulations halted and, in many cases, reversed serious and irreparable damage. Likewise, the struggle to change the focus from end-of-pipe means of prevention to point-of-generation means has improved the effectiveness of pollution and waste management. Of even more significance, however, this policy shift has served to clarify the more fundamental systemic causes of environmental risks.

It is now possible to see that the basic materials and processes of industrial production often are incompatible with environmental or public health goals. Thus, to move forward, the prevention efforts of the future need to focus centrally on the basic resources and processes of production and on the lifecycle impacts of those materials and processes as they interact with people and the environment over time. With this longer, more fundamental, and more politically compelling view, it is possible to see that by choosing to move (in small steps) from control strategies to source reduction strategies to production strategies, the prevention approach of the future might embrace the more forward-looking orientation of cleaner production. At that point, pollution prevention would be compatible with cleaner production's espoused commitment to sustainable development.

Hirschhorn is right in his critique. To be successful, proponents of pollution prevention must cast a big and bold vision. In essence, the prevention movement needs to recapture the inspirational vision of its founders. To date, it largely has been a vision waylaid by the incremental proclivities of those who eventually implemented that vision, by powerful interests for whom the financial incentives of more limited approaches were not obvious, and by the absence of a politically compelling agenda to support more aggressive action. Establishing this agenda, however, will require walking a fine line.

In daily practice, pollution prevention needs to be implemented as a site-specific and detailed set of technical tasks bent on improving the efficiency of existing regulatory regimes. It also must offer clearly specified and demonstrable market incentives that upper-level managers and professionals understand and value. At a national political level, however, advocacy for prevention must take on an ambitious and transformative edge, one embodying a visible and well-articulated national commitment to cleaner production as an antidote to the inherent incompatibilities between industrial production and broader environmental goals.

At a minimum, leaders in national and state offices must choose to dedicate themselves to promoting pollution prevention. Nor will any one set of government policy or program instruments be effective. What is more, proponents must link the promotion of pollution prevention to tightening regulations and enforcement. In turn, effective enforcement needs to be coupled with plenty of professional education and training, technical assistance, and support for research, testing, and piloting. All of this, of course, requires money. Government pollution prevention programs need to be reasonably funded and adequately staffed. Most definitely, the international experiences with cleaner production demonstrate the value of well-targeted economic assistance programs and private financial and insurance services that offer market-based economic incentives.

Even all this, however, will not be enough. As noted earlier, reformers advocating change must persistently choose to make reform economically advantageous to regulatory targets. Pollution prevention needs to be about industrial modernization and the economic benefits derivable from it. It needs to promote new materials and new equipment. It needs to go beyond merely touting the cost savings for pollution generators and on to promoting the economic benefits that greener chemistries and cleaner technologies will accrue to pollution generators, material suppliers, and technology vendors.

Furthermore, if international experiences in the environmental and health policy arenas are any guide, pollution prevention must be cast in the language of process innovation, product enhancement, and production efficiencies. Here again, these changes must yield improvements that production and business managers can understand and appreciate. At the firm level, and as Jan Mazurek describes in chapter 13, policymakers need to encourage the utilization of environmental management systems that promote and measure pollution prevention outcomes. Moreover, these systems must be "sold" to companies as adjuncts to conventional business management systems that measure economic outcomes. Finally, pollution prevention must address products and the organization of consumption at the community and national levels. The use of products and their disposal needs to be organized so as to minimize waste and eliminate pollution over the entire product lifecycle. Put simply, to reach its full potential, pollution prevention needs to be more like cleaner production.

In sum, as we struggle to determine how to achieve the sustainable economy that Robert Paehlke and Gary Bryner discuss in greater depth in chapters 1 and 2, prevention can continue to be a valuable tool. But prevention alone will not get us there. A prevention approach that focuses on reducing risks and avoiding hazards must be accompanied by an assertive approach such as cleaner production that promotes health and encourages the safest and most environmentally compatible forms of production and consumption. Otherwise, the potential for pollution prevention to become a tool for building a results-based sense of common purpose in environmental governance will die aborning.

All this, however, leads to a final and particularly daunting strategic challenge for the United States. Preventing pollution, as noted, fits within the cleaner production approach, but the latter offers a much more ambitious vision. The two approaches, in turn, grow out of and respond to different social and economic perspectives on the role of government in the countries where they have been adopted. The more centralist planning and prescriptive orientation among European governments and among countries with national development plans encourages the cleaner production approach. It fits comfortably into national industrial development policymaking. In contrast, the more minimalist orientation toward government in the United States has discouraged broad national industrial policies and, instead, has encouraged the more limited pollution prevention approach that so far has prevailed in the nation.

Will the realities that conventional approaches to pollution prevention have exposed about the incompatibility between industrial production and broader environmental goals be compelling enough to overcome the formidable obstacles to adopting cleaner production in the United States? Can the nation overcome what Paehlke calls its "cowboy culture" of economic development? Can it eventually embrace what Bryner calls a "thick" or "strong" notion of ecological sustainability? This task will be a difficult one, and its result is presently unclear. But, not unlike the chapters by Fiorino and Mazurek that discuss market-based and corporate-driven ENR approaches, this chapter has offered the rudiments of a strategy and tactics for advancing reforms that are grounded in the market-driven and political realities of the U.S. economy and government.

One thing *is* clear, however. If the United States continues to choose a conventional pollution prevention strategy, that strategy will be too ad hoc, piecemeal, and uninspiring to be effective. It will continue to lose its capacity to become a vehicle for building a results-based sense of common purpose in environmental governance. Like a boat without a rudder, conventional pollution prevention approaches may stay afloat, but they will not reach the desired destination. The way forward toward sustainability requires a prevention approach that is nested carefully in a more positive and more goal-informed strategy for cleaner production and sustainable consumption.

Notes

1. See J. Clarence Davies and Jan Mazurek, *Pollution Control in the United States: Evaluating the System* (Washington, D.C.: Resources for the Future, 1998); U.S. Environmental Protection Agency (EPA), Office of Air Quality Planning and Standards Research, *National Air Pollutant Emissions Trends, 1900–1995* (Washington, D.C.: EPA, 1996); U.S. EPA, Office of Water, *National*

Water Quality Inventory, 1994 Report to Congress (Washington, D.C.: EPA, 1995).

2. In employing the paradigm shift metaphor, the early pollution prevention proponents drew on Thomas Kuhn's description of shifts in ways of thinking that mark critical revolutions in scientific explanations. Kuhn argued that science advanced through recognizable and discontinuous "paradigm shifts," and pollution prevention advocates used this concept to characterize the discontinuous and revolutionary way in which this new approach might void and substitute for the older approach. See Thomas Kuhn, *The Structure of Scientific Revolutions,* 2d ed. (Chicago: University of Chicago Press, 1970).

3. See U.S. Congress, Office of Technology Assessment, *Serious Reduction of Hazardous Waste: For Pollution Prevention and Industrial Efficiency* (Washington, D.C.: Government Printing Office, September 1986). For a compilation of pollution prevention techniques, see Harry M. Freeman, ed., *Industrial Pollution Prevention Handbook* (New York: McGraw-Hill, 1995).

4. See Thomas W. Zosel, "How 3M Makes Pollution Prevention Pay Big Dividends," *Pollution Prevention Review* 1(1) (winter 1990–91): 67–68; Larry J. Nielsen, "How Digital Uses Measurement Techniques in Managing Packaging Waste," *Pollution Prevention Review* (summer 1991): 247–256; Jeffrey R. Kirk, "A Methodology for Waste Minimization Project Selection at a Hoechst Celanese Manufacturing Facility," *Pollution Prevention Review* (spring 1994): 191–198.

5. See U.S. EPA, Science Advisory Board, *Future Risks: Research Strategies for the 1990s,* SAB-EC-88-40 (Washington, D.C.: EPA, September 1988); U.S. Congress, *Pollution Prevention Act of 1990,* P.L. 101-508, 42 U.S.C.A. sec. 13101–13109.

6. See U.S. EPA, *Pollution Prevention Strategy* (Washington, D.C.: EPA, May 1992). For reviews of EPA initiatives, see Harry M. Freeman, "Pollution Prevention: The U.S. Experience," *Environmental Progress* 14(4) (November 1995): 214–219; U.S. EPA, Office of Pollution Prevention and Toxics, *Pollution Prevention 1997: A National Progress Report,* 742-R-97-00 (Washington, D.C.: EPA, 1997).

7. Joel S. Hirschhorn, "Why the Pollution Prevention Revolution Failed—and Why It Ultimately Will Succeed," *Pollution Prevention Review* 5(2) (winter 1997), p. 11.

8. Ibid.

9. Warren Muir, "Facing Facts," in U.S. EPA, *Pollution Prevention 1997,* p. 242.

10. Robert Gottlieb, *Environmentalism Unbound: Exploring New Pathways for Change* (Cambridge, Mass.: MIT Press, 2001), p. 79.

11. For similar arguments, see Ken Geiser, "Can the P2 Revolution Be Restated?" *Pollution Prevention Review* 8(3) (summer 1998): 71–80.

12. U.S. EPA, *Preventing Pollution Through Regulations: The Source Reduction Review Project* (Washington, D.C.: EPA, February 1996).

13. Nicholas Ashford has argued that it is the consistency and stringency of regulations that drive innovations in environmental technologies. See N. Ashford, C. Ayers, and R. Stone, "Using Regulations to Change the Market for Innovation," *Harvard Environmental Law Review* 9(2) (1985): 419–466. For more detailed arguments, see U.S. General Accounting Office (GAO), *Environmental Protection: EPA Should Strengthen Its Efforts to Measure and Encourage Pollution Prevention*, GAO-01-283 (Washington, D.C.: GAO, February 2001); Thomas Eggert, "Moving Forward by Looking Back: The Role of Enforcement in Promoting P2," *Pollution Prevention Review* 9(2) (spring 1999): 1–5.

14. United Nations Environment Program (UNEP), Industry and Environment Program, *Cleaner Production Program,* brochure (Paris: UNEP, 1992), p. 1.

15. John S. Dryzek and David Schlosberg, eds., *Debating the Earth: The Environmental Politics Reader* (New York: Oxford University Press, 1998), p. 299.

16. "Sustainable Consumption and Cleaner Production: Two Sides of the Same Coin," *Industry and Environment* (a UNEP periodical) 24(1–2) (January–June 2001): 37–40.

17. Per Bakken, "Using Cleaner Production to Achieve Implementation of MEAs," *Industry and Environment* 24(1–2) (January–June 2001): 54–56.

18. For the early arguments of cleaner production advocates, see Kim Christiansen and John Kryger, "Promotion and Implementation of Cleaner Technologies in Danish Industries," *Environmental Professional* 11(3) (1989): 199–208; L. W. Baas, M. van der Belt, D. Huisingh, and F. Neumann, "Cleaner Production: What Some Governments Are Doing and What All Governments Can Do to Promote Sustainability," *European Water Pollution Control* 2(1) (1992): 10–25. For the role of regulations, see UNEP, Industry and Environment Program Activity Center, *Government Strategies and Policies for Cleaner Production* (Paris: UNEP, 1994). For cleaner production in industrializing countries, see UNEP, Industry and Environment Program Activity Center, *Cleaner Production Worldwide* (Paris: UNEP, 1993); UNEP, Industry and Environment Program Activity Center, *Cleaner Production in the Asia Pacific Economic Cooperation Region* (Paris: UNEP, 1994).

19. Joseph J. Romm, *Lean and Clean Management: How to Boost Profits and Productivity by Reducing Pollution* (New York: Kodansha, 1994).

20. The Dutch first launched their national program in 1985 from the central Office on Clean Technologies, and the Thai government recently restructured its national technology transfer office into the Office for Clean Technology Transfer.

21. Lemuel Shattuck, N. P. Banks, and Jeheil Abbott, *Report of a General Plan for the Promotion of Public and Personal Health* (Boston: Dutton and Wentworth State Printers, 1850; reprint, New York: Arno and the *New York Times*, 1972), p. 228.

22. Virginia Aita and Benjamin Crabtree, "Historical Reflections on Current Preventive Practice," *Preventive Medicine* 30 (2000): 5–16; Steven H. Woolf and

David Atkins, "The Evolving Role of Prevention in Health Care: Contributions of the U.S. Preventive Health Services Task Force," *American Journal of Preventive Medicine* 20(3S) (2001): 13–20.

23. Primary and secondary prevention typically are seen in a hierarchy of preference, with primary preferred to secondary and with medical treatment (tertiary prevention) seen as the least-preferred form of intervention. For a description and illustration, see H. O. Adami, N. E. Day, D. Trihopoulos, and W. C. Willett, "Primary and Secondary Prevention in the Reduction of Cancer Morbidity and Mortality," *European Journal of Cancer* 37 (2001): S118–S127.

24. U.S. Preventive Services Task Force, *Guide to Clinical Preventive Services*, 2d ed. (Washington, D.C.: Office of Disease Prevention and Health Promotion, U.S. Government Printing Office, 1996), p. 10.

25. World Health Organization (WHO), *Ottawa Charter for Health Promotion* (Geneva: WHO, 1986), p. 1.

26. See Don Nutbeam, "Evaluating Health Promotion—Progress, Problems and Solutions," *Health Promotion International* 13(1) (1998): 27–44.

27. Colin Sindall, "Health Promotion and Chronic Disease: Building on the Ottawa Charter, Not Betraying It?" *Health Promotion International* 16(3) (2001): 215–217.

28. Ibid., p. 217.

13

Third-Party Auditing of Environmental Management Systems

Jan Mazurek

As Ken Geiser argues in chapter 12 in this volume, proponents of pollution prevention in the United States initially envisioned a very comprehensive, ambitious, and proactive agenda that moved away from traditional end-of-pipe approaches to fundamental changes in business production processes. As he also contends, however, a variety of factors derailed this originally very ambitious agenda. Included among these factors were the departure of early visionaries from positions of power, the magnitude of the changes necessary to production processes, and the perverse incentives (professional, business, and organizational) preventing businesses from pursuing the necessary changes. Together, they wrought formidable resistance to all but incremental changes. Thus, in arguing for a return to that more ambitious agenda embodied in the "cleaner production movement," Geiser points out how important it is for reformers to reframe their vision less in terms of business problems to be avoided and more in terms of business advantages for the bottom line to be gained.

Perhaps nowhere are these dynamics more at work or is the logic of Geiser's argument better illustrated for the regulatory *and* regulated communities than in the international movement toward adopting environmental management systems (EMSs) as tools for building a results-based sense of common purpose in environmental governance. Unlike ad hoc efforts to control pollution, an EMS is a formalized set of management procedures and measurement tools designed to improve an organization's environmental performance. Patterned after business systems to improve product quality, an EMS is comprised of a set of iterative housekeeping and accounting procedures. In general, these steps require firms to develop an environmental management plan and a set of actions to implement that plan. The planning stage typically requires firms to assess all of the environmental impacts—regulated and unregulated—generated by their business activity. The EMS plan thus becomes a set of actions designed to minimize these impacts. Then, to promote continuous environmental improvement, EMSs typically put into place a set of procedures to verify that the management plan is working and, where necessary, to develop a set of corrective actions to ensure that the plan is reducing the firm's environmental impacts.

Because EMS adoption is voluntary, why would any organization (public or private) adopt such a system? Motivations for an individual organization to adopt an EMS may include greater assurance that it is in compliance with all applicable environmental laws and regulations or that it can minimize legal liability. Other motives include saving money by employing resources more efficiently and achieving more uniform environmental reporting, documentation, and employee training procedures. On a larger scale, and as globalization of raw materials extraction and manufacturing expanded rapidly in the 1990s, large businesses faced growing public pressure to assume responsibility for the impacts of their activities on the environment. They also faced disparate environmental and natural resources (ENR) compliance standards in different countries. These standards sorely complicated their ability to market their products internationally unless they made significant and costly changes to their production lines to meet them. At the same time, many businesses operated in less-developed countries, where standards for performance can be highly varied, sometimes absent, or, more often, codified on paper but inconsistently or ineffectively enforced.

Thus, to facilitate the exchange of goods and services worldwide, businesses in recent years have developed international standards to make their EMSs more uniform. They have done so in part in the hope of gaining market advantage by persuading customers that they are more socially responsible industries and corporations than are their competitors. But they have also done so in the hope of shifting regulators' focus away from traditional enforcement of compliance standards for pollutants and toward the "greening" of the *processes* that produce them. More precisely, businesses have developed their own EMS standards, created various third-party auditing mechanisms to certify compliance with them, and tried to persuade nations and states to accept these mechanisms as evidence of regulatory compliance.

In some cases, specific firms unilaterally have implemented a set of ENR goals and practices (for example, the Home Depot's policy to use third-party verification to ensure its wood products promote more sustainable forestry practices). In other cases, industry trade associations have developed codes of conduct that apply to the entire sector. One such example is the chemical industry's Responsible Care Program, developed by industry trade associations after the 1984 disaster that killed 3,000 people at a Union Carbide subsidiary plant in Bhopal, India. The most widely adopted EMS to date, however, is the so-called 14001 series of international voluntary environmental standards issued by the International Organization for Standardization (ISO). Regardless of which approach is taken, however, auditing (either self-auditing or third-party auditing) is critical to the process.

For their part, regulators in various nations see virtue in third-party auditing approaches such as ISO 14001. Thus, although largely businesses develop these types of certification approaches, some government officials see them as a potentially promising public policy tool. In the United States, for example, a small but growing number of federal and state regulators see auditing of a firm's EMS as a way to direct scarce public resources toward the most pressing health and environmental risks. If EMSs can assure regulators that entities can manage environmental impacts effectively, regulators can redirect their resources toward other less well-managed facilities that might pose greater hazards. In part with these gains in mind, the U.S. Environmental Protection Agency (EPA), with strong backing by the George W. Bush administration, issued in 2002 several landmark policy statements that offer a strong endorsement of third-party EMS auditing strategies for the regulated community.[1]

Despite the growing popularity of third-party EMS auditing initiatives, however, their prospects as public policy tools for helping avoid adversarial regulatory processes are clouded by a variety of factors. Prominent among these factors is confusion among different stakeholders about the ultimate purposes of this approach to environmental governance. Some environmental regulators, for example, consider third-party EMS auditing to be privatized regulation, substituting—to a manageable yet significant degree—for compliance monitoring and inspection in some facilities. Some environmental groups perceive these programs as a business-controlled, and therefore not credible, substitute for compliance verification. Other environmentalists, however, see them in a positive light, as yet another environmental cop or unannounced inspector to catch facilities that violate regulatory requirements. Meanwhile, although some businesses envision EMS auditing as justification for regulatory or public-recognition benefits, others prefer that it remain a strictly voluntary, "by-business-for-business" framework for management improvement. Finally, and further complicating the matter, concern has arisen about auditors' rigor in evaluating whether a company's EMS practices conform to the ISO 14001 series standards.[2] Such concerns are fueled by recent disclosures in the financial securities industry involving the auditing inaccuracies of prominent U.S. companies such as Enron, WorldCom, and Xerox.

This chapter argues that the source of these different expectations and concerns regarding third-party EMS auditing stems from confusing it with other types of financial, environmental, and voluntary auditing so that all the shortcomings of those other types of auditing are applied to third-party EMS auditing as well. Consequently, the future of third-party auditing as a politically viable, effective, and credible tool for building a results-based sense of common purpose in environmental governance depends on the extent to which proponents can do two things: incorporate into it the strengths of other types of auditing and remedy their shortcomings. To understand better how these differing expectations have emerged and persisted, as well as what the future might hold for certification as a tool of environmental governance if they are left unresolved, the chapter first reviews the logic and forces driving the movement to adopt EMSs worldwide. It chronicles a variety of social, economic, and political forces that have prompted businesses worldwide to see certification as an attractive alternative to traditional reactive approaches to ENR regulation.

The chapter turns next to chronicling the commonalities and differences among third-party EMS auditing, financial auditing, compliance auditing, and voluntary auditing programs. Because analyzing all of the permutations of different EMS systems is beyond the scope of the chapter, the analytical focus of this section is one increasingly popular form of third-party EMS certification in the United States: ISO 14001. The analysis also holds lessons more broadly for those interested in third-party certification processes used worldwide and for environmental managers who contemplate the use of independent auditors in other contexts as well.

The chapter concludes by discussing the implications of these conflicting expectations and concerns for the future of third-party EMS auditing in particular and for certification programs in general. It suggests what proponents of third-party EMS auditing as a tool for building a results-based sense of common purpose in environmental governance will have to do to advance their cause. It also emphasizes three sets of formidable strategic challenges, choices, and opportunities for using third-party auditing of EMSs: proponents must distinguish it better from existing types of auditing; build trust in its operations, embracing the strengths and avoiding the weaknesses of other types of auditing; and persuade stakeholders that third-party EMS auditing has both managerial and public interest-oriented purposes.

Third-Party EMS Auditing: From Reaction to Proaction in the Regulatory Community

The third-party auditing movement and its most prominent variant, ISO 14001, may be understood as industry's effort during the past two decades to stop simply reacting to environmental laws and regulations. The aim instead is to take a more *proactive* approach in which businesses seek to manage environmental impacts more effectively and efficiently. Not only has this movement drawn momentum from the globalization of world markets, but the challenges to that market system have helped to shape its contours as well. In particular, the globalization of raw materials extraction, supply, and manufacturing, as well as international efforts to promote sustainability, spawned industry efforts at self-regulation. These efforts, in turn, have come packaged in a variety of approaches to EMSs. What these approaches share in common, however, is the need for accurate, credible, and understandable information. In the United

States and abroad, this need has created political controversy over third-party EMS auditing initiatives, especially as to their merits as tools of environmental governance in the twenty-first century.

The Political Economy of Third-Party Auditing

The advent and proliferation of industry self-regulation with third-party auditing approaches came in response to several political and economic factors. At one level, self-regulation is a response by businesses to public pressure to improve environmental management. Responsible Care, for example, was designed to improve how chemical companies manage their environmental activities. Participants are required to adopt and implement six management practice codes that govern activities ranging from pollution prevention to product stewardship. To ensure that management practices are consistent with Responsible Care's requirements, participants are encouraged to undertake informal verification exercises.

At another level, self-regulation initiatives may be viewed as part of an international effort to address uneven economic, legal, and institutional capacities. As Robert Paehlke and Gary Bryner discuss more extensively in chapters 1 and 2, the Brundtland Commission launched the concept of "sustainability" in its 1987 report *Our Common Future*. This seminal report popularized the concept of sustainability as a way to reconcile what formerly were perceived as the competing objectives of economic development and environmental protection. Some business organizations with operations worldwide reacted to the report by adopting voluntary codes. For instance, the International Chamber of Commerce (ICC) adopted the Business Charter for Sustainable Development.[3] The charter sought to promote continual improvements in how businesses managed their environmental impacts.

In turn, the use of EMSs as an especially appropriate way to achieve these goals was popularized in response to the 1992 United Nations (UN) Conference on Environment and Development, also known as the Rio "Earth Summit." In the early 1990s, the ICC began to require its member companies to adopt EMSs as a way to promote the objectives advanced in Rio.[4] To ensure further that these EMSs were designed to advance the goals of sustainable development, it required participating companies to conduct periodic audits. Nor has the salience of this approach diminished in recent years, as shown by several related initiatives at the 2002 UN World Summit on Sustainability in Johannesburg, South Africa.

In addition to these initiatives, a separate but related movement arose during the same period to improve public reporting of environmental performance. Among the most notable was an initiative designed to leverage the power of the financial industry to promote socially responsible corporate behavior. The Coalition for Environmentally Responsible Economies (CERES) was established in 1989 by investor, environmental, and advocacy groups to promote sustainability through more systematic reporting of firms' environmental management practices. The CERES principles not only encouraged firms to undergo periodic self-audits, but also launched the Global Reporting Initiative (GRI). GRI is designed to find agreement among businesses, environmental groups, accounting firms, and others on guidelines for standardized environmental management and sustainability reporting. To this end, it has adopted a hierarchy for organizing and presenting information in sustainability reports.[5]

Using an EMS as a Basis for Certification

Although the use of EMSs and independent auditors is not an explicit requirement of most of the initiatives covered in the previous section, all of the initiatives at least implicitly encouraged the use of self-audits to make corporate environmental practices more rigorous and more uniform. Not surprisingly, when EMSs were first developed, the absence of a consensus on the desired ends and on what constituted an effective EMS led to various approaches. Indeed, each system developed was as unique as the company or public agency that put it into place. In recent years, however, several industry-based and international harmonization efforts have been launched to make EMSs more uniform and to advance substantive public policy goals (for example, to reduce the problems of dealing with different compliance regulations in different nations).

In this respect, two initiatives that may be considered ISO 14001's most direct antecedents are the British Standard (BS) 7750 Specification for Environmental Management Systems and the European Union's Eco-Management and Audit Scheme (EMAS). As a way to promote

EMS harmonization, the British Standards Institute published BS 7750 in 1992. BS 7750 was designed to apply to all types of organizations, both public and private, large and small, rather than to an individual firm or industry sector. The standard required organizations to develop an environmental policy and an inventory of the actual and potential effects of its activities on the environment.

In contrast to BS 7750, which was designed more to promote harmonization of various EMSs, the EMAS may be considered the first EMS initiative designed to advance public policy goals. Developed by the European Union, the EMAS is a voluntary regulation mechanism designed to use EMSs as a way to promote the principles of sustainability. Like BS 7750, the EMAS requires participating businesses to develop an environmental policy and an EMS. Unlike BS 7750, the EMAS also requires participants to prepare a public environmental statement that has to be audited by independent third-party auditors to verify its content and to ensure that it advances sustainability goals. But what was third-party auditing supposed to deliver in the way of ENR performance? What criteria were auditors to apply in conducting audits? What methods were they to use to advance these purposes? The EMAS was decidedly unclear in its answers to any of these questions. Indeed, significant efforts to answer them had to wait until the members of the ISO met to develop the ISO 14001 series.

The Advent of ISO 14001

ISO 14001, developed in 1996, reflects many of the features of its predecessors. The ISO fundamentally designed it as a way for businesses worldwide to harmonize their EMSs. Harmonization would give companies that operated in varied regulatory regimes a consistent set of environmental management practices. To the degree that ISO 14001 promotes consistent practices that conform to one universal standard, it also promotes trade.

In terms of specific requirements, ISO 14001, like a number of its predecessors, requires participants to develop an environmental policy. Moreover, like the EMAS, it also requires firms to develop a public environmental statement. At its heart, ISO 14001 consists of a set of management practices to promote such environmental goals as prevention of pollution and continual environmental improvement. To achieve these ends, ISO 14001 directs participating companies to initiate an elaborate planning process that identifies all environmental aspects and impacts of a facility's operations, products, and services, along with other applicable legal and nonbinding requirements.

Finally, to bring rigor and discipline to EMSs, ISO 14001 gives implementing organizations the option—not a mandatory requirement—to use third-party auditors to assess whether the EMS continually is improving. In the United States, the American National Standards Institute and the Registrar Accreditation Board jointly administer the National Accreditation Program, a private program designed to ensure that EMS auditing methods conform to national and international standards.

Despite this attempt at discipline, expectations surrounding what third-party auditing is supposed to deliver stem in part from ambiguities in the ISO 14001 standard. The requirements drafted originally in the early 1990s for organizations and auditors who checked EMS conformance were the product of considerable disagreement among the delegations from around the world that drafted them. This disagreement was particularly acute concerning the definitions and interpretations of "continual environmental improvement" and "prevention of pollution." According to one author, there existed "a deep chasm [on these points] between various ISO 14001 . . . authors."[6]

European delegations, influenced by the EMAS, wanted to measure environmental improvement in terms of reduced environmental *impacts,* such as reduced toxic pollutants. However, the U.S. delegation argued that continual improvement should be measured on enhancements to the *performance* of the EMS itself, such as internal auditors' performance in identifying nonconformances. To date, the entities charged with accrediting third-party EMS auditors in the United States largely have refrained from developing specific guidance on how auditors should assess continual improvement and prevention of pollution.[7]

In sum, a variety of forces have propelled the salience and use of third-party EMS auditing as an alternative to traditional regulation worldwide. In turn, a variety of approaches to self-regulation lie within the general rubric of audit-based initiatives, each experiencing various levels of success. To date, however, one of the major dilemmas plaguing the widespread acceptance of third-party EMS auditing systems is the existence and persistence of differing expectations about what it is supposed to accomplish, in what ways, and how other tools of environmental governance can leverage its strengths and compensate for its weaknesses.

Trust, Transparency, and Third-Party EMS Auditing: A Comparative Perspective

To show more fully why differing expectations exist, and why these expectations generate concerns about using third-party auditing approaches as tools for building a results-based sense of common purpose in environmental governance, this section focuses on the travails of adopting ISO 14001 in the United States. Confusion over the relationship between ISO 14001 and three prior and existing models of auditing is arguably most responsible for this dilemma. The first model, related to auditing in general, is the standard financial auditing model. The other two models, both predecessors in the ENR policy arena, are environmental compliance audits and voluntary ENR programs based on audits. Almost inevitably, proponents and opponents of third-party EMS auditing conceptualize its strengths and weaknesses differently, depending on which of the three prior auditing models they have in mind.

Financial Audits
One highly touted model for EMS auditing was until recently the widely used independent audit of public corporations' and nonprofit organizations' financial statements. Owing to recent scandals involving a few high-profile corporations and their financial accounting firms, however, the promise of this model now has been cast into doubt. During the late 1990s, a small but growing group of state and federal environmental regulators looked to this "financial" or "Securities and Exchange Commission (SEC)" model as a way to make public environmental policies more effective and efficient. To them, it offered hope that a public agency could harness private third parties to conduct EMS auditing and oversight. Some government programs also have used EMS audits on a pilot basis as potential tools for assuring environmental performance. For example,

EPA New England's Star Track initiative, which includes EMS implementation and auditing as an element, was patterned in part after methods the SEC employed.

The EMS third-party auditing system is designed not only to ensure conformity and adherence to the ISO 14001 standard, but also to provide assurance of conformity to stakeholders who are external to the audited organization. In this latter regard, EMS auditing resembles financial auditing; the performance of one firm is not measured relative to others. It differs strikingly from financial auditing, however, in that EMS auditors, unlike financial accountants, are not required to adhere to externally defined professional standards. For example, the SEC places two requirements on certified public accountants (CPAs) who audit an organization's financial statement. They must be licensed and in good standing with a state board of accountancy, and they must be professionally independent of the organization they audit.[8] These requirements by themselves obviously do not confirm fully the quality of financial audits. Thus, to monitor and assure the quality-control systems for CPAs, the SEC also relies on private organizations. Thus, 97 percent of U.S. organizations are audited by CPA firms that themselves undergo periodic "peer reviews."[9]

Also unlike the SEC model, third-party EMS auditing in the United States remains primarily a *private* system. Whereas the public SEC registers financial auditing systems and oversees auditing practice standards, a private organization—the National Accreditation Program—oversees the EMS third-party auditing system. One major consequence of this difference is a disparity in the approaches that the two systems take to transparency. Because the SEC's purpose is to assure investors of the truthfulness of financial disclosures, financial audit findings—unlike EMS audit findings—are accompanied by a detailed public report of financial performance.

Were these differences not enough to raise concerns about this tool of environmental governance, many critics argue that third-party auditing approaches also suffer from guilt by association with the financial audit model. Most salient here are concerns related to auditor independence. Critics of ISO 14001 auditing, for example, routinely note that the financial accounting profession does not always set an ideal example. As the Arthur Anderson fiasco so vividly illustrates, financial accounting firms have built lucrative consulting businesses that sometimes conflict with the required independence of their financial audits. The profitable nature of consulting has led to its increase because accounting firms tend to earn more from it than from auditing. Since 1993, for example, the auditing revenues of accounting firms have grown at only 9 percent annually, but their fees for consulting and similar services have grown at a 27 percent rate.[10]

Thus, well before Enron, some analysts—including former SEC chairman Arthur Leavitt—were concerned about this potential conflict of interest wherein accounting firms also sell consulting services.[11] Over the years prior to Enron, in fact, the SEC brought hundreds of lawsuits and other actions based on accounting rule violations, many of which involved questions about auditor independence.[12] The SEC more recently (yet still prior to Enron) had focused on the amount of wealth that accounting firms and employees derived from their consulting business. In all cases, however, the concern was (and remains) whether accountants will audit rigorously those numbers that their own firm (as consultants) produces, as a truly independent auditor would.[13]

Also prior to Enron, the SEC established conflict-of-interest rules that govern financial auditor independence. Similar limitations in the ISO 14001 standards for EMS auditors and auditing firms prevent them from selling consulting services to audited clients. Yet, under SEC rules, independence refers primarily to the specific principle that auditors must not have any *ownership interests* in the companies audited. Moreover, these SEC rules until recently have been applied only to accounting firms that derive a significant share of their income through services other than auditing.[14]

It was, however, the Enron scandal and the travails of its equally troubled accounting firm, Arthur Anderson, that brought vividly to the public's imagination the reality of this conflict of interest. Anderson's auditors were alleged to have failed on a variety of occasions to report to the investing public a number of financial irregularities that masked Enron's overstatement of earnings by more than $580 million. In response, many critics of the system have encouraged the SEC to *require* accounting firms to divest or separate the two functions. Yet, as of this writing, the U.S. Congress has not made separation of these two functions a mandatory requirement.

As recent events at Enron, WorldCom, and Xerox (among others) suggest, however, even financial attestation, random system checks, and conflict-of-interest rules do not mean that the information reported is accurate or that deliberate malfeasance is avoided. Indeed, the information chicanery may be startling. Even when mischief is not afoot, financial attestation and random system checks cannot guarantee that the information contained in one company's financial statements is more accurate than the information disclosed in another's report.

These caveats notwithstanding, however, the need to pursue efforts like these to ensure the transparency, integrity, and honesty of the EMS auditing system cannot be overstated. Whether in conventional financial auditing or third-party EMS auditing, stakeholder trust is critical. To this end, financial audits of publicly traded businesses are *mandatory* and *externally driven*. Yet EMS auditing remains a *voluntary, internally driven* practice. Thus, whereas auditing the financial statements of SEC-regulated companies (warts and all) is intended to assure the truthfulness and full disclosure of financial information, EMS auditing remains largely a voluntary initiative by business for business. As a consequence, businesses perceive it merely as yet another *optional* tool in the sound management of an organization's operations, along with best practices, compliance with applicable laws, and the general duty to safeguard the public against corporate negligence. And this, fairly or unfairly, makes many ENR stakeholders and members of the public highly skeptical of the EMS auditing model.

Compliance Audits

A second model of auditing that has exacerbated confusion over the strengths and weaknesses of ISO 14001 certification is environmental compliance audits. Many regulated businesses in the United States began to undertake compliance audits (or environmental audits) voluntarily during the 1970s, in part in response to the spate of federal statutes enacted during that period. Companies saw these audits as a means to evaluate compliance with environmental regulation, to assess their potential liability for noncompliance, and to correct these problems to avoid fines.

Compliance auditing then accelerated during the 1980s and 1990s in response to the strict liabilities associated with Superfund. Lending institutions and insurance firms began to require due-diligence audits in financial transactions involving real estate. Thus, by the late 1990s, 75 percent of all U.S. industry was engaged in some form of internal environmental auditing.[15] In turn, as reliance on compliance audits increased, professional organizations, consulting firms, and standards organizations began to develop auditing procedures, guidelines, and standards.[16] They were joined in 1986 by the EPA as it began to develop its own audit policies.

The EPA defined environmental auditing as a "systematic, documented, periodic and objective review by regulated entities of facility operations and practices related to meeting environmental requirements."[17] Under the EPA's definition, auditing can meet several objectives: verifying compliance with environmental laws and regulations, evaluating the effectiveness of systems in place to manage environmental responsibilities, and assessing the risks from regulated and unregulated activities in facility operations.

Despite the apparent straightforwardness of these aims, one of the most vexing problems regarding compliance audits has been the regulated community's fear about how the information collected will be used. An audit by its very nature is designed to find violations. Thus, producing such information and making it available to a third-party auditor may trigger legal consequences, such as immediate disclosure, lawsuits, and sanctions. Consequently, businesses maintain that they face an untenable Hobson's choice: they can choose to hide the information and hope environmental regulators will not find it, or they can report the violation and face stiff penalties. Such fears are, of course, equally germane to ISO 14001 auditing practices.

Responding to this dilemma in the 1990s, both the EPA and state environmental agencies addressed what happens when a company's compliance audit detects violations. They sometimes did so, however, in ways that sent conflicting signals to industry. On the one hand, some states adopted audit privilege and immunity laws, which would grant businesses, municipalities, and other entities "safe passage" to conduct self-audits and then disclose and correct any violations. Approximately twenty states have enacted these laws, and ten more considered them during 2001. On the other hand, the EPA has tried to dissuade state legislatures from adopting some versions of these laws, especially those laws that may allow businesses to hide information about violations rather than make them public. Together, these actions not only send mixed signals, but also can undercut the states' ability to carry out their delegated responsibilities for enforcement of federal environmental statutes.

At the same time, since 1995 the EPA also has initiated a series of policies targeted at firms to promote compliance auditing, ranging from reduced penalties to increased rewards such as public recognition. It also has developed and recently updated its own compliance-oriented audit policy for encouraging firms to self-disclose violations voluntarily. Included are such incentives as eliminating or substantially reducing the gravity of civil penalties and recommending against criminal prosecution of the disclosing entity. The updated audit policy also restates the EPA's long-standing practice of not using requests for copies of voluntary audit reports as triggers for federal enforcement actions.[18] Some states, in response, have adopted this approach rather than create audit-privilege and use-immunity laws for self-disclosure of environmental violations.

The rub remains, however, that whenever a facility invites a third-party auditor to review its operations, it accepts the possibility that the auditor will discover problems that otherwise would not have been identified. In this respect, an EMS audit is similar to compliance auditing. As in a compliance audit, the auditor's job is to look for weaknesses, including evidence demonstrating whether the firm understands its legal obligations and is capable of identifying and fixing any actual or potential noncompliance situations. Companies that genuinely seek to carry out consistent and superior environmental management welcome these findings as a key step toward correcting and improving deficiencies. Companies that only want to be reassured or certified for what they already are doing may find these discoveries unwelcome.

It is also important to note, however, that compliance audits and EMS audits have different yet intersecting purposes. The former are designed to ensure that an organization complies with all regulatory requirements, whereas the latter seek to make certain that an organization's EMS conforms to ISO 14001 standards. These standards require an organization to commit to legal and regulatory compliance and to demonstrate that it has a continuously improving EMS that will implement and fulfill effectively its commitment to compliance. However, ISO 14001 does *not* require an organization to maintain compliance with regulatory requirements. In fact, EMS auditors are neither trained nor expected to serve as compliance auditors. Nor do they take responsibility for assuring that effective management systems are in place to prevent recurrence of violations.

This difference also means that, in principle, compliance audits are somewhat more straightforward than EMS audits. The compliance auditor's task, after all, is a relatively more *objective* one: to determine compliance with specific regulations. To be sure, not unlike an EMS audit, a compliance audit requires detailed familiarity with complex federal and state regulations, as well as with the performance of environmental monitoring and control technologies used for achieving and maintaining compliance. Moreover, as in EMS auditing, compliance is not always based on a single event, but more likely on a series of events over an extended period of time. EMS audits, however, require the auditor to make more *subjective* decisions because there are few clearly right or wrong ways for managing and demonstrating continuous improvements in an EMS.

The EMS auditor's *duties* are, however, quite straightforward: to determine conformance or nonconformance with all elements of the ISO standards that apply to a firm's scope of operations. In so doing, EMS auditors do *not* judge regulatory compliance or noncompliance in a particular instance, nor do they systematically evaluate all possible sources of regulatory noncompliance. Rather, they try to identify actual and potential noncompliance situations and to ensure that an EMS system is in place that is capable of correcting, anticipating, and making these situations less likely to occur or recur in the future.

Not surprisingly, then, the different purposes of compliance audits and EMS audits mean that they also use different measures to gauge success. A compliance audit judges the organization's behavior in terms of its compliance with externally driven regulations, whereas an EMS audit charts the organization's behavior against its *own* professed aims (for example, standards and processes) in creating the EMS. Thus, at one level, the success of a compliance audit is based on reducing the number of noncompliance findings identified in a report; the success of an EMS audit is based on the clarity and accuracy of the findings identified so that problems in the EMS that may be precluding continuous ENR improvements can be addressed.[19] Nor can a third-party EMS audit, including ISO 14001 certification, be characterized as an environmental compliance inspection or performance assessment.[20] In contrast to those auditing approaches, it is predicated in part on the organization's own goals and objectives for its EMS, including its commitment to an effective system for fulfilling regulatory compliance.

Finally, the scope of an EMS audit differs significantly from the scope of a compliance audit. The range of applicable regulations and the processes and pollution sources subject to them determine the parameters of a compliance audit. In contrast, the scope of an EMS audit might be determined solely by the elements required under the ISO 14001 standards and by the environmental goals, objectives, and targets set by the company. A firm, of course, might go beyond ISO 14001 requirements if it chooses. An EMS audit, for example, might encompass the full range of a facility's activities, processes, functions, and products that have significant environmental aspects and impacts. Alternatively, however, a firm might opt instead to *limit* the audit to a defined subset of these operations or products.

Despite these differences in purpose, scope, measurement, and outcome, the perceived shortcomings of compliance audits have unduly colored the perceptions and expectations of those who may be inclined to mistrust EMS audits using ISO 14001. Most especially, environmental organizations and some regulators worry that state audit-privilege laws might shield regulated facilities from liability for potential wrongdoing, negligence, or noncompliance. Meanwhile, businesses worry about the inherent subjectivity of the process and about the uses that third parties will make of the data provided. In the process, and not unlike the confusion of third-party EMS auditing with financial auditing, the implementation dilemmas associated with compliance audits are inaptly equated with the ISO 14001 process as well.

Voluntary Programs Based on Audits

Further fostering conflicting expectations about ISO 14001 audits by proponents and opponents is their association with voluntary government incentive programs based on audits. These programs, some of which Daniel Fiorino discusses in greater detail in chapter 11, have grown in number and visibility in recent years. They also have been greeted with skepticism in many environmental quarters—and even in some quarters in the EPA—for allegedly tilting too far in the direction of corporate self-regulation. The EPA's voluntary self-disclosure and audit policy, for example, was accompanied by an offer to decrease inspections for firms that conduct voluntary self-audits, adopt EMSs, or engage in mentoring and public education. The Environmental Leadership Program (ELP), for example, was one approach to rewarding corporate efforts that went "beyond compliance" by offering reduced EPA enforcement activities.

Initiatives such as the EPA's Star Track initiative in New England and the National Environmental Performance Track Program also fit comfortably within an auditing framework. The former is a variation on the ELP, and the latter is a two-tiered program that incorporates some of Star Track's features and those of similar leadership initiatives in New Jersey, Oregon, Wisconsin, and other states. In turn, the EPA's National Environmental Performance Track Program offers an opportunity to innovate with third-party auditing on a broader scale, with a subset of high-performing facilities.

Notable differences existed, however, in the purposes and means of auditing across these voluntary programs. Although the ELP and Star Track initiatives were related, for example, they served very different purposes. The EPA's Star Track audit policy program promoted *voluntary* self-auditing and disclosure in exchange for more flexibility, whereas the ELP reduced inspections as an incentive for firms to use compliance audits and EMSs. Moreover, although the ELP did not refer specifically to ISO 14001, the standard was embedded in it. In contrast, Star Track *required* both compliance audits and EMS audits to promote the concept of third-party verification. Like the ELP, it was based on the notion that recognition and rewards would provide participants with incentives to improve performance. But, unlike the ELP, Star Track proposed that increasing the number of more compliance-minded firms would allow the EPA to focus its inspectors and other enforcement resources on firms with greater likelihood of violations.

At the same time, however, these voluntary programs were rife with issues that some readily equated with third-party EMS auditing initiatives such as ISO 14001. Consider, for example, the Star Track initiative. At the same time that ISO 14001 was developed in 1996, EPA's New England region initiated its Star Track program. What drew environmentalists' attention to this effort, however, was the motivation given by former EPA regional administrator John DeVillars for launching Star Track: he was particularly interested in determining whether third-party compliance audits—similar to financial audits done by independent CPAs and relied on by the federal SEC—"could begin to privatize EPA's enforcement operations."[21]

Equally disturbing to environmentalists, Star Track envisioned replacing inspectors with a firm's chosen compliance auditors, who were to validate and certify the results. The presumed public benefit would be reduced demands on agency resources; the benefit to firms would be decreased frequency and scope of inspections. To be sure, environmental performance reports would be provided, including data on unregulated elements of facility operations. Publishing these reports, coupled with the firm's commitment to verify performance, presumably would spur additional improvement and enhanced performance beyond required standards. Yet when the amount of auditing information that may be released to the public became contentious, environmentalists worried as well about the ultimate transparency of the program.

In sum, unqualified support—either within or outside the EPA and state regulatory agencies—was lacking for each of these initiatives. And being linked directly or tangentially with these programs, third-party EMS auditing initiatives associated with ISO 14001 became equally suspect in important quarters. State regulators and representatives of the EPA's Office of Enforcement and Compliance Assurance, for example, viewed with deep suspicion the idea that enforcement can be privatized.[22] It is important to note that programs such as the ELP and Star Track did *not* envision EMS auditing under ISO 14001 as a means for privatizing enforcement. Yet DeVillar's comments helped heighten existing anxieties among many of the EPA's stakeholders, anxieties that remain strong today.

Third-Party Auditing of EMSs: Challenges, Choices, and Opportunities

The preceding discussion chronicled how and why industries and corporations turned to EMS-based auditing initiatives during the 1990s as a way to promote trade and create a standard set of environmental management practices in the face of disparate international enforcement capacities. It focused on the centrality of auditing—especially third-party auditing—to making EMS-based auditing approaches work. In the process, and using ISO 14001 for illustrative purposes, it looked at how association of third-party EMS auditing with prior auditing models (especially financial, compliance, and voluntary programs) has led to both confusion and concerns over third-party audit initiatives in the United States.

From this analysis, one discerns how precarious the prospects are for third-party EMS auditing initiatives such as ISO 14001 to become widely accepted tools capable of building a results-based sense of common purpose in environmental governance, particularly in the United States. Thus, proponents of ISO 14001 and other audit-based initiatives face three sets of analytically distinct, but interrelated strategic challenges, choices, and opportunities if they are to prevail in the years ahead: they must (1) better distinguish third-party EMS-based auditing from existing types of auditing; (2) adopt reforms that build trust; and (3) persuade stakeholders that EMS-based auditing has both managerial and public interest-oriented purposes.

Making Distinctions

The first major strategic challenge is distinguishing third-party EMS auditing initiatives such as ISO 14001 from other forms of auditing in the minds of the public, key stakeholders, and many regulators. This challenge is particularly acute when they are associated with financial securities accounting, which has come under heavy fire in the wake of the scandals mentioned earlier. Although some environmental regulators look to the SEC model as a potential way for the EPA to harness the private sector's ability to promote better environmental performance, the preceding discussion outlined how these two auditing systems differ in important respects. To the extent to which policymakers and stakeholders inaccurately associate EMS self-certification with the weaknesses of and the potential for mischief in financial securities accounting, the more likely resistance to EMS auditing will arise from environmentalists. Proponents of third-party EMS auditing must disabuse opponents of these (mis)perceptions if they are to prevail.

In turn, proponents must clarify and emphasize the differences between the ends and means of compliance audits and third-party EMS auditing initiatives such as ISO 14001. As noted, compliance audits judge the organization's behavior in terms of its compliance with externally driven regulations, whereas EMS auditing charts the organization's behavior against its own professed aims in creating the EMS. Indeed, ISO 14001 is geared toward continuous process improvement in the EMS; it is not concerned with compliance in the traditional sense of one-time assessments of an organization's behavior relative to existing regulations. To the extent that proponents allow EMS auditing initiatives to be confused with the worries that compliance auditing has occasioned among businesspersons and environmental critics regarding how information is going to be used, the less likely ISO 14001 and other EMS auditing initiatives will flourish in the future. In particular, proponents must resolve issues regarding audit-privilege and use-immunity laws for self-disclosure of environmental violations.

Finally, to the extent that policymakers and stakeholders see EMS auditing initiatives as a privatization of regulation, the same kinds of resistance that have plagued other voluntary programs will haunt them, especially among regulators. For example, if regulators and environmentalists continue to link EMS auditing to programs such as the ELP and Star Track, they most likely will see EMS auditing as an effort to privatize regulation. Thus, proponents must do two things: clarify misperceptions that those other programs *were* intended to privatize regulation, and decouple EMS auditing from these perceptions. Otherwise, neither voluntary nor EMS auditing initiatives will become widely accepted public policy tools for environmental governance.

Trust Building

By the same token, *distinctions* among the three types of audits ironically cast third-party EMS audit initiatives such as ISO 14001 in a decidedly negative light, especially when it comes to building trust in the process. As a consequence, a second major strategic challenge confronts proponents of these initiatives: they must persuade policymakers and stakeholders that they are willing to address these issues in ways that make EMS audits more *like* financial, compliance, and voluntary audit programs in certain ways. In this vein, proponents must do five interrelated things if they are to have any hope of building the levels of public trust necessary for ISO 14001 and other EMS auditing initiatives to become important tools of environmental governance. The EMS auditing community must (1) choose to improve peer review systems, (2) enhance the transparency of certification systems, (3) ensure auditor independence, (4) promote the complementarity of auditing approaches, and (5) distinguish certification programs from related programs.

Peer Review   In terms of developing a peer review system, proponents seriously should consider adopting a system similar to the one accounting firms use to maintain uniform professional norms of interpretation and practice. To be sure, such a system is not foolproof, as the cases of Enron and several other prominent public companies have demonstrated. Even the SEC's additional safeguards were not up to the job of ensuring transparency through reporting requirements and auditor independence. But without a system that the public perceives as affording peer review at least equal to what is provided by the financial auditing community, the prospects seem bleak for widespread acceptance of third-party audit-based systems in the United States. Even better, of course, would be the choice to establish a peer review system that addresses the shortcomings that have come to light in the financial sector.

Transparency   At the same time, proponents of EMS auditing initiatives such as ISO 14001 must persuade the audit community to address the unresolved conflict of expectations regarding public reporting of environmental performance indicators and outcomes. Most significant with regard to its impact on transparency and trust building, the EMS audit under ISO 14001 is a confidential report to an organization's management. Yet, to have credibility with the public, the goal of such an audit, of course, must provide assurance to citizens that conformity with operant standards has been certified. That certification and report, moreover, must be made available to the public.

ISO 14001 shortcomings in this regard are not accidental and thus will not be resolved easily. European and U.S. drafters of these standards differed significantly over whether the auditing process should be designed to foster internal management improvements or to impart information to the public. The resulting standard is thus a hybrid that is useful to managers, but less informative to the public and less clear about what third-party auditing represents. The confusion rendered by this choice contrasts sharply with the openness of financial auditing and reporting, and it has to be resolved more in favor of public reporting if ISO 14001 auditing has any chance of building the level of trust necessary for building common purpose in the future.

All is not bleak on this front, however, if one looks to other developments regarding public reporting in environmental governance. Extensive public reporting on environmental and social performance *has* occurred. The Global Reporting Initiative is one example. Arguments for such initiatives focus on public and investor interest, as well as on the benefits to businesses of having a single, widely accepted, and credible reporting format. Given these developments, U.S. bodies that develop ISO 14001 or other third-party audit standards face two important strategic challenges and choices. One is figuring out how best to involve public interest groups, corporations, and smaller businesses as they tackle the challenge of bridging the gap between the public's need to know and the private sector's proprietary and legal interests.

Auditor Independence   Yet another strategic challenge relevant to trust building is ensuring that the public is confident that auditor independence exists. As noted, the EMS auditing system in the United States presently restricts auditors from providing both consulting and EMS auditing services to the same client. As long as the system remains largely private, with little or no public policy function, this restriction is probably adequate. If state and federal agencies wish to use EMS auditing to advance public policy goals, however, policymakers *must* choose stronger measures to ensure auditor independence.

Complementarity   Proponents also must alert policymakers to how third-party EMS auditing approaches can complement other auditing approaches. Consider, for example, the potential for complementarity between third-party EMS auditing and traditional compliance auditing. If properly conducted by independent auditors, an ISO 14001 audit can provide independent and verifiable evidence about the abilities of a polluter to improve its environmental performance, evidence about which the public can be confident. Discernible as well in such an audit is whether or not a firm has an effective compliance management system in place to prevent noncompliance, to detect and correct noncompliance situations promptly, and to prevent recurrences. Policymakers thus must appreciate how aspects of third-party EMS auditing initiatives such as ISO 14001 audits and strict compliance audits can be complementary. Together they can create an opportunity to strengthen the overall assurance of environmental compliance, reduce adverse environmental impacts, *and* build public trust.

Differentiation   Yet trust building also will require proponents and policymakers to ensure that the aims and requirements of third-party EMS auditing approaches such as ISO 14001 are carefully *distinguished* from those of other policy initiatives. Take, for example, initiatives providing administrative or regulatory benefits or relief in exchange for merely having an EMS in place. Policymakers must understand that the related policy goals (for example, compliance with ENR standards) that they seek will not be achieved through voluntary third-party EMS auditing alone. As Geiser and other authors in this book correctly point out, much-maligned command-and-control regulation creates necessary financial incentives for moving toward voluntary compliance with ENR laws. To forget this truism by relaxing ENR standards or enforcement can diminish public trust in two ways: by rendering the initiative vulnerable to charges of privatization and by diminishing respect for the initiative if ENR degradation occurs after EMSs are in place.

Toward Public Interest Auditing?

A third and related major strategic challenge facing proponents of third-party EMS auditing is persuading stakeholders that it serves both managerial and public interest purposes. As noted, EMS auditors and their clients continue to choose for the most part to view third-party certification approaches such as ISO 14001 auditing as being strictly by business for business. Yet they also recognize that this view, even among some in industry, is changing. Government—including state and federal regulatory agencies—thus has an opportunity to build on and expand this mindset by seizing and creating opportunities to inform the public and other parties about how third-party EMS auditing approaches work to advance both managerial *and* civic purposes. By commissioning research, publishing public reports, and incorporating their findings in public policy statements, they can show the positive synergistic results of EMS-based auditing for the bottom line and for public health, safety, and the environment. The EPA recently has undertaken such efforts, and it would be well advised to assess periodically the degree to which these efforts are serving to clarify expectations about what third-party EMS auditing can and cannot deliver.[23]

Although government can play an important role in clarifying expectations, proponents of third-party EMS auditing initiatives also must try to get those inside the system—EMS auditors and their clients—to play a greater role in managing the expectations of the public. In the United States, the National Accreditation Program is offering public forums for state regulators who are interested in learning more about ISO 14001 auditing. These efforts are laudable and should continue. EMS auditors also can help to shape more accurate and realistic public expectations in several ways: by choosing to promote greater uniformity in their auditing procedures, by adopting effective peer review, and by communicating high professional auditing standards more clearly during public policy discussions and debates over EMS-based auditing approaches. Trade associations traditionally have performed this function in other industries, and EMS auditors should consider giving their own association sufficient resources to undertake this vital trust-building function.

In sum, actors and organizations outside the EMS auditing system will benefit from clearly understanding and directly experiencing how third-party EMS auditing systems such as ISO 14001 work in theory and in practice. Nonparticipants' expectations are, in many ways, both too high and too low today. They are too high because they link third-party EMS auditing with enforcement of environmental compliance or verification of performance. Yet they also are too low because they underestimate the continual improvements in environmental performance that well-functioning and carefully audited EMSs can produce. Disabusing stakeholders of these misperceptions affords strategic challenges, choices, and opportunities that proponents of third-party auditing as a tool for building a results-based sense of common purpose ignore at their peril.

Notes

1. U.S. Environmental Protection Agency (EPA), "Position Statement on Environmental Management Systems," http://www.epa.gov/ems/policy/position.htm, signed by Administrator Christine Todd Whitman on May 15, 2002; U.S. EPA, "Environmental Management System Implementation Policy," http://www.epa.gov/ems/policy/own.htm, signed by Administrator Christine Todd Whitman on May 17, 2002.

2. National Academy of Public Administration (NAPA), *Environment.gov: Transforming Environmental Protection for the 21st Century* (Washington, D.C.: NAPA, 2000); NAPA, *Third-Party Auditing of Environmental Management Systems: U.S. Registration Practices for ISO 14001* (Washington, D.C.: NAPA, 2001).

3. Naomi Roht-Arriaza, "Shifting the Point of Regulations: The International Organization for Standardization and Global Lawmaking on Trade and the Environment," *Ecology Law Quarterly* 22(3) (1995): 479–539.

4. Pacific Institute for Studies in Development, Environment, and Security, *Managing a Better Environment: Opportunities and Obstacles for ISO 14001 in Public Policy and Commerce* (Oakland, Calif.: Pacific Institute for Studies in Development, Environment, and Security, 2000).

5. Begun in 1997 by the CERES, the GRI became an independent institution in 2002 and is today an official collaborating center of the UNEP involved in the Secretary General's Global Compact.

6. David Burdick, "Opportunities to Strengthen the Registration and Accreditation System for ISO 14001 Certification," www.ecologicresources.com/pdf/paper2lw.pdf, June 28, 2001, p. 3.

7. NAPA, *Third-Party Auditing of Environmental Management Systems.*

8. The standards by which the CPA obtains a certificate and how an audit is conducted depend on state boards of accountancy. The SEC, however, establishes the Generally Accepted Accounting Principles and the Generally Accepted Auditing

Standards. The latter were developed by the American Institute of Certified Public Accountants (AICPA), a private standard-setting, professional organization of CPAs. Financial consultants also are certified, unlike in the EMS field where there is no certification requirement for consultants who help firms to design and administer their EMSs.

9. AICPA estimates that 400,000 CPAs are practicing in the United States and that, of those, 331,000 are members of AICPA (AICPA, *"Peer Review" Fact Sheet* [Washington, D.C.: AICPA, 1997], www.aicpa.org).

10. B. Barker, "Are Auditors Independent?" TMF Max News Service, September 8, 2000, www.fool.com/portfolios/rulemaker/2000/rulemaker000908.htm?ref= prevreg.

11. Lynn Turner, "Independence 'Matters,'" paper presented at the Twenty-Eighth Annual National Conference on Current SEC Developments, Washington, DC, December 6, 2000.

12. J. Bryant Quinn, "Investors Rely on Independent Auditors," *Washington Post,* October 1, 2000, p. H2.

13. Thomas M. Gardner, *Testimony Before the U.S. Securities and Exchange Commission* (Washington, D.C.: U.S. SEC, 2000).

14. *Independence* means that the CPA, the CPA's firm, or a firm member cannot during the time of a professional engagement have any financial interest in the financial statements of the CPA's client or be an underwriter, voting trustee, or employee of the client. Further explanation is provided in Rule 2-01, Qualifications of Accounts, www.law.uc.edu/CCL/regS-X/SX2-01.html.

15. S. Petie Davis, "Managing the ISO 14000 Revolution: A Comparative Look at Compliance and EMS Audits," *International Environmental Systems Update* 4(4) (April 1997): 17–19, www.nsf-isr.org/info/article_iso_revolution.html.

16. Tom Tibor with Ira Feldman, *ISO 14000: A Guide to New Environmental Management Standards* (Chicago: Irwin Professional, 1996).

17. U.S. EPA, *Incentives for Self-Policing: Discovery, Disclosure, Correction, and Prevention of Violations* (Washington, D.C.: EPA, Office of Enforcement and Compliance Assistance, 2000), p. 36.

18. Ibid.

19. Davis, "Managing the ISO 14000 Revolution."

20. Nicholas Schnee, *Observations on the ISO 14001 Registration System and the Registrar's Role in Encouraging Environmental Performance* (Washington, D.C.: EPA, Office of Policy Development, 1999).

21. NAPA, *Environment.gov.,* p. 43.

22. Ibid.

23. See, for example, NAPA, *Third-Party Auditing of Environmental Management Systems;* U.S. EPA, "Position Statement on Environmental Management Systems"; U.S. EPA, "Environmental Management System Implementation Policy."

Conclusion

Robert F. Durant, Daniel J. Fiorino, and Rosemary O'Leary

We editors hope that the chapters in this volume have aided readers in drawing their own conclusions about how enduring the individual elements informing or complicating reformers' agendas for building a results-based sense of common purpose in environmental governance will *or* should be in the years ahead. We also hope that readers now have a more comprehensive, conceptually grounded, and thematically integrated understanding and assessment of the logic, promise versus performance, and likely future of these major reform initiatives than they had when they began this book. We hope as well that they have a better appreciation of environmental governance as a combination of important, inter-related, and complex issues involving environmental policy, economics, democratic theory, political science, and public administration.

As promised, each of the authors has taken stock of and assessed the strategic challenges, choices, and opportunities facing proponents of these reforms. Each also has had much to say about the prospects and problems facing the three key themes informing reformers' agendas today: reconceptualizing purpose, reconnecting with citizens, and re-defining administrative rationality. In the process, they collectively have offered students an intensive "seminar" on thirteen key reform proposals related to environmental governance in the twenty-first century. Proffered as well to scholars and researchers have been propositional inventories suitable for testing, elaborating, and refining in future research. And by offering the latest research insights regarding the conditions under which most of the reforms are more or less likely to succeed (as well as the obstacles and facilitating factors affecting their implementation), the authors have offered a compass by which reformers might craft strategies and tactics for pursuing their own goals in the future.

Reviewing in detail what each author had to say to these various audiences seems unnecessarily repetitive at this point. The consistent format used across the chapters makes locating, comparing, and synthesizing the authors' thoughts on the logic, implementation lessons, and likely futures readily locatable and accessible to readers. A more valuable project here would be to aid readers further in making their own informed judgments by doing three things: (1) summarizing why it is likely that the salience of building a results-based sense of common purpose will persist well into the future; (2) highlighting several paradoxes that are important for students, scholars, and practitioners to appreciate; and (3) culling in broad strokes from the chapters a research agenda commensurate with the strategic challenges, choices, and opportunities they raise for building common purpose in the twenty-first century.

Built to Last?

How widespread, formidable, and enduring is the salience of the results-based reform agenda likely to be? As Robert Durant, Young-Pyoung Chun, Byungseob Kim, and Seongjong Lee argue elsewhere, a variety of primary, interrelated, and enduring secular trends are likely to ensure the future salience to environmental governance of reconceptualizing purpose, reconnecting with citizens, and redefining administrative rationality.[1] First, the identification and trumpeting of certain *and* speculative risks will grow increasingly more prevalent and pronounced with new technical and scientific breakthroughs. Second, the recognition of the interdependency of the sources and victims of these risks will spiral apace. Third, the rise of postmaterialist philosophies is likely to continue as economic development proceeds, thus raising the salience of and public consciousness regarding risk. Fourth, awareness of the shrinking costs of spreading both information and disinformation that politically can arouse networked activists worldwide will exacerbate these concerns further.

Fifth, ongoing changes in governance philosophy will continue unabated in the future, a phenomenon that can only emphasize further the salience of building a results-based sense of common purpose in environmental governance. Sixth, enough success has occurred with results-based environmental governance to suggest that pressures for it will continue, pressures that will be informed by research that specifies the conditions under which it is more or less likely to be successful. Seventh, any success in building a results-based sense of common purpose in environmental governance will be affected by how well governments handle the "graying" of the federal workforce in the United States. Finally, despite the travails well documented in the chapters, pressures will continue, as market globalization proceeds, for greater reliance on international partnerships and transparency as interrelated tools for building a results-based sense of common purpose in environmental governance.

Risk Awareness

The future, of course, yet may bring technoscientific advances that offer an opportunity to attenuate the risk concerns noted throughout the chapters in this volume. Moreover, as Jack Hollander, professor emeritus of energy and resources at the University of California at Berkeley, forcefully has argued, technological advances also can help to reduce the poverty in developing nations that leads to environmental degradation.[2] Developing nations, he argues, can take advantage of "leap-frog" technologies to avoid the environmentally degrading path that plagued economic growth in the developed world during the nineteenth and early twentieth centuries. And when rising levels of affluence are coupled with democratic reform, these nations may follow the historical patterns so prevalent in the developed world: increased affluence leads to growing public health, safety, and environmental concerns among broader segments of societies, concerns that get translated in democracies into more aggressive environmental and natural resources (ENR) protection.

Many of these advances, however, also will raise a new set of challenging legal, ethical, financial, and scientific questions that will become the grist of political conflict among various stakeholders. Consider, for example, technological breakthroughs in agriculture (aside from the biotechnological breakthroughs noted by Durant with Boodphetcharat) that have wrought concerns worldwide about the safety of food supplies. Pesticides, for example, have helped to multiply crop yields, thus raising hopes of attenuating hunger and nutrition problems in many developing nations. Yet that increase came at a high price. For example, researchers at the University of Essex have demonstrated how costly high technology farming can be to the environment.[3] They found that subsidies from the British government tend mostly to support these methods. Yet the negative externalities that they produce cost approximately £2.34 billion annually in water pollution, soil erosion, and habitat loss. With the identity of polluters frequently unknown, obvious ENR damage delayed for years, and farm prices not internalizing these negative externalities, calls for revamping perverse market incentives should continue to mount.

So-called factory farms (for example, poultry farms) or concentrated animal feed operations also offer economic and supply advantages to farmers and citizens. Yet the inordinate amounts of fetid waste runoff from these farms prompt calls for regulatory action by those living downwind and downstream from them. Other critics contend that these operations are much too conducive to outbreaks of disease. Thousands of genetically uniform animals are raised in unhygienic warehouses where dangerous microbes can breed. Factory farms then recycle animal manure and slaughterhouse waste as feed for the animals. Meat processing done at breakneck speed follows, often in the presence of blood, feces, and other contagions. Long-distance transport of food then offers additional opportunities for contamination.

Nor, many critics claim, does it help that farm animals consume roughly ten times as many antibiotics as do humans. Antibiotic overuse in factory farms has led to drug-resistant microbes, including *Salmonella*, *E. coli,* and *Camplyobacter*. Still, industrial animal farming is the fastest-growing form of animal production worldwide, increasing by a third since 1990 and contributing to nearly half the world's meat production. Though concentrated in North America and Europe, feedlots are sprouting up near urban centers in Brazil, China, India, the Philippines, and elsewhere in the developing world where demand for meat and animal products is soaring. Soaring, as well, are concerns about health hazards in the food supply.

The future also may bring technoscientific advances that offer an opportunity to attenuate some of the world's most debilitating diseases. Again, however, many of these advances will raise a new set of challenging legal, ethical, and scientific questions that will become the grist of political conflict among various stakeholders. Consider, for example, one promising yet potentially conflictual advance in the area of risk assessment and management: *toxicogenomics*. As defined by the National Institute of Environmental Health Sciences, toxicogenomics strives to take advantage of recent research on gene sequencing from the genome project to study scientifically "how genomes respond to environmental stressors/toxicants."[4] With these data, regulators might be able to determine the precise mechanism causing harm (for example, tumors) and thus predict whether particular exposures in humans will result in health problems in particular subpopulations (for example, children with particular gene traits, rather than children in general). Conversely, genomic data showing characteristic gene expression changes from stressors might facilitate decidedly less expensive, more effective, and much earlier toxicity screening than conventional screening today.

All this, however, only raises additional questions for environmental governance to answer.[5] For example, should ENR regulatory standards apply to those subpopulations that are genetically most susceptible to harm? Should "disproportionate genetic risk" replace "disproportionate exposure" as the criterion for evaluating environmental justice claims? Should today's generic regulatory standards (for example, "x"-parts-per-million or billion exposure levels) be replaced in part by more information-based regulatory approaches predicated on individuals knowing their genotype for relevant genes and avoiding exposure to products (for example, chemicals) that express (that is, turn on or off) those genes? Might citizens with particular genetic disorders go to court demanding more stringent regulation? For example, should persons with the genetic disorder known as Alpha-1, which makes them more highly susceptible to emphysema and other lung diseases when exposed to smoke or dust, sue for greater regulation of emissions of particulate matter? Can toxicogenomic studies create political pressure to eliminate present assumptions that there is a threshold level of exposure below which no harm occurs? These questions only begin to scratch the surface.

But whether or not toxicogenomic research becomes the wave of the regulatory future, the nature of risk assessment and risk management means continuing conflict over the rights to protection to which citizens of the world are entitled. As with the other technological breakthroughs discussed in this book, calls for reconceptualizing purpose, reconnecting with citizens, and redefining administrative rationality will continue apace. Nor, as the next section discusses, will this trend attenuate in the wake of growing awareness of risk interdependency in the United States and abroad.

Awareness of Risk Interdependency

Perceptions that complex risks exist, often are interrelated, and will need a sense of common purpose to be dealt with also are likely to prove enduring. Absent alternatives, for example, subsistence farmers left to eke out livings on marginal croplands will continue to entertain burning as a way to enrich soils and clear forest lands. Cash-strapped governments and profit-seeking private companies are likely to find legal and illicit clear-cutting of tropical rain forests attractive and profitable. Threats such as soil erosion, deforestation, and desertification will thus continue apace, energizing national and international bodies and nongovernmental organizations (NGOs) to pressure governments and private actors regarding the risks these threats entail for society. In their wake may emerge further indications of global warming that protagonists will debate. Included among these indications will be alteration of weather patterns and water supplies, the spread of disease-carrying insects into new climes, the melting of polar ice caps at unprecedented rates, and the transport of choking smoke and haze into neighboring regions and nations (as happens when smoke wafts from Indonesian forest fires into Southeast Asia).

In the process, a continuing sense of global interdependence should grow apace, along with cross-border, cross-regional, and international debates over the precautionary steps that governments and international regimes should take to attenuate the negative externalities these global activities occasion. In response, developing nations' resentment of "outside interference" in their domestic affairs (for example, with regard to halting deforestation in the tropics) and of threats to their economic or food security (for example, with regard to corporate patenting of genetically modified [GM] cash crops such as Thai jasmine rice and Indian basmati rice, and of indigenous plants discovered during "bioprospecting" by pharmaceutical companies) will continue to rise as well.

Nor are conflicts over these issues and the ENR risks they may pose to public health, safety, and the ecology likely to dwindle in the future. The U.S. Energy Department, for example, projects that world oil demand will increase 56 percent by the year 2025, with most of that demand related to transportation costs.[6] Consequently, proposals for drilling and transporting carbon-based fuels forebode continuing confrontations between consumptive users and conservationists or preservationists the world over. Nuclear power plants offer the promise of clean power production to meet these energy needs, a promise that several nations are seizing. Japan, for example, envisions cutting carbon dioxide emissions 18 percent below 1990 levels by 2010 by increasing the nation's reliance on nuclear power from 34 percent to 40 percent. Even in Great Britain, where the Blair government plans to develop eighteen wind farms to help meet carbon dioxide reduction targets under the Kyoto Protocol, the chairman of the Royal Society says these goals cannot be met without new nuclear power plants.[7]

In the United States, however, nuclear power long has been anathema to most environmentalists for a variety of risk-related reasons, including the technically and politically formidable dilemma of nuclear waste storage and disposal. Resistance also has mounted more recently in Europe and Japan as Green parties and NGOs have rallied against nuclear power with some success.[8] Moreover, even when nonnuclear sources of energy are involved, controversies over site locations can produce the same passions and "not-in-my-backyard" reactions that controversies over the risks associated with solid, toxic, and hazardous-waste disposal have occasioned.[9] These efforts, moreover, frequently run pell-mell into an increasingly resistant, vocal, and sometimes litigious environmental justice movement.[10]

Energy conservation, of course, is an obvious approach to resolving supply dilemmas, especially if the true social costs of producing electricity can be incorporated into prices (for example, carbon taxes) or if precepts of the ecological modernization movement become widespread in business. But meaningful carbon taxes like those proposed in the United States by the Clinton administration in the early 1990s proved politically unpalatable as too risky for the economy and have faded in salience on political agendas. Moreover, with exceptions in some corporations, conservation efforts in the United States typically ebb and flow with crises.[11] Consequently, the future of conservation efforts—as well as of the larger ecological modernization movement in the United States and abroad—depends on whether political leaders persistently embrace, NGOs promote, and business leaders see competitive advantage in such efforts.

Nor will a sense of interdependence in solutions to risks, real or imagined, diminish on a national scale. For example, risk-related disputes over property rights and regulatory takings are likely to remain salient in the western United States, in suburban and pastoral areas slated for development, and whenever the U.S. Congress is reauthorizing statutes such as the Endangered Species Act. Gridlocked highways, in turn, will continue to spawn all the ENR risks associated with suburban sprawl, including those associated with higher gasoline consumption, traffic congestion, critical habitat destruction, and fragmentation of ecosystems.

Together, these negative externalities will induce escalating risk-related battles among developers, environmentalists, and NGOs over what constitutes prudent land-use planning. Moreover, even proposed solutions to these problems are likely to initiate conflict, requiring the building of common purpose in environmental governance. New mass-transit systems, for example, will pit preservationists, neighborhood groups, developers, property rights proponents, and environmental justice groups against each other. And each of these mitigation efforts will reveal further how existing single-pollutant, single-media, and single-pathway risk assessment approaches and statutes pose formidable obstacles to resolving metropolitan risk issues that require holistic approaches.[12]

The Postmaterialist Challenge

Changes in the voting predispositions of persons in developed democracies worldwide also are likely to make enduring the salience of conflict resolution through reconceptualizing purpose, reconnecting with citizens, and redefining administrative rationality. One of the most prominent yet controversial theoretical perspectives on public-opinion formation in this regard is political scientist Ronald Inglehart's postmaterialist thesis.[13] Inglehart argues that a "silent revolution" in value orientations has occurred that corresponds to levels of economic affluence and physical security. As a rule, the higher the income and education levels of a nation, he avers, the greater the level of concern its citizens have about ENR risks and the more prone they are to support initiatives to reduce them.[14]

Consider recent trends in the United States. For decades, conventional political wisdom was that the higher the educational and income levels of Americans, the more likely they were to vote Republican. Yet a new fault line differentiating voters in the 2000 elections was consonant with Inglehart's postmaterialist thesis.[15] Following a decade-long and accelerating realignment trend, well-educated, higher-income, and non-church-attending white professionals (for example, academics, doctors, lawyers, and scientists) are now among the Democratic Party's most reliable voters. In contrast, lower-income whites without college degrees who attend church regularly are among the most reliable Republican voters. Moreover, among the postmaterialist concerns animating this reversal of partisan fortunes are issues associated with risk and government's responsibility for allaying it for their citizens (for example, gun control and abortion), with ENR issues most prominent among these concerns.

With the United States increasingly divided demographically and politically on the basis of postmaterialist values such as ENR policy, the political stage is set for a continuation of conflict over risk and against the political economy that has both propelled and constrained reform to date. Moreover, when these developments are contrasted with the evolving political economy of ENR management globally and regionally in the world, the prognosis is similar for the international arena as well. Consider, for example, the representation of the Green Party as members or junior partners in coalition governments in major democracies in the world over the past decade. This trend has occurred most notably in the European Parliament and in those countries with proportional rather than first-past-the-post representational systems (for example, in Australia, Belgium, Finland, France, Germany, the Netherlands, and New Zealand). As Director Christopher Rootes of the Center for the Study of Social and Political Movements at the University of Kent notes, "The Greens represent a new agenda in Western politics, one that is peculiarly appropriate to the new era of global politics in which issues of environmental sustainability, intergenerational and international equity, human rights, and social justice are intertwined."[16]

Granted, purists and antiglobalization protesters are apt to be disappointed in the performance of Greens in office. As coalition partners with left-of-center governments, they have had to make compromises on both hypothetical and speculative risk that will strike purists as betrayals (for example, with regard to promises to phase out nuclear power and to promote ecotaxes in Germany). Nevertheless, they *have* had a decided impact in seeing that existing ENR laws are implemented effectively and by facilitating the implementation of initiatives launched by Green ministers because of the even higher level of representation of Green politicians at subnational levels of government. They presently also are represented disproportionately on environmental policy committees in the European Parliament. Moreover, with many of the party's strategists seeing involvement with consumer protection issues as a way to expand the Greens' electoral base (for example, the commercialization of GM foods), their pursuit to ensure the viability of the precautionary principle is likely to grow accordingly. International political tensions over risk are thus likely to continue in debates over issues such as sustainability, international governance regimes, environmental justice, and market-based solutions to ENR management problems.

At the same time, both postmaterialist and materialist values are likely to continue arousing NGOs' passions to incorporate environmental and labor values into trade agreements such as the North American Free Trade Agreement and the Free Trade Area of the Americas. Meanwhile, at the local level, both sets of values—plus political stalemates at the national level—are likely to stimulate the furtherance of self-organizing and self-regulatory institutions so that indigenous peoples who are already calling for political empowerment can manage better their common-pool resources for sustainability.

Reduced Costs of Political Mobilization

Continuing to ensure that conflict-provoking perceptions of ENR risk are well, widely, and quickly known are advances in telecommunications. These advances have dramatically lowered the costs of gathering and sharing ENR information, of communicating concerns, and of organizing political movements the world over.[17] Last year, for example, the United Nations Food and Agriculture Organization used its Forest Information System to assess the overall health of the world's silviculture. Likewise, advances in direct-mail solicitation, telemarketing, the Internet, and news broadcasting permit the sending of provocative messages and riveting images almost instantaneously to targeted or mass audiences around the world.

As several of the authors in this volume have pointed out, these advances have helped to create new NGOs or have helped existing ones communicate their concerns worldwide at little cost. The Internet, for example, allows continuous interaction among widely scattered audiences once they are aroused, which facilitates the arranging, planning, coordination, and implementation of grassroots strategies, movements, and demonstrations. In recent years, protesters coordinated activities via cell phones, pagers, and instant messaging devices in demonstrations against the World Trade Organization (WTO), the World Bank, and the International Monetary Fund. Likewise, the Internet has been effective in the anti–GM food campaign that Greenpeace has led internationally since the late 1990s, in recent demonstrations in Quebec involving the Free Trade Area of the Americas, and in a successful international campaign to boycott lumber from British Columbia unless the Canadian province preserved large areas of the Great Bear Rain Forest from harvesting.[18]

On a less confrontational yet no less important scale, the Internet also allows government agencies and private companies to report and frequently update toxic release inventories, air and water quality measures, wetlands assessments, desertification measures, and other ecosystem and watershed quality efforts.[19] As such, information reporting strategies by ENR agencies and private companies are quite attractive as alternatives to command-and-control regulation. Moreover, with no end in sight to telecommunication advances in general, pressures from NGOs for progressively greater transparency of corporate operations are unlikely to abate soon. In turn, calls from the business community for more flexibility in order to produce improvements more cost-effectively are also likely to continue. Future struggles among these protagonists thus can be expected over pollution prevention, accountability for results, and market and quasi-market alternatives to regulation. So, too, are calls likely to accelerate for equity in the sharing of the benefits and burdens of economic development as data regarding them are analyzed in both the developed and developing worlds.

Finally, globalization of both technology and markets will continue to pose challenges related to the politics of precaution, perhaps making these politics even more conflictual and vulnerable to switches in political regimes than previously understood. As political ecology theory predicts, the environment can become a "legitimating discourse" comprising a whole host of issues (especially in developing nations) that governments or their citizens otherwise might not discuss out of fear, ignorance, or political will. In the process, debates over environmental issues become surrogates for issues previously off the table. These issues most notably involve the state's role in determining (with economic interests) who has control over natural resources and the wealth they create, destroy, or redistribute. In some developing nations, for example, discussions over risk management in reality are surrogates for battles over Western versus European versus Asian models of economic development.[20] ENR issues also can become proxy issues for long-standing rural versus urban tensions and conflicts, and for long-standing and seemingly intractable cultural battles. Most notable in this regard are protracted battles between, on the one hand, forces of traditional wisdom and community self-reliance and, on the other hand, forces of modern nationalism, internationalism, and globalization.

Changes in Public Philosophy

Major shifts in broader public philosophy promise to continue reinforcing elements of the political economy that have propelled cries to reconceptualize purpose, reconnect with citizens, and redefine administrative rationality. Nor are these tendencies toward devolution, deliberation, and collaboration likely to abate soon, either in general or in particular in the arena of environmental governance. Political clashes that have both prompted these calls for reform and constrained their ability to reconstitute first-generation command-and-control ENR management regimes will continue as well. Especially noteworthy among these clashes will be evolving philosophical shifts related to governance, the privatization of regulation, and the potential renaissance of community.

Shifts in Governance Philosophy   At least four analytically distinct yet interrelated models of governance exist today that challenge established administrative arrangements worldwide: the market, participatory state, flexible government, and deregulated government models.[21] Nor is there any evidence that this broader, postmodern agenda will flag in salience in the immediate future, either generally or as it applies to environmental governance in the United States or abroad in the ways outlined by the authors in this volume. As political scientist Stephen Skowronek argues, crises, class conflicts, and complexity arising in any era can demonstrate that the "arrangements established to facilitate the collective management of the state apparatus [are] now no longer appropriate for effective government."[22] And as nearly all the authors note, perceptions have abounded in the United States and abroad that precisely such a disjunction has existed for some time in environmental governance.

Yet, as Skowronek also argues, the existence of "historical-structural impasses" like these are not sufficient on their own to generate comprehensive reforms. Issues of who wins and loses power and control over administration are inherent in these types of reform and must be resolved in the political arena. This is true even when historical needs, policies, and structural mismatches are so blatant that only a fundamental reconstitution of the existing order seems necessary and inevitable. What is more, even when reform does take place, ambiguous authority relationships typically are left in its wake, making implementation highly problematic.[23] Enacting reforms always requires compromise with those who benefit from the status quo and who struggle mightily with reformers to retain their access, influence, and power.

In addition, these beneficiaries usually have enough power to stymie reforms unless, and until, the reforms are crafted to preserve the beneficiaries' access, influence, and power. Confronted by these realities, reformers typically sacrifice the clarity of authority relationships in order to give their reforms a foothold in the old administrative order. In the process, the forces of opposition to reform are left to fight another day. Wrought by these machinations is a halting, halfway, and patchworked system of reform, one within which battles over the next wave of reform will occur.[24] ENR policymakers, as a result, largely can expect to confront what Fritz Sharpf calls the daunting task of "networking in the shadow of hierarchy." Moreover, they must expect to do so against a leit-motif of challenging national rivalries, ethnic clashes, and underdeveloped international regimes.[25]

Privatizing Regulation?   The international standards movement sum-marized so ably by Jan Mazurek in this volume also gained substantial momentum by the end of the twentieth century. Whether designed for polluters to meet minimum international ENR standards (for example, to become a member of the European Union), to comply voluntarily with environmental management system (EMS) standards developed by inter-national bodies (for example, the ISO 14001 series), or to embrace as principles developed by NGOs in conjunction with business, the salience of this approach is likely to remain. Many polluters feel that standardiz-ing environmental regulations is necessary for global markets to function effectively, and many regulators anticipate that standards will ease their enforcement and compliance costs.

Policy debates nonetheless rage over the wisdom of pursuing these kinds of accountability mechanisms. On the one hand, international standards may be useful in breaking down protectionist barriers to trade in a global economy. Moreover, they ultimately may have a leavening ef-fect on lax product and environmental standards in both developed and developing countries by making regulatory compliance a marketing ad-vantage. On the other hand, critics argue that this approach has inherent risks: a lack of regulatory vigilance may harm public health; a tendency may develop to compromise standards to the lowest common denomina-tor of quality or safety; and a strategy may develop to drive smaller com-petitors out of business by setting standards that are too costly for them to meet. Moreover, questions of efficacy aside, shifting regulatory standard-setting responsibilities to supranational bodies while devolving many regulatory responsibilities to states and localities also raises the specter of a loss of democratic accountability and state sovereignty to firms and international bureaucratic elites.[26] Although there is little evi-dence to suggest that this has happened—for example, in the European Union—vigilance is required more broadly.[27]

A Rebirth of Community?   Public confidence in many national govern-ments has fallen dramatically. Between 1933 and 1999 in the United

States, for example, belief that too much power is concentrated in Washington has risen in public-opinion polls from one-third agreeing with the statement to two-thirds routinely agreeing.[28] Approximately 60 percent of respondents in a 1999 survey agreed that "the best government is that which governs least," compared to only 32 percent agreeing in 1973. Indeed, of those voting in the 2000 election, 53 percent surveyed said that government should do less, not more.[29] Since 1973, trust in the federal government "to do the right thing" also has dropped by half. Meanwhile, as judges across the world began confronting corruption on massive scales within their countries, governments have fallen (for example, in Indonesia, Mexico, and Thailand) after years and sometimes generations of one-party control. And although trust in government increased dramatically in polls taken in the aftermath of the tragedy of September 11, 2001, it (along with trust in institutions generally) declined again fairly rapidly as time passed.

Yet evidence also abounds in surveys that citizens wish to *reframe* government's role in meeting society's needs, not to cut it back significantly. Respondents also tend overwhelmingly to be unconvinced that either business or volunteerism (individually or in cooperation) are capable by themselves of meeting society's needs.[30] Nearly three-quarters of respondents agree, for example, that social problems facing Americans are addressed best when government and voluntary associations (be they secular or faith based) cooperate with business. Nor are these attitudes limited to the United States. Grassroots networks in developing countries have linked NGOs and "people's organizations" to form powerful extra-constitutional political movements that join environmental and social activists in a common cause (for example, BIOTHAI and the Assembly of the Poor, respectively, in Thailand). As such, the fundamentals underpinning the civic environmentalism, collaboration, and deliberation elements of today's reform agenda seem strong, albeit controversial, in the absence of crises.

The Continuing Salience of Results-Based Environmental Governance

As many of the authors in this volume ably demonstrate, reformers face a daunting exercise in cultural change as they try to move existing ENR regimes from "rule-based" (that is, in compliance with rules and regulations) to "ruler-based" (that is, results-based) environmental governance.[31] They effectively ask regime members to think about results in the long term, across functions, and across networks of collaborating public, private, and nonprofit organizations. Yet they ask them to do so within a largely intact bureaucratic context. Within that context, reforms are grafted on rather than replace existing and perverse incentive structures that focus regime participants instead on the short term; on single media; on individual programs and organizations; and on inputs, procedures, and outputs untethered to outcomes.

As Durant summarizes elsewhere,[32] implementing results-oriented management requires agencies to have an uncommon ability to do several critical things well: (1) see policy problems through clients' eyes; (2) drop their defensive protection against program attacks that functional rather than problem-based implementation structures (or "regimes") afford (for example, the "it's not our problem" syndrome); (3) thrive in unaccustomed "regimes"[33] or "networks"[34] where coordination and cooperation are negotiated and brokered rather than dictated by third parties; and (4) abandon turf consciousness in favor of collective responsibility for outcomes. Moreover, they paradoxically are told frequently to do all this by elected officials who themselves still think in terms of short-run results geared to campaign cycles, of overseeing single programs and functions (or tasks), and of focusing on one set of programs or a single agency at a time.

Thus, the conclusions of Don Moynihan of the Maxwell School's Government Performance Project regarding the fate of state and local government efforts at managing for results today are typical:

Governments at all levels are devoting significant energy to creating and distributing performance information. Problems in the creation of these performance information systems are common, however. Frequently, governments engage in multiple types of planning that are not well coordinated. Translating high-level goals into quantitative measures also proves problematic. A broader challenge is ensuring that performance information, once created, is actually used for decision-making.[35]

Nevertheless, many theoreticians, researchers, and elected officials are convinced that going through the process and developing results-based measures for both organizations and partnerships afford a better "conversation" for policymakers to have than traditional debates over inputs and outputs.[36] Why is this the case? For starters, evidence exists that ENR agencies are getting better at implementing results-based management approaches.[37] Each successive National Environmental Performance Partnership System (NEPPS) agreement negotiated by the U.S. Environmental Protection Agency (EPA; see the chapter by Denise Scheberle), for example, has been better than the previous one, showing a promising trend toward increased use of information about environmental conditions as the basis for decision making.[38] In addition, an increasing number of states are beginning to produce reports showing environmental quality trends.[39]

Evidence also exists from "best practices" research that when agencies at all levels of government integrate performance goals and measures into their planning and operations, they can realize significant performance gains.[40] Much of that evidence supports many of the pillars of logic that Shelley Metzenbaum identifies in her research regarding the motivational contributions that results-based approaches can make to environmental governance. Identifying goals and tracking results specifically allows organizations and networks to: set clear organizational direction; energize participants; enhance learning about problems that need to be fixed, about the effectiveness of various intervention strategies, and about more effective ways to reach their goals; and advance accountability and the building of civic capital.[41]

Not only is this focus on results likely to continue, but a more strategic understanding of the conditions under which it is more or less likely to succeed is available to guide future applications. Research[42] suggests, for example, that success is less likely whenever goals are

- too unclear or vague to draw the public's attention;
- too numerous for the public to focus on;
- not place or time specific;
- not inspirational or meaningful to participants, citizens, or the media;
- not prioritized.

Research[43] also suggests that the interaction of results-based systems with other accountability mechanisms, the kinds of technical support afforded to these efforts, and their credibility have major influences on success. Results-based initiatives are less likely to be successful whenever

- opportunities are great for existing accountability mechanisms to clash with outcomes-based performance goals (for example, with procedural mechanisms designed to deter government corruption and promote fairness);[44]

• policymakers do not give priority and technical support to subordinates for outcomes-based performance measures;

• data are neither collected nor audited independently;

• redundancy in the production of outcomes measures is not used to combat fudging of data or merely to compensate for the possibility of unintentional measurement errors;

• public reporting of the data is not compulsory;

• participants do not believe that the measurement data will be used to encourage learning rather than incur punishment if goals are not met.

The literature on results-based management[45] also suggests that outcomes-focused incentive systems are not only necessary, but also more likely to be successful whenever they

• offer very high rewards or threaten serious consequences;

• monitor measurement closely and penalize falsification;

• avoid penalizing agencies or networks for failing to meet goals;

• hold agencies and networks accountable for relentlessly focusing on outcomes, developing cogent strategies, learning from experience, sharing easy-to-understand information about progress, and discussing strategies openly and regularly with the public;

• reward teams rather than individuals when people need to work together to achieve a goal;

• do not arbitrarily limit the number of people or teams rewarded when cooperation is vital.

As noted, however, the obstacles to becoming a results-based (or "learning") organization that does all these things are formidable. What dynamics typically accompany attempts by public agencies in general to shift toward results-oriented behaviors and accountability structures? In addition to those factors Schlager and John identify in chapters 4 and 6, prior research on results-based initiatives generally identifies sets of facilitating and inhibiting preconditions for success.[46] Researchers suggest that progress toward becoming outcomes-based organizations is likely to be more difficult whenever

- central administrative agencies are unsupportive of this effort;
- legislators view inputs rather than results as critical;
- a lack of external pressures exists for results orientation;
- no statutory requirement exists (for example, the Government Performance and Results Act of 1993);
- strong leadership favoring results orientation is absent;
- coalitions supporting a results orientation do not exist throughout organizations;
- "milestones" do not exist to chart progress toward goals;
- measures are not linked to consequences;
- measures constrain flexibility;
- employees do not know the difference between inputs, outputs, and outcomes;
- employee training in outcomes measurement is lacking;
- agencies and legislators are mutually suspicious about the "gaming" of measures;
- employees fear that their responsibility is incommensurate with their authority.[47]

Likewise for partnering networks, a review of the literature on results, cultural change, and partnerships[48] involving public agencies suggests that implementation of results-oriented management will be more difficult whenever

- no history of trust exists among potential partners;
- partners do not focus on the long term;
- the opaqueness of the partnership makes monitoring difficult;
- divergence of interests among partners is likely;
- harm to citizens is likely if the partnership breaks down;
- prospects for future interaction among partners are minimal;
- partners do not view dependence as critical or complementary;
- opportunities to leave the partnership are attractive;
- rewards to partners are not linked to cooperation;
- opportunities for partners to logroll are not available;
- large program goals cannot be broken into smaller ones to avoid defection of partners.[49]

Demography as Destiny?

As political philosopher James Harrington wrote in his classic *The Commonwealth of Oceana,* "Laws are but words and paper without the hands and swords of men." As the chapters in this book have demonstrated amply, a recognition has emerged over the past three decades that the "first generation" of regulatory laws and "swords" wielded by ENR agencies may be too Lilliputian to deal with contemporary threats to subnational, national, regional, and global ecosystems.[50] Garnering considerably less attention until recently, however, has been the extent to which the quantity and quality of the "hands" wielding these regulatory swords can joust effectively with today's and tomorrow's ENR threats.

Most responsible for crystallizing the salience of this issue in many policymakers' minds in the United States today are rather striking projections of impending retirement eligibility rates in ENR agencies. To be sure, the U.S. Office of Personnel Management recently has found that federal employees generally retired during 2001 and 2002 at rates approximately 20 percent less than projected only two years earlier.[51] Nonetheless, even if projected retirements in ENR agencies are adjusted downward by 20 percent, they still pose significant challenges, choices, and opportunities for environmental management. Each year, after all, larger percentages of federal employees are retiring or becoming eligible for retirement. In 1996, for example, 32.3 percent of federal workers were employed for twenty years or more, but that percentage is now 38.5 percent. Moreover, these projections come after a nearly decade-long downsizing of the federal bureaucracy that was done largely without paying attention to its effects on ENR agencies' capacities to perform their missions. Further fomenting these concerns since the tragic events of September 11 is the war on terrorism in the United States. Wrought in its wake are homeland security responsibilities for ENR agencies that depend for their success on getting persons with the right skills into critical jobs in timely ways with adequate resources.

A graying workforce, of course, offers both threats and opportunities. If addressed strategically by aligning agency recruitment, training, succession planning, and outsourcing initiatives with evolving ENR missions, retirements conceivably may be a boon to efficient, effective, and equitable ENR management. Yet if handled reactively, opportunistically, or ham-handedly by the George W. Bush administration (and its successors), the Congress, and federal agencies, the graying of the workforce will combine with fiscal constraints, new governance responsibilities, administrative systems misaligned with these responsibilities, and homeland security challenges to put both traditional *and* evolving ENR responsibilities decidedly at risk. Despite the progress ENR agencies have made over the past two years, however, the General Accounting Office (GAO) still characterizes strategic human capital management systems in all federal agencies as "not appropriately constituted to meet [these] current and emerging [mission] challenges."[52] Much the same situation is rife in ENR agencies within the states and localities in the United States.

Consider the gaps between mission and human capital facing the EPA as a result of these trends over the past decade. Although the EPA experienced an increase in personnel of approximately 16 percent between fiscal year 1990 and fiscal year 2002, the GAO reports in 2003 that the "EPA hired thousands of employees [during the 1990s] without systematically considering the workforce impact of the changes in environmental laws and regulations, the technological advances, or the expansion in state environmental staff that occurred during [that decade]."[53] Today, more than one-quarter of the agency's workforce is eligible for retirement over the next four years. By the end of fiscal year 2008, more than 60 percent of the EPA's senior executives will be eligible to retire, with all EPA regions facing at least a 40 percent rate of retirement eligibility and with five regions facing 70 percent plus eligibility rates. In addition, by the end of fiscal year 2008, nearly 45 percent of EPA toxicologists, approximately 35 percent of its health physicists, more than 30 percent of its biological scientists, and nearly 30 percent of its environmental protection specialists will be eligible for retirement.

The EPA's chief financial officer and the GAO also have highlighted how shortcomings in the agency's personnel succession and training programs are putting its diverse missions at risk. Cited, among other critical needs, are developing leadership, management, technical, and science skills at the EPA that are commensurate with the expanded responsibilities it has assumed over the past decade in major amendments to the Clean Air Act, the Safe Drinking Water Act, and the Food Quality Protection Act. Between 1993 and 1998, for example, the number of states accepting responsibility for effecting various aspects of the Safe Drinking Water Act soared from eight to thirty-six. This development, however, only exacerbated shortages (which continue today) of EPA personnel with the skills necessary to afford technical assistance to the states and to review how well state programs are implemented.

Likewise, the EPA's chief financial officer has reported that staff implementing the Superfund and hazardous-waste programs need better training if they are to perform quality assurance adequately at these sites or to calculate fines and penalties to levy against responsible parties. Threatened as well by retirements and training deficiencies, the EPA inspector general reports, are the integrity of two innovative and celebrated EPA initiatives: the NEPPS nationwide and the Supplemental Environmental Projects in particular EPA regions. Were these problems not challenging enough for human capital management at the EPA, post–September 11 terrorist threats prompted Congress in the Public Health Security and Bio-Terrorism Response Act of 2002 to charge the EPA with such new responsibilities as funding and conducting vulnerability assessments of water supply systems across the United States.

Similarly striking is the gap between mission and human capital facing the Interior Department. Since 1985, the number of wildlife refuges managed by the Fish and Wildlife Service (FWS) has grown by 100, and visits have increased by 60 percent; visits to national parks and their accompanying natural resource impacts have spiraled, as fifty new units have been added (for a total of 385); Bureau of Land Management (BLM) lands in protective service have risen by twenty million acres, while recreational visits have increased by 40 percent; and the number of FWS threatened or endangered species consultations have quadrupled each year (37,500 annually). Nonetheless, the Interior Department's overall retirement and attrition rate for the next five years will track governmentwide levels (that is, approximately 20 percent). Moreover, the U.S. Geological Survey, the BLM, the National Park Service (NPS), and the FWS will absorb even higher rates of retirement and attrition in valuable technical career groupings (for example, computer operators and engineers). Meanwhile, the FWS expects a combined retirement and attrition rate of 13 percent between 2001 and 2005, and the Office of Surface Mining and the Minerals Management Service are projected to show combined retirement and attrition rates of 44 and 23 percent, respectively.

The GAO also reports that Department of Energy headquarters and field staffs already cannot adequately oversee cleanup of hazardous and radioactive waste sites because they lack contract management skills; that the Nuclear Regulatory Commission's new "risk-informed" regulatory approach is being jeopardized by a lack of skilled personnel in this area; that the NPS lacks the skills necessary to hold park superintendents accountable for the progress they make toward meeting natural resource goals; and that building "sustainable biological communities" will require the BLM, the FWS, the NPS, and the Bureau of Indian Affairs to select, train, and evaluate a coterie of employees possessing collaborative negotiation, alternative dispute resolution, and team-building skills. Especially in light of terrorist threats, insufficient funding for and focus on succession planning and training at the Department of Agriculture portend the continuation of such problems as problematic deployment of resources, insufficient coordination, and inconsistent oversight of the nation's food safety system.

Nor are the challenges facing mission and human capital management any less daunting at the National Oceanic and Atmospheric Administration (NOAA). According to the GAO, the NOAA will jeopardize its three major priorities (namely, understanding climate variability and change, advancing ecosystem management, and creating a global environmental observation system) if the agency cannot increase the quantity and quality of the cost-benefit and forecasting analyses it produces. Necessary as a result are the hiring and retention of economists, decision analysts, risk managers, and social science analysts, along with succession planning for these positions. Also, because many of these positions will have to be outsourced, skills in grants management, financial management, contract management, and budget and performance integration will need considerable buttressing and improvement in the years ahead.

Nevertheless, demographics need not be destiny. Wilson's "29th day" metaphor for ecosystem collapse (see Preface) need not find a counterpart in the mission capabilities of federal ENR agencies to advance a results-based sense of common purpose in environmental governance. Avoiding this scenario, however, requires that presidents, the Congress, and ENR agencies themselves marshal the political, organizational, and financial wherewithal to use the graying of the federal workforce as leverage for efficient, effective, responsive, and equitable ENR governance. The words of a U.S. president never associated with aggressive ENR protection sum up the situation best: "I do not believe in a fate that will fall on us no matter what we do," said Ronald Reagan in his 1981 Inaugural Address, "but I do believe in a fate that will fall on us if we do nothing."

International Partnering and "Regulation by Revelation"
As authors such as Gary Bryner and Robert Paehlke aptly have demonstrated, global interdependence has brought in its wake a host of positive and negative externalities that go beyond the capacity of national governments to cope effectively. Nor does global interdependence show any signs of slowing down. In the early 1990s, for example, researchers could identify a globalization of markets involving 35,000 multinational corporations affiliated with approximately 170,000 foreign suppliers. By the late 1990s, they could identify the affiliation of more than 60,000 multinational corporations with more than 500,000 foreign companies, producing nearly one-quarter of total global economic output. Indeed, transnational corporations have literally "reengineered" the globalization of production lines worldwide over the past decade.[54]

At the same time, international institutions such as the United Nations increasingly look to these transnational corporations to "partner" with them to address some of the world's most serious environmental threats (see, for example, Bryner's discussion of the emphasis on partnerships at the 2003 Johannesburg World Summit in South Africa). As Ann Florini of the Brookings Institution puts the situation wryly, "The halls of the United Nations used to ring with calls for international regulation of those dreaded evil-doers, the multinational corporations. Now the UN instead implores business to join with it in a voluntary Global Compact to ensure respect for internationally agreed environmental, labor, and human rights standards."[55] Meanwhile, these transnational actors' influence on domestic ENR policies is likely to grow as well. As students of emerging international governance structures that incorporate partnerships have observed perceptively, "given that the state of the environment in any country is not merely the result of intranational forces, it is not sufficient to emphasize . . . domestic matters [when talking about environmental management] to the exclusion of other international factors."[56]

All these issues will continue to provoke a commensurate movement on the part of some industries, governments, international bodies, and NGOs to embrace various tools for "regulation through revelation." These tools may be of the aspirational variety that require no confirmation of conduct by outsiders (for example, the Caux Principles, offering a set of normative principles such as human rights). They alternatively may include commitments to principles that are checked by outsiders (for example, the labor and environmental standards incorporated in the Social Accountability 8000 code of conduct designed by the Council on Economic Priorities). They also may be technical (for example, the sustainability analysis tools Paehlke discusses in chapter 1); informational (for example, the Toxics Release Inventory reporting Fiorino discusses in chapter 11); or procedural (for example, third-party auditing of EMSs as Mazurek discusses in chapter 13). All, however, will succeed or fail on the extent to which they can afford sufficient transparency to inoculate themselves against what Shang-Jin Wei and Heather Milkiewicz call "Enron-itis" in the years ahead.[57]

Missing Links, Links Gone Missing, and the Paradoxes of Reform

Although the salience of building the results-based sense of common purpose chronicled in this book is likely to continue, its ability to transcend the forces that have constrained the widespread application of that purpose is decidedly less clear.[58] One of the most persistent lessons the authors communicate involves the significant and difficult extent of attitudinal and behavioral change that its elements require of citizens, organizations (public, private, and nonprofit), nations, and international bodies. Also pervasive in their chapters is the theme of contingency.

Recall, for example, how many of the reforms seem to be more or less difficult to implement under different conditions (see, for instance, the chapters by Schlager and John on self-regulating communities and civic environmentalism, respectively). Other reforms appear dependent for success on various contingencies arising in the future (see, for instance, Paehlke on the need for a North American shift away from "cowboy capitalism," and Fiorino and Mazurek on the importance of trust and capacity building). Discernible from the chapters, as well, is a set of paradoxes within this reform agenda that its implementers will be challenged to resolve in practice and under varying circumstances in the future. These paradoxes essentially are paradoxes of the state, modernity, bureaucracy, participation, and sustainability. They merit the serious attention of students, scholars, and practitioners who seek to understand, research, or pursue these reforms in the future.

The Paradox of the State

A major theme running throughout the chapters in this volume is how much rethinking is required about the roles that nation-states play in building a results-based sense of common purpose in environmental governance. None of the authors argues, of course, that national governments will or should wither away. Nevertheless, most of them (for example, Bryner, Scheberle, John, Durant with Boodphetcharat, and Schlager) see many environmental responsibilities being pushed upward to international bodies (for example, ISO 14001 standards, the Codex Alimentarius Commission, and the WTO), downward to states and localities (for example, devolution, place-based regulation, regulatory takings decisions, and common-pool resource agreements), and outward to the private and nonprofit sectors (for example, the Coalition for Environmentally Responsible Economies).

Most also insinuate, however, that capacity building at the national level has become, if anything, even more important. This occurs as first-generation approaches to environmental governance fall short of their aims, as the challenges of networking in the shadow of hierarchy proceed apace, and as the international standardization movement gets its bearing as a tool of environmental governance. Some (for example, Paehlke, Durant with Boodphetcharat, and John) see research and regulatory capacity building as central to rebuilding public trust in public agencies charged with both promoting and protecting public health and safety in the developed and developing world. Otherwise, promising technoscientific advances will continue to be debated in deliberatively and democratically dysfunctional ways. Still others (for example, Geiser, Ringquist, and Fiorino) see regulatory capacity building at the national level as critical, viewing the national "stick" and the threat of strict standards as vital to many of the flexibility-granting tools envisioned by reformers. And still others (for example, Paehlke) see the building of national capacity to perform sustainability analyses (among other things) as vital to making sustainability a central animating principle of environmental governance at national, subnational, and international levels.

Thus, at one *proactive* extreme, national governments must take on novel and difficult tasks such as catalyzing, arranging, coordinating, nurturing, and evaluating the performance and outcomes produced by networks or partnerships of public, private, nonprofit, and civic society actors. At a more *reactive* extreme, they must learn not to get in the way of emergent grassroots initiatives associated with common-pool resource management, civic environmentalism, and deliberative democracy (for example, by failing to seize opportunities to eliminate the stove-piping and procedural kudzu that gets in the way of allowing these collaborative ventures to work effectively). In between these extremes, national governments must ensure that local variations in commitments do not undermine such goals as measuring outcomes, achieving environmental justice, and protecting the rights of property owners from unconstitutional regulatory takings, while simultaneously protecting the public interest in wise stewardship.

The Paradox of Modernity

A second discernible theme indicating the depth of change the authors in this volume identify either explicitly or implicitly relates to a need to reevaluate many of the central metanarratives of the affluent, industrialized, Western world. Again, however, a bit of a paradox runs through the chapters as contributors identify how best to build a results-based sense of common purpose in environmental governance: although many of the tools and assumptions of modernity cause problems, some of the solutions to these problems lie with these tools themselves. On the negative side, some of the authors (for example, Bryner, Geiser, and Paehlke) indicate that significant changes in key modernist metanarratives and their assumptions are necessary for progress. Either questioned or cited as obstacles to prudent environmental governance in the United States are such things as the so-called "Washington consensus" on economic development, the Western fixation on technocratic rationality and scientific methodology, the embrace in North America of consumerism as the linchpin of life quality, the use of a materialistic felicific calculus to operationalize the public interest, and enduring faith in markets over governments.

Some authors (see Paehlke), for example, indict Western—in particular, North American—materialism, overconsumption, and "cowboy economics" as dominant and pernicious sources of humanity's global ecological woes, even as they find reasons for both optimism and pessimism that these attitudes might change in the future (for example, through the rise of post-materialism). Others (see Durant with Boodphetcharat) illustrate how non-Western views of economic development (for example, the Asian model), environmentalism (for example, Buddhist economics, "traditional wisdom" in resource management, or configurations of the environment as a legitimating discourse for otherwise marginalized debates over power and control), and technocratic solutions (for example, biotechnology) both induce conflict and beg for philosophical and behavioral changes by persons, organizations, and governments in the West. Still others (Bryner, Paehlke, Ringquist, and Wise) discern the necessity and appropriateness of linking ENR concerns to livelihood issues. They believe that equity and fairness in the distribution of environmental harms and benefits for present and future generations must become central animating premises of local, national, and international environmental governance (for example, in property rights, environmental justice, international trade, and food security). Others (Geiser and Bryner), in turn, argue that a more audacious focus in the United States and elsewhere on the benefits to corporate "bottom lines" of ecological modernization and dematerialization is necessary to make progress on such values as pollution prevention and ecological sustainability.

At the same time, however, other authors (see Fiorino) find components of modernity as absolutely critical to building sustainable, equitable, and prudential solutions to many of humanity's most pressing environmental governance challenges. They see market incentives, for example, as the ultimate tools for gaining the flexibility so badly needed by regulators and the regulated community. Moreover, proponents of this position (for example, Fiorino; Geiser; and O'Leary, Nabatchi, and Bingham) see clear, ambitious, and unambiguous regulatory standards set by regulatory bureaucracies—the epitome of the postmodern problematic—as essential complements to market and mediation incentives. Otherwise, polluters will have little incentive to move toward ecological modernization, the reframing of industrial production processes, and environmental conflict resolution (ECR). Relatedly, approaches incorporating tradable emission and discharge rights require bureaucracies with adequate capacities to determine initial allocations and to supervise markets in these rights. Likewise, other authors in this volume (see Wise) consider it critical for regulators to be sensitive to property rights, to establish reasons for better stewardship by local indigenous communities in emergent self-regulatory regimes, and to coax better stewardship of common-pool resources more generally (see Schlager). Here again, however, regulatory bureaucracies have a key role to play in deciding what these rights are, how to allocate them equitably, and how best to police future stewardship of them.

Finally, some authors (for example, Meadowcroft, John, and Fiorino) consider technocracy as potentially conducive to effective, equitable, and democratically informed environmental governance. This is the case, for example, when technocracy takes the form of compatible computer technology and software for collecting and analyzing the data necessary to move toward outcomes measurements; to get information to decision makers in timely and understandable formats; to inform sustainability analyses or pollution prevention programs; to improve the quality of third-party EMS auditing; to devise marketable permits, emission fees, mandatory information disclosures, challenge programs, and EMSs; and to make citizens and stakeholders better informed in deliberative democracy, civic environmentalism, or ECR exercises. It is also the case when, for instance, international NGOs test the claims of those promoting technoscientific advances with their own expert (and inexpert) analyses, when advocacy rather than peer-reviewed research attempts to dominate ENR decision making, and when property rights and legal analyses must better inform regulatory takings decisions in order to avoid adverse legal decisions that compromise effective environmental governance.

The Paradox of Bureaucracy

A related and equally paradoxical theme discernible from this collection is the simultaneous need to reduce the pathological elements of conventional bureaucratic structures, processes, and cultures. However, building a results-based sense of common purpose in this fashion concomitantly entails protecting and improving the ability of government bureaucracies to manage third-party deliverers of ENR services (for example, contractors), ensure trust in the integrity of accountability systems (for example, third-party auditing of EMS systems), and promote technological advances (see the chapters by Scheberle, John, Mazurek, and Durant with Boodphetcharat). Moreover, all this must be done in ways consonant with the disparate and often competing values that David Rosenbloom associates with the managerial, political, and legal traditions of public administration: efficiency, economy, effectiveness, responsiveness, accountability, equity, and due process.[59] Indeed, the greater the amount of deregulation, debureaucratization, devolution, and load shedding to the private and nonprofit sector envisioned for environmental governance, the more necessary will be the maximization or trade-off of these values. These include eliminating arbitrary and capricious decisions, institutionalizing continuity and expertise, protecting substantive and constitutional rights, and ensuring accountability.

The bureaupathologies that the authors in this volume identify and the extent of behavioral change reformers require to address them are appreciated best by reviewing the culturally redefining catchwords and phrases that critics associate with reform. Some of the most challenging among these are prescriptions that learning organizations become *priority based, information driven, results oriented, customer focused, cross-media centered,* and *seamless.* All this, in turn, requires a distinctive, sustained, and persistent focus on *dialogue, trust building, transparency, information sharing, outcomes-focused goals, flexibility,* and *intra-* and *interorganizational collaboration* (see, for example, the chapters by Meadowcroft; Schlager; Scheberle; and O'Leary, Nabatchi, and Bingham).

The authors also suggest that the building of linkages is critical—linkages that bureaucracies have been known to slight or avoid in the past. Civic environmentalism, for example, requires local actors to link their actions (at least in their own minds) to larger national, regional, and global causes. Effectiveness depends on linking bold visions with day-to-day operations, measuring progress, and designing reward structures accordingly. The prospects for technoscientific advances require a linkage in proponents' minds between bureaucratic expertise, on the one hand, and cultural sensitivity, openness, and collaboration, on the other (see, for example, the Meadowcroft, Durant with Boodphetcharat, Paehlke, and Bryner chapters). Deliberative democracy requires the linking of bureaucrats and citizens in unconventional ways; the former must develop a coproduction service ethic that eschews one-way flows of communications between agencies and their stakeholders (see, for example, the John and Meadowcroft chapters). Various forms of deliberative democracy and ECR require bringing others together to talk and deliberate in unaccustomed and challenging ways for bureaucracies accustomed to legal adversarialism in the procedural republic (see, for example, the chapter by O'Leary, Nabatchi, and Bingham). Put most simply, agencies and their legislative overseers must learn to listen and not just talk, a behavioral change that will be painful for many of them.

Yet even if these adjustments are made, one thing will *not* change: reforms designed in part to advance the building of a results-based sense of common purpose must proceed without jeopardizing the values associated with the three traditions of public administration noted earlier. The rub, paradoxically, is this: the conventional administrative orthodoxy of hierarchy, rules and regulations, and functionally based organization that is the target of reform has served many of these values *very* well over the years. As James Q. Wilson argues, if public agencies are the institutionalization of red tape that critics bemoan, it is because citizens do not want to compromise certain values—namely, constitutional rights, administrative due process, and equal treatment under the law. Likewise, although ENR bureaucracies are typically assailed for being too responsive to particularistic interests, many of the reforms discussed in this volume appear equally vulnerable. Consequently, citizens must be assured that responsiveness does not entail undue, inappropriate, or even corrupt influence by legislators, contractors, auditors, self-regulating common-pool resource regimes, protectionist governments, or participants in ECR initiatives.

Policymakers thus have to achieve a fine balance: they will have to ensure that these values are protected without imposing inordinate unfunded mandates on subnational and supranational regulators; without "governmentalizing" the private and nonprofit sectors; without discouraging a focus on outcomes in favor of process or outputs; and without using existing or new international regimes or bureaucracies (for example, the Codex Alimentarius Commission, the Convention on Biological Diversity, or the new European Food Safety Authority) to write biosafety regulations constituting nontariff barriers to trade.

The Paradox of Participation

A fourth equally paradoxical theme discernible in the chapters and requiring significant attitudinal and behavioral changes to build a results-based sense of common purpose involves stakeholder participation in environmental governance. Put most directly, the more that *traditional* modes of stakeholder participation in environmental governance are pursued, the less likely that civic trust, deliberative democracy, and the building of common purpose can prosper. Some of the authors (see, for example, Meadowcroft, Bryner, Schlager, Ringquist, and Wise) suggest that conventional "tell-and-defend" strategies of participation are disastrously inadequate in a networked world of vocal and litigious, or civil disobedience-prone, citizens and NGOs. In an uncertain, complex era when environmental issues are morphed into economic livelihood issues, solutions will require broad consensus, equitable impact, and heavy doses of social learning to gain acceptance. To these ends, several authors (for example, Meadowcroft) argue that only group-based collaborative and cross-sectoral (public, private, and nonprofit) deliberative mechanisms will suffice.

Standard efforts to boost participation also are incapable of promoting what several authors (including Meadowcroft, John, and Schlager) discuss as a singularly important participative end in its own right: the development of civic capital. Whether pursued through environmental covenants, negotiated regulations, common-pool resource strategies, or mediation, civic capital building premised on probative rather than prejudicial policy deliberations is considered critical to building a results-based sense of common purpose (see, for example, the arguments by Schlager; Fiorino; and O'Leary, Nabatchi, and Bingham). Each approach requires a greater, timelier, and more persistent stakeholder role in policy formulation, implementation, and evaluation than historically has been the preference of government policymakers. Yet without an unprecedented level of participation and transparency, citizens will doubt that flexibility can be granted while still keeping pressure on polluters to improve their environmental performance (see, for example, the Fiorino chapter).

Several authors (Meadowcroft, Ringquist, Paehlke, Bryner, and Durant with Boodphetcharat) also imply that participation is unlikely to advance common purpose in environmental governance if it proceeds in three dysfunctional ways. First, progress will not be made if participation is structured in ways that eschew cultural sensitivity (whether, for example, in crafting and implementing environmental justice policies in the United States; in Europe's worries that growing GM crops will have adverse affects on biodiversity [because most European farms are located near national forests]; or in developing nations' embrace of the Asian rather than Washington consensus model of development). Second, participation will be counterproductive if it fails to incorporate "voice" for future generations (that is, if it ignores intergenerational equity). Third, it will fall short of its aims if policymakers fail to appreciate that environmental issues are about more than environmental protection and "good science"; these issues have become legitimating discourses for a broader set of power and control issues that otherwise might be marginalized in policy debates, especially in developing nations transitioning to democracy. This development means that debates and the positions that participants take in them are informed as much or more by resource redistribution issues as they are by regulatory disagreements.

The Paradox of Sustainability

A fifth paradoxical theme discernible in the collection relates to what many reformers wish to see become the central animating principle of environmental governance: sustainability. Some of the authors (Paehlke, Bryner, and Geiser) embrace the ideas of "contextual economics" and "ecological sustainability" as offering an environmental ethic that should inform both domestic statutes and international laws, regimes, treaties, and accords. What is more, they see these concepts as offering ways to link local-level action to global concerns, to help build community, and to gain commitment for action on transboundary problems. They maintain this view, in fact, despite formidable concerns about the concepts' ambiguity, analytical challenges, and ideological underpinnings (some critics, for example, portray proponents of the concepts as "fellow travelers" of the earlier "limits to growth" movement).[60]

The merits or demerits of sustainability as an animating principle of environmental governance aside, the paradox of sustainability for the building of a results-based sense of common purpose lies in the "triple bottom line" of economic prosperity, social well-being, and environmental protection that it seeks to promote. In linking these three elements of well-being into a calculus for decision making, sustainability also helps morph environmental issues into the decidedly more conflictual politics of livelihood issues. In the process, it does two things. First, it (like environmental justice) converts ENR policies, which traditionally were framed and seen largely as public interest–oriented initiatives to help broad segments of the population, into policies targeted more to particular segments of domestic or foreign populations (see, for example, the Ringquist chapter). Second, and because of this conversion, the politics of sustainability shift into the decidedly more conflictual realm of redistributive politics, either within or across nations and within and across the developed and developing worlds.

Thus, a concept that some hope will become an environmental ethic uniting presently disparate and often conflictual national and international actors is quite vulnerable to its opponents' portrayal that it is less about the environment and more about redistributing resources on broad social scales. Such a portrayal is neither without merit in terms of its redistributive implications nor so compelling as to be beyond its proponents' abilities to counter it effectively. It does, however, immensely complicate the building of common purpose, especially when proposals for sustainability require significant shifts of resources from the developed world. Nor is the challenge reduced when proposals are filtered through the cultural prisms of developing nations worried about Western technocratic solutions to environmental problems, about technology transfers creating a new "colonialism" or "dependency" relationship with the developed world, or about globalism and its impacts on traditional cultural values (see, for example, the chapter by Durant with Boodphetcharat).

A Paperweight Lifted?

One of the most striking impressions that one gets from reading the chapters in this volume is the dearth of theoretically grounded, methodologically rigorous, and empirically informed research that can be marshaled in evaluating the claims of both reformers and their critics. As the authors have illustrated, the fate of any of the reforms that inform the reconceptualizing of purpose, the reconnecting of citizens, and the redefining of administrative rationality in environmental governance is likely to vary widely. Yet with few exceptions (most notably, common-pool resource theory), understanding the conditions under which various initiatives in the reformers' arsenals are more or less likely to succeed depends largely, as the authors suggest, on best practices literatures, participant observations and insights, and anecdotal information.

To be sure, compiling these insights, sifting through them for common concepts and patterns, and considering their lessons for practice are worthwhile endeavors. As such, the authors' work in collating what practitioners and scholars know about the contingencies of each of the concepts discussed in this volume is a significant contribution to our understanding. Yet as these authors also point out, their efforts are only a beginning. Some indicate, for example, that the future viability of the concepts they discuss for building a results-based sense of common purpose depends even more basically on researchers sorting out the validity of broad, competing, and as yet unresolved claims. Illustrative here is the need to assess more empirically the true relationship between such things as: (1) economic growth and environmental quality; (2) ECR interventions and environmental outcomes; (3) threats of regulatory takings and regulators' responses to those threats (adaptation or risk aversion?); (4) self-regulatory mechanisms such as EMSs or common-pool resource management and the quality of ENR stewardship; (5) different participatory modes and both the quality of the decisions produced and the civic capacity derived from them; (6) the precautionary principle and both redistributive politics and delays in promising technoscientific innovations; and (7) various flexibility tools (for example, marketable permits and emissions fees) and the degree of adaptability, reflexivity, and social learning they afford without compromising such values as environmental justice.

More narrowly, but nonetheless important, the propositional inventories offered by many of the authors in this volume beg more rigorous testing, refinement, and elaboration in future research. As some of them painstakingly point out, the lack of solid empirical support for the effectiveness of these results-based reforms threatens to undermine their appeal in the future (see, for example, the chapters by Scheberle; Ringquist; and O'Leary, Nabatchi, and Bingham). Without more empirical research, they claim, reforms will beach on the shoals of cultural, bureaucratic, political, and economic perceptions of self-interest. The argument here is straightforward: without data and analyses rebutting opponents' claims (real or contrived), these reforms stand little chance of overcoming formidable resistance to them. Nor do the prospects for scholars advancing theory building in any of these areas seem promising absent more systematic research.

In addition to the broad-based questions just noted and the subset of questions marbled throughout the volume, what might a research agenda suitable for informing debates about the building of a results-based sense of common purpose in environmental governance look like? As we noted in the introduction to this volume, a major question for researchers to pursue is whether or not this set of reforms is internally coherent. To some extent, some of the paradoxes described previously call this assumption into question. Other related questions remain, however. For example, will outcomes-based accountability, transparency, and more democratically deliberative initiatives make it easier or more difficult to build consensus? Under what conditions are they more or less likely to do so? Using what policy tools? Will market-based approaches really increase flexibility, increase transparency, improve deliberative capacities, prompt civic engagement, and develop civic capital? How, when, and under what conditions are they most likely to do so? Likewise, will sustainability analyses inflame environmental disputes and diminish trust building by degenerating into disputes over measures, data manipulation, and motives? How, when, and under what circumstances is this likely to occur? Does the internal logic of these reforms differ between parliamentary and presidential systems, between the developed and developing worlds, and among different types of ENR policies regardless of context?

As the authors in this volume indicate, answers to the questions raised here are timely, important, and ripe for exploration by researchers. The authors collectively have offered an impressive, robust, and challenging research agenda for scholars and practitioners to ponder and pursue in the years ahead. Regardless of the research questions they ultimately pursue, however, three things are clear: data collection and analysis demands will be daunting; both cross-sectional and longitudinal studies must inform this research enterprise; and rigorous comparative analyses must drive both qualitative and quantitative analyses of these topics. Rigor, of course, will not guarantee the successful, widespread, and effective adoption and implementation of any tools for building a results-based sense of common purpose in environmental governance. As two prominent scholars in public administration suggest, the fate of reform movements generally is determined less by their logic than by their consonance with broader sociopolitical trends.[61]

Nevertheless, as policy theorists now widely recognize, social learning *can* be a critical component of those broader trends, with epistemic communities over time demonstrating to policymakers precisely what they ought to prefer.[62] The authors in this volume have summarized what scholars and practitioners know and do not know about reconceptualizing purpose, reconnecting with citizens, and redefining administrative rationality. They have offered, in the process, a compass rather than a roadmap suggesting what students, scholars, and practitioners need to know additionally to cope successfully with the strategic challenges, choices, and opportunities facing anyone trying to advance a results-based sense of common purpose in environmental governance in the future. Hopefully, researchers will find this compass informative, thought-provoking, and ripe for refining, elaborating, and testing in future research as the importance of building common purpose spirals apace in the twenty-first century. Lifted in the process, as H. G. Wells might say, could be one of the great paperweights—namely, uncertainty—that made the incipient transition from first-generation approaches to environmental governance so halting, halfway, and patchworked in the twentieth century.

Notes

1. This section is based heavily on Robert F. Durant, Young-Pyoung Chun, Byungseob Kim, and Seongjong Lee, "Toward a New Governance Paradigm in Environmental and Natural Resource Management in the 21st Century?" *Administrative and Society* 35(6) (2004): 643–682.

2. Jack M. Hollander, *The Real Environmental Crisis: Why Poverty, Not Affluence, Is the Environment's Number One Enemy* (Berkeley: University of California Press, 2003).

3. Jules Pretty, "The Real Costs of Modern Farming," *Agricultural Systems Journal,* http://www.gn.apc.org/resurgence/issues/pretty205.htm, accessed March 16, 2001.

4. National Institute of Environmental Health Sciences, "NIEHS Toxicogenomics Research and Environmental Health Introduction," June 1, 2001, http://www.niehs.nih.gov/dert/rograms/tgintro.htm.

5. See Gary Marchant for an excellent and more extensive treatment of these issues (Gary Marchant, "Ten Ways Genomics Could Change Environmental Policy," paper presented at the Environmental Law Institute Associates Seminar, March 7, 2002, Washington, D.C.).

6. Tom Doggett, "World Oil Demand Seen Up 56 Percent by 2020," *Environmental News Network,* March 29, 2001, http://www.enn.com/news/wire-stories/2001/03/03292001/reu_oil_42787.asp.

7. "UK to Get 18 Wind Farms," *BBC News,* April 5, 2001, http://www.news.bbc.co.uk/hi/english/uk_politics/newsid_1261000/1261759.stm. Even in Japan and Great Britain, however, the cause of nuclear power has suffered setbacks of late. In Japan, for example, a number of accidents and scandals over the past 10 years have compromised citizens' trust in the industry (see, for example, "Six Sentenced over Japan's Worst Nuclear Accident," *Planet Ark,* March 4, 2003, www.planetark.com/dailynewsstory.cfm/newsid/20020, accessed March 26, 2003). Likewise, the British government decided in 2002 to delay decisions relating to building new nuclear plants after a series of embarrassments for the industry. Most notable among those incidents that have buoyed the spirits of the antinuclear lobby is the "financial meltdown" of the privatized nuclear power firm British Energy (see, for example, "UK Balks at Building New Nuclear Reactors," *Planet Ark,* December 20, 2002, www.planetark.com/dailynewsstory.cfm/newsid/19148, accessed March 26, 2003).

8. "Anti-nuclear Protestors Attack German Railways," *BBC News,* March 21, 2001, http://www.news.bbc.co.uk.

9. Michael B. Gerrard, *Whose Backyard, Whose Risk: Fear and Fairness in Toxic and Nuclear Waste Siting* (Cambridge, Mass.: MIT Press, 1994).

10. Scott Disavino, "Environmentalists Rally to Stop NYC Power Plants," *Environmental News Network,* March 16, 2001, http://www.enn.com/news/wire-stories.

11. Joseph Kahn, "Energy Efficiency Programs Are Set for Bush Budget Cut," *New York Times,* April 5, 2001, http://www.nytimes.com/2001/04/05/politics/05BUDG.html.

12. Eileen R. Larence, "Do Federal Environmental Laws Help or Hinder Localities Who Want to Curb Urban Sprawl?" paper presented at the National Conference of the American Society for Public Administration, March 10–13, 2001, Newark, N.J.

13. Ronald Inglehart, *Culture Shift* (Princeton, N.J: Princeton University Press, 1990).

14. But see Philip Hirsch for a decidedly different perspective on this dynamic in developing nations (Philip Hirsch, *Seeing Forests for Trees: Environment and Environmentalism in Thailand* [Chiang Mai, Thailand: Silkworm, 1996]).

15. Thomas B. Edsall, "Voter Values Determine Political Affiliation," *Washington Post,* March 26, 2001, p. A1.

16. Christopher Rootes, "It's Not Easy Being Green: Green Parties: From Protest to Power," *Harvard International Review* 23(4) (winter 2002), p. 82.

17. James Q. Wilson, *Bureaucracy* (New York: Basic, 1989); Jeffrey M. Berry, *The New Liberalism: The Rising Power of Citizen Groups* (Washington, D.C.: Brookings Institution Press, 1999).

18. "Canadian Rainforest 'Saved' after Timber Deal," *BBC News,* April 5, 2001, http://news.bbc.co.uk/hi/english/world/Americas/newsid_1261000/1261688.stm.

19. "Citizens Can View Refinery Emissions Data Online," *CNN Online,* March 21, 2001, http://www.commodities-now.com/news/pr_technology/pr_20010321a.shtml.

20. Pasuk Phongpaichit and Chris Baker, *Thailand's Crisis* (Chiang Mai, Thailand: Silkworm, 2002).

21. H. Brinton Milward, "Symposium on the Hollow State: Capacity, Control, and Performance in Interorganizational Settings," *Journal of Public Administration Research and Theory* 6(2) (1996): 193–314; B. Guy Peters, *The Future of Governing: Four Emerging Models* (Lawrence: University Press of Kansas, 1996); Robert F. Durant, "Agenda Setting, the 'Third Wave,' and the Administrative State," *Administration and Society* 30(3) (1998): 211–247; Donald F. Kettl, "The Transformation of Governance: Globalization, Devolution, and the Role of Government," discussion paper prepared for a meeting of the National Academy of Public Administration, Washington D.C., June 1–3, 2000.

22. Stephen Skowronek, *Building a New American State: The Expansion of National Administrative Capacities, 1877–1920* (Cambridge: Cambridge University Press, 1982), p. 13.

23. John Clarke and Janet Newman, *The Managerial State: Power, Politics, and Ideology in the Remaking of Social Welfare* (Thousand Oaks, Calif.: Sage, 1997).

24. Skowronek, *Building a New American State.*

25. Fritz W. Sharpf, "Games Real Actors Could Play: Positive and Negative Coordination in Embedded Negotiations," *Journal of Theoretical Politics* 6(1) (1994): 27–53.

26. Robert A. Dahl, *On Democracy* (New Haven, Conn.: Yale University Press, 1999).

27. See, for example, Regina Axelrod and Norman J. Vig, "The European Union as an Environmental Governance System," in Norman J. Vig and Regina S. Axelrod, eds., *The Global Environment: Institutions, Law, and Policy,* 72–97 (Washington, D.C.: Congressional Quarterly, 1999).

28. Joseph S. Nye Jr., Philip D. Zelikow, and David C. King, *Why People Don't Trust Government* (Cambridge, Mass.: Harvard University Press, 1997); Mark J. Penn, "The Community Consensus," *Blueprint* 3 (spring 1999): 44–56.

29. Al From, "Building a New Progressive Majority," *Blueprint,* special issue: *Election 2000* (2001): 4–11.

30. William A. Galston, "Where We Stand," *Blueprint* 3 (spring 1999): 6–13; Penn, "The Community Consensus."

31. Robert F. Durant, "The Political Economy of Results-Oriented Management in the 'Neoadministrative State': Lessons Learned from the MCDHHS Experience," *American Review of Public Administration* 29(4) (1999): 1–16.

32. Ibid.

33. Robert P. Stoker, "A Regime Framework for Implementation Analysis: Cooperation and Reconciliation of Federalist Imperatives," *Policy Studies Review* 9(1) (1989): 29–49.

34. Laurence J. O'Toole Jr., "Treating Networks Seriously: Practical and Research-Based Agendas in Public Administration," *Public Administration Review* 57(1) (1997): 45–52; Laurence J. O'Toole Jr., "Implementing Public Innovations in Network Settings," *Administration and Society* 29(2) (1997): 115–138.

35. See Don Moynihan, "Managing for Results," in *Government Performance Project, Paths to Performance in State and Local Government: A Final Assessment from the Maxwell School of Citizenship and Public Affairs* (Syracuse, N.Y.: Maxwell School of Citizenship and Public Affairs, 2003), p. 153.

36. Donald F. Kettl, "Reinventing Government: Past, Present, But Is There a Future?" lecture, University of Baltimore, May 5, 1997.

37. Also see Moynihan, "Managing for Results."

38. See http://www.epa.gov/ocirpage/nepps/agreements.htm.

39. See, for example, "Illinois Annual Environmental Conditions Report 2000," http://www.epa.state.il.us/environmental-conditions/2000/index.html.

40. Few formal evaluations are available comparing performance of programs that use performance measures and those that do not. Evidence from government agencies that have begun managing more intensively with detailed performance measures—especially those such as precincts that apply measures to locational subunits of the larger organization—provides additional support for the conclusion that skilled management with performance goals and measures leads to performance gains. See Executive Session on Public Sector Performance Management, *Get Results Through Performance Management: An Open Memorandum to Government Executives,* Visions of Governance for the 21st Century Program (Cambridge, Mass.: Kennedy School of Government, Harvard University, 2001).

41. For an excellent and insightful review of the logic and application of results-based accountability mechanisms in the environmental governance arena, see Shelley H. Metzenbaum, "Measurement That Matters: Cleaning Up the Charles River," in Donald F. Kettl, ed., *Environmental Governance: A Report on the Next Generation of Environmental Policy, 58–117* (Washington, D.C.: Brookings Institution Press, 2002). Many of the points in this section are culled from Metzenbaum's insights on outcomes-based performance measures.

42. See, for example, Metzenbaum, "Measurement That Matters." Data scarcity also is a common problem. For example, water quality has been assessed for only 23 percent of the nation's river miles, 43 percent of its lakes, and 32 percent of its estuaries. Water quality data are available for only 5 percent of ocean shorelines (U.S. Environmental Protection Agency [EPA], *Water Quality Conditions in the United States: A Profile from the 1998 National Water Quality Inventory Report,* EPA-841-F-00-006 [Washington, D.C.: EPA, June 2000], p. 1). For points regarding public availability of measures, see Robert F. Durant, Jerome S. Legge Jr., and Antony Moussios, "People, Profits, and Service Delivery: Lessons from the Privatization of British Telecom," *American Journal of Political Science* 42(1) (1998): 117–140. For points regarding the related difficulties and lessons learned from the EPA Performance Partnership Grant Program, see U.S. EPA, "Performance Partnership Grants for State and Tribal Environmental Program: Revised Interim Guidance; Notice," *Federal Register,* 63(193) [Notices] (October 6, 1998): 53763–53774, http://www.epa.gov/fedrgstr/EPA-AIR/1998/October/Day-06/a26459.htm.

43. See Metzenbaum, "Measurement That Matters"; also see footnote 44.

44. For example, tracking inputs to programs slowed states' transition to outcomes-focused management as envisioned in NEPPS.

45. The difficulty of structuring effective reward systems has received great attention over the years. Edward Deming, the father of total quality management, warned against misuse of measurements to create fear in the workforce. See W. Edwards Deming, *Out of the Crisis* (Cambridge, Mass.: MIT Press, 1986), pp. 73–74, 76. See also Thomas B. Wilson, *Innovative Reward Systems for the Changing Workplace* (New York: McGraw-Hill, 1995); Rick Kowalski, *Using Outcome Information to Redirect Programs: A Case Study of the Coast Guard's*

Pilot Project under the Government Performance and Results Act (Washington, D.C.: United States Coast Guard, Office of Marine Safety, Security, and Environmental Protection, April 1996); Lee Ross and Richard E. Nisbett, *The Person and the Situation: Perspectives of Social Psychology* (New York: McGraw-Hill, 1991), p. 66, referring to M. R. Lepper, D. Greene, and R. E. Nisbett, "Undermining Children's Intrinsic Interest with Extrinsic Reward," *Journal of Personality and Social Psychology* 28 (1973): 129–137.

46. See, for example, Southern Growth Policies Board and the Southern Consortium of University Public Service Organizations, *Results-Oriented Government: A Guide to Strategic Planning and Performance Measurement in the Public Sector* (Research Triangle Park, N.C.: Southern Growth Policies Board, 1996); David N. Ammons, ed., *Accountability for Performance: Measurement and Monitoring in Local Government* (Washington, D.C.: International City/Council Management Association, 1995); M. D. Campbell, *Building Results: New Tools for an Age of Discovery in Government* (Washington, D.C.: Council of Governors' Policy Advisors, 1994); S. S. Grifel, "Organizational Culture: Its Importance in Performance Measurement," *Public Management* (September 1994): S19–S20; A. Halachami and G. Bouchaert, eds., *Organizational Performance and Measurement in the Public Sector: Toward Service, Effort, and Accomplishment Reporting* (Westport, Conn.: Quorum, 1996); U.S. General Accounting Office (GAO), *Managing for Results: Critical Actions for Measuring Performance,* GAO/T-GGD/AIMD-95-187 (Washington, D.C.: GAO, June 1995); U.S. GAO, *Executive Guide: Effectively Implementing the Government Performance and Results Act,* GAO/GGD-96-118 (Washington, D.C.: GAO, June 1996); J. S. Wholey and K. E. Newcomer, *Improving Government Performance: Evaluation Strategies for Strengthening Public Agencies and Programs* (San Francisco: Jossey-Bass, 1989); J. S. Wholey, H. P. Hatry, and K. E. Newcomer, eds., *Handbook of Practical Program Evaluation* (San Francisco: Jossey-Bass, 1994).

47. These factors are taken from a summary of the literature in Robert F. Durant, "Whither the Neoadministrative State: Toward a Polity-Centered Theory of Administrative Reform," *Journal of Public Administration Research and Theory* 10(1) (2000): 79–109.

48. Ibid.

49. Ibid.

50. This section relies heavily on Robert F. Durant, "Demographics as Destiny? 'Graying,' 'Greening,' and the '29th Day' in Environmental Management," *PA Times* (April 2003): 4–5.

51. Brian Friel, "Federal Retirements Fall Short While Hiring Booms," *Government Executive Magazine,* February 20, 2003, www.govexec.com/dailyfed/0203/022003bl.htm, accessed February 24, 2003. Comparable figures for specific ENR agencies are not yet available as of this printing.

52. U.S. GAO, "What GAO Found," *High-Risk Series: Strategic Human Capital Management,* GAO-03-120 (Washington, D.C.: GAO, January 2003), p. 29.

53. U.S. GAO, *Performance and Accountability Series: Environmental Protection Agency,* GAO-03-112 (Washington, D.C.: GAO, January 2003), p. 21.

54. Ann Florini, "Business and Global Governance," *Brookings Review* 21(2) (spring 2003), p. 5.

55. Ibid.

56. Laurence J. O'Toole Jr. and Kenneth I. Hanf, "American Public Administration and Impacts of International Governance," *Public Administration Review* 62, special edition (September 2002), p. 160.

57. Shang-Jin Wei with Heather Milkiewicz, "A Global Crossing for Enronitis? How Opaque Self-Dealing Damages Financial Markets Around the World," *Brookings Review* 21(2) (spring 2003): 28–31.

58. The phrasing in the heading for this section is adapted from Benny Hjern, "Implementation Research—The Link Gone Missing," *Journal of Public Policy* 2 (1982): 301–308.

59. David Rosenbloom, "Public Administrative Theory and the Separation of Powers," *Public Administration Review* 43(3) (1983): 219–227. Rosenbloom writes of a managerial tradition stressing economy, efficiency, and effectiveness; a political tradition emphasizing responsiveness, representativeness, and accountability; and a legal tradition upholding constitutional rights and substantive due process.

60. See, for example, Vaclav Smil, *Feeding the World: A Challenge for the 21st Century* (Cambridge, Mass.: MIT Press, 2000).

61. David H. Rosenbloom and Bernard H. Ross, "Administrative Theory, Political Power, and Government Reform," in Patricia W. Ingraham, Barbara S. Romzek, and Associates, eds., *New Paradigms for Government: Issues for the Changing Public Service,* 145–167 (San Francisco: Jossey-Bass, 1994).

62. Craig W. Thomas, "Public Management as Interagency Cooperation: Testing Epistemic Community Theory at the Domestic Level," *Journal of Public Administration Research and Theory* 7(2) (1998): 221–246; Paul A. Sabatier and Hack C. Jenkins-Smith, eds., *Policy Change and Learning: An Advocacy Coalition Approach* (Boulder, Colo.: Westview, 1993).

About the Contributors

Lisa B. Bingham is Keller-Runden Professor of Public Service and director of the Indiana Conflict Resolution Institute at the Indiana University School of Public and Environmental Affairs, Bloomington, Indiana. Professor Bingham cofounded the institute, which conducts applied research and program evaluation on mediation, arbitration, and other forms of dispute resolution.

Thanit Boodphetcharat is a faculty member at Payap University in Chiang Mai, Thailand, and a research associate at the Payap Research and Development Institute. She specializes in environmental and natural resources policy.

Gary C. Bryner is professor of political science and director of the Public Policy Program at Brigham Young University. He teaches courses on natural resource policy, environmental regulation, and international development. He is author of *Blue Skies, Green Politics: The Clean Air Act of 1990 and Its Implementation* (1995, 2d ed.) and *From Promise to Performance: Achieving Global Environmental Goals* (1997).

Robert F. Durant is professor of public administration in the School of Public Affairs at American University. His research has focused on environmental policy, public management, and executive branch politics. He is the author of *When Government Regulates Itself: EPA, TVA, and Pollution Control in the 1970s* (1985) and *The Administrative Presidency Revisited: Public Lands, the BLM, and the Reagan Revolution* (1992), as well as a coauthor of *Managing for the Environment: Understanding the Legal, Organizational, and Policy Challenges* (1999). He has received five research and three teaching awards and was given the 2003 Charles H. Levine Memorial Award for excellence in teaching, research, and service from the American Society for Public Administration and the National Association of Schools of Public Affairs and Administration.

Daniel J. Fiorino holds a Ph.D. in political science from the Johns Hopkins University and is currently director of the Performance Incentives Division, Office of Policy, Economics, and Innovation, at the U.S. Environmental Protection Agency in Washington, D.C. He directs projects to encourage strong environmental performance in the business sector. He is a principal architect and the first director of the agency's National Environmental Performance Track Program, which integrates several agency innovations. He is the author of *Making Environmental*

Policy (1995) and a coauthor of *Managing for the Environment: Understanding the Legal, Organizational, and Policy Challenges* (1999). He has published articles in several policy, law, and social science journals.

Ken Geiser is director of the Massachusetts Toxics Use Reduction Institute, a multidisciplinary research, education, training, and policy center at the University of Massachusetts–Lowell, where he is professor of work environment. He also is codirector of the university's Lowell Center for Sustainable Production. He serves on the U.S. Environmental Protection Agency's Toxics Data Reporting Committee of the National Advisory Council for Environmental Policy and Technology and has worked on the agency's Common Sense Initiative for Regulatory Reinvention. Geiser previously served on the core advisory group for the United Nations Environment Program's Cleaner Production Program. He is the author of *Materials Matter: Toward a Sustainable Materials Policy* (2001).

Dewitt John is Thomas F. Shannon Director of the Environmental Studies Program and senior lecturer in government at Bowdoin College in Brunswick, Maine. Before joining the Bowdoin faculty, he worked in state governments and in Washington, D.C. His interests include civic environmentalism, management of federal environmental and natural resource agencies, new approaches to regulation, and community development.

Jan Mazurek directs the Center for Innovation and Environment at the Progressive Policy Institute in Washington, D.C. Her work focuses on ways in which to update first-generation environmental management strategies to reflect such new economic realities as industry restructuring and short product life cycles. Prior to working at the institute, Mazurek served as an analyst in the Clean Air Markets division of the U.S. Environmental Protection Agency. An expert on voluntary environmental agreements, she has evaluated their effectiveness for organizations such as Resources for the Future, the National Academy of Public Administration, and the Organization for Economic Cooperation and Development. Mazurek is the author of *Making Microchips: Policy, Restructuring, and Globalization in the Semiconductor Industry* (1999) and a coauthor of *Pollution Control in the United States: Evaluating the System* (1998).

James Meadowcroft is a reader in the Department of Politics at the University of Sheffield. He has a B.A. in political science from McGill University and a D.Phil. in politics from the University of Oxford. He has a number of publications on the politics of the environment and sustainable development, including *Implementing Sustainable Development: Strategies and Initiatives in High Consumption Societies,* edited with William Lafferty (2000), and *Planning Sustainability,* edited with Michael Kenny (1999). He is coeditor of *International Political Science Review* and associate editor of *Journal of Political Ideologies.*

Tina Nabatchi is a doctoral candidate in the public affairs program at Indiana University's School of Public and Environmental Affairs. Her research interests include public management, public policy, and law, particularly in relation to conflict resolution and sustainable development administration.

Rosemary O'Leary is professor of public administration and director of the Ph.D. program at the Maxwell School of Citizenship and Public Affairs, Syracuse University. O'Leary previously was cofounder and codirector of the Indiana Conflict Resolution Institute. She has won six national awards and one international award for her research.

Robert C. Paehlke has taught political science and environmental policy at Trent University in Peterborough, Ontario, since 1970. He is the author of *Environmentalism and the Future of Progressive Politics* (1989), *Democracy's Dilemma: Environment, Social Equity, and the Global Economy* (2003), several shorter monographs, and more than 100 journal articles and book chapters. He edited *Conservation and Environmentalism: An Encyclopedia* (1995) and coedited *Managing Leviathan: Environmental Politics and the Administrative State* (1991; 2d. ed. forthcoming).

Evan J. Ringquist is a professor in the School of Public and Environmental Affairs at Indiana University, where he specializes in environmental policy, policy evaluation, bureaucratic behavior, and quantitative methodology. He received undergraduate degrees in political science, economics, and biology, and graduate degrees in political science and environmental studies from the University of Wisconsin. He has published roughly three dozen refereed articles, books, and book chapters in areas such as the effectiveness of state pollution control programs, the distribution of environmental risk and the policy contributions to this distribution, and the factors affecting bureaucratic discretion in policymaking. He has served as a consultant to such organizations as the National Park Service, the Texas Governor's Energy Office, the Wisconsin Commission for the Study of Administrative Values and Efficiency, and the Sierra Club.

Denise Scheberle is professor of public and environmental affairs at the University of Wisconsin–Green Bay. Her research focuses on the implementation of environmental laws, environmental federalism, and U.S. government. She has written several articles on environmental policy and currently is working on a new edition of her book *Trust and the Politics of Implementation: Federalism and Environmental Policy* (1997).

Edella Schlager is an associate professor in the Department of Political Science and the School of Public Administration and Policy at the University of Arizona. Her research has focused on self-organizing institutions for governing common-pool resources, the politics of structural choice, and property rights regimes in environmental governance.

Charles R. Wise is professor of public and environmental affairs at Indiana University. On three separate occasions, his articles have received the William Mosher and Frederick Mosher Award for best academic article published in *Public Administration Review*. His research focuses on the intergovernmental and interorganizational dimensions of environmental policy.

Index